"Amazingly easy to use. Very portable, very complete."

—*Booklist*

◆

"The only mainstream guide to list specific prices. The Walter Cronkite of guidebooks—with all that implies."

—*Travel & Leisure*

◆

"Complete, concise, and filled with useful information."

—*New York Daily News*

◆

"Hotel information is close to encyclopedic."

—*Des Moines Sunday Register*

Frommer's®

1st Edition

Washington State

by Karl Samson with Jane Aukshunas

Macmillan • USA

ABOUT THE AUTHORS

Karl Samson and **Jane Aukshunas,** husband-and-wife travel-writing team, make their home in the Northwest, where they've never been able to decide which city they like best, Seattle or Portland. Together they also cover the rest of Washington and Oregon for Frommer's, and Karl is also the author of *Outside Magazine's Adventure Guide to the Pacific Northwest* (which is published by Frommer's).

MACMILLAN TRAVEL

A Simon & Schuster Macmillan Company
1633 Broadway
New York, NY 10019

Find us online at **www.frommers.com**

Copyright © 1998 by Simon & Schuster, Inc.
Maps copyright © by Simon & Schuster, Inc.

ISBN 0-02-861828-9
ISSN 1093-7455

Editor: Margot Weiss
Production Editor: Robyn Burnett
Design by Michele Laseau
Digital Cartography by XNR Productions, Inc., and John Decamillis

SPECIAL SALES

Bulk purchases (10+ copies) of Frommer's and selected Macmillan travel guides are available to corporations, organizations, mail-order catalogs, institutions, and charities at special discounts, and can be customized to suit individual needs. For more information write to Special Sales, Macmillan General Reference, 1633 Broadway, New York, NY 10019.

Manufactured in the United States of America

Contents

List of Maps

AN INVITATION TO THE READER

In researching this book, we discovered many wonderful places—hotels, restaurants, shops, and more. We're sure you'll find others. Please tell us about them, so we can share the information with your fellow travelers in upcoming editions. If you were disappointed with a recommendation, we'd love to know that, too. Please write to:

Karl Samson & Jane Aukshunas
Frommer's Washington 1st Edition
Macmillan Travel
1633 Broadway
New York, NY 10019

AN ADDITIONAL NOTE

Please be advised that travel information is subject to change at any time—and this is especially true of prices. We therefore suggest that you write or call ahead for confirmation when making your travel plans. The authors, editors, and publisher cannot be held responsible for the experiences of readers while traveling. Your safety is important to us, however, so we encourage you to stay alert and be aware of your surroundings. Keep a close eye on cameras, purses, and wallets, all favorite targets of thieves and pickpockets.

WHAT THE SYMBOL MEANS

✪ Frommer's Favorites

Our favorite places and experiences—outstanding for quality, value, or both.

The following abbreviations are used for credit cards:

AE	American Express	EURO	Eurocard
CB	Carte Blanche	JCB	Japan Credit Bank
DC	Diners Club	MC	MasterCard
DISC	Discover	V	Visa
ER	enRoute		

The Best of Washington

Planning a trip to Washington involves making lots of decisions, so we've tried to give you some direction. We've traveled the state extensively and have chosen what we feel is the very best that Washington has to offer—the places and experiences you won't want to miss. Most are written up in more detail elsewhere in this book; this chapter will give you an overview and get you started.

1 The Best Natural Attractions

- **The San Juan Islands:** Although overrun with tourists in the summer months and slowly becoming a favorite retirement locale, the San Juan Islands still maintain much of their natural beauty. Forested mountains rise up from the cold waters north of Puget Sound. Bald eagles wheel overhead while orca whales dive for salmon below. See chapter 6.
- **Olympic National Park:** This park contains the only rain forests in the contiguous United States, and they comprise a fascinating ecosystem—living plants stake out almost every square inch of space, from towering Sitka spruce trees to mosses and lush ferns. The park also preserves miles of pristine, fog-shrouded beaches and beautiful alpine and subalpine scenery dotted with lush meadows. Shy Roosevelt elk also populate the park. See chapter 8.
- **The North Cascades National Park Complex:** Actually comprised of one national park and two national recreation areas, this remote and rugged region is among the least explored in the state. Most visitors view the park from the North Cascades Scenic Highway, from which there are stupendous views on clear days. However, this highway is closed by snow for half the year. See chapter 10.
- **Mount Rainier National Park:** With its glaciers and easily accessible alpine meadows, Mount Rainier is Washington's favorite mountain. Sunrise and Paradise are the two best vantage points for viewing the massive bulk of Mount Rainier, and from these locations you'll also find some of the best hiking trails. See chapter 10.
- **Mount St. Helens National Volcanic Monument:** Mount St. Helens is slowly recovering from the 1980 volcanic blast that turned one of the Cascades' most beautiful peaks into a scarred landscape of fallen trees and fields of ash. Several visitor centers

relate the events of the eruption and what has been happening on the mountain since. See chapter 10.

- **Columbia Gorge National Scenic Area:** Carved by ice-age floods that were as much as 1,200 feet deep, the Columbia Gorge is a unique feature of the Northwest landscape. Waterfalls by the dozen cascade from the basalt cliffs on the Oregon side of the Gorge, but the best wide-angle views are from the Washington side, where you'll also find one of the largest monoliths in the world. See chapter 10.

2 The Best Outdoor Activities

- **Sea Kayaking in the San Juan Islands:** Emerald islands, clear water, remote campsites that can only be reached by boat, orca whales, and bald eagles lure sea kayakers to the San Juan Islands. You can paddle the islands on your own (if you're experienced) or go out with a guide for a few hours or a few days. See chapter 6.
- **Hiking the Olympic Coast:** Within the contiguous United States, there are very few miles of wilderness coastline left. Among the longest, and most spectacular, are those of Olympic National Park along the west side of the Olympic Peninsula. Whether you just want to do a good long day hike, or spend several days backpacking along the beach, you've got several options along this coast. See chapter 8.
- **Cross-Country Skiing in the Methow Valley:** This valley on the east side of Washington's North Cascades has more than 105 miles of immaculately groomed trails, making it one of the premier cross-country ski destinations in the country. Skiers can ski from one lodge to the next down the valley, or use one of the luxurious lodges as a base for doing day skis. See chapter 10.
- **Hiking on Mount Rainier:** Fed by huge amounts of melting snow each summer, the wildflowers of the alpine meadows on the flanks of Mount Rainier burst into bloom each year in July. Through these hillsides of color meander miles of hiking trails that are among the most memorable in the state. Sure you'll encounter crowds, but the wildflower displays with Mount Rainier for a backdrop, far outweigh the inconvenience of dealing with hordes of other hikers. See chapter 10.
- **Climbing Mount St. Helens:** Though it isn't the highest peak in the Washington Cascades, Mount St. Helens is certainly the most interesting mountain to climb (you'll need a permit and numbers of climbers are limited). You don't need any technical climbing skills for this one, just plenty of stamina and a tolerance for hiking in dusty conditions; you'll likely be hiking in volcanic ash. See chapter 10.
- **Boardsailing at Hood River:** Winds that rage through the Columbia Gorge whip up whitecapped standing waves and have turned this area into the boardsailing capital of the United States, attracting boardsailors from around the world. See chapter 10.

3 The Best Beaches

- **Alki Beach (Seattle):** Located in West Seattle, this is the closest Washington comes to a Southern California–style beach scene. There's a sandy beach; a paved path crowded with in-line skaters, walkers, and cyclists; and lots of cheap restaurants and places to buy sunglasses across the street that parallels the beach. See chapter 5.
- **Obstruction Pass State Park (Orcas Island):** Set at the end of a half-mile-long trail through the woods, this tiny cove is barely big enough for a dozen sea

kayakers to beach their boats on, but therein lies this beach's charm. This is the quintessential little San Juan Islands cove beach, and you don't have to have a boat to get to it. See chapter 6.

- **Deception Pass State Park Beaches (Whidbey Island):** There's a reason this is the most popular state park in Washington—the many miles of beach, spread out on two sides of Deception Pass, are among the prettiest in the Puget Sound area. See chapter 6.
- **Dungeness Spit (Dungeness):** With 6 miles of windswept sand stretching out to a lighthouse in the Strait of Juan de Fuca, Dungeness is a hikers' beach, and the reward for hiking several miles out this narrow strip of sand is the chance to see some of the area's resident harbor seals. See chapter 8.
- **Rialto Beach (Olympic National Park outside Forks):** Located on the north side of the Quillayute River, this beach is the southern terminus of a 29-mile-long stretch of wilderness beach. However, most visitors simply walk a mile up the beach to Hole in the Wall, a huge monolith through which the ocean's waves have bored a tunnel. See chapter 8.
- **Third Beach (Olympic National Park outside Forks):** It's difficult to pick the best beach in the national park, since they are almost all so ruggedly beautiful, but Third Beach, at the end of a 1 1/2-mile trail, is one of our personal favorites. Here you can listen to the calls of the eagles and gulls and contemplate the sheer vastness of the Pacific. See chapter 8.

4 The Best Hikes

- **Trails Out of Hurricane Ridge:** Hurricane Ridge is the most easily accessible alpine region of Olympic National Park, and from here, and nearby Obstruction Peak, there are several possible hikes of varying durations that will give you a glimpse of a superb part of the Olympic wilderness. See chapter 8.
- **Hall of Mosses Trail/Hoh River Trail (Hoh River Valley):** Whether you're only up for a short walk in the woods or want to do a multiday backpacking trip, this is the best place to experience the Olympic Peninsula's famed rain forest. Just don't forget your rain gear. See chapter 8.
- **Cascade Pass Trail:** This is the single most popular and rewarding hike in North Cascades National Park. Before you even start hiking there are stupendous vistas of jagged granite peaks all around, and as you climb up to the pass, the views just get better. The energetic can continue up to the foot of a glacier. See chapter 10.
- **The Maple Pass Loop Trail:** You simply won't find a more rewarding hike anywhere along the North Cascades Scenic Highway than this one. The trail climbs nearly 2,000 feet from Rainy Pass to a ridge with an astounding view of seemingly all the mountains in Washington. See chapter 10.
- **Trails out of Sunrise:** The Sunrise area, on the northeast flanks of Washington's Mount Rainier, offers fabulous unobstructed views of both the mountain and Emmons Glacier, the largest glacier in the contiguous 48 states. From Sunrise more than a dozen trails of different lengths head off to viewpoints and lakes. Take your pick. See chapter 10.
- **The Beacon Rock Trail (Columbia Gorge West of Stevenson):** Although this hike is less than 2 miles long, it makes up for its short length with its steep pitch. In fact much of the trail is on metal stairs bolted to the shear cliff face of Beacon Rock, a massive monolith that rivals the Rock of Gibraltar in size. The view from the top is superb. See chapter 10.

5　The Best Scenic Drives

- **Chuckanut Drive:** This road winds south from Bellingham through the Chuckanut Mountains, which rise straight up from the waters of Chuckanut and Samish bays. Across the water lie the San Juan Islands, and the sunsets are spectacular. Larrabee State Park provides an opportunity to get out of your car and walk down to a pretty little beach. See chapter 6.
- **The North Cascades Scenic Highway:** Passing through the most rugged and spectacular mountains in the Northwest, this highway was not opened until 1972 because of the difficulty of building any sort of road through Washington's glacier-carved North Cascades. Even now it is closed for half of every year due to heavy snows and avalanches. See chapter 10.
- **The Columbia River Highway:** Wash. 14 parallels the Columbia River from Vancouver, Washington, eastward through the Columbia Gorge and along its length provides some of the most awe-inspiring vistas in the Northwest. Across the river, in Oregon, can be seen not only the south side of the Gorge, with its many waterfalls, but also the snow-clad summit of Mount Hood. See chapter 10.
- **The Palouse:** This wheat-farming region in southeastern Washington is a convoluted landscape of steep hills and narrow valleys, and a meandering drive through the region is a trip into another time. Small towns and boldly striped hillsides make this the most fascinating farm country in the state. See chapter 11.
- **Soap Lake to the Grand Coulee Dam:** Although today the landscape of central Washington is that of a desert, vast floodwaters once poured across this landscape. Today a drive up the Grand Coulee provides a glimpse into one of the most fascinating events in Northwest geologic history. Canyons, mineral lakes, caves, and a huge dry waterfall provide the roadside distractions. See chapter 11.

6　The Best Bed-and-Breakfast Inns

- **Gaslight Inn** (Seattle; ☎ 206/325-3654): Beautifully decorated with lots of original Stickley furniture, this inn consists of two houses in the Capitol Hill neighborhood. One house is done in a more contemporary style if you don't happen to be a fan of Arts-and-Crafts style. There's also a swimming pool. See chapter 5.
- **Chestnut Hill Inn** (Orcas Island; ☎ 360/376-5157): Tucked between forest and pastures in a secluded corner of Orcas Island, this country retreat has rapidly become known as one of the best B&Bs in the San Juan Islands. Each of the rooms has its own fireplace, as well as a canopy bed, it's obvious that this inn is all about romantic getaways. See chapter 6.
- **Spring Bay Inn** (Orcas Island; ☎ 360/376-5531): Not only is this secluded waterfront inn a luxurious island retreat, but a stay here includes not only a bed-and-breakfast, but brunch and a daily sea kayak excursion as well. In-room fireplaces and a hot tub right on the beach add a touch of romance. See chapter 6.
- **The Inn at Swifts Bay** (Lopez Island; ☎ 360/468-3636): Though the superb breakfasts here alone would be enough to qualify this place as one of the best B&Bs in the state, the secluded setting on laid-back Lopez Island and the large suites make this a superb getaway spot. See chapter 6.
- **The Wild Iris** (La Conner; ☎ 800/477-1400 or 360/466-1400): Although with 20 rooms, this inn is large for a B&B, the guest rooms are luxurious and romantic, and out the back door of the inn is a dahlia farm. Most rooms have whirlpool tubs. See chapter 6.

- **Manor Farm Inn** (Poulsbo; ☎ 360/779-4628): With all the luxuries of a manor house and the quaintness of a farm, this B&B between Scandinavian Poulsbo and the Hood Canal Bridge offers the best of both worlds to anyone seeking a romantic getaway. See chapter 7.
- **Ann Starrett Mansion** (Port Townsend; ☎ 800/321-0644 or 360/385-3205): This is the premier Victorian B&B in the Northwest. The outrageously ornate Queen Anne–style mansion is packed to the rafters with antiques, and staying here is a bit like being in a museum. See chapter 8.
- **Domaine Madeleine** (Port Angeles; ☎ 360/457-4174): Situated on a bluff overlooking the Strait of Juan de Fuca, this inn is perfect both for exploring Olympic National Park and for romantic getaways. Most guest rooms have fireplaces, whirlpool tubs, and VCRs. See chapter 8.
- **Abendblume Inn** (Leavenworth; ☎ 800/669-7634 or 509/548-4059): Of all the many alpine chalet accommodations in Leavenworth, this is the most luxurious. The attention to detail shown in the construction of this chalet makes the inn an especially enjoyable place to spend a romantic weekend. See chapter 10.
- **Run of the River Bed & Breakfast** (Leavenworth; ☎ 800/288-6491 or 509/548-7171): Set amid beautiful rock gardens on a side channel of the Wenatchee River, this rustic yet contemporary log inn is as tranquil a place to stay as you'll find in the region. The innkeepers are extremely helpful and eager to share their love of the area with guests. See chapter 10.

7 The Best Mountain Lodges/Resorts/Retreats

- **Lake Crescent Lodge** (Olympic National Park west of Port Angeles; ☎ 360/928-3211): Set on the shore of Lake Crescent, a landlocked fjord, in Olympic National Park, is the best base for exploring the north side of the park. The lodge has simple rooms in the old main lodge building and larger though less memorable rooms in various newer buildings around the property. See chapter 8.
- **Lake Quinault Lodge** (Lake Quinault; ☎ 800/562-6672 or 360/288-2900): This gracefully aging lodge on the shore of Lake Quinault has the most character of any of the lodges scattered around the perimeter of Olympic National Park. It's something of a cross between mountain lodge and a classic lake resort. See chater 8.
- **Sun Mountain Lodge** (Winthrop ☎ 800/572-0493 or 509/996-2211): Perched atop a mountain and overlooking the remote Methow Valley, this is Washington's premier mountain resort. Luxurious and rustic at the same time, the lodge is a base for cross-country skiing in winter and hiking and mountain biking in summer. See chapter 10.
- **Freestone Inn** (Mazama; ☎ 800/639-3809 or 509/996-3906): This impressive log lodge beside a small trout lake at the west end of the Winthrop Valley is not as extensive a place as nearby Sun Mountain Lodge (there are, however, big plans for the future), but the guest rooms here are among the most luxurious in the state. See chapter 10.
- **Mountain Home Lodge** (Leavenworth; ☎ 800/414-2378 or 509/548-7077): Set in the middle of a large pasture high on the slopes above the town of Leavenworth, this lodge enjoys a breathtaking view of the Stuart Range, and in winter is only accessible by snow cat (complimentary transport provided by the lodge). See chapter 10.
- **Sleeping Lady** (Leavenworth; ☎ 800/574-2123 or 509/548-6344): Although primarily a conference resort, this place on the outskirts of Bavarian Leavenworth

is far too pleasant to be reserved for those in town for business. With the feel of an upscale summer camp, the lodge is tucked amid granite boulders and ponderosa pines. See chapter 10.

- **Salish Lodge & Spa** (North Bend; ☎ **800/826-6124**, 800/2SALISH, or 425/888-2556): Perched on the brink of Snoqualmie Falls near the town of North Bend, this elegant country lodge is a favorite weekend getaway for Seattleites who now come to be pampered at the spa as much as to enjoy the nearby farm country, mountain trails, and ski slopes. See chapter 10.
- **Paradise Inn** (Mt. Rainier National Park; ☎ **360/569-2275**): Perched high on the slopes of Washington's Mount Rainier, this classic mountain lodge was built in 1917, and though it's a bit faded from hard use, it's always packed throughout its short May to October season. You just can't beat the location. See chapter 10.
- **Skamania Lodge** (Stevenson; ☎ **800/221-7117** or 509/427-7700): Set amid the grandeur of the Columbia Gorge, this modern mountain resort makes the ideal base for exploring the Gorge. The resort's golf course has a very distracting view of the Oregon side of the Columbia Gorge. See chapter 10.
- **Wellspring** (Ashford; ☎ **360/569-2514**): A little bit funky, a little bit fun, this casual spa retreat just outside Mount Rainier National Park consists of several cabins, including a few modern log cabins. Wood-fired hot tubs and a sauna make this a very relaxing place to return to after a day of hiking or cross-country skiing. See chapter 10.

8 The Best Waterfront/Beach Resorts & Lodges

- **The Woodmark Hotel on Lake Washington** (Kirkland; ☎ **800/822-3700** or 425/822-3700): Set on spacious grounds on the eastern shore of Lake Washington, this luxurious hotel is the Seattle area's finest waterfront hotel and has a very resortlike feel. See chapter 5.
- **Friday Harbor House** (Friday Harbor; ☎ **360/378-8455**): OK, so this one isn't right on the water. Still, it's the most luxurious accommodation on San Juan Island, and the guest rooms have views of the water and distant island peaks. See chapter 6.
- **Rosario Resort** (Orcas Island; ☎ **800/562-8820** or 360/376-2222): With new owners and a complete renovation of the guest rooms and main lodge, this resort is once again living up to its position as the premier San Juan Islands resort. See chapter 6.
- **The La Conner Channel Lodge** (La Conner; ☎ **360/466-1500**): Set on the shore of the Swinomish Channel, this inn is steeped in Northwest styling. River rocks and weathered wood siding lend an air of age to the exterior, which is brightened by lovely perennial gardens. In the guest rooms, balconies, fireplaces, fir accents, and slate floors yield an unexpected sophistication. See chapter 6.
- **The Inn at Langley** (Whidbey Island; ☎ **360/221-3033**): The setting alone, overlooking the Saratoga Passage, would be enough to rank this place firmly among the best small inns in the region. However, Japanese-influenced styling, soaking tubs with water views, and fireplaces all add up to uncommon luxuries at this romantic retreat. See chapter 6.
- **The Inn at Semiahmoo** (Blaine; ☎ **800/770-7992** or 360/371-2000): Located on a spit of land looking across the water to Canada, this is one of Washington's top two golf resorts. It also happens to be on a long stretch of beach, which makes this a great place to get away from it all whether you want to play golf or tennis or just walk on the beach. See chapter 6.

- **The Captain Whidbey Inn** (Whidbey Island; ☎ **800/366-4097** or 360/ 678-4097): This unusual inn was built in 1907 of local madrona-tree logs, which give it a thoroughly unique appearance. The island's seafaring history is evoked throughout the inn, and the seat in front of the lobby's beach-stone fireplace is a wonderful spot to while away a gray afternoon. See chapter 6.
- **Inn at Ludlow Bay** (Port Ludlow; ☎ **360/437-0411**): Located a few miles south of Port Townsend, this small, luxury inn offers all the best aspects of the San Juan Islands without the hassles of the ferries. A superb restaurant and an adjacent golf course keep guests contented. See chapter 8.
- **Kalaloch Lodge** (Kalaloch; ☎ **360/962-2271**): Comprised primarily of bluff-top cabins overlooking a wild and windswept beach, this is Olympic National Park's only oceanfront lodge. As such it is extremely popular See chapter 8.
- **Ocean Crest Resort** (Moclips; ☎ **800/684-VIEW** or 360/276-4465): Perched high on a forested bluff above the crashing waves of the Pacific Ocean, this casual resort enjoys the most spectacular setting of any lodging on the Washington coast. There's also an excellent restaurant on the premises. See chapter 9.

9 The Best Seattle Restaurants

- **Canlis** (☎ **206/283-3313**): For decades this has been *the* special occasion restaurant in Seattle. Set high on Queen Anne Hill overlooking Lake Union, the restaurant recently underwent a major make-over to give it a more contemporary appeal. See chapter 5.
- **Chez Shea** (☎ **206/467-9990**): Tucked away in a secluded corner of Pike Place Market, this romantic little restaurant makes superb use of all the very freshest ingredients from the market. If the fixed-price dinners are out of your price range, Chez's Lounge offers much more affordable dining in the same atmosphere. See chapter 5.
- **Etta's Seafood** (☎ **206/443-6000**): Chef Tom Douglas has for years been one of Seattle's restaurant wizards, and while it's difficult to choose between his three downtown restaurants, Etta's, which is located in the Pike Place Market area and specializes in seafood, is a pretty good bet. It was in this same spot (then called Cafe Sport) that Douglas first made a name for himself years ago. See chapter 5.
- **Fuller's** (Seattle; ☎ **206/447-5544**): This elegant and refined restaurant in the Sheraton Seattle Hotel has managed to maintain its enviable reputation for many years now, despite changes in chefs. Dishes are beautifully presented and draw on the bounty of the Northwest for their inspiration. See chapter 5.
- **The Georgian** (☎ **206/621-1700**): You simply will not find a more rarefied atmosphere in any Seattle restaurant. Having dinner at The Georgian is a bit like dining in a palace, with sumptuous meals and a pianist performing on a grand piano. are See chapter 5.
- **Il Terrazzo Carmine** (☎ **206/467-7797**): Tucked in the back of an office building in the Pioneer Square area, this upscale Italian restaurant attracts a very well-heeled clientele. While contemporary Italian restaurants have sprung up on seemingly every other street corner in Seattle in recent years, none serve food like this. See chapter 5.
- **Palisade** (☎ **206/285-1000**): While there are lots of waterfront restaurants around Seattle these days, few come even remotely close to matching Palisade's lush setting. A saltwater stream flows through the middle of the dining room and a curving wall of glass takes in plenty of waterfront views. See chapter 5.

- **Rover's** (☎ 206/325-7442): This little cottage restaurant in an unassuming neighborhood east of downtown Seattle is a stage for the French-Northwest culinary fusions of chef Thierry Rautureau. Every course here surprises with flavors both subtle and bold. See chapter 5.
- **Virazon** (☎ 206/233-0123): Located near Pike Place Market, this upmarket French restaurant foregoes the simpler flavors of nouvelle French for more traditional fare, including truffles, foie gras, and frog legs. This is definitely not the sort of place for dilettantes in the world of French cuisine. See chapter 5.
- **Wild Ginger** (☎ 206/623-4450): Wild Ginger pioneered Asian-influenced cuisine here in Seattle quite a few years back and its satay bar is still one of the most fun and authentic in town. While the flavors of Asia are beginning to dominate in the kitchens of fine restaurants all over town, this attractive restaurant near Pike Place Market is still one of the best. See chapter 5.

10 The Best Restaurants Outside Seattle

- **The Place by the Ferry** (San Juan Island; ☎ 360/378-8707): In a small waterfront building beside the ferry landing in Friday Harbor, you'll find one of the finest restaurants in the San Juan Islands. Contemporary cuisine is served amid contemporary art, but the view of the ferries coming and going keeps most diners distracted. See chapter 6.
- **Christina's** (Orcas Island; ☎ 360/376-4904): Located on the second floor of an old waterfront building in the village of Eastsound, this is Orcas Island's long-time favorite restaurant. In summer, dinner on the deck is an experience not to be forgotten. See chapter 6.
- **Bay Café** (Lopez Island; ☎ 360/468-3700): Small and casual, this cafe on quiet Lopez Island has become a local institution that sums up the Lopez experience. Fresh seafood and local wines combine for memorable meals. See chapter 6.
- **Inn at Langley** (Langley; ☎ 360/221-3033): This quintessentially northwestern inn on Whidbey Island is one of the state's most luxurious accommodations and also serves, on weekends only, some of the best multicourse gourmet dinners in Washington. Make reservations early. See chapter 6.
- **Inn at Ludlow Bay** (Port Ludlow; ☎ 360/437-0411): Operated by the same company that runs the Inn at Langley, this equally elegant little inn opts for a more New England style, though the menu in the dining room is strictly Northwest gourmet. See chapter 8.
- **The Ark** (Nahcotta; ☎ 360/665-4133): Oyster lovers take note, this restaurant on the Long Beach Peninsula offers and all-you-can-eat oyster dinner. Garlic lovers rejoice, this place revels in its use of the stinking rose. See chapter 9.
- **Sun Mountain Lodge** (Winthrop ☎ 800/572-0493 or 509/996-2211): If you get vertigo easily, you may want to forego meals at this precipitously perched dining room overlooking the Methow Valley. However, if you relish creative cooking, seek out a table away from the window. See chapter 10.
- **The Herbfarm** (Fall City; ☎ 206/784-2222): This restaurant, located east of Seattle near Issaquah, in the Cascade foothills, started out as a roadside herb farm but has since grown to become the most highly acclaimed (and most expensive) restaurant in the state. See chapter 10.
- **Patit Creek Restaurant** (Dayton; ☎ 509/382-2625): The small town of Dayton seems an unlikely place for one of the state's best restaurants, but the reliable French-inspired fare served at this unpretentious place draws diners from miles around. See chapter 11.

- **Patsy Clark's Mansion** (Spokane; ☎ 509/838-8300): Housed in one of the most magnificent Victorian mansions in Spokane, this elegant restaurant has long been the favored dining establishment of the city's wealthiest residents. Classic continental fare dominates the menu. See chapter 11.

11 The Best Brew Pubs

- **Elysian Brewing Company** (Seattle; ☎ 206/860-1920): Located on Capitol Hill, this locals' brew pub is a big space with an industrial, warehouse feel. Elysian has one of the smallest outputs of any brew pub in town, and does exceptional strong ales and stouts. See chapter 5.
- **The Pike Pub & Brewery** (Seattle; ☎ 206/622-6044): While Seattle is home to plenty of big breweries that can no longer be called "micro," there are still some small places where real craft ales are still produced. Here at this Pike Place Market brew pub, cask-conditioned ales are a specialty. See chapter 5.
- **Grant's Brewery Pub** (Yakima; ☎ 509/575-2922): Located in a restored railroad depot in downtown Yakima, which is hops country as well as wine country, Grant's claims to be the first brew pub in the country pub and specializes in Scottish-style ales. See chapter 11.
- **Winthrop Brewing Company** (Winthrop; ☎ 509/996-3183): Winthrop, which sports false-fronted cow town facades just wouldn't be complete without a classic Western saloon, and in this case, it's the Winthrop Brewing Company that fits the bill. Wedged into a triangular space on the town's main street, this brew pub is the après–cross-country ski spot. See chapter 10.
- **The Leavenworth Brewery Restaurant & Pub** (Leavenworth; ☎ 509/548-4545): How could a Bavarian theme town not have a decent beer hall? Luckily not all the beers here are strictly Munich-style lagers. Unusual seasonal ales are anxiously anticipated by locals and happily enjoyed by tourists. See chapter 10.

12 The Best Museums

- **Seattle Art Museum**: Although the temporary exhibits are usually fascinating, an outstanding collection of Northwest Coast Native American art and artifacts is the highlight of this museum. The African art exhibit is equally impressive, and the 20th-century art collection includes a respectable exhibition of works by regional artists. See chapter 5.
- **Museum of Flight** (Seattle): As the home of Boeing, Seattle has played a historic role in the history of flight, and this museum reflects this heritage with its diverse collection of planes. The location, adjacent to Boeing Field, allows visitors to watch planes taking off and landing as they study the museum displays. See chapter 5.
- **Museum of Northwest Art** (La Conner): The historic Skagit Valley fishing town of La Conner began attracting artists in the middle part of this century and so is a fitting location for a museum dedicated to the work of Northwest artists. The large, open museum changes its exhibits regularly. See chapter 6.
- **Washington State History Museum** (Tacoma): It's big. It's high tech. It's fun. As the archive of state history, this museum works hard to entertain visitors while exploring the state's past. There are lots of interactive exhibits as well as displays on little known and often controversial aspects of Washington history. See chapter 7.
- **Makah Cultural and Resource Center** (Neah Bay): This museum is located on the extreme northwest tip of the Olympic Peninsula and contains artifacts

recovered from a nearby archaeological site. In the museum are totem poles, dugout canoes, and even a mock-up of a native longhouse complete with smoked salmon hanging from the rafters. See chapter 8.

- **Columbia Gorge Interpretive Center** (Stevenson): With historical photos, quotations from pioneers, and exhibits on various aspects of historic and prehistoric life in the Columbia Gorge, this museum serves as a valuable introduction to one of the Northwest's scenic wonders. See chapter 10.

13 The Best Family Attractions

- **Seattle Center** (Seattle): As the site of the Space Needle, Seattle Center is one of the city's required stops. However, families will also find here a children's museum, a children's theater, amusement park rides, and an arcade area. See chapter 5.
- **Enchanted Village and Wild Waves** (Federal Way): Kids of all ages have a blast at this combination water park and children's amusement park south of Seattle. There are water slides as well as roller coasters. See chapter 5.
- **Whale-Watching Tours in the San Juan Islands:** Sure you can see orca whales perform at marine parks, but in the San Juan Islands during the summer, you can see genuinely free Willies, lots of them during whale-watching tours that usually also include sightings of minke whales, harbor seals, and bald eagles. See chapter 6.
- **Point Defiance Park** (Tacoma): This gigantic city park at the north end of Tacoma packs in more fun stuff for kids to see and do than a family could ever hope to do in one day. There's a zoo, a storybook land, a reconstructed historic trading fort, and an old-time logging camp. See chapter 7.
- **Long Beach:** With minigolf, horseback riding, miles of wide beaches, and perfect winds for kite flying, this beach community on the southern Washington coast is the state's best family beach. See chapter 9.

14 The Best Small Towns

- **La Conner:** Surrounded by tulip fields and filled with art galleries and interesting shops, this former fishing and farming town gets jammed on weekends, but if you stop by on a weekday or in the off-season, you can easily be seduced by its vintage charm. See chapter 6.
- **Langley:** Located near the south end of Whidbey Island, this former fishing village has taken on the trappings of an upscale arts community in recent years. There are several excellent art galleries, upscale fashion boutiques, and several good restaurants. All this right on the shore of Saratoga Passage. Some buildings even rise straight out of the water. See chapter 6.
- **Port Townsend:** Late in the 19th century, this town on the Olympic Peninsula was poised to become the region's most important city, but when the railroad passed it by, it slipped into obscurity. Today Port Townsend is obscure no more. With block after block of Victorian homes and a waterfront setting, it has become a favorite weekend destination for Seattleites. See chapter 8.
- **Leavenworth:** Lederhosen? Dirndls? Polka parties? Sounds like someplace to steer clear of, but actually, the Bavarian theme town of Leavenworth works. Maybe there are too many cuckoo clocks and nutcrackers for sale, but those mountains on the edge of town are the genuine article. See chapter 10.
- **Winthrop:** If you saw an 1890s photo of Winthrop, you might think the town had been caught in a time warp. It just doesn't look much different then it did back then. See chapter 10.

Getting to Know Washington

While this state in the upper left-hand corner of the country shares a name with the nation's capital and itself has a state capitol that looks like the one back east, there the similarities end. This Washington, despite not having the long history, politics, and monumental buildings, is infinitely more varied.

In fact, it could have served as a model for the song "America the Beautiful." Out in the eastern high desert country, there are beautiful spacious skies as big as Montana's. In the Cascades, it has mountains that turn majestically purple at sunset. In the Palouse country of the southeastern corner of the state, amber waves of grain stripe the steep hillsides. In the Yakima, Wentachee, and Chelan valleys, the fruited plains produce the world's most familiar apples. Out on the Pacific Coast, there are beaches white with foam, and with an inland sea across the Olympic Peninsula from the Pacific, the sun in Washington shines from sea to shining sea. From its mountains to its valleys, Washington is beautiful country.

But the diversity of this state goes far beyond mere song lyrics. There's an island archipelago as beautiful as the coast of Maine (though without the harsh winters). There are beaches as long and sandy as those of North Carolina's Outer Banks (though the waters are too cold for swimming). There are granite mountains as rugged as the Sierra Nevada (though not as crowded with hikers). There are desert canyons like those of the Southwest (though not nearly as hot). There are vineyard-covered hillsides like those of the Napa Valley (though without the crowds). There's even a bay-front city with dauntingly steep streets (no cable cars, though).

This, then, is a glimpse of the complex landscape of Washington state. To learn more about this state, read on. Within this chapter you'll find information that will help you plan your trip to this, the other, Washington.

1 The Natural Environment

The state of Washington encompasses a vast area that contains within its boundaries an amazing diversity of natural environments—not only lush forests, but glacier-covered peaks, alpine meadows, grasslands, sagebrush-covered hills, and even a high desert. Together these diverse environments support a surprisingly wide variety of natural life that has evolved to fill the many niches created by Northwest geography.

While Washington's Pacific Ocean coastline stretches for only about 150 miles, from the Columbia River to the tip of the Olympic Peninsula, inland waters including Puget Sound, the Strait of Juan de Fuca, and the myriad of channels through the San Juan Islands add hundreds of miles of coastline. Consequently, this extensive shoreline provides a habitat not only for large populations of seabirds such as cormorants, tufted puffins, and pigeon guillemots, but also several species of marine mammals. The largest and most impressive marine mammals to frequent these shores are the more than 20,000 Pacific gray whales that pass by Washington each year between December and April as they make their annual migration south to their breeding grounds off Baja California. These whales can often be seen from shore at various points along the coast, and numerous whale-watching tours operate out of Grays Harbor. More frequently spotted, however, are harbor seals and Steller and California sea lions, which are frequently seen lounging on rocks, especially in the San Juan Islands. Off the remote beaches of the Olympic Peninsula, there's a small population of sea otters, and river otters are frequently sighted in the San Juan Islands and Puget Sound.

Washington's Pacific coastline is roughly divided into a wild and rugged northern coast, at the base of the Olympic Mountains, and a more developed southern coast characterized by long sandy beaches backed by low dunes. However, even more than the mountains, rain gives the Pacific coastline its distinctive character. As moist winds from the Pacific Ocean rise up and over the coastal mountain ranges, they drop their moisture as rain and snow. In the northwest corner of Washington state, on the western slopes of the Olympic Mountains, rain is measured not by the inch but by the foot; and annual rainfall can exceed 12 feet! This tremendous amount of rain has produced the country's only temperate rain forests and some of the largest trees on earth. Although the Sitka spruce is the most characteristic tree of these rain forests, it is the Douglas-fir, common throughout the Northwest and second only to the coast redwood of northern California in overall size, that's the most impressive, sometimes reaching 300 feet in height. Other common trees of the rain forest include western hemlocks, Alaska cedars, western red cedars, and big-leaf maples. These latter trees are often draped with thick mats of moss.

More than a century of intensive logging has, however, left the region's forests of centuries-old trees shrunken to remnant groves scattered in often remote and inaccessible areas. How much exactly is still left is a matter of hot debate between the timber industry and environmentalists, and the battle to save the remaining old-growth forests continues, with both sides claiming victories and losses with each passing year. Among this region's most celebrated and controversial wild residents is the northern spotted owl, which, because of its large requirements for undisturbed old-growth forest and its listing as a federally threatened species, brought logging of old-growth forests to a virtual halt in the early 1990s. Today concern is also focused on the marbled murrelet, a small bird that feeds on the open ocean but nests exclusively in old-growth forests.

The Olympic Mountains, which rise to 7,965 feet at the top of Mount Olympus, are a rugged range capped with alpine meadows, glaciers, and ice fields. Although black-tailed deer are the most common large mammals of these mountains, there is also a population of mountain goats in Olympic National Park. However, these goats are not native to this area and attempts are being made to remove them because of the damage they cause the fragile high-elevation meadows. This removal program has proven controversial and expensive. The Roosevelt elk, the largest commonly

Washington

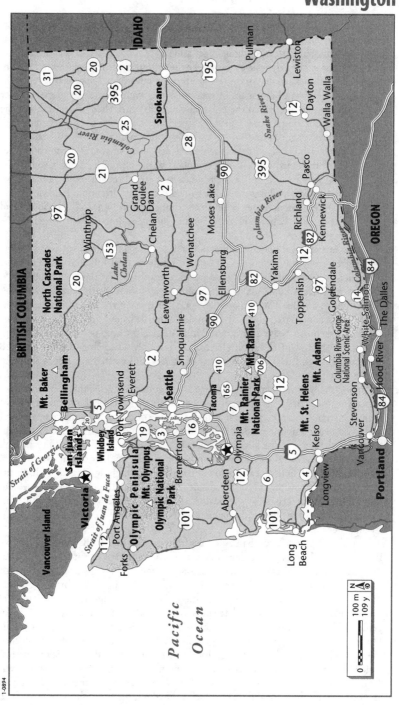

encountered land mammal in the state, can be found here and throughout the western regions of the state. It was to protect these animals that the land now known as Olympic National Park was originally set aside.

To the east of the Olympic Peninsula lie the lowlands of the Puget Sound region. Because of the mild climate of this area, this is the most densely populated region of the state. Puget Sound is a maze of waterways that were formed by glacial activity during the last Ice Age, when the polar ice sheets that stretched southward into the region carved out long narrow valleys that were later flooded as the glaciers retreated.

Just north of Puget Sound, in the waters surrounding the San Juan Islands, live some of the Northwest's most celebrated residents—orca whales, also known as killer whales. Once maligned, these largest members of the porpoise family have become a symbol of the region. With the plight of captive orcas brought to the public attention by the Free Willy films, orcas have gained even more attention. Bald eagles also flock to this area. Though they can be seen throughout the year in Puget Sound and throughout the San Juan Islands, they gather in large numbers each winter on the nearby Skagit River.

To the east of Puget Sound rise the mountains of the 700-mile-long Cascade range, which stretches from northern California to southern British Columbia. The most prominent features of the Cascades are its volcanic peaks: Baker, Glacier Peak, Rainier, St. Helens, and Adams. The eruption of Mount St. Helens on May 18, 1980, vividly reminded Washingtonians that this is still a volcanically active region.

The same rainfall that gives the Olympic Peninsula its rain forests leaves the Cascades with frequent heavy snows and dozens of glaciers, among which are the largest glacier, the lowest elevation glacier, and the only advancing glacier in the 48 contiguous states. In 1972, Mount Rainier set a record when 93$^1/_2$ feet of snow fell in one winter.

Among the wild residents of the Cascades are mountain goats that can sometimes be seen in the North Cascades, along the shores of Lake Chelan, and in Mount Rainier National Park. Picas and marmots are some of the high country's smaller but more visible and audible residents. The former is a mouse-sized relative of the rabbit, while the latter is the largest member of the squirrel family. Both live in high meadows and rocky slopes and both can be recognized by their distinctive whistles. The pica's is small and squeaky, while the marmot's is high, loud, and shrill. In the remote northern section of North Cascades National Park there are even wolves and grizzly bears, though these large predators are almost never encountered by humans. Cougars also roam the forests throughout the Northwest and are as elusive as the grizzly and the wolf.

East of the Cascades, less than 200 miles from the rain forest valleys of the Olympic Peninsula, the landscape becomes a desert. The Columbia Plateau region is a vast, dry, high desert region that stretches eastward to the Rockies, a side range of which actually reaches into the northeast corner of the state. The Columbia Plateau was formed by sheets of lava flowing over the land and covering more than 100,000 square miles. Through this desolate landscape flows the Columbia River, which, together with its tributary the Snake, forms the second-largest river drainage in the United States. During the last Ice Age, roughly 15,000 years ago, a glacier blocked the flow of the Columbia, forming a huge lake behind its ice dam. This vast prehistoric lake repeatedly burst its ice dam, sending massive and devastating walls of water flooding down the Columbia. These floodwaters were sometimes 1,000 feet high and carried with them ice and rocks, which scoured out the Columbia Gorge in much the same way that glaciers scoured out the Yosemite Valley in California. In both places the results were similar—tall, narrow waterfalls. These same floodwaters also scoured the landscape of eastern Washington, leaving in their wake abandoned river channels known as coulees and channeled scablands. The most famous of these coulees is Grand Coulee, site of one of the largest dams on earth.

This and the dozens of other dams on the Columbia and Snake rivers have become the focus of one of the region's current environmental battles. Though many of these dams have fish ladders to allow salmon to return upriver to spawn, salmon populations have been steadily dwindling for more than a century. Overfishing for salmon canneries in the late 19th century struck the first major blow to salmon populations, and the large dams, mostly built during the middle part of this century, created further barriers both to returning adults and to young salmon headed downstream to the Pacific. Among the obstacles faced by these young salmon are slower river flow in the reservoirs behind the dams, turbines that kill fish by the thousands, and irrigation canals that often confuse salmon into swimming out of the river and into farm fields. Compounding the problem has been the use of fish hatcheries to supplement wild salmon populations (hatchery fish tend to be less vigorous than wild salmon). A salmon recovery plan adopted to save threatened runs of native salmon has yet to be fully implemented; as farmers, electricity producers, shipping companies, and major users of hydroelectric power continue to fight its requirements, including lowering water levels in reservoirs to speed the downstream migration of young salmon.

2 The Regions in Brief

The state of Washington covers 68,139 square miles—roughly the same area as all of New England. Within this geographically diverse landscape lie an inland sea dotted with hundreds of islands, temperate rain forests where rainfall is measured in feet, a high desert of sagebrush and junipers, several distinct mountain ranges, volcanoes both dormant and extinct, the West's most important river, and of course, hundreds of thousands of acres of coniferous forests (hence the state's nickname—the Evergreen State).

Puget Sound   Puget Sound, a convoluted maze of waterways, is a vast inland sea that stretches for more than 80 miles. Created when glaciers receded at the end of the last ice age, the Sound is characterized by hilly forested terrain. However, because the Sound's protected waters make such good harbors and are so full of fish and shellfish, this area has been the most densely populated region of the state since before the first Europeans sailed into these waters and named it Puget Sound. Today, the eastern shore of the Sound has become one huge Pugetopolis that includes Seattle, Tacoma, Olympia, and dozens of smaller cities and bedroom communities that together form the largest metropolitan area in the state. The western and southernmost reaches of the Sound are much less developed. These rural areas are popular weekend escapes for Seattleites and Tacomans but are much less familiar to visitors from out of state, who, though they might appreciate the Sound and Rainier vistas, tend to overlook this region because of its lack of major attractions.

The San Juan Islands   Lying just to the north of Puget Sound, the San Juan Islands (also called the San Juans) are a lush, mountainous archipelago, home to orca whales, harbor seals, and bald eagles. Of the 175 or so named San Juan Islands, only four are accessible by public ferry, and of these only three have accommodations (the fourth does have a campground). The mild climate, watery vistas, and quiet, rural character of these islands have made the San Juans Washington's favorite summer vacation destination. As such the islands are packed to overflowing throughout the summer and it can be impossible to get a hotel reservation at the last minute. A summer trip to the San Juans definitely requires plenty of advance planning. It also requires a great deal of patience, as waits for ferries can mount into hours. To avoid the crowds, consider visiting in spring or fall, when the weather is often just as good as in the summer. Because the San Juans lie within the rain shadow of the Olympic Mountains, they get far less rain than Seattle (and therein lies much of their appeal for Seattleites).

The Olympic Peninsula Aside from a thin necklace of private land around its perimeter, this huge peninsula, wedged between Puget Sound and the Pacific Ocean, is almost entirely public land. At the heart of the peninsula is Olympic National Park, which encompasses almost the entirety of the Olympic Mountains. Surrounding the park is Olympic National Forest. The western slopes of the Olympic Mountains contain the contiguous United States' only temperate rain forests, where rainfalls of 150 inches per year are common. Over the past 100 years, these forests, and others on the peninsula, have seen some of the most intensive logging in the nation. Rugged remote beaches separated by rocky headlands characterize the Pacific shore of the peninsula, while along the north coast, there are several large towns, including the historic Victorian seaport of Port Townsend. Just remember when planning a vacation out here that you're likely to get rained on even in the summer; be prepared to get wet.

Southwest Washington The southwest corner of the state is, for the most part, a sparsely populated region of huge tree farms. However, along the southern coast, there are long sandy beaches and numerous beach resorts and towns, which, though popular with Portlanders and the residents of Puget Sound, lack a distinctly Northwest character. Inland, up the Columbia River, lies the city of Vancouver (not to be confused with Vancouver, British Columbia), which though rich in regional history, has been overshadowed by Portland, Oregon, directly across the Columbia River.

The Cascade Range Dividing the state roughly into eastern and western regions, the Washington Cascades are actually two very distinct mountain ranges. The North Cascades are jagged, glaciated granite peaks, while the central and southern Washington Cascades are primarily volcanic in origin. Mount St. Helens, which erupted with awe-inspiring force in 1980, is the only one of these volcanoes to be active in recent years, but even Mount Rainier, the highest mountain in the state, is merely dormant and is expected to erupt again some time in the next few hundred years. Within this mountain range are North Cascades National Park, Mount Rainier National Park, Mount St. Helens National Volcanic Monument, the third deepest lake in the country (Lake Chelan), half a dozen ski areas, and a couple of interesting little theme towns. If you're thinking about a summer vacation in these mountains, keep in mind that the snow at higher elevations (where you'll find the beautiful wildflower meadows) often doesn't melt off until well into July.

Eastern Washington While to the west of the Cascade Range all is gray skies and green forests, to the east the sun shines 300 days a year and less than 10 inches of rain falls each year. Consequently, the high desert of eastern Washington is a sparsely populated region of little interest to out-of-state visitors but highly valued by waterlogged residents of western Washington. Irrigation waters from the Columbia River have allowed the region to become an agricultural powerhouse. In the Yakima, Wenatchee, and Chelan valleys, apple orchards produce the bulk of the nation's apple crop, while in the southeast corner of the state lie the rolling Palouse Hills, whose rich soils sustain the most productive wheat fields in the nation. Spokane, close to the Idaho state line, is the region's largest metropolitan area.

3 Washington Today

While there are signs that Seattle's domination of mass-market media hype has begun to wear off, both Seattle and the state continue to attract visitors in unprecedented numbers. To understand the state's popularity, it is only necessary to lift one's eyes. From almost anywhere in the western Washington it's possible to gaze up at forests and mountains or out across sparkling waters. The fact that the tourist season is confined to western Washington's all-too-brief summer months, when Seattle, the San Juan Islands, Mount St. Helens National Volcanic Monument, and the state's three national parks—Mount Rainier, North Cascades, and Olympic—are all at their best, doesn't hurt things either. If you're averse to crowds, however, consider visiting in the spring or fall when you might luck into a sunny week and won't have to deal with high hotel rates and long lines for ferries.

Washingtonians for the most part don't let the weather stand between them and the outdoors. The temptation is too great to head for the hills, the river, the beach, the Sound, or the islands. Consequently, life in Washington's cities tends to revolve as much around parks, gardens, waterfronts, and other outdoor spaces as it does around such traditional urban pastimes as shopping, the performing arts, and dining. And when such green spaces as Seattle's Discovery and Green Lake parks, Tacoma's Point Defiance Park, and Spokane's Riverfront and Minto parks aren't wild enough to satisfy the craving for an outdoor experience, most of the state's population is within an hour or two of a national park, and even closer to a national forest or state park. These parks are where people find tranquillity, where summer festivals are held, where locals take their visiting friends and relatives.

As of 1997, however, it has gotten more expensive to enjoy Washington's mountains. National park entry fees have doubled, user fees were instituted for the first time at Mount St. Helens National Volcanic Monument (where a new visitor center with a head-on view of the volcano's crater opened at Johnston Ridge), and trailhead parking permits were instituted on almost all national forests. However, despite the increased fees, the Washington mountains are still a bargain.

The region's outdoors aesthetic does not, however, preclude a strong support of the arts. The Seattle Opera is one of the finest companies in the country (well known for its stagings of Wagner's Ring series), as is the Seattle Symphony, and both will get a new home in 1998 with the opening of the new Benaroya Hall adjacent to the Seattle Art Museum. In recent years, Seattle has also become a center for live theater. Tacoma, Olympia, and Spokane all have large, modern, and active performing arts centers as well. During the summer months, numerous festivals around the state take music, theater, and dance outdoors. These festivals feature everything from chamber music to polka bands to the grunge sound that first put Seattle on the alternative rock map several years ago.

The visual arts are not overlooked either. In 1997, three Seattle museums—the Henry, the Frye, and the Burke—underwent extensive renovations and expansions. Tacoma's Washington State Historical Museum, now just a few years old, has also made the state's history extremely accessible with its innovative interactive exhibits. Ground was also broken in 1997 for the Music Experience, a museum of rock 'n' roll that was inspired by Seattle resident and Microsoft cofounder Paul Allen's obsession with Jimi Hendrix, who was also a Seattle native. The design of this museum, by avant-garde architect Frank Gehry, promises to give the Space Needle serious competition. Plans are also now on the drawing boards to build a new and much larger Seattle Aquarium.

While the state may not be as popular with Hollywood as it was a few years ago, when *Sleepless in Seattle*, *Northern Exposure*, and *Twin Peaks* were all filmed here, film and television producers continue to head this way to shoot their productions (although competition from British Columbia, where the dollar goes further, has been stiff of late). Even though it isn't actually filmed here, NBC's current hit *Frasier* brings a slice of Seattle life to TV viewers each week and keeps the city in the national eye.

The major league mania that has been sweeping the nation has also descended on Washington. Despite the controversies surrounding private dollars being spent to hold a special statewide stadium election and public tax dollars being spent to construct new stadiums for both the Seattle Seahawks football team and the Seattle Mariners baseball team, most Washingtonians are happy that their teams will be staying put for a while (and nobody is really going to miss the Kingdome). The Seattle Supersonics NBA basketball team also got a new arena recently (without controversies), and women's professional basketball arrived in the form of the Seattle Reign.

Everyone has heard about the Seattle espresso scene that has now spread to most of the rest of the country. Once an urban phenomenon, the demand for rich, strong espresso has reached small towns throughout the state, and travelers exploring even the most remote parts of Washington can usually find an espresso stand parked by the side of the road somewhere nearby. However, high prices for coffee beans may be dampening the state's appetite for espresso.

The demand for only the best has also spread to the realm of malt beverages. Today Washington is one of the leading states in the realm of craft brewing of beers and ales. Small breweries and brew pubs throughout Washington are producing delicious and unique ales that range from light, fruit-flavored wheat beers to hearty barley wines. Not to be left behind, the state's wineries are giving California a run for its money. However, the ascendancy of martinis has given microbreweries cause for concern, and several have cut back production due to a shrinking market.

With the pronounced urban population growth over the past few years, politics has taken a very pronounced urban-rural split, with politicians in rural districts arguing that cities such as Seattle and Olympia are dictating the politics for rural regions that have little in common with the cities. In Whatcom County, home to Bellingham and liberal Western Washington University, there are even secession movements underway that are trying to create new counties from the rural reaches of Whatcom County.

However, despite differences of opinions and politics, Washingtonians share a common interest in the outdoors, and it is this interest that dominates the character of the region. Nowhere else in the country is such a diverse natural beauty so close at hand, even for those who live in the cities. And if winters are long, gray, and rainy, well, you just put on a colorful rain jacket, fill the travel mug with a double tall raspberry latte, and head for the hills, mountains, rivers, or coast regardless.

4 A Look at the Past

Dateline

- **13,000 b.c.** Massive floods, as much as 1,000 feet deep, rage down Columbia River and carve the Columbia Gorge.

continues

EARLY HISTORY   Native Americans inhabiting present-day Washington developed very distinct cultures depending on the food-gathering constraints of their territory. It is estimated that before the arrival of Euro-Americans in the region, there were 125 Northwest tribes speaking 50 languages. However, between the 1780s, when white explorers and traders began frequenting the Northwest coast, and the 1830s, when the first settlers began arriving, the Native American population of the Northwest was reduced to perhaps a tenth of its historic numbers. It was not war that wiped out these people, but diseases such as smallpox, measles, malaria, and influenza. Native Americans had no resistance to these diseases and entire tribes were soon decimated by fast-spreading epidemics.

THE AGE OF EXPLORATION Though a Spanish ship reached what is now southern Oregon in 1542, the Spanish had no interest in the gray and rainy coast. Nor did famed British buccaneer Sir Francis Drake, who in 1579 sailed his ship the *Golden Hind* as far north as the mouth of Oregon's Rogue River. Drake called off his explorations in the face of what he described as "thicke and stinking fogges."

Though the Spanish laid claim to all of North America's west coast, they had little interest in the lands north of Mexico. However, when the Spanish found out that Russian fur traders were establishing themselves in Alaska and along the North Pacific coast, Spain took a new interest in the Northwest. Several Spanish expeditions sailed north from Mexico to reassert the Spanish claim to the region. In 1775, Spanish explorers Bruno de Heceta and Francisco de la Bodega y Quadra charted much of the Northwest coast, and though they found the mouth of the Columbia River, they did not enter it.

Within a few years the Spanish found their claims to the region also being challenged by English traders. Capt. James Cook, on a voyage of discovery that began in 1776, spent time at Nootka Sound on Vancouver Island, where the native peoples were eager to trade furs. Though Cook was killed in Hawaii later in the same voyage, his crew discovered en route back to England that the Chinese would pay astronomical prices for Northwest furs, especially sea otter.

By 1785, the fur trade between the Northwest and China was underway, with the British now asserting a claim to the Pacific Northwest. The Spanish and English teetered on the brink of war, but a compromise was worked out and the Spanish agreed to allow continued English trade in the area.

The negotiations of this settlement took place in 1792 at Nootka Sound (in present-day British Columbia), with Capt. George Vancouver serving as English envoy. Before reaching Nootka Sound,

- **10,000 b.c.** Earliest known human inhabitation of the Northwest.
- **1774** Spanish explorer Juan Perez sails to 54° north latitude; Bruno de Heceta and Francisco de la Bodega y Quadra chart the Northwest coast.
- **1785** James Hanna becomes the first fur trader to ship pelts from the Northwest to China.
- **1805–06** Expedition led by Meriwether Lewis and William Clark crosses the continent and spends the winter at the mouth of the Columbia River.
- **1810** Spokan House is established as a fur-trading post near present-day Spokane.
- **1819** Spain cedes all lands above 42° north latitude.
- **1824** Russia gives up claims to land south of Alaska; Fort Vancouver is founded by Hudson's Bay Company.
- **1833** The Hudson's Bay Company's Fort Nisqually becomes the first nonnative settlement on Puget Sound.
- **1845** Pioneers from Missouri establish New Market, the first town in Washington, at present-day Tumwater.
- **1846** The 49th parallel is established as the boundary between American and British territories in the Northwest.
- **1847** Marcus and Narcissa Whitman and several other residents of their mission are massacred by the Cayuse.
- **1853** Washington becomes a U.S. territory.
- **1859** U.S. and Britain come to the brink of war over a pig killed on San Juan Island; Oregon becomes a state.
- **1883** Northern Pacific Railroad connects Puget

continues

Sound with St. Paul, Minnesota.

- **1889** Washington becomes a state.
- **1897** Klondike gold rush begins, bringing prosperity to Seattle.
- **1916** William Boeing launches his first airplane on the waters of Seattle's Lake Union.
- **1928** Washington's domed capitol building, the tallest domed state capitol in the nation, is completed.
- **1940s** Boeing airplane plants turn out thousands of B-17s and B-29s.
- **1943** In eastern Washington, U.S. government builds top-secret plutonium-manufacturing plant that produces the nuclear material for the bomb dropped on Nagasaki; JapaneseAmericans are relocated to internment camps.
- **1962** Seattle's Century 21 world's fair gives the city its most identifiable structure: the Space Needle.
- **1980** Mount St. Helens erupts violently on May 18.
- **1994** Speaker of the U.S. House of Representatives Tom Foley of Washington voted out of office.
- **1997** In a controversial election funded by Paul Allen, Washingtonians vote to replace Seattle's King-dome. Boeing merges with competitor McDonnell Douglas.

Vancouver spent time exploring and mapping much of the Northwest. Though he passed the Columbia River off as unimportant, he sailed up the Strait of Juan de Fuca and discovered a large inland sea that he named Puget Sound, after one of his lieutenants. Vancouver's negotiations at Nootka failed to establish a firm British claim to the land, but with sea otter populations decimated by several intense years of trading, interest in the Northwest was waning both in England and Spain.

Now a new player entered the Northwest arena of trade and exploration in the person of American trader Robert Gray. Risking a passage through treacherous sandbars, Gray sailed his ship, *Columbia Rediviva,* into the mouth of the long-speculated-upon Great River of the West, which he named Columbia's River after his ship. This discovery established the first American claim to the region.

When news of the Columbia's discovery reached the United States and England, both countries began speculating on a northern water route across North America. Such a route, if it existed, would facilitate trade with the Northwest. In 1793, Scotsman Alexander MacKenzie made the first overland trip across North America north of New Spain. Crossing British Canada on foot, MacKenzie arrived somewhere north of Vancouver Island.

After reading MacKenzie's account of his journey, Thomas Jefferson decided that the United States needed to find a better route overland to the Northwest. To this end he commissioned Meriwether Lewis and William Clark to lead an expedition up the Missouri River in hopes of finding a single easy portage that would lead to the Columbia River. Beginning in 1804, the members of the Lewis and Clark expedition paddled up the Missouri, crossed the Rocky Mountains on foot, and then paddled down the Columbia River to its mouth. A French Canadian trapper and his Native American wife, Sacajawea, were enlisted as interpreters, and it was the presence of Sacajawea that helped the expedition gain acceptance among western tribes. After the very dismal, wet winter of 1805–06 spent at the mouth of the Columbia, the expedition headed back east. Discoveries made by the expedition added greatly to the scientific and geographical knowledge of the continent.

In 1819 the Spanish relinquished all claims north of the present California-Oregon state line, and the Russians gave up their claims to all lands south of Alaska. This left only the British and Americans dickering for control of the Northwest.

SETTLEMENT   Only 6 years after Lewis and Clark spent the winter at the mouth of the Columbia, employees of John Jacob Astor's Pacific Fur Company managed to establish themselves at a site they called Fort Astoria, on the Oregon side of the mouth of the Columbia River. The War of 1812 between the United States and Britain produced no firm decision about possession of the Northwest. The British still dominated the region, but American trade was tolerated.

With the decline of the sea otter population, British fur traders turned to the beaver and headed inland up the Columbia River. For the next 30 years or so, fur-trading companies would be the sole authority in the Northwest. Fur-trading posts (including Spokan House, which was established in 1810 near present-day Spokane) were established throughout the region, though most were on the eastern edge of the territory in the foothills of the Rocky Mountains. The powerful Hudson's Bay Company (HBC) eventually became the single fur-trading company in the Northwest.

In 1824, the HBC established its Northwest headquarters at Fort Vancouver, 100 miles up the Columbia near the mouth of the Willamette River. Between 1824 and 1846, when the 49th parallel was established as the boundary between British and American northwestern lands, Fort Vancouver was the most important settlement in the region.

By the 1830s the future of the Northwest had arrived in the form of American missionaries. The first was Jason Lee, who established his mission in the Willamette Valley near present-day Salem, Oregon. Two years later, in 1836, Marcus and Narcissa Whitman, along with Henry and Eliza Spaulding, made the overland trek to Fort Vancouver, then backtracked into what is now eastern Washington and Idaho, to establish two missions. This journey soon inspired other settlers to make the difficult overland crossing.

In 1840, a slow trickle of American settlers began crossing the continent, a 2,000-mile journey. Their destination was the Oregon country, which had been promoted as a veritable Eden with wide expanses of land just waiting to be claimed. In 1843, Marcus Whitman, after traveling east to plead with his superiors not to shut down his mission, headed back west, leading 900 settlers on the Oregon Trail. Before these settlers arrived, the small population of retired trappers, missionaries, and HBC employees who were living at Fort Vancouver and in nearby Oregon City, had formed a provisional government in anticipation of the land-claim problems that would arise with the influx of settlers to the region.

Oregon City became, in 1844, the first incorporated town west of the Rocky Mountains. This outpost in the wilderness, a gateway to the fertile lands of the Willamette Valley, was the destination of the wagon trains that began traveling the Oregon Trail, each year bringing more and more settlers to the region. As the land in the Willamette Valley was claimed, settlers began fanning out to different regions of the Northwest so that during the late 1840s and early 1850s many new towns, including Seattle and Portland, were founded.

Many wagon trains stopped at the Whitman mission near present-day Walla Walla, and it was one of these groups of pioneers that brought the measles to the region. The Cayuse tribe, many of whom lived at the Whitman mission, had no resistance to the disease, and soon their population was decimated. Whitman and his family seemed immune to the disease. In retribution for Whitman's inability to cure the Native Americans of this horrible disease, several Cayuse attacked the mission and killed the Whitmans and several other whites who were staying there. It was the Whitman massacre and the subsequent demand for territorial status and U.S. military protection that brought about the establishment of the first U.S. territory west of the Rockies. Though the line between American and British land in the Northwest had been established at the 49th parallel (the current Canadian-American border) in 1846, it was not until 1848, in the wake of the Whitman massacre, that Oregon was finally given U.S. territorial status. Washington, however, would have to wait another five years, until 1853, to officially become a territory.

The establishment of the 49th parallel as the boundary between U.S. and British territories extended only as far as the main channel between the mainland and Vancouver Island, which was firmly in the hands of the British. However, because there was disagreement over where the main channel was, American and British troops jointly occupied San Juan Island. When, in 1859, a British pig rooting in an American soldier's potato patch was shot and killed, the two nations came to the brink of war. It took international arbitration to settle the disagreement, which was finally resolved by turning San Juan Island over to U.S. control.

In 1881, the first transcontinental railroad reached Spokane, in eastern Washington, and finally linked the Northwest with the eastern United States. In 1883, Tacoma became the end of the line for the Northern Pacific Railroad tracks that originated in St. Paul, Minnesota. With the arrival of the railroads, Washington took a great leap forward in its development. No longer a remote wilderness, the region began to attract industry, and in 1889 Washington gained statehood.

INDUSTRIALIZATION & THE 20TH CENTURY   From the very beginning of Euro-American settlement in the Northwest, the region based its growth on an extractive economy. When, in 1848, gold was discovered in California, the Northwest benefited from the sudden demand for lumber and wheat. Even oysters were shipped from the Washington waters to the tables of San Francisco restaurants. In 1897, another gold rush, this time in Alaska and the Klondike, brought sudden prosperity to Seattle, where merchants enjoyed a thriving business supplying hopeful miners with the tools of the trade.

Lumber and salmon, the two natural resources that Washington had in the greatest concentrations, were both exploited relentlessly. The history of the timber and salmon-fishing industries have run parallel for more than a century and have each led to similar results in the 1990s.

Nurtured on steady rains, such trees as Douglas-fir, Sitka spruce, western red cedar, Port Orford cedar, and hemlock grew tall and straight, sometimes as tall as 300 feet. The first sawmill in the Northwest began operation near present-day Vancouver, Washington, in 1828. Between the 1850s and 1870s, Northwest sawmills supplied the growing California market as well as a limited foreign market. When the transcontinental railroads arrived in the 1880s, a whole new market opened up and mills began shipping to the eastern states.

In the early years of logging in the region, sawmills and logging companies would level a forest and then move on to greener forests. By the turn of the century the government had gained more control over public forests in an attempt to slow the destruction of the region's forestlands, and sawmill owners were buying up huge tracts of land. At the outbreak of World War I, more than 20% of the forestland in the Northwest was owned by three companies—Weyerhaeuser, the Northern Pacific Railroad, and the Southern Pacific Railroad—and more than 50% of the workforce labored in the timber industry.

The timber industry has always been extremely susceptible to fluctuations in the economy and experienced a roller-coaster ride of boom and bust throughout the 20th century. Boom times in the 1970s brought on record-breaking production that came to a screeching halt in the 1980s, first with a nationwide recession, and then with the listing of the northern spotted owl as a threatened species. When the timber industry was born in the Northwest, there was a belief that the forests of the region were endless. However, by the latter half of this century, big lumber companies had realized that the forests were dwindling. Tree farms had been planted, but the large old trees continued to be cut. By the 1980s, environmentalists, shocked by vast clear-cuts on public lands, began trying to save the last old-growth trees. Today the battle between the timber industry and environmentalists continues.

Salmon was the mainstay of the diet for Northwest Indians for thousands of years before the first whites arrived, but within 10 years of the opening of the first salmon cannery in the Northwest, the fish population was severely depleted. In 1877, the first fish hatchery was developed to replenish dwindling runs of salmon, and that same year Washington canceled the salmon-fishing season. Salmon canning reached a peak on the Columbia River in 1895 and on Puget Sound in 1913. Later in the 20th century, salmon runs would be further reduced by the construction of numerous dams on the Columbia and Snake rivers. Though fish ladders help adult salmon make their journeys upstream, the young salmon heading downstream have no such help and a large percentage are killed by the turbines of hydroelectric dams. One solution to this problem has been barging and trucking young salmon downriver. Today the salmon population of the Northwest is so diminished that entire runs of salmon have been listed as threatened or endangered.

In 1916, William Boeing launched a small seaplane from the waters of Seattle's Lake Union and laid down the foundation for what would become the Seattle area's single largest employer: Boeing. The company became a major employer in Seattle when it began manufacturing B-17s and B-29s for the war effort and today continues to be one of the largest employers in the state. However, this has had its drawbacks for Seattle. The city's fortunes have been so closely linked to the aircraft manufacturer that in the past any cutback in production at Boeing had a devastating ripple effect on the local economy. However, with the global ascendancy in recent years of Bill Gates's software giant Microsoft (based just outside Seattle), the Seattle economy has begun to diversify. With many more high-tech companies locating in the area, and trade with Asian countries growing, Seattle has become one of the major players on the Pacific Rim.

5 Northwest Cuisine

The cuisine of the Northwest features such regional produce as salmon, oysters, halibut, raspberries, blackberries, apples, pears, and hazelnuts. Classic Northwest dishes include raspberry chicken, and oysters with a hazelnut crust, both of which provocatively pair meat and fruit.

Fresh seafood is a major element of regional cuisine, and salmon is the king of Northwest fish (though now it's more likely to come from Alaska). It's prepared in seemingly endless ways, the most traditional being smoked over alderwood. You'll find such smoked salmon for sale at gourmet food shops, at better grocery stores, and in restaurants.

With plenty of clean, cold water in its bays and estuaries, Washington raises an astounding array of oysters. Stop in at an oyster bar and you'll find the succulent bivalves introduced by their first names: Kumamoto, Quilcene, Willapa Bay. Then there are the mussels and clams. Two local clams of particular note are the razor clam, which can be tough and chewy if not prepared properly, and the gargantuan geoduck (pronounced *gooey* duck), which generally only shows up minced in clam chowders. The Dungeness crab is the region's other great seafood offering. Though not as large as an Alaskan king crab, the Dungeness is usually big enough to make a meal for one person.

Washington's combination of climate and abundant irrigation waters has helped make this one of the nation's major fruit-growing regions. The state is known the world over for its apples, which are grown on the east side of the Cascades near

Yakima, Wenatchee, and Chelan. The Yakima Valley is also known for its cherry orchards, though it is wine grapes that are this valley's main claim to fame. Strawberries, raspberries, and numerous varieties of blackberries are also grown throughout the Puget Sound region. All these fruits show up in the summer months at farm stands all over the state. These stands make a drive through Washington in the summer a real treat. Pick-your-own farms are also fairly common.

One last Northwest food that we should mention is the wild mushroom. As you'd expect in such a rainy climate, mushrooms abound in Washington. The most common wild mushrooms are morels, which are harvested in spring, and chanterelles, which are harvested in the autumn. We don't suggest heading out to the woods to pick your own unless you or a companion are experienced mushroom hunters. However, you will find wild mushrooms showing up on menus of better restaurants throughout the region, so by all means try to have some while you're here.

Washington has a thriving wine industry, which has for quite a few years been producing award-winning varietal wines. The state is on the same latitude as the French wine regions of Burgundy and Bordeaux and produces similar wines. Washington's vineyards are primarily on the dry east side of the Cascades, where irrigation is used to produce very reliable and consistent vintages. Wineries throughout the Northwest are open to the public for tastings and better restaurants also tend to stock plenty of local wines. Fruit-flavored wines and fruit-based distilled liqueurs are also produced around the state. Whidbey's loganberry liqueur is one such drink.

The microbrewery business that has swept the country in recent years had its start in the Northwest, where such tiny local breweries as those of the Grant's Brewery in Yakima and the Red Hook Brewery in the Seattle area started brewing rich, flavorful ales and beers the likes of which had not been brewed in the United States since before Prohibition. Today nearly every city in the region, and even some fairly small towns, boasts at least one microbrewery.

Coffee, however, is what keeps the Northwest going through long gray winters—and even through hot sunny summers, for that matter. Coffee in Washington is not the standard bottomless cup of insipid black liquid that's passed off as coffee in the rest of the country. The coffee that has become a statewide obsession is rich, dark, flavorful espresso, often served as a latte, with a generous portion of steamed milk. In Seattle it's almost impossible to walk a block without passing an espresso purveyor of some sort.

6 Recommended Books

GENERAL The single best introduction to the Northwest, both past and present, is Timothy Egan's *The Good Rain* (Vintage Departures, 1991), which uses a long-forgotten Northwest explorer as the springboard for an exploration of all the forces that have made the Northwest what it is today. *The Final Forest* by William Dietrich (Simon & Schuster, 1992) objectively addresses the conflicting views of the logging industry and environmentalists, who are locked in a battle for the last old-growth forests in the Northwest. In *Stepping Westward* (Henry Holt and Company, 1991), Sallie Tisdale blends memoir, travel, and history in an evocation of the landscapes and life of Washington, Oregon, and Idaho.

The Journals of Lewis and Clark (Mentor, 1964), compiled by Meriwether Lewis and William Clark during their 1804–06 journey across the continent, is a fascinating account of a difficult journey and includes a wealth of observations on Native Americans and North American flora and fauna. David Freeman Hawke's *Those Tremendous Mountains: The Story of the Lewis and Clark Expedition* (W.W. Norton &

Company, 1980) is a more readable form of the journals and also has a considerable amount of background information.

For a complete history of the Northwest, try *The Pacific Northwest: An Interpretive History* by Carlos A. Schwantes (University of Nebraska Press, 1989) or *The Great Northwest: The Story of a Land and Its People* (America West Publishing, 1973).

FICTION The Northwest has not inspired a great deal of fiction, though Tom Robbins, a Northwest resident, does manage to work a bit of the Northwest into most of his novels. In 1995, the Puget Sound region served as the backdrop for David Guterson's critically accalimed *Snow Falling on Cedars* (Harcourt Brace, 1994), which won the PEN/Faulkner Award in 1995. Ernest Callenbach's *Ecotopia* (Bantam, 1975) is a novel of the near future in which the Northwest secedes from the United States to pursue its own environmentally conscious beliefs (unfortunately much has changed in the Northwest since the idealistic early 1970s when this novel was written).

Other novels set in the Northwest include Ken Kesey's *Sometimes a Great Notion* (Viking Penguin, 1977) and *One Flew Over the Cuckoo's Nest* (Viking Penguin, 1977). The former, in its portrayal of a logging family, is more evocative of the region. In 1936 H.L. Davis won the Pulitzer Prize for his novel *Honey in the Horn* (Larlin, 1975), a realistic portrayal of homesteading in the Northwest in the early 1900s.

TRAVEL The outdoors is a way of life in the Northwest and enjoying it might require a specialized guidebook to get you to the best places. One such guide to outdoor sports in Washington is co-author Karl Samson's *Outside Magazine's Adventure Guide to the Pacific Northwest* (Macmillan, 1997). Depending on your interests, you might want to check out some of the following: *Ancient Forests of the Pacific Northwest* by the Wilderness Society and Elliot A. Norse (Island Press, 1990); *A Waterfall Lover's Guide to the Northwest* by Gregory A. Plumb (The Mountaineers, 1989); and *Garden Touring in the Pacific Northwest* by Jan Kowalczewski Whitner (Alaska Northwest Books, 1993).

3

Planning a Trip to Washington

Before any trip, you need to do a bit of advance planning. When should I go? What is this trip going to cost me? Can I catch a festival during my visit? And where should I head to pursue my favorite sport? We'll answer these and other questions for you in this chapter.

1 Visitor Information & Money

SOURCES OF INFORMATION

For information on Washington, call the **Washington State Tourism Office,** 101 General Administration Building (P.O. Box 42500), Olympia, WA 98504-2500 (☎ **800/544-1800**). For information on Seattle and vicinity, contact the **Seattle–King County Convention & Visitors Bureau,** 520 Pike St., Suite 1300, Seattle, WA 98101 (☎ **206/461-5800**).

Also keep in mind that most cities and towns in Washington have either a tourist office or a chamber of commerce that can provide you with information. When approaching cities and towns, watch for signs along the highway directing you to these information centers. See the individual chapters for specific addresses.

CityNet keeps excellent hot lists of many city, and some regional, Web sites. Log onto **www.city.net/countries/united stateswashington** for cities in Washington. For another hot list of Washington resources, check out **Washington State Department of Tourism's** site at **www.tourism.wa.gov**, or **City Web USA** at **www.scescape.com/cityweb/wash.html** or **www.travel-in-wa.com/**.

You can also get travel information covering Washington from the **American Automobile Association (AAA)** if you're a member.

To get information on outdoor recreation in national parks and national forests of Washington, write or call the **National Park Service,** Outdoor Recreation Information Center, which is located at REI's main store in Seattle at 223 Yale Ave. N., Seattle, WA 98109 (☎ **206/470-4060**). To make reservations to camp at a national forest, call ☎ **800/280-CAMP.**

For information on Washington state parks, contact **Washington State Parks and Recreation,** 7150 Cleanwater Lane (P.O. Box 42650), Olympia, WA 98504-2650 (☎ **800/233-0321**). For state campsite reservations, call **Reservations Northwest** (☎ **800/452-5687**).

What Things Cost in Seattle	U.S. $
Taxi from the airport to the city center	28.00
Bus ride between any two downtown points	Free
Local telephone call	0.25
Double at Alexis Hotel (very expensive)	195.00–210.00
Double at Pacific Plaza Hotel (moderate)	80.00–125.00
Double at Seattle City Center Travelodge (inexpensive)	59.00–70.00
Lunch for one at Salty's on Alki (expensive)	25.00
Lunch for one at Queen City Grill (moderate)	12.00
Lunch for one at Emmett Watson's Oyster Bar (inexpensive)	8.00–12.00
Dinner for one, without wine, at Fuller's (expensive)	50.00
Dinner for one, without wine, at Etta's (moderate)	35.00
Dinner for one, without wine, at Belltown Pub (inexpensive)	12–20.00
Pint of beer	3.50
Coca-Cola	1.00
Cup of coffee (latte)	1.90
Roll of ASA 100 Kodacolor film, 36 exposures	5.50
Movie ticket	7.00
Theater ticket to Seattle Repertory Theater	10.00–40.00

For information on ferries, contact **Washington State Ferries,** Colman Dock, Seattle, WA 98104-1487 (☎ **800/843-3779** in Washington, or 206/464-6400).

MONEY

What will a vacation in Washington cost? That depends on your tastes. If you drive an RV or carry a tent, you can get by very inexpensively and find a place to stay almost anywhere in Washington. On the other hand, you can easily spend a couple of hundred dollars a day on a room at one of Washington's resorts. However, if you want to stay in clean, modern motels at interstate highway off-ramps, expect to pay $45 to $65 a night for a double room in most places. When it comes time to eat, you can get a great meal almost anywhere in the Northwest for under $25, but if you want to spend more or less, of course that's usually possible as well.

Automatic teller machines (with Plus, Cirrus, Star, Visa, and MasterCard networks widely available) are nearly ubiquitous throughout Washington, so you can get cash as you travel; however, some small town banks still do not have ATMs.

2 When to Go

Though gray skies and mild temperatures are what Washington is known for, the region is actually characterized by a wide range of climates. For the most part, moist winds off the Pacific Ocean keep temperatures west of the Cascade Range mild year-round. In the Puget Sound area you're likely to need a sweater or light jacket at night even in August. The Northwest rains that are so legendary fall primarily as light-but-almost-constant drizzle between October and early July. There are windows of sunshine during these months, but they usually last no more than a few days. There are also, unfortunately, occasional wet summers (with rain sometimes falling in both August and September), so be prepared for wet weather whenever you plan to visit. Winters usually include one or two blasts of Arctic air that bring snow and freezing weather to the Seattle area.

There are several exceptions to Washington's mild and rainy climate. If you visit the coast, expect grayer, wetter weather than in the Seattle area. The Olympic Peninsula in northwest Washington is the rainiest spot in the mainland United States, with rainfall reaching 140 inches per year.

On the other hand, some regions east of the Cascades are effectively a high desert and are characterized by lack of rain and temperature extremes. These high desert areas can be very cold in the winter and can get moderate amounts of snow in the foothill regions. In summer the weather can be blazing hot, though nights are often cool enough to require a sweater or light jacket.

In the Cascades, Olympics, and other smaller mountain ranges, snowfall is heavy in the winter and skiing is a popular sport.

Seattle's Average Monthly Temperatures & Rainfall

	Jan	Feb	Mar	Apr	May	June	July	Aug	Sept	Oct	Nov	Dec
Temp. (°F)	46	50	53	58	65	69	75	74	69	60	52	47
Temp. (°C)	8	10	11	15	18	21	24	23	21	16	11	9
Days of Rain	19	6	17	14	10	9	5	7	9	14	18	20

WASHINGTON CALENDAR OF EVENTS

February

- **Northwest Flower & Garden Show,** Washington State Convention Center, Seattle. The largest flower and garden show in the Northwest, with beautiful displays and hundreds of vendors. (☎ **800/229-6311** or 206/224-1700). Mid- to late February.
- **Spam Carving Contest,** Doc Maynard's Club, Seattle. A rowdy get-together where the participants attempt to carve that wonder food from the fifties, Spam. (☎ **206/682-4649**). The Tuesday before Lent, Fat Tuesday.

March

- **Irish Festival/St. Patricks Day Celebration,** Seattle. Traditional Irish dancing, music, and contests.☎ 206/684-7200. Days before and including March 17.
- **Whale Fest,** Westport. Kickoff celebration for whale-watching season, when 20,000 gray whales migrate along the Washington coast from Baja California to the Bering Sea. ☎ **800/345-6223** or 360/268-9422. March 1 through the end of May.

April

- **Skagit Valley Tulip Festival,** Skagit Valley. View a rainbow of blooming tulip fields. ☎ **360/428-5959.** First two weeks in April.
- **Spring Barrel Tasting,** Yakima Valley. Straight-from-the-barrel wine tasting of spring-release wines at Yakima Valley wineries. ☎ **509/829-6027.** Late April.
- **Washington State Apple Blossom Festival,** Wenatchee. Many different events, including a parade and activities for families. ☎ **509/662-3616.** End of April to early May.

May

- **Opening Day of Boating Season,** Lake Union and Lake Washington, Seattle. A parade of boats and much fanfare as Seattle boaters bring out everything from kayaks to yachts. (☎ 206/325-1000). First Saturday in May.
- **Irrigation Festival,** Sequim. The oldest continuous festival in Washington, with a grand parade, logging show, dancing, arts and crafts. ☎ 360/683-8058. Early May.
- **Viking Fest,** Poulsbo. Norwegian heritage on display in picturesque Poulsbo, with a parade and entertainment. ☎ 360/779-4848. Mid-May.
- **Spokane Lilac Festival,** Spokane. A 55-year tradition celebrating the blooming of the lilacs. ☎ 509/326-3339. Mid-May.
- ✪ **Northwest Folklife Festival,** Seattle. This is the largest folklife festival in the country, with dozens of national and regional folk musicians performing on numerous stages. In addition, craftspeople from all over the Northwest show and sell. Lots of good food and dancing too. ☎ 206/684-7300. Memorial Day weekend.

June

- **Mural-in-a-Day,** Toppenish. The small town of Toppenish has covered its blank walls with murals and each June one more is added in a day of intense painting. ☎ 509/865-3262. Early June.
- **Seattle to Portland Bicycle Classic,** Seattle. Cyclists challenge themselves with this 200-mile bike ride accomplished in 2 days. ☎ 206/522-BIKE. Third weekend in June.
- **Fort Vancouver Days,** Vancouver. Riverside jazz concert, chili cook-off, and arts and crafts. ☎ 360/696-8031. Late June.

July

- **Fourth of July Fireworks,** Vancouver. The biggest fireworks display west of the Mississippi. July 4.
- **Slug Festival,** Eatonville. The native banana slug is celebrated with slug races and the wearing of antennae, among other activities, at this town located between Tacoma and Mt. Rainier. ☎ 360/832-6117. Early July.
- **Seafair Indian Days Pow Wow,** Seattle. Salmon bake, dancing, singing and drumming are some of the activities held at the Daybreak Star Cultural Center. ☎ 206/285-4425. Last weekend in July.
- **Pilchuck Open House,** Stanwood. The Pilchuck Glass School, founded by internationally renowned glass artist Dale Chihuly, is located in the foothills of the Cascade Mountains 50 miles north of Seattle. The school opens its doors once a year for visitors and reservations are necessary. ☎ 206/621-8422, ext. 44. Last weekend in July.
- **Pacific Northwest Arts and Crafts Fair,** Bellevue. This is the largest arts and crafts fair in the Northwest. (☎ 425/454-4900). Last weekend in July.
- ✪ **Seafair,** Seattle. The biggest event of the year, with festivities every day, including parades, hydroplane boat races, performances by the navy's Blue Angels, a Torchlight Parade, ethnic festivals, sporting events, and open houses on naval ships. This one really packs in the out-of-towners and sends Seattleites fleeing on summer vacations. Call ☎ 206/728-0123 for details on events and tickets. Third weekend in July to the first weekend in August.

August

- **International Accordion Celebration,** Leavenworth. Accordion competitions and a parade are held against the backdrop of this town which is reminiscent of a Bavarian village. ☎ 509/548-5807. Early August.

- **Omak Stampede/World Famous Suicide Race/Indian Encampment,** Omak. Rodeo and horse race down a cliff face. ☎ **800/933-6625.** Early August.
- **Chief Seattle Days,** Suquamish. Celebration of Northwest Native American culture across Puget Sound from Seattle. ☎ **360/598-3311.** Third weekend in August.
- **Washington State International Kite Festival,** Long Beach. World-class kite flying competition. ☎ **360/665-5495.** Third week in August.

September

○ **Bumbershoot, the Seattle Arts Festival,** Seattle. Seattle's second most popular festival derives its peculiar name from a British term for umbrella—an obvious reference to the rainy weather. Lots of rock music and other events pack Seattle's youthful set into Seattle Center and other venues. You'll find plenty of arts and crafts on display, too. For a schedule, call ☎ **206/281-8111.** Labor Day weekend.

- **Ellensburg Rodeo,** Ellensburg. The state's biggest rodeo, with a carnival and country and rock bands. ☎ **509/962-7831.** Labor Day weekend.
- **Wooden Boat Festival,** Port Townsend. Historic boats on display, demonstrations. ☎ **360/385-4742.** Early September.
- **Western Washington Fair,** Puyallup. One of the 10 largest fairs in the nation. ☎ **206/841-5045.** Third week in September.
- **Annual Washington State Autumn Leaf Festival,** Leavenworth. Bavarian costumes, food, music, and autumn foliage. ☎ **509/548-5807.** Late September to early October.

October

- **Salmon Days Festival, Issaquah.** This festival in a town 15 miles east of Seattle celebrates the annual return of salmon that spawn within the city limits. ☎ **425/392-0661.** First full weekend in October.
- **Kinetic Sculpture Race,** Port Townsend. The two rules of this race are (1) the vehicle must be people-powered and (2) the wackier the contraption the better. ☎ **888/365-6978.** First weekend in October.
- **Great Northwest Microbrewery Invitational,** Seattle. Dozens of microbrews to sample here, plus entertainment. ☎ **206/232-2982.** Mid-October.
- **Cranberrian Fair,** Ilwaco, Long Beach Peninsula. Cranberry bog tours, cranberry products, arts and crafts. ☎ **360/642-3446.** Mid-October.

November

- **Thanksgiving in Wine Country,** Yakima Valley. Foods and the wines that complement them are offered for tasting by Yakima-area wineries. ☎ **509/829-6027.** Thanksgiving weekend.
- **Yule Fest,** Poulsbo. Traditional Norwegian customs including lighting the yule log and the arrival of Father Christmas. ☎ **360/779-4848.** End of November.
- **Zoolights,** Tacoma. The Point Defiance Zoo is decorated with thousands of sparkling lights. ☎ **253/591-5337.** End of November through December.

December

- **Victorian Holidays,** Port Townsend. Santa arrives in this historic Victorian town in an unusual conveyance: the state ferry from Whidbey Island. (☎ **888/365-6978**). First weekend in December.
- **Seattle Christmas Ships,** various locations. Boats decked out with imaginative Christmas lights parade past various waterfront locations. Argosy Cruises offers tours. ☎ **206/623-1445.** Through December.

3 The Active Vacation Planner

The abundance of outdoor recreational activities is one of the reasons people choose to live in Washington. With both mountains and beaches within an hour's drive of the major metropolitan areas, there are numerous choices for the active vacationer.

Outdoor enthusiasts with Web access will want to check out **GORP's** resource listings for on-line information on area parks and activities from fishing to skiing to kayaking. Head for **www.gorp.com/gorp/location/wa/wa.htm** to get to the Washington hot list.

ACTIVITIES A TO Z

BICYCLING/MOUNTAIN BIKING   The San Juan Islands, with their winding country roads and Puget Sound vistas, are the most popular bicycling locale in the state. Of the four main San Juan Islands (San Juan, Orcas, Lopez, and Shaw), Lopez has the easiest and Orcas the most challenging terrain for bikers. Here you can pedal for as many or as few days as you like, stopping at parks, inns, and quaint villages.

Other popular road biking spots include Bainbridge and Vashon islands, with their easy access to Seattle; the Olympic Peninsula, with its scenic vistas and campgrounds; and the Long Beach Peninsula, with its miles of flat roads. Seattle, Tacoma, Spokane, and Yakima also all have many miles of easy bicycle trails that are either in parks or connect parks. The longest of these are in Seattle and Spokane.

The region's national forests provide miles of logging roads and single-track trails for mountain biking. However, the state's premier mountain-biking destination is the Methow Valley, where miles of cross-country ski trails are opened to bicycles in the summer.

For information on bicycle routes in Washington, contact the **Bicycle Program,** Washington State Department of Transportation, P.O. Box 47393, Olympia, WA 98504-7393 (☎ **360/705-7277**).

If you're interested in participating in an organized bicycle tour, there are a couple of companies you might want to contact. **Backroads,** 801 Cedar St., Berkeley, CA 94710-1740 (☎ **800/462-2848** or 510/527-1555; fax 510/527-1444), offers road bike trips in the San Juan Islands and the Olympic Peninsula. Tour prices range from $749 to $1,498. **Bicycle Adventures,** P.O. Box 11219, Olympia, WA 98508 (☎ **800/443-6060** or 360/786-0989; fax 360/786-9661), offers biking trips in the San Juan Islands, Olympic Peninsula, and the Washington Cascades. Tour prices range from $950 to $1,500.

BIRD WATCHING   With a wide variety of habitats, Washington offers many excellent bird-watching spots. Each winter in January, bald eagles flock to the Skagit River, north of Seattle, to feast on salmon. Birders can observe from shore or on a guided raft trip. Migratory shorebirds make annual stops at Bowerman Basin in the Gray's Harbor Wildlife Refuge outside the town of Hoquiam. One of Washington's best birding excursions is a ride through the San Juan Islands on one of the Washington State Ferries. From these floating observation platforms, birders can spot bald eagles and numerous pelagic birds.

BOARDSAILING   The Columbia River Gorge is one of the most renowned boardsailing spots in the world. Here, high winds and a strong current come together to produce radical sailing conditions. As the winds whip up the waves, skilled sailors rocket across the water and launch themselves skyward to perform aerial acrobatics. On calmer days and in spots where the wind isn't blowing so hard, there are also opportunities for novices to learn the basics. Summer is the best sailing season, and the town of Hood River, Oregon is the center of the boarding scene with plenty of windsurfing schools and rental companies. Windsurfing is also popular on Lake Union in Seattle and Vancouver Lake in Vancouver, Washington.

CAMPING   Public and private campgrounds abound all across Washington, with those in Mount Rainier National Park and Olympic National Park being the most popular. North Cascades National Park has campgrounds as well. Camping is on a first-come, first-served basis at all three national parks. To get information on outdoor recreation in Washington's national parks and forests, write or call the **National Park Service,** Outdoor Recreation Information Center, which is located at REI's main store in Seattle at 223 Yale Ave. N., Seattle, WA 98109 (☎ 206/470-4060).

Washington also has 80 state parks with campgrounds. Moran State Park on Orcas Island and Deception Pass State Park have two of the most enjoyable campgrounds. For information on Washington state parks, contact **Washington State Parks and Recreation,** 7150 Cleanwater Lane (P.O. Box 42650), Olympia, WA 98504-2650 (☎ 800/233-0321).

For state park campsite reservations, call **Reservations Northwest** (☎ 800/452-5687). To make campsite reservations at national forest campgrounds, call the **National Forest Reservation Service** (☎ 800/280-CAMP).

If you're interested in renting an RV for your trip around the state, contact **Western Motorhome Rentals,** 19303 Hwy. 99, Lynnwood, WA 98036 (☎ 800/800-1181 or 425/775-1181), or **Motorhome America RV Rentals,** 6011 E. Lake Sammamish Rd. SE, Issaquah, WA 98027 (☎ 425/392-9226).

CANOEING/KAYAKING   White-water kayakers in Washington head for such rivers as the Wenatchee around Leavenworth, the Methow near Winthrop, the Skagit and Skykomish rivers north of Seattle, and the White Salmon River near Trout Lake. On the Olympic Peninsula, the Queets, Hoh, and Elhwa rivers are the main kayaking rivers. One of the most popular canoeing lakes in Washington is Lake Ozette in Olympic National Park.

FISHING   For information on freshwater fishing in Washington, contact the **Department of Wildlife,** 600 Capitol Way N., Olympia, WA 98501 (☎ 360/902-2200).

GOLFING   Although the rainy weather in western Washington puts a bit of a damper on golfing, the mild temperatures mean that it's possible to play year-round. The state has only a handful of resorts with golf courses, but most larger cities have public courses.

HIKING & BACKPACKING   Washington has an abundance of hiking trails, including the Pacific Crest Trail, which runs along the spine of the Cascades from Canada to the California line (and onward all the way to Mexico). Elsewhere in Washington, you'll find hikes along the beach, up rain forest valleys, and through alpine meadows in Olympic National Park, through forests and the state's most beautiful meadows in Mount Rainier National Park (hikes from Sunrise and Paradise are the most spectacular), and through the state's most rugged scenery in North Cascades National Park. The Alpine Lakes region outside Leavenworth is breathtakingly beautiful, but so popular that advance-reservation permits are required. Another popular hike is to the top of Mount St. Helens. Lesser known are the hiking trails on Mount Adams in southern Washington. In the Columbia Gorge, the hike up Dog Mountain is strenuous but rewarding.

If you'd like to hike the wild country of Washington state with a knowledgeable guide, you've got some good options. **Sierra Club Outings,** 85 Second St., 2nd

Floor, San Francisco, CA 94105 (☎ **415/977-5630**; Web site: www.sierraclub.org/ outings) offers several trips each year in the Cascades and the Olympic Peninsula. The **Olympic Park Institute,** 111 Barnes Point Rd., Port Angeles, WA 98363 (☎ **360/ 928-3720**), also offers a variety of hiking and backpacking trips.

MOUNTAINEERING   While Mount Rainier, Mount Adams, Mount Baker, Glacier Peak, Mount St. Helens, and Mount Olympus are the most popular mountaineering peaks in the state, there are countless other peaks throughout the Cascades, North Cascades, and Olympic Mountains that attract climbers. The state's peaks offer challenging mountain climbing and rock climbing for both novices and experts.

If you're interested in learning some mountain-climbing skills or want to hone your existing skills, you can do so on Mount Rainier and other Cascade peaks. **Rainier Mountaineering,** 535 Dock St., Suite 209, Tacoma, WA 98402 (☎ **253/ 627-6242** or 360/569-2227 in summer; fax 253/627-1280), which operates out of Paradise inside Mount Rainier National Park, offers 1-day classes for $85, three-day summit climbs for $457, and five-day mountaineering seminars for $695.

SCUBA DIVING   Though the waters of Puget Sound are cold, they are generally quite clear and harbor an astounding variety of life, including giant octopi and wolf eels. Consequently, the sound is popular with dry-suited divers. There are underwater parks for scuba divers at Fort Worden, Kopachuck, Blake Island, Saltwater, and Tolmie state parks. For more information, contact the **Washington Scuba Alliance,** 120 State Ave., Suite 18, Olympia, WA 98501-8212. For a list of dive shops in Washington and additional information, visit Web site **www.travel-in-wa.com/ OUTDOOR/scuba.html.**

SEA KAYAKING   Sea kayaks differ from river kayaks in that they are much longer, more stable, and able to carry gear as well as a paddler or two. There are few places in the country that offer better sea kayaking than the waters of Puget Sound and around the San Juan Islands, and therefore this sport is especially popular in the Seattle area. The protected waters of Puget Sound offer numerous spots for a paddle of anywhere from a few hours to a few days. There's even a water trail under development that will link camping spots throughout the Sound.

The San Juan Islands are by far the most popular sea-kayaking spot in the region, and several tiny islands, accessible only by boat, are designated state campsites. In the Seattle area, Lake Union and Lake Washington are both popular kayaking spots. Willapa Bay, on the Washington coast, is another popular paddling spot.

If you'd like to explore Puget Sound or Seattle's Lake Union in a sea kayak, contact the **Northwest Outdoor Center,** 2100 Westlake Ave. N., Seattle, WA 98109 (☎ **206/281-9694**). This center rents kayaks and also offers various classes and guided trips. Day trips are $70 to $75, three-day trips are about $240, and 5-day trips are $450. **San Juan Kayak Expeditions,** P.O. Box 2041, Friday Harbor, WA 98250 (☎ **360/378-4436**), and **Shearwater Adventures,** P.O. Box 787, Eastsound, WA 98245 (☎ **360/376-4699**), also offer multiday kayak trips. Three-day trips range in price from around $270 to $290. **Sea Quest Expeditions/Zoetic Research,** P.O. Box 2424, Friday Harbor, WA 98250 (☎ **360/378-5767**; Web site: www.sea-quest-kayak.com), is a nonprofit organization that sponsors educational sea-kayaking trips through the San Juans.

SKIING   Washington has more than a dozen ski areas spread across its many mountain ranges, from Hurricane Ridge in the Olympic Mountains to Mount Spokane near the Idaho border, and from Mount Baker Ski Area near the Canadian border to White Pass outside Mount Rainier National Park. The most popular ski areas are Mount Baker (a snowboarding mecca) near Bellingham, Stevens Pass near

Leavenworth, Alpental/Ski Acres/Snoqualmie/Hyak near Seattle, and Crystal Mountain just outside Mount Rainier National Park. Smaller and more remote ski areas include White Pass, southeast of Mount Rainier National Park; Mission Ridge, near Wenatchee; Mount Spokane and 48 Degrees North, both north of Spokane; and Ski Bluewood, near Walla Walla. Tiny ski locals-only ski areas with only a handful of runs include Hurricane Ridge, in Olympic National Park; Loup Loup, near Winthrop; Echo Valley, near Lake Chelan; and Sitzmark, in central Washington near the Canadian border. There's also heli-skiing available in the Methow Valley.

Many downhill ski areas also offer groomed cross-country ski trails. The most popular cross-country areas in Washington include the Methow Valley (one of the largest trail systems in the country), Leavenworth, Ski Acres/Hyak, White Pass, Stevens Pass, and near Mount St. Helens and Mount Adams.

WHALE WATCHING   Orca whales, commonly called killer whales, are a symbol of the Northwest and are often seen in Puget Sound and around the San Juan Islands, especially during the summer. Dozens of companies offer whale-watching trips from the San Juans. You can also spot orcas from San Juan Island's Lime Kiln State Park. Out on the Washington coast, migrating gray whales can be seen March through May. In the town of Westport, there are both viewing areas and companies operating whale-watching excursions.

WHITE-WATER RAFTING   Plenty of rain and lots of mountains combine to produce dozens of good white-water rafting rivers, depending on the time of year and water levels. In the Washington Cascades, some of the popular rafting rivers include the Wenatchee outside Leavenworth, the Methow near Winthrop, the Skagit and Skykomish rivers north of Seattle, and the White Salmon River near Trout Lake. On the Olympic Peninsula, the Queets, Hoh, and Elhwa rivers are the main rafting rivers. See the respective chapters for information on rafting companies operating on these rivers. Rates generally range from $45 to $75 for a day of rafting.

Throughout the state there are dozens of rafting companies operating on as many rivers. Many of these companies offer trips on several different rivers with trips offered throughout most of the year. Among these companies are Alpine Adventures (☎ **800/926-RAFT**), Cascade Adventures (☎ **800/RAFT-FUN**), Downstream River Runners (☎ **800/234-4644**), North Cascades River Expeditions (☎ **800/ 634-8433**), River Recreation, (☎ **800/464-5899**), River Riders (☎ **800/ 448-RAFT**), and Wildwater River Tours (☎ **800/522-WILD**).

4 Educational & Volunteer Vacations

On the Olympic Peninsula, the **Olympic Park Institute,** 111 Barnes Point Rd., Port Angeles, WA 98363 (☎ **360/928-3720**), offers a wide array of summer field seminars ranging from painting classes to bird-watching trips to multiday backpacking trips.

The **North Cascades Institute,** 2105 State Route 20, Sedro-Woolley, WA 98284-9394 (☎ **360/856-5700,** ext. 209), is a nonprofit organization that offers field seminars focusing on natural and cultural history in the North Cascades.

In its Seminars Afloat Program, the **Resource Institute,** 2319 N. 45th St., Suite 139, Seattle, WA 98103-6953 (☎ **206/784-6762**), offers programs about the culture, ecology, and arts of the Northwest that reflect the interconnection between the human community and nature. Their trip to the San Juan Islands takes 5 days.

Sound Experience, 2730 Washington St., Suite D, Port Townsend, WA 98368 (☎ **360/379-0438**), offers sailing trips of 3 to 10 days on the *Adventuress,* a two-masted schooner. The program is open to both children and adults, and focuses on hands-on learning and environmental education.

Umiak Adventure School, 274 Welch Lane, Anacortes, WA 98221 (☎ 360/299-0804), uses umiaks, open boats constructed in the style of Inuit and Aleut skin kayaks, to transport participants throughout the San Juan Islands for educational outdoor seminars. Three-day trips include, among others, workshops on ethnobotany and photography.

Island Institute, P.O. Box 358, Eastsound, WA 98245 (☎ 800/956-6722 or 360/376-6720), located on Orcas Island in the San Juans, offers multiday programs focusing on snorkeling, kayaking, whale watching, and the natural history of the San Juan Islands. Accommodations are in wood-floored tents or cottages. Rates are all-inclusive and range from $399 for 3 days to $895 for a week's stay.

The Nature Conservancy is a nonprofit organization dedicated to the global preservation of natural diversity, and to this end it operates educational field trips and work parties to their own nature preserves and those of other agencies. For information about field trips in Washington, contact the **Nature Conservancy,** 217 Pine St., Suite 1100, Seattle, WA 98101 (☎ 206/343-4344).

If you enjoy the wilderness and want to get more involved in preserving it, consider a Sierra Club Service Trip. These trips are for the purpose of building, restoring, and maintaining hiking trails in wilderness areas. It's a lot of work, but it's also a lot of fun. For more information on Service Trips, contact **Sierra Club Outings,** 85 Second St., 2nd Floor, San Francisco, CA 94105 (☎ 415/977-5630; Web site www.sierraclub.org/outings). Alternatively, you can call your local chapter of the Sierra Club or Washington's Cascade Chapter (☎ 206/523-2147).

Earth Watch, P.O. Box 9104, Watertown, MA 02172 (☎ 617/926-8200), sends volunteers on scientific research projects. Contact them for a catalog listing trips and costs. Projects have included studies of orca whales and chimpanzee communication.

Habitat for Humanity is an organization that enlists volunteers to help build homes for people within the fifty states and around the world who could not otherwise afford them. Contact David Minich, 121 Habitat St., Americus, Georgia, 31709-3423 (☎ 800/422-5913, ext. 547).

Older travelers who want to learn something from their trip to Washington or who simply prefer the company of like-minded older travelers should look into programs by **Elderhostel,** 75 Federal St., Boston, MA 02110 (☎ 617/426-7788). To participate in an Elderhostel program, either you or your spouse must be 55 years old. In addition to 1-week educational programs, Elderhostel offers short getaways with interesting themes.

5 Travel Insurance

Before going out and spending money on various sorts of travel insurance, check your existing policies to see if they'll cover you while you're traveling. Make sure your health insurance will cover you when you're away from home. Most credit and charge cards offer automatic flight insurance when you purchase an airline ticket with that card. These policies insure against death or dismemberment in the case of an airplane crash. Also, check your cards to see if any of them pick up the loss-damage waiver (LDW), and if so what the deductible is, when you rent a car. The LDW can run as much as $15 a day and can add 50% or more to the cost of renting a car. Check your automobile insurance policy too; it might cover the LDW as well. If you own a home or have renter's insurance, see if that policy covers off-premises theft and loss wherever it occurs. If you're traveling on a tour or have prepaid a large chunk of your travel expenses, you might want to ask your travel agent about trip-cancellation insurance.

If, after checking all your existing insurance policies, you decide that you need additional insurance, a good travel agent can give you information on a variety of different options. **Travelex,** P.O. Box 9408, Garden City, NY 11530-9408 (☎ **800/228-9792**), offers several different types of travel insurance policies for one day to six months. These policies include medical, baggage, trip-cancellation or interruption insurance, and flight insurance against death or dismemberment. **Travel Guard International,** 1145 Clark St., Stevens Point, WI 54481-9970 (☎ **800/826-1300**), also offers similar types of coverage.

6 Tips for Special Travelers

FOR TRAVELERS WITH DISABILITIES   Almost all hotels and motels in the Northwest, aside from bed-and-breakfast inns and older or historic lodges, offer disabled-accessible accommodations. However, when making reservations be sure to ask.

The public transit systems found in most Northwest cities have either disabled-accessible regular vehicles or offer special transportation services for the disabled.

If you plan to visit any national parks or monuments, you can avail yourself of the **Golden Access Passport.** This lifetime pass is issued free to any U.S. citizen or permanent resident who has been medically certified as disabled or blind. The pass permits free entry into national parks and monuments.

Rick Crowder of the **Travelin' Talk Network,** P.O. Box 3534, Clarksville, TN 37043-3534 (☎ **615/552-6670** Monday through Friday between noon and 5pm central time), organizes a network for travelers with disabilities. A directory listing people and organizations around the world who are networked to provide travelers with disabilities with firsthand information about a chosen destination is available for $35.

FOR GAY & LESBIAN TRAVELERS   Seattle is well known as one of the most gay-friendly cities in the country, and has a large gay-and-lesbian community that is centered around the Capitol Hill neighborhood. The *Seattle Gay News* (☎ **206/324-4297**) is the community's newspaper and is available at gay bars and nightclubs. For a guide to Seattle's gay community, get a copy of the *Greater Seattle Business Association (GSBA) Guide Directory.* It's available at the GSBA's office at 2033 Sixth Ave., Suite 804 (☎ **206/443-4722**). The **Pink Pages,** a free directory to gay-and lesbian-friendly businesses, available at 1122 E. Pike St., Suite 1226 (☎ **206/328-5850**), is another good resource. Both of these publications are available at the **Pink Zone,** 211 Broadway Ave. E. (☎ **206/325-0050**), a gay-oriented shop on Capitol Hill. The **Lesbian Resource Center,** 1808 Bellevue Ave., Suite 204 (☎ **206/322-3953**), is a community resource center providing housing and job information, therapy, and business referrals.

FOR SENIORS   When making airline and hotel reservations, always mention that you are a senior citizen. Many airlines and hotels offer discounts. Also be sure to carry some form of photo ID with you when touring Seattle. Most attractions, some theaters and concert halls, tour companies, and the Washington State Ferries all offer senior-citizen discounts. These can add up to substantial savings, but you have to remember to ask for the discount.

If you are planning on visiting either Mount Rainier National Park or Olympic National Park while in the Seattle area, you can save on park admissions by getting a **Golden Age Passport,** which is available for $10 to U.S. citizens and permanent residents age 62 and older. This federal government pass allows lifetime entrance privileges. You can apply in person for this passport at a national park, national forest, or other location where it's honored, and you must show reasonable proof of age.

Also, if you aren't already a member of the **American Association of Retired Persons (AARP),** 601 E. St. NW, Washington, DC 20077-1214 (☎ **800/424-3410**), you should consider joining. This association provides discounts at many lodgings and attractions throughout the Seattle area, although you can sometimes get a similar discount simply by showing your ID.

If you'd like to do some studying while on vacation, consider Elderhostel (see "Educational & Volunteer Vacations," earlier in this chapter).

FOR FAMILIES Families traveling in Washington should be sure to take note of family admission fees at many museums and other attractions. These admission prices are often less than what it would cost for individual tickets for the whole family.

At hotels and motels, children usually stay free if they share their parents' room and no extra bed is required.

FOR STUDENTS If you don't already have one, get an official student ID from your school. Such an ID will entitle you to discounts to museums and performances at different theaters and concert halls around town.

Seattle International Hostel is at 84 Union St., Seattle, WA 98101 (☎ **206/622-5443**). Besides being a place to stay, this hostel has a bulletin board with information on rides, other hostels, camping equipment for sale, and the like. There are six other affiliated Hosteling International hostels in western Washington, including hostels in Port Townsend, Bellingham, on Vashon Island, and in Fort Flagler and Fort Columbia state parks.

7 Getting There

BY PLANE

The Major Airlines Sea-Tac Airport is Washington's main airport and is served by about 30 airlines. The major carriers include **Alaska Airlines** (☎ 800/426-0333); **American Airlines** (☎ 800/433-7300); **America West** (☎ 800/235-9292); **Continental** (☎ 800/523-3273); **Delta** (☎ 800/221-1212); **Horizon Air** (☎ 800/547-9308); **Northwest** (☎ 800/225-2525); **Reno Air** (☎ 800/736-6247); **Southwest** (☎ 800/435-9792); **TWA** (☎ 800/221-2000); **United** (☎ 206/441-3700 or 800/241-6522); and **USAirways** (☎ 800/428-4322).

Seaplane service between Seattle and the San Juan Islands and Vancouver and Victoria, British Columbia, is offered by **Kenmore Air** (☎ 800/543-9595 or 206/486-1257), which has its Seattle terminals at the south end of Lake Union and at the north end of Lake Washington.

There is also now helicopter service to Seattle's Boeing Field from Victoria and Vancouver, British Columbia, on **Helijet Airways** (☎ 800/665-4354). The flights, of which there are three a day, take only 35 minutes from Victoria and 90 minutes from Vancouver. The round-trip airfare is $170 between Victoria and Seattle and $299 between Vancouver and Seattle.

Finding the Best Airfare The way airline ticketing is going these days, finding the best fare on a flight to Seattle is mostly about paying attention to special sales on tickets. If you are flexible about when you fly and start checking with a travel agent or watching the newspapers for sale ads, you may be able to get a bargain on a flight.

Cyber Deals for Net Surfers

It's possible to get some great deals on airfare, hotels, and car rentals via the Internet. So go grab your mouse and start surfing—you could save a bundle on your trip. The Web sites we've highlighted below are worth checking out, especially since all services are free (but don't forget that time is money when you're on line).

Microsoft Expedia (www.expedia.com)   The best part of this multipurpose travel site is the "Fare Tracker": You fill out a form on the screen indicating that you're interested in cheap flights to Washington from your hometown, and, once a week, they'll e-mail you the best airfare deals. The site's "Travel Agent" will steer you to bargains on hotels and car rentals, and you can book everything, including flights, right on line. This site is even useful once you're booked: Before you go, log on to Expedia for oodles of up-to-date travel information, including weather reports and foreign exchange rates.

Preview Travel (www.reservations.com and www.vacations.com)   Another useful travel site, "Reservations.com" has a "Best Fare Finder," which will search the Apollo computer reservations system for the three lowest fares for any route on any days of the year. Say you want to go from Chicago to Seattle and back between December 6th and 13th: Just fill out the form on the screen with times, dates, and destinations, and within minutes, Preview will show you the best deals. If you find an airfare you like, you can book your ticket right on line—you can even reserve hotels and car rentals on this site. If you're in the preplanning stage, head to Preview's "Vacations.com" site, where you can check out the latest package deals for destinations around the world by clicking on "Hot Deals."

Travelocity (www.travelocity.com)   This is one of the best travel sites out there. In addition to its "Personal Fare Watcher," which notifies you via e-mail of the lowest airfares for up to five different destinations, Travelocity will track the three lowest fares for any routes on any dates in minutes. You can book a flight right then and there, and if you need a rental car or hotel, Travelocity will find you the best deal via the SABRE computer reservations system (a huge database used by travel agents worldwide). Click on "Last Minute Deals" for the latest travel bargains, including a link to "H.O.T. Coupons" (**www.hotcoupons.com**), where you can print out electronic coupons for travel in the United States and Canada.

Any time of year you may be able to save some money on your ticket by shopping the discount ticket brokers that advertise in major newspapers. Also, don't forget to ask for a student or senior discount if either of these happens to apply to you.

If you happen to be flying from another city on the West Coast or somewhere else in the West, check with Shuttle by United, Alaska Airlines, Horizon Airlines, Reno Air, or Southwest. These airlines often have the best fares between western cities.

BY CAR

The distance from Los Angeles to Seattle is 1,190 miles; from Salt Lake City, 835 miles; from Spokane, in the eastern part of Washington, 285 miles; and from Vancouver, British Columbia, 110 miles.

If you're driving up from California, I-5 runs up through the length of the state and continues up toward the Canadian border; it will take you through both

Trip.Com (**www.thetrip.com**): This site is really geared toward the business traveler, but vacationers-to-be can also use Trip.Com's valuable fare-finding engine, which will e-mail you every week with the best city-to-city airfare deals on your selected route or routes.

Discount Tickets (**www.discount-tickets.com**)   Operated by the ETN (European Travel Network), this site offers discounts on airfares, accommodations, car rentals, and tours. It deals in flights between the United States and other countries, not domestic U.S. flights, so it's most useful for travelers coming to Washington from abroad.

E-Savers Programs   Several major airlines offer a free e-mail service known as **E-Savers,** via which they'll send you their best bargain airfares on a weekly basis. Here's how it works: Once a week (usually Wednesday), subscribers receive a list of discounted flights to and from various destinations, both international and domestic. Now here's the catch: These fares are only available if you leave the very next Saturday (or sometimes Friday night) and return on the following Monday or Tuesday. It's really a service for the spontaneously inclined and travelers looking for a quick getaway. But the fares are cheap, so it's worth taking a look. If you have a preference for certain airlines (in other words, the ones you fly most frequently), sign up with them first. Another caveat: You'll get frequent-flier miles if you purchase one of these fares, but you can't use miles to buy the ticket.

Here's a list of airlines and their Web sites, where you can not only get on the e-mailing lists, but also book flights directly:

• **American Airlines:** www.americanair.com
• **Alaska Airlines/Horizon Air:** www.alaska-air.com
• **Continental Airlines:** www.flycontinental.com
• **TWA:** www.twa.com
• **Northwest Airlines:** www.nwa.com
• **US Airways:** www.usairways.com

Epicurious Travel (**travel.epicurious.com**), another good travel site, allows you to sign up for all of these airline e-mail lists at once.

—Jeanette Foster

Portland, Oregon and Seattle. If you're coming from the east, I-90 runs from Montana and Idaho into Washington, eventually hitting Seattle.

BY TRAIN

Seattle and cities along the north-south I-5 corridor are served by **Amtrak** (☎ **800/872-7245**), as are several Washington cities east to Spokane. Trains that serve the region are: the *Coast Starlight,* which operates between Los Angeles and Seattle with stops in San Francisco and Portland, as well as at smaller towns and cities; The *Empire Builder,* which connects the Northwest with Chicago, following a northern route through North Dakota and Montana; and trains running through the Pacific Northwest Corridor which provide service between Eugene, Oregon and Vancouver, British Columbia, with stops in Seattle and Portland. At press time the round-trip fare between San Francisco and Seattle was between $180 and $332.

BY BUS

Greyhound Lines buses and **Northwest Trailways** (☎ 800/231-2222) offer service to the Northwest from around the country. These buses operate primarily along the Interstate corridors (I-5, I-84, I-90, and I-82) and to a few other towns and cities on major highways. The fare between San Francisco and Seattle at press time was $90 round-trip.

BY FERRY

If you are traveling between Victoria, British Columbia, and Seattle, there are several options available from **Victoria Clipper,** Pier 69, 2701 Alaskan Way (☎ 800/888-2535, 206/448-5000 or 250/382-8100 in Victoria). Throughout the year, a catamaran passenger ferry taking 3 to 5 hours and a high-speed turbo-jet passenger ferry taking only 2 hours make the trip ($79 to $109 round-trip for adults). This latter ferry is the fastest passenger boat in the western hemisphere. The lower fare is for advance-purchase tickets. Some scheduled trips also stop in the San JuanIslands.During the summer months, this company also operates a car ferry, the *Princess Marguerite III,* from Pier 48 in Seattle ($49 one way for car and drive, $29 for passengers).

Bellingham, north of Seattle, is the port for Alaska ferries and cruise ships.

PACKAGE TOURS

Gray Line of Seattle, 720 S. Forest St., Seattle (☎ 800/426-7505), offers 3- to 7-day bus and cruise tours that include Seattle, Mt. Rainier, Vancouver, and Victoria. Prices range from about $150 for a 3-day trip to $830 for a 7-day trip. **Alaska Sightseeing Cruise West,** Fourth and Battery Building, Suite 700, Seattle (☎ 800/426-7702 or 206/441-8687), offers an 8-day cruise from Portland on the Columbia and Snake rivers, and 8-day cruises from Seattle to British Columbia and the San Juan Islands. Fares range from about $795 to $3,395 per person.

If you prefer traveling on your own, but would like to have a custom itinerary planned for your trip to Washington or the Northwest, consider consulting **Pacific Northwest Journeys,** 6036 41st Ave. SW, Seattle, WA 98136 (☎ 800/935-9730 or 206/935-1091). They can tailor a trip that suits your personal traveling style.

8 Getting Around

BY CAR

A car is by far the best way to see the state of Washington. There just isn't any other way to get to the more remote natural spectacles or to fully appreciate such regions as the Olympic Peninsula.

RENTALS   Prices at car-rental agencies in Seattle tend to be lower than elsewhere in Washington, so if at all possible, try to rent your car in Seattle. It always pays to shop around for a rental car and to call the same companies a few times over the course of a couple of weeks (rates change depending on demand). For the very best deal on a rental car, make your reservation at least one week in advance. If you decide on the spur of the moment that you want to rent a car, check to see whether there are any weekend or special rates available. If you are a member of a frequent-flier program, be sure to mention it: You might get mileage credit for renting a car. At press time, daily rates for a compact were between $30 and $54, with weekly rates running between $150 and $250. Expect lower rates between October and April.

All the major car-rental agencies have offices in Seattle and at or near Seattle-Tacoma International Airport. These include **Alamo** (☎ 800/327-9633,

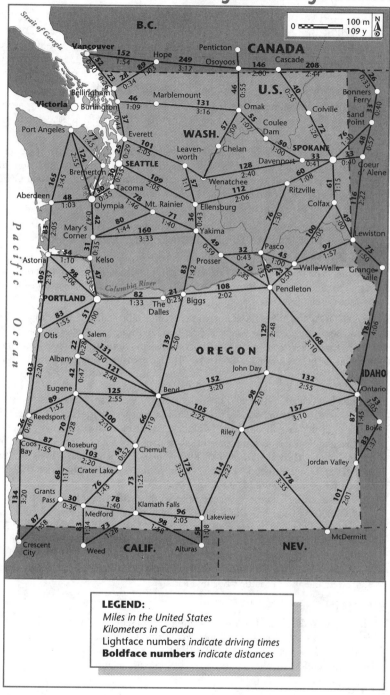

Washington Driving Distances

LEGEND:
Miles in the United States
Kilometers in Canada
Lightface numbers *indicate driving times*
Boldface numbers *indicate distances*

206/433-0812 or 206/292-9770), **Avis** (☎ **800/831-2847,** 206/433-5231, or 206/ 448-1700), **Budget** (☎ **800/527-0700** or 206/682-2277), **Dollar** (☎ **800/ 800-4000,** 206/433-6777, or 206/682-1316), **Enterprise** (☎ **800/325-8007,** 206/ 246-1953, or 206/382-1051), **Hertz** (☎ **800/654-3131,** 206/433-5275, or 206/ 682-5050), **National** (☎ **800/227-7368,** 206/433-5501, or 206/448-7368), and **Thrifty** (☎ **800/367-2277,** 206/246-7565, or 206/625-1133).

GASOLINE   Washington is a big state, so keep your gas tank as full as possible when traveling in the mountains or on the sparsely populated east side of the Cascades.

MAPS   Maps are available at most highway tourist information centers, at the tourist information offices listed earlier in this chapter, and at gas stations throughout the region. For a free map of Washington call the **Washington State Tourism Office** (☎ **800/544-1800**). Members of the AAA can get detailed road maps of the Northwest by calling their local AAA office.

AAA   If you're a member of the American Automobile Association and your car breaks down, call **800/AAA-HELP** for 24-hour emergency road service.

DRIVING RULES   A right turn on red is permitted after first coming to a complete stop. You may also turn left on a red light if you're in the far-left lane of a one-way street and are turning into another one-way street. Seat belts are required, as are car seats for children.

BREAKDOWNS/ASSISTANCE   In the event of a breakdown, stay with your car, lift the hood, turn on your emergency flashers, and wait for a police patrol car. *Do not leave your vehicle.* If you're a member of the American Automobile Association and your car breaks down, call **800/AAA-HELP** for 24-hour emergency road service.

BY PLANE

Washington is a large state, and if you're trying to see every corner of it in a short time, you may want to consider flying. There are airports with regularly scheduled commercial flights at Bellingham, Whidbey Island, Port Townsend, Port Angeles, Yakima, and Spokane. Airlines operating short hops between most of these towns and cities include **Alaska Airlines** (☎ **800/426-0333**), **America West** (☎ **800/ 235-9292**), **Horizon Air** (☎ **800/547-9308**), **Southwest** (☎ **800/435-9792**), and **United Express** (☎ **800/241-6522**).

Seaplane service between Seattle and the San Juan Islands is offered by **Kenmore Air** (☎ **800/543-9595** or 206/486-1257), which has its Seattle terminals at the south end of Lake Union and at the north end of **Lake Washington. Harbor Airlines** (☎ **800/359-3220**) flies between Sea-Tac International Airport in Seattle and Whidbey, San Juan and Orcas Islands, as well as Port Angeles on the Olympic Peninsula. **West Isle Air** (☎ **800/874-4434**) flies to the San Juans from Bellingham and Anacortes, and also to Seattle's Boeing Field.

BY TRAIN

There is **Amtrak** (☎ **800/872-7245**) passenger rail service linking Los Angeles, San Francisco, Portland, Seattle, and Vancouver, British Columbia, and from Seattle eastward to Spokane. The run between Portland and Seattle takes about four hours and costs between $31 to $60 round-trip (reservations are required).

BY FERRY

Washington State Ferries (☎ **800/84-FERRY** in Washington, or 206/464-6400) operates the most extensive ferry network in the United States. There are ferries connecting Seattle to Vashon Island, Bremerton, Southworth, and Bainbridge Island; Tacoma to Vashon Island; Edmonds to Kingston; Mukilteo to Clinton; Keystone to Port Townsend; and Anacortes to San Juan, Orcas, Lopez, and Shaw Islands, and Sidney, British Columbia (for Victoria).

There are also a number of smaller county or private ferries. The most important of these are the **Black Ball Transport** (☎ **360/457-4491** or 250/386-2202 in Victoria) and **Victoria Rapid Transit** (☎ **800/633-1589** in Washington, 360/452-8088, or 250/361-9144 in Victoria) ferries that operate between Port Angeles and Victoria, British Columbia. Victoria Rapid Transit runs only between Memorial Day weekend and the end of September. There's also passenger-ferry service between Seattle and Friday Harbor on San Juan Island, and between Seattle and Victoria, British Columbia, on the **Victoria Clipper** ferries (☎ **800/888-2535,** 206/448-5000, or 250/382-8100 in Victoria).

BY RV

An economical way to tour the Northwest is with a recreational vehicle. If you're considering renting an RV, look under "Recreational Vehicles—Rent and Lease" in the yellow pages of the local phone book. They can be rented for a weekend, a week, or longer. One company to try is **Western Motorhome Rentals,** 19303 Hwy. 99, Lynnwood, WA 98036 (☎ **800/800-1181** or 425/775-1181). If you're going to be traveling in the peak season of summer, it's important to make reservations for your RV at least 3 months ahead of time.

9 Cruising the Columbia River

Paddle-wheel steamboats played a crucial role in the settling of the Northwest, shuttling people and goods down the Columbia River before railroads came to the region. Today, the *Queen of the West,* a paddle-wheel cruise ship operated by the **American West Steamboat Company,** 601 Union St., Suite 4343, Seattle, WA 98101 (☎ **800/434-1232**) is cruising the Columbia offering a luxury never before known in Columbia River paddlewheelers. Fares for the 7-night cruise range from $1,050 to $4,050 per person. Shorter cruises are also available.

If you'd rather cruise aboard a smaller vessel, consider a trip with **Alaska Sightseeing Cruise West,** Fourth and Battery Building, Suite 700, Seattle (☎ **800/426-7702** or 206/441-8687), which offers an eight-day cruise from Portland, Oregon on the Columbia and Snake rivers. Fares range from $795 to $3,395 per person. Similar trips, though with naturalists and historians on board, are offered by **Special Expeditions** (☎ **800/762-0003** or 212/765-7740); their rates range from $1990 to $3090.

FAST FACTS: Washington

AAA   If you're a member of the American Automobile Association and your car breaks down, call ☎ **800/AAA-HELP** for 24-hour emergency road service.

American Express   In Seattle, the Amex office is in the Plaza 600 building at 600 Stewart St. (☎ **206/441-8622**). The office is open Monday through Friday from 9am to 5pm. Call this office for information on American Express services in other outlying towns. To report lost or stolen traveler's checks, call ☎ **800/221-7282.**

Area Code   The telephone area code in Seattle is 206. The area code for the Eastside (including Kirkland and Bellevue) is 425. The area code for Tacoma and surrounding areas is 253. Other parts of western Washington use area code 360, while east of the Washington Cascades the area code is 509.

Banks and ATM Networks   The most commonly used ATM networks in Washington are the Plus, Cirrus, Star, Visa, and MasterCard networks.

Car Rentals   See "Getting Around," earlier in this chapter.

Climate   See "When to Go," earlier in this chapter.

Embassies and Consulates   See "Fast Facts: For the Foreign Traveler" in Chapter 4.

Emergencies   Call **911** for fire, police, and ambulance.

Information   See "Visitor Information & Money," earlier in this chapter, and individual city chapters for local information offices.

Liquor Laws   The legal drinking age in Washington is 21. Bars can legally stay open until 2am.

Maps   See "Getting Around," earlier in this chapter.

Pets   Many hotels and motels in the Northwest accept small, well-behaved pets. However, there's often a small fee charged to allow them into guest rooms. Many places, in particular bed-and-breakfast inns, don't allow pets at all. On the other hand, many bed-and-breakfasts have their own pets, so if you have a dog or cat allergy, be sure to mention it when making a bed-and-breakfast reservation. Two good resources for dog owners are *Frommer's on the Road Again with Man's Best Friend: Northwest and Frommer's America on Wheels: Northwest* (both from Macmillan), which will steer you toward dog-friendly accommodations. Pets are usually restricted in national parks for their own safety, so call each park's ranger station to check before setting out.

Police   To reach the police, dial **911.**

Taxes   The state of Washington makes up for its lack of an income tax with its sales tax of between 6.5% and 8.2%. Hotel-room tax is 15.2% in Seattle.

Time Zone   The Northwest is on Pacific standard time (PST) and observes daylight saving time from the last Sunday in October to the first Sunday in April, making it consistently 3 hours behind the East Coast.

Weather   If you can't tell what the weather is by looking out the window, or you want to be absolutely sure that it's going to rain the next day, call the Seattle Times Info Line ☎ **206/464-2000,** ext. 9900.

For Foreign Visitors 4

This chapter will provide some specifics about getting to the United States as economically and effortlessly as possible, plus some helpful information about how things are done in Washington—from receiving mail to making a local or long-distance telephone call.

1 Preparing for Your Trip

ENTRY REQUIREMENTS

DOCUMENT REGULATIONS   Citizens of Canada and Bermuda may enter the United States without visas, but they will need to show proof of nationality, the most common and hassle-free form of which is a passport.

The U.S. State Department has a Visa Waiver Pilot Program allowing citizens of certain countries to enter the United States without a visa for stays of fewer than 90 days of vacation travel. At press time these included Andorra, Argentina, Australia, Austria, Belgium, Brunei, Denmark, Finland, France, Germany, Iceland, Ireland, Italy, Japan, Liechtenstein, Luxembourg, Monaco, the Netherlands, New Zealand, Norway, San Marino, Spain, Sweden, Switzerland, and the United Kingdom. (The program as applied to the United Kingdom refers to British citizens who have the "unrestricted right of permanent abode in the United Kingdom," that is, citizens from England, Scotland, Wales, Northern Ireland, the Channel Islands, and the Isle of Man; and not, for example, citizens of the British Commonwealth of Pakistan.)

Citizens from these countries need only a valid passport and a round-trip air or cruise ticket in their possession upon arrival. If they first enter the United States, they may then visit Mexico, Canada, Bermuda, and/or the Caribbean islands and return to the United States without needing a visa. Further information is available from any U.S. embassy or consulate.

Citizens of countries other than those specified above, or those traveling to the United States for reasons or length of time outside the restrictions of the Visa Waiver program, or those who require waivers of inadmissibility must have two documents: (1) a valid passport, with an expiration date at least 6 months later than the scheduled end of the visit to the United States (Some countries are exceptions to the six-month validity rule. Contact any U.S. embassy or consulate for complete information); and (2) a tourist visa, available from the nearest U.S. consulate. To obtain a visa, the traveler must submit a completed application form (either in person or by mail) with a 1½-inch square photo and the required application fee. There may also be an issuance fee, depending on the type of visa and other factors. Usually you can obtain a visa right away or within 24 hours, but it may take longer during the summer rush period (June to August). If you cannot go in person, contact the nearest U.S. embassy or consulate for directions on applying by mail. Your travel agent or airline office may also be able to provide you with visa applications and instructions. The U.S. consulate or embassy that issues your visa will determine whether you will be issued a multiple- or single-entry visa. The Immigration and Naturalization Service officers at the port of entry in the United States will make an admission decision and determine your length of stay.

MEDICAL REQUIREMENTS   No inoculations are needed to enter the United States unless you are coming from, or have stopped over in, areas known to be suffering from epidemics, particularly of cholera or yellow fever.

If you have a disease requiring treatment with medications containing narcotics or drugs requiring a syringe, carry a valid signed prescription from your physician to allay any suspicions that you are smuggling drugs.

CUSTOMS   Every adult visitor may bring in free of duty: one liter of wine or hard liquor; 200 cigarettes or 100 cigars (but no cigars from Cuba) or 3 pounds of smoking tobacco; $100 worth of gifts. These exemptions are offered to travelers who spend at least 72 hours in the United States and who have not claimed these exemptions within the preceding 6 months. It is altogether forbidden to bring into the country foodstuff (particularly cheese, fruit, cooked meats, and canned goods) and plants (vegetables, seeds, tropical plants, and so on). Foreign tourists may bring in or take out up to $10,000 in U.S. or foreign currency with no formalities; larger sums must be declared to Customs on entering or leaving.

INSURANCE

There is no national health system in the United States. Because the cost of medical care is extremely high, we strongly advise every traveler to secure health coverage before setting out.

You may want to take out a comprehensive travel policy that covers (for a relatively low premium) sickness or injury cost (medical, surgical, and hospital); loss or theft of your baggage; trip-cancellation costs; guarantee of bail in case you are arrested; costs of accident, repatriation, or death. Such packages (for example, "Europe Assistance" in Europe) are sold by automobile clubs at attractive rates, as well as by insurance companies and travel agencies.

MONEY

CURRENCY & EXCHANGE   The U.S. monetary system has a decimal base: 1 American dollar ($1) = 100 cents (100¢).

Dollar bills commonly come in $1 ("a buck"), $5, $10, $20, $50, and $100 denominations (the last two are not always welcome when paying for small purchases and are not accepted in taxis or subway ticket booths). There are also $2 bills (seldom encountered).

There are six denominations of coins: 1¢ (one cent, or "penny"), 5¢ (five cents, or "a nickel"), 10¢ (ten cents, or "a dime"), 25¢ (twenty-five cents, or "a quarter"), 50¢ (fifty cents, or "a half dollar"), and the rare $1 piece.

TRAVELER'S CHECKS   Traveler's checks in U.S. dollar denominations are readily accepted at most hotels, motels, restaurants, and large stores; but the best place to change traveler's checks is at a bank. Do not bring traveler's checks denominated in other currencies, with the possible exception of those in Canadian dollars. Because of the proximity of the Canadian border, many hotels, restaurants, and shops will accept Canadian currency.

CREDIT & CHARGE CARDS   The method of payment most widely used is the credit card: VISA (BarclayCard in Britain), MasterCard (EuroCard in Europe, Access in Britain, Charges in Canada), American Express, Diners Club, Discover Card, and Carte Blanche. You can save yourself trouble by using "plastic money," rather than cash or traveler's checks in most hotels, motels, restaurants, and retail stores (a growing number of food and liquor stores now accept credit cards). You must have a credit card to rent a car. It can also be used as proof of identity (often carrying more weight than a passport), or as a "cash card," enabling you to draw money from banks that accept them.

Note: The "foreign-exchange bureaus" so common in Europe are rare except at airports in the United States, and nonexistent outside major cities. Try to avoid having to change foreign money or traveler's checks not denominated in U.S. dollars at a small-town bank, or even a branch in a big city; in fact, leave any currency other than U.S. dollars at home—it may prove to be more of a nuisance to you than it's worth.

SAFETY

GENERAL   While tourist areas are generally safe, crime is on the increase everywhere, and U.S. urban areas tend to be less safe than those in Europe or Japan. Visitors should always be alert. This is particularly true of large U.S. cities. It is wise to ask the city's or area's tourist office if you are in doubt about which neighborhoods are safe.

Avoid deserted areas, especially at night. Don't enter a city park at night unless there is an event that attracts crowds. Generally speaking, you can feel safe in areas where there are many people, and many open establishments.

Avoid carrying valuables with you on the street, and don't display expensive cameras or electronic equipment. Hold on to your pocketbook, and place your billfold in an inside pocket. In restaurants, theaters, and other public places, keep your possessions in sight.

Remember also that hotels are open to the public, and in a large hotel, security personnel may not be able to screen everyone entering. Always lock your room door—don't assume that once inside your hotel you are automatically safe and need no longer be aware of your surroundings.

DRIVING   Safety while driving is particularly important. Question your car-rental agency about personal safety, or ask for a brochure of traveler safety tips when you pick up your car. Obtain written directions, or a map with the route marked in red, from the agency showing how to reach your destination. And, if possible, arrive and depart during daylight hours.

Recently, more and more crime has involved cars and drivers. If you drive off a highway into a neighborhood that seems threatening, leave the area as quickly as possible. If you have an accident, even on a highway, remain inside your car with the doors locked until you assess the situation, or until the police arrive. If you are bumped from behind on the street or are involved in a minor accident with no injuries and the situation appears to be suspicious, motion to the other driver to follow you. Never get out of your car in such situations.

You can also keep a premade sign in your car which reads: Please follow this vehicle to report the accident. Show the sign to the other driver and go directly to the nearest police precinct, well-lighted service station, or all-night store.

If you see someone on the road who indicates a need for help, do not stop. Take note of the location, drive on to a well-lighted area, and telephone the police by dialing 911.

Park in well-lighted, well-traveled areas if possible. Always keep your car doors locked, whether attended or unattended. Look around you before you get in or out of your car, and never leave packages or valuables in sight. If someone attempts to rob you or steal your car, do not try to resist the thief/carjacker—report the incident to the police department immediately.

2 Getting to & Around the U.S.

GETTING TO THE U.S.

Travelers from overseas can take advantage of **APEX** (advance purchase excursion) fares offered by all major U.S. and European carriers. Aside from these, attractive values are offered by **Icelandair** on flights from Luxembourg to New York and by **Virgin Atlantic Airways** from London to New York/Newark.

From Toronto, there are flights to Seattle on Air Canada (☎ **800/268-7240** in Ontario, or 800/776-3000 in the U.S.), American, Continental, Delta, Northwest, TWA, and United. There are flights **from Vancouver, British Columbia,** to Seattle on Air Canada and Horizon.

In addition, Seattle is served by **Amtrak** (☎ **800/872-7245**) Pacific Northwest Corridor trains which connect Vancouver, British Columbia, with Seattle and Spokane, Washington. Vancouver to Seattle takes about 4 hours and the fare is $19. This route includes a bus segment.

Seaplane service between Seattle and the San Juan Islands and Vancouver and Victoria, British Columbia is offered by **Kenmore Air** (☎ **800/543-9595** or 206/486-1257).

There is also now helicopter service to Seattle's Boeing Field from Victoria and Vancouver, British Columbia on Helijet Airways (☎ **800/665-4354**). The flights, of which there are three a day, take only 35 minutes from Victoria and 90 minutes from Vancouver. The round-trip airfare is $170 between Victoria and Seattle and $299 between Vancouver and Seattle.

Airlines traveling **from London** to Seattle are American, Delta, Northwest, TWA, and United. British Airways flies directly to Seattle from London.

You can make reservations by calling the following numbers in Britain: **American** (☎ 0181/572-5555), **British Airways** (☎ 0345/222-111), **Delta** (☎ 0800/414-767), **Northwest** (☎ 0990/56-1000), **TWA** (☎ 0181/814-0707), and **United** (☎ 0181/990-9900). **From Ireland,** you can also try **Aer Lingus** (☎ 01/705-3154 in Ireland).

From New Zealand and Australia, there are flights to Los Angeles on **Quantas** (☎ 131211 in Australia) and **Air New Zealand** (☎ 0800/737-000 in Auckland, or 3/379-5200 in Christchurch). **United** flies to Seattle from New Zealand and Australia, with a stop in Los Angeles or San Francisco.

The visitor arriving by air, no matter what the port of entry, should cultivate patience and resignation before setting foot on U.S. soil. Getting through Immigration control may take as long as two hours on some days, especially summer weekends. Add the time it takes to clear Customs and you'll see that you should make very generous allowance for delay in planning connections between international and domestic flights—an average of 2 to 3 hours at least.

In contrast, travelers arriving by car, rail, or ferry from Canada will find border-crossing formalities streamlined to the vanishing point. And air travelers from Canada, Bermuda, and some places in the Caribbean can sometimes go through Customs and Immigration at the point of departure, which is much quicker and less painful.

For further information about travel to and around Washington, see "Getting There" and "Getting Around" in chapter 3.

GETTING AROUND THE U.S.

BY PLANE   Some large airlines (for example, **American, Delta, Northwest, TWA,** and **United**) offer transatlantic and transpacific travelers special discount tickets under the name **Visit USA,** allowing travel between any U.S. destinations at minimum rates. These tickets are not on sale in the United States and must therefore be purchased before you leave your foreign point of departure. This system is the best, easiest, and fastest way to see the United States at a low cost. You should obtain information well in advance from your travel agent or the office of the airline concerned, since the conditions attached to these discount tickets can be changed without advance notice.

BY TRAIN   International visitors can buy a **USA Railpass,** good for 15 or 30 days of unlimited nationwide travel on **Amtrak** (☎ **800/872-7245**). The pass is available through many foreign travel agents and at any staffed Amtrak station in the U.S. The price at press time for a 15-day peak period pass was $375, and for a 15-day off-peak period pass $260; a 30-day peak period pass cost $480, and a 30-day off-peak period pass was $350. (With a foreign passport, you can also buy passes at major Amtrak offices in the United States, including locations in San Francisco, Los Angeles, Chicago, New York, Miami, Boston, and Washington, D.C.) Reservations are generally required and should be made for each part of your trip as early as possible. Amtrak also offers a program called **Amtrak Vacations,** which allows you to travel both by train and plane and includes hotel bookings; for information call ☎ **800/ 321-8684.**

Visitors should also be aware of the limitations of long-distance rail travel in the United States. With a few notable exceptions (for instance, the Northeast Corridor line between Boston and Washington, D.C.), service is rarely up to European standard: Delays are common, routes are limited and often infrequently served, and fares are rarely significantly lower than discount airfares. Thus, cross-country train travel should be approached with caution.

BY BUS   The cheapest way to travel the United States is by bus. **Greyhound** (☎ **800/231-2222**), the nation's nationwide bus line, offers an **Ameripass** for unlimited travel for 7 days (for $179), 15 days (for $289), and 30 days (for $399). Bus travel in the United States can be both slow and uncomfortable, so this option is not for everyone.

BY CAR   The United States is a nation of cars, and the most cost-effective, convenient, and comfortable way to travel through the country is by driving. The Interstate highway system connects cities and towns all over the country, and in addition to these high-speed, limited-access roadways, there is an extensive network of federal, state, and local highways and roads. Another convenience of traveling by car is the easy access to inexpensive motels at interstate highway off-ramps. Such motels are almost always less expensive than hotels and motels in downtown areas.

FAST FACTS: For the Foreign Traveler

Accommodations   It is always a good idea to make hotel reservations as soon as you know your trip dates. Reservations require a deposit of one night's payment. Seattle is particularly busy during summer months, and hotels book up in advance—especially on weekends when there is a festival on. If you do not have reservations, it is best to look for a room in the midafternoon. If you wait until evening, you run the risk that hotels will be filled. Major downtown hotels, which cater primarily to business travelers, commonly offer weekend discounts of as much as 50% to entice vacationers to fill up the empty hotel rooms. However, resorts and hotels near tourist attractions tend to have higher rates on weekends.

Automobile Organizations   Auto clubs will supply maps, suggested routes, guidebooks, accident and bail-bond insurance, and emergency road service. The major auto club in the United States, with 955 offices nationwide, is the American Automobile Association (AAA). Members of some foreign auto clubs have reciprocal arrangements with the AAA and enjoy its services at no charge. If you belong to an auto club, inquire about AAA reciprocity before you leave. If your driver's license isn't in English, check with your foreign auto club to see if they can provide you with an International Driving Permit validating your foreign license in the United States. You may be able to join the AAA even if you are not a member of a reciprocal club. To inquire, call ☎ **800/AAA-HELP.** In addition, some automobile rental agencies now provide these services, so you should inquire about their availability when you rent your car.

Automobile Rentals   To rent a car you need a major credit card and a valid driver's license. Sometimes a passport or an international driver's license is also required if your driver's license is in a language other than English. You usually need to be at least 25; although some companies do rent to younger people, they may add a daily surcharge. Be sure to return your car with the same amount of gasoline you started out with as rental companies charge excessive prices for gas. Keep in mind that a separate motorcycle-driver's license is required in most states. See "Getting Around" in chapter 3 for specifics on auto rental in Washington.

Business Hours   Banks are open weekdays from 9am to 5pm, with later hours on Friday; many banks are now open on Saturday also. There is also 24-hour access to banks through automatic teller machines at most banks and other outlets. Most offices are open weekdays from 9am to 5pm. Most post offices are open weekdays from 8am to 5pm, with shorter hours on Saturday. In general, stores open between 9 and 10am and close between 5 and 6pm, Monday through Saturday; stores in malls generally stay open until 9pm; some department stores stay open till 9pm on Thursday and Friday evening; and many stores are open on Sunday from 11am to 5 or 6pm.

Climate   See "When to Go" in chapter 3.

Currency   See "Money" in "Preparing for Your Trip," above.

Currency Exchange   You will find currency exchange services in major airports with international service (including Seattle-Tacoma International Airport). Elsewhere, they may be quite difficult to come by.

To exchange money in Seattle, go to **American Express,** 600 Stewart St. (☎ **206/441-8622**), or **Thomas Cook,** 906 Third Ave. (☎ **206/623-4012**) or **Westlake Center** (☎ **206/682-4525**).

Drinking Laws The legal drinking age in Washington is 21. The penalties for driving under the influence of alcohol are stiff.

Electricity The United States uses 110 to 120 volts AC (60 cycles), compared to 220 to 240 volts AC (50 cycles), in most of Europe. In addition to a 110-volt converter, small appliances of non-American manufacture, such as hair dryers or shavers, will require a plug adapter with two flat, parallel pins.

Embassies & Consulates All embassies are located in the national capital, Washington, D.C. Some consulates are located in major cities, and most nations have a mission to the United Nations in New York City. Listed here are embassies and consulates of some major English-speaking countries. If you are from another country, you can obtain the telephone number of your embassy or consulate by calling Information in Washington, D.C. (☎ **202/555-1212**).

- **Australia** The embassy is at 1601 Massachusetts Ave. NW, Washington, DC 20036 (☎ **202/797-3000**). The nearest consulate is in San Francisco at 1 Bush St., San Francisco, CA 94104-4425 (☎ **415/362-6160**).
- **Canada** The embassy is at 501 Pennsylvania Ave. NW, Washington, DC 20001 (☎ **202/682-1740**). The regional consulate is at 412 Plaza 600 Building, Sixth Ave. and Stewart St., Seattle, WA 98101-1286 (☎ **206/ 443-1777**).
- **Ireland** The embassy is at 2234 Massachusetts Ave. NW, Washington, DC 20008 (☎ **202/462-3939**). The nearest consulate is in San Francisco at 44 Montgomery St., Suite 3830, San Francisco, CA 94104 (☎ **415/392-4214**).
- **New Zealand** The embassy is at 37 Observatory Circle NW, Washington, DC 20008 (☎ **202/328-4800**). The nearest consulate is in Los Angeles at 12400 Wilshire Blvd., Suite 1150, Los Angeles, CA 90025 (☎ **310/ 207-1605**).
- **United Kingdom** The embassy is at 3100 Massachusetts Ave. NW, Washington, DC 20008 (☎ **202/462-1340**). There is a consulate in Seattle at 999 Third Ave., Suite 820, Seattle, WA 98104 (☎ **206/622-9255**).

Emergencies Call **911** to report a fire, call the police, or get an ambulance. This is a toll-free call (no coins are required at a public telephone).

Gasoline (Petrol) One U.S. gallon equals 3.75 liters, while 1.2 U.S. gallons equals one Imperial gallon. You'll notice there are several grades (and price levels) of gasoline available at most gas stations. And you'll also notice that their names change from company to company. The unleaded ones with the highest octane are the most expensive (most rental cars take the least expensive "regular" unleaded) and leaded gas is the least expensive, but only older cars can take this any more, so check if you're not sure. In Washington you are allowed to pump your own gasoline.

Holidays On the following legal national holidays, banks, government offices, post offices, and many stores, restaurants, and museums are closed:

January 1 (New Year's Day)
Third Monday in January (Martin Luther King Jr. Day)
Third Monday in February (Presidents' Day, Washington's Birthday)
Last Monday in May (Memorial Day)
July 4 (Independence Day)
First Monday in September (Labor Day)
Second Monday in October (Columbus Day)

November 11 (Veterans Day/Armistice Day)
Fourth Thursday in November (Thanksgiving Day)
December 25 (Christmas Day)

The Tuesday following the first Monday in November is Election Day, and is a legal holiday in presidential-election years.

Languages Major hotels may have multilingual employees. Unless your language is very obscure, they can usually supply a translator on request.

Legal Aid If you are stopped for a minor driving infraction (for example, of the highway code, such as speeding), never attempt to pay the fine directly to the police officer; you may wind up arrested on the much more serious charge of attempted bribery. Pay fines by mail, or directly into the hands of the clerk of the court. If accused of a more serious offense, it is wise to say and do nothing before consulting a lawyer. Under U.S. law, an arrested person is allowed one telephone call to a party of his or her choice. Call your embassy or consulate.

Mail If you want to receive mail on your vacation and you aren't sure of your address, your mail can be sent to you, in your name, c/o General Delivery at the main post office of the city or region where you expect to be. The addressee must pick it up in person and produce proof of identity (driver's license, credit card, passport, etc.).

Generally to be found at intersections, mailboxes are blue with a red-and-white stripe and carry the inscription U.S. mail. If your mail is addressed to a U.S. destination, don't forget to add the five-figure postal code, or ZIP (zone improvement plan) code, after the two-letter abbreviation of the state to which the mail is addressed (WA for Washington, OR for Oregon, CA for California, and so on).

Medical Emergencies Dial **911** for an ambulance.

Newspapers & Magazines National newspapers include *The New York Times, USA Today,* and the *Wall Street Journal.* National news weeklies include *Newsweek, Time,* and *U.S. News and World Report.* For local news publications, see "Fast Facts" for Seattle in chapter 5.

Radio & Television Radio and TV, with four coast-to-coast networks—ABC, CBS, NBC, and Fox—joined by the Public Broadcasting System (PBS) and the cable network CNN, play a major part in American life. In big cities, viewers have a choice of about a dozen channels (including the UHF channels), most of them transmitting 24 hours a day, without counting the pay-TV channels showing recent movies or sports events. All options are usually indicated on your hotel TV set. You'll also find a wide choice of local radio stations, each broadcasting particular kinds of talk shows and/or music—classical, country, jazz, pop, gospel—punctuated by news broadcasts and frequent commercials.

Safety See "Safety" in "Preparing for Your Trip," above.

Taxes In the United States there is no value-added tax (VAT) or other indirect tax at a national level. Every state, and each city in it, can levy a local tax on all purchases, including hotel and restaurant checks, airline tickets, and so on. In Seattle and King County the sales tax rate is 8.6%; in the rest of Washington, the sales tax varies.

Telephone, Telegraph, Telex & Fax The telephone system in the United States is run by private corporations, so rates, especially for long distance service, can vary widely—even on calls made from public telephones. Local calls in the United States usually cost 25¢.

Generally, hotel surcharges on long-distance and local calls are astronomical. You are usually better off using a public pay telephone, which you will find clearly marked in most public buildings and private establishments as well as on the street. Outside metropolitan areas, public telephones are more difficult to find. Stores and gas stations are your best bet.

Most long-distance and international calls can be dialed directly from any phone. For calls to Canada and other parts of the United States, dial 1 followed by the area code and the seven-digit number. For international calls, dial 011 followed by the country code, city code, and the telephone number of the person you wish to call.

For reversed-charge or collect calls, and for person-to-person calls, dial 0 (zero, not the letter "O"), followed by the area code and number you want; an operator will then come on the line, and you should specify that you are calling collect, or person-to-person, or both. If your operator-assisted call is international, ask for the overseas operator.

For local directory assistance ("information"), dial ☎ **555-1212;** for long-distance information, dial 1, then the appropriate area code and ☎ **555-1212.**

Like the telephone system, telegraph and telex services are provided by private corporations like ITT, MCI, and, above all, Western Union. You can bring your telegram to the nearest **Western Union** office (there are hundreds across the country), or dictate it over the phone (a toll-free call, ☎ **800/325-6000**). You can also telegraph money, or have it telegraphed to you very quickly over the Western Union system.

If you need to send a fax, almost all shops that make photocopies offer fax service as well. Many hotels also offer faxing service.

Telephone Directory   There are two kinds of telephone directories available to you. The general directory is the so-called White Pages, in which private and business subscribers are listed in alphabetical order.

The inside front cover lists emergency numbers for police, fire, and ambulance, as well as other vital numbers (coast guard, poison control center, crime-victims hot line, and so on). The first few pages are devoted to community-service numbers, including a guide to long-distance and international calling, complete with country codes and area codes.

The second directory, printed on yellow paper (hence its name, Yellow Pages), lists local services, businesses, and industries by type, with an index at the back. The listings cover not only such obvious items as automobile repair services by make of car, or drugstores (pharmacies)—often by geographical location—but also restaurants by type of cuisine and geographical location, bookstores by special subject and/or language, places of worship by religious denomination, and other information that the tourist might otherwise not readily find. The Yellow Pages also include city plans or detailed area maps, often showing postal zip codes and public transportation.

Time   The United States is divided into four time zones (six, if Alaska and Hawaii are included). From east to west, these are: eastern standard time (EST), central standard time (CST), mountain standard time (MST), Pacific standard time (PST), Alaska standard time (AST), and Hawaii standard time (HST). Always keep changing time zones in mind if you are traveling (or even telephoning) long distance in the United States. For example, noon in Seattle (PT) is 1pm in Denver (MT), 2pm in Chicago (CT), 3pm in New York City (ET), 11am in Anchorage (AT), and 10am in Honolulu (HT). Daylight saving time is in effect from 2am on the last Sunday in April until 2am on the last Sunday in October except in

Arizona, Hawaii, part of Indiana, and Puerto Rico. Daylight saving time moves the clock one hour ahead of standard time.

Tipping   This is part of the American way of life, on the principle that you must expect to pay for any service you get. Here are some rules of thumb:

Bartenders: 10% to 15%.

Bellhops: at least 50¢ per piece; $2 to $3 for a lot of baggage.

Cab drivers: 15% of the fare.

Cafeterias, fast-food restaurants: no tip

Chambermaids: $1 a day.

Checkroom attendants (restaurants, theaters): $1 per garment.

Cinemas, movies, theaters: no tip.

Doormen (hotels or restaurants): not obligatory.

Gas-station attendants: no tip.

Hairdressers: 15% to 20%.

Redcaps (airport and railroad stations): at least 50¢ per piece, $2 to $3 for a lot of baggage.

Restaurants, nightclubs: 15% to 20% of the check.

Sleeping-car porters: $2 to $3 per night to your attendant.

Valet parking attendants: $1.

Toilets   Foreign visitors often complain that public toilets (or "restrooms") are hard to find in most U.S. cities. True, there are none on the streets, but the visitor can usually find one in a bar, restaurant, hotel, museum, department store, or service station and it will probably be clean (although the last-mentioned sometimes leaves much to be desired).

Note, however, that some restaurants and bars display a notice that "Toilets Are for the Use of Patrons Only." You can ignore this sign, or better yet, avoid arguments by ordering a cup of coffee or a soft drink, which will qualify you as a patron. The cleanliness of toilets at railroad stations and bus depots may be questionable; some public places are equipped with pay toilets, which require you to insert one or more coins into a slot on the door before it will open.

Seattle 5

You can get a latte almost anywhere in the country these days, and it's been years since Tom Hanks was sleepless in Seattle. Grunge music has lost its rock 'n' roll preeminence, and Seattle's fringe theater is looking a bit frayed around the edges. Martinis are replacing the Northwest microbrews that helped reacquaint the nation with the flavor of real beer, and the flavors of Asia have replaced those of the Northwest on restaurant menus all over the city.

Could it be that the shine has worn off the Emerald City? Don't bet on it. Seattle may have stepped out of the national limelight for the moment, but in 1996, *Conde Naste Traveler, Travel & Leisure, Money, Fortune,* and the American Society of Travel Agents all ranked this city among the top 10 cities in the United States to live in or visit. Seattleites would love it if magazines would quit publishing such polls, but the accolades continue to roll in year after year.

Seattle's popularity and rapid growth, though it has brought fine restaurants, a new symphony hall, new downtown hotels, rock-music fame, and national recognition of the city's arts scene, has not been entirely smooth. Far from being the Emerald City at the end of the yellow brick road, Seattle has its share of urban problems. The city government has a penchant for spending tax dollars on sports arenas rather than on education or street repairs. Housing costs are approaching those of California. The streets and highways have reached critical mass, and commuting has become almost as nightmarish as down in California, from whence so many of the city's commuters once fled partly because of the traffic congestion (go figure). But when the sun is setting across Puget Sound and the great snowy bulk of Mount Rainier is glowing salmon pink in the waning light, it's almost impossible not to order up a double tall raspberry latte and enjoy the show.

1 Orientation

ARRIVING
BY PLANE

Seattle-Tacoma International Airport (☎ **800/544-1965** or 206/431-4444), known as Sea-Tac, is located about 14 miles south of Seattle. It's connected to the city by I-5. Generally, allow 30 minutes for the trip between the airport and downtown, and more during rush hour.

Gray Line Airport Express (☎ 206/626-6088) provides service between the airport and downtown Seattle daily from about 4:40am to 10:40pm. This shuttle van stops at the Madison Hotel, Crowne Plaza, Four Seasons Olympic, Sheraton Seattle, Westin Hotel, and the Warwick Hotel. Rates are $7.50 one way and $13 round-trip.

Shuttle Express (☎ 800/487-RIDE or 206/622-1424) provides 24-hour service between Sea-Tac and the Seattle, North Seattle and Bellevue areas. Their rates vary from $13 to $19. You need to make a reservation to get to the airport, but to leave the airport, just call when you arrive. Push 48 on one of the courtesy phones outside the baggage-claim area.

Metro Transit (☎ 800/542-7876 or 206/553-3000) operates three buses between the airport and downtown. It's a good idea to call for the current schedule when you arrive in town. At this writing, **no. 194** operates (to Third Avenue and Union Street or the bus tunnel, depending on the time of day) every 30 minutes weekdays from about 5:30am to 8:30pm, and weekends from about 6:30am to 6:30pm. **No. 174** operates (to Second Avenue and Union Street) every 30 minutes weekdays from about 5:30am to 1:20am, and weekends from about 6:30am to 1:20am. **No. 184** has two runs from the airport (to Second Avenue and Union Street) in the early morning 7 nights a week. The first bus leaves for the airport at 2:15am and the second leaves at 3:30am. Bus trips take 30 to 40 minutes depending on conditions. The fare is $1.10 during off-peak hours and $1.60 during peak hours.

A **taxi** into downtown Seattle will cost you about $28. There are usually plenty of taxis around, but if not, call **Yellow Cab** (☎ 206/622-6500) or **Farwest Taxi** (☎ 206/622-1717). The flag-drop charge is $1.80; after that, it's $1.80 per mile.

BY CAR

I-5 is the main north-south artery through Seattle, running south to Portland and north to the Canadian border. I-405 is Seattle's eastside bypass and accesses the cities of Bellevue, Redmond, and Kirkland on the east side of Lake Washington. I-90, which ends at I-5, connects Seattle to Spokane, in the eastern part of Washington. Wash. 520 connects I-405 with Seattle just north of downtown and also ends at I-5. Wash. 99, the Alaskan Way Viaduct, is another major north-south highway through downtown Seattle; it passes through the waterfront section of the city.

BY FERRY

Seattle is served by the Washington State Ferries (☎ 800/84-FERRY in Washington State, or 206/464-6400 in Seattle), the most extensive ferry system in the United States. Car ferries travel between both Bainbridge Island and Bremerton (on the Kitsap Peninsula) and downtown Seattle at Pier 52. A passenger-only ferry from Vashon Island uses the adjacent Pier 50. Car ferries also cross between both Vashon Island and Southworth (on the Kitsap Peninsula) and Fauntleroy in West Seattle. One-way fares for a car and driver from Bainbridge Island to Seattle (a 35-minute crossing) are $5.90 ($7.10 from mid-May to mid-October). Car passengers and walk-ons only pay fares on westbound ferries. Fares from Bremerton to Seattle (a 60-minute crossing), Vashon Island to Seattle (a 15-minute crossing), Kingston to Edmonds (a 30-minute crossing), and Southworth to Fauntleroy (a 35-minute crossing) are the same.

If you are traveling between Victoria, British Columbia, and Seattle, there are several options available from **Victoria Clipper,** Pier 69, 2701 Alaskan Way (☎ 800/888-2535, 206/448-5000, or 250/382-8100 in Victoria). Throughout the year, a catamaran passenger ferry taking 3 to 5 hours and a high-speed turbo-jet passenger ferry taking only 2 hours make the trip ($79 to $109 round-trip for adults). This

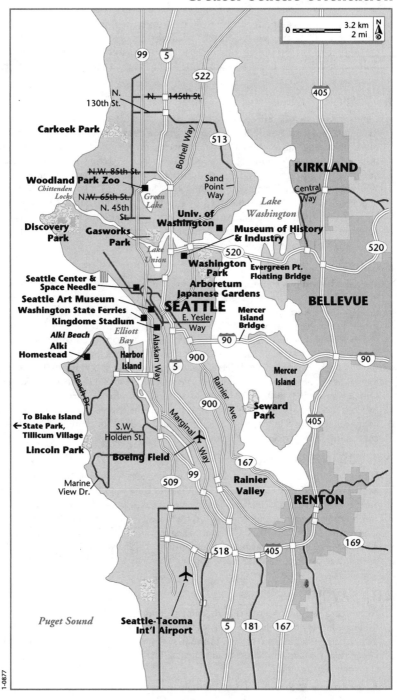

Carkeek Park

N. 130th St.

N. 145th St.

99 5

522

513

KIRKLAND

Bothell Way

Sand Point Way

Central Way

Lake Washington

405

N.W. 85th St.

Woodland Park Zoo

Chittenden Locks

N.W. 65th St.

N. 45th St.

Green Lake

Discovery Park

Gasworks Park

Univ. of Washington

Museum of History & Industry

Lake Union

520

Evergreen Pt. Floating Bridge

520

Washington Park

Seattle Center & Space Needle

Seattle Art Museum

Washington State Ferries

Kingdome Stadium

Arboretum Japanese Gardens

SEATTLE

E. Yesler Way

Mercer Island Bridge

BELLEVUE

Elliott Bay

Alki Beach

Alki Homestead

Harbor Island

Beach Dr.

Alaskan Way

5

900

900

Rainier Ave.

Mercer Island

Seward Park

90

90

405

To Blake Island State Park, Tillicum Village

Lincoln Park

S.W. Holden St.

Boeing Field

Marginal Way

167

99

509

Rainier Valley

RENTON

Marine View Dr.

169

518

405

Puget Sound

Seattle-Tacoma Int'l Airport

5 181 167

1-0877

57

latter ferry is the fastest passenger boat in the western hemisphere. The lower fare is for advance-purchase tickets. Some scheduled trips also stop in the San Juan Islands. During the summer months, this company also operates a car ferry, the *Princess Marguerite III,* from Pier 48 in Seattle ($49 one way for car and drive, $29 for passengers).

BY TRAIN

There is **Amtrak** (☎ **800/872-7245**) service to Seattle from Vancouver, British Columbia; Spokane and points east on the *Empire Builder;* and Portland and points south (including San Francisco and Los Angeles) on the *Coast Starlight.* The trains stop at King Street Station (☎ **206/382-4125**), Third Avenue South and Jackson Street, near the Kingdome and the south entrance to the downtown bus tunnel. The Waterfront Streetcar also stops near King Street Station.

Several trains run daily between Seattle and both Portland, Oregon; and Vancouver, British Columbia. Portland to Seattle takes about four hours and fares range from $15.50 to $29 one way. Vancouver to Seattle takes about four hours and the fare is $19. This route includes a bus segment.

BY BUS

The **Greyhound bus station,** Eighth Avenue and Stewart Street (☎ **800/231-2222** or 206/628-5530), is located a few blocks northeast of downtown Seattle. Greyhound bus service provides connections to almost any city in the continental United States. From the bus station it is only a few blocks to several budget chain motels.

Gray Line of Seattle (☎ **800/426-7505** or 206/624-5813) also offers scheduled shuttle service between Victoria and Seattle. The trip takes a little more than 8 hours (by way of the San Juan Islands ferry) and the one-way fare is $30 for adults and $15 for children. There is also continuing service to Seattle-Tacoma International Airport. **Quick Shuttle** (☎ **800/665-2111** or 604/244-3744) offers express bus service between Vancouver, British Columbia, and Seattle. The trip takes about 4 hours and the one-way fare is $28 for adults, $26 for seniors, and $14 for children. There is also continuing service to Sea-Tac Airport.

VISITOR INFORMATION

Visitor information on Seattle and the surrounding area is available by contacting the **Seattle-King County Convention and Visitors Bureau,** 520 Pike St., Suite 1300, Seattle, WA 98101 (☎ **206/461-5840;** www.seeseattle.org), which operates a Visitor Information Center in the Washington State Convention and Trade Center, 800 Convention Place, Level 1, Galleria, at the corner of Eighth Avenue and Pike Street. There is also a **Visitor Information Center** in the baggage-claim area at Sea-Tac Airport. It's across from carousel no. 8 (open daily from 9:30am to 7:30pm; ☎ **206/ 433-5218**).

CITY LAYOUT

Although downtown Seattle is fairly compact and can easily be navigated on foot, finding your way through this area by car can be frustrating. The Seattle area has been experiencing phenomenal growth in the past few years, and this has created traffic congestion problems that must be anticipated. Here are some guidelines to help you find your way around.

Main Arteries & Streets   There are three interstate highways serving Seattle. I-90 comes in from the east and ends downtown. I-405 bypasses the city completely, traveling up the east shore of Lake Washington through Bellevue, Redmond, and Kirkland. The main artery is I-5, which runs through the middle of Seattle. Take the

James Street exit west if you're heading for the Pioneer Square area; take the Seneca Street exit for Pike Place Market; or the Olive Way exit for Capitol Hill.

Downtown is roughly defined as extending from the Kingdome on the south to Denny Way on the north and from Elliott Bay on the west to Broadway on the east. Within this area avenues are numbered, whereas streets have names. The exceptions to this rule are the first two roads parallel to the waterfront. They are Alaskan Way and Western Avenue. Spring Street is one way eastbound, and Seneca Street one way westbound. Likewise, Pike Street is one way eastbound, and Pine Street, one way westbound. First Avenue and Third Avenue are both two-way streets, but Second and Fifth are one way southbound. Fourth Avenue and Sixth Avenue are one way northbound.

To get from downtown to Capitol Hill, take Pike Street or Olive Way. Yesler Way or S. Jackson Street will get you over to Lake Washington on the east side of Seattle. If you are heading north across town, Westlake Avenue will take you to the Fremont neighborhood and Eastlake Avenue will take you to the University District. These two roads diverge at the south end of Lake Union.

There is an irreverent little mnemonic device locals use for remembering the names of Seattle's downtown streets, and since most visitors spend much of their time downtown, this little phrase could be useful to you as well. It goes like this: "Jesus Christ made Seattle under protest." What this stands for is all the downtown east-west streets north of Yesler Way and south Olive Way/Stewart Street—**J**efferson, **J**ames, **C**herry, **C**olumbia, **M**arion, **M**adison, **S**pring, **S**eneca, **U**niversity, **U**nion, **P**ike, **P**ine.

Finding an Address   After you become familiar with the streets and neighborhoods of Seattle, there is really only one important thing to remember to find an address: Pay attention to the compass point of the address. Downtown streets have no directional designation attached to them, but when you cross I-5 going east, most streets and avenues are designated "East." South of Yesler Way, which runs through Pioneer Square, streets are designated "South." West of Queen Anne Avenue, streets are designated "West." The University District is designated "NE" (Northeast); the Ballard neighborhood, "NW" (Northwest). Therefore, if you are looking for an address on First Avenue South, head south of Yesler Way.

Another helpful hint is that odd-numbered addresses are likely to be on the west and south sides of streets, whereas even-numbered addresses will be on the east and north sides of streets. Also, in the downtown area, address numbers increase by 100 with each block as you move away from Yesler Way going north or south, and as you go east from the waterfront.

Street Maps   Even if the streets of Seattle seem totally unfathomable to you, rest assured that even longtime residents sometimes have a hard time finding their way around. Don't be afraid to ask directions. You can obtain a free map of the city from the Seattle-King County Convention and Visitors Bureau and the Visitor Information Centers (see above).

You can buy a decent map of Seattle in most convenience stores and gas stations around the area, or for a greater selection, stop in at **Metsker Maps,** 702 First Ave. (☎ **206/623-8747**).

NEIGHBORHOODS IN BRIEF

Partly because it is divided by bodies of water, Seattle is a city of neighborhoods.

International District   The most immediately recognizable of Seattle's neighborhoods, the International District is home to a large Asian population. Here you'll find the Wing Luke Museum, Nippon Kan Theatre, Hing Hay Park (with an ornate pagoda), Uwajimaya (an Asian supermarket), and many other small shops and restaurants. The International District begins around Fifth Avenue South and S. Jackson Street. While this neighborhood is interesting for a stroll, there really isn't a lot to do here.

Pioneer Square   The Pioneer Square Historic District, known for its restored 1890s buildings is centered around the corner of First Avenue and Yesler Way. The tree-lined streets and cobblestone plazas make this one of the prettiest downtown neighborhoods. Pioneer Square, which refers to the neighborhood and not a specific square, is full of antiques shops, art galleries, restaurants, and bars, but is also home to a large population of street people. After dark, this is the most unsafe neighborhood in which Seattle visitors are likely to find themselves.

Downtown   This is Seattle's main business district and can roughly be defined as the area from Pioneer Square in the south to around Pike Place Market in the north and from First Avenue to Eighth Avenue. It's characterized by high-rise office buildings, luxury hotels, and the city's greatest diversity of retail shops and steep streets. This is also where you'll find the Seattle Art Museum and the new Benaroya Hall, which, when completed, will be the home of the Seattle Symphony. Because hotels in this area are convenient to both Pioneer Square and Pike Place Market, this is a good neighborhood to stay in.

Belltown   Located in the blocks north of Pike Place Market between Western and Third or Fourth avenues, this area once held mostly warehouses, but now is rapidly gentrifying and contains lots of restaurants, nightclubs, and high-rise condominiums. The area is popular with a young, hip crowd, and is becoming another art gallery district.

First Hill   Known as Pill Hill by Seattleites, this hilly neighborhood, just east of downtown across I-5, is home to several hospitals as well as the Frye Art Museum. There are a couple of hotels in this neighborhood and the blocks along Pike and Pine streets are becoming known for their nightclubs and stores selling mid-century collectibles.

Capitol Hill   To the northeast of downtown, centered along Broadway near Volunteer Park, Capitol Hill is Seattle's cutting-edge shopping district and gay community. Broadway sidewalks are always crowded and it is nearly impossible to find a parking place in the neighborhood. While there are lots of inexpensive restaurants in the area, few are really worth recommending. However, the city's two best dessert spots are here. This is also city's main hangout for runaways and street kids, many of whom have gotten involved in the city's infamous heroin scene.

Queen Anne Hill   Queen Anne is located just northwest of Seattle Center and offers great views of the city. This affluent neighborhood, one of the most prestigious in Seattle proper, is where you'll find some of Seattle's oldest homes, several of which are now bed-and-breakfast inns. Today the neighborhood is divided into the Upper Queen Anne and Lower Queen Anne neighborhoods, with the lower area, adjacent to Seattle Center, having a more urban feel and the upper area having a more neighborhood feel. There are several excellent restaurants in the neighborhood.

Ballard   In northwest Seattle, bordering the Lake Washington Ship Canal and Puget Sound, you'll find Ballard, a former Scandinavian community now known for its busy nightlife, but with remnants of its past still visible. While Ballard does have a bustling business district, it is mostly geared toward the needs of area residents.

University District   As the name implies, this neighborhood surrounds the University of Washington in the northeast section of the city. The U District, as it's known to locals, provides all the amenities of a college neighborhood—cheap ethnic restaurants, bars and pubs, and music stores.

Wallingford   This neighborhood is one of Seattle's up-and-comers. Located just west of the University District and adjacent to Lake Union, it's filled with small, inexpensive but good restaurants. There are also interesting little shops and an old school that has been renovated and is now filled with boutiques and restaurants.

Fremont   Located north of the Lake Washington Ship Canal between Wallingford and Ballard, Fremont is home to Seattle's best-loved piece of public art— *Waiting for the Interurban*—as well as the famous *Fremont Troll* sculpture. This is Seattle's wackiest neighborhood and is filled with eclectic shops, ethnic restaurants, and artists' studios. During the summer, there's a Sunday flea market and almost-free Saturday night outdoor movies. If you have time to visit only one neighborhood outside of downtown, make it Fremont.

Madison Park   One of Seattle's more affluent neighborhoods, it fronts on the western shore of Lake Washington, northeast of downtown. The centerpiece is the University of Washington Arboretum, including the Japanese Gardens. There are several excellent restaurants here at the end of E. Madison Street.

2 Getting Around

BY PUBLIC TRANSPORTATION

Because downtown Seattle is quite compact, a car is a liability when exploring this part of the city, so until you decide to start exploring the city's outlying neighborhoods or take a trip out from the city, you'll be better off leaving your car parked in a garage somewhere. By utilizing the monorail, waterfront streetcar and free downtown buses, you can explore from Seattle Center to the International District without ever having to get into your car. You can even head out of the city on a ferry and explore Bremerton and downtown Bainbridge Island on the far side of the Puget Sound.

By Bus   The best thing about Seattle's **Metro** (☎ **206/553-3000**) bus system is that as long as you stay within the downtown area, you can ride for free between 4am and 9pm. The Ride Free Area is between Alaskan Way (the waterfront) in the west, Sixth Avenue in the east, Battery Street in the north, and South Jackson Street in the south. Within this area are Pioneer Square, the waterfront attractions, Pike Place Market, and almost all the city's major hotels. Two blocks from South Jackson Street is the Kingdome, and six blocks from Battery Street is Seattle Center. Keeping this in mind, you can visit nearly every tourist attraction in Seattle without having to spend a dime on transportation.

The Ride Free Area also encompasses the Bus Tunnel, which allows buses to drive underneath downtown Seattle, thus avoiding traffic congestion. The tunnel extends from the International District in the south to the Convention Center in the north, with three stops in between. Commissioned artworks decorate each of the stations, making a trip through the tunnel more than just a way of getting from point A to point B. It's open Monday through Friday from 5am to 7pm, on Saturday from 10am to 6pm (closed on holidays). When the Bus Tunnel is closed, buses operate on surface streets. Because the tunnel is within the Ride Free Area, there is no charge for riding through it, unless you are traveling to or from outside of the Ride Free Area.

If you travel outside the Ride Free Area, fares range from 85¢ to $1.60, depending on the distance and time of day. Keep in mind that you pay when you get off the bus when traveling out of the Ride Free Area. When traveling into the Ride Free Area, you pay when you get on the bus. Exact change is required.

Discount Passes   On Saturday, Sunday, and holidays, you can purchase an All Day Pass for $1.70; it's available on any Metro bus or the Waterfront Streetcar.

By Water Taxi   In the summer of 1997, a pilot water taxi service was operating on a fixed route between the downtown Seattle waterfront (with stops at Pier 66 and Pier 55) and Seacrest Park in West Seattle. This service was aimed both at commuters and visitors and provided access to the popular Alki Beach and adjacent bike/foot path in West Seattle. The water taxi was running between 6am and 8pm and the fare was $2 each way for adults and $1 for children ages 5 to 12. To see if the water taxi is running when you visit, call **Elliott Bay Water Taxi** (☎ **206/684-0224**).

By Monorail   If you are planning a visit to Seattle Center, there is no better way to get there from downtown than on the monorail. It leaves from Westlake Center shopping mall (Fifth Avenue and Pine Street). The once-futuristic elevated trains cover the 1.2 miles in 90 seconds and provide a few nice views along the way. The monorail leaves every 15 minutes daily from 9am to midnight during the summer; the rest of the year, Sunday through Thursday from 9am to 9pm, and Friday and Saturday until midnight. The one-way fare is only $1 for adults, 50¢ for senior citizens and people with disabilities, and 75¢ for children 5 to 12.

By Waterfront Streetcar   Old-fashioned streetcars run along the waterfront from Pier 70 to the corner of Fifth Avenue South and South Jackson Street on the edge of the International District. These streetcars are more tourist attraction than commuter transportation, and actually are much more useful to visitors than are most of the city's buses. Tourist sites along the streetcar route include Pioneer Square, the Seattle Aquarium, Omnidome Film Experience, and Pike Place Market. In summer streetcars operate Monday through Friday from around 7am to around 11pm, departing every 20 to 30 minutes; on Saturday, Sunday, and holidays from around 9am to almost midnight (shorter hours in other months). One-way fare is 85¢ in off-peak hours and $1.10 in peak hours. If you plan to transfer to a Metro bus, you can get a transfer good for 70 minutes. Streetcars are wheelchair accessible.

BY CAR

Before you venture into downtown Seattle in a car, whether your own or a rental, keep in mind that traffic congestion is bad, parking is limited (and expensive), and streets are almost all one way. You'll avoid a lot of frustration and aggravation by leaving your car outside the downtown area.

Depending on what your plans are for your visit, you might not need a car at all. If you plan to spend your time in downtown Seattle, a car is a liability. With public buses free in the downtown area, the monorail from downtown to Seattle Center, and the Waterfront Streetcar connecting Pike Place Market and Pioneer Square, the city center is well serviced by public transport. You can even take the ferries over to Bainbridge Island or Bremmerton for an excursion out of the city. Most Seattle neighborhoods of interest to visitors are also well served by public buses. However, if your plans include any excursions out of the city, say to Mount Rainier or the Olympic Peninsula, you'll definitely need a car.

Car Rentals   It always pays to shop around for a rental car and call the same companies a few times over the course of a couple of weeks (rates change depending on demand). For the very best deal on a rental car, make your reservation at least one week in advance. If you decide on the spur of the moment that you want to rent a car, check to see whether there are any weekend or special rates available. If you are a member of a frequent-flier program, be sure to mention it: You might get mileage credit for renting a car. In the summer of 1997, daily rates for a subcompact were between $36 and $54, with weekly rates running between $150 and $300. Expect lower rates between October and April.

All the major car-rental agencies have offices in Seattle and at or near Seattle-Tacoma International Airport. These include **Alamo** (☎ **800/327-9633,** 206/433-0812, or 206/292-9770), **Avis** (☎ **800/831-2847,** 206/433-5231, or 206/448-1700), **Budget** (☎ **800/527-0700** or 206/682-2277), **Dollar** (☎ **800/800-4000,** 206/433-6777, or 206/682-1316), **Enterprise** (☎ **800/325-8007,** 206/246-1953, or 206/382-1051), **Hertz** (☎ **800/654-3131,** 206/433-5275, or 206/682-5050), **National** (☎ **800/227-7368,** 206/433-5501, or 206/448-7368), and **Thrifty** (☎ **800/367-2277,** 206/246-7565, or 206/625-1133).

Parking   On-street parking in downtown Seattle is expensive, extremely limited, and, worst of all, rarely available near your destination. Downtown parking decks (either above or below ground) charge from $7 to $16 per day. Many lots offer early bird specials that, if you park before a certain time in the morning (usually around 9am), allow you to park all day for $6 to $7. With the purchase of $20 or more, many downtown merchants offer Easy Streets tokens that can be used toward parking fees in many downtown lots. Look for the black and yellow signs.

You'll also save money by parking near the Space Needle, where parking lots charge around $6 per day. The Pike Place Market parking garage, accessed from Western Avenue under the sky bridge charges only $1 from 4 to 11pm, which makes this a good choice if you are headed downtown for dinner or a show. If you don't mind a bit of a walk, try the parking lot off Jackson Street between Eighth and Ninth avenues in the International District. This lot charges only $3 to park all day on weekdays and $1 on weekends. Also in the International District you'll find free 2-hour on-street parking.

Driving Rules   A right turn at a red light is permitted after coming to a full stop. A left turn at a red light is permissible from a one-way street onto another one-way street. If you park your car on a sloping street, be sure to turn your wheels to the curb—you may be ticketed if you don't. When parking on the street, be sure to check the time limit on your parking meters. Some allow only as little as 15 minutes of parking, while others are good for up to four hours. Also be sure to check whether or not you can occupy a parking space during rush hour.

BY TAXI

If you decide not to use the public-transit system, call **Yellow Cab** (☎ **206/622-6500**) or **Farwest Taxi** (☎ **206/622-1717**). Taxis can be difficult to hail on the street in Seattle, so it's best to call or wait at the taxi stands at major hotels. The flag-drop charge is $1.80; after that, it's $1.80 per mile. **Graytop Cab** (☎ **206/282-8222**), which operates only within the Seattle city limits, charges $1.20 for the flag-drop and $1.40 per mile.

ON FOOT

Seattle is a surprisingly compact city. You can easily walk from Pioneer Square to Pike Place Market and take in most of downtown. Remember, though, that the city is also very hilly. When you head in from the waterfront, you will be climbing a very steep hill. If you get tired of walking around downtown Seattle, remember that between 6am and 7pm you can always catch a bus for free as long as you plan to stay within the Ride Free Area. Cross streets only at corners and only with the lights in your favor. Jaywalking, especially in the downtown area, is a ticketable offense

FAST FACTS: Seattle

Airport   See "Arriving" earlier in this chapter.

American Express   In Seattle, the Amex office is in the Plaza 600 building at 600 Stewart St. (☎ 206/441-8622). The office is open Monday through Friday from 9am to 5pm.

Area Code   The telephone area code in Seattle is 206. The area code for the Eastside (including Kirkland and Bellevue) is 425.

Baby-Sitters   Check at your hotel first if you need a sitter. If they don't have one available, contact **Best Sitters** (☎ **206/682-2556**).

Business Hours   Banks are generally open weekdays from 9am to 5pm, with later hours on Friday; some have Saturday morning hours. Offices are generally open weekdays from 9am to 5pm. Stores typically open Monday through Saturday between 9 and 10am and close between 5 and 6pm. Some department stores have later hours on Thursday and Friday evenings until 9pm and are open on Sunday from 11am to 5 or 6pm, and stores in malls are usually open until 9pm. Bars stay open until 1 or 2am; dance clubs often stay open much later.

Car Rentals   See "Getting Around" earlier in this chapter.

Climate   See "When to Go" in chapter 3.

Dentist   If you need a dentist while you're in Seattle, contact the **Dentist Referral Service,** the Medical Dental Building, 509 Olive Way (☎ **206/448-CARE**).

Doctor   To find a physician in Seattle, check at your hotel for a reference, or call the **Medical Dental Building** line (☎ **206/448-CARE**).

Driving Rules   See "Getting Around" earlier in this chapter.

Drugstores   See "Pharmacies" below.

Embassies/Consulates   See chapter 4, "For Foreign Visitors."

Emergencies   For police, fire, or medical emergencies, phone **911**.

Eyeglass Repair   Market Optical in Pike Place Market (☎ **206/448-7739**) is located next to Starbucks.

Hospitals   Virginia Mason Hospital and Clinic, 925 Seneca St. (☎ **206/583-6433** for emergencies, or 206/624-1144 for information), is on First Hill just outside downtown Seattle. There's also the **Virginia Mason Fourth Avenue Clinic,** 1221 Fourth Ave. (☎ **206/223-6490**), open Monday through Friday from 7am to 4:30pm, Saturday from 10am to 1:30pm, which provides medical treatment for minor ailments without an appointment.

Hotlines   The local rape hotline is ☎ **206/632-7273**.

Information   See "Visitor Information" earlier in this chapter.

Libraries   The main branch of the Seattle Public Library is at 1000 Fourth Ave. (☎ **206/386-4636**).

Liquor Laws   The legal minimum drinking age in Washington is 21.

Lost Property If you left something on a Metro bus, call ☎ **206/553-3090,** if you left something at the airport, call ☎ **206/433-5312.**

Luggage Storage/Lockers Most hotels will let you store your bags if you arrive before check-in or won't be departing until late in the day that you check out. Some will also store extra bags if you are going off on an overnight excursion but plan to return to the hotel. **Ken's Baggage,** Room MT3080B, Sea-Tac Airport (☎ **206/433-5333**) will store your extra bags at the airport. There is also a luggage-storage facility at Amtrak's King Street Station, as well as lockers at the Greyhound bus station, 811 Stewart St.

Maps See "City Layout" earlier in this chapter.

Newspapers/Magazines The *Seattle Post-Intelligencer* is Seattle's morning daily, and the *Seattle Times* is the evening daily. *Seattle Weekly* is the city's free arts-and-entertainment weekly.

Pharmacies **Pacific Drugs,** 822 First Ave. (☎ **206/624-1454**), is open Monday through Friday from 7am to 6:30pm, on Saturday from 10am to 5pm. There is also a **Payless Drugs** at 319 Pike St. (☎ **206/223-1128**).

Photographic Needs **Cameras West,** 1908 Fourth Ave. (☎ **206/622-0066**), is the largest-volume camera and video dealer in the Northwest. Best of all, it's right downtown and also offers 1-hour film processing. It's open Monday through Saturday from 10am to 6pm, and on Sunday from noon to 5pm.

Police For police emergencies, phone **911.**

Post Office Besides the main post office, 301 Union St., there are also convenient postal stations in Pioneer Square at 91 Jackson St. S., and on Broadway at 101 Broadway E. All stations are open Monday through Friday with varying hours; the Broadway station is open Saturday from 9am to 1pm as well. For more information, call the Postal Service's toll-free phone number ☎ **800/275-8777.**

Radio For National Public Radio (NPR), tune to 94.9 FM or 88.5 FM.

Restrooms There are public restrooms in Pike Place Market, Westlake Center, Seattle Center, and the Washington State Convention and Trade Center. You'll also find restrooms in most hotel lobbies in downtown Seattle.

Safety Although Seattle is rated as one of the safest cities in the United States, it has its share of crime. The least safe neighborhood you're likely to be in is the Pioneer Square area, which is home to more than a dozen bars and nightclubs. By day this area is quite safe, but take extra precaution late at night when the bars are closing. Also be extra careful with your wallet or purse when you're in the crush of people at Pike Place Market—this is a favorite spot of pickpockets. Whenever possible try to park your car in a garage, not on the street, at night.

Taxes The state of Washington makes up for its lack of an income tax with a 6.5% sales tax; King County adds another 1.7% for 8.2% total. Hotel-room tax is 15.2% in Seattle.

Taxis See "Getting Around" earlier in this chapter.

Television Local television channels include 4 (ABC), 5 (NBC), 7 (UPN), 9 (PBS), 11 (CBS), and 13 (Fox).

Time Seattle is on Pacific time (PT), and daylight saving time, depending on the time of year, making it 3 hours behind the East Coast.

Transit Information For 24-hour information on Seattle's Metro bus system, call ☎ **206/553-3000.** For information on the Washington State Ferries, call

☎ **206/464-6400** or **800/84-FERRY.** For Amtrak information, call ☎ **800/ 872-7245.** To contact the King Street Station (trains), call ☎ **206/382-4125.** To contact the Greyhound bus station, call ☎ **206/628-5530.**

Useful Telephone Numbers   For a wide variety of local information on topics that range from personal health to business news, from entertainment listings to the weather report and marine forecast, call the *Seattle Times* Info Line at ☎ **206/ 464-2000.**

Weather   If you can't tell what the weather is by looking out the window, or you want to be absolutely sure that it's going to rain the next day, call the Seattle Times Info Line ☎ **206/464-2000,** ext. 9900.

3 Accommodations

Seattle has become such a popular summer destination in the past few years, that the city has been unable to keep up with the demand for hotel rooms. As of the summer of 1997, most downtown hotels were staying completely full, and were in fact often overbooking reservations and having to send guests as far away as the airport or even Tacoma when they showed up to check in. To handle the crowds that continue to descend on Seattle each summer, several new luxury hotels have recently opened downtown and others are either under construction or in the planning stages. Still other hotels are busy expanding.

What this all means is that visitors now have a broader spectrum of accommodations choices here in Seattle, but concurrent with new construction has been an escalation in room rates that has brought Seattle hotel prices up to par with hotels in other major cities throughout the nation. However, Seattle is still a seasonal destination and in the winter months hotel rooms are a real bargain.

Seattle's largest concentrations of hotels are in downtown and near the airport, with a few good hotels in the University District and also over in the Bellevue/Kirkland area. If you don't mind high prices, the downtown hotels are most convenient for the majority of visitors. However, if your budget won't allow for a first-class business hotel, you'll have to stay near the airport or elsewhere on the outskirts of the city. Also, be sure to make reservations as far in advance as possible, especially if you plan a visit during Seafair or another major Seattle festival (see "Washington Calendar of Events" in chapter 3 for dates of festivals).

In the following listings, price categories are based on the rate for a double room (most hotels charge the same for a single or double room) in high season and are as follows: "Very Expensive," more than $175 per night; "Expensive," $126 to $175 per night; "Moderate," $75 to $125 per night; and "Inexpensive," under $75 per night. Keep in mind that these rates do not include taxes, which add up to 15.2% in Seattle.

Also remember that these are what hotels call "rack rates," or walk-in rates. Various discounts on these rates are often available, so be sure to ask if there are any specials or discounted rates available. At inexpensive chain motels, there are almost always discounted rates for AAA members and senior citizens. You'll also find that room rates are almost always considerably lower from October through April (the rainy season), and downtown hotels often offer substantially reduced prices on weekends throughout the year. A few hotels include breakfast in their rates; others offer complimentary breakfast only on certain deluxe floors. Most all hotels in the Seattle area now offer nonsmoking rooms, and, in fact, most bed-and-breakfast inns are exclusively nonsmoking establishments. Most hotels also offer wheelchair-accessible rooms.

There are plenty of fine bed-and-breakfast establishments in Seattle, and we have listed a few of our favorites. To find out about other good B&Bs in Seattle, contact the **Bed and Breakfast Association of Seattle,** P.O. Box 31772, Seattle, WA 98103-1772. (☎ **206/547-1020**). Alternatively, you can contact **A Pacific Reservation Service,** P.O. Box 46894, Seattle, WA 98146 (☎ **206/439-7677;** fax 206/431-0932), which offers many accommodations, mostly in bed-and-breakfast homes, in the Seattle area. Rates range from $45 to $200 for a double and a small booking fee may be charged. They charge $5 for a directory of members.

DOWNTOWN, THE WATERFRONT & PIONEER SQUARE
VERY EXPENSIVE

✪ **Alexis Hotel.** 1007 First Ave. (at Madison St.), Seattle, WA 98104. ☎ **800/426-7033** or 206/624-4844. Fax 206/621-9009. 65 rms, 44 suites. A/C TV TEL. $195–$210 double; $240–$380 suite. Rates include continental breakfast. AE, CB, DC, MC, V. Valet parking $18.

This elegant little hotel has an enviable location halfway between the Pike Place Market and Pioneer Square. Throughout the hotel there's a pleasant mix of the contemporary and the antique that gives the Alexis a very special atmosphere. Each room is furnished with antique tables, overstuffed chairs, and brass reading lamps. In your black-tiled bath, you'll find a marble counter, terry-cloth robes, and a telephone. The nicest rooms are the fireplace suites, which have raised king-size beds, whirlpool baths, and wet bars. If you need more space, there's a varied assortment of suites available.

Dining: The hotel's main dining room, the Painted Table, serves highly creative meals (see "Dining," later in this chapter, for details). Just off the lobby is the Bookstore Bar, which serves light lunches as well as drinks.

Services: Concierge, room service, valet/laundry service, complimentary evening sherry, shoeshine service.

Facilities: Steam room, small fitness room (and privileges at two sports clubs), Aveda day spa, business center.

Four Seasons Olympic Hotel. 411 University St., Seattle, WA 98101. ☎ **800/332-3442,** 800/821-8106 in Washington State), 800/268-6282 in Canada, or 206/621-1700. Fax 206/682-9633. 240 rms, 210 suites. A/C MINIBAR TV TEL. $260–$290 double; $310–$1,250 suite. AE, CB, DC, ER, JCB, MC, V. Valet parking $20; self-parking $16.

The Four Seasons Olympic Hotel, an Italian Renaissance palace, is without a doubt the grandest hotel in the city. Gilt-and-crystal chandeliers hang from the arched ceiling, and ornate moldings grace the glowing hand-burnished oak walls and pillars. Unfortunately, what you seem to be paying for here are the hotel's public areas and the service, not the guest rooms, some of which are rather small and even a bit worn around the edges.

Dining: In keeping with the overall character of the hotel, The Georgian is the most elegant (and most expensive) restaurant in Seattle. The menu combines creative Northwest and continental cuisines. (See listing in section 4 later in this chapter for details.) For much more economical meals, there is the casual Garden Court, and downstairs from the lobby, there is Shuckers, an English pub featuring fresh seafood.

Services: 24-hour room service, concierge, valet/laundry service, 1-hour pressing, complimentary shoeshine, massages available.

Facilities: Indoor pool, whirlpool spa, sauna, sundeck, health club, exclusive shopping arcade, business center.

Hotel Monaco. 1101 Fourth Ave., Seattle, WA 98101. ☎ **800/945-2240** or 206/621-1770. Fax 206/621-7779. 144 rms, 45 suites. A/C TV TEL. $210–$230 double; $250–$900 suite. AE, CB, DC, DISC, JCB, MC, V.

Seattle Accommodations & Dining—Downtown including First Hill

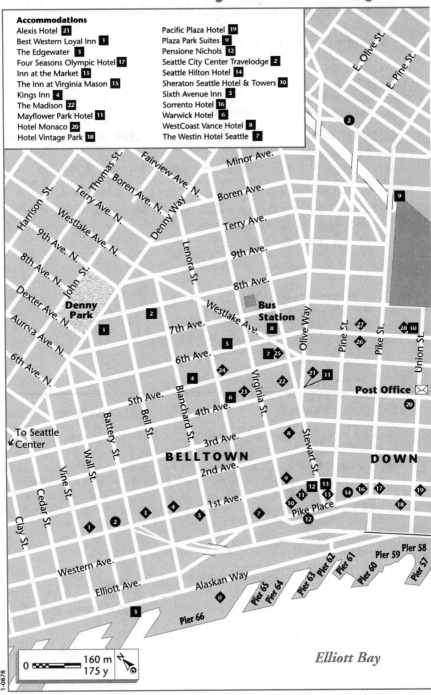

Accommodations

Alexis Hotel 21
Best Western Loyal Inn 1
The Edgewater 3
Four Seasons Olympic Hotel 17
Inn at the Market 13
The Inn at Virginia Mason 15
Kings Inn 4
The Madison 22
Mayflower Park Hotel 11
Hotel Monaco 20
Hotel Vintage Park 18

Pacific Plaza Hotel 19
Plaza Park Suites 9
Pensione Nichols 12
Seattle City Center Travelodge 2
Seattle Hilton Hotel 14
Sheraton Seattle Hotel & Towers 10
Sixth Avenue Inn 5
Sorrento Hotel 16
Warwick Hotel 6
WestCoast Vance Hotel 8
The Westin Hotel Seattle 7

Elliott Bay

0   160 m
     175 y

1-0878

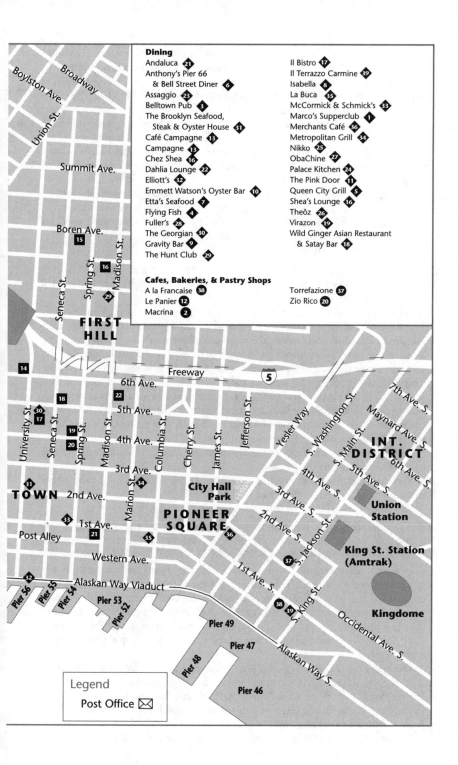

Dining

Andaluca 21
Anthony's Pier 66
  & Bell Street Diner 6
Assaggio 23
Belltown Pub 3
The Brooklyn Seafood,
  Steak & Oyster House 31
Café Campagne 13
Campagne 13
Chez Shea 16
Dahlia Lounge 22
Elliott's 32
Emmett Watson's Oyster Bar 10
Etta's Seafood 7
Flying Fish 4
Fuller's 28
The Georgian 30
Gravity Bar 9
The Hunt Club 29

Il Bistro 17
Il Terrazzo Carmine 39
Isabella 8
La Buca 35
McCormick & Schmick's 33
Marco's Supperclub 1
Merchants Café 36
Metropolitan Grill 34
Nikko 25
ObaChine 27
Palace Kitchen 24
The Pink Door 11
Queen City Grill 5
Shea's Lounge 16
Theôz 26
Virazon 19
Wild Ginger Asian Restaurant
  & Satay Bar 18

Cafes, Bakeries, & Pastry Shops

A la Francaise 38
Le Panier 12
Macrina 2

Torrefazione 37
Zio Rico 20

Boylston Ave.
Broadway
Union St.
Summit Ave.
Boren Ave.
15
Spring St.
Madison St.
Seneca St.
16
29

FIRST HILL

14
Freeway
6th Ave.
5
18
22
5th Ave.
7th Ave. S.
University St.
30
17
Seneca St.
Spring St.
19
20
4th Ave.
Madison St.
Columbia St.
Cherry St.
James St.
Jefferson St.
Yesler Way
S. Washington St.
Maynard Ave. S.
S. Main St.
INT. DISTRICT
6th Ave. S.
3rd Ave.
4th Ave. S.
31
TOWN 2nd Ave.
Marion St.
34
City Hall Park
3rd Ave. S.
5th Ave. S.
Union Station
33
1st Ave.
21
PIONEER SQUARE
2nd Ave. S.
S. Jackson St.
King St. Station (Amtrak)
Post Alley
35
36
Western Ave.
37
S. Jackson St.
32
Pier 56
Pier 55
Pier 54
Alaskan Way Viaduct
Pier 53
Pier 52
1st Ave. S.
King St. S.
38
39
Kingdome
Occidental Ave. S.
Pier 49
Pier 48
Pier 47
Alaskan Way S.
Pier 46

Legend
Post Office ✉

This is one of Seattle's newest hotels and is a bright new addition to the city's hotel scene. Billing itself as the coolest hotel in town, and adopting a classic 1940s style for its logo, the hotel is boldly styled throughout its public areas and guest rooms. Reproductions of ancient Greek murals adorn the lobby. From the outside, however, it is difficult to tell what is hidden within. The hotel building used to be a telephone company office building and switching center. Expect wild color schemes and bold striped wallpaper in your room, and if you happen to opt for a Monte Carlo suite, your bed will be tucked behind heavy draperies. Some of the suites have whirlpool tubs. All the rooms and suites have fax machines and all the other requirements of modern business.

Dining: Sazerac, the hotel's restaurant, serves upscale southern cuisine inspired by Cajun cooking styles. It's open for three meals a day, and also has a lively bar.

Services: 24-hour room service, concierge, complimentary morning newspaper and coffee, complimentary evening wine receptions.

Facilities: Fitness center, business center.

✪ **Hotel Vintage Park.** 1100 Fifth Ave., Seattle, WA 98101. ☎ **800/624-4433** or 206/624-8000. Fax 206/623-0568. 126 rms, 1 suite. A/C MINIBAR TV TEL. $190–$220 double, $370 suite. AE, CB, DC, DISC, JCB, MC, V. Valet parking $17.

Small and classically elegant, the Vintage Park is a must for oenophiles interested in Washington wines. Every guest rooms is named for a Washington winery and each evening in the library-like lobby, there is a complimentary wine tasting featuring Washington wines. Throughout the hotel, you'll likely spot other homages to the grape, and even the minibars are stocked with Washington wines. Rooms vary quite a bit here, but if you opt for a deluxe room, you'll likely want to spend your days luxuriating in the elegant canopied bed. Deluxe rooms also have the best views (including some views of Mount Rainier). Standard rooms, though smaller and less luxuriously appointed, are still very comfortable, and surprisingly the bathrooms are larger than in the deluxe rooms.

Dining: The adjacent Tulio Restaurant serves good Tuscan Italian meals. A small bar adjoins the restaurant.

Services: Room service, concierge, access to health club, complimentary daily newspaper and morning coffee, valet/laundry service.

Facilities: Limited in-room fitness equipment is available.

The Westin Hotel Seattle. 1900 Fifth Ave., Seattle, WA 98101. ☎ **800/228-3000** or 206/728-1000. Fax 206/728-2259. 822 rms, 43 suites. A/C MINIBAR TV TEL. $240–$280 double ($169 weekends); $240–$1,100 suite. AE, CB, DC, DISC, JCB, MC, V. Valet $18; self-parking $15.

The Westin caters primarily to conventions and tour groups and consequently can be crowded and impersonal. This said, it's still one of the better downtown choices, especially if you want a view from your room. The hotel's twin cylindrical towers provide interesting vistas from most of the higher floors. With their curved walls of glass and beds that face out to the views, guest rooms here are some of the nicest in town. For the best views, ask for a room on the west side as high up as possible (there are 47 floors here).

Dining: The cuisine at Roy's can only be described as creative Euro-Asian, while at Nikko you'll find superb Japanese meals and high-tech decor (See "Dining" below for details.) For breakfast and quick meals, there's the Gold Bagel, which serves everything from espresso to bagels to wraps to foccacia sandwiches. Much of the lobby is set aside as a quiet lounge area.

Services: Concierge, 24-hour room service, valet/laundry service.

Facilities: Large indoor pool, exercise room with new equipment, whirlpool spa, sauna, gift shops, business center.

EXPENSIVE

✪ **The Edgewater.** Pier 67, 2411 Alaskan Way, Seattle, WA 98121. ☎ **800/624-0670** or 206/728-7000. Fax 206/441-4119. 230 rms, 3 suites. A/C TV TEL. $129–$250 double; $275–$750 suite. AE, CB, DC, DISC, MC, V. Valet parking $12; self-parking $10.

Built on a pier, The Edgewater, Seattle's only waterfront hotel, is incongruously designed to resemble a deluxe mountain lodge—somehow it works. A vaulted ceiling, deer-antler chandelier, a river-stone fireplace, and a wall of glass that looks out on busy Elliott Bay all combine to make the lobby a great place to hang out for a while. The mountain-lodge theme continues in the rooms, which feature rustic lodgepole pine furniture. Half the rooms have balconies over the water.

Dining: The hotel's restaurant is a woodsy retreat that could have been designed by Eddie Bauer. The menu features somewhat pricey Northwest cuisine, but it's the view of Elliott Bay and the Olympic Mountains that's the real main course here. In the pine-walled Lobby Lounge, there are more great views and a fireplace.

Services: Room service, concierge, same-day laundry/valet service, courtesy shuttle to downtown locations.

Facilities: Gift shop, access to nearby athletic club.

Inn at the Market. 86 Pine St., Seattle, WA 98101. ☎ **800/446-4484** or 206/443-3600. 65 rms, 9 suites. A/C MINIBAR TV TEL. $130–$210 double; $225–$325 suite. AE, CB, DC, DISC, MC, V. Parking $15.

French country decor is the theme at this inconspicuous little luxury hotel in the middle of Pike Place Market. A small lobby with a fireplace and a few pieces of antique furniture gives the impression that you've stepped into the living room of a French country home and this theme continues in the guest rooms. Up on the roof you'll find a deck overlooking the harbor. The water-view rooms, with antique furniture and huge bathrooms, are definitely the ones to opt for if you can afford the $185 to $210 rates. If you need more room than a standard hotel room offers, consider the two-floor townhouse suites. Unfortunately this hotel has been looking quite threadbare of late.

Dining/Entertainment: Bacco, the hotel's little bistro, serves fresh juices, breakfast, and lunch. Café Campagne offers French country-style meals, while the more formal Campagne, serves excellent southern French fare (see "Dining" below for details).

Services: Limited room service, concierge, valet/laundry service, complimentary limousine service in downtown Seattle.

Facilities: Health spa, privileges at athletic club.

The Madison—A Renaissance Hotel. 515 Madison St., Seattle, WA 98104. ☎ **800/468-3571** or 206/583-0300. Fax 206/622-8635. 553 rms, 78 suites. A/C MINIBAR TV TEL. $129–$210 double; $250–$2,000 suite. AE, CB, DC, DISC, JCB, MC, V. Parking $13.

Despite its large size, The Madison manages to stay quieter and less hectic than most convention hotels, and with its roof-top restaurant and swimming pool with a view, it is a good choice for leisure travelers as well as those in town on business. All rooms are larger than average and many have views of either the Puget Sound or the Cascade Range. For the best views, ask for a room on the west side of the hotel. The Club Floors provide more luxurious accommodations and a lounge in which a continental breakfast and afternoon snacks are served.

Dining/Entertainment: Prego, on the 28th floor, serves northern Italian cuisine amid eye-catching views. There's live jazz here several nights a week. The hotel also has a casual cafe. A convivial lounge spills out onto an outdoor terrace, complete with waterfall, when the weather permits.

Services: 24-hour room service, concierge, complimentary morning coffee and newspaper, valet/laundry service, complimentary shoeshine, massages available.

Facilities: The roof-top indoor pool is this hotel's best selling point. There are also a whirlpool tub, sauna, fitness room, and gift shop.

✪ **Mayflower Park Hotel.** 405 Olive Way, Seattle, WA 98101. ☎ **800/426-5100,** 206/382-6990, or 206/623-8700. Fax 206/382-6997. 172 rms, 20 suites, A/C TV TEL. $150–$180 double; $190 suite. AE, CB, DC, DISC, MC, V. Valet parking $9.

If either shopping or sipping martinis is among your favorite recreational activities, there's no question of where to stay in Seattle. The Mayflower Park Hotel is connected to the upscale shops of Westlake Center and is flanked by Nordstrom and The Bon Marché. In Oliver's Lounge, the hotel also serves up the best martinis in Seattle. Most rooms are furnished with an eclectic blend of contemporary Italian and traditional European furnishings. Some rooms have bathrooms that are small and old-fashioned but have large old tubs that are great for soaking. If you crave space, ask for one of the large corner rooms or a suite. The smallest rooms here are very cramped.

Dining: Andaluca is currently one of Seattle's hottest restaurants (see "Dining" below for details). Oliver's Lounge, which was once a pharmacy, is martini central for Seattle and also serves light lunches and free hors d'oeuvres in the evening.

Services: 24-hour room service, valet/laundry service.

Facilities: There's a small well-equipped fitness room, but guests can also use a nearby health club.

Seattle Hilton Hotel. Sixth Ave. and University St., Seattle, WA 98101. ☎ **800/426-0535** or 206/624-0500. Fax 206/682-9029. 237 rms. 6 suites. A/C TV TEL. $160–$230 double; $250–$475 suite. AE, CB, DC, DISC, MC, V. Parking $16.

What you'll find at this downtown high-rise are very comfortable rooms, all of which have been recently redecorated in a sort of plush Italianate style with contemporary accents. These are now some of the prettiest rooms downtown. Perhaps because this hotel caters primarily to convention crowds, you won't find a swimming pool here.

Dining/Entertainment: Up on the top floor at Asgard Restaurant, there is Continental cuisine with a Northwest accent, as well as a piano bar. The views are superb. Macaulay's Restaurant and Lounge is a casual spot serving familiar American food, though without any views to accompany it.

Services: 24-hour room service, concierge, valet/laundry service.

Facilities: Gift shop, small exercise room (plus access to nearby health club for $10).

✪ **Sheraton Seattle Hotel & Towers.** 1400 Sixth Ave., Seattle, WA 98101. ☎ **800/325-3535** or 206/621-9000. Fax 206/621-8441. 798 rms, 42 suites. A/C MINIBAR TV TEL. $165–$250 double; $250–$650 suite. AE, CB, DC, DISC, ER, JCB, MC, V. Valet parking $17; self-parking $14.

From the collection of art glass in the lobby to the top-of-the-line fitness center, the Sheraton has figured out what travelers want. King rooms are spacious and are designed for business travelers, and if you book a room on the Club or Tower Level, you'll get the kind of service you would expect only from a boutique hotel. Fresh from a complete remodeling, the rooms here are looking better than ever.

Dining/Entertainment: Fuller's has long been one of Seattle's most talked about restaurants (see "Dining" below for details). For casual meals, there's the Pike Street Cafe, with its 27-foot dessert bar. There's also a tiny oyster bar, a quick Italian lunch place, and a nautical-theme sports bar. The Gallery Lounge features live jazz on weekends.

Services: 24-hour room service, concierge, valet/laundry service, tour desk.

Facilities: The 35th-floor fitness center provides some of the best views in the city and includes an indoor pool, whirlpool spa, sauna, and exercise room. The hotel also has a business center, art-glass gallery, a gift shop, and a currency exchange desk.

Warwick Hotel. 401 Lenora St., Seattle, WA 98121. ☎ **800/426-9280** or 206/443-4300. Fax 206/448-1662. 229 rms, 4 suites. A/C MINIBAR TV TEL. $160–210 double ($119 weekends); $375–$475 suite. AE, CB, DC, DISC, MC, V. Parking $12.

The Warwick offers European charm and exceptional service in a convenient location. The best rooms here are those on the north side of the hotel. These have views of the Space Needle and are particularly popular when there are fireworks at the Seattle Center, such as New Year's Eve and the Fourth of July.

Corner rooms are a bit smaller than others, many of which have king beds and sofa beds. Modern furnishings, a desk for working, and a couch or an easy chair for relaxing round out the amenities that will help you settle in. Lots of marble adds a touch of class to the bathrooms.

Dining/Entertainment: Liaison is the hotel's distinctive dining room, serving Northwest-influenced Pacific Rim cuisine. There is live piano music several nights a week in the adjacent lounge.

Services: 24-hour room service, concierge, valet/laundry service, complimentary shuttle service to downtown Seattle.

Facilities: Indoor pool, whirlpool spa, sauna, fitness room.

MODERATE

Best Western Loyal Inn. 2301 Eighth Ave., Seattle, WA 98121. ☎ **800/528-1234** or 206/ 682-0200. Fax 206/467-8984. 91 rms, 12 suites. A/C TV TEL. $80–$102 double; $150–$200 suite. Rates include continental breakfast. AE, DC, DISC, MC, V. Free parking.

Located only a few blocks from Seattle Center and the Space Needle, this motel is a good city-center choice for anyone on a budget, especially families. Deluxe rooms have wet bars, coffeemakers, remote-control TVs, king-size beds, and two sinks in the bathrooms. Facilities here include a 24-hour sauna and a whirlpool spa, but there is no pool or restaurant.

Pacific Plaza Hotel. 400 Spring St., Seattle, WA 98104. ☎ **800/426-1165** or 206/623-3900. Fax 206/623-2059. 160 rms. A/C TV TEL. $80–$104 double. Rates include continental breakfast. AE, DC, DISC, MC, V. Parking $9.

There aren't too many choices left for economical accommodations in downtown Seattle, but this fairly well maintained hotel, built in 1928, offers economical rooms and a prime location. You're halfway between Pike Place Market and Pioneer Square, and just about the same distance from the waterfront. Rooms are small and sometimes cramped, but overall they're fairly comfortable and generally clean. If you aren't too fussy, this is as good a choice as any of the chain motels near the Space Needle.

✪ **Sixth Avenue Inn.** 2000 Sixth Ave., Seattle, WA 98121 ☎ **800/648-6440** or 206/ 441-8300. Fax 206/441-9903. 166 rms. A/C TV TEL. $80–$135 double. AE, CB, MC, V. Free parking.

Located close to Pike Place Market and the Westlake Center monorail station, this low-rise hotel is convenient and economically priced for downtown Seattle. This is more than your standard budget hotel. In the guest rooms you'll find a brass bed, old photos of Seattle, and a small wall shelf with a selection of old hardcover books and *Readers Digest* condensed books. The hotel's Sixth Avenue Bar and Grill serves breakfast, lunch, and dinner and overlooks a Japanese garden. There's also a quiet lounge, and room service is available.

WestCoast Vance Hotel. 620 Stewart St., Seattle, WA 98101. ☎ **800/426-0670** or 206/ 441-4200. Fax 206/441-8612. 165 rms. A/C TV TEL. $115–$149 double. AE, DC, DISC, MC, V. Parking $11.

Built in the 1920s, this hotel has a very elegant little lobby with wood paneling, marble floors, Oriental carpets, and ornate plasterwork moldings. However, with neither a fitness room nor a swimming pool, it's obvious that this hotel caters to business travelers simply looking for a convenient place to sleep at night. Accommodations vary in size and style and some are quite small; the corner rooms compensate with lots of windows. Furniture is in keeping with the style of the lobby, and for the most part is fairly elegant. Bathrooms are uniformly small. The hotel's Salute in Città Ristorante is a bright and popular Italian restaurant.

INEXPENSIVE

Seattle City Center Travelodge. 2213 Eighth Ave., Seattle, WA 98121. ☎ **800/578-7878** or 206/624-6300. Fax 206/233-0185. 73 rms. A/C TV TEL. $59–$99 double. AE, CB, DC, DISC, MC, V. Free parking.

This conveniently located and moderately priced downtown motel is about midway between the Westlake Center shopping mall and Seattle Center which makes it a fairly convenient choice if you don't mind doing a bit of walking. The rooms are attractive and some even have balconies and views of the Space Needle.

BED & BREAKFASTS

Pensione Nichols. 1923 First Ave., Seattle, WA 98101. ☎ **800/440-7125** or 206/441-7125. 8 rms (none with private bath). 2 suites (both with private bath). $85 double; $160 suite. Two-night minimum on summer weekends. Rates include breakfast. AE, MC, V.

This European-style city-center bed-and-breakfast is up two flights of stairs from the street, and though it is only a block from Pike Place Market, it is also upstairs from a porno theater. The B&B is a touch expensive for what you get (some of the furniture is getting quite worn), though it is hard to beat the location. Only two of the guest rooms have windows (the two rooms facing the street), but all the rest have skylights. High ceilings and white bedspreads brighten the rooms and make them feel spacious. The two suites on the other hand are huge and have full kitchens as well as large windows overlooking the bay. These suites have a few antiques, as does the inn's living room, which also overlooks the water.

⊕ Family-Friendly Hotels

Sheraton Seattle Hotel & Towers *(see pg. 72)*　With a 35th floor swimming pool, a little snack shop selling pizza and pasta, and a 27-foot-long dessert bar in another of the hotel's restaurants, this downtown convention hotel is a good choice for families.

Seattle Sea-Tac Marriott *(see pg. 81)*　With a huge jungly atrium containing a swimming pool and whirlpool spas, kids can play Tarzan and never leave the hotel. There is also a game room that will keep the young ones occupied for hours if need be.

LAKE UNION & QUEEN ANNE HILL

EXPENSIVE

Seattle Downtown—Lake Union Marriott Residence Inn. 800 Fairview Ave. N., Seattle, WA 98109. ☎ **800/331-3131** or 206/624-6000. Fax 206/223-8160. 234 suites. A/C TV TEL. $110–$200 one-bedroom suite; $170–$300 two-bedroom suite. Rates include continental breakfast. AE, DC, DISC, JCB, MC, V. Parking $9.

Located just across the street from Lake Union, this seven-story atrium hotel is within a block or two of several waterfront restaurants. All accommodations here are suites, so you'll buy quite a bit more space for your money. The suites include full kitchens, so you can fix your own meals if you like, though the buffet breakfast down in the lobby shouldn't be missed. Though the suites here are generally quite spacious, they don't have much in the way of character. However, they do have phones and televisions in bedrooms and living rooms and there are large desks as well.

Dining: Though the hotel has no restaurant of its own, there are several restaurants right across the street, and one of these provides the hotel's room service.

Services: Complimentary cookies and coffee, evening dessert, Wednesday night guest reception, grocery shopping service, complimentary morning newspaper, valet/laundry service, free downtown shuttle service.

Facilities: Indoor lap pool, children's pool, steam room, sauna, whirlpool spa, exercise room.

MODERATE

Houseboat Hideaways. Boat World Marina, 2144 Westlake Ave., Seattle, WA 98109 (mailing address: c/o Kent Davis, P.O. Box 782, Edmonds WA 98020) ☎ **206/323-5323.** Two houseboats. TV. $105–$135 double. AE, MC, V.

Located at a marina on the west shore of Lake Union, these two houseboats are nothing like the place Tom Hanks was living in *Sleepless in Seattle*. Much smaller, they still offer a chance to sample the Seattle houseboat life. If you're prone to sea sickness, you might want to pass on these, since boat wakes tend to keep these houseboats rocking throughout the day. While both houseboats have galleys and sundecks, one is 28 feet long and sleeps up to four people and the other is 40 feet long and sleeps up to six people. Both have great views of the lake.

○ **The M.V. Challenger.** 1001 Fairview Ave. N., Seattle, WA 98109. ☎ **206/340-1201.** Fax 206/621-9208. 15 rms (12 with private bath). $75–$200 double. Rates include full breakfast. Children by reservation only. AE, CB, DC, DISC, MC, V. Free parking.

If you love ships and the sea and want a taste of Seattle's water-oriented lifestyle, don't pass up an opportunity to spend the night on board a restored and fully operational old tugboat (or one of this inn's other boats). If, however, you need lots of space, this place is definitely not for you. Guest rooms are as small as you would expect berths to be on any small boat. However, you're welcome to visit the bridge of the *Challenger* for a great view of Lake Union and the Seattle skyline or simply hang out in the conversation pit in the cozy main cabin. The location, at the south end of Lake Union, puts you a bit of a walk (or a short bus ride) from downtown, but there are lots of waterfront restaurants within walking distance.

A BED & BREAKFAST

B.D. Williams House Bed & Breakfast. 1505 Fourth Ave. N., Seattle WA 98109-2902. ☎ **800/880-0810** or 206/285-0810. 5 rms (all with private or dedicated bathroom). $75–$150 double. Rates include full breakfast. AE, DC, MC, V.

Located high atop Queen Anne Hill, yet within walking distance of Seattle Center, this restored historic home dates back to the turn of the century. Colorful flower

Seattle Accommodations & Dining—
Capitol Hill, Lake Union, Queen Anne & U. District

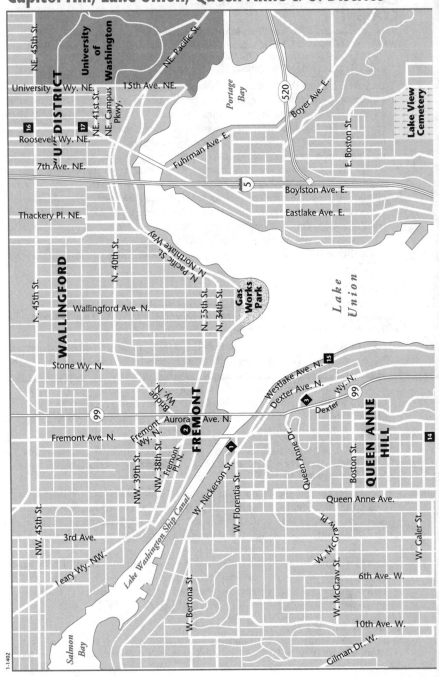

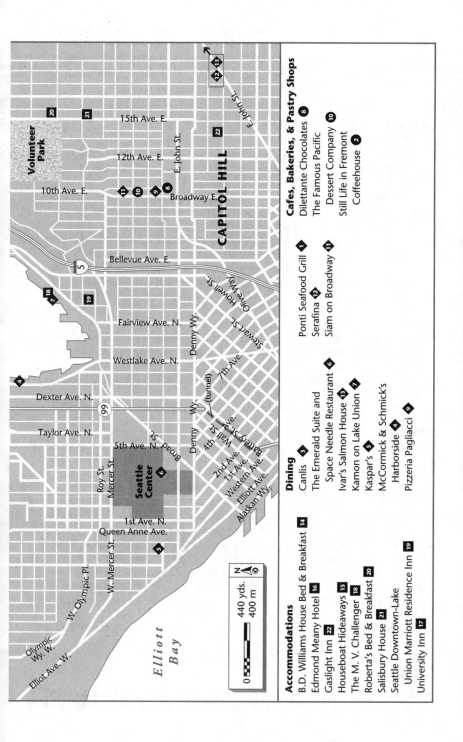

Accommodations

B.D. Williams House Bed & Breakfast **14**
Edmond Meany Hotel **16**
Gaslight Inn **22**
Houseboat Hideaways **15**
The M. V. Challenger **18**
Roberta's Bed & Breakfast **20**
Salisbury House **21**
Seattle Downtown–Lake
Union Marriott Residence Inn **19**
University Inn **17**

Dining

Canlis **3**
The Emerald Suite and
Space Needle Restaurant **6**
Ivar's Salmon House **13**
Kamon on Lake Union **7**
Kaspar's **5**
McCormick & Schmick's
Harborside **4**
Pizzeria Pagliacci **9**

Ponti Seafood Grill **1**
Serafina **12**
Siam on Broadway **11**

Cafes, Bakeries, & Pastry Shops

Dilettante Chocolates **8**
The Famous Pacific
Dessert Company **10**
Still Life in Fremont
Coffeehouse **2**

77

gardens surround the inn, and a vegetable garden provides produce for the inn's gourmet breakfasts. An enclosed sunporch and an open veranda are pleasant spaces in which to relax at any time of year and no matter what the weather. Most rooms here have excellent views of either Puget Sound, Lake Union, or the downtown city skyline. Both the rooms and the neighborhood are extremely quiet, and walkers will appreciate the nearby parks.

FIRST HILL & CAPITOL HILL
VERY EXPENSIVE

✪ **Sorrento Hotel.** 900 Madison St., Seattle, WA 99104-1297. ☎ **800/426-1265** or 206/622-6400. Fax 206/343-6155. 34 rms, 42 suites. A/C MINIBAR TV TEL. $200–$220 double; $240–$1,200 suite. AE, CB, DC, DISC, MC, V. Valet parking $16.

An old-world atmosphere reigns at this hotel high on First Hill overlooking downtown Seattle. From the wrought-iron gates and palm trees of the courtyard entrance to the plush seating of the octagonal lobby, the Sorrento whispers style and elegance. No two rooms are alike here, but all are luxuriously appointed and set up for business travelers (rooms even have their own fax machines). More than half the accommodations are suites, with the least expensive of these going for only $20 more than a deluxe room. West-side rooms have a view of the city and Puget Sound.

Dining/Entertainment: The Hunt Club, a dark restaurant with an appropriately clubby atmosphere, serves superb Northwest cuisine (see "Dining" below for details), and in the adjacent Fireside Room bar, you can get lighter and less expensive meals. Several nights a week a pianist plays in the lounge. Afternoon tea and weekend meals are served in the lobby and Fireside Room. In the summer, there's an Italian "street" cafe in the hotel's courtyard.

Services: Room service, concierge, valet/laundry service, complimentary limousine service to downtown, massages.

Facilities: Exercise room with the latest Nautilus equipment, salon, flower shop.

EXPENSIVE

Plaza Park Suites. 1011 Pike St., Seattle, WA 98101. ☎ **800/426-0670** or 206/682-8282. Fax 206/682-5315. 26 rms, 168 suites. A/C TV TEL. $125 double; $180–$340 suite. Rates include continental breakfast. AE, DC, DISC, MC, V. Valet parking $13.

Located just a block uphill from the Washington State Convention and Trade Center, this hotel caters primarily to business travelers who need a bit of extra room for getting work done while in town. However, because it is about equidistant between the waterfront and Capitol Hill, it makes a good choice if you are planning on doing a bit of bar hopping or nightclubbing on the hill. While not all the accommodations here are suites, they are definitely the better choice. However, even the suites here are not as big as you would expect, although they do have two TVs, two phones, and two-poster, king-size beds. Lots of rooms here have good views that take in the Space Needle, but many also get a lot of traffic noise from both the freeway and Pike Street.

Services: Room service, valet/laundry service, complimentary downtown shuttle.

Facilities: Small outdoor pool (seasonal), whirlpool spa, fitness room (plus access to nearby athletic club for $7), deli.

MODERATE

The Inn at Virginia Mason. 1006 Spring St., Seattle, WA 98104. ☎ **800/283-6453** or 206/583-6453. Fax 206/223-7545. 79 rms, 3 suites. A/C TV TEL. $98–$155 double; $155–$215 suite. AE, CB, EC, DISC, MC, V. Parking $4.

This hotel takes its name from the Virginia Mason Hospital, which is next door and is connected to the hotel. Regardless of the fact that most of the guests here are either here on hospital business or to visit relatives who are in the hospital, the hotel is a good choice for its economical rates, its quiet location, and its proximity to downtown. The hotel also keeps good company; the Sorrento Hotel is only a block away. Because this is an old building, room sizes vary a lot, but most have large closets, modern bathrooms, and wing-back chairs. Most deluxe rooms and suites are quite large, and some have whirlpool baths, fireplaces, dressing rooms, and refrigerators.

Dining/Entertainment: The Rhododendron Restaurant serves Northwest and traditional cuisine, and there is live piano music several nights a week.

Services: Valet/laundry service, concierge, room service.

Facilities: Privileges at nearby fitness center.

BED & BREAKFASTS

✪ **Gaslight Inn.** 1727 15th Ave., Seattle, WA 98122. ☎ **206/325-3654.** 9 rms (5 with private bath), 1 studio and 6 suites (all with private bath). TV. $68–$108 double; $98 studio; $128–$148 suite. Rates include continental breakfast. AE, MC, V. Off-street parking only if staying in studio or suite.

Anyone who is a fan of the Arts-and-Crafts movement of the early-20th-century will enjoy a stay at this 1906 vintage home. Throughout the inn, there are numerous pieces of Stickley furniture, and everywhere you turn, oak trim frames doors and window. The common rooms are spacious and attractively decorated with a combination western and northwestern flare, and throughout the inn's two houses there are lots of art-glass pieces. In summer, guests can swim in the backyard pool or lounge on the deck. Guest rooms include lots of oak furnishings and heavy, peeled-log beds in some rooms. An annex next door has a studio and six suites. One of these suites, done in a contemporary style with an art-glass chandelier, has a fireplace and an outstanding view of the city. Another has a hot tub and its own private garden. Innkeepers Steve Bennet, Trevor Logan, and John Fox can provide a wealth of information about Seattle and the inn's Capitol Hill environs.

Roberta's Bed & Breakfast. 1147 16th Ave. E., Seattle, WA 98112. ☎ **206/329-3326.** Fax 206/324-2149. 5 rms (4 with private bath). $85–$125 double. Rates include full breakfast. MC, V.

This turn-of-the-century home is on a beautiful tree-lined street just around the corner from Volunteer Park. A big front porch stretches across the front of the house, while inside there are hardwood floors and a mix of antique and modern furnishings. Bibliophiles will be certain to develop an instant rapport with this B&B's namesake innkeeper. Roberta is, to say the least, fond of books and has filled shelves in nearly every room with books both old and new. Our favorite room is the attic hideaway, which has angled walls, painted wood paneling, lots of skylights, and a claw-foot bathtub. The overall effect of this room is that of a ship's cabin or artist's garret. Breakfast starts with tea or coffee left at your door and continues downstairs in the dining room with a hearty meal that includes home-baked treats.

Salisbury House. 750 16th Ave. E., Seattle, WA 98112. ☎ **206/328-8682.** Fax 206/720-1019. 4 rms (all with private bath). $75–$125 double. Rates include full breakfast. AE, MC, V.

This grand old house on tree-lined 16th Avenue East has a wide porch that wraps around two sides. Inside there's plenty to admire as well. Two living rooms (one with a wood-burning fireplace) and a second-floor sunporch provide plenty of spots for relaxing and meeting other guests. On sunny summer days, breakfast may even be served in the small formal garden in the backyard. Guest rooms all have queen-sized beds with down comforters, and one of the rooms has an old claw-foot tub in the bathroom. Breakfasts here are deliciously filling and might include fresh fruit, juice, quiche, fresh-baked muffins or bread, or oatmeal pancakes. Cathryn and Mary Wiese, mother and daughter, are the friendly innkeepers.

THE UNIVERSITY DISTRICT

Located 15 to 20 minutes from downtown Seattle, the U District will likely appeal to younger travelers. The neighborhood offers less-expensive accommodations than downtown, yet is still fairly convenient to Seattle's major attractions. Also nearby are the Burke Museum, Henry Art Gallery, the Woodland Park Zoo, and, of course, the University of Washington. As you would expect in a university neighborhood, there are lots of cheap restaurants in the neighborhood, and this fact, combined with the lower hotel rates here, makes this a good choice for anyone on a budget.

EXPENSIVE

✪ **Edmond Meany Hotel.** 4507 Brooklyn Ave. NE, Seattle, WA 98105. ☎ **800/899-0251** or 206/634-2000. 155 rms. A/C TV TEL. $129–$169 double. AE, DC, MC, V. Free parking.

Fresh from a complete renovation, the Edmond Meany Hotel is now one of Seattle's hippest hotels, and the modern art deco styling will surround you in retro style unlike anything you'll find anywhere else in the city. Every room here is a large corner room, which means plenty of space to spread out and plenty of views of downtown Seattle, distant mountains, and various lakes and waterways from the higher floors. Boldly styled furnishings will appeal to anyone with an appreciation for contemporary furniture design. Tiled combination baths are small.

Dining/Entertainment: The Pleiades Restaurant, down in the basement, is as brashly contemporary in styling as the rest of the hotel and serves moderately priced creative meals with a northwestern slant. There's a bar to one side of the restaurant, and just off the lobby is a stylish little cafe where you can get your espresso fix throughout the day.

Services: Room service, valet/laundry service, complimentary newspaper.

Facilities: Unfortunately, there's no swimming pool here but there is a fitness room.

MODERATE

✪ **University Inn.** 4140 Roosevelt Way NE, Seattle, WA 98105. ☎ **800/733-3855** or 206/632-5055. Fax 206/547-4937. 102 rms, 12 junior suites. A/C TV TEL. $102–$112 double; $132 junior suite. Rates include continental breakfast. AE, DC, DISC, MC, V.

Located within easy walking distance of the university, this renovated 1960s vintage hotel offers surprisingly attractive rooms, many of which have views of Lake Union. Although the standard rooms have only showers in their bathrooms, these rooms compensate for this lack with small balconies. The deluxe rooms are more spacious and those on the west side of the hotel have unusual pushed-out windows that provide glimpses of Lake Union. For even more room and the best views, opt for one of the junior suites, which have large windows, microwaves, small refrigerators, coffeemakers, and telephones in the bathrooms (ask for room 331; it's got a view of Mount Rainier). Facilities include a small outdoor pool (seasonal), whirlpool spa, and a tiny exercise room. Along with your simple breakfast, you can grab a free copy of the paper. More filling breakfasts, as well as lunch are available in the inn's Portage Bay Cafe.

NEAR SEA-TAC AIRPORT
EXPENSIVE

✪ **Seattle Sea-Tac Marriott.** 3201 S. 176th St., Seattle, WA 98188. ☎ **800/228-9290** or 206/241-2000. Fax 206/248-0789. 459 rms, 5 suites. A/C TV TEL. $144 double ($89–$144 weekends); $225–$550 suite. AE, CB, DC, DISC, MC, V. Free parking.

With its steamy atrium garden full of tropical plants, a swimming pool, and two whirlpool tubs, this resortlike hotel may keep you so enthralled you won't want to leave. The atrium even has waterfalls and totem poles for that Northwest outdoorsy feeling, and best of all, it's always sunny and warm in here. In the lobby, a huge stone fireplace and moose head hanging on the wall conjure up images of a remote mountain lodge. To get the most out of your stay here, try to get one of the rooms with a view of Mount Rainier.

Dining: Yukon Landing Restaurant sports a gold rush decor with stone pillars; rough-hewn beams and wooden walls; moose, deer, and elk heads on the walls; and deer-antler chandeliers. The Lobby Lounge is its own little greenhouse overlooking the atrium.

Services: Room service, free airport shuttle, car-rental desk, valet/laundry service.

Facilities: Indoor swimming pool, whirlpool spa, health club, sauna, game room.

Wyndham Garden Hotel Seattle-Tacoma Airport. 18118 International Blvd., Seattle, WA 98188. ☎ **800/WYNDHAM** or 206/244-6666. Fax 206/244-6679. 204 rms, 24 suites. A/C TV TEL. $125–$139 double ($69–$89 weekends); $139–$159 suite. AE, CB, DC, DISC, MC, V. Free parking.

This hotel caters primarily to business travelers, but the ease of airport access makes it a good place to stay if you are arriving late or leaving early. Guest rooms are set up with business travelers in mind (two phones, work desks, coffeemakers, irons and ironing boards). Try to get a room with a view of the adjacent small lake.

Dining/Entertainment: A casual cafe is located right in the lobby, and there's also a library-like lounge with chairs gathered around a fireplace.

Services: Evening room service, complimentary airport shuttle, laundry/valet service.

Facilities: Indoor pool, whirlpool, exercise room.

MODERATE

WestCoast Sea-Tac Hotel. 18220 International Blvd., Seattle, WA 98188. ☎ **800/426-0670** or 206/246-5535. Fax 206/246-9733. 146 rms. A/C TV TEL. $90–$114 double. AE, CB, DC, DISC, MC, V. Free parking.

Located almost directly across from the airport's main entrance, this modern hotel was renovated recently and provides comfortable accommodations designed for business travelers. European styling prevails and there's a grand piano in the lobby. The guest rooms have queen- or king-size beds, work desk, and are generally quite large (if you need space, this is the place). In superior king rooms, you get evening turndown service, coffee and a newspaper in the morning, terry-cloth robes, hairdryers, and an honor bar. The hotel backs to a small lake, but only a few rooms have lake views.

Dining: Gregory's Bar and Grill, a moderately priced restaurant with unremarkable food, is across the parking lot from the main hotel facility. The attached lounge features an aeronautical theme.

Services: Room service, free airport shuttle, valet/laundry service.

Facilities: Seasonal outdoor pool, whirlpool spa, sauna.

INEXPENSIVE TO MODERATE

Among the better and more convenient inexpensive chain motel choices are **Motel 6 (Sea-Tac South),** 18900 47th Ave. S., Seattle, WA 98188 (☎ 206/241-1648), charging $37 to $48; **Super 8 Motel,** 3100 S. 192nd St., Seattle, WA 98188 (☎ 206/433-8188), charging $69 to $82 for a double; and **Travelodge Seattle Airport,** 2900 S. 192nd St., Seattle, WA 98188 (☎ 206/241-9292), charging $39 to $85 double.

THE EASTSIDE

Home to Bill Gates, Microsoft, countless high-tech spin-off companies, and seemingly endless suburbs, the Eastside lies across Lake Washington from Seattle proper and is comprised of the fast-growing cities of Kirkland, Bellevue, Redmond, Bothell, and a few other smaller communities. As can be attested by Bill Gates's media-hyped mansion, there are some pretty wealthy neighborhoods here on the Eastside, but wealth doesn't necessarily equal respect, and the Eastside is still much derided by Seattle citizens as uncultured and nothing more than a bedroom community for the city. However, Seattlites' attitudes aside, should you be out this way on high-tech business or visiting friends, you may find an eastside hotel more convenient than one in downtown Seattle, and surprisingly, two of the most luxurious hotels in the entire Seattle area are here on this side of Lake Washington. If it isn't rush hour, you can usually get from the Eastside to downtown Seattle in about 20 minutes via the famous floating I-90 and Wash. 520 bridges.

VERY EXPENSIVE

✪ **Bellevue Club Hotel.** 11200 SE Sixth St., Bellevue, WA 98004. ☎ **800/579-1110** or 425/454-4424. Fax 425/688-3101. 64 rms, 3 suites. A/C TV TEL. $190–$230 double; $370–$995 suite. AE, DC, MC, V.

This hotel epitomizes contemporary Northwest styling in its gardens, architecture, and interior design, and you won't find more elegant rooms anywhere in Seattle. Style, however, is only part of the story here. The "club" in this hotel's name refers to a state-of-the-art health club. Guest rooms are outrageously plush, with the high-ceilinged garden rooms among our favorites. These come with a floor-to-ceiling wall of glass, massive draperies, and a private patio facing onto a beautiful garden. Luxurious European fabrics are everywhere, giving rooms a very romantic feel. In most bathrooms, resplendent in granite and glass, you'll find whirlpool tubs. Three telephones, fax machines, irons and ironing boards, in-room safes, and hair dryers are all standard.

Dining: The same elegant contemporary styling seen in the lobby is to be found in the Polaris Restaurant, which is part of the club complex. Northwest flavors predominate on the menu here. There's also a lounge.

Services: Concierge, 24-hour room service, valet/laundry service, complimentary morning newspaper and overnight shoeshine.

Facilities: The "Club" in this hotel's name is a massive full-service health club that has everything from an indoor running track to a 50-meter pool to squash courts and tennis courts. At press time, there were plans to add a spa.

✪ **The Woodmark Hotel on Lake Washington.** 1200 Carillon Point, Kirkland, WA 98033-7351. ☎ **800/822-3700** or 425/822-3700. Fax 425/822-3699. 100 rms, 25 suites. A/C MINIBAR TV TEL. $180–$230 double; $250–$1,250 suite. AE, DC, JCB, MC, V. Valet parking $11; self parking $9.

Located 20 minutes from downtown Seattle (on a good day), this is the metro area's premier waterfront lodging and is located on the shore of Lake Washington. While there are plenty of lake-view rooms here, you'll pay as much as a $50 premium for these rooms. Creek-view rooms, which are the least expensive, actually offer pleasant views of a salmon stream. In the guest rooms you'll find such welcome features as floor-to-ceiling windows, a tiny television in the bathroom, and large work desks.

Dining/Entertainment: At Waters, an upscale lake-view bistro, you can dine on an eclectic melange of flavors. For afternoon tea, and cocktails throughout the day, there is the cozy Library Bar, which often has live piano music in the evenings. In addition, there are complimentary late-night snacks and drinks available.

Services: Room service, concierge, courtesy local shopping van, shoeshine service, laundry/valet service, complimentary use of laptop computer, cellular phone, pager.

Facilities: Exercise room, day spa, marina, business center.

MODERATE

Best Western Bellevue Inn. 11211 Main St., Bellevue, WA 98004. ☎ **800/421-8193** or 425/455-5240. Fax 206/455-0654. 179 rms. $100–$140 double. AE, DC, DISC, JCB, MC, V. Free parking.

The Bellevue is one of the few hotels in the Seattle area that captures the feel of the Northwest in design and landscaping. The sprawling two-story hotel is roofed with cedar shingles and lushly planted with rhododendrons, ferns, azaleas, and fir trees. Try to book a poolside first-floor room. These rooms, though a bit dark, have sunken, rock-walled patios. Bathrooms include plenty of counter space, and there are built-in hairdryers. The hotel's lackluster restaurant serves standard American fare, and the adjoining bar is an after-work hang-out for business travelers. Complimentary passes to a local athletic club and complimentary local van service are available. There's also an outdoor pool and an exercise room.

4 Dining

Over the past few years Seattle has begun to develop a reputation as one of the country's top restaurant cities. This reputation has brought in the likes of Planet Hollywood and a restaurant by California celebrity chef Wolfgang Puck (with a second on the way at press time). The city has also been drawing more and more top-notch chefs eager to make a start.

While Seattle's reputation has risen on the shoulders of its creative Northwest cuisine, the past few years saw the city in the throes of the Mediterranean/rustic Italian dining trend that swept the nation. Although there still seems to be an Italian restaurant on every corner in Seattle, and new ones are still opening, a new trend is slowly developing—pan-Asian or Euro-Asian restaurants with boldly contemporary interior decor.

Although a few years back this style of cooking might have been dubbed Pacific Rim (another name for Northwest cuisine), the new moniker is more appropriate. Pan-Asian restaurants such as Seattle's own Wild Ginger and Wolfgang Puck's ObaChine spread the flavors of Asia across their menus and, in the case of ObaChine, mix them all up together. In the Westin Hotel, Hawaiian restaurateur Roy Yamaguchi has opened a mainland outpost serving his highly creative Euro-Asian cuisine. Part of the basis for this trend is the setting of the restaurant, and the basic idea is, why not take Asian food out of low-budget and characterless settings and transform it into haute cuisine by dressing up the surroundings. Of course, in the hands of accomplished chefs, the food itself also leaps out of the realm of the mundane. A few more Seattle restaurants have been hopping on the pan-Asian bandwagon this year, and still others are acknowledging the trend by incorporating plenty of

Asian dishes into the their menus. So, are you ready for sushi egg rolls with fiery Burmese dipping sauce on a bed of Sumatran smoked eel curry? Just kidding.

One Seattle dining trend that has been unchanged by the passing of time has been the city's near obsession with seafood. You may be aware that wild salmon in the Northwest are rapidly disappearing from the region's rivers, but this doesn't prevent salmon from showing up on nearly every menu in the city. Much of it is now hatchery fish, or imported from Canada or Alaska. There are also nearly a dozen varieties of regional oysters available. Dungeness crabs are another Northwest specialty, which though not as large as king crabs, are quite a bit heftier than the blue crabs of the eastern United States. You may also run across such unfamiliar clams as the razor clam or the geoduck (pronounced "gooey duck"). The former is shaped like a straight razor and can be chewy if not prepared properly, and the latter is a bivalve of prodigious proportions (up to 12 pounds) that usually shows up only in stews and chowders.

With so much water all around, you would be remiss in your duties if you didn't eat at a waterfront restaurant while in Seattle. You'll find **waterfront restaurants** on virtually every body of water in the Seattle area, and they offer views of everything from marinas to Mount Rainier, the Olympic Mountains to the Space Needle. We have listed waterfront restaurants in appropriate neighborhood categories below. Downtown, you'll find Anthony's Pier 66 and Elliott's; in the Queen Anne Hill/Lake Union area, you'll find McCormick's Harborside, Kamon on Lake Union, and Palisade; in the north Seattle section, you'll find Ivar's Salmon House, Ponti, and Ray's Boathouse; in West Seattle, you'll find Salty's on Alki; in east Seattle, you'll find Leschi Lakecafe; and on the Eastside, you'll find Yarrow Bay Grill.

If you're looking for someplace to eat past midnight, there are ever more decent options in Seattle (especially downtown) for **late-night dining.** In the listings below, check out Flying Fish, Palace Kitchen, Trattoria Mitchelli, and 13 Coins.

Want to do **brunch?** No problem, there are some great options around the city. Try Cafe Flora, Ivar's Salmon House, McCormick & Schmick's Harborside, Palisade, Ponti Seafood Grill, Salty's on Alki, the Space Needle, or, over on the Eastside, Yarrow Bay Grill.

Pricing categories in this chapter are as follows: expensive, over $40; moderate, $20 to $40; inexpensive, under $20. These prices are in most cases based on a three-course meal and do not include the cost of beer, wine, or cocktails.

DOWNTOWN (INCLUDING THE WATERFRONT, PIONEER SQUARE, BELLTOWN & THE INTERNATIONAL DISTRICT)
EXPENSIVE

✪ **Anthony's Pier 66 & Bell Street Diner.** 2201 Alaskan Way ☎ **206/448-6688.** Reservations recommended (and only accepted) upstairs at Pier 66. Main dishes $17–$27 (Pier 66), $9–$22 (Bell Street Diner). AE, DISC, MC, V. Pier 66 Sun–Thurs 5–9:15pm; Fri–Sat 5–10:15pm; Bell Street Diner Sun–Thurs 11am–10pm, Fri–Sat 11am–11pm. SEAFOOD.

There are a lot of mediocre restaurants on the Seattle waterfront, but if you head up to the north end of the waterfront you'll find not only excellent food but an exceedingly stylish restaurant with lots of art glass and boldly contemporary styling throughout. This is actually two restaurants (three if you count the walk-up window out front), with the up-market crowd heading upstairs for the likes of apple-wood grilled salmon, and the more cost-conscious staying downstairs at the Bell Street Diner where meals are much easier on the wallet. Here, we recommend the fish tacos (also served at the walk-up window) or crab cakes that are 100% crab meat. For the higher prices, you also get the better views, but as long as you don't get stuck at the counter that overlooks the exhibition kitchen you'll be fine. In summer, the decks are the place to be.

The Brooklyn Seafood, Steak & Oyster House. 1212 Second Ave. ☎ **206/224-7000.** Reservations recommended. Main courses $13–$33. AE, DC, DISC, MC, V. Mon–Fri 11am–3pm; Mon–Thurs 5–10pm, Fri 5–10:30pm, Sat 4:30–10:30pm, Sun 4:30–10pm. SEAFOOD.

Designed to look as if it's been here for decades, The Brooklyn is housed in one of the city's oldest buildings. The specialty here is definitely oysters, with about 10 different types piled up at the oyster bar on any given night. If oysters on the half shell don't appeal to you, there are plenty of other tempting appetizers ranging from grilled salmon sausages to roasted garlic and goat cheese. Alder-planked meats and fishes are another specialty here. This type of cooking is similar to smoking or grilling and originated with the Native Americans of the Northwest. In addition, there are simply prepared grilled steaks, and such dishes as seafood pasta in parchment, and grilled black tiger prawns with a vanilla bean and lime sauce.

Campagne. Inn at the Market, 86 Pine St. ☎ **206/728-2800.** Reservations recommended. Main dishes $20–$30; tasting menu $55; 3-course family dinners for two or three persons, $30 per person; for four or more, $25 per person. AE, CB, DC, MC, V. Daily 5:30–10pm (cafe dining until midnight). FRENCH.

On the far side of the fountain that bubbles in the courtyard of the Inn at the Market, French country decor continues inside the aptly named Campagne. Large windows let in precious sunshine and provide a view of Elliott Bay over the top of Pike Place Market. The menu here leans toward country French, with such dishes as house-cured duck prosciutto with a chilled fig and melon timbale, arugula and shaved Reggiano cheese; grilled lamb; and roasted baby chicken stuffed with basmati rice and fava beans. Family dinners are available, and change daily. Cheerful and unpretentious, Campagne is one of the most enjoyable French restaurants in Seattle.

۞ Chez Shea. Corner Market Building, Suite 34, 94 Pike St., Pike Place Market. ☎ **206/467-9990.** Reservations highly recommended. Main dishes $25–$26 (à la carte dishes available Tues–Thurs and Sun); fixed-price four-course dinner $39. AE, MC, V. Tues–Sun 5:30–10pm. NORTHWEST.

Quiet, dark, and intimate, Chez Shea is one of the finest restaurants in Seattle, and while there are other equally fine restaurants in the city, none has quite the quintessential Seattle atmosphere as this Pike Place hideaway. A dozen candlelit tables with views across Puget Sound to the Olympic Mountains provide the perfect setting for a romantic dinner. The menu changes seasonally, and ingredients come primarily from the market below. On a recent spring evening, dinner started with an asparagus-watercress flan and then moved on to a carrot bisque. There were five choices of entrees, including rabbit braised in wine with balsamic vinegar, sweet peppers, leeks, and rosemary, and halibut sautéed with blood orange coulis with gaeta olives, red onion, coriander, white wine, and garlic. Though dessert is à la carte, you'll find it impossible to let it pass you by.

۞ Fuller's. Sheraton Seattle Hotel & Towers, 1400 Sixth Ave. ☎ **206/621-9000.** Reservations recommended. Main dishes $18–$30; tasting menu $55; lunches $10–$15. AE, CB, DC, DISC, JCB, MC, V. Mon–Fri 11:30am–2pm; Mon–Sat 5:30–10pm. NORTHWEST.

Fuller's, named for the founder of the Seattle Art Museum, is dedicated to both the culinary and the visual arts of the Northwest. Each dish is as artfully designed as it is superbly prepared, and surrounding you in this elegant and newly renovated dining room are works of art by the Northwest's best artists. Fuller's menu changes seasonally, but Asian and Mediterranean flavors seem to be predominating of late.

A recent menu included an appetizer of smoked Ahi tuna with cucumber wasabi vinaigrette and daikon sprouts and such main dishes as saffron and coriander marinated demi rack of lamb or grilled veal chop with morel mushrooms. Lunch, with its lower prices, is especially popular. The wine list reflects the seasonal changes on the menu.

✪ **The Georgian.** Four Seasons Olympic Hotel, 411 University St. ☎ **206/621-1700.** Reservations recommended. Main dishes $20–$36. AE, CB, DC, MC, V. Mon–Fri 6:30–11am, Sat 6:30am–noon, Sun 7am–1pm; Mon–Thurs 5:30–10pm, Fri–Sat 5:30–10:30pm. CONTINENTAL/ NORTHWEST.

Nowhere in Seattle is there a more elegant restaurant—to dine at The Georgian is to dine in a palace. The soaring ceiling is decorated with intricate moldings, and the huge windows are framed by luxurious curtains. The excellent service will convince you that your table is the only one being served. Menu offerings are a mingling of Northwest and Continental cuisines, but veal or New York tenderloin with mushrooms and aged Black Angus steak are the signature dishes. As you would expect, the wine list is well suited to both the food and the restaurant's ambience.

Il Bistro. 93-A Pike St. and First Ave. (inside Pike Place Market). ☎ **206/682-3049.** Reservations recommended. Pastas $10–$16; main dishes $16–$26.50. AE, CB, DC, MC, V. Mon–Sat 11:30am–3pm; Sun–Thurs 5:30–10pm, Fri–Sat 5:30–11pm; bar nightly until 2am. ITALIAN

Il Bistro, located to the left of the famous Pike Place Market sign, and with the atmosphere of a wine cellar, takes Italian cooking very seriously. Long before you arrived, the choice of which main dish to order was decided by the hundreds of loyal fans who insist that the rack of lamb with wine sauce is the best in Seattle. Don't take their word for it—decide for yourself. The menu also lists such mouthwatering starters as calamari sautéed with fresh basil, garlic vinegar, and white wine; and pastas here can be a genuine revelation when served with the likes of shiitake mushrooms, hot pepper flakes, vodka, and tomato cream. A wine list featuring Italian, Northwest, and California wines, and a selection of single-malt scotches and grappas round out the experience.

✪ **Il Terrazzo Carmine.** 411 First Ave. S. ☎ **206/467-7797.** Reservations recommended. Pastas $9.50–$14; main dishes $18.50–$26. AE, DC, DISC, MC, V. Mon–Fri 11:30am–2:30pm and 5:30–10pm, Sat 5:30–10pm. ITALIAN.

Considered by many to be the finest Italian restaurant in Seattle, Il Terrazzo Carmine is tucked into the back of an office building in the Pioneer Square area and overlooks a hidden waterfall terrace. This is a big-time power lunch spot and suits are de rigueur for men. What the wealthy come for is a rarefied atmosphere, professional service, and reliable fine Italian fare. Nowhere else in town will you find the likes of sweetbreads ragout and both beef and tuna carpaccio. Among the pastas, you're likely to encounter venison-stuffed ravioli and pappardelle with duck. If you're a steak eater, consider the *bistecca piemontese,* made with dry-aged black angus New York steak and served with truffle oil, radicchio, and endive.

✪ **Metropolitan Grill.** 818 Second Ave. ☎ **206/624-3287.** Reservations recommended. Main dishes lunch $7.50–$20, dinner $17–$35. AE, CB, DC, DISC, JCB, MC, V. Mon–Fri 11am–3:30pm and 5–11pm; Sat 4–11pm, Sun 4:30–10pm. STEAK.

Another reliable restaurant for aspiring financial whiz kids and their mentors, the Metropolitan is dedicated to carnivores. When you walk in, you'll see various cuts of meat, from filet mignon to triple-cut lamb chops, displayed on ice. Green-velvet booths and floral-design carpets strike the keynote of the sophisticated atmosphere, and mirrored walls and a high ceiling trimmed with elegant plasterwork make the dining room feel larger than it actually is. Perfectly cooked steaks are the primary attraction here. A baked potato and a pile of thick cut onion rings complete the perfect steak dinner.

✪ **Virazon.** 1329 First Ave. ☎ **206/233-0123.** Reservations recommended. Main dishes $16–$39; five-course tasting menu $49. AE, DC, MC, V. Mon 11:30am–2:30pm, Tues–Thurs 11:30am–2:30pm and 5:30–9:30pm, Fri–Sat 11:30am–2:30pm and 6–10pm. FRENCH.

There are several French restaurants in the Pike Place Market vicinity, but none is as authentic as Virazon. This is high-end French, the cuisine of legend, with truffles making frequent appearances (a black and white soup of black truffles and celery root; a salad with truffles, peas, white corn, and poached quail eggs; crab and lobster cakes with peas, basil, truffles, and a champagne sauce). Foie gras caviar, squab, and frogs legs also show up. While the classic dishes on the menu will be tempting to gastronomes, it is the tasting menu that is the restaurant's biggest draw; let chef Astolfo Rueda create a truly memorable dinner for you. Though the restaurant is located on busy First Avenue, inside you'll find a quiet, refined atmosphere perfect for a romantic dinner or other special occasion.

MODERATE

✪ **Andaluca.** Mayflower Park Hotel, 407 Olive Way. ☎ **206/382-6999.** Reservations recommended. Main dishes $14.50–$23. AE, CB, DC, DISC, MC, V. Mon–Thurs 11:30am–2:30pm and 5–10pm, Fri–Sat 11:30am–2:30pm and 5–11pm, Sun 4–9pm. NORTHWEST/MEDITERRANEAN.

Located in the basement of the Mayflower Park Hotel, this sumptuous restaurant mixes traditional and the contemporary like no other restaurant in town. To step into the restaurant is to enter a world of vibrant artistry, both in decor and cuisine. Chef Don Curtiss continues to build his reputation with such dishes as traditional Spanish zarzuela shellfish stew and, at press time, paella on Sunday nights. The menu is divided into small plates and large plates, so no matter the size of your hunger, you'll find something to fill it. Although the menu changes frequently, you might find a spicy octopus dish on the small plate menu. The Dungeness crab tower, made with avocado, palm hearts, and gazpacho salsa, has taken Seattle diners by storm. Don't miss it.

Assaggio. 2010 Fourth Ave. ☎ **206/441-1399.** Reservations recommended. Pastas $9–$15, main dishes $14–$20. AE, DC, DISC, MC, V. Mon–Fri 11:30am–2:30pm and 5–10pm, Sat 5–10pm. ITALIAN.

Located on the ground floor of the Hotel Claremont, Assaggio has become one of Seattle's favorite Italian restaurants. This large, casual restaurant has an Old World feel, with a high ceiling, arches, Roman-style murals on the walls, and a wait staff in white aprons and loud ties (definitely an American touch). However, what really recommends this place is the excellent food. For a starter, you might try the grilled radicchio wrapped in pancetta (Italian ham) and topped with a red onion-balsamic vinaigrette. Pastas come from all over Italy, but it's hard to beat the *pappardella boscaiola* with prosciutto, wild mushrooms, Marsala and Barolo wine and a touch of cream. Of course there are traditional pizzas, and also other standbys like osso buco and veal saltimboca.

Dahlia Lounge. 1904 Fourth Ave. ☎ **206/682-4142.** Reservations highly recommended. Main dishes $16–$22. AE, DC, DISC, MC, V. Mon–Fri 11:30am–2:30pm; Mon–Thurs 5:30–10pm, Fri–Sat 5:30–11pm, Sun 5–9pm. NORTHWEST.

The neon chef holding a flapping fish may suggest that the Dahlia is little more than a roadside diner, but a glimpse inside at the stylish decor will likely have you thinking otherwise. One look at the menu, one bite of any dish, will convince you that this is one of Seattle's finest restaurants. Mouth-watering and succulent Dungeness crab cakes, a bow to Chef Tom Douglas's Maryland roots, are the house specialty and should not be missed. Lobster-shiitake potstickers are also a perennial favorite. The menu, influenced by the far side of the Pacific Rim, changes regularly. The lunch menu features many of the same offerings at slightly lower prices.

Elliott's. Pier 56, Alaskan Way. ☎ **206/623-4340.** Reservations recommended. Main dishes $14–$30. AE, DISC, MC, V. Sun–Thurs 11am–11pm, Fri–Sat 11am–11:30pm (the oyster bar stays open later). SEAFOOD.

While most of its neighbors are content to coast along on tourist business, Elliott's actually aims to keep locals happy by serving some of the best seafood in Seattle. Although the restaurant is right on the waterfront, the view really isn't that great, so if that's what you're looking for, try elsewhere. However, if you're looking for superbly prepared fresh seafood, Elliott's is a good bet. The oyster bar, which *Fortune* magazine called one of the five best in the country, does usually have a great selection of fresh oysters. If you prefer your oysters cooked, consider the pan-seared oyster sampler, which includes a trio of boldly flavored dipping sauces.

✪ Etta's Seafood. 2020 Western Ave. ☎ **206/443-6000.** Reservations recommended. Main dishes $8.50–$23. AE, DC, DISC, MC, V. Mon–Thurs 11:30am–10pm, Fri 11:30am–11pm, Sat 9am–11pm, Sun 9am–10pm. SEAFOOD

This, Seattle chef Tom Douglas's makeover of his original Cafe Sport, is located in the Pike Place Market area and, of course, serves Douglas's signature crab cakes (crunchy on the outside, creamy on the inside), which are not to be missed. However, the menu, almost exclusively seafood, has much else to offer as well. Consider the seared ahi tuna if it should be on the menu; this almost-sushi has a wonderful texture. Don't ignore your side dishes, either; they can be exquisite and are usually enough to share around the table. Stylish contemporary decor sets the mood and assures that this place is as popular with locals as it is with tourists.

✪ Flying Fish. 2234 First Ave. ☎ **206/728-8595.** Reservations recommended. Main dishes $9–$20. AE, MC, V. Daily 5pm–midnight. NORTHWEST.

Chef Christine Keff has been on the Seattle restaurant scene for many years now and in Flying Fish has hit on something the city really wants. Not only are there the bold combinations of vibrant flavors demanded by the city's well-traveled palates, but the hip Belltown restaurant serves dinner until midnight every night, keeping late-night partiers from going hungry. Every dish here is a work of art, and with small plates, large plates, and platters for sharing, diners are encouraged to sample a wide variety of the kitchen's creations. On a recent night, the smoked rock shrimp spring rolls were positively sculpted, and the hot and sour squid salad was a fiery melange of flavors that alone make this restaurant worth coming back to again and again. Desserts are often so decorated that they're almost parties in their own right.

Isabella. 1909 Third Ave. ☎ **206/441-8281.** Reservations recommended. Pastas $9.50–$15, main dishes $17.50–$26.50. AE, DISC, MC, V. Mon–Thurs 11:30am–10pm, Fri 11:30am–11pm, Sat 5–11pm. ITALIAN.

Although Isabella is on a block just out of the mainstream of downtown traffic, it has developed a loyal following for its romantic setting and bold flavors. The sumptuous decor goes against the local trend toward hard-edged contemporary designs, and the menu flaunts the vibrant flavors of fresh herbs. Although the menu is primarily southern Italian in focus, don't be surprised to see the likes of grilled lamb chops with a Dijon peppercorn sauce or a mixed seafood grill. However, it is the restaurant's rich and creamy risottos that are Isabella's real claim to fame. The wine list, unfortunately, sticks strictly to Italian wines and doesn't offer much in a low price range. Lunches, mostly pastas and pizzas, are very reasonably priced.

La Buca. 102 Cherry St. ☎ **206/343-9517.** Reservations recommended on weekends. Lunch $7–$10, dinner $10–$16. AE, DC, DISC, MC, V. Mon–Sat 11:30am–2:30pm; Mon–Sun 5–10pm. SOUTHERN ITALIAN.

Walk down the flight of stairs into this Pioneer Square area and you'll be dining in the Seattle underground. Dark and cavernous with brick arches supporting the ceiling, La Buca is reminiscent of a huge wine cellar. The menu is primarily southern Italian, but goes far beyond spaghetti and meatballs. Such dishes as pan-roasted chicken breast served with a Gorgonzola and toasted pistachio sauce; polenta with a topping of lamb ragout; rigatoni with roasted chicken and roasted pepper sauce; and beef rollantina stuffed with provolone cheese, Italian parsley and garlic and roasted with a red wine, rosemary, and tomato sauce are just a few examples of the mouthwatering fare that comes out of La Buca's kitchen.

McCormick & Schmick's. 1103 First Ave. ☎ **206/623-5500.** Reservations recommended. Main dishes $7–$27. AE, DC, DISC, MC, V. Mon–Fri 11:30am–11pm, Sat 4:30–11pm, Sun 4:30–10pm. SEAFOOD.

Force your way past the crowds of business suits at the bar and you'll find yourself in a classic fish house—cafe curtains, polished brass, leaded glass, wood paneling, waiters in black bow ties. Daily fresh sheets featuring well-prepared seafood dishes like Louisiana catfish with bay shrimp creole sauce, traditional crab cakes with tartar sauce, or blue marlin grilled with Hunan barbecue sauce and crispy leeks have made McCormick and Schmick's extremely popular. Late afternoons and late evenings, bar appetizers are only $1.95, and early dinner specials ($12.95) are available weekdays from 3 to 5:30pm and Sunday between 5 and 6pm. If the restaurant is crowded and you can't get a table, consider sitting at the counter and watching the cooks perform feats with fire.

Marco's Supperclub. 2510 First Ave. ☎ **206/441-7801.** Reservations highly recommended. Main courses lunch $7–$11, dinner $11–$17. AE, MC, V. Mon–Fri 11:30am–2pm; daily 5:30–11pm. INTERNATIONAL.

This Belltown restaurant, furnished with thrift-store crockery and reupholstered yardsale furnishings, has a casual ambience that belies the high-quality meals that emanate from the kitchen. The menu draws on cuisines from around the world, so even jaded gourmands may find something unfamiliar here. A recent menu included such unusual offerings as fried sage leaves with a medley of dipping sauces, Thai-style mussels, and Korean barbecue with spicy soba noodle salad for appetizers. Among the entrees, you're likely to find such memorable dishes as Jamaican jerk chicken with sautéed greens and sweet potato puree or sesame-crusted ahi tuna with stir-fried veggies and ginger-steamed rice. If you enjoy creative cookery at reasonable prices, check this place out.

Palace Kitchen. 2030 Fifth Ave. ☎ **206/448-2001.** Reservations recommended. Main dishes $14–$19. AE, ED, DISC, MC, V. Daily 5pm–1am. NORTHWEST.

This, chef Tom Douglas's third restaurant (Dahlia Lounge and Etta's Seafood are the other two), is also the most casual. The atmosphere is urban chic, with cement pillars, simple wood booths, and a few tables in the window, which overlooks the monorail tracks. The menu is short and features a nightly selection of unusual cheeses and a different preparation from the apple-wood grill each night of the week (North Carolina ribs on Monday, cured pork loin with ricotta ravioli on Thursday, pheasant with porcini risotto on Sunday). Any night of the week you can start a meal with goat cheese fondue or salt cod cakes on sorrel, but it's the olive poppers that are the biggest hit. Night owls will be glad to know they have the Palace Kitchen to turn to for a decent meal after midnight.

The Pink Door. 1919 Post Alley. ☎ **206/443-3241.** Reservations recommended. Pastas $10–$12.50; main dishes $13–$18. AE, MC, V. Tues–Sat 11:30am–10pm (bar food Tues–Thurs until 11:30pm, Fri–Sat until 1am). ITALIAN.

If we didn't tell you about this one, you'd never find it. There's no sign out front, only the pink door for which the restaurant is named (look for it between Stewart and Virginia streets). On the other side of the door stairs lead down to a cellarlike space, which in summer is almost always empty because people would rather dine on the deck with a view of Elliott Bay. What makes this place so popular the rest of the year is not just the good food, but the fun goings on. Tuesday through Thursday, there's a tarot card reader in residence, and on weekends there's usually an accordionist. Sometimes there are even magicians. Be sure to start your meal with the fragrant roasted garlic and ricotta-Gorgonzola spread or the *bagna cauda*, a hot anchovy, herb, and olive oil dipping sauce.

Queen City Grill. 2201 First Ave. ☎ **206/443-0975.** Reservations recommended. Main dishes $9–$20. AE, DC, DISC, MC, V. Mon–Thurs 11:30am–11pm, Fri 11:30am–midnight, Sat 5pm–midnight, Sun 5–11pm. INTERNATIONAL.

Battered wooden floors that look as if they were salvaged from an old hardware store and high-backed wooden booths give the Queen City Grill the look of age. If you didn't know better, you'd think this place had been here since the Great Fire of 1889. The spare decor and sophisticated lighting underscore an exciting menu. Some people come here just for the crab cakes (with just the right amount of roasted pepper/garlic aioli) but everything else is just as inspired. Seafood is the specialty, so you might start with tuna carpaccio accompanied by a lime, ginger, and mustard sauce. The chicken–wild rice gumbo is an unusual and tasty soup.

Theôz. 1523 Sixth Ave. ☎ **206/749-9660.** Reservations recommended. Main dishes $10.50–$24. AE, MC, V. Mon–Thurs 11am–2pm and 5–10pm, Fri 11am–2pm and 5–11pm, Sat 5–11pm, Sun 5–10pm. NORTHWEST.

With chef Emily Moore, former chef of The Painted Table, at the helm, Theôz has become an instant hit. Its location directly across the street from Wolfgang Puck's much touted ObaChine, hasn't hurt things either. With a very spare, though sophisticated interior, Theôz lets the food make all the architectural statements—it's layered and dressed and decorated until each plate is a work of art (sound like The Painted Table?). The menu, which is broken into small and large plates, is overwhelmingly tempting, and laced with the unfamiliar. How about some beautiful little lotus chips or banana leaf tamales? Or try something from the clay oven, perhaps pork loin and ribs with red chile-banana sauce, Tehuantepec mashed potatoes, and garlic greens. However, whatever you do, don't eat so much that you can't fit in a dessert like the chocolate piano, a tiny baby grand with brownies for legs, cake for a body, and chocolate mouse where the wires should be. Astounding!

✪ Wild Ginger Asian Restaurant & Satay Bar. 1400 Western Ave. ☎ **206/623-4450.** Reservations not necessary. Satay $2–$8; main dishes $8.50–$18. AE, DC, DISC, MC, V. Mon–Thurs 11:30am–3pm and 5–11pm, Fri 11:30am–3pm and 5pm–midnight, Sat 11:30am–3pm and 4:30pm–midnight, Sun 4:30–11pm. Satay until 1am. CHINESE/SOUTHEAST ASIAN.

With chef Jeem Han Lock winning the 1997 "Best Chef of the Northwest" award from the James Beard Foundation, Wild Ginger has gone from being a long-time local favorite to national stardom. Even celebrity chef Wolfgang Puck copied Wild Ginger's concept at ObaChine, his first Seattle restaurant.

Pull up a comfortable stool around the large satay grill and watch the cooks grill little skewers of anything from fresh produce to fish to pork to prawns to lamb. Each skewer is served with a small cube of sticky rice and a dipping sauce. Order three or four satay sticks and you have a meal. If you prefer to sit at a table and have a more traditional dinner, you might want to try the Panang beef curry (flank steak in pungent curry sauce of cardamom, coconut milk, Thai basil, and peanuts). The lunch menu contains many of the dinner entrees at lower prices.

INEXPENSIVE

✪ Belltown Pub. 2322 First Ave. ☎ **206/728-4311.** Reservations not accepted. Main dishes $7–$17. AE, MC, V. Sun–Thurs 11:30am–11pm, Fri–Sat 11:30am–midnight. INTERNATIONAL.

Located in an old sleeping bag factory in Belltown, this lively pub serves a surprisingly varied menu. However, what people really come here for are the burgers, which are the best in Seattle—thick, juicy, well flavored, and set on thick, chewy rolls. Accompany your burger with a pint from one of the 20 microbrew taps. There are tables on the sidewalk in summer, and huge wooden booths for when the weather is inclement.

Café Campagne. 1600 Post Alley. ☎ **206/728-2233.** Reservations not accepted. Main dishes $8–$15. AE, MC, V. Mon–Sat 8am–11pm, Sun brunch 8am–3pm. FRENCH.

This cozy little cafe is an offshoot of the Inn at the Market's popular Campagne, and though it is located in the heart of the Pike Place Market neighborhood, it is a world away from the market madness. The menu changes with the season but might include a hearty country-style pâté or baked marinated goat cheese on the appetizer menu. Entrees include filling sandwiches such as the popular lamb burger with aioli or roast pork tenderloin on foccacia with apricot mustard. Main courses are served à la carte, so if you're particularly hungry, peruse the list of side dishes, which might include baby artichokes stewed in olive oil with lemon and garlic. The cafe also doubles as a wine bar and has a good selection of reasonably priced wines by the glass or by the bottle.

Emmett Watson's Oyster Bar. 1916 Pike Place No. 16. ☎ **206/448-7721.** Reservations not accepted. Soups $2–$7; main dishes $5–$9. No credit cards. Summer Mon–Thurs 11:30am–9pm, Fri–Sat 11:30am–10pm, Sun 11:30am–8pm. Winter Mon–Thurs 11:30am–8pm, Fri–Sat 11:30am–9pm, Sun 11:30am–6pm. SEAFOOD.

Tucked away in a rare quiet corner of Pike Place Market (well, actually, it's across the street in the market overflow area), Emmett Watson's exudes regional character and local color. The battered booths are tiny, but there's also courtyard seating. Named for a famous Seattle newspaper columnist, there are clippings and photos all over the walls of the restaurant. Oysters on the half shell are the raison d'être for this little place, but the fish dishes are often memorable as well. Service is infamously slow, but it's worth the wait for such tasty treats as a bowl of garlicky salmon chowder, a meal in itself.

✪ Gravity Bar. 113 Virginia St. ☎ **206/448-8826.** Reservations not necessary. Meals $4–$7.25; juices $2–$4.75. MC, V. Downtown: Mon–Thurs 11am–9pm, Fri 11am–10pm, Sat 10am–10pm, Sun 10am–8pm; Broadway: Sun–Thurs 10am–10pm, Fri–Sat 10am–11pm. NATURAL.

If you're young and hip and concerned about the food that you put into your body, this is the place you frequent in downtown Seattle. The postmodern, neoindustrial decor (lots of sheet metal on the walls, bar, and menus) is the antithesis of the wholesome juices and meals they serve here. The juice list includes all manner of unusual combinations, all with catchy names like Martian Martini or Seven Year Spinach. In spite of what you might think after reading this description, you'll also encounter espresso, beer, and wine here—sometimes in unique combinations, Guinness with apple juice, for example. Be there or be square. There's another Gravity Bar on Capitol Hill at 415 E. Broadway (☎ **206/325-7186**).

Merchants Café. 109 Yesler Way. ☎ **206/624-1515.** Reservations not necessary. Main dishes and sandwiches $5–$15. AE, DISC, MC, V. Mon 11am–4pm, Tues–Thurs 11am–9pm, Fri 11am–2pm, Sat 10am–2pm. AMERICAN.

Merchants Café is Seattle's oldest restaurant and looks every bit of its 100-plus years. A well-scuffed tile floor surrounds the bar, which came around the Horn in the 1800s. An old safe and gold scales are left over from the days when Seattle was the first, or last, taste of civilization for Yukon prospectors. At one time the restaurant's basement was a card room and the upper floors were a brothel. In fact, this may be the original Skid Row saloon (Yesler Way was the original Skid Road down which logs were skidded to a sawmill). Straightforward sandwiches and steaks are the mainstays of the menu.

✪ **ObaChine.** 1518 Sixth Ave. ☎ **206/749-9653.** Reservations recommended. Main courses $8.25–$16.50. AE, DC, MC, V. Daily 11:30am–midnight. ASIAN.

Celebrity chef Wolfgang Puck moved into Seattle in early 1997 with this pan-Asian restaurant and satay bar. The main dining room, with its more formal, though still very reasonably priced menu is upstairs, while the satay bar, with its exhibition kitchen, is the lively street-level space. As you would expect of a chef who made his name keeping the jaded citizens of Los Angeles and Santa Monica happy, ObaChine is a very stylish place, the sort of restaurant where you're not sure whether to ogle the decor or peruse the menu. While the menu is short and at first seems similar to those at countless other Asian restaurants, closer inspection reveals that the flavors of Asia are all mixed up here. There are tandoori shrimp egg rolls, seared scallops with plum wine-black bean sauce and yam-wasabi puree, and tea-leaf baked 10-spice salmon. Whatever else you order, however, don't miss the banana and walnut spring rolls with caramel dipping sauce.

Shea's Lounge. Corner Market Building, Suite 34, 94 Pike St., Pike Place Market. ☎ **206/467-9990.** Reservations for 6 or more people only. Main courses $8.50–$13. AE, MC, V. Tues–Sun 4:30pm–10 or 11pm. NORTHWEST/INTERNATIONAL.

This is the lounge for the ever-popular Chez Shea, one of the Pike Place Market's hidden treasures, and is one of the most sophisticated little spaces in Seattle. Romantic lighting and a view of the bay make this a popular spot with couples, and whether you just want a cocktail and an appetizer or a full meal, you can get it here. The menu features gourmet pizzas (green apple, bleu cheese, and walnuts, for example), sandwiches, combination appetizer plates, a few soups and salads, and five nightly specials such as Moroccan chicken pie. You might start with an asparagus-watercress flan with red pepper-shallot confetti. The desserts, though pricey, are divinely decadent. This is a great spot for a light meal.

LAKE UNION, QUEEN ANNE HILL & MAGNOLIA
EXPENSIVE

✪ **Canlis.** 2576 Aurora Ave. N. ☎ **206/283-3313.** Reservations highly recommended. Main dishes $20–$32. AE, CB, DC, DISC, MC, V. Mon–Sat 5–11pm. AMERICAN/CONTINENTAL.

Canlis has been in business since 1950, and has become a Seattle tradition. However, traditions tend to lose their appeal for younger generations, and to reconnect with the movers and shakers of today's Seattle, this restaurant recently went through a major remodeling. With a mix of contemporary styling and Asian antiques, the restaurant definitely seems poised to take on the 21st century. The mix of Asian and classic American and Continental fare keeps both traditionalists and more adventurous diners content. If so inclined you could start with sashimi or escargots and then go on to a filet mignon from the restaurant's famed copper grill or Dungeness crab cakes with orange butter. This is the perfect place to close a big deal or celebrate a very special occasion. To finish why not go all the way and have the Grand Marnier soufflé. While jackets are no longer required for men, this is still the sort of special occasion place that just makes you want to get dressed up.

Space Needle Restaurant and The Emerald Suite. Seattle Center, 219 Fourth Ave. N. ☎ 206/443-2100. Reservations required. Main dishes $25–$48. Sun brunch $18–$24. AE, CB, DC, MC, V. Mon–Sat 8–10:30am, 11am–3:30pm, and 4–10:30pm; Sun 8am–2:45pm and 5–10:30pm. NORTHWEST.

While Seattleites will be quick to tell you that the prices here are outrageous and the food is not nearly as good as that served at dozens of other less high profile restaurants around town, both the Emerald Suite and Space Needle Restaurant stay packed day in and day out. People come simply because it's such a unique experience to dine 500 feet above the city in a revolving restaurant. The Space Needle Restaurant offers the same views as the Emerald Suite, but in a more casual setting. Menus at both restaurants are almost identical (prices are a bit higher in the Emerald Suite). The best thing about eating here is you don't have to pay for the elevator ride!

Kaspar's. 19 W. Harrison St. ☎ **206/298-0123.** Reservations recommended. Main courses $15–$20; Vintners dinners $35–$45; chef's table dinners $50 for 5-course and $75 for 7-course; wine bar appetizers $2.50–$7.50. AE, MC, V. Tues–Sat 4:30–10pm. NORTHWEST/SEAFOOD.

Located in the Lower Queen Anne neighborhood, Kaspar's has long been a favorite with Seattleites, and offers many dining options for various appetites and budgets. For the connoisseur and oenophile there are vintner's dinners; for the ultimate in personal service, try a chef's table dinner and dine in the kitchen with chef Kaspar Donier. For light meals, drinks, and desserts, there's the wine bar. The menu here places an emphasis on seafood and draws on worldwide influences, such as an Asian antipasto plate that includes a crab sushi roll, smoked ahi, and a vegetable spring roll. Alaskan halibut might come with crab-corn cannelloni and sun-dried tomato sauce. Kaspar's is also rightly famous for its desserts.

MODERATE

McCormick & Schmick's Harborside. 1200 Westlake Ave. N. ☎ **206/270-9052.** Reservations recommended. Main dishes $7.50–$20. AE, DC, JCB, MC, V. Mon–Sat 11:30am–11pm; Sun 10am–11pm. SEAFOOD.

This is the best location of any of Seattle's McCormick & Schmick's restaurants and overlooks the marinas on the west side of Lake Union. The menu, which changes daily, includes seemingly endless choices of appetizers, sandwiches, salads and creative entrees. Just be sure to order something with seafood in it, like a seared rare ahi with Asian cucumber salad, a crab cake sandwich, or grilled halibut topped with a hazelnut butter and tart cherry chutney. Sure, there are meat dishes on the menu, but why bother, unless it's just that you came here as much for the excellent view. There are early dinner specials ($13.95) between 3 and 6:30pm.

✪ **Palisade.** Elliott Bay Marina, 2601 W. Marina Place. ☎ **206/285-1000.** Reservations recommended. Main dishes $14–$30. AE, DC, DISC, MC, V. Mon–Thurs 11:30am–2pm and 5–9:30pm, Fri 11:30am–2pm and 5–10pm, Sat 11:30am–2pm and 4:30–10pm, Sun 10am–2pm and 4:30–9pm. NORTHWEST.

🎈 Family-Friendly Restaurants

Ivar's Salmon House *(see pg. 96)*   This restaurant is built to resemble a Northwest Coast Native American longhouse and is filled with artifacts that kids will find fascinating. If they get restless, they can go out to the floating patio and watch the boats passing by.

Gravity Bar *(see pg. 91)*   If you're traveling with teenagers, they'll love this place where Seattle's young and hip and health-conscious crowd comes to dine. The decor is postmodern neoindustrial and the food is wholesome, with juices called Martian Martini and 7 Year Spinach.

With a view that sweeps from downtown to West Seattle and on across the sound to the Olympic Mountains, Palisade has one of the best views of any Seattle waterfront restaurant. It also happens to have great food and the most unique interior design of any restaurant in town (a salt-water pond complete with fish, sea anemones, and starfish, is in the middle of the dining room). The building itself is a cross between an old lighthouse and Chinese palace. The extensive menu features dishes prepared on a searing grill, in a wood-fired oven, in a wood-fired rotisserie, and in an apple-wood broiler. What this all adds up to is lots of choices of very flavorful seafoods and meats. Palisade is not easy to find, but it is more than worth the trouble to find it. Call for directions.

✪ **Serafina.** 2043 Eastlake Ave. E. ☎ **206/323-0807.** Reservations recommended. Pastas $9.50–$15; entrees $13–$19. MC, V. Mon–Thurs 11:30am–2pm and 5:30–10pm, Fri 11:30am–2pm and 5:30–11pm, Sat 5:30–11pm, Sun 5:30–10pm. ITALIAN.

The atmosphere is rustic and serves to underscore the earthy Italian country-style dishes served here. This is one of our favorite dining spots, with just a touch of sophistication and a casual ambience. In the summer, try to get a table in the romantic garden courtyard. The antipasti Serafina is always a good choice for a starter and changes daily, though it's hard to resist prosciutto and figs. Among the pastas you might find the likes of penne with leeks, pears, and prawns. For a main dish try a classic Umbrian preparation of roasted Italian sausages with grapes served over soft polenta.

INEXPENSIVE

Cucina! Cucina! Chandler's Cove, Fairview Ave. N. ☎ **206/447-2782.** Reservations accepted at lunch only. Main dishes $6–$15. AE, DISC, MC, V. Sun–Thurs 11:30am–11pm, Fri–Sat 11:30am–midnight. ITALIAN.

Although it is part of a chain headquartered in Bellevue, Cucina! Cucina! is popular not only for its waterfront view but also for its lively party atmosphere. Located at the south end of Lake Union, this restaurant is also a favorite of Seattle families because of all the special attention kids are given here. But just because families are welcome doesn't mean this place isn't fun for adults, too. In summer, the deck is the place to be.

FIRST HILL, CAPITOL HILL & EAST SEATTLE
EXPENSIVE

The Hunt Club. Sorrento Hotel, 900 Madison St. ☎ **206/343-6156.** Reservations recommended. Main dishes $24–$33. AE, CB, DC, DISC, MC, V. Mon–Thurs 7–10am, 11am–2:30pm, and 5:30–10pm; Fri 7–10am, 11am–2:30pm, and 5:30–11pm; Sat 7am–2:30pm, 5:30–11pm; Sun 7am–2:30pm, 5:30–10pm. NORTHWEST.

The Hunt Club is just the sort of place its name would indicate—dark, intimate, well suited to business lunches and romantic celebrations. Mahogany paneling lines the walls, and if you need a little privacy, folding louvered doors can create private dining areas. The menu, which changes weekly, balances French, Italian, and Asian influences while stirring in a generous helping of Northwest ingredients. Whether you're having a quick meal in the lounge, a light lunch, or a four-course dinner, you'll find creativity a keystone of the menu. The best way to start a meal is with the Sorrento seafood appetizer plate, which includes a trio of delicately flavored preparations. You might then move onto something as unusual as spice grilled ostrich fillet with blackberries or something more familiar like filet mignon with merlot beef essence. Just be sure to save room for one of the outstanding desserts.

✪ **Rover's.** 2808 E. Madison St. ☎ **206/325-7442.** Reservations required. Main dishes $23–$39; five-course tasting menu $49.50–$59.50; chef's grand menu $89.50. AE, DC, DISC, MC, V. Tues–Sat 5:30–9:30pm. NORTHWEST.

Tucked away in a quaint clapboard house behind a chic little shopping center in the Madison Valley neighborhood is one of Seattle's most acclaimed restaurants. Rover's chef, Thierry Rautureau, received classic French training before falling in love with the Northwest and all the wonderful ingredients it has to offer an imaginative chef. Voil´á! Northwest cuisine with a French accent. The menu changes frequently, and its delicacies are enough to send the most jaded of gastronomes into fits of indecision. To make life easier, many guests simply opt for one of the five-course dinners and leave the decision making to a professional—the chef. Rest assured you won't be disappointed. If on the other hand you must have the seared sea scallops with foie gras and a chestnut puree or roasted guinea-fowl with green lentils, cherry chutney, and huckleberry vinegar sauce, by all means order from the menu.

MODERATE

✪ **Café Flora.** 2901 E. Madison St. ☎ **206/325-9100.** Reservations taken for 8 or more. Main dishes $7.25–$14. MC, V. Tues–Fri 11:30am–10pm, Sat 9am–2pm and 5–10pm, Sun 9am–2pm and 5–9pm. VEGETARIAN.

Big, bright, and airy, this Madison Valley cafe will dispel any ideas about vegetarian food being boring. This is meatless gourmet cooking and draws on influences from around the world—a vegetarian's dream come true. While the menu changes weekly, unusual pizzas are always on the menu. Just to get you in the mood, consider these recent offerings: a Provençal appetizer plate that included a tapenade (kalamata olives, orange zest, and capers), herbed goat cheese, roasted eggplant pâté, and crostini; portobello Wellington with a mushroom-pecan pâté and sautéed leeks in a puff pastry; and a pea and gorgonzola risotto with a ragout of morels, tomatoes, roasted garlic, thyme, and sherry. Of course, completely different items will probably be available when you visit, but you get the picture.

Leschi Lakecafe. 102 Lakeside Ave. ☎ **206/328-2233.** Reservations recommended. Main dishes $9–$20. AE, DISC, MC, V. Mon–Thurs 11:30am–2pm and 5–9pm, Fri 11:30am–2pm and 5–10pm, Sat 11:30am–3pm and 5–10pm, Sun 9am–2pm and 5–9pm. AMERICAN.

While views across Elliott Bay from the downtown waterfront, are all well and good, they don't include a view of Mount Hood. Leschi Lakecafe does, however, at least when The Mountain is out. This casual restaurant on the shore of Lake Washington was the ferry terminal for Eastside ferries back before they built the floating bridges. While the view's the thing here, the menu offers enough variety to satisfy most people and the specials can be real winners. The menu includes such contemporary offerings as Northwest bouillabaisse and peach-soy marinated chicken, but it also includes ale-battered fried seafood for those who like to keep things simple. Be sure to try the Leschi's ice cream, even if you only get a petite serving, although when we were last there, the chocolate mousse in a chocolate tulip cup was irresistible.

INEXPENSIVE

Pizzeria Pagliacci. 426 Broadway E. ☎ **206/324-0730.** Reservations not accepted. Pizza $9–$17. AE, MC, V. Sun–Thurs 11am–11pm, Fri–Sat 11am–1am. PIZZA.

Pagliacci's pizza was voted the best in Seattle, and they now have three popular locations. Although you can order a traditional cheese pie, there are much more interesting choices like pesto pizza or the sun-dried tomato primo. It's strictly counter service here, but there are plenty of seats at each of the bright restaurants. For those in a hurry or who just want a snack, there is pizza by the slice. Pagliacci is also at 550 Queen Anne Ave. N. (☎ 206/285-1232) and at 4529 University Way NE (☎ 206/632-0421).

Siam on Broadway. 616 Broadway E. ☎ **206/324-0892.** Reservations recommended on weekends. Main dishes lunch $5.50–$9, dinner $6.50–$10.50;. AE, MC, V. Mon–Thurs 11:30am–10pm, Fri 11:30am–11pm, Sat 5–11pm, Sun 5–10pm. THAI.

At the north end of Broadway, on Capitol Hill, you'll find one of Seattle's best Thai restaurants, the small and casual Siam on Broadway. The tom yum soups, made with either shrimp or chicken, are the richest and creamiest I've ever had—and some of the spiciest. If you prefer your food less fiery, let your server know. Just remember that they mean it when they say superhot. The phad Thai (fried noodles with egg, shrimp and tofu) is excellent, and the nua phad bai graplau (spicy meat and vegetables) is properly fragrant with chiles and basil leaves. A second much larger restaurant, Siam on Lake Union, is located at 1880 Fairview Ave. E. (☎ 206/323-8101).

NORTH SEATTLE (FREMONT, WALLINGFORD & THE UNIVERSITY DISTRICT)

MODERATE

Ivar's Salmon House. 401 NE Northlake Way. ☎ **206/632-0767.** Reservations recommended. Main dishes $11–$27; fish bar $4.50–$7.50. AE, MC, V. Main restaurant, Mon–Fri 11:30am–2:30pm and 4:30–11pm, Sat noon–11pm, Sun 10am–2pm and 4–10pm. Fish bar, Sun–Thurs 11:30am–10pm, Fri–Sat 11am–11pm. SEAFOOD.

This Ivar's commands an excellent view of the Seattle skyline from the north end of Lake Union, and floating docks out back act like magnets for weekend boaters who abandon their own galley fare in favor of the restaurant's clam chowder and famous alder-smoked salmon. The theme here is Northwest Coast Indian, and the building has even won an award from the Seattle Historical Society for its replica of a tribal longhouse. Inside are many artifacts, including long dugout canoes and historic photographic portraits of Native American chiefs. Kids, and adults, love this place.

Ponti Seafood Grill. 3014 Third Ave. N. ☎ **206/284-3000.** Reservations recommended. Main dishes $12.50–$23.50. AE, DC, MC, V. Mon–Thurs 11:30am–2:30pm and 5–10pm, Fri 11:30am–2:30pm and 5–11pm, Sat 5–11pm, Sun 10am–2:30pm and 5–10pm. SEAFOOD.

Situated at the south end of the Fremont Bridge overlooking the Lake Washington Ship Canal, Ponti is one of Seattle's most elegant and sophisticated restaurants. The menu here has an international flavor, though it also offers some solidly northwestern creations. On a recent evening, the appetizers list included a decadent dish of smoked salmon served with a corn pancake, vodka crème fraîche, chives, and caviar. The pasta menu always includes some highly creative dishes such as Thai curry penne with broiled scallops, Dungeness crab meat, ginger-tomato chutney, and fresh basil chiffonade, and the daily listing of fresh seafoods might include the likes of grilled Copper River salmon with a subtle ginger buerre blanc and mushroom salsa. If possible, save room for a piece of the Chocolate Lover's torte, with chocolate mousse and ganache, in a pool of raspberry sauce. Three-course early dinners ($13.95) are served between 5 and 6pm. Lunches are less expensive than dinner and equally well prepared.

Ray's Boathouse and Cafe. 6049 Seaview Ave. NW. ☎ **206/789-3770.** Reservations not accepted upstairs; recommended on weekends downstairs. Main dishes $14–$32 (in Boathouse), $9–$16 (in Cafe). AE, CB, DC, DISC, MC, V. Daily 11:30am–10pm. SEAFOOD/STEAK.

If you're looking for a waterfront restaurant with reliably good food and a different perspective than what's available from the Seattle downtown waterfront, head out to Ballard, where you'll find Ray's at the mouth of the Lake Washington Ship Canal. Instead of seeing the city, you'll see the bluff in Discovery Park, a marina, and the Olympic Mountains across the sound. Ray's is actually two distinctly different restaurants (as are several Seattle waterfront restaurants). Upstairs, where you'll find a boisterous crowd of suntanned boating types, are the cafe and lounge. Waits of up to an hour for a table here are not unusual, but no one seems to mind. Downstairs, everything is quiet, cozy, and sophisticated.

WEST SEATTLE
MODERATE

Salty's on Alki. 1936 Harbor Ave. SW. ☎ **206/937-1600.** Reservations recommended. Main dishes $10–$37. AE, DISC, MC, V. Mon–Fri 11am–2:30pm and 4:30–10pm, Sat noon–3pm and 4–10pm, Sun 4–10pm. SEAFOOD.

Although the prices are almost as out of line as those at the Space Needle and the service can be abysmal, this restaurant has *the* waterfront view in Seattle, and the food is usually pretty good. You're definitely paying for the view here. Because it is set on the northeast side of the Alki Peninsula, it faces downtown Seattle on the far side of Elliott Bay. Come for a sunset dinner and watch the setting sun sparkle off the windows of skyscrapers as the lights of the city twinkle on. Monday through Friday there are sunset dinner specials starting at 4:30pm. On sunny summer days, lunch on one of the two decks is a sublimely Seattle experience.

CAFES, BAKERIES & PASTRY SHOPS
CAFES & COFFEE BARS

Unless you've been on Mars the past few years, you're likely aware that Seattle has become the espresso capital of America. Seattleites are positively rabid about coffee. Coffee isn't just a hot drink or a caffeine fix anymore, it's a way of life. Espresso and its creamy cousin latte (made with one part espresso to three parts milk) are the stuff that this city runs on, and you will never be more than about a block from your next cup. There are espresso carts on the sidewalks, drive-through espresso windows, espresso bars, espresso milk shakes, espresso chocolates, even eggnog lattes at Christmas. The ruling coffee king is Starbucks, a chain of dozens of coffee bars where you can buy your java by the cup or by the pound. They sell some 36 types and blends of coffee, and you can find their shops all over the city. SBC, formerly Stewart Brothers Coffee and also known as Seattle's Best Coffee, doesn't have as many shops as Starbucks, but it does have a very devoted clientele. Rapidly gaining ground in the Seattle coffee wars is the Tully's chain, which seems to be opening an espresso bar on every corner that doesn't already have a Starbucks or an SBC. However, serious espresso junkies swear by Torrefazione and Cafe Apassionato. If you see one of either of these chains, check it out and see what you think.

Coffee bars and cafes are now almost as popular as bars as places to hang out and visit with friends. Among our favorite Seattle cafes are the following:

Still Life in Fremont Coffeehouse, 709 N. 35th St. (☎ **206/547-9850**). Fremont is Seattle's most eclectic neighborhood, and Still Life reflects this eclecticism. It's big and always crowded. Good vegetarian meals.

Torrefazione, 320 Occidental Ave. S. (☎ **206/624-5773**), and also at 622 Olive Way (☎ **206/624-1429**). With its hand-painted Italian crockery, Torrefazione has the feel of a classic Italian cafe. The one in the Pioneer Square area has much more atmosphere. Great pastries.

Zio Rico, 1415 Fourth Ave. (☎ **206/467-8616**). This is the most elegant cafe in Seattle, with big, comfortable easy chairs and lots of dark, wood paneling. A great place to sit and read the Wall Street Journal.

BAKERIES & PASTRY SHOPS

A la Francaise, 415 First Ave. S. (☎ **206/624-0322**). This Pioneer Square French bakery has the most authentic feel of any bakery or pastry shop in Seattle, right down to the sidewalk tables surrounded by a low wall with flower-filled planters on top. Great breads and pastries!

Dilettante Chocolates, 416 Broadway E. (☎ **206/329-6463**). This chocolate shop turned pastry bakery also happens to be Seattle's leading proponent of cocoa as the next drink to take the country by storm. If you don't order something with chocolate here, you're missing the point. Can you say, "To die for"? We knew you could.

The Famous Pacific Dessert Company, 516 Broadway E. (☎ **206/328-1950**). At this Capitol Hill pastry extravaganza, you can indulge in more than 30 cakes and tortes.

Le Panier, 1902 Pike Place (☎ **206/441-3669**). Located in the heart of Pike Place Market, this French bakery is a great place to get a croissant and a latte and watch the market action.

Macrina, 2408 First Ave. (☎ **206/448-4032**). This Belltown bakery is a great place for a quick and cheap breakfast or lunch. In the morning, the smell of baking bread wafts down First Avenue and draws in many a passing stranger.

5 Seeing the Sights

In the past few years, as Seattle has become one of the nation's most talked about and popular cities, life on the city's cultural front has changing dramatically. However, despite new and renovated museums, Seattle's natural surroundings are still the city's primary attraction. You can easily cover all of Seattle's museums and major sights in 2 or 3 days, and with the help of the itineraries below, you should have a good idea of what not to miss. The outlined itineraries will provide a good overview of the history, natural resources, and cultural diversity that have made Seattle the city it is today.

Once you've seen what's to see indoors, you can begin exploring the city's outdoor life. A car is helpful, though not entirely necessary, for sampling the city's outdoor activities. However, if you want to head farther afield, say to Mount Rainier, the Olympic Mountains, or a Puget Sound or ocean beach, you'll definitely need a car.

Seattle Attractions

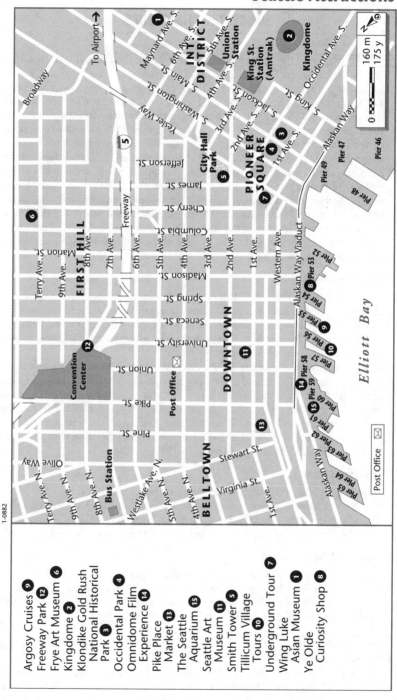

Argosy Cruises **9**
Freeway Park **12**
Frye Art Museum **6**
Kingdome **2**
Klondike Gold Rush
National Historical
Park **3**
Occidental Park **4**
Omnidome Film
Experience **14**
Pike Place
Market **13**
The Seattle
Aquarium **15**
Seattle Art
Museum **11**
Smith Tower **5**
Tillicum Village
Tours **10**
Underground Tour **7**
Wing Luke
Asian Museum **1**
Ye Olde
Curiosity Shop **8**

SUGGESTED ITINERARIES

If You Have 1 Day

Day 1 Start your day in the historic Pioneer Square District and take the earliest **Seattle Underground Tour** you can. You'll have fun and get a good idea of Seattle's early history. From Pioneer Square, walk down to the waterfront and head north. You'll pass numerous overpriced seafood restaurants, as well as quite a few fish-and-chip counters. At Pier 55 you can get a 1-hour harbor tour cruise, and at Pier 59 you'll find the Seattle Aquarium, where you can learn about the sea life of the region. Directly across from the aquarium is the Pike Hill Climb, which leads from the waterfront up the hill to Pike Place Market. In the market you can buy fresh salmon and Dungeness crabs packed to go, peruse the produce and flower vendors, and explore the dark depths of the market for unusual shops. From Pike Place Market, walk to the monorail station in Westlake Center shopping mall, which is at the corner of Pine Street and Fourth Avenue. The monorail will take you to Seattle Center, where you can ride an elevator to the top of the Space Needle. Seattle's best-known landmark. Finish the day with dinner at one of the city's many restaurants serving seafood or Northwest cuisine.

If You Have 2 Days

Day 1 Start your first day in Pioneer Square, as outlined above. After the Seattle Underground Tour, head over to the nearby International District (Chinatown) and have lunch in a Chinese restaurant. Hing Loon is our favorite. After lunch, head over to the waterfront for a harbor cruise, a stop at the aquarium and Ye Olde Curiosity Shop, and dine at one of the seafood restaurants.

Day 2 Start your second day at Pike Place Market, and be sure to arrive early as the fruit, vegetable, flower, and fish vendors are opening. You'll likely be in the company of several of the city's finest chefs, many of whom do their shopping here. From the market it is only two blocks to the new Seattle Art Museum. After touring the museum, take the lunch tour to Tillicum Village. You'll see Northwest Native American dances while dining on alder-smoked salmon. When you return to Seattle, head for Seattle Center and the Space Needle.

If You Have 3 Days

Days 1–2 Follow the 2-day strategy outlined above.

Day 3 Do something very Seattle. Rent a sea kayak on Lake Union or go in-line skating at Green Lake. Wander around the funky Fremont neighborhood and maybe go to the Woodland Park Zoo or the Burke Museum depending on your interests.

If You Have 5 Days or More

Days 1–3 Follow the 3-day strategy, as outlined above.

Days 4–5 Take a trip out of the city to Mount Rainier, Mount St. Helens, Snoqualmie Falls, Bainbridge Island, the Olympic Peninsula, or the San Juan Islands. All these trips can be turned into overnighters or longer.

THE TOP ATTRACTIONS

THE WATERFRONT

The Seattle waterfront is the city's single most popular attraction, and much as in San Francisco's Fishermen's Wharf area, there is much to recommend both for and against the waterfront. Yes it's very touristy, with tacky gift shops, saltwater taffy, T-shirts galore, and lots of overpriced restaurants, but it's also home to the Seattle

Aquarium, the Omnidome Film Experience, and Ye Olde Curiosity Shop (king of the tacky gift shops). Several cruise boat companies dock here, and there are also companies offering sailboat and sea kayak tours. The waterfront is also the best place to hire a horse-drawn carriage for a spin around the downtown.

At the south end of the waterfront, near Pioneer Square, you'll find the Washington State Ferries terminal at Pier 52 (a ferry ride makes for a cheap cruise). At Pier 54, you'll find companies offering sea kayak tours, sportfishing trips, jet-boat tours, and bicycle rentals. At Pier 55, boats leave for 1 1/2-hour harbor cruises, as well as on the Tillicum Village excursions to Blake Island. At Pier 57, you'll find the Bay Pavilion, which has a vintage carousel and a video arcade to keep the kids busy. At Pier 59, you'll find the Seattle Aquarium and the Omnidome Film Experience and a waterfront park. Continuing up the waterfront, you'll find Pier 66, the Bell Street Pier, which has a rooftop park with free binoculars. This is also where you'll find Anthony's, the hippest restaurant on the waterfront, and by the summer of 1998, the Odyssey Maritime Discovery Center, dedicated to the history of shipping and fishing in Puget Sound should be open. At Pier 67, you'll find the Edgewater hotel, which is a great place to take in the sunset over a drink or dinner. Next door, at Pier 69, is the dock for the ferries that ply between Seattle and Victoria. Sunset and jazz cruises also leave from this pier. At Pier 70, you'll find the Spirit of Puget Sound cruise ship, as well as a nightclub. Just north of this pier is grassy Myrtle Edwards Park, a nice finale to a very pleasant waterfront. This park has a popular bicycling and skating trail, and is the northern terminus for the Waterfront Streetcar, which can take you back to your starting point.

OTHER TOP ATTRACTIONS

✪ **Pike Place Market.** Between Pike St. and Pine St. (at First Ave.). ☎ **206/682-7453.** Free admission (tours $5). Mon–Sat 9am–6pm, Sun 11am–5pm. Closed New Year's Day, Easter, Memorial Day weekend, July 4, Labor Day, Thanksgiving, Christmas. Bus: 15 or 18. Waterfront Streetcar: To Pike Place Market stop.

Pike Place Market, originally a farmers' market, was founded in 1907 when housewives complained that middlemen were raising the price of produce too high. The market allowed shoppers to buy directly from producers, and thus save on grocery bills. By the 1960s, however, the market was no longer the popular spot it had once been. World War II had deprived it of nearly half its farmers when Japanese Americans were moved to internment camps. The postwar flight to the suburbs almost spelled the end for the market, and the site was being eyed for a major redevelopment project. However, a grassroots movement to save the nine-acre market culminated in its being declared a National Historic District.

Today it bustles once again, but the 100 or so farmers and fishmongers who set up shop here are only a small part of the attraction. More than 200 local craftspeople and artists can be found selling their creations throughout the year. There are excellent restaurants, and hundreds of shops fill the market area. Street performers—including mimes, a pianist, and hammered-dulcimer players—serenade milling crowds. There is an information booth almost directly below the large Pike Place Market sign where you can pick up a free map and guide to the market. Watch for Rachel the giant piggy bank and the flying fish at Pike Place Fish.

For a glimpse behind the scenes at the market, you can take a Market Classroom Tour on Wednesday mornings in summer or on Saturday mornings other months. On these tours you'll learn about the market's history, get tips on shopping here, and maybe meet a restaurant chef or two as they shop for fresh market ingredients. Call the above number for information on scheduled tours and to make a reservation.

The Space Needle. 203 Sixth Ave. N., Seattle Center. ☎ **206/443-2111.** Admission $8.50 adults, $7 seniors, $4 ages 5–12, ages 4 and under free (no charge if dining in rotating restaurant). Daily 8am–midnight. Valet parking $5. Bus: 1, 15 or 18. Monorail: From Westlake Center at Pine St. and Fourth Ave.

From a distance it resembles a flying saucer on top of a tripod, and when it was built it was meant to suggest future architectural trends. Erected for the 1962 World's Fair, the 600-foot-tall Space Needle is the quintessential symbol of Seattle. At 518 feet above ground level, the views from the observation deck are stunning. There are displays identifying more than 60 sites and activities in the Seattle area, and high-powered telescopes let you zoom in on distant sights. You'll also find a history of the Space Needle, a lounge, and two very expensive restaurants. If you don't mind standing in line and paying quite a bit for an elevator ride, make this your first stop in Seattle so you can orient yourself (there are, however, cheaper alternatives if you just want a view of the city; see "Panoramas" below for details).

✪ Seattle Art Museum. 100 University St. ☎ **206/654-3100.** Admission $6 adults, $4 seniors and students, ages 12 and under free. Free first Thurs of each month (free for seniors on first Fri of each month). Admission ticket also valid at Seattle Asian Art Museum if used within 1 week. Tues–Sun 10am–5pm (Thurs until 9pm). Also open on Martin Luther King Day, Presidents' Day, Memorial Day, and Labor Day. Closed Thanksgiving, Christmas, and New Year's Day. Bus: 15, 18 or any bus using the bus tunnel.

Located only two blocks from Pike Place Market and presenting a stark cement facade to the street, the Seattle Art Museum is a repository for everything from African masks to old masters to Andy Warhol. No matter what your taste in art, you're likely to find a few rooms here to interest you. To see the museum's most striking piece of art you don't even have to buy a ticket; outside the front door stands Jonathon Borofsky's *Hammering Man,* an animated three-story steel sculpture that hammers unceasingly and at first glance appears to be nothing more than a shadow. Inside you'll find one of the nation's premier collections of Northwest Coast Indian art and artifacts and an equally large collection of African art. There is also a small collection of Asian art at this museum, but Seattle's main collection of Oriental art is at the Seattle Asian Art Museum in Volunteer Park (see below for details). Up on the museum's top floor, you'll find European and American art, covering the ancient Mediterranean to the medieval, Renaissance, and Baroque periods in Europe. A large 18th-century collection and a smaller 19th-century exhibition lead up to a large 20th-century collection that includes a room devoted to Northwest contemporary art. Throughout the year there are special exhibits mounted here, as well as a film and music series.

✪ The Seattle Aquarium. 1483 Alaskan Way, Pier 59, Waterfront Park. ☎ **206/386-4320.** Admission $7.75 adults, $7 seniors, $5.15 ages 6–18, $1.95 ages 3–5 (joint Aquarium-Omnidome tickets also available). Labor Day to Memorial Day, daily 10am–5pm; Memorial Day to Labor Day, daily 10am–7pm. Bus: 15 or 18; then walk through Pike Place Market to the waterfront. Waterfront Streetcar: To Pike Place Market stop.

Although not nearly as large and impressive as either the Monterey Bay Aquarium or the Oregon Coast Aquarium, the Seattle Aquarium is still quite impressive and presents well-designed exhibits dealing with the water worlds of the Puget Sound region. One of the aquarium's most popular exhibits is an interactive tide pool and discovery lab that re-creates Washington's wave-swept intertidal zone. As part of the exhibit, a video microscope provides a magnified glimpse of the seldom-seen world of plankton. From the underwater viewing dome, you get a fish's-eye view of life beneath the waves, and each September, you can watch salmon return up a fish ladder to spawn. Of course there are also plenty of small tanks that allow you to familiarize yourself with the many fish of the Northwest. In 1998, an exhibit on waterways from the Puget Sound to the mountains is scheduled to open.

In addition to exhibits on the sealife of the region, there is a beautiful large coral-reef tank, as well as many smaller tanks that exhibit fish from distant waters.

✪ **Museum of Flight.** 9404 E. Marginal Way S. ☎ **206/764-5720.** Admission $8 adults, $7 seniors, $4 ages 6–15, free for ages 5 and under. Free first Thurs of the month from 5 to 9pm. Daily 10am–5pm (until 9pm Thurs). Closed Thanksgiving and Christmas. Take exit 158 off I-5. Bus: 174.

Located right next door to busy Boeing Field, 15 minutes south of downtown Seattle, this museum will have aviation buffs walking on air. Displayed within the six-story glass-and-steel repository are some of history's most famous planes. There's a replica of the Wright brothers' first glider to start things off, and then the exhibits progress up through modern flight. Suspended in the Great Hall are 20 planes, including a DC-3 and the first air force F-5 supersonic fighter. You'll also see the famous Blackbird spy plane, which was once the world's fastest jet. A rare World War II Corsair fighter rescued from Lake Washington and restored to its original glory is on display. Visitors also get to board the original Air Force One presidential plane. An exhibit on the U.S. space program features an Apollo command module. And while any air-and-space museum lets you look at mothballed planes, not many have their own air-traffic control tower and let you watch aircraft taking off and landing at an active airfield.

✪ **Woodland Park Zoo.** 5500 Phinney Ave. N. ☎ **206/684-4800.** Admission $8 adults; $7.25 seniors, college students and travelers with disabilities; $5.50 children ages 6–17; $3.25 ages 3–5; ages 2 and under free. Mar 15–Oct 30 daily 9:30am–6pm; Oct 31–Mar 14 daily 9:30am–4pm. Parking $3.50. Bus: 5.

Located in north Seattle, this sprawling zoo has outstanding exhibits focusing on such bioclimatic zones as Alaska, tropical Asia, the African savanna, and the tropical rain forest. The brown bear enclosure is an amazing reproduction of an Alaskan stream and hillside, and in the savanna, zebras gambol as antelopes and giraffes graze contentedly. An elephant forest provides plenty of space for the zoo's pachyderms. The tropical nocturnal house has fascinating exhibits that allow visitors to see nocturnal creatures when they are at their most active. Gorilla and orangutan habitats also are memorable. For the little ones, there is a farm animal area.

Omnidome Film Experience. Pier 59, Waterfront Park. ☎ **206/622-1868.** Admission $6.95 adults, $5.95 seniors and ages 6–18, $4.95 ages 3–5, under age 3 free (a second film costs only $3 more; Omnidome-Aquarium combination tickets available). Sun–Thurs 10am–9pm, Fri–Sat 10am–11pm. Closed Thanksgiving and Christmas. Bus: 15 or 18; then walk through Pike Place Market to the waterfront. Waterfront Streetcar: To Pike Place Market stop.

The Omnidome, for those who have never experienced it, is a movie theater with a 180° screen that fills your peripheral vision and puts you right in the middle of the action—people with hangovers or who get motion sickness should stay away! This huge wraparound theater is located adjacent to the Seattle Aquarium, and for many years now has featured a film about the eruption of Mount St. Helens. In late 1997, a feature on whales was scheduled to open and various other special features are shown throughout the year.

MORE ATTRACTIONS
ART MUSEUMS

✪ **Seattle Asian Art Museum.** 1400 E. Prospect St., Volunteer Park (14th Ave. E. and E. Prospect St.). ☎ **206/654-3100.** Admission $6 adults, $4 students and seniors, ages 12 and under free. Free to all on first Thurs of each month (free for seniors on first Fri of each month).

Admission ticket also valid at Seattle Art Museum if used within 1 week. Tues–Sun 10am–5pm (Thurs until 9pm). Closed Thanksgiving, Christmas, and New Year's Day. Bus: 10.

Housed in the renovated art deco building that once served as the city's main art museum, the Asian art collection has an emphasis on Chinese and Japanese art but also includes pieces from Korea, Southeast Asia, South Asia, and the Himalayas. The Chinese terra-cotta funerary art, snuff bottles, and Japanese netsukes (belt decorations) are among the more notable collections. One room is devoted almost exclusively to Japanese screens and painting while another holds Japanese folk art, including several old kimonos. The central hall is devoted to the stone religious sculptures of South Asia (primarily India). Special exhibits change every six months and there are frequent lectures and concerts.

Frye Art Museum. 704 Terry Ave. (at Cherry St.). ☎ **206/622-9250.** Free admission. Tues–Sat 10am–5pm (Thurs until 9pm), Sun noon–5pm. Closed Thanksgiving, Christmas, and New Year's Day. Bus: 3, 4, or 12.

Located on First Hill, this recently renovated and expanded museum is primarily an exhibit space for the extensive personal art collection of Charles and Emma Frye, Seattle pioneers who began collecting art in the 1890s. The collection focuses on late 19th-century and early-20th-century representational art by European and American painters. There are works by Thomas Hart Benton, Edward Hopper, Albert Bierstadt, and Pablo Picasso, as well as a large collection of engravings by Winslow Homer. In the museum's new wings, you'll find special exhibits that change monthly. The special exhibitions are often in striking contrast to the styles seen in the permanent collection.

✪ Henry Art Gallery. University of Washington, 15th Ave. NE and NE 41st St. ☎ **206/543-2280.** Admission $5 adults, $3.50 students and seniors, ages 12 and under free. Free Thurs 5–8pm. Tues–Sun 11am–5pm (Thurs until 8pm). Closed Thanksgiving, Christmas, and New Year's Day. Bus: 7, 43, 70, 71, 72, or 73.

This museum on the University of Washington campus was greatly expanded in 1997 and now has nearly three times the exhibit space that it once had. This new space has loads of potential and is well lit by pyramidal and cubic skylights that can be seen near the main museum entrance. Expect the museum to stage more and more interesting exhibits in the years to come. The focus here is on contemporary art with retrospectives of individual artists, as well as exhibits focusing on specific themes or media. Photography and video are both well represented, and for the most part, the exhibits here are the most daring that can be seen in the Seattle area. There's also a cafe and a small sculpture courtyard.

HISTORY AND CULTURE MUSEUMS

Burke Museum. 17th Ave. NE and NE 45th St. ☎ **206/543-5590.** Donation, $3 adults, $2 students and seniors, $1.50 ages 6–18. Daily 10am–5pm. Closed July 4, Thanksgiving, Christmas, and New Year's Day. Bus: 70, 71, 72, or 73.

Located in the northwest corner of the University of Washington campus, the Burke Museum features exhibits on the natural and cultural heritage of the Pacific Rim. It is noteworthy primarily for its Northwest Coast Indian art collection and an active schedule of special exhibits. Down in the basement, there is a large collection of minerals and fossils. In front of the museum stand replicas of totem poles carved in the 1870s and 1880s. There is also an ethnobotanical garden displaying plants used by northwestern tribes. At press time the museum was about to reopen after an extensive renovation aimed at providing better space and all new exhibits. Campus parking is very expensive on weekdays and Saturday mornings, so try to visit on a Saturday afternoon or a Sunday.

Museum of History & Industry. 2700 24th Ave. E. ☎ **206/324-1126.** Admission $5.50 adults, $3 seniors and ages 6–12, $1 for ages 2–5, under age 2 free. Tues by donation. Daily 10am–5pm. Closed Thanksgiving, Christmas, and New Year's Day. Bus: 25, 43, or 48.

If the Seattle Underground Tour's vivid description of prefire life has you curious about what the city's more respectable citizens were doing back in the 1880s, you can find out here, where re-created storefronts provide glimpses into their lives. Located at the north end of Washington Park Arboretum, this museum explores various aspects of Seattle's history, with frequently changing exhibits on more obscure aspects of the city's past. While many of the exhibits will be of greatest interest to Seattle residents, anyone wishing to gain a better understanding of the history of Seattle and the Northwest will find the displays here of interest. There is a Boeing mail plane from the 1920s, plus an exhibit on the 1889 fire that leveled the city. This museum also hosts touring exhibitions that address Northwest history.

Klondike Gold Rush National Historical Park. 117 S. Main St. ☎ **206/553-7220.** Free admission. Daily 9am–5pm. Closed Thanksgiving, Christmas, and New Year's Day. Waterfront Streetcar: To Occidental Park stop. Bus: 15, 18, 21, 22, or 23.

It isn't in the Klondike (which isn't even in the United States) and it isn't really a park (it's a single room in an old store), but it is a fascinating little museum. "At 3 o'clock this morning the steamship Portland, from St. Michaels for Seattle, passed up [Puget] Sound with more than a ton of gold on board and 68 passengers." When the *Seattle Post-Intelligencer* published that sentence on July 17, 1897, they started a stampede. Would-be miners heading for the Klondike goldfields in the 1890s made Seattle their outfitting center and helped turn it into a prosperous city. When they struck it rich up north, they headed back to Seattle, the first U.S. outpost of civilization, and unloaded their gold, making Seattle doubly rich. It seems only fitting that this museum should be here. Film buffs can catch a free screening of Charlie Chaplin's film *The Gold Rush* the first Sunday of each month. Another unit of the park is in Skagway, Alaska.

NW Seaport/Maritime Heritage Center. 1002 Valley St. ☎ **206/447-9800.** Admission free. Mon–Sat 10am–4pm, Sun noon–4pm (until 5pm daily in summer).

Although this marine heritage center at the south end of Lake Union is currently little more than a shipyard for the restoration of three historic ships, there are grand plans for the future. If you're a fan of tall ships and the age of sail, you can pay a visit to the 1897 schooner *Wawona,* which is currently under restoration. Most months of the year, there are Friday lunchtime folk music concerts on the deck of this boat. Nearby, in Chandler's Cove, you'll find the **Puget Sound Maritime Museum Exhibit,** 901 Fairview N. (☎ **206/624-3028**), with more exhibits on Northwest maritime heritage. Together these two centers are working to turn the adjacent Navy Reserve Training Center into a maritime museum.

Wing Luke Asian Museum. 407 Seventh Ave. S. ☎ **206/623-5124.** Admission $2.50 adults, $1.50 students and seniors, 75¢ ages 5–12, under 5 free. Free on Thurs. Tues–Fri 11am–4:30pm, Sat–Sun noon–4pm. Closed New Year's Day, Easter, July 4, Veteran's Day, Thanksgiving, Christmas eve, and Christmas day. Bus: Any bus using the bus tunnel.

Located in the heart of Seattle's International District (Chinatown) and named for the first Asian American to hold public office in the Northwest, this museum explores the role various Asian cultures have played in the settlement and development of the Northwest. Despite much persecution over the years, Asians, primarily Chinese and Japanese, have played an integral role in developing the Northwest, and today the connection of this region with the far side of the Pacific is opening up both economic and cultural doors. Many of the museum's special exhibits are meant to help explain Asian customs to non-Asians.

SCIENCE MUSEUMS

Pacific Science Center. 200 Second Ave. N., Seattle Center. ☎ **206/443-2001.** Admission $7.50 adults, $5.50 ages 6–13 and seniors, $3.50 ages 2–5, under 2 free. IMAX $5.50 adults, $4.50 ages 6–13 and seniors, $3.50 ages 2–5. Laser show $6 for evening performances ($3 on Tues). Various discounted combination tickets available. June–Sept, daily 10am–6pm; Oct–May, Mon–Fri 10am–5pm, Sat–Sun and holidays 10am–6pm. Closed Thanksgiving and Christmas. Bus: 1, 2, 3, 4, 6, 13, 15, 16, 18, 19, 24, or 33. Monorail: To Seattle Center.

Although exhibits are aimed primarily at children, the Pacific Science Center is fun for all ages. The main goal of this sprawling complex at Seattle Center is to teach kids about science and to instill a desire to study it. To that end, there are dozens of fun hands-on exhibits addressing the biological sciences, physics, and chemistry. Kids learn how their bodies work, blow giant bubbles, and experiment with robots. There is a planetarium for learning about the skies (plus laser shows for the fun of it). Even more interesting are the many special exhibits, so be sure to check the schedule when you're in town. There are also special events, including a bubble festival. An IMAX theater has daily showings of short films on its $3\frac{1}{2}$-story-high screen.

NEIGHBORHOODS

The **International District,** which is centered between Fifth Avenue S. and Eighth Avenue S. (between S. Main Street and S. Lane Street, is Seattle's large and prosperous Asian neighborhood. Called the International District rather than Chinatown, because so many Asian nationalities call this area home, this neighborhood has been the center of the city's Asian communities for more than 100 years. You can learn about the district's history at the Wing Luke Museum (see above), where you can also pick up a walking-tour map of the area. There are of course lots of restaurants, import stores, and food markets. In fact, the huge **Uwajimaya** (see "Markets" later in this chapter for details) is all of these rolled up in one. Both the **Nippon Kan Theatre,** 628 S. Washington St. (☎ 206/467-6807), and the **Northwest Asian-American Theater,** 409 Seventh Ave. S. (☎ 206/340-1049), feature performances with an Asian flavor. At the corner of Maynard Avenue S. and S. King Street, you'll find Hing Hay Park, the site of an ornate and colorful pavilion given to the city by Taipei, Taiwan.

The **Fremont District,** which begins at the north end of the Fremont Bridge near the intersection of Fremont Avenue N. and N. 36th Street, is Seattle's funkiest, funnest, and most unusual neighborhood. "Welcome to the Center of the Universe" reads the sign on the Fremont Bridge, and from that point onward, you know you are in a very different part of Seattle (maybe even a different dimension). This funky neighborhood also goes by the name Republic of Fremont, and has as its motto "De Libertas Quirkas," which roughly translated means "free to be peculiar." At this crossroads business district, you'll find unusual outdoor art, the Fremont Sunday Market, several vintage clothing and furniture stores, a brew pub, and many more unexpected and unusual shops, galleries, and cafes. On summer Saturday nights there are outdoor movies, and in June, there is the wacky Solstice Parade, a countercultural promenade with giant puppets, wizards, fairies, face paint, and hippies of all ages. Among the public artworks in the neighborhood are *Waiting for the Interurban* (at the north end of the Fremont Bridge), the *Fremont Troll* (under the Aurora Bridge on N. 36th Street) *The Rocket at the Center of the Universe* (at the corner of Evanston Ave. N. and N. 35th Street), and *Lenin* (at the corner of Fremont Place and N. 36th Street).

Good Times in Bad Taste

If you love bad jokes and have a fascination with the bizarre (or maybe this describes your children), you won't want to miss Bill Speidel's Underground Tour and a visit to Ye Olde Curiosity Shop. Together these two should reassure you that espresso, traffic jams, and stadium controversies aside, Seattle really does have a sense of humor.

Bill Speidel's Underground Tour, 610 First Ave. (☎ **206/682-4646**), will entertain and enlighten anyone who has an appreciation for off-color humor and is curious about the seamier side of Seattle history. The tours lead down below street level in the Pioneer Square area where vestiges of Seattle businesses built before the great fire of 1889 can still be found. Learn the low-down dirt on early Seattle, a town where plumbing was problematic and a person could drown in a pothole. (Tours held daily; $6.50 adults, $5.50 seniors, $5 students ages 13 to 17, $2.75 children ages 6 to 12).

Ye Olde Curiosity Shop, 1001 Alaskan Way, Pier 54 (☎ **206/682-5844**), is a cross between a souvenir store and Ripley's Believe It or Not! It's weird! It's tacky! It's always packed! See Siamese-twin calves, a natural mummy, the Lord's Prayer on a grain of rice, a narwhal tusk, shrunken heads, a 67-pound snail, fleas in dresses, walrus and whale oosiks (the bone of the male reproductive organ)—in other words, all the stuff that fascinated you as a kid. The collection of oddities was started in 1899 by Joe Standley, who had developed a more-than-passing interest in strange curios.

TOTEM POLES

Totem poles are the quintessential symbol of the Northwest, and although this Native American art form actually comes from farther north (in British Columbia), there are quite a few totem poles around Seattle. In Occidental Park, just off Pioneer Square at Occidental Avenue South and South Washington Street you'll find four totem poles that were carved by local artist Duane Pasco. The tallest is the 35-foot-high *The Sun and Raven,* which tells the story of how Raven brought light into the world. Next to this pole is *Man Riding a Whale.* This type of totem pole was traditionally carved to help villagers during their whale hunts. The other two figures that face each other are symbols of the Bear Clan and the Welcoming Figure.

A block away, in the triangular park of Pioneer Place, you can see Seattle's most famous totem pole. The pole you see here now is actually a copy of the original, which arrived in Seattle in 1890 after a band of drunken men stole it from a Tlingit village up the coast. In 1938, the pole was set afire by an arsonist. The Seattle city fathers sent a $5,000 check to the Tlingit village requesting a replacement. Supposedly, the response from the village was, "Thanks for paying for the first totem pole. If you want another, it will cost another $5,000." The city of Seattle paid up, and so today Pioneer Square has a totem pole and the city has a clear conscience.

Up near Pike Place Market, at Victor Steinbrueck Park, which is at the intersection of Pike Place, Virginia Street, and Western Avenue, are two 50-foot-tall totem poles. To see a large concentration of authentic totem poles, visit the University of Washington's Burke Museum (see above for details).

PANORAMAS

If you've ever seen a photo of the Space Needle framed by the high-rises of downtown Seattle, then you've probably seen a photo taken from **Kerry Viewpoint** on

Queen Anne Hill. If you want to take your own drop-dead photo of the Seattle sky-line from this elevated perspective, head north from Seattle Center on Queen Anne Avenue N. and turn left on W. Highland Drive. When you reach the park, you'll immediately recognize the view—it's on the cover of virtually every Seattle tourist booklet available.

For a more far-reaching panorama that takes in everything from the Cascades to the Olympics, head up to **Volunteer Park** on Capitol Hill. Here you'll find an old water tower surrounded by attractive gardens. A winding staircase leads to the top of the water tower, from which you get 360° of views. To find the water tower, park near the Se-attle Asian Art Museum if you can and walk back out of the parking lot to where the road splits. The view from directly in front of the museum isn't bad either.

If you don't want to deal with the crowds at the Space Needle, but still want an elevated downtown view, head to the big, black **Columbia Seafirst Center** at the cor-ner of Fourth Avenue and Columbia Street. At 943 feet, this is the tallest building in Seattle (twice as tall as the Space Needle) and the tallest building (by number of stories) west of the Mississippi. Up on the 73rd floor, you'll find an observation deck. Admission is $5 for adults and $3 for seniors and children.

PUBLIC GARDENS

In addition to the gardens listed here, you'll find the Carl S. English Jr. Ornamen-tal Gardens adjacent to the Hiram M. Chitteneden Locks in the Ballard neighbor-hood of north Seattle (see "Salmon Viewing" below for details).

Washington Park Arboretum. 2300 Arboretum Dr. E. ☎ **206/543-8800.** Free admission. Daily dawn to dusk; visitors center Mon–Fri 10am–4pm, Sat–Sun 10am–4pm. Enter on Lake Washington Blvd. off E. Madison St. or take Wash. 520 off I-5 north of downtown, take the Montlake exit, and go straight through the first intersection. Bus: 11, 43, or 84.

Acres of trees and shrubs stretch from the far side of Capitol Hill all the way to the Montlake Cut, a canal connecting Lake Washington to Lake Union. Within the 200-acre arboretum, there are 5,000 varieties of plants and quiet trails that, although most beautiful in spring when azaleas, cherry trees, rhododendrons, and dogwoods are all in flower, are pleasant throughout the year. Sadly though, much of the arboretum has been neglected over the decades since it was created and plants and paths are no longer as well maintained as they ought to be. The north end of the arboretum, a marshland that is home to ducks and herons, is popular with kayakers, canoeists (see below for where you can rent a canoe or kayak) and bird watchers. A boardwalk meanders along the water in this area providing views across the waters of Lake Washington.

Japanese Gardens. Washington Park Arboretum, Lake Washington Blvd. E. (north of E. Madison St.). ☎ **206/684-4725.** Admission $2 adults; $1 seniors, the disabled, and ages 6–18. Mar–Apr, daily 10am–6pm; May, daily 10am–7pm; June–Aug, daily 10am–8pm; Sept–Oct, daily 10am–6pm; Nov, daily 10am–4pm. Closed Dec–Feb. Bus: 11.

Situated on 3¹/₂ acres of land, the Japanese Gardens are a perfect little world unto themselves. Babbling brooks, a lake rimmed with Japanese irises and filled with col-orful koi (Japanese carp), and a cherry orchard (for spring color) are peaceful any time of year. Unfortunately, noise from a nearby road can be distracting at times. A spe-cial Tea Garden encloses a Tea House, where, between April and October, on the third Saturday of each month at 1:30pm, you can attend a traditional tea ceremony.

Volunteer Park Conservatory. E. Prospect St. and 14th Ave. E. ☎ **206/322-4112.** Free admission. May 1–Sept 15, daily 10am–7pm; Sept 16–Apr 30, 10am–4pm. Bus: 10.

This stately old Victorian conservatory, built in 1912, houses a large collection of tropical and desert plants, including palm trees, orchids, and cacti.

On the Trail of Dale Chihuly

For many years now Northwest glass artist Dale Chihuly, one of the founders of the Pilchuck School for glass art north of Seattle, has been garnering nationwide media attention for his fanciful and color-saturated contemporary glass art. From tabletop vessels to massive window installations, his creations in glass have a depth and richness of color that have captured the attention of collectors across the country. Sensuous forms include vases within bowls that are reminiscent of Technicolor birds' eggs in giant nests. His ikebana series, based on the traditional Japanese flower-arranging technique, are riotous conglomerations of color that twist and turn like so many cut flowers waving in the wind.

So where do you go to see the works of this master of molten glass? There's no one place in Seattle to see a collection of his work, but there are numerous public displays around the city. Up on the third floor of the Washington State Convention and Trade Center, Pike Street and Eighth Avenue, there is a case with some beautifully lighted vases. In the lobby of the Sheraton Seattle Hotel, 1400 Sixth Ave., there are works by Chihuly and other Northwest glass artists from the Pilchuck School. If you want to dine surrounded by art glass, including work by Chihuly, make a reservation at the Sheraton's ever-popular Fuller's. The City Centre shopping arcade, 1420 Fifth Ave., has displays by numerous glass artists, including Chihuly. Don't miss the large wall installation that is beside this upscale shopping arcades lounge (out the back door of FAO Schwartz). Also here at City Centre, you'll find the **Foster/White Gallery,** which represents Chihuly in Seattle and always has a few of his pieces on display (and yes they are for sale). The main Foster/White Gallery, 311¹/₂ Occidental Ave. S., is down in Pioneer Square, and another satellite gallery is located in Kirkland at 126 Central Way.

If you're willing to drive to Chihuly's home town of Tacoma, 32 miles south Seattle, you can see the largest museum exhibit of Chihuly's work at the **Tacoma Art Museum**, 1123 Pacific Ave. (☎ **253/272-4258**); Tuesday, Wednesday, Friday, and Saturday 10am to 5pm, Thursday 10am to 7pm (until 8pm on the third Thursday of each month), Sunday noon to 5pm. Just up the street from here, at Tacoma's restored Union Station (now the federal courthouse), some of the artist's larger pieces have been installed.

SALMON VIEWING

While numbers of salmon in the Puget Sound region have dwindled dangerously low in recent years, it is still possible in various places to witness the annual return of salmon.

In the autumn, on the waterfront, you can see returning salmon at the **Seattle Aquarium.** At **Hiram M. Chittenden Locks,** 3015 NW 54th St. (☎ **206/783-7059**), between July and August, you can view salmon both as they leap up the locks' fish ladder and through underwater observation windows. These locks, which are used primarily by small boats, connect Lake Union and Lake Washington with the waters of Puget Sound, and depending on the tides and lake levels, there is a difference of 6 to 26 feet on either side. The Carl S. English Jr. Botanical Gardens, which contains more than 500 species of plants, is adjacent to the locks. The locks and park are open daily from 7am to 9pm and the visitors center is open June through September daily from 10am to 7pm and October through May Thursday through Monday from 11am to 5pm (closed Thanksgiving, Christmas, and New

Year's Day). Take bus 17 or 46. East of Seattle, in downtown **Issaquah,** there is a salmon hatchery at 125 Sunset Way (☎ 425/391-9094), where salmon can be seen year-round. However, it is in October that adult salmon can be seen returning to the hatchery. Each year in October, the city of Issaquah holds a Salmon Days Festival to celebrate the return of the natives.

ESPECIALLY FOR KIDS

Listed below you'll find several attractions that are aimed almost exclusively at kids, however, for a few other attractions that will appeal to both kids and adults, see "The Top Attractions" and "More Attractions," above, for the following Seattle attractions: **Pacific Science Center, The Seattle Aquarium, Omnidome Film Experience,** and **Woodland Park Zoo.** And if your kids are fascinated by the bizarre, don't leave town without visiting **Ye Olde Curiosity Shop.** And what could be more fun than exploring the creepy world of the **Seattle Underground?** (See the boxed feature on page 107.)

You can also take the kids to a sports event. Seattle supports professional football, basketball, and baseball teams (see section 8 below). You might also be able to catch a performance at the Seattle Children's Theatre or the Northwest Puppet Center. See "Children's Theater" later in this chapter for details.

✪ **Enchanted Village and Wild Waves.** 36201 Enchanted Pkwy. S., Federal Way. ☎ **206/661-8000.** Enchanted Village, $11 adults, $9 children ages 3–9, free for children 2 and under, $7 seniors; Enchanted Village and Wild Waves together, $19.95 adults, $17.95 children ages 3–9, free for children 2 and under, $10 seniors. Mid-May to early Sept; call for hours. By car from Seattle, take I-5 south to Exit 142-B, Puyallup.

The littlest kids can watch the clowns and ride on miniature trains, merry-go-rounds, and the like at Enchanted Village. The older kids, teenagers, and adults will want to spend the hot days of summer riding the wild waves, tubing down artificial streams, and swooshing down water slides.

✪ **Seattle Center.** 305 Harrison St. ☎ **206/684-7200** or 206/728-1585. Free admission; pay per ride or game (various multiride tickets available). June to Labor Day, daily noon–11pm; Labor Day to June, weekends noon–11pm (schedule sometimes varies in winter months). Bus: 15 or 18. Monorail: from Westlake Center at the corner of Pine St. and Fourth Ave.

If you want to keep the kids entertained all day long, spend the day at Seattle Center. This 74-acre amusement park and cultural center was built for the Seattle World's Fair in 1962 and stands on the north edge of downtown at the end of the monorail line. The most visible building at the center is the Space Needle (see above), which provides an outstanding panorama of the city from its observation deck. However, of much more interest to children are the Fun Forest rides (a roller coaster, log flume, merry-go-round, and Ferris wheel), arcade games, and minigolf. Seattle Center is also the site of the Children's Museum and Seattle Children's Theatre (see map above). This is Seattle's main festival site, and in the summer months hardly a weekend goes by without some festival or another filling its grounds.

The Children's Museum. Center House, Seattle Center. ☎ **206/298-2521.** Admission $4.50. Daily 10am–5pm. Closed Thanksgiving, Christmas, and New Year's Day. Bus: 15 or 18. Monorail: from Westlake Center at the corner of Pine St. and Fourth Ave.

Seattle's Children's Museum is located in the basement of the Center House at Seattle Center. The museum includes plenty of hands-on cultural exhibits, a child-size neighborhood, an imagination station, a mountain wilderness area, a global village, and other exhibits to keep the little ones busy learning and playing for hours.

WALKING TOUR
Pioneer Square Area

Start: Pioneer Place at the corner of Yesler Way and First Avenue.
Finish: Washington Street Public Boat Landing.
Time: Approximately 2 hours, not including shopping, dining, and museum and other stops.
Best Times: Weekdays, when the neighborhood and the Seattle Underground Tour are not so crowded.
Worst Times: Weekends, when the area is very crowded.

In the late 19th century, the Pioneer Square area was the heart of downtown Seattle, so when a fire raged through these blocks in 1889, the city was devastated. However, residents and merchants quickly began rebuilding and set about to remedy many of the infrastructure problems that had faced Seattle in the years prior to the fire. Today this small section of the city is all that remains of old Seattle, and due to the fact that one architect, Elmer Fisher, was responsible for the design of many of the buildings constructed after the fire, the neighborhood has a distinctive uniformity of architectural style.

While wandering these streets, don't bother looking for a place called Pioneer Square, you won't find it. The name actually applies to the whole neighborhood, not a park surrounded by four streets as you would surmise. However, what you should keep your eye out for is old man-hole covers, many of which were cast with maps of Seattle or Northwest Coast Indian designs.

Start your tour of this historic neighborhood at the corner of Yesler Way and First Avenue on:

1. **Pioneer Place,** the triangular park at the heart of Pioneer Square. The totem pole here is a replacement of one that burned in 1938. The original pole had been stolen from a Tlingit village up the coast in 1890. Legend has it that after the pole burned the city fathers sent a check for $5,000 requesting a new totem pole. The Tlingit response was, "Thanks for paying for the first one. Send another $5,000 for a replacement." The cast-iron pergola in the park was erected in 1905 as a shelter for a large underground lavatory. Facing the square are several historic buildings, including the gabled Lowman Building and three others noteworthy for their terra cotta facades. One of these,

2. **the Pioneer Building,** is one of the architectural standouts of this neighborhood. It houses an antiques mall and:

3. **Doc Maynard's,** 610 First Ave. (☎ **206/682-4649**), a nightclub featuring live rock bands. By day this is also the starting point of the Underground Tour, which takes a look at the Pioneer Square area from beneath the sidewalks. The tour is a great introduction to the history of the area (if you don't mind off-color jokes) and actually spends quite a bit of time above ground (duplicating much of the walking tour outlined here). Forming the south side of Pioneer Place is:

4. **Yesler Way,** the original Skid Row. In Seattle's early years, logs were skidded down this road to a lumber mill on the waterfront, and the road came to be known as Skid Road. These days it's trying hard to live down its reputation, but there are still quite a few people down on their luck here.

☕ **TAKE A BREAK**   Across Yesler Way from the pergola is **Merchants Cafe,** 109 Yesler Way (☎ **206/624-1515**), the oldest restaurant in Seattle. If it happens to be time for lunch or dinner, this makes a good place to stop. Meals are moderately priced and well prepared.

From Pioneer Place, walk up James Street past a triangular parking deck (a monstrosity of urban renewal that prompted the movement to preserve the rest of this neighborhood). At the corner of Second Avenue, turn left to reach:

5. **Ruby Montana's Pinto Pony,** 603 Second Ave. (☎ **206/621-PONY**), a cluttered shop selling (and displaying) all manner of retro-kitsch both new and vintage. If pink flamingos and Elvis clocks are your style, Ruby's is your store. Right next door is:

6. **Laguna,** 609 Second Ave. (☎ **206/682-6162**), which specializes in mid-century pottery, primarily from California. Fiesta, Bauer, and Weller are all well represented. Across the street and half a block toward Yesler Way, you'll come to:

7. **the Linda Cannon Gallery,** 520 Second Ave. (☎ **206/233-0404**), which among other things sells early works by popular comic artist Lynda Barry. Right next door is:

8. **Smith Tower,** which when completed in 1914 was the tallest building west of the Mississippi. The ornate lobby and elevator doors are reason enough for a visit to this building, but there is also a great view of the city from an observatory near the top of the building. However, the observatory is only open to the public if you happen to be on a Seattle Underground tour.

From Smith Tower, continue down Second Avenue on the opposite side of the street (keeping right when Second Avenue S. Extension forks to the left). At the corner of Main Street, you'll find the shady little:

9. **Waterfall Park,** with a roaring waterfall that looks as if it had been transported here straight from the Cascade Range. The park is built on the site of the original United Parcel Service (UPS) offices and makes a wonderful place for a rest or a picnic lunch. Turn right onto Main Street and in one block you'll come to cobblestoned:

10. **Occidental Park,** with four totem poles carved by Northwest artist Duane Pasco. This shady park serves as a gathering spot for homeless people, so you may not want to linger. However, on the west side of the park is the:

11. **Grand Central Arcade,** a shopping and dining center created from a restored brick building. Inside, there are craft and antique stores as well as art galleries. Across Main Street from Occidental Park is a unit of:

12. **Klondike Gold Rush National Historical Park,** 117 S. Main St. (☎ **206/553-7220**). The small museum is dedicated to the history of the 1897–98 Klondike gold rush, which helped Seattle grow from an obscure town into a booming metropolis. The waterfront streetcar, which connects Pioneer Square with Pike Place Market and other waterfront attractions, stops in front of the historical park. Around the corner from this small museum is Occidental Mall, where you'll find a couple of Seattle's best galleries.

13. **Davidson Gallery,** 313 Occidental Ave. S. (☎ **206/624-7684**), sells everything from 16th-century prints to contemporary art by Northwest artists. You never know what to expect when you walk through the front door here. Right upstairs from this gallery is:

14. **Foster/White Gallery,** 311¹/₂ Occidental Ave. S. (☎ **206/622-2833**), which is best known for its art glass. This is famed glass artist Dale Chihuly's Seattle gallery and always has several of his works on display.

Walking Tour—Pioneer Square Area

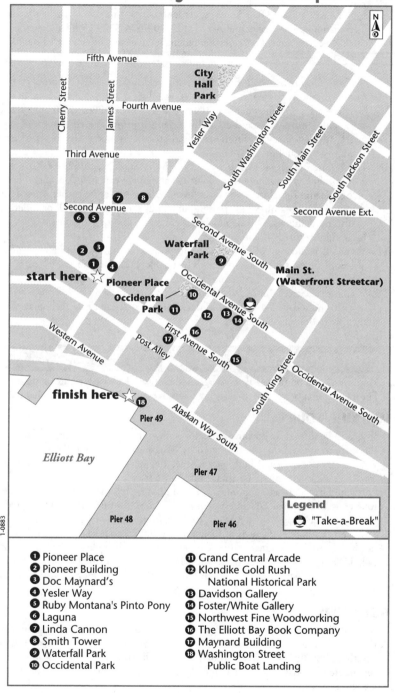

Legend

🌀 "Take-a-Break"

1. Pioneer Place
2. Pioneer Building
3. Doc Maynard's
4. Yesler Way
5. Ruby Montana's Pinto Pony
6. Laguna
7. Linda Cannon
8. Smith Tower
9. Waterfall Park
10. Occidental Park
11. Grand Central Arcade
12. Klondike Gold Rush National Historical Park
13. Davidson Gallery
14. Foster/White Gallery
15. Northwest Fine Woodworking
16. The Elliott Bay Book Company
17. Maynard Building
18. Washington Street Public Boat Landing

☕ **TAKE A BREAK**   Across Occidental Park from these two galleries is **Torrefazione,** 320 Occidental Ave. S. (☎ 206/624-5773), which many people claim serves the best coffee in Seattle. Be sure to get your coffee in one of the hand-painted cups.

From Occidental Mall, turn right onto Jackson Street. At the corner of First Avenue on the opposite side of the street, you'll see:

15. **Northwest Fine Woodworking,** 101 S. Jackson St. (☎ 206/625-0542), a large store selling exquisite, hand-crafted wooden furniture, as well as some smaller pieces. Well worth a visit. From here, head up First Avenue to the corner of Main Street, where you'll find:

16. **The Elliott Bay Book Company,** 101 S. Main St. (☎ 206/624-6600), which is one of the city's most popular bookstores and has an extensive selection of books on Seattle and the Northwest. From here, walk north to the corner of First Avenue and Washington Street, passing numerous shops and bars, all of which are in historic buildings. On the northwest corner of this intersection you'll see the beautifully restored:

17. **Maynard Building,** which is named for Seattle founding father David "Doc" Maynard and was the site of the city's first bank. Turn left here and in one block, you'll come to the waterfront and the:

18. **Washington Street Public Boat Landing.** This iron open-air building was erected in 1920 and today serves as a public dock where people can tie up their boats while they are in Seattle.

6 Organized Tours

For information on the Seattle Underground tour, see the boxed feature on page 107. For information on touring the Boeing plant, see section 11 later in this chapter.

WALKING TOURS

If you'd like to explore downtown Seattle with a knowledgeable guide, join one of the informative walking tours offered by **See Seattle Walking Tours** (☎ 425/226-7641). The tours visit Pike Place Market, the waterfront, the Pioneer Square district, and the International District. Prices range from $15 to $30.

If you'd like an insider's glimpse of life in Seattle's International District, book a tour with **Chinatown Discovery Tours** (☎ 206/236-0657). On these walking tours, which last from 1¹/₂ to 3 hours, you'll learn the history of this colorful and historic neighborhood. A Touch of Chinatown ($9.95) is a brief introduction to the neighborhood. The Chinatown by Day tour ($24.95) includes a six-course lunch. Nibble Your Way Through Chinatown ($14.95) provides a sampling of flavors from around the International District. The Chinatown by Night tour ($34.95) includes an eight-course banquet.

BUS TOURS

If you'd like an overview of Seattle's main tourist attractions, or if you're pressed for time during your visit, you can pack in a lot of sights on a tour with **Gray Line of Seattle** (☎ 800/426-7532 or 206/626-5208). Half-day tours are $24 for adults, $12 for children; full-day tours are $33 for adults, $16.50 children. Tours outside the city are also available.

From May through October, Gray Line also offers a Trolley Tour on one of those buses made up to look like an old trolley. The tour is actually a day pass to use the trolley, which follows a set route around downtown Seattle. The trolley goes along the waterfront and also stops at Seattle Center, Pike Place Market, the Seattle Art Museum, and Pioneer Square. A 2-day pass is $13 for adults and $6.50 for children. Because buses in downtown are free, the Waterfront Streetcar is less than $1 most of the day, and the monorail will get you to Seattle Center for $1, the trolley is not a very good deal.

BOAT TOURS

In addition to the boat tours and cruises mentioned below, you can do your own low-budget cruise simply by hopping on one of the ferries operated by Washington State Ferries. Try the Bainbridge Island or Bremmerton ferries out of Seattle for a 2-hour round-trip. For a longer and more scenic trip, drive north to Anacortes and ride the ferries through the San Juan Islands, perhaps spending a few hours in the town of Friday Harbor before returning. It's also possible to take the first ferry of the day from Anacortes, ride all the way to Sidney, British Columbia, and then catch the next ferry back to Anacortes.

Located at Blake Island State Marine Park across Puget Sound from Seattle and only accessible by tour boat or private boat, Tillicum Village was built in conjunction with the 1962 Seattle world's fair. The "village" is actually just a large restaurant and performance hall fashioned after a traditional Northwest Coast Indian longhouse, but with totem poles standing vigil out front, the forest encircling the longhouse, and the waters of Puget Sound stretching out into the distance, Tillicum Village is a beautiful spot. **Tillicum Village Tours,** Pier 56. (☎ 206/443-1244), operates tours that include the scenic boat ride to and from the island, a dinner of alder-smoked salmon, and a performance of traditional masked dances. After the dinner and dances, you can strike out on forest trails to explore the island (returning on a later boat if you want to spend a couple of extra hours hiking). There are even beaches on which to relax. Tours cost $50.25 for adults, $46.50 for seniors, $32.50 for children ages 13 to 19, $20 for children ages 6 to 12, and $10 for children ages 4 to 5. Tours are offered daily from May to October; other months the schedule varies. If you were going to opt for one tour only while in Seattle, this should be it—unique and truly northwestern.

Seattle is a city surrounded by water, and if you'd like to see it from various aquatic perspectives, you can take one of the cruises offered by **Argosy Cruises,** Pier 55 (☎ 206/623-4252), which offers the widest array of cruises in the Seattle area. There's a Seattle harbor cruise (departs from Pier 55; $13.40 adults, $6.45 children ages 5 to 12); a cruise through the Hiram Chittenden Locks to Lake Union (departs from Pier 57; $21.70 adults, $11.10 children ages 5 to 12), and two cruises around Lake Washington (one departs from Chandler's Cove at the south end of Lake Union and the other departs from downtown Kirkland on the east side of the lake; $17.10 adults, $8.75 children ages 5 to 12). These latter two cruises will take you past the fabled Xanadu built by Bill Gates on the shore of Lake Washington.

From June through August **Clipper Navigation,** Pier 69 (☎ **800/888-2535,** 206/448-5000, or 250/382-8100 in Victoria), operates 2-hour sunset cruises that circumnavigate Bainbridge Island. Fares are $16 for adults and $8 for children. In July and August, some of the cruises also include live jazz music ($20 for adults, $10 for children).

You can explore the mazelike waterways of the Puget Sound on an all-day cruise aboard the *San Juan Explorer,* which is also operated by Clipper Navigation. This cruise heads up the east side of Whidbey Island and through Deception Pass before reaching the San Juan Islands. You then get four hours in the town of Friday

Harbor before starting the return trip to Seattle. The round-trip fare is $59 for adults, $54 for seniors, and $29.50 for children. Discounted advance purchase fares are also available, and overnight stays can be arranged.

Various *Victoria Clipper* ferries, operated by Clipper Navigation, ply the waters between Seattle and Victoria, British Columbia, with several departures daily in summer. A high-speed catamaran passenger ferry takes three to five hours to reach Victoria, and a turbo-jet passenger ferry takes only 2 hours (this is the fastest passenger boat in the western hemisphere). If you leave on the earliest ferry, you can spend the better part of the day exploring Victoria and be back in Seattle for a late dinner. Round-trip fares range from $88 to $109 for adults, $78 to $99 for seniors, and $44 to $54.50 for children ages 1 to 11. Discounted advance-purchase tickets are also available. Some scheduled trips also stop in the San Juan Islands. Various tour packages are also available, including an add-on tour to Butchart Gardens.

Clipper Navigation also operates a car ferry, the *Princess Marguerite III,* between Seattle and Victoria during the summer months. This ship takes 4^1/$_2$ hours to make the journey and the round-trip fare is $98 for a car and driver and $58 for adult passengers, $50 for seniors, and $29 for children ages 1 to 11.

If you'd like a bit of dining and dancing with your cruise around Puget Sound, book a cruise on the **Spirit of Puget Sound,** Pier 70 (☎ **206/443-1442**). This big sleek yacht does lunch and dinner cruises. Adult fares range between $31.50 and $33 for lunch and between $55.50 and $59.25 for dinner.

Want a boat tour that's really all about raw power? Try a ride on the turbo-charged *Rocket,* a 70-foot tour boat operated by **Pier 54 Adventures,** Pier 54 (☎ **206/ 623-6364**). Powered by twin V-12 engines, this boat absolutely flies over the waters of Puget Sound. Fares for the 30-minute outings are $10 for adults, $9 for seniors, and $7 for children.

Looking for a quieter way to see Seattle from the water? Pier 54 Adventures also offers sailboat rides in their replica of the *Spray,* the sailboat Joshua Slocum used in his 1895 solo voyage around the world (the first such trip ever). Cruises are $15 to $25 for adults, $13.50 to $22.50 for seniors, and $10 to $15 for children. The higher fare is for the sunset cruise. **Let's Go Sailing,** Pier 56 (☎ **206/624-3931**), offers 1^1/$_2$- and 2^1/$_2$-hour sailboat cruises. The longer excursions are at sunset. Cruises are $20 to $35 for adults, $18 to $32 for seniors, and $15 to $28 for children under age 12. Over on Lake Union, **Sailing in Seattle,** 1900 Westlake Ave. N. (☎ **206/ 298-0094**), offers 2^1/$_2$-hour cruises for $35.

SCENIC FLIGHTS

Seattle is one of the few cities in the United States where floatplanes are a regular sight in the skies and on the lakes of the area. If you'd like to see what it's like to take off and land from the water, you've got a couple of options. **Seattle Seaplanes,** 1325 Fairview Ave. E. (☎ **800/637-5553** or 206/329-9638), which takes off from the southeast corner of Lake Union, offers 20-minute scenic flights over the city for $42.50. **Sound Flight,** 243 W. Perimeter Rd., Renton (☎ **800/825-0722**), which leaves from the south end of Lake Washington, offers a variety of scenic flights of varying lengths, with rates starting at $59. You could also book a flight on **Kenmore Air** (☎ **800/543-9595** or 206/486-1257) for an excursion to the San Juan Islands or Victoria. This company flies from Lake Union at 950 Westlake Ave. N. and from the north end of Lake Washington.

You can go up in a 1927 biplane with **Galvin Flying Service** (☎ **206/763-9706**), which flies out of Boeing Field. A 20-minute flight along the Seattle waterfront costs $79 for one person and $89 for two.

A RAILWAY EXCURSION

If you happen to be a fan of riding the rails, consider the **Spirit of Washington Dinner Train,** 625 S. Fourth St., Renton (☎ **800/876-RAIL** or 206/227-RAIL). Running from Renton, at the south end of Lake Washington, to the Columbia Winery near Woodinville, at the north end of the Lake, this train rolls past views of the lake and Mount Rainier. Along the way, you're fed a tasty and filling lunch or dinner. At the turn-around point, you get to tour a winery and taste some wines. Dinner tours range from $57 to $69; lunch tours range from $47 to $59. The higher prices are for seatings in the dome car, which definitely has finer views.

A COUPLE OF UNUSUAL TOURS

If you're interested in tapping into Seattle's microbrew scene, consider taking a **Brew Hops Tour** (☎ 206/283-8460). This company offers both lunch and dinner tours to several Seattle breweries and brew pubs. Tours are $35 per person.

If your tastes run to the macabre, you might be interested in the Private Eye on Seattle tour offered by **Windsor and Hatten Legal Investigators** (☎ 206/ 622-0590). These somewhat bizarre van tours are led by a retired private investigator who shares his stories of interesting and unusual cases he handled over the 40 years he was a private dick in the Emerald City. Tours are $20 per person.

7 Outdoor Activities

BEACHES **Alki** (rhymes with sky) **Beach,** across Elliott Bay from downtown Seattle, is Seattle's most popular beach and is the nearest approximation you'll find in the Northwest to a Southern California beach scene. The paved path that runs along this 2^{1}/2-mile-long beach is popular with skaters, walkers, and cyclists, and the road that parallels the beach is lined with shops and restaurants. However, the views across Puget Sound to the Olympic Mountains confirm that this is indeed the Northwest.

For a more northwestern beach experience (which usually includes a bit of hiking or walking), head to one of the area's many waterfront parks. Lincoln Park, south of Alki Beach in West Seattle has bluffs and forests backing the beach. Northwest of downtown Seattle, you'll find **Discovery Park,** where miles of beaches are the primary destination of most park visitors. North of Ballard, on Seaview Avenue NW, **Golden Gardens Park** has lawns and shade trees. There are also several parks along the shores of Lake Washington that have small stretches of beach, many of which are actually popular with swimmers. **Mount Baker Beach** and **Seward Park,** both of which are southeast of downtown Seattle along Lake Washington Boulevard, are two good places to hang out by the water and do a little swimming.

BICYCLING During the summer, **Terrene Tours** (☎ 206/325-5569) rents bicycles from Pier 54 on the waterfront. Rental rates are $10 for two hours and $16 for up to four hours. This company also offers guided bicycle tours around both the immediate Seattle vicinity and farther afield in Washington.

Gregg's Green Lake Cycle, 7007 Woodlawn Ave. NE (☎ **206/523-1822**); and the **Bicycle Center,** 4529 Sand Point Way NE (☎ **206/523-8300**) both rent bikes by the hour, day, or week. Rates range from $3 to $5 per hour and $15 to $30 per day. These shops are both convenient to the **Burke-Gilman Trail** and the **Sammamish River Trail.** The former is a 12^{1}/2-mile trail created from an old railway bed. It starts at **Gasworks Park** and continues to **Kenmore Logboom Park** at the north end of Lake Washington by way of the University of Washington. Serious riders can then connect to the Sammamish River Trail, which leads to Marymoor Park at the north end of Lake Sammamish. Linking the two trails together adds up to a 50-mile round-trip ride. Marymoor Park is the site of Seattle's velodrome. There are lots of great picnicking spots along both trails. Bicycles can also be rented on the Seattle waterfront at Pier The West Seattle bike path along **Alki Beach** is another good place to ride.

From spring through early fall Lake Washington Boulevard between **Seward Park** and **Mount Baker Beach** is closed to motor vehicles on the second Saturday and third Sunday of each month for Bicycle Saturdays and Sundays.

BOARDSAILING   Local Seattle waters are ideal for boardsailing, and depending on conditions can be excellent for beginners or the experienced. **Urban Surf,** 2100 N. Northlake Way (☎ 206/545-WIND), will rent you a board and give you lessons if you need them. Rates are $35 per day for a board. Lessons are $100 for two 3-hour sessions. Magnuson Park, on Lake Washington north of the University District, and Gasworks Park on Lake Union, Alki Beach in West Seattle, and Golden Gardens Park north of Ballard are some of the area's popular boardsailing spots.

FISHING   While salmon and steelhead runs have dwindled dangerously low all over the Northwest, it is still possible to do a lot of fishing in the waters off Seattle. **Sport Fishing of Seattle,** Pier 54 (☎ 206/623-6364) offers year-round fishing for both salmon and bottom fish. For a half day of fishing, they charge $65 for adults and $50 for children. If you'd rather do some saltwater fly-fishing, contact **A Spot Tail Salmon Guide** (☎ 206/283-6680), a guide service operated by Keith Richards, who charges $350 for one or two people for a full day of angling.

GOLF   While Seattle isn't a name that springs immediately to mind when one thinks of golf, the sport is as much a passion here as it is all across the country these days. There are more than a dozen public golf courses in the Seattle area. Seattle also has three conveniently located municipal golf courses: **Jackson Park Golf Course,** 1000 NE 135th St. (☎ 206/363-4747); **Jefferson Park Golf Course,** 4101 Beacon Ave. S. (☎ 206/762-4513); and **West Seattle Golf Course,** 4470 35th Ave. SW (☎ 206/935-5187), all three of which charge very reasonable greens fees of $18.50.

Harbour Pointe, 11817 Harbour Pointe Blvd., Mukilteo (☎ 800/233-3128 or 206/355-6060), the number-two ranked public golf course in Washington state, is just a few miles north of Seattle near the city of Everett. This course abounds in water hazards (each of the first 10 holes has water), and on the 11th hole you're treated to a fine view of Puget Sound. Greens fees range from $30 to $45. One hour north of Seattle, in the town of Stanwood, you'll find the **Kayak Point Golf Course,** 15711 Marine Dr. (☎ 800/562-3094), which Golf Digest Magazine rated the best public course in the Northwest. Greens fees range from $23 to $27.

HIKING   Within the environs Seattle itself, there are several large natural parks that are laced with enough trails to allow for a few good long walks. Among these are Seward Park on Lake Washington Boulevard southeast of downtown and Lincoln Park south of Alki Beach in West Seattle. However, the city's largest natural park, and Seattleites' favorite quick dose of nature, is Discovery Park, northwest of downtown at the western tip of the Magnolia neighborhood. This park covers more than 500 acres and has many miles of trails and beaches to hike. There are gorgeous views, forest paths, and meadows for lazing in after a long walk.

HOT-AIR BALLOONING   Seattle really isn't known as a hot-air ballooning center, but if you'd like to try floating over the Northwest landscape not far outside the city, contact **Over the Rainbow** (☎ 206/364-0995), which flies over the vineyards of the Woodinville area. Fares range from $110 for a weekday breakfast flight with

In case you want to see the world.

At American Express, we're here to make your journey a smooth one. So we have over 1,700 travel service locations in over 120 countries ready to help. What else would you expect from the world's largest travel agency?

do more

Travel

In case you want to be welcomed there.

We're here to see that you're always welcomed at establishments everywhere. That's why millions of people carry the American Express® Card – for peace of mind, confidence, and security, around the world or just around the corner.

do more

Cards

In case you're running low.

We're here to help with more than 118,000 Express Cash locations around the world. In order to enroll, just call American Express before you start your vacation.

do more

Express Cash

And just in case,

We're here with American Express® Travelers Cheques and Cheques *for Two*® They're the safest way to carry money on your vacation and the surest way to get a refund, practically anywhere, anytime.

Another way we help you...

do more®

Travelers Cheques

champagne and continental breakfast to $140 for a weekend flight with a picnic dinner at the end of the flight.

IN-LINE SKATING   Seattle has developed a reputation as one of the nation's hot in-line skating destinations. Throughout the city there are dozens of miles of paved paths that are perfect for skating. You can rent in-line skates at **Gregg's Green Lake Cycle,** 7007 Woodlawn Ave. NE (☎ **206/523-1822**) for about $12 per day or $4 per hour. The trail around Green Lake in north Seattle and the Burke-Gilman trail (see the description under "Bicycling," above) are both good places for skating and are convenient to Gregg's. Other place to try include Myrtle Edwards Park and the waterfront, and the paved path along Lake Washington Boulevard north of Seward Park.

JOGGING   The waterfront, from Pioneer Square north to Myrtle Edwards Park, where a paved path parallels the water, is a favorite downtown jogging route. The residential streets of Capitol Hill when combined with roads and sidewalks through Volunteer Park are another good choice. If you happen to be staying in the University District, you can access the 12½-mile-long Burke-Gilman Trail or run the ever-popular trail around Green Lake.

PARKS   For much of Seattle's population, it is the city's many parks that make this such a livable place. In the downtown area, **Myrtle Edwards Park,** at the north end of the waterfront, provides a great spot for enjoying sunsets over Puget Sound and the Olympic Mountains. **Freeway Park**, at Sixth Avenue and Seneca Street, is one of Seattle's most unusual parks. Built right on top of busy Interstate 5, this green space is more a series of urban plazas, with lots of terraces, waterfalls, and cement planters creating walls of greenery. You'd never know there's a roaring freeway beneath your feet.

For serious communing with nature, however, nothing will do but **Discovery Park.** Occupying a high bluff and sandy point jutting into Puget Sound, this is Seattle's largest and wildest park. You can easily spend a day wandering the trails and beaches here.

Up on Capitol Hill, you'll find one of Seattle's largest and most popular parks. **Volunteer Park,** E. Prospect Street and 14th Avenue E., is surrounded by the elegant mansions of Capitol Hill and is a popular spot for suntanning and playing Frisbee. The park is also home to the Seattle Asian Art Museum, an amphitheater, a water tower with a superb view of the city, and a conservatory filled with tropical and desert plants.

On the east side of Seattle, along the shore of Lake Washington, you'll find not only swimming beaches but also large **Seward Park,** which has in recent years been home to a pair of bald eagles. While this park's waterfront area's are its biggest attraction, it also has a dense forest with trails wandering through it.

In north Seattle, you'll find several parks worth visiting. These include the unique **Gasworks Park** at the north end of Lake Union on N. Northlake Way and Meridian Avenue N. This park has, in the middle of its green lawns, the rusting hulk of an old industrial plant; and its Kite Hill is the city's favorite kite-flying spot. North of here, on Green Lake Way N. near the Woodland Park Zoo, you'll find **Green Lake Park,** which is a center for exercise buffs who jog, bicycle, and skate around the park on a paved path. It's also possible to swim in the lake, and there are plenty of grassy areas. Due east of Green Lake several miles, on the shore of Lake Washington at Sand Point, is the large **Magnusson Park.** This park is a former military base and for that reason doesn't have the feel of other Seattle parks. However, the meadows, beaches, and adjacent Sound Garden (a series of aural sculptures for which

Seattle's famous grunge rock band was named) make this an interesting spot to visit. The park is off Sand Point Way NE.

North of the Ballard district, you'll find two very pleasant waterfront parks: **Golden Gardens** and **Carkeek.** The former, on Seaview Avenue NW, is best known as the site of one of Seattle's best beaches, but it is also a very pleasant spot for a sunset stroll. Carkeek Park, on NW Carkeek Park Road, is farther north and is a wild bit of forest surrounded by suburbia. Within the park, trails meander among the trees and lead down to a beach (which is unfortunately backed by railroad tracks).

SEA KAYAKING, CANOEING, ROWING & SAILING   On the waterfront, at Pier 54, **Outland Adventures** (☎ 206/623-6364) offers guided 1¹/₂-hour sea kayak tours. Tours are $35 per person and are in very stable double kayaks.

If you'd rather head out on your own, try **Northwest Outdoor Center,** 2100 Westlake Ave. N. (☎ 206/281-9694), is located on Lake Union and will rent you a sea kayak for between $8 and $12 per hour. You can also opt for guided paddles lasting from a few hours to several days, and there are plenty of classes available for those who are interested.

Moss Bay Rowing and Kayak Center, 1001 Fairview Ave. N. (☎ 206/682-2031) rents sea kayaks at the south end of Lake Union near Chandler's Cove. Rates range from $8 per hour for a single to $12 per hour for a double.

The **University of Washington Waterfront Activities Center,** on the university campus behind Husky Stadium (☎ 206/543-9433), is open to the public and rents canoes and rowboats for $5 per hour. With the marshes of the Washington Park Arboretum directly across a narrow channel from the boat launch, this is an ideal place for the inexperienced to rent a boat.

The **Center for Wooden Boats,** 1010 Valley St. (☎ 206/382-BOAT), a museum that rents classic boats, is at Waterway 4 at the south end of Lake Union. Dedicated to the preservation of historic wooden boats, the center is unique in that many exhibits can be rented and taken out on Lake Union. There are rowboats and large and small sailboats. Rates range from $15 to $38 per hour. Individual sailing instruction is also available. From June 1 to Labor Day, the center is open daily from 11am to 7pm; the rest of the year, Wednesday through Monday from noon to 6pm.

TENNIS   Seattle Parks and Recreation operates dozens of outdoor tennis courts all over the city. The most convenient are at **Volunteer Park,** 15th Ave. East and East Prospect St., and at **Lower Woodland Park,** West Green Lake Way North. If it happens to be raining and you had your heart set on playing tennis, there are indoor public courts at the **Seattle Tennis Center,** 2000 Martin Luther King Jr. Way S. (☎ 206/684-4764). Rates here are $14 for singles and $18 for doubles for 1¹/₄ hours. This center also has outdoor courts for $4 for 1¹/₂ hours.

8 Spectator Sports

With professional football, baseball, basketball, women's basketball, and ice hockey teams, as well as the various University of Washington Huskies teams, Seattle is obviously a city of sports fans. However, even sports fans have their limits, and the stadium battles of the past few years have tried the patience of both sports fans and Seattleites who couldn't care less who's in the National League playoffs or heading to the Super Bowl. First there was the partial collapse and restoration of the Kingdome roof, paid for by tax payers. Then the Mariners demanded a new stadium. Seattle voters said no they wouldn't pay for a new stadium, but the state legislature figured out a way to get the stadium built (and keep the Mariners in town) without

---

Treat Yourself

If you prefer being pampered to paddling a kayak, facials to fishing, or massages to mountain climbing, then you'll be glad to know that Seattle has plenty of day spas scattered around the metro area. These facilities offer such treatments as massages, facials, seaweed wraps, mud baths, and the like. Seattle day spas include **Aveda,** Alexis Hotel, 1015 First Ave. (☎ **206/628-9605**); **Le Salon Paul Morey,** Rainier Square Concourse, 1301 Fifth Ave. (☎ **206/624-4455**); **Marketplace Salon & Day Spa,** 2001 First Ave. (☎ **206/441-5511**); **Robert Leonard,** 2033 Sixth Ave. (☎ **206/441-9900**); and **Ummelina,** 1523 Sixth Ave. (☎ **206/624-1370**); and, over in Kirkland at Carillon Point, **Spa Csaba,** 1250 Carillon Point (☎ **206/803-9000**). At these spas, a wide variety of treatments is available. Expect to pay at least $150 for a half day of pampering and $300 or more for a full day.

---

raising Seattle property taxes. Then the owner of the Seahawks football team started talking about moving his team somewhere else because he didn't want to play in the Kingdome either. When Microsoft cofounder Paul Allen stepped in and offered to buy the Seahawks if the city would build a new stadium, the entire state got to vote on whether to build a separate football stadium. By a slim margin the citizens of Washington state voted to tax themselves so that they could keep the Seahawks in Seattle. As things now stand, the Kingdome will soon be torn down to make way for the new football stadium. The Seattle Supersonics basketball team, by the way, got a new arena (actually a renovated existing arena) with no controversy at all.

So, as it currently stands, in a few years there will be two new stadiums, one for baseball and one for football, standing side by side where the Kingdome now stands. And the Kingdome, alas, will be torn down. But, as they say, it ain't over till the fat lady sings, and it is likely that the latest stadium vote will be challenged in court.

TicketMaster (☎ **206/628-0888**) sells tickets to almost all sporting events in the Seattle area. If they're sold out, try **Pacific Northwest Ticket Service** (☎ **206/232-0150**).

BASEBALL   Of all of Seattle's major league sports teams, none is more popular than the American League's **Seattle Mariners** (☎ **206/628-9400**). The team would probably be almost as popular even without Ken Griffey Jr., but with this powerhouse hitter slamming in the home runs with astounding regularity, the team has developed a devoted following. For the time being (until their new stadium is completed) the Mariners play in the Kingdome. Ticket prices range from $5 to $22 and are usually fairly readily available. Expect these prices to go up when the new stadium is finally completed. Tickets are available at the Kingdome box office or through TicketMaster (☎ **206/622-HITS**). Parking is next to impossible in the Kingdome neighborhood, so plan to leave your car behind.

BASKETBALL   The NBA's **Seattle SuperSonics** (☎ **206/281-5800**) have been putting in good showings in the past few years, but haven't quite gotten their act together. They play in the completely remodeled and updated Key Arena in Seattle Center. Tickets are $8 to $60 and are available at the arena box office and through TicketMaster (☎ **206/628-0888**). Tickets can generally be had even on short notice.

With an instant following among women's basketball fans weaned on the University of Washington Huskies women's basketball team, the **Seattle Reign**

(☎ 206/285-5225), of the newly formed American Basketball League, was an instant hit in Seattle. The women of the Reign play ball at the Mercer Arena at Seattle Center. Tickets are available through TicketMaster and cost $8 to $35.

If not for the popularity of the University of Washington Huskies women's basketball team, Seattle might not have gotten a pro women's basketball team. For information on the women's and men's Huskies basketball games, contact University of Washington Sports (☎ 206/543-2200).

FOOTBALL With five bad seasons in a row, the NFL's **Seattle Seahawks** (☎ 206/827-9777) are the least loved of Seattle's pro ball teams. Nevertheless, the people of the state obviously didn't want to see the Seahawks leave town or they wouldn't have voted for a new stadium. Until the new stadium is built, they'll likely be playing in the Kingdome. Tickets, at $19 to $38. Parking in the Kingdome area is nearly impossible during games, so take the bus if you can.

Not surprisingly, the **University of Washington Huskies** (☎ 206/543-2200), who play in Husky Stadium on the university campus, have a more loyal following. Big games (Nebraska or Washington State) sell out as soon as tickets go on sale in the summer. Other games can sell out in advance, but there are usually obstructed-view tickets available on the day of the game. Ticket prices range from $28 to $30.

HOCKEY The Western Hockey League's **Seattle Thunderbirds** (☎ 206/448-PUCK) play at the Key Arena in Seattle Center. While Seattle isn't really a hockey town, the Thunderbirds have quite a following. Tickets are available by calling the above number or TicketMaster (☎ 206/628-0888).

HORSE RACING The new **Emerald Downs** (☎ 888/931-8400 or 206/288-7711) race track has brought horse racing and pari-mutuel betting back to the Seattle area after an absence of several years (since the closure of Longacres Race Track). This new, state-of-the-art track is in the city of Auburn off Wash. 167, which is reached from I-405 at the south end of Lake Washington. To reach the track, take the 15th Avenue NW exit. Admission prices range from $3 to $5.50. The season runs from March to September.

MARATHON The **Seattle Marathon** takes place in November. There's a runners' hot line in Seattle that you can call for more information on this and other races in the area (☎ 206/524-RUNS).

9 Seattle Shopping

As the largest U.S. city in the region, Seattle has always been where the Northwest shops. Nordstrom, Eddie Bauer, and REI (all of which were founded in Seattle) have become familiar to shoppers all across the country and these stores remain some of the busiest in the city. However, in the past few years as Seattle has developed a national reputation as a great place to put down roots, the retail face of the city has begun to change considerably.

National retailers have been taking over the storefronts of downtown Seattle, opening up flashy new stores, and cashing in on the city's newfound popularity. The names and merchandise at these stores are often familiar both from stores in other cities as well as from mail-order catalogs. Banana Republic, Nike, Levi Strauss, Ann Taylor, FAO Schwartz, Barney's New York, and others have stores in Seattle now, so if you forgot to pick up that dress in Chicago or those running shoes in New York, have no fear, you can find them here.

Seattle does, however, have one last bastion of local merchandising: Pike Place Market. Whether shopping is your passion or merely an activity in which you occasionally indulge, you should not miss this historic market, which is actually one of Seattle's top tourist attractions. Once the city's main produce market, this sprawling collection of buildings is today filled with hundreds of unusual shops, including quite a few produce vendors' stalls.

After tasting the bounties of the Northwest, it's hard to go back to Safeway, Sanka, and Chicken of the Sea. Sure you can get coffee, wine, and seafood where you live, but do a little food shopping in Seattle and you'll be tapping the source. Washington state wines, coffee from the original Starbucks, and fish that flies—these are a few of the culinary treats awaiting you here.

THE SHOPPING SCENE

Although Seattle is a city of neighborhoods, and even out in the 'hoods you'll find great little shops. Ground zero of the Seattle shopping scene is the **corner of Pine Street and Fifth Avenue.** Within one block of this intersection are two major department stores, Nordstrom and The Bon Marché, and an upscale urban shopping mall. Fanning out from this intersection both east and south are blocks of upscale shopping that over the past few years have begun to take on a very familiar look. Small local shops are rapidly being replaced by national and international boutiques and megastores. In this neighborhood you'll now find the Ann Taylor, Barney's New York, Niketown, the Original Levi's Store, the Warner Bros. Studio Store, Banana Republic, and FAO Schwartz. However, you'll also still find a few local stores in the neighborhood.

The city's main tourist shopping district is the **Pike Place Market** neighborhood where you'll find dozens of T-shirt and souvenir shops, as well as import shops and stores appealing to teenagers and 20-somethings. Pike Place Market itself is a fascinating warren of cubby holes that pass for shops. While produce usually isn't something you stock up on while on vacation, there are several market shops that sell ethnic cooking supplies that are not as perishable as say a dozen oysters or a geoduck clam. While you may never find anything here you really need, it's fun to look (at least that's what millions of Seattle visitors each year seem to think). Just west of Pike Place Market is the Seattle waterfront, where you'll find lots more gift and souvenir shops.

In the **Pioneer Square** area, Seattle's historic district, you'll find the city's greatest concentration of art galleries, some of which specialize in Native American art. This neighborhood also has several antique stores.

As the center of both the gay community and the city's youth culture, **Capitol Hill** has the most eclectic selection of shops in the city. Beads, imports, CDs, vintage clothing, politically-correct merchandise, and gay-oriented goods fill the shops along Broadway. The neighborhoods main shopping plaza is the Broadway Market, which has lots of small shops.

Even funkier than Capitol Hill, the **Fremont** neighborhood just north of Lake Union, has lots of retro stores selling vintage clothing, mid-century furniture and collectibles, and curious crafts. A couple of miles east of Fremont is the **Wallingford** neighborhood, which is anchored by an old schoolhouse that has been converted into a shopping arcade with interesting crafts, fashions, and gifts. The **University District,** also in north Seattle, has everything necessary to support a student population, but it also now has the upscale University Village shopping center, which has all sorts of upscale shops.

SHOPPING A TO Z

Hours   Shops in Seattle are generally open Monday through Saturday from 9 or 10am to 5 or 6pm, with shorter hours on Sunday. The major department stores usually stay open later on Friday evenings, and many shopping malls stay open until 9pm Monday through Saturday.

ANTIQUES & COLLECTIBLES

For an absolutely astounding selection of antiques, head north of Seattle to the town of Snohomish (near Everett),where you'll find more than 150 antiques shops.

Clarke & Clarke Tribal Arts. 524 First Ave. S. ☎ **206/447-7017.**

This small shop near the Kingdome specializes in tribal antiques and art from around the world. Antique silk Chinese robes, Japanese samurai swords, Africa wood carvings, masks from Oaxaca, Mexico, and Middle Eastern copper pots are just some of the items you'll find here.

The Crane Gallery. 100 W. Roy St. ☎ **206/622-7185.**

Chinese, Japanese, and Korean antiquities are the focus of this shop in the Queen Anne neighborhood, which prides itself on selling only the best pieces. Imperial Chinese porcelains, bronze statues of Buddhist deities, rosewood furniture, Japanese ceramics, netsukes, snuff bottles, and Chinese archaeological artifacts are just some of the quality antiques you'll find here. Some Southeast Asian and Indian objects are also available.

Honeychurch Antiques. 1008 James St. ☎ **206/622-1225.**

For high-quality Asian antiques, including Japanese wood-block prints, textiles, furniture, and ivory and wood carvings, few Seattle antiques stores can approach Honeychurch Antiques. Regular special exhibits give this shop the feel of a tiny museum. An annex, called **Glenn Richards/The Honeychurch Warehouse** (☎ **206/287-1877**), is located at 964 Denny Way and specializes in new and old architectural elements from Asia.

Laguna. 609 Second Ave. ☎ **206/682-6162.**

Twentieth-century art pottery is the specialty of this shop near Pioneer Square. Pieces by such mid-century pottery factories as Catalina, Roseville, Bauer, Weller, and Franciscan are stacked on the shelves here. Lots of dinnerware and vintage tiles.

Manifesto Vintage Posters. 2030 First Ave. ☎ **206/269-0898.**

This Belltown gallery specializes in vintage posters from around the world, and usually has more than 2,000 posters in stock. Subjects include travel, movies, and advertising. Posters aren't cheap, but even if you can't afford to buy, the shop is fun to visit.

ANTIQUE MALLS & FLEA MARKETS

The Downtown Antique Market. 2218 Western Ave. ☎ **206/448-6307.**

Housed in a turn-of-the-century warehouse three blocks north of Pike Place Market, this antique mall houses more than 80 dealers and a wide variety of antiques and collectibles.

Fremont Sunday Market. 600 N. 34th St. ☎ **206/282-5706.**

Crafts, imports, antiques, collectibles, fresh produce, and live music all combine to make this Seattle's second favorite public market (after Pike Place Market). The market is open from the end of April through Christmas.

Pioneer Square Antique Mall. 602 First Ave. ☎ **206/624-1164.**

This underground antiques mall is in the heart of Pioneer Square right beside the ticket booth for the Seattle Underground tour and contains 80 stalls selling all manner of antiques and collectibles. Lots of glass, old jewelry, and small collectibles.

ART GALLERIES

The Pioneer Square area has for many years been Seattle's main art gallery district, and although there are still quite a few galleries in the neighborhood, over the past few years many galleries have moved to other locations around the metropolitan area. Still, there are enough galleries left around Pioneer Square that anyone interested in art should be sure to wander around south of Yesler Way.

GENERAL ART GALLERIES

Carolyn Staley. 313 First Ave. S. ☎ **206/621-1888.**

A wide range of old prints, including a large collection of Japanese wood-block prints, are on view at this Pioneer Square gallery. Whatever your personal interest, you'll likely find something in the gallery's large collection to interest you.

Davidson Galleries. 313 Occidental Ave. S. ☎ **206/624-7684.**

Located in the heart of the Pioneer Square neighborhood, this gallery is divided into three different areas of focus—contemporary paintings and sculptures, often by Northwest artists; contemporary prints by American and European artists; and antique prints, some of which date from the 1500s.

Greg Kucera Gallery. 608 Second Ave. ☎ **206/624-0770.**

A low-key setting in the Pioneer Square area serves as one of Seattle's most reliably cutting-edge galleries in Seattle. Both emerging artists and those with international reputations find their way into this gallery, often in the same show.

Linda Cannon Gallery. 520 Second Ave. ☎ **206/233-0404.**

This gallery near Pioneer Square sells, among many other new works, older pieces by now-famous cartoonist Lynda Barry. Because these latter pieces are resales of works from early in Barry's career, you never know what you might find.

Lisa Harris Gallery. 1922 Pike Place. ☎ **206/443-3315.**

Landscapes and figurative works, by both expressionist and realist Northwest and West Coast artists, are a specialty of this gallery, which is located on the second floor of a building in Pike Place Market.

GLASS ART

Edge of Glass Gallery. 513 N. 36th St. ☎ **206/547-6551.**

Located in the Fremont district, this gallery doubles as a studio. There are glass-blowing demonstrations Thursday through Sunday afternoons.

Foster/White Gallery. 311^1/$_2$ Occidental Ave. S. ☎ **206/622-2833.**

If you are enamored of art glass, as we are, be sure to stop by one or all of the three Foster/White galleries. These galleries represent Dale Chihuly in Seattle and always have a few works by this master glass artist for sale. Some of Chihuly's pieces even sell for less than $10,000! Other glass artists who have trained at the Pilchuck School of Glass are also represented.

Another Foster/White Gallery is located in the City Centre shopping mall, 1420 Fifth Ave. (☎ **206/340-8025**), and a third is in Kirkland at 126 Central Way (☎ **206/822-2305**).

The Glass Eye. 1902 Post Alley, Pike Place Market. ☎ **206/441-3221.**

The Glass Eye is one of Seattle's oldest art-glass galleries and specializes in glass made from Mount St. Helens' ash. These hand-blown pieces all contain ash from the volcano's 1980 eruption. Works by artists from around the country are available and many pieces are small enough to carry home.

Vetri. 1408 First Ave. ☎ **206/667-9608.**

With a wide variety of art glass by dozens of artists, some of whom have studied at the Pilchuck School, this gallery is riotously colorful and will give you a good idea of the broad spectrum of work being created by contemporary glass artists. They also represent William Morris, whose works have the look of ancient artifacts.

NATIVE AMERICAN ART

Flury & Company. 322 First Ave. S. ☎ **206/587-0260.**

This Pioneer Square gallery specializes in prints by photographer Edward S. Curtis, who is known for his portraits of Native Americans. The gallery also has an excellent selection of antique Native American Art.

✪ **The Legacy.** 1003 First Ave. ☎ **800/729-1562** or 206/624-6350.

The Legacy is Seattle's oldest and finest gallery of contemporary and historic Northwest Coast Indian and Alaskan Eskimo art and artifacts. You'll find a large selection of masks, boxes, bowls, baskets, ivory artifacts, jewelry, prints, and books. For the serious collector.

Northwest Tribal Art. 1417 First Ave. ☎ **206/467-9330.**

Located next to Pike Place Market, this is one of Seattle's most important galleries selling Northwest Coast Indian and American Eskimo art. Traditional and contemporary wood carvings, masks, fossilized ivory carvings, soapstone carvings, scrimshaw, jewelry, drums, and even totem poles are available.

Stonington Gallery. 2030 First Ave. ☎ **206/443-6580.**

This is one of Seattle's top galleries specializing in contemporary Native American art and crafts. Here you'll find a good selection of Northwest Coast Indian masks, totem poles, mixed-media pieces, prints, and carvings. There is also a good selection of books about Northwest Native American art.

BOOKS

Bowie & Company Booksellers. 314 First Ave. S. ☎ **206/624-4100.**

Located in the Pioneer Square area, this bookstore specializes in old, rare, out-of-print, and hard-to-find books. Lots of signed editions in stock. A recent catalog listed such books as a 1945 edition of *The Oregon Trail* (illustrated and signed by Thomas Hart Benton; $150), a 1921 *The Boy's Life of Edison* (signed by Thomas Edison; $1,450), and a first edition of Tom Robbins's *Another Roadside Attraction* ($150). Books on cooking are a specialty here.

Elliott Bay Book Company. 101 S. Main St. ☎ **206/624-6600.**

With battered wooden floors and a maze of rooms full of books, this is the bookstore of choice for Seattle book lovers. There's an excellent selection of books on Seattle and the Northwest, so if you want to learn more or are planning further excursions around the region, stop by. The store is located just south of Pioneer Square.

Shorey's Book Store. 1109 N. 36th St. ☎ **206/633-2990.**

Shorey's has been in business since 1890, and will be happy to find you books from the year they opened (or any other year for that matter). Rare, antiquarian, and out-of-print books are their specialty. With more than a million items in stock, Shorey's is sure to have that obscure tome you've been seeking for years. If they don't have it, they'll search the world to find it for you. The store's motto is "The oldest, the biggest, the best!" You'll find the store north of Lake Union to the east of Fremont off Stone Way.

COFFEE

All over the city, almost every corner, you'll find espresso bars, cafes, and coffeehouses, and while you can get coffee back home, you just might want to pick up some of whichever local coffee turns out to be your personal favorite. If you are a latte junkie, you might want to make a pilgrimage to the shop that started it all.

✪ **Starbucks.** Pike Place Market, 1912 Pike Place. ☎ **206/448-8762.**

Seattle has developed a reputation as a city of coffeeholics, and Starbucks is one reason why. This company has coffeehouses all over town, but this is the original. With some 36 types of coffee available by the cup or by the pound, you can do a bit of taste testing before making a decision.

CRAFTS

The Northwest is a leading center for craftspeople, and one of the places to see what they are creating is Pike Place Market. Although there are quite a few permanent shops within the market that sell local crafts, you can meet the artisans themselves on weekends when they set up tables on the main floor.

Crackerjack Contemporary Crafts. Wallingford Center, 1815 N. 45th Ave. ☎ **206/547-4983.**

With colorful and imaginative crafts by more than 250 artists from around the country, this shop in the eclectic Wallingford Center shopping arcade (an old schoolhouse) is a great place to check for something interesting and unique to bring home from a trip to Seattle.

✪ **Fireworks Fine Crafts Gallery.** 210 First Ave. S. ☎ **206/682-8707.**

Playful, outrageous, bizarre, beautiful—these are just some of the terms that can be used to describe the eclectic collection of Northwest crafts on sale at this Pioneer Square–area gallery. Cosmic clocks, wildly creative jewelry, and artistic picture frames are some of the fine and unusual items you'll find here. Other stores are at Westlake Center, 400 Pine St. (☎206/682-6462); Belleuve Square, Bellevue Way, Bellevue (☎ **425/688-0933**); and the University Village shopping plaza in the University District at the junction of Montlake Blvd. NE and NE 45th Street. (☎ **206/527-2858**).

John Page Pottery/Page and Thorbeck Studio. 604 N. 34th St. ☎ **206/632-6178.**

Billing themselves as the potters to the stores, the owners of this Fremont pottery studio and retail shop specialize in dinnerware with classic Western ranch motifs. Clients have included Oprah Winfrey, Robin Williams, and Darryl Hannah. You can pick up a single piece of pottery or commission an entire set of dishes.

✪ **Northwest Fine Woodworking.** 101 S. Jackson St. ☎ **206/625-0542.**

This store is a showcase for some of the most amazing woodworking you'll ever see. Be sure to stroll through here while in the Pioneer Square area. The warm hues of the exotic woods are soothing and the designs are beautiful. Furniture, boxes, sculptures, vases, bowls, and much more are created by more than 35 Northwest artisans. A second shop is at 122 Central Way, Kirkland (☎ **206/889-1513**).

DEPARTMENT STORES

The Bon Marché. Third Ave. and Pine St. ☎ **206/506-6000.**

Seattle's other department store is every bit as well-stocked as next-door neighbor Nordstrom and with such competition in the neighborhood tries every bit as hard to keep its customers happy. You'll find nearly anything you could possibly want at this store.

✪ **Nordstrom.** 1501 Fifth Ave. ☎ **206/628-2111.**

Known for personal service, Nordstrom stores have gained a reputation for being among the premier department stores in the United States. The company originated here in Seattle (opening its first store in 1901), and its customers are devotedly loyal. Whether it's your first visit or your 50th, the knowledgeable staff will help you in any way they can. Prices are comparable to those at other department stores, but you also get the best service available. There are very popular sales in January (for men), June (for women and children), July (for men and women), and November (for women and children). In August 1998, a Nordstrom is scheduled to open at 500 Pine Street in what used to be the Frederick & Nelson department store. There are other Nordstroms at area shopping malls.

DISCOUNT SHOPPING

✪ **The Rack.** 1601 Second Ave. ☎ **206/448-8522.**

This is the Nordstrom overflow shop where you'll find discontinued lines as well as overstock, and all at greatly reduced prices. Women's fashions make up the bulk of the merchandise here.

SuperMall. 1101 SuperMall Way. ☎ **800/SAY-VALU** or 206/833-9500.

Sort of the outlet mall to end all outlet malls, SuperMall has upper-end fashion outlets including Nordstrom Rack, Off 5th–Saks Fifth Avenue Outlet, Eddie Bauer Outlet, and Ann Taylor Loft. In 1997, they were even offering a free bus shuttle from downtown Seattle, so if you need a ride, call and see if they're still offering this deal.

FASHION

In addition to the stores listed below, you'll find quite a few familiar names in downtown Seattle.

Eddie Bauer. Fifth Ave. and Union St. ☎ **206/622-2766.**

Eddie Bauer got his start here in Seattle back in 1922 and today is one of the country's foremost purveyors of upscale outdoor fashions. A visit to this store is a must for anyone who likes the Eddie Bauer look. Other Eddie Bauer stores can be found at Bellevue Square mall, University Village mall, Northgate mall, and Southcenter mall.

Niketown. 1500 Sixth Ave. ☎ **206/447-6543.**

Around the country, there are currently eight Niketowns selling all things Nike and only things Nike. If you don't live near one of these high-tech megastores and you do wear swooshes, then this store should definitely be on your shopping itinerary, even if you aren't in the market for a new pair of basketball shoes.

Mario's. 1513 Sixth Ave. ☎ **206/223-1461.**

If you happen to be able to spend $300 for a shirt, then you'll want to be sure to visit this top-of-the-line clothing store while you're in town. Mario's sells both men's and women's fashions, with Giorgio Armani and Calvin Klein well represented.

Seattle Pendleton. 1313 Fourth Ave. ☎ **206/682-4430.**

For northwesterners, and many other people across the nation, Pendleton is and always will be the name in classic wool fashions. This store features tartan plaids and Indian-pattern separates, accessories, and blankets. Other Pendleton stores are at Southcenter Mall, Bellevue Square, and Tacoma Mall.

CLOTHING

Men's

The Forum. 95 Pine St. ☎ **206/624-4566.**

Located in the Pike Place Market neighborhood, The Forum features sophisticated fashions from the likes of Perry Ellis, Girbaud, and Robert Comstock. A second store is in Bellevue Square mall.

Women's

Ardour. 1115 First Ave. ☎ **206/292-0660.**

The fashions here are romantic without being fussy and are something of a cross between the Seattle and the Paris looks. There are lots of soft, natural-looking fabrics and handmade sweaters. There are also shoes, jewelry, and other accessories. You can put together a very nice ensemble here, though it won't be cheap.

Baby & Co. 1936 First Ave. ☎ **206/448-4077.**

Claiming stores in Seattle and on Mars, this up-to-the-minute store stocks fashions that can be trendy, outrageous, or out of this world. Whether you're into earth tones or bright colors, you'll likely find something you can't live without.

Local Brilliance. 1535 First Ave. ☎ **206/343-5864.**

This shop carries a wide selection of casual and fun fashions by designers from around the Northwest and the rest of the country. Fashions here will appeal to a wide range of age groups, and there are also artist-designed hats and jewelry.

Passport. 123 Pine St. ☎ **206/628-9799.**

Soft and easy-going styles are the current style at this large store near Pike Place Market. Velvet, cotton, rayon, and natural fibers are the fabrics of choice here.

✪ Ragazzi's Flying Shuttle. 607 First Ave. ☎ **206/343-9762.**

Fashion becomes art and art becomes fashion at this chic boutique-cum-gallery on Pioneer Square. Hand-woven fabrics and hand-painted silks are the specialties here, but of course such sophisticated fashions require equally unique body decorations in the form of exquisite jewelry creations. Designers and artists from the Northwest and the rest of the nation find an outlet for their creativity at the Flying Shuttle.

GIFTS/SOUVENIRS

Pike Place Market is the Grand Central Station of Seattle souvenirs, with stiff competition from Seattle Center and Pioneer Square.

Made in Washington. Pike Place Market (Post Alley at Pine St.). ☎ **206/467-0788.**

Whether it's salmon, wine, or Northwest crafts, you'll find a selection of Washington State products in this shop, which is an excellent place to pick up gifts for all those who didn't get to come with you on your visit to Seattle. Other Made in Washington locations include Westlake Center (☎ **206/623-9753**); Bellevue Square, Bellevue (☎ **206/454-6907**); Gilman Village, Issaquah (☎ **206/392-4819**); and Northgate Shopping Center (☎ **206/361-8252**).

Ruby Montana's Pinto Pony. 603 Second Ave. ☎ **206/621-PONY.**

Definitely not your run-of-the-mill souvenir shop, Ruby Montana's bills itself as the "Outfitters for the Cosmic Cowpoke." Retro-kitsch is the name of the game at this Pioneer Square–area shop, with wind-up robots, pig lights to hang from your Christmas tree, wacky salt-and-pepper shakers, Betty Boop stuff, lava lamps, pink flamingos, and, yes, even some cowboy motif items.

JEWELRY

Fox's Gem Shop. 1341 Fifth Ave. % 206/623-2528.

This is Seattle's premier jeweler, and among other elegant lines, they feature the Tiffany Collection. Displays here, including an 11,000-year-old mastodon skeleton, make shopping here a bit like visiting a museum.

MALLS/SHOPPING CENTERS

Bellevue Square. Bellevue Way and NE 8th Ave., Bellevue. ☎ **206/454-2431.**

Over in Bellevue, on the east side of Lake Washington, you'll find one of the area's largest shopping malls, with more than 200 stores. There's even an art museum, the Bellevue Art Museum, here in the mall.

Broadway Market. 401 Broadway E. ☎ **206/322-1610.**

Located in the stylish Capitol Hill neighborhood, the Broadway Market is a trendy little shopping center with a decidedly urban neighborhood feel. The mall houses numerous small shops and restaurants with reasonable prices.

City Centre. Sixth Ave. and Union St. ☎ **206/223-8999.**

This upscale downtown shopping center is the Seattle address of such familiar high-end retailers as Barneys New York, Benetton, FAO Schwartz, and Ann Taylor. There is also a Foster/White Gallery selling works by Dale Chihuly and other Northwest glass artists, and works of art by these and other glass artists are on display throughout City Centre. Bernard C. chocolaterie is also here, and there is a very comfortable lounge where you can rest your feet out of the Seattle weather.

Westlake Center. 400 Pine St. ☎ **206/467-1600.**

This is Seattle's premier downtown, upscale, urban shopping mall and is in the heart of Seattle's main shopping district. Under this roof are more than 80 specialty shops, including Godiva Chocolatier, Cache, Victoria's Secret, The Limited, and Made in Washington. Tehre's also an extensive food court here. This mall is also the southern terminus for the monorail to Seattle Center.

MARKETS

✪ Pike Place Market. Pike St. and First Ave. ☎ **206/682-7453.**

Pike Place Market is one of Seattle's most famous landmarks and tourist attractions. Not only are there produce vendors, fishmongers, and butchers, but also artists, craftspeople, and performers. There are also hundreds of shops and dozens of restaurants (including some of Seattle's best) tucked away in hidden nooks and crannies on the numerous levels of the market. With so much to see and do, a trip to the market can easily turn into an all-day affair.

Uwajimaya. 519 Sixth Ave. S. ☎ **206/624-6248.**

Typically, your local neighborhood supermarket has a section of Chinese cooking ingredients; it's probably about 10 feet long, with half that space taken up by various brands of soy sauce. Now imagine your local supermarket with nothing but Asian foods, housewares, produce, and toys. That's Uwajimaya, Seattle's Asian supermarket in the heart of the International District.

RECREATIONAL GEAR

The North Face. 1023 First Ave. ☎ **206/622-4111.**

The North Face is one of the country's best-known names in the field of outdoor gear, and here in their downtown shop, you can choose from their diverse selection.

Patagonia Seattle. 2100 First Ave. ☎ **206/622-9700.**

Patagonia has built up a very loyal clientele based on the durability of its outdoor gear and clothing. Sure the prices are high, but these clothes are built to last.

REI. 222 Yale Ave. N. ☎ **206/223-1944.**

Recreational Equipment, Incorporated (REI) was founded here in Seattle back in 1938 and today is the nation's largest co-op selling outdoor gear. In 1996, REI opened an awesome flagship store just off I-5 not far from Lake Union. The store, a cross between a high-tech warehouse and a mountain lodge is massive and houses not only anything you could ever need for pursuing your favorite outdoor sport, but also has a 65-foot climbing pinnacle, a rain room for testing rain gear, a mountain-bike trail for test driving bikes, a footwear test trail, even a kids' play area. With all this under one roof, who needs to go outside?

SALMON

If you think the fish at Pike Place Market looks great, but you could never get it home on the plane, think again. Any of the seafood vendors in Pike Place Market will pack your fresh salmon or Dungeness crab in an airline-approved container that will keep it fresh for up to 48 hours. Alternatively, you can buy vacuum-packed smoked salmon that will keep for years without refrigeration.

✪ **Pike Place Fish.** 86 Pike Place, Pike Place Market. ☎ **800/542-7732** or 206/682-7181.

Located just behind Rachel, the life-sized bronze pig, this fishmonger is famous for flying fish. Pick out a big silvery salmon, ask them to fillet it, and watch the show. They'll also deliver your packaged order to your hotel, ready to carry onto your plane.

Port Chatham Smoked Seafood. Rainier Square, 1310 Fourth Ave. ☎ **800/872-5666** or 206/623-4645.

Northwest Coast Indians relied heavily on salmon for sustenance, and to preserve the fish they used alder-wood smoke. This tradition is still carried on today to produce one of the Northwest's most delicious food products. This store sells smoked sockeye, king salmon, rainbow trout, and oysters—all of which will keep without refrigeration until the package is opened.

Other stores are in Bellevue Square mall and Southcenter mall.

Totem Smokehouse. Pike Place Market, 1906 Pike Place ☎ **800/972-5666** or 206/443-1710.

Located at street level in Pike Place Market, this is another good source of vacuum-packed smoked salmon, and while prices aren't cheap, it sure is tasty fish.

TOYS

Archie McPhee. 3510 Stone Way N. ☎ **206/545-8344.**

You may already be familiar with this temple of the absurd through its mail-order catalog. Now imagine wandering through aisles full of goofy gags. Give yourself plenty of time and take a friend.

✪ **Magic Mouse.** 603 First Ave. ☎ **206/682-8097.**

Adults and children alike have a hard time pulling themselves away from this, the funnest toy store in Seattle. It is conveniently located on Pioneer Square and has a good selection of European toys.

Wood Shop Toys. 320 First Ave. S. ☎ **206/624-1763.**

Just two blocks away from Magic Mouse is another Seattle favorite, this one selling wooden toys, puppets, and lots of nostalgia toys that will appeal to adults as much as they appeal to kids. This place is worth a look even if you're not in the market for toys.

WINE

The Northwest is rapidly becoming known as a producer of fine wine. The relatively dry summer with warm days and cool nights provides a perfect climate for growing grapes. After you have sampled Washington or Oregon vintages, you might want to take a few bottles home.

Pike & Western Wine Merchants. 1934 Pike Place, Pike Place Market. ☎ **206/441-1307.**

Visit this shop for an excellent selection of Washington and Oregon wines, as well as those from California, Italy, and France. The extremely knowledgeable staff will be happy to send you home with the very best wine available in Seattle.

10 Seattle After Dark

Though Seattleites spend much of their free time enjoying the city's natural surroundings, they have not overlooked the more cultured evening pursuits. In fact, winter weather that keeps people indoors and a long-time desire to be the cultural mecca of the Northwest have fueled a surprisingly active and diverse nightlife here. In recent years, Seattle has become something of an arts mecca. The Seattle Opera is ranked one of the top operas in the country and its stagings of Wagner's Ring series have achieved near-legendary status. The Seattle Symphony also receives accolades, and the Seattle Repertory Theatre has received Tony awards for its productions. There are more equity theaters in Seattle than in any U.S. city other than New York, and a thriving fringe theater keeps the city's lovers of avant-garde theater contentedly discoursing in cafes about the latest hysterical or thought-provoking performances. Music lovers will also find a plethora of classical, jazz, and rock music offerings.

The biggest news on the Seattle performing arts scene is the construction of the new Benaroya Hall performing arts center downtown adjacent to the Seattle Art Museum. This state-of-the-art performance hall will serve as home for the Seattle Symphony and Seattle Opera and will move classical music performances back downtown from the Seattle Center Opera House. Benaroya Hall is scheduled to open in 1998.

Much of the evening entertainment is clustered in the Seattle Center and Pioneer Square areas, with the former hosting theater, opera, and classical music performances and the latter being a nightclub district. The Belltown area north of Pike Place Market also has quite a few bars and nightclubs and a few alternative performance spaces.

While winters are a time for enjoying the performing arts, summers are a time of outdoor festivals, and while these take place during daylight hours as much as they do after dark, you'll find information on these festivals and performance series in this chapter.

For half-price, day-of-show tickets to a wide variety of performances all over the city, stop by **Ticket/Ticket** (☎ 206/324-2744), which has two sales booths—one in Pike Place Market and one on Capitol Hill. The Pike Place Market location, First

Avenue and Pike Street, is open Tuesday through Sunday from noon to 6pm. The other booth is on the second floor of the Broadway Market, 401 Broadway E., and is open Tuesday through Saturday from 10am to 7pm and Sunday from noon to 6pm. Ticket/Ticket levies a service charge of 50¢ to $3 depending on the ticket price. If you want to pay full price with your credit card, call **TicketMaster Northwest** (☎ **206/292-ARTS** or 206/628-0888).

To find out what's going on when you are in town, pick up a free copy of *Seattle Weekly*, which is Seattle's weekly arts-and-entertainment newspaper. You'll find it in bookstores, convenience stores, grocery stores, newsstands, and other places around the city. On Friday, the *Seattle Times* includes a section called "Tempo," which is a guide to the week's arts and entertainment offerings.

THE PERFORMING ARTS

Although a new downtown symphony hall was under construction at press time, the main venues for the performing arts in Seattle are still primarily clustered in Seattle Center, the special events complex that was built for the 1962 Seattle world's fair. Here, in the shadow of the Space Needle, you'll find the Opera House, Bagley Wright Theater, Intiman Playhouse, Seattle Children's Theatre, Seattle Center Coliseum, and Memorial Stadium.

OPERA & CLASSICAL MUSIC

The **Seattle Opera** (☎ 206/389-7676), which currently performs at the Seattle Center Opera House but which will move to the new Benaroya Hall when it opens in 1998, is considered one of the finest opera companies in the country and is *the* Wagnerian opera company. The stagings of Wagner's four-opera *The Ring of the Nibelungen* are breathtaking spectacles that draw crowds from around the country. In addition to classical operas, the season usually includes a more contemporary musical. Ticket prices range from $30 to $97.

Each year under the baton of Gerard Schwarz, the **Seattle Symphony** (☎ 206/215-4747), which also performs at the Seattle Center Opera House and will later move to Benaroya Hall, offers an amazingly diverse musical season that runs from September to May. There are evenings of classical, light classical, and pops, plus morning concerts, children's concerts, guest artists, and much more. Ticket prices range from $8 to $65.

The **Northwest Chamber Orchestra** (☎ 206/343-0445), a perennial favorite with Seattle classical music fans, is a showcase for Northwest performers. The annual Baroque Festival in the autumn is the highlight of the season, which runs from September to April. Performances are held primarily in Kane Hall on the University of Washington campus, although there is also a series of concerts at the Seattle Art Museum. Ticket prices range from $18 to $25.

Other classical music companies to keep an eye and ear out for while in town include the **Bellevue Philharmonic Orchestra** (☎ 425/455-4171), the **Early Music Guild** (☎ 206/325-7066), and **Philharmonia Northwest** (☎ 206/392-7694).

THEATER

Mainstream Theaters

The **Seattle Repertory Theater** (☎ 206/443-2222), which performs at the Bagley Wright Theater, Seattle Center, 155 Mercer St., has been around for more than 30 years and as Seattle's top professional theater, stages the most consistently entertaining productions in the city. In 1997, the Rep cranked up its reputation another two notches with the addition of the new Leo K. Theatre and the hiring of Sharon Ott right after she won a Tony for leading the Berkeley Rep to become the best regional theater in the country. Expect lots of good things to come out of these additions. The season here runs from October to May with six plays performed in the main theater and three more in the more intimate Leo K. Theatre. Productions range from classics to world premieres to Broadway musicals. Ticket prices range from $10 to $40.

With a season that runs from May to October, the **Intiman Theatre Company** ☎ 206/269-1900), which performs at the Intiman Playhouse, Seattle Center, 201 Mercer St., picks up where the Seattle Rep leaves off, effectively filling in the gap left by those months when the Seattle Rep's lights are dark. The fact that the two theaters are side by side at Seattle Center makeps it easy to remember where to head to on performance nights. Ticket prices range from $18.50 to $31; $10 for standing room only.

Performing in the historic Eagles Building theater adjacent to and accessed from the Washington State Convention and Trade Center, **A Contemporary Theater (ACT),** 700 Union St. (☎ 206/292-7676), offers slightly more adventurous productions than the other major theater companies in Seattle. However, it is not nearly as avant-garde as some of the smaller companies. The season runs from the end of April to mid-November. Ticket prices range from $16.25 to $30.50.

Located on the shore of Green Lake in north Seattle, **The Bathhouse Theatre,** 7312 W. Green Lake Way N. (☎ 206/524-9108), is known for its revivals of classic musicals and stagings of old radio revues. Ticket prices range from $12.60 to $25.

Fringe Theaters

With such a burgeoning mainstream performing-arts community, it is not at all surprising that Seattle has also developed the sort of fringe theater life once only associated with such cities as New York, London, and Edinburgh. The city's more avant-garde performance companies have been grabbing their share of the limelight with daring, outrageous, and thought-provoking productions.

A perusal of a few local entertainment publications recently turned up the following fringe theater performances (all taking place in the same two-week period): *The Shadow of Drek* (which included a *Star Trek* send-up), *Lucky Stiff* (a musical about a Monte Carlo competition for $6 million), *Wuthering! Heights! The! Musical!* (a spoof of small-town musicals), *The whY Files* (a parody of the hit TV show), *Lady Chatterly's Lover,* and *The Return of the Sirens of Swing* (a cabaret piece about three singing sisters).

Seattle's newfound interest in fringe theater finds its greatest expression each spring, when the **Seattle Fringe Theater Festival** (☎ 206/320-9588), a showcase for small, self-producing theater companies, takes over various Capitol Hill venues. There are usually performances by more than 70 theater groups from around the country.

Even if you don't happen to be in town for Seattle's annual fringe binge, check out the following venues for way-off Broadway productions, performance art, poetry jams, and spoken word performances:

- **Annex Theater,** 1916 Fourth Ave. (☎ 206/728-0933)—thought-provoking dramas and comedies, cabaret theater.
- **Book-It Theater,** 1219 Westlake Ave., Suite 301. (☎ 206/216-0833)—works by local playwrights.
- **Empty Space Theatre,** 3509 Fremont Ave. N. (☎ 206/547-7500)—mostly comedy, popular with a young crowd.
- **The Group Theater,** Seattle Center House, 305 Harrison St. (☎ 206/441-1299)—multicultural theater.
- **New City Theater,** 1634 11th Ave. (☎ 206/323-6800)—performance art, works by local playwrights.

- **Northwest Asian-American Theater,** Theatre Off Jackson, 409 Seventh Ave. S. (☎ 206/340-1049)—works by Asian American writers, actors, and musicians.
- **Theater Schmeater,** 1500 Summit St. (☎ **206/324-5801**)—best known for its stage adaptations of *The Twilight Zone* episodes.
- **Velvet Elvis Arts Lounge Theatre,** 107 Occidental Ave. S. ☎ **206/624-8477**)—performance art, poetry nights, alternative video productions, jazz.

Children's Theater

If it's a rainy day and you'd like to keep the kids entertained for a couple of hours, there are a couple of excellent options in downtown Seattle. The **Seattle Children's Theatre,** Charlotte Martin Theatre at Seattle Center, Second Ave. N. and Thomas St. (☎ **206/441-3322**), stages both entertaining classics and thought-provoking dramas. Shows appeal to children of different ages, so call to see what's being staged (tickets $11.50 to $17.50). Drawing on international themes and traditional tales from around the world, the innovative **Northwest Puppet Center,** 9123 15th Ave. NE. (☎ **206/523-2579**), stages performances that will appeal to adults as well as children. Puppet companies from around the world perform throughout the year. There is also a puppet museum here (tickets $7.50 adults, $5.50 children).

DANCE

Although Seattle has a well-regarded ballet company and a theater dedicated to contemporary dance and performance art, Seattle is not nearly as devoted to dance as it is the theater and classical music. However, this said, there is hardly a week that goes by without some sort of dance performance being staged somewhere in the city. Touring companies of all types, the University of Washington Dance Department faculty and student performances, UW World Dance series (see below for details), and the Northwest New Works Festival (see below for details) each spring all bring plenty of creative movement to the stages of Seattle. When you're in town, check *Seattle Weekly* or the *Seattle Times* for a calendar of upcoming performances.

The **Pacific Northwest Ballet,** Seattle Center Opera House, 321 Mercer St. (☎ **206/441-2424** for information, or 206/292-ARTS for tickets), is Seattle's premier dance company. During the season, which runs from September to June, the company presents a wide range of classics, new works, and (the company's specialty) pieces choreographed by George Balanchine (tickets $14–$69). If you happen to be in Seattle in December, try to get a ticket to this company's performance of *Nutcracker.* In addition to outstanding dancing, you'll enjoy sets and costumes by children's book author Maurice Sendak.

Much more adventurous choreography is the domain of **On the Boards,** 153 14th Ave. (☎ **206/325-7901**), which, although it stages a wide variety of performance art, is best known as Seattle's premier modern-dance venue (tickets $8 to $22). In addition to dance performances by Northwest artists, there are a variety of productions each year by internationally known artists. The Northwest New Works Festival, a barrage of contemporary dance and performance art held every spring, is the season's highlight.

MAJOR PERFORMANCE HALLS

With ticket prices for shows and concerts as high as they are these days, it pays to be choosy about what you see, but sometimes where you see it is just as important. Seattle has two restored historic theaters that are as much a part of a performance as what goes on up on the stage.

The **5th Avenue Theatre,** 1308 Fifth Ave. (☎ **206/625-1418**), which first opened its doors in 1926 as a vaudeville house, is a loose re-creation of the imperial throne room in Beijing's Forbidden City. In 1980, the theater underwent a complete renovation that restored this Seattle jewel to its original splendor, and today the astounding interior is as good a reason as any to see a show here. Don't miss an opportunity to attend a performance here. Broadway shows are the theater's mainstay (tickets $20 to $65).

The **Paramount Theatre,** Pine St. and Ninth Ave. (☎ **206/682-1414**), one of Seattle's few historic theaters, has been restored to its original beauty and today shines with all the brilliance it did when it first opened. New lighting and sound systems have brought the theater up to contemporary standards. The theater stages everything from rock concerts to Broadway musicals (tickets $20 to $65).

PERFORMING ARTS SERIES

When Seattle's own resident performing arts companies aren't taking to the dozens of stages around the city, various touring companies from around the world are. If you're a fan of Broadway shows, check the calendars at the Paramount Theatre and the 5th Avenue Theatre, both of which regularly serve as Seattle stops for touring shows.

The **International Music Festival of Seattle,** P.O. Box 2166, Seattle, WA 98111-2166 (☎ **206/233-0993**), usually held in late June and early July, is a classical music series focusing primarily on chamber music. Performances are held at Meany Hall, the Seattle Art Museum, and the Meydenbauer Center in Bellevue (tickets $23 to $24).

The **UW World Series** (☎ **206/543-4880**), held at Meany Hall on the University of Washington campus, is actually several different series including a chamber music series, a classical piano series, a world dance series, and a world music and theater series. Together these four series keep the Meany Hall stage busy between October and April. Special events are also scheduled. Tickets are $21 to $40.

Seattle loves the theater and each spring, the city binges on the fringes with the **Seattle Fringe Theater Festival** (see Fringe Theaters earlier in this chapter for details).

Summer is a time of outdoor festivals and performance series in Seattle, and should you be in town during the sunny months, you'll have a wide variety of al fresco performances from which to choose. The city's biggest summer music festivals are the Northwest Folklife Festival over Memorial Day weekend and Bumbershoot over Labor Day weekend. See section 3 of chapter 2 for details.

THE CLUB & MUSIC SCENE

If you have the urge to do a bit of nightclubbing and barhopping while in Seattle, there's no better place to start than in Pioneer Square. Good times are guaranteed whether you want to hear a live band, hang out in a good old-fashioned bar, or dance. The Belltown neighborhood, north of Pike Place Market is another good place to stumble from one club to the next, although here you'll get a bit more exercise and cover a few more blocks.

FOLK, COUNTRY & ROCK

While the distinctive Seattle sound has lost its hold on the American consciousness, Seattle is still a lively city if you're into rock 'n' roll. Currently, as elsewhere in the country, lounge music and 1970s nostalgia are all the rage. Martinis are being sipped as much as microbrews are being quaffed, and Frank Sinatra wannabes are showing up in clubs all over town.

The Pioneer Square area is Seattle's main live music neighborhood (almost everything but classical) and the clubs have banded together to make things easy on music fans. The "Joint Cover" plan lets you pay one admission to get into 10 or so clubs.

The charge is $5 on weeknights and $8 on weekends (occasionally $12 for national-act nights). Participating clubs currently include The Fenix/Fenix Underground, Doc Maynard's, The Central Saloon, Colourbox, The Bohemian Cafe, and a few other night spots. Most of these clubs are short on style and hit-or-miss when it comes to music (which makes the joint cover a great way to find out where the good music is on any given night).

A few noteworthy Pioneer Square clubs include **The Central Saloon,** 207 First Ave. S. (☎ **206/622-0209**), which was established in 1892 and is the oldest saloon in Seattle; **Doc Maynard's,** 610 First Ave. (☎ **206/682-4649**), which by day is the starting point of the family-oriented Underground Tour; and **Fenix/Fenix Underground,** 315 and 323 Second Ave. (☎ **206/467-1111**), two clubs that together book what usually is the best music in Pioneer Square.

✪ **The Backstage.** 2208 NW Market St. ☎ **206/781-2805.** Cover $6–$20.

This is Seattle's top venue for contemporary music of all kinds and packs in the crowds most nights. The audience ranges from drinking age up to graying rock 'n' rollers. The music runs the gamut from Afro pop to zydeco, with lots of national acts, both new and old hitting the stage.

Ballard Firehouse. 5429 Russell St. ☎ **206/784-3516.** Cover $3–$20.

A similarly eclectic assortment of musical styles finds its way onto the bandstand of this converted firehouse in the old Scandinavian neighborhood of northwest Seattle. Now it's just the music that's hot, and that's the way they want to keep it. Performers run the gamut from the up-and-coming to revival bands back on tour to cash in on 1970s nostalgia. People having dinner here get the best tables.

Crocodile. 2200 Second Ave. ☎ **206/728-0316.** Cover $2–$9.

With its rambunctious, wild decor, this Belltown establishment is a combination nightclub, bar, and restaurant. There's live rock Tuesday through Sunday nights; and the music calendar is an eclectic mix of everything from rock to folk to jazz. In the summer of 1997, the Crocodile staged Lounge-a-Palooza I with lots of lounge acts crooning for the lounge lizards.

Showbox. 1426 First Ave. ☎ **206/628-3151.**

Located across the street from Pike Place Market, this club used to be a comedy venue but has been booking a lot of name rock acts lately. You never know who might be playing here; maybe Rickie Lee Jones, maybe George Clinton, maybe Better than Ezra. Definitely *the* downtown rock venue for performers with a national following.

JAZZ & BLUES

✪ **Dimitriou's Jazz Alley.** 2033 Sixth Ave. ☎ **206/441-9729.** Cover $10–$18.50.

This is Seattle's premier jazz club. Cool and sophisticated, Dimitriou's books only the very best performers, including plenty of name acts, and is reminiscent of New York jazz clubs.

New Orleans Creole Restaurant. 114 First Ave. S. ☎ **206/622-2563.** No cover weeknights (unless there's a national act playing); weekends $8 (joint cover).

If you like your food and your jazz hot, check out the New Orleans. Tuesday is Cajun night, but the rest of the week you can hear Dixieland, R&B, jazz, and blues.

Prego. Madison Hotel, 512 Madison St. ☎ **206/583-0300.** No cover.

How about jazz with a view? Prego, an Italian restaurant at the top of the Madison Hotel, features live jazz several nights a week. Although this is meant as music to dine by, it's still fun to have a drink in the lounge and listen to a little light music while gazing out over the city.

COMEDY, CABARET & DINNER THEATER

Cabaret de Paris. Rainier Square, Fourth Ave. and Union St. ☎ **206/623-4111.** $37–$39 for dinner and show.

Throughout the year this club stages a wide variety of entertaining programs of music, dance, and humor. Updated torch songs and numbers from classic musicals assure that the shows here will appeal to both young and old alike. The Christmas shows are especially funny. Over the years the cabaret's satirical musical reviews poking fun at Seattle have been big hits.

Comedy Underground. 222 S. Main St. ☎ **206/628-0303.** Admission $4–$10.

Located in the Pioneer Square area, where the Seattle Underground tour has proved that too much time beneath the city streets can lead even normal people to tell bad jokes, this is Seattle's most convenient comedy club.

Entros. 823 Yale St. N. ☎ **206/624-0057.** Game pass $10 to $15.

This place is part dinner theater, part weird-and-wacky game center. Housed in an old industrial building near Lake Union, Entros entertains with all kinds of strange games before, during, and after meals. In fact, you don't even have to eat here to enjoy the games. The games defy categorization, but they're all loads of fun; you just have to check it out yourself.

Mystery Cafe Dinner Theatre. The Bon Marché, Third Avenue and Stewart Street. ☎ **206/324-8895.** $38 for dinner and show.

The patented formula of allowing the audience to become part of the staged murder mystery has been around for a while now and remains a fun way to spend an evening if you're a fan of murder mysteries or games. Here the suspects also serve the three-course meal. Shows are Friday and Saturday night at 8pm. The Mystery Cafe had plans to move at press time, but you should still be able to track them down by calling the above number.

DANCE CLUBS

Downunder. 2407 First Ave. ☎ **206/728-4053.** No cover on Thurs, $5 Fri and Sat.

Located in the Belltown neighborhood north of Pike Place Market, the Downunder doesn't necessarily play underground music, but it is down a flight of stairs from street level. Wild decor, light shows, and high-energy music attract a Gen-X crowd. Techno to grunge. Open Thursday, Friday and Saturday 9pm to 4am.

Iguana Cantina. 2815 Alaskan Way. ☎ **206/728-7071.** Cover $5–$9.

Over on the waterfront is a cavernous place popular with Seattle's singles set. There's live Top 40 dance music most nights, and the restaurant has great views of Elliott Bay. Closed Monday and Tuesday.

Kid Mohair. 1207 Pine St. ☎ **206/625-4444.** Cover $4

Billing itself as a cigar bar and nightclub, this classy little dance club is currently one of Seattle's hot dance spots. Things don't start happening here until late.

THE BAR & PUB SCENE

BARS

Art Bar. 1516 Second Ave. ☎ **206/622-4344.** No cover to $3.

With funky thrift-store decor and very eclectic taste in art, this bar is a Bohemian hangout par excellence. Some nights there is live jazz and other nights a DJ spins tunes (not necessarily jazz), but mostly, the Art Bar is just someplace for the city's more artistic types to get together.

FX McRory's. 419 Occidental Ave. S. ☎ **206/623-4800.**

The clientele is upscale and you're likely to see members of the Seahawks or the SuperSonics at the bar. The original Leroy Neiman paintings on the walls lend class to this sports bar. You'll also find Seattle's largest selection of bourbon (more than 140 varieties) and microbrew beers and ales. There's also an oyster bar and good food.

McCormick & Schmick's. 1103 First Ave. ☎ **206/623-5500.**

The mahogany paneling, sparkling cut glass, and waiters in bow ties lend this restaurant bar a touch of class, but otherwise this place could have been the inspiration for *Cheers.* Very popular as an after-work watering hole of Seattle money-makers, McCormick & Schmick's is best know for its excellent and inexpensive happy-hour snacks.

Oliver's. Mayflower Park Hotel, 405 Olive Way. ☎ **206/623-8700.**

Oliver's is martini central for Seattle, and year after year bartender Mike Rule keeps winning the award for best martini in town in the Martini Classic Challenge (which also happens to be sponsored by the Mayflower Park Hotel). Only you can decide whether Oliver's shakes up the perfect martini.

The Pink Door. 1919 Post Alley ☎ **206/443-3241.**

Better known as Pike Place Market's unmarked restaurant, the Pink Door has a very lively after-work bar scene, and while a lot of people sipping Campari-laced martinis may just be waiting for a table on the deck, others are waiting to have their palms read. There aren't too many bars with their own resident palm reader.

The Virginia Inn. 1937 First Ave. ☎ **206/728-1937.**

Of all the bars in Belltown, that oh-so-stylish neighborhood north of Pike Place Market, the Virginia Inn has long been a favorite of everyone from artists to grunge rockers to the after-work crowd. With lots of burnished wood and a few tables out on the sidewalk, it's a comfortable place to sip a martini or microbrew.

PUBS & BREW PUBS

Big Time Brewery and Alehouse. 4133 University Way NE. ☎ **206/545-4509.**

Located in the University District and decorated to look like a turn-of-the-century tavern complete with 100-year-old back bar and wooden refrigerator, the Big Time serves as many as 12 of its own brews at any given time, and some of these can be pretty unusual.

✪ **Elysian Brewing Company.** 1221 E. Pike St. ☎ **206/860-1920.**

Although the brewery at this Capitol Hill brew pub is one of the smallest in the city, the pub itself is quite large and has a industrial feel that says local brewpub all over it. The stout and strong ales are especially good.

Hales Ales Brewery & Pub. 4301 Leary Way NW. ☎ **206/782-0737.**

Located about a mile west of the Fremont Bridge heading toward Ballard, this is the area's *other* brew pub, and while Red Hook Ales' Trolleyman gets most of the attention, Hales brews fine ales as well. This brewery, which has a second brew pub over in downtown Kirkland on the Eastside, doesn't bottle any of its brews, so if you want to try a Hales, you'll just have to stop by a pub.

Hart Brewery Pub. 1201 First Ave. S. ☎ **206/682-3377.**

Located south of the Kingdome in a big old warehouse, this pub is part of the brewery that makes Thomas Kemper lagers and Pyramid ales. Brewery tours and beer tastings are offered, but it's most popular as a place for dinner and drinks. Before and after sporting events at the Kingdome, the place is packed. There's good pub food, too.

✪ **Kells.** 1916 Post Alley, Pike Place Market. ☎ **206/728-1916.** Cover Fri–Sat only, $3.

This friendly Irish pub has the look and feel of a casual Dublin pub and stays absolutely packed most nights of the week. They pull a good Guinness stout and feature live traditional Irish music Wednesday through Saturday. This is also a restaurant serving traditional Irish meals.

✪ **The Pike Pub & Brewery.** 1415 First Ave. ☎ **206/622-6044.**

Located in an open, central space inside Pike Place Market, this brew pub does excellent stout and pale ale and on Thursdays taps a cask and offers $1.50 pints. There's live instrumental music a couple of nights a week, and, with its comfortable couches, the Pike makes a great place to get off your feet after a day of exploring the market.

Trolleyman Pub/Red Hook Ale Brewery. 3400 Phinney Ave. N. ☎ **206/548-8000.**

This is the taproom of the Redhook Ale Brewery, one of the Northwest's most celebrated microbreweries, and is located in a restored trolley barn on the Lake Washington Ship Canal. You can sample the ales brewed here, have a bite to eat, and even tour the brewery if you're interested. Red Hook has a second brewery and pub at 14300 NE 145th St. (☎ **206/483-3232**) in Woodinville on the east side of Lake Washington.

THE GAY & LESBIAN NIGHTLIFE SCENE

Capitol Hill is Seattle's main gay neighborhood, and it is here that you'll find the greatest concentration of gay & lesbian bars and dance clubs. The *Seattle Gay News* (☎ **206/324-4297**) is the community's newspaper and is available at gay bars and nightclubs.

DANCE CLUBS

The Easy. 916 E. Pike St. ☎ **206/323-8343.**

This Capitol Hill bar is popular with the lesbian singles crowd and doubles as a dance club.

Neighbours. 1509 Broadway. ☎ **206/324-5358.** Cover Sun–Thurs, $1; Fri–Sat, $5.

This has been the favorite dance club of Capitol Hill's gay community for years, and recently word has gotten out to straights. Still, the clientele is primarily gay. Friday and Saturday buffets are extremely popular. As at other clubs, different nights of the week feature different styles of music.

Re-Bar. 1114 Howell St. ☎ **206/233-9873.** Cover $3–$10

Each night there's a different theme, with the DJs spinning everything from world beat to funk and soul. Although this club isn't strictly a gay club, Thursday is currently Queer Disco night. Saturday nights also attract a primarily gay crowd.

Timberline. 2015 Boren Ave. ☎ **206/622-6220.**

If the boot-scootin' boogie is your favorite dance, the Timberline is the place to be. You'll find more men line dancing here than in any other club in town.

BARS

Thumpers. 1500 E. Madison St. ☎ **206/328-3800.**

Perched high on Capitol Hill with an excellent view of downtown Seattle, Thumpers is a classy bar done up with lots of oak. The seats by the fireplace are perfect on a cold and rainy night.

C.C. Attle's. 1501 E. Madison St. ☎ **206/726-0565.**

Located across the street from Thumpers, this bar has a 1940s look and is known for its cocktails.

Wildrose. 1021 E. Pike St. ☎ **206/324-9210.**

This friendly restaurant/bar is another long-time favorite with the Capitol Hill lesbian community and claims to be the oldest women's bar on the West Coast. Nonsmokers take note, there are smoke-free sections here.

MORE ENTERTAINMENT
MOVIES

Movies come close behind coffee and reading as a Seattle obsession. The city supports a surprising number of theaters showing foreign, independent, and nonmainstream films, as well as first-run movies. These include the **Varsity,** 4329 University Way NE (☎ 206/632-3131); **Grand Illusion,** NE 50th Ave. and University Way NE (☎ 206/523-3935); **Neptune,** NE 45th Ave. and Brooklyn St. NE (☎ 206/633-5545); **Harvard Exit,** 807 E. Roy St. (☎ 206/323-8986); and the **Egyptian,** 801 E. Pine St. (☎ 206/323-4978).

The Seattle International Film Festival is held each May and early June, with around 150 films shown at various theaters. Check the local papers for details.

A GAME CENTER

Techies would like to have us all believe that game centers (basically video arcades raised to the highest level) are the entertainment world's wave of the future. These parlors of virtual reality appeal primarily to teens and offer a noisy escape into the high-tech world of virtual reality.

Gameworks. 1511 Seventh Ave. ☎ **206/521-0952.**

Feeling more like a nightclub than a video arcade on steroids, this much-hyped entertainment center is hoping to be the wave of the future for the video-game generation. The Indy race car game, with racers sitting in cars that bounce and bank in conjunction with the view on the screen ahead, is a favorite here. However, Vertical Reality is the game that has people standing in line. In this one, you're strapped into a chair that rises and falls depending on how many bad guys you shoot or hits you take.

ONLY IN SEATTLE

While Seattle has plenty to offer in the way of performing arts, some of the city's best after-dark offerings have nothing to do with the music. There's no better way to start the evening (that is if the day has been sunny or only partly cloudy) than to catch the **sunset from the waterfront.** The Bell Street Pier and Myrtle Edwards Park are two of the best and least commercial vantages for taking in the nature's evening light show. Keep in mind that sunset can come as late as 10pm in the middle of summer.

Want the best view of the city lights? Hold off on your splurge elevator ride to the top of the **Space Needle** until after dark. Alternatively, you can hop a ferry and sail off into the night. Now, what could be more romantic?

Perhaps a **carriage ride.** Carriages are to be found parked and waiting for customers—couples and families alike—on the waterfront.

For a cheap date, nothing beats the **first Thursday art walk.** On the first Thursday of each month, galleries in Pioneer Square and Belltown stay open until 8 or 9pm. There are usually appetizers and drinks available and sometimes live music. On those same first Thursdays, the Seattle Art Museum, the Seattle Asian Art Museum, the Henry Art Gallery, and the Museum of Flight all stay open late and waive their usual admission charge. With the exception of the Museum of Flight, all of these art museums, as well as the Frye Art Museum, are open late every Thursday, though you'll have to pay on those other nights (except at the Frye, which never charges an admission).

Elliott Bay Book Co., 101 S. Main St. (☎ 206/624-6600), is not only a great place to hang out after dark (or during the day for that matter), but it also schedules frequent readings by touring authors. Stop by or call to check the schedule. There are also frequent art lectures at the Seattle Art Museum and Seattle Asian Art Museum.

Want to learn to dance? Up on Capitol Hill, there are **brass dance steps** inlaid into the sidewalk along Broadway. Spend an evening strolling the strip and you and your partner could teach yourselves several classic dance steps in between noshing a piroshky and savoring a chocolate torte.

11 An Excursion North of the City: Jumbo Jets, Wine & Antiques

This driving excursion takes in the world's largest building, a town full of antique stores, wineries, and a picturesque lakeshore community.

Roughly 30 miles north of Seattle on I-5 on the shore of Puget Sound, is the city of Everett. Though for the most part it has become a bedroom community for Seattle commuters, it is also home to the region's single largest employer: Boeing. It is here in Everett that the aircraft manufacturer has its main assembly plant. This is the single largest building, by volume, in the world and easily could hold 911 basketball courts, 74 football fields, 2,142 average homes, or all of Disneyland (with room left over for covered parking). Free guided 1-hour tours of the facility are held Monday through Friday throughout the year. The schedule varies with the time of year, so be sure to call ahead for details and directions to the plant. Children under 50 inches tall are not allowed, and the tours are first-come, first-served. For more information, contact the **Boeing Tour Center,** Wash. 526, Everett (☎ 800/464-1476 or 206/544-1264).

A few miles east of Everett off U.S. 2, you can jump from the jet age to horse-and-buggy-days in the historic town of Snohomish. Established in 1859 on the banks of the Snohomish River, this historic town was, until 1897 the county seat. However, when the county seat was moved to Everett, Snohomish lost its regional importance and development slowed considerably. Today, an abundance of turn-of-the-century buildings are the legacy of the town's early economic growth. By the 1960s these old homes began attracting people interested in restoring them to their original condition, and soon antique shops began proliferating in historic downtown Snohomish. Today the town has more than 400 antique dealers and is without a doubt the antique capital of the northwest. Surrounding the town's commercial core of antique stores are neighborhoods full of restored Victorian homes. Each year in September, you can get a peek inside some of the town's most elegant homes on the annual Historical Society Home Tour. You can pick up a copy of a guide to the town's antiques stores and its historic homes by stopping by or contacting the **Snohomish Chamber of Commerce**, P.O. Box 135, Snohomish, WA 98291 (☎ **360/568-2526**).

While in town, you may want to visit the **Blackman Museum**, 118 Avenue B (☎ **360/568-5235**), which is housed in an 1879 Queen Anne Victorian that has been restored and filled with period furnishings. The museum is open daily from noon to 4pm in summer (Wednesday through Sunday from noon to 4pm other months), and admission is $1 for adults and 50¢ for seniors and children. For another glimpse into the town's past, head over to Pioneer Village, a collection of restored cabins and other old buildings on Second Street. Each of the buildings is furnished with period antiques. Pioneer Village is open the same hours as the Blackman Museum and admission is $1.50 for adults and $1 for seniors and children.

Heading south from Snohomish to Woodinville on Wash. 9, and then Wash. 522, brings you into the Puget Sound's small wine region. The first winery you're likely to encounter here is the tiny **Silver Lake Sparkling Cellars**, 17721 132nd Ave. NE, Woodinville (☎ **425/486-1900**), which is located in an industrial area near the junction of Wash. 522 and Wash. 202. Although this place lacks character, they craft some excellent red wines. From here, head south on Wash. 202 (Woodinville-Redmond Road), where you'll come to **Facelli Winery**, 16120 Woodinville-Redmond NE no. 1 (☎ **206/488-1020**), which is open for tastings only on the weekends. Largest and most famous of the wineries in the area is **Chateau Ste. Michelle**, 14111 NE 145th St., Woodinville (☎ **425/488-3300**), which is located in a grand mansion on a historic estate that was established in 1912. The winery, which is the largest in Washington, is known for the consistent quality of its wines. An amphitheater on the grounds stages music performances throughout the summer. To reach the winery, head south from Woodinville on Wash. 202 and watch for signs. Right across the road from Chateau Ste. Michelle, you'll find **Columbia Winery**, 14030 NE 145th St. (☎ **425/488-2776**), which, unfortunately doesn't seem to have the same touch with wines that its neighbor does. If beer is more to your tastes, you can stop in at the large **Red Hook Brewery**, 14030 NE 145th St. (☎ **425/483-3232**), which is home to the Forecaster's Pub and is right next door to Columbia Winery.

Finish your day with a walk around downtown Kirkland, which is along the Moss Bay waterfront. You can stroll along the waterfront and stop in at interesting shops and any of more than a dozen art galleries. There are also several decent restaurants in the area. We like **Bistro Provençal**, 212 Central Way (☎ **425/827-3300**), a very reasonably priced French restaurant in downtown Kirkland. To get back to Seattle, take I-405 south to I-90.

6

The San Juan Islands, Skagit Valley & the Bellingham Area

When English explorer Capt. George Vancouver first sailed down the Strait of Juan de Fuca in 1792, he discovered a vast inland sea he named the Puget Sound. To the north of this sound, within a convolution of twisting channels, narrow straits, and elongated bays, lay an archipelago of islands, and rising to the east in a magnificent backdrop stood a range of snowcapped peaks. Several of the archipelago's islands—San Juan, Lopez, Fidalgo, and Guemes—had already been named by earlier Spanish explorers, but Vancouver's 2 months of exploring and charting the waters of the Sound left Northwest maps with many new names, such as Deception Pass, Whidbey Island, Bellingham Bay, and Mount Baker.

Washingtonians have made northern Puget Sound and the San Juan Islands their favorite summer playground and weekend getaway. Shimmering waters, mountain vistas, and tranquil islands are the ingredients of the tonic that revives the weary souls of vacationing urbanites from the densely populated and industrialized southern Puget Sound. Though it's only 30 miles from Seattle to Whidbey Island and 85 to the San Juans, the distance is multiplied by the serenity that descends as you cross the sound by ferry and leave the mainland behind.

However, this corner of the state isn't all about island life. On the mainland, the historic fishing village of La Conner has become one of the most charming little towns in the state. Surrounding the town are the Skagit Valley bulb fields, which burst into bloom each spring with acres and acres of tulips and daffodils.

Farther north, the town of Bellingham serves as a base for exploring the Emerald Coast, one of the least visited (the San Juans seem to siphon off all the traffic) stretches of coastline in the state. However, though there are few crowds here, the vistas (and the oysters) are as good as any you'll find in the islands. It is also on this coast that you will find the state's premier waterfront golf resort.

1 La Conner & the Skagit Valley

70 miles N of Seattle, 10 miles E of Anacortes, 32 miles S of Bellingham

Although the name sounds as if it's a combination of Spanish and Irish, La Conner is actually named for Louisa A. (LA) Conner, who helped found the town in the 1870s. La Conner dates from a time when Puget Sound towns were connected by water and not by road,

The Northwest Washington Coast

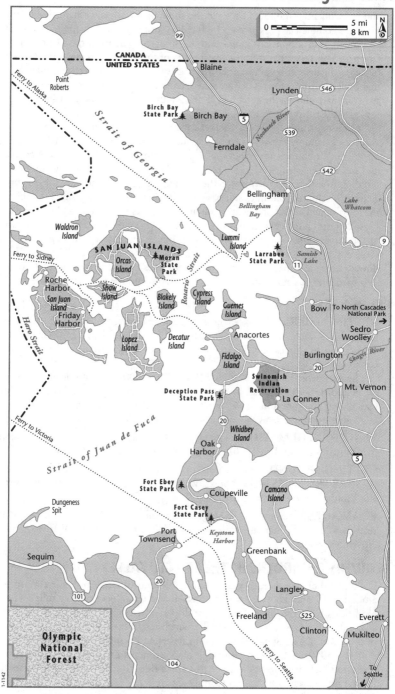

0   5 mi
8 km

N

99

CANADA
UNITED STATES

Blaine

Point
Roberts

Lynden

546

Birch Bay
State Park

Birch Bay

5

Nooksack River

Strait of Georgia

Ferndale

539

542

Bellingham

Bellingham
Bay

Lake
Whatcom

Waldron
Island

SAN JUAN ISLANDS

Lummi
Island

Larrabee
State Park

Samish
Lake

9

Ferry to Alaska

Ferry to Sidney

Orcas
Island

Moran
State
Park

Rosario Strait

11

Roche
Harbor

Shaw
Island

Blakely
Island

Cypress
Island

Bow

To North Cascades
National Park

San Juan
Island

Friday
Harbor

Guemes
Island

Sedro
Woolley

Haro Strait

Lopez
Island

Decatur
Island

Anacortes

Burlington

Skagit River

20

Fidalgo
Island

Mt. Vernon

Swinomish
Indian
Reservation

Deception Pass
State Park

La Conner

20

Whidbey
Island

Ferry to Victoria

Strait of Juan de Fuca

Oak
Harbor

5

Dungeness
Spit

Fort Ebey
State Park

Coupeville

Camano
Island

Fort Casey
State Park

Sequim

Port
Townsend

Keystone
Harbor

Greenbank

101

Langley

20

Freeland

525

Everett

Clinton

Mukilteo

104

Olympic
National
Forest

Ferry to Seattle

To
Seattle

1-1142

and consequently, the town clings to the shore of Swinomish Channel. The town reached a commercial peak around 1900 (when steamers made the run to Seattle) and continued as an important grain- and log-shipping port until the Depression. La Conner never recovered from the hard times of the 1930s, and when the highways bypassed the town it became a neglected backwater. The wooden false-fronted buildings built during the town's heyday were spared the waves of progress that swept over the Northwest during the latter half of this century, and today these quaint old buildings give the town its charm.

Beginning in the 1940s, La Conner's picturesque setting attracted several artists and writers, and by the 1970s La Conner had become known as an artists' community (Tom Robbins wrote about the area in his novel *Another Roadside Attraction*), and tourism began to revive the economy. Today, the 19th-century commercial buildings that line the town's waterfront have been restored and are filled with art galleries, boutiques, antiques stores, and crafts shops. For most visitors shopping is the town's main attraction—and on summer weekends the crowds can be formidable.

Adding still more color to this vibrant little town are the commercial flower farms of the surrounding Skagit Valley. In the spring, tulips and daffodils carpet the surrounding farmlands with great swaths of red, yellow, and white. These wholesale flower farms have given rise to quite a few nurseries and garden stores in La Conner, so if gardening is your passion, don't miss this quaint little waterfront town.

ESSENTIALS

GETTING THERE   From I-5, take U.S. 20 west toward Anacortes. La Conner is south of U.S. 20 on La Conner–Whitney Road. Alternatively, take the Conway exit off I-5 and head west on Fir Island Road to Chilberg Road, which leads into La Conner.

The **Airporter Shuttle** (☎ **800/235-5247** or 360/679-0600) operates between the Anacortes ferry terminal and Sea-Tac Airport, stopping at the Farmhouse Inn, which is at the junction of Wash. 20 and La Conner–Whitney Road, north of La Conner (one-way fares: $27 for adults, $24 for seniors, $14 for children).

VISITOR INFORMATION   Contact the **La Conner Chamber of Commerce,** 315 Morris St. (P.O. Box 1610), La Conner, WA 98257 (☎ **360/466-4778**).

GETTING AROUND   Public transit in Skagit County is provided free of charge on **SKAT** (☎ **360/757-4433**) buses, which make stops in La Conner, Anacortes, and Mount Vernon among other places.

FESTIVALS   In addition to the Skagit Valley Tulip Festival (see below), La Conner celebrates its artistic heritage with the **Art's Alive!** festival on the first weekend in November.

FLOWERS & GARDENS IN THE SKAGIT VALLEY

For a few short weeks each year, from late March to mid-April, the countryside around La Conner is awash with color as 2,000 acres of Skagit Valley tulip and daffodil fields burst into bloom in a floral display that rivals that of the Netherlands. These flowers are grown for their bulbs, which each fall are shipped to gardeners all over the world. The **Skagit Valley Tulip Festival** (☎ **360/424-3228,** ext. 2100, or 360/428-5959), held each year during bloom time, is La Conner's biggest annual event and includes dozens of events from bike rides to a brew festival. Contact the festival office or stop by the **La Conner Chamber of Commerce,** 315 Morris St. (☎ **360/466-4778**), for a scenic tour map of the flower fields. On festival weekends area roads are clogged with cars, so you should consider opting to ride the Tulip

Transit buses that loop through the flower fields. Contact the festival office to find out about these buses.

Whether you're here in tulip time or not, you might want to stop by some of the area's farms, gardens, and nurseries. **Roozengaarde Flowers & Bulbs,** 1587 Beaver Marsh Rd. (☎ **800/732-3266** or 360/424-8531), has a gift shop open daily March to May and Monday through Saturday in other months. At **Christianson's Nursery & Greenhouse,** 1578 Best Rd. (☎ **360/466-3821**), you'll find more than 600 varieties of roses and lots of other plants as well. Located on Swinomish Channel at the end of Downey Road, **West Shore Acres** (☎ **360/466-3158**), boasts one of the finest spring bulb display gardens in the valley. Back in town, there's the **Tillinghast Seed Company,** 623 Morris St. (☎ **360/466-3329**), which is the oldest seed company in the Northwest and now includes a country store, nursery, gardening supply store, and florist.

EXPLORING LA CONNER & ITS ENVIRONS

✪ The **Museum of Northwest Art,** 121 S. First St. (☎ **360/466-4446**), was formerly housed in the Gaches Mansion, but now occupies a large contemporary building in downtown La Conner. The museum features works by Northwest artists, including Morris Graves, Mark Tobey, and Guy Anderson, all of whom once worked in La Conner, and mounts a variety of exhibits throughout the year. This museum would be right at home in downtown Seattle, so it comes as a very pleasant surprise to find it in this tiny town. It's open Tuesday through Sunday from 10am to 5pm; admission is $3.

High atop a hill in the center of town, you can learn about the history of this area at the **Skagit County Historical Museum,** 501 S. Fourth St. (☎ **360/466-3365**). It's open Tuesday through Sunday from 11am to 5pm; admission is $2 for adults, $1 for children. A few blocks away, you'll find the **La Conner Quilt Museum,** 703 S. Second St. (☎ **360/466-4288**), which is housed in the historic Gaches Mansion. On the first floor of this museum, you'll find rooms furnished with turn-of-the-century antiques, while on the second floor, there are quilt displays. The museum is open Wednesday through Sunday from 11am to 5pm, and admission is $3. Two blocks down the street from the Gaches Mansion is the much less pretentious **Magnus Anderson Cabin,** built in 1869 by the area's first white settler. Beside the cabin is the **La Conner Town Hall,** which is housed in a triangular bank building that was built in 1886. Across the street from these two buildings is **Totem Pole Park,** which in addition to having a totem pole, has a dugout canoe carved by local Swinomish artisans, whose reservation is just across the Swinomish Channel.

There is excellent bird watching around the Skagit Valley, especially during the winter months when migratory waterfowl, including trumpeter swans and snow geese, and various raptors, including peregrine falcons and bald eagles, flock to the area's marshes, bays, and farm fields. Eight miles north of La Conner at the **Padilla Bay National Estuarine Research Reserve and Breazeale Interpretive Center,** 1043 Bayview-Edison Rd. (☎ **360/428-1558**), you can bird watch and learn about the importance of estuaries. Interpretive exhibits explore life in Padilla Bay and its salt marshes. The reserve is open daily; the interpretive center, Wednesday through Sunday from 10am to 5pm. Admission is free. The Skagit Wildlife Area, south of La Conner and west of Conway, is another good winter birding area.

Viking Cruises, 109 N. First St. (☎ **360/466-2639**), offers various cruises to see wildlife, including birds and whales (tours run $20 to $79).

Shopping is the most popular pastime in La Conner, and as you wander up and down First Street, stop in at **The Wood Merchant,** 709 S. First St. (☎ **360/**

466-4741), which features handcrafted wooden furniture and accent pieces; and **Earthenworks,** 713 S. First St. (☎ **360/466-4422**), which has fine crafts in ceramic, glass, wood, and other media.

WHERE TO STAY

✪ **The La Conner Channel Lodge.** 205 N. First St., La Conner, WA 98257. ☎ **360/466-1500.** 40 rms. TV TEL. $149–$215 double (lower rates in off-season). Rates include continental breakfast. AE, DISC, MC, V.

Luxurious accommodations, Northwest styling, and views of Swinomish Channel from all but seven of the rooms make this a truly memorable lodge. A flagstone entry, cedar-shake siding, and a river-rock fireplace in the lobby set the tone for the rest of the lodge. Most guest rooms are large and all have small balconies and gas fireplaces. Fir accents and a combination of slate flooring and carpeting give the rooms a natural richness. Nautical accent pieces, wooden venetian blinds, and wrought-iron bed frames tie the rooms to La Conner's seafaring past and add touches of Italianate styling. The elegant buffet breakfast is served on the mezzanine above the lobby. If you have your own boat, you can tie up at the hotel's dock.

La Conner Country Inn. 107 S. Second St., La Conner, WA 98257. ☎ **360/466-3101.** 28 rms. TV TEL. $93–$150 double. Rates include continental breakfast. AE, DISC, MC, V.

Under the same management as the La Conner Channel Lodge, the Country Inn is a much more casual, folksy sort of place. It's set back a block from the water but is still right in downtown, so it's very convenient for shopping. The exterior looks as if this were a mountain lodge, though the interior is more country than mountain. In the cozy lobby there's a huge stone fireplace, and every guest room also has its own fireplace. Some rooms have brass beds and most have rustic pine furniture.

The White Swan Guest House. 1388 Moore Rd., Mount Vernon, WA 98273. ☎ **360/445-6805.** 3 rms (all with shared baths); 1 cottage. $80 double; $135 cottage. Rates include continental breakfast. MC, V.

If you're here for the tulip blossoms or if you're a gardener, make this your first choice. Located out in the country, this restored Victorian farmhouse is set beneath ancient poplar trees and is surrounded by stunning perennial gardens. Of the guest rooms in the main house, we like the one with the turret, though all are comfortable enough. For more space and privacy, opt for the rustic little cottage set on the far side of the gardens. Peter, the owner, bakes up some of the best chocolate chip cookies around.

✪ **The Wild Iris.** 121 Maple Ave. (P.O. Box 696), La Conner, WA 98257. ☎ **800/477-1400** or 360/466-1400. Fax 360/466-1221. www.ncia.com/~wildiris. 20 rms, 12 suites. TV TEL. $90–$115 double; $120–$180 suite. Rates include full breakfast. AE, MC, V.

The Wild Iris is a modern Victorian inn on the edge of town, and directly behind the inn is a dahlia farm. Ask for a second-floor room with a view in late summer and you'll have not only dahlias out your window, but a view of Mount Baker as well. The inn was designed for romantic weekends, and many of the rooms have double whirlpool tubs. In some the whirlpool tub is in the room, while in others it's on the balcony. Breakfasts are large and are served buffet style. Dinners are also served on Friday and Saturday nights.

WHERE TO DINE

If you dare go against the Northwest coffee aesthetic and opt for a cup of tea, try **The Rose and Thistle,** 606 E. Morris St. (☎ **360/466-3313**). If it's baked goodies you need, stop by **Georgia's Bakery,** 109 N. First St. (☎ **360/466-2149**), in the Lime Dock Building. For locally brewed beers in a contemporary setting, drop by the **La Conner Brewing Company,** 117 S. First St. (☎ **360/466-1415**).

La Conner Seafood and Prime Rib House. 614 S. First St. ☎ **360/466-4014.** Reservations recommended. Main courses $9–$20. AE, DC, DISC, MC, V. Sun–Thurs 11:30am–10pm, Fri–Sat 11:30am–11pm (closes an hour earlier off-season). SEAFOOD/PRIME RIB.

With a long menu of reliable choices at mostly moderate prices, this is your best bet in La Conner for a waterfront meal. This place keeps getting voted best seafood in the county, and if you like oysters, we recommend Grandma Lou's oysters or the sautéed oysters. Although seafood is the real forte here you can still get the likes of prime rib, either traditional or Cajun. The lunch menu is as long as the dinner menu and includes plenty of seafood salads and sandwiches.

✪ Palmer's. In the La Conner Country Inn, 205 E. Washington Ave. ☎ **360/466-4261.** Reservations recommended. Main courses $14–$21; pub entrees $6–12. AE, MC, V. Pub daily 11:30am–10pm, dining room daily 5–10pm. INTERNATIONAL.

La Conner's finest meals are to be had at Palmer's, a cozy little restaurant attached to the La Conner Country Inn. In the dining room, elegant furnishings are a contrast to the rustic, mountain-lodge styling. The menu here is basically traditional gourmet with an occasional twist. A recent appetizer list included gravlax served with a shot of single-malt whiskey and curried scallops. On the entree menu were pheasant, roast duckling, and filet mignon. For less expensive meals in a casual atmosphere, you can dine in the pub, which is a good rendition of a cramped 19th-century English pub.

2 Anacortes

75 miles N of Seattle, 39 miles S of Bellingham, 92 miles S of Vancouver

Founded in the 1850s by Amos Bowman, this town was named after Bowman's wife, Annie Curtis, but over the years the spelling and pronunciation was slowly corrupted to its current Spanish-sounding pronunciation (in keeping with such local Spanish names as San Juan, Lopez, and Guemes). While most people only pass through Anacortes on their way to catch a ferry to the San Juan Islands or Vancouver Island (Victoria), the town is slowly becoming something of a destination in its own right. A restored downtown business district, residential neighborhoods full of old Victorian homes, and a large, forested waterfront park are all worth a look. The town made its early fortunes on lumbering and fishing, and today commercial fishing, as well as boatbuilding, are important to the town's economy. This marine orientation has given the town its character, which can be seen in the many restored buildings along Commercial Avenue.

Anacortes also makes a good base for exploring the San Juans if you either can't get or can't afford a room on the islands. Using Anacortes as a base and leaving your car here on the mainland, you can travel as a passenger on the ferries and, by using public transit, mopeds, or bicycles, still manage to see plenty of the San Juan Islands. In any event, Anacortes is also on an island, Fidalgo Island. From here you can also explore Whidbey Island and La Conner.

ESSENTIALS

GETTING THERE From I-5 at Mount Vernon or Burlington, take Wash. 20 west to the Wash. 20 Spur. South of Anacortes, Wash. 20 connects to Whidbey Island by way of the Deception Pass Bridge.

See "Getting There" under "The San Juan Islands" below for details on airporter service to Anacortes from Seattle Tacoma International Airport and for information on ferry connections to Anacortes from the islands and Vancouver Island, British Columbia.

VISITOR INFORMATION   For information on Anacortes, contact the **Anacortes Chamber of Commerce,** 819 Commercial Ave., Suite G, Anacortes, WA 98221 (☎ 360/293-3832).

GETTING AROUND   Public transit in Skagit County is provided free of charge on **SKAT** (☎ 360/757-4433) buses, which make stops in Anacortes, La Conner, and Mount Vernon among other places.

EXPLORING ANACORTES

Any walking tour of downtown should be sure to include a visit to the historic **sternwheeler** *W. T. Preston,* which was built in the 1890s to clear log jams on Puget Sound and now sits on dry land in a little park at the corner of Seventh Street and R Avenue. Tours are offered on summer weekends. For more information, contact the Anacortes Museum, 1305 Eight St. (☎ 360/293-1915).

Right next door is the terminal for the **Anacortes Steam Railway,** a working miniature train that makes a short run through town on summer weekends and holidays. At this same corner is **The Depot** (☎ 360/293-3663), a restored 1911 railway depot that now serves as an arts center. For a glimpse of an old-fashioned hardware store, stop by **Marine Supply and Hardware,** 202 Commercial St., which is the oldest continuously operating store in Anacortes (and some say on the West Coast). **Murals** are a mainstay of the Northwest's historic towns, and here in Anacortes they take the shape of more than 50 life-size cutouts of the town's forebears. The murals, based on historic photos, are done by artist Bill Mitchell. Also, several totem poles can be seen at 2102 Ninth Street in the yard of Paul Luvera Sr., who has carved more than 2,600 totem poles over the years.

If you want to learn more about local history, stop by the **Anacortes Museum,** 1305 Eighth St. (☎ 360/293-1915), housed in a former Carnegie Library. It's open Thursday through Monday from 1 to 5pm; admission is free. Across the street from the museum is **Causland Memorial Park,** the town's most unusual attraction. Built in 1919 to honor servicemen who died in World War I, the park contains rock walls that were constructed as giant mosaics. It's a piece of folk art that reflects a much simpler era.

Nature lovers can head to **Washington Park,** just a short distance past the ferry terminal. The park contains not only a campground and several miles of hiking trails, but tranquil **Sunset Beach,** which looks out across Rosario Strait to the San Juan Islands. For even more spectacular views, head up to **Mount Erie Park** on the summit of 1,270-foot Mount Erie. From here, on a clear day you can see Mount Rainier, Mount Baker, and the Olympic Mountains. You'll find this park by heading south out of Anacortes on Commercial Avenue, turning right on 29th Street, which becomes I Avenue and then Heart Lake Road, and then taking Erie Mountain Drive to the top of the mountain.

You don't have to go all the way to the San Juans if you want to go fishing or whale watching. **Island Adventure Cruises** (☎ 800/465-4604 or 360/293-2428), which operates out of Cap Sante Marina, offers both. Sea Kayak rentals are available at **Eddyline Watersports Center,** 1019 Q Ave. (☎ 360/299-2300).

WHERE TO STAY

Channel House. 2902 Oakes Ave., Anacortes, WA 98221. ☎ **800/238-4353** or 360/293-9382. Fax 360/299-9208. www.channel-house.com. 6 rms. $69–$105 double. Rates include full breakfast. AE, DISC, MC, V.

Located right on the busy road to the ferry landing, this restored 1902 Victorian home has good views across the water to the San Juan Islands. Our favorite room has a view of the water from both the bedroom and the claw-foot tub in the bathroom. If you're a light sleeper, you might find that the rooms in the rose cottage are a bit quieter than those in the main house; these rooms also have whirlpool tubs. Out in the attractive gardens you'll find a hot tub overlooking the water.

Islands Motel. 3401 Commercial Ave., Anacortes, WA 98221. ☎ **360/293-4644.** 36 rms. A/C TV TEL. Summer, $65–$75 double; other months, $48–$58 double. Rates include Dutch breakfast. AE, DC, DISC, MC, V.

Located right at the end of U.S. 20, the Islands may look just like any other aging strip motel from the street, but after you check in you'll find that there are some differences. First of all, this is a bed-and-breakfast motel, and the breakfast is not just a doughnut and a cup of weak coffee. Instead you get a traditional Dutch breakfast complete with ham and cheese. Some of the rooms have fireplaces, and all have tiled entries and bathrooms. You may even find a second telephone in the bathroom. On top of all this, there's a pool in the summer and the motel's La Petite restaurant, one of the best in town, serves delicious European dishes with an emphasis on Dutch cooking. Entree prices range from $16 to $25.

✪ **The Majestic Hotel.** 419 Commercial Ave., Anacortes, WA 98221. ☎ **360/293-3355.** Fax 360/293-5214. 23 rms. TV TEL. $98–$166 double; $215 minisuite. Rates include continental breakfast. AE, DISC, MC, V.

Throughout this elegant antique-filled hotel you'll find beautiful and unusual works of art that hearken back to the turn of the century. Outside there's a little English garden, and up on the roof an observatory provides a splendid panorama of the city. The guest rooms are furnished with antiques and down comforters. Just off the lobby you'll find an opulent restaurant , The Salmon Run, serving excellent Northwest cuisine, (see below). Through another door you'll find the hotel's casually elegant lounge, a sort of Victorian pub complete with wicker furniture and marble bar. The Majestic gets our vote for most elegant hotel in the area.

WHERE TO DINE

If you love good pastries and baked goodies, be sure to drop by **La Vie En Rose,** 418 Commercial Ave. (☎ **360/299-9546**), is a great little French pastry shop. For good deli fare, try **Gere-a-Deli,** 502 Commercial Ave. (☎ **360/293-7383**). If you're looking for a microbrew and some pub grub, check out the **Anacortes Brewhouse,** Fourth street and Commercial Avenue (☎ **360/293-2444**).

La Petite Restaurant. Islands Motel, 3401 Commercial Ave. ☎ **360/293-4644.** Reservations recommended. Main dishes $16–$25. AE, DC, DISC, MC, V. Tues–Sun 5–10pm. DUTCH.

Dutch cuisine is not something you run across all that often in the United States, so should you be the least bit curious, here is a prime opportunity to find out what it's all about. Actually, the menu, which changes regularly, is not entirely Dutch; you'll find pasta dishes and the likes of red snapper with tarragon-caper butter sauce. However, you'll also find pork tenderloin with an apple brandy sauce and, usually, an Indonesian-influenced dish. The menu is short and entrees come with both soup and salad.

The Salmon Run. The Majestic Hotel, 419 Commercial Ave. ☎ **360/299-2923.** Reservations recommended. Main dishes $7–$17. MC, V. Sun–Mon 5:30–10pm, Tues–Sat 11:30am–2pm and 5:30–10pm. INTERNATIONAL.

By far the most elegant restaurant in town, the Salmon Run occupies a sumptuous space off the lobby of the aptly named Majestic Hotel. Seafood is the focus of the menu here, and there are daily specials prepared from whatever happened to look good at the market that day. Preparations tend to be straightforward (grilled salmon with wild mushrooms, cedar-planked salmon) but occasional bursts of creativity (sturgeon with three-citrus sauce) show up as well. For a more casual, yet no less atmospheric, setting you can dine in the Victorian pub across the lobby from the Salmon Run. The food comes from the same kitchen.

3 The San Juan Islands

On a late afternoon on a clear summer day, the sun slants low, suffusing the scene with a golden light. The fresh salt breeze and the low rumble of the ferry's engine lulls you into a half-waking state. All around you are emerald green islands, the tops of glacier-carved mountains flooded at the end of the last Ice Age, rise from a shimmering sea. A bald eagle swoops from its perch on a twisted madrona tree. Off the port bow, two knifelike fins slice the water. You catch a glimpse of black and white orca whales. As the engine slows, you glide toward a narrow wooden dock with a simple sign above it that reads "San Juan Island." With a sigh of contentment, you step out onto the San Juan Islands and a slower pace of life.

There's something magical about traveling to the San Juans. Some people say it's the light, some say it's the sea air, some say it's the weather (temperatures are always moderate and rainfall is roughly half what it is in Seattle). Whatever it is that so entrances, the San Juans are indeed magical. They have become the favorite getaway of urban Washingtonians, and if you make time to visit these idyllic islands, we think you, too, will fall under their spell.

There is, however, one caveat. The San Juans have been discovered. In summer, there can be waits of several hours to get on ferries if you're driving a car. One solution is to leave your car on the mainland and either come over on foot or with a bicycle. If you choose to come over on foot, you can rent a car, moped, or bicycle, take the San Juan or Orcas island shuttle bus, or use taxis to get around. Then again, you can just stay in one place and really relax. Along with crowded ferries come hotels, inns, and campgrounds that can get booked up months in advance and restaurants that can't seat you unless you have a reservation. If it's summer, don't come out here without a reservation expecting to find a place to stay. Outside the summer months it's a different story. Spring and fall are often clear, and in spring, the islands gardens and hedgerows of wild roses burst into bloom, making this one of the best times of year to visit. Perhaps best of all, in spring and fall room rates are much less than they are in the summer.

Depending on who you listen to there are between 175 and 786 islands in the San Juans. The lower number constitutes those islands large enough to have been named, while the larger number represents all the islands, rocks, and reefs that poke above the water on the lowest possible tide. However, of all these islands, only four (San Juan, Orcas, Lopez, and Shaw) are serviced by the Washington State Ferries and of these, only three (San Juan, Orcas, and Lopez) have anything in the way of tourist accommodations (Shaw does have a campground).

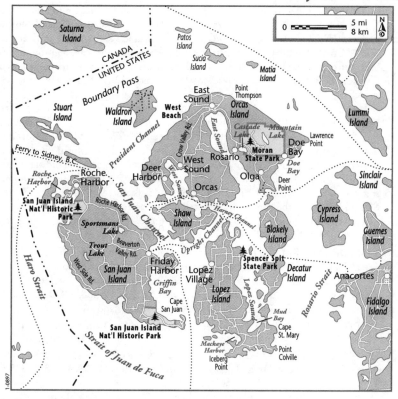

The San Juan Islands

ESSENTIALS

GETTING THERE   Washington State Ferries (☎ 800/84-FERRY in Washington, or 206/464-6400) operates ferries between Anacortes and four of the San Juan Islands—Lopez, Shaw, Orcas, and San Juan. One ferry a day also connects the San Juans with Sidney, British Columbia (on Vancouver Island near Victoria). The fare for a vehicle and driver from Anacortes to Lopez is $12.30 to $14.75, to Shaw or Orcas is $14.70 to $17.65, to San Juan is $16.80 to $20.30, and to Sidney is $29.70 to $35.65; the fare for passengers from Anacortes to any of the islands is $4.95 and to Sidney is $6.90. The fare for a vehicle and driver on all westbound interisland ferries is $7 to $8.25, and foot passengers ride free. Except for service from Sidney, fares are not collected on eastbound ferries. If you plan to explore the islands by car, you'll save some money by starting your tour on San Juan Island and making your way back east through the islands. During the summer you may have to wait several hours to get on a ferry, so plan to arrive early. In fare ranges above, the higher fares reflect the summer surcharge.

There are also passenger-ferry services from several cities around the region. Victoria Clipper's ***San Juan Explorer*** (☎ 800/888-2535 or 206/448-5000) travels between Seattle and both Friday Harbor and Rosario Resort. The fare to Friday Harbor is $39 one way and $59 round-trip; the fare to Rosario Resort is $43 one way and $67 round-trip. Between late March and early October, **P.S. Express** (☎ 360/385-5288) operates between Port Townsend and Friday Harbor and carries bicycles and sea kayaks as well as passengers. Fares are $31 to $34.50 one way and $45 to $49 round-trip. Summer passenger service is also offered from Bellingham to Friday Harbor, as well as Lieber Haven Resort on Orcas Island, on **San Juan Island Shuttle Express** (☎ **800/373-8522** or 360/671-1137), which leaves from the Fairhaven Station & Cruise Terminal, 335 Harris Ave. The fare is $20 one way, $33 round-trip. Service from Bellingham to Roche Harbor Resort is offered by **Victoria–San Juan Cruises** (☎ **800/443-4552** or 360/738-8099), which charges $21 one way and $39 round-trip.

If you're flying in to Sea-Tac Airport and continuing on to the San Juans, **Harbor Airlines** (☎ **800/359-3220**) is the most convenient airline to fly. It flies between Sea-Tac Airport and Friday Harbor. **Kenmore Air** (☎ **800/543-9595** or 206/486-1257) operates small floatplanes between Seattle and the San Juans. Flights leave from both Lake Union, north of downtown Seattle, and the north end of Lake Washington and stop at Friday Harbor and Roche Harbor on San Juan Island, Rosario Resort on Orcas Island, the Lopez Islander on Lopez Island. **West Isle Air** (☎ **800/874-4434**) flies to the San Juans from Bellingham and Anacortes.

The **Airporter Shuttle** (☎ **800/423-4219**) makes trips between Sea-Tac International Airport in Seattle and the Anacortes ferry terminal. The cost is $27 for adults.

VISITOR INFORMATION   Contact the **San Juan Info Center**, P.O. Box 2809, Friday Harbor, WA 98250; the **San Juan Island Chamber of Commerce**, P.O. Box 98, Friday Harbor, WA 98250 (☎ **360/378-5240**); the **Orcas Island Chamber of Commerce**, P.O. Box 252, Eastsound, WA 98245-0252 (☎ **360/376-2273**); or the **Lopez Chamber of Commerce**, P.O. Box 102, Lopez Island, WA 98261.

GETTING AROUND   Car rentals are available on San Juan Island from **Inn at Friday Harbor** (☎ **800/752-5752** or 360/378-4351) and **M&W Auto Sales** (☎ **360/378-AUTO**). On Orcas Island, contact **Rosario Resort** (☎ **800/562-8820** or 360/376-2222) or **Orcas Island Taxi and Car Rental** (☎ **360/376-8294**). Expect to pay between $40 and $60 per day.

For a taxi on San Juan, call **San Juan Transit** (☎ **360/378-3550**); on Orcas, call **Orcas Island Taxi** (☎ **360/376-8294**); on Lopez, call **Angie's Cab Courier** (☎ **360/468-2227**).

San Juan Transit (☎ **800/887-8387**, 360/378-8887 on San Juan, or 360/376-8887 on Orcas) operates shuttle buses on both San Juan and Orcas islands during the summer. These shuttles can be boarded at the ferry terminal and operate frequently throughout the day, stopping at all the major attractions on both islands, which makes these shuttles a great way to get around if you came out without a car. Day passes on either island are $10, and one-way and round-trip tickets are also available.

FESTIVALS   Each summer in late July, the **San Juan Island Jazz Festival** brings in jazz bands from all over the country. Each year on the first weekend in August the **Orcas Fly-In** attracts numerous antique airplanes to Orcas Island.

SAN JUAN ISLAND
EXPLORING FRIDAY HARBOR

Although not the largest, San Juan Island is the most populous and touristy of the San Juan Islands. **Friday Harbor,** where the ferry docks, is the county seat for San Juan County and is the only real town on all of the islands. As such it is home to numerous shops, restaurants, motels, and bed-and-breakfast inns that cater to tourists, as well as such necessities of island life as grocery and hardware stores. With its well-protected, large marina, it's also one of the most popular places in the islands for boaters to drop anchor.

❓ Did You Know?

- With 375 miles of saltwater shoreline, Island County, which encompasses the San Juan Islands, has more shoreline than any other county in the United States.
- Channels between the San Juan Islands range between 600 and 1,000 feet deep.
- Water temperatures off the San Juan Islands range between 45°F in winter and 52°F in summer.

If you arrived by car, you'll first want to find a parking space, which can be difficult in the summer. Once on foot, stroll around town admiring the simple wood-frame shop buildings built back at the turn of the century. At that time, Friday Harbor was referred to as the southernmost port in Alaska and was a busy harbor. Schooners and steamships hauled the island's fruit, livestock, and lime (for cement) off to more populous markets. Today these pursuits have all died off, but reminders of the island's rural roots linger on, and these memories have fueled the island's new breadwinner—tourism.

Whale watching is one of the most popular summer activities in the San Juans, and before you head out to spot some spouts, you should stop by the **Whale Museum,** 62 First St. N. (☎ **360/378-4710**). Here you can see whale skeletons and models of whales and learn all about the area's pods of orcas (also known as killer whales). The museum is open daily from 10am to 6pm (until 7pm in summer); admission is $4 for adults, $2.50 for seniors, and $1 for children 5 to 18.

Here in Friday Harbor, you'll also find the headquarters of the **San Juan National Historic Park** (☎ **360/378-2240**), which is at the corner of Spring and First streets. This park commemorates the San Juan Island Pig War, one of North America's most unusual and least remembered confrontations. Way back in 1859, San Juan Island nearly became the site of a battle between the British and the Americans. The two countries had not yet agreed upon the border between the United States and Canada when a British pig on San Juan Island decided to have dinner in an American garden. The owner of the garden didn't take too kindly to this and shot the pig. The Brits, rather than welcoming this succulent addition to their evening's repast, threatened redress. In less time than it takes to smoke a ham, both sides were calling in reinforcements. Luckily, this pigheadedness was defused and a more serious confrontation was avoided. While the park's headquarters is here in Friday Harbor, the main historic sites are English Camp, at the north end of the island, and American Camp, at the south end of the island. At both camps, you can visit historic buildings that are much as they might have looked in 1859.

If you're interested in island history, stop by the **San Juan Historical Museum,** 405 Price St. (☎ **360/378-3949**), where you can pick up a walking map to Friday Harbor's historic buildings. May to September the museum is open Wednesday through Saturday from 1 to 4:30pm; October to April the museum is open Thursday and Friday from 1 to 4:30pm. Admission is by donation.

Friday Harbor is also home to quite a few good art galleries. At **Annikin,** 165 First St. (☎ **360/378-7286**), **Waterworks Gallery,** 315 Spring St. (☎ **360/378-3060**), and **Island Studios,** 270 Spring St. (☎ **360/378-6550**), you'll find fine art and contemporary crafts by local and regional artists. At **Arctic Raven Gallery,** 1 Front St. (☎ **360/378-3433**) and **Nat-sa-la-né,** 285 Spring St. (☎ **360/378-8580**), you'll find contemporary Native American art and crafts.

If you need some wine for your vacation or want to take some home with you, be sure to stop by the tasting room at **Island Wine Company,** Cannery Landing (☎360/378-3229), which is the only place you can buy San Juan Cellars wines (made in the Yakima Valley). You'll find the wine shop on the immediate left as you leave the ferry.

SEEING THE REST OF THE ISLAND

Most of the island's main attractions can be seen on a long loop drive around the perimeter of the island. Start the drive by following Roche Harbor signs north out of Friday Harbor. On the way north, you might stop in at **Giannangelo Farms,** 5500 Limestone Point Rd. (☎ 360/378-4218), an organic herb farm and garden off Rouleau Road. You can stroll through the gardens and perhaps buy some herbs or herbed vinegar.

Continuing north, you'll soon come to **Roche Harbor Resort.** Roche Harbor was once the site of large limestone quarries that supplied lime to much of the West Coast. Today many of the quarries' old structures are still visible, giving this area a decaying industrial look, but amidst the abandoned machinery stands the historic Hotel de Haro, a simple whitewashed wooden building with verandahs across its two floors. Stop and admire the old-fashioned marina and colorful gardens. The deck of the hotel's lounge is one of the best places on the island to linger over a drink. Back in the woods near the resort you'll find an unusual **mausoleum** that was erected by the founder of the quarries and the Hotel de Haro.

Continuing south on what is now West Valley Road, you'll soon come to **English Camp.** Set amid shady trees and spacious lawns, the camp is the picture of British civility. There's even a formal garden surrounded by a white picket fence. You can look inside the reconstructed buildings and imagine the days when this was one of the most far-flung corners of the British Empire. If you're full of energy, hike up to the top of 650-foot **Mount Young** for a panorama of the island. An easier hike is out to the end of **Bel Point.**

As you head south on West Valley Road, watch for the Bay Road turnoff. This connects to the Westside Road, which leads down the island's west coast. Along this road, you'll find **San Juan County Park,** a great spot for a picnic. A little farther south you'll come to **Lime Kiln State Park,** the country's first whale-watching park.

At the far south end of the island is the windswept promontory on which stood the **American Camp** during the Pig War. Here you'll find a visitor center and a few reconstructed buildings. Before the American Camp was built here, this was the site of a Hudson's Bay Company farm. The meadows sweeping down to the sea were once grazed by sheep and cattle, but today you'll see only rabbits browsing amid the high grasses and wildflowers. There are several **hiking trails** along the bluffs and down to the sea. One trail leads through a dark forest of Douglas firs. At the end of the trail you'll find **Jackle's Lagoon,** which is a great spot for bird watching. Keep your eyes peeled for bald eagles which are relatively plentiful around here.

SPORTS & OUTDOOR ACTIVITIES

BICYCLING   Bicycling is another favorite sport of island visitors. Winding country roads are almost ideal for leisurely trips. If you didn't bring your own bike, you can rent one from **Island Bicycles,** 380 Argyle St., in Friday Harbor (☎ 360/378-4941), which charges $3 to $10 per hour and $15 to $50 per day. Here on San Juan Island (and on no other of these islands) you can rent scooters and mopeds. They're available by the hour or by the day from **Island Scooter & Bike Rental,** 85 Front St. (☎ 360/378-8811) or **Susie's Mopeds** (☎ 800/532-0087 or 360/378-5244), which is located at the top of the ferry lanes.

The Truth About Killer Whales

Killer whales, once maligned as the wolves of the deep and dreaded as ruthless marauders of the sea, have been going through a change of image over the past decade. As more has been learned about these highly intelligent members of the porpoise family, an unofficial public-relations campaign has been waged to convince people that these are not killer whales, but orca whales. The more one learns about these intelligent, family oriented animals, the more evident it becomes that past images of this whale are misinformed.

Orcas can be found in every ocean, but one of their highest concentrations is in the waters stretching north from Puget Sound along the coast of British Columbia. This has become one of the most studied and most publicized populations of orcas in the world.

Orcas, which can grow to 30 feet long and weigh almost 9,000 pounds, are the largest member of the porpoise family. In the wild, they can live for up to 80 years, with female orcas commonly living 20 to 30 years longer than males. Orcas are among the most family-oriented animals on earth, and related whales will often live together for their entire lives, sometimes with three generations present at the same time. These family groups frequently band together with other closely related groups into extended families known as pods. A community of orcas consists of several pods, and in this area these communities number around 100 individuals. There are three populations of orcas living in the waters off Vancouver Island, British Columbia. These are known as the northern and southern resident communities and the transient community. It's the southern resident community that whale watchers in the San Juan Islands are most likely to encounter.

As predators, orcas do live up to the name "killer," and have been known to attack other whales much larger than themselves. Some orcas off the coast of Argentina even swim up onto the shore, beaching themselves to attack resting sea lions, then thrashing and twisting their way back into the water. However, not all orcas feed on other marine mammals. Of the three communities in this area, only the transients feed on mammals. The two resident communities feed primarily on salmon, which are abundant in these waters, especially off the west side of San Juan Island during the summer.

BOAT CHARTERS   If you and a few friends would just like to get out on the water for a leisurely cruise, there are always boats to be chartered in Friday Harbor. Check around the marina for notices. The upmarket **Mariella Inn & Cottages** (☎ 800/700-7668 or 360/378-6868) also offers a variety of day cruises aboard their 1927 yacht the *Arequipa*. Prices range from $115 per person for a lunch cruise to $195 per person for a candlelight dinner cruise with wine. You can also try contacting **Cap'n Howard's Sailing Charters** (☎ 360/378-3958).

FISHING   If you want to try catching some salmon, contact **Buffalo Works** (☎ 360/378-4612), **Trophy Charters** (☎ 360/378-2110), or **Roche Harbor Resort** (☎ 800/451-8910, ext. 505, or 360/378-2155, ext. 505), all of which also offer bottom-fishing trips.

GOLF   Golfers will find nine holes at the **San Juan Golf Club** (☎ 360/378-2254). Greens fees are $17.50 for nine holes and $25 for 18.

SCUBA DIVING   Believe it or not, scuba diving is also extremely popular in the San Juans. Though the water stays frigid year-round, it's also exceedingly clear. If you're a diver and want to rent equipment or go on a guided dive, or if you want to take a diving class while you're here, contact **Emerald Seas Dive Center,** 2-A Spring St., Spring St. Landing, Friday Harbor (☎ 360/378-2772). Two dives will cost you $65.

SEA KAYAKING Three- to 4-hour sea kayak tours ($35 to $39) are offered by **Roche Harbor Resort** (☎ 800/451-8910, ext. 505, or 360/378-2155, ext. 505), **Leisure Kayak Adventures** (☎ 800/836-1402 or 360/378-5992), **San Juan Kayak Expeditions** (☎ 360/378-4436), and **Crystal Seas Kayaking** (☎ 360/378-7899). Most of these companies also offer full-day and overnight trips.

WHALE WATCHING When it's time to spot some whales, you have two choices. You can take a whale-watching cruise or head over to **Lime Kiln State Park,** where a short trail leads down to a rocky coastline from which orca whales, minke whales, Dall's porpoises, and sea lions can sometimes be seen. The best months to see orcas are June to September, but it's possible to see them throughout the year. Whale-watching cruises lasting from 4 to 6 hours are offered in the summer by **Western Prince Cruises** (☎ 800/757-6722 or 360/378-5315) and **San Juan Excursions** (☎ 800/80-WHALE or 360/378-6636), both of which operate out of Friday Harbor. Cruises are $45 for adults and $32 for children 4 to 12. Three-hour whale-watching trips from Roche Harbor Resort, on the north side of the island, are offered by the **Marine Activity Center** (☎ 800/451-8910, ext. 505, or 360/378-2155, ext. 505), which charges $39 for adults and $29 for children 17 and under. Should you happen to see a whale on your travels through the San Juans, report the sighting to the **Whale Sighting Hotline** (☎ 800/562-8832).

WHERE TO STAY

Expensive

✪ **Friday Harbor House.** 130 West St. (P.O. Box 1385), Friday Harbor, WA 98250. ☎ **360/ 378-8455.** Fax 360/378-8453. 20 rms. TV TEL. May–Oct, $187–$197 double; $277 suite. Nov–Apr, $167–$187 double; $257 suite. Rates include continental breakfast. AE, DC, DISC, MC, V.

With its contemporary, yet distinctly northwestern architecture, this luxurious little boutique hotel brings urban sophistication to Friday Harbor. The hotel's bluff-top location assures excellent views of the ferry landing and adjacent marina, as well as Orcas Island in the distance. With their fireplaces and double whirlpool tubs, guest rooms are designed for romantic getaways. Only a curtain separates the tub from the bedroom, so you can gaze out at the view or the fire while soaking. Slate foyers, lots of glowing wood, and neutral, beachy tones are accented by contemporary furnishings. Most rooms have decks or balconies. If you enjoy contemporary styling, these are the best rooms on all the San Juan Islands. The dining room here is one of the best on the island and has a seasonal menu with an emphasis on Northwest cuisine (see "Where to Dine," below).

Mariella Inn & Cottages. 630 Turn Point Rd., Friday Harbor, WA 98250. ☎ **800/700-7668** or 360/378-6868. Fax 360/378-6822. 8 rms, 3 suites, 12 cabins and cottages. Mid-June–late Sept, $125–$215 double; $235–$275 suite; $175–$375 cottage or cabin. Lower rates in other months, rates include full breakfast. AE, MC, V.

Although the estatelike waterfront setting here is the quintessence of island life, the prices are surprisingly high for what you get. While some of the guest rooms are small, a few have rooftop decks. The suites have solariums with whirlpool tubs and are probably the most comfortable accommodations. The waterfront cottages, though they all have great views, vary considerably in style and comfort level. Because maintenance on this old house isn't all it should be, try to get one of the newer cottages. The inn's spacious lawns are set up for badminton, volleyball, and croquet in summer, and bike rentals and guided sea kayak tours are also available. The first floor of the inn is taken up by a restaurant that leans toward traditional preparations in its seasonal menus.

Moderate

Duffy House Bed & Breakfast Inn. 760 Pear Point Rd., Friday Harbor, WA 98250. ☎ 800/972-2089 or 360/378-5604. Fax 360/378-6535. 5 rms. $95–$105 double. MC, V.

Don't despair when you find yourself in a gravel pit as you try to find this B&B. Keep going and you'll come out the other side of the gravel pit to find a secluded point on the slopes of which stands this 1920s Tudor home. Surrounded by a small farm, the inn has a great view over the water. The country-style guest rooms can be a bit cramped but are still comfortable enough. Our favorite is the one with the view of the eagle's nest.

Hillside House Bed & Breakfast. 365 Carter Ave., Friday Harbor, WA 98250 ☎ 800/232-4730 or 360/378-4730. 7 rms (5 with private baths). Fax 360/378-4715. $85–$175 double. Lower rates off-season. Rates include full breakfast. AE, DISC, MC, V.

Located less than a mile from the ferry landing, this contemporary home sits atop a hill and has good views of both Mount Baker and the water from many of its guest rooms. The inn's best room is the Eagle's Nest, which takes up the entire top floor and has a bird's-eye view of the harbor. This room also has a whirlpool tub and balcony. Other rooms are much smaller and less luxurious but comfortable nonetheless.

Lonesome Cove Resort. 5810-A Lonesome Cove Rd., Friday Harbor, WA 98250. ☎ 360/378-4477. 6 cabins. $95 cabin for two. Minimum stay 2 nights Sept–May, 5 nights June–Aug. MC, V.

If you want to be alone, there's no better place on San Juan Island than Lonesome Cove. This is the sort of place your grandparents might have frequented on summer vacation 50 years ago. Forests hide the 6-acre property from the rest of the world, while lawns and orchards surround the waterfront cabins. Each of the rustic cabins has a large deck, stone fireplace, and full kitchen. There's a quarter mile of private beach, a trout pond, friendly ducks, romantic sunsets, and more peace and solitude than you'll find anywhere else on the island.

✪ Olympic Lights Bed and Breakfast. 4531-A Cattle Point Rd., Friday Harbor, WA 98250. ☎ 360/378-3186. Fax 360/378-2097. 5 rms, 1 with bath. $70–$105 double. Rates include full breakfast. No credit cards.

Located at San Juan's dry southwestern tip, the Olympic Lights is a yellow Victorian farmhouse surrounded by windswept meadows. If you couldn't see Puget Sound from here, it would be easy to mistake the setting for the prairies of the Midwest. There are colorful gardens, an old barn, even some hens to lay the eggs for your breakfast. The ocean breezes, nearby beach, and friendliness of innkeepers Christian and Lea Andrade lend a special feel to this American classic. If you seek creature comforts, opt for the Garden Room, which has a king-size bed and private bathroom. However, our personal favorite is the Ra Room, which is named for the Egyptian sun god and features a bay window in front of which are arranged two wicker chairs. The view out the windows is enough to settle the most stressed-out soul.

Roche Harbor Resort. P.O. Box 4001, Roche Harbor, WA 98250. ☎ 800/451-8910 or 360/378-2155. Fax 360/378-6809. 16 rms (all with shared baths); 3 suites; 20 condos; 9 cottages. TEL. May–Sept, $79–$85 double with shared bath; $115–$130 suite; $145–$245 condo; $130–$195 cottage. Lower rates Oct–Apr. AE, MC, V.

Located at the north end of the island, the Roche Harbor Resort is steeped in island history, with the historic Hotel de Haro, established in 1886, serving as the resort's centerpiece. A brick driveway and manicured gardens provide the foreground for the two-story, white hotel, which overlooks the marina and has porches running the length of both floors. Unfortunately maintenance of the guest rooms in the old Hotel de Haro has been somewhat lax in recent years, so, though it has plenty of character, you won't necessarily want to stay here. For more reliable accommodations, you'll need to opt for one of the condos or cottages.

The resort's dining room (open May to September only) serves continental and Northwest cuisine and has a view of the marina. The deck is a great spot for a sunset cocktail.

Services include whale-watching cruises, sea kayaking, and fishing charters; there is an outdoor pool, tennis court, marina, and general store.

Wharfside Bed & Breakfast. Slip K-13, Port of Friday Harbor (P.O. Box 1212), Friday Harbor, WA 98250. ☎ **360/378-5661.** 2 rms, neither with bath. $90–$95 double. Rates include full breakfast. AE, MC, V.

Formerly of Portland, Oregon, Betty and Clyde Rice decided to leave their city ways and opted for life on a 60-foot ketch-rigged motorboat. Before long they turned the boat into a bed-and-breakfast with two spacious yet cozy cabins. The cabins are comfortably furnished (one has space for two children), and the skylit main saloon is decorated with antiques and memorabilia. Listening to the soothing sound of water lapping against the boat's hull, you'll get a peaceful night's sleep here; and a filling breakfast on the sunny deck in the summer is a great way to begin a day.

Campgrounds

Lakedale Campground, 2627 Roche Harbor Rd., Friday Harbor, WA 98250 (☎ **800/617-CAMP** or 360/378-2350), is 4 miles north of Friday Harbor. With 82 acres, several lakes, and campsites for tents as well as RVs, this private campground makes an ideal spot for a family vacation. There are also a few modern log cabins for rent.

Our personal favorite campground, though, is **San Juan County Park,** 380 Westside Rd. N., Friday Harbor, WA 98250 (☎ **360/378-2992**), which is set on the site of an old waterfront farm. The views are unbeatable. This is a great spot for bicyclists. If you're heading up here in summer, make reservations as early as January.

WHERE TO DINE

In addition to the restaurants listed below, there are several other places in Friday Harbor where you can get a quick, simple meal. **Katrina's,** 135 Second St. (☎ **360/378-7290**), has long been a locals' favorite for good, mostly vegetarian lunches. At the top of the ferry lanes, you'll find **Madelyn's Bagel Bakery** (☎ **360/378-4545**), a small bagel and sandwich shop, and the **Garden Path Cafe,** (☎ **360/378-6255**), which usually has a good selection of pasta salad. The latter two are on A Street, across the street from each other.

Duck Soup Inn. 3090 Roche Harbor Rd. ☎ **360/378-4878.** Reservations highly recommended. Main courses $18–$25. DISC, MC, V. Summer, Wed–Sun 5:30–10pm; spring and fall, Fri–Sat 5:30–10pm. Closed Nov–Mar. NORTHWEST.

North of Friday Harbor 4$^{1}/_{2}$ miles you'll find the Duck Soup Inn, a barnlike restaurant beside a pond frequented by—you guessed it—ducks. Inside this quintessentially northwestern building you'll find lots of exposed wood, a fieldstone fireplace, paintings by local artist Malcolm Ross, and more ducks—this time on the menu. Dishes include such local favorites as duck confit and apple-wood–smoked oysters. The menu changes frequently, depending on the availability of fresh produce, but is always very creative.

Friday Harbor House Dining Room. 130 West St. ☎ **360/378-8455.** Reservations recommended. Main courses $14–$18. AE, DC, DISC, MC, V. Daily 5:30–9pm. Closed Tues–Wed in winter. NORTHWEST.

Located in the luxurious Friday Harbor House boutique hotel, this is the most sophisticated restaurant on San Juan Island. Striking contemporary decor sets the tone, but can't distract diners from the harbor views out the glass walls. The menu is short and relies heavily on local ingredients, including island-grown greens and Westcott Bay oysters. The chef draws on diverse inspirations for the dishes served here, which are always attractively presented as well as carefully prepared. A recent menu included grilled pork tenderloin with a double-mustard glaze, as well as a green curry with prawns, oysters, mussels, clams, scallops, and fish.

✪ The Place by the Ferry. 1 Spring St. ☎ **360/378-8707.** Main dishes $15–$19. MC, V. Tues–Sat 5:30–9pm (longer hours in summer). NORTHWEST/INTERNATIONAL.

Located on the waterfront to the right as you get off the ferry in Friday Harbor, this aptly named establishment, in a small wooden building was once part of a Coast Guard station, is San Juan Island's finest waterfront restaurant. With lots of local art on the wall, this place aims to attract the upscale Seattle market and seems to be successful at doing just that. A recent menu included such flavorful dishes as pork tenderloin in a Madeira sauce and a southwestern black bean ravioli lime, garlic, cilantro, basil, and tiger shrimp flamed in tequila. The Place has rapidly become one of the most popular restaurants on the island and sometimes seems slightly overwhelmed by its own popularity.

Roberto's Restaurant. At the corner of First and A sts. ☎ **360/378-6333.** Reservations highly recommended. Main courses $9–$16.50. DISC, MC, V. June–Aug daily 5:30–9pm, other months Tues–Sat 5:30–9pm. Closed Jan–Feb. SOUTHERN ITALIAN.

Located in an old house that sits a bit above street level, the restaurant has about a dozen tables jammed into a tiny room that luckily opens onto a deck for summer overflow. Coral walls and relaxed lighting create a relaxed atmosphere belied by the bustling waitresses. We recommend chopped clams, bay shrimp, and linguine; and our cod with anchovy, garlic, caper, and parsley sauce, accompanied by perfectly grilled summer squash, was delicious.

✪ Springtree Eating Establishment and Farm. 310 Spring St. ☎ **360/378-4848.** Reservations recommended. Main courses $15–$19. MC, V. Summer, daily 11:30am–2pm and 5:30–9pm; winter, Tues–Sat 11:30am–2pm and 5:30–8:30pm. NORTHWEST.

Tucked in behind a white picket fence and a beautiful weeping elm tree at the top of Spring Street, the Springtree restaurant is a perennial island favorite. The menu changes regularly, and seafood usually takes the fore, with the crab cakes a specialty. Local oysters and mussels also make regular appearances, accompanied by whatever new sauce strikes the chef's fancy (roasted poblano and cilantro butter recently). There's an excellent selection of wines, and desserts often feature local fruits.

ORCAS ISLAND
EXPLORING THE ISLAND

Named for the whales and shaped like a horseshoe, Orcas Island has long been a popular summer-vacation spot. The island is a particular favorite of nature lovers who come to enjoy the views of green rolling pastures, forested mountains, and fjordlike bays. **Eastsound** is the largest town on the island and has several interesting shops and good restaurants. Other, smaller villages include Deer Harbor, West Sound, and Olga.

To learn a little about the history of Orcas Island, drop by the **Orcas Island Historical Museum,** North Beach Road, Eastsound (☎ 360/376-4849). The museum is open mid-May to October, Monday through Saturday from 1 to 4pm and Friday 1 to 8pm. Admission is $1. A second historical museum, the **Crow Valley School Museum** (☎ 360/376-4260), an old one-room schoolhouse, is located 3 miles southwest of Eastsound on Crow Valley Road. The museum is open Memorial Day to Labor Day only, Thursday through Saturday from 1 to 4pm. At the **Lambiel Home Museum** (☎ 360/376-3222) on Horseshoe Highway southeast of Eastsound, you can view a private collection of artwork by artists from around the San Juan Islands. The museum is open daily from 9am to 5pm by appointment and admission is $5.

Around the island you'll find quite a few interesting shops worth visiting. In Eastsound, **Darvill's Rare Print Shop,** Horseshoe Highway, (☎ 360/376-2351), sells antique prints and maps and is adjacent to **Darvill's Book Shop** (☎ 360/376-2135), which specializes in Northwest fiction, history, and guidebooks. **Shinola Jewelry,** North Beach Road (☎ 360/376-4508) is also worth checking out. A few miles west of Eastsound off Enchanted Forest Road, you'll find **Orcas Island Pottery** (☎ 360/376-2813), the oldest pottery studio in the Northwest; and, on West Beach across from the West Beach Resort, **The Right Place Pottery Shop** (☎ 360/376-4023) and **The Naked Lamb Wool Shop** (☎ 360/376-4606). Between Eastsound and Orcas on Horseshoe Highway, you'll find **Crow Valley Pottery** (☎ 360/376-4260), which is in an 1866 log cabin. On the east side of the island, **Orcas Island Artworks** (☎ 360/376-4408) is full of beautiful work by island artists.

Although there aren't any vineyards on Orcas Island, **Orcas Wine Company** (☎ 360/376-6244), with tasting rooms both at the ferry landing and in Eastsound on Horseshoe Highway, features its own Madrona Cellars wines (grown and bottled in the Yakima Valley).

SPORTS & OUTDOOR ACTIVITIES

Moran State Park (☎ 360/376-2326), which covers 5,175 acres of the island, is the largest park in the San Juans and the main destination of most visitors to the island. If the weather is clear, you'll find great views from the summit of Mount Constitution, which rises 2,409 feet above Puget Sound. There are also five lakes, 32 miles of hiking trails, and an environmental learning center. Fishing, hiking, boating, mountain biking, and camping are all popular park activities. The park is off Horseshoe Highway, approximately 12½ miles from the ferry landing.

AIRPLANE RIDES   For a very fun overview of Orcas Island, try a scenic biplane ride with pilot Rod Magner who flies a restored 1929 Travelair. Thirty-minute flights with his **Magic Air Tours** (☎ 800/FLY-1929 or 360/376-2733) cost $199 for two people.

BICYCLING   Although Orcas is considered the most challenging of the San Juan Islands for bicycling, plenty of cyclists still pedal the island's roads. Bike rentals here are available from **Dolphin Bay Bicycles** (☎ 360/376-4157), located just to the right as you get off the ferry, and **Wildlife Cycles,** North Beach Road, Eastsound (☎ 360/376-4708). Bikes rent for between $5 and $8 per hour or $20 to $60 per day. Dolphin Bay Bicycles also offers guided bike trips for $45 to $100 per day. If you're exploring the island by mountain bike, you may want to take the unpaved Dolphin Bay Road to Eastsound, otherwise, take the Crow Valley Road.

BOAT CHARTERS If you're interested in heading out on the water in a 33-foot sailboat, contact **Amante Sail Tours** (☎ 360/376-4231), which charges $35 per person (with a two-person minimum) for a half-day sail. **Quarter Moon Cruises** (☎ 360/376-2878), on the other hand will take you out in a 55-foot motor yacht. A lunch cruise to the Wasp Islands is $65 per person. Cruises to Sucia Island or Stuart Island are $125 per person.

GOLF Golfers can head to the nine-hole **Orcas Island Country Golf Club** (☎ 360/376-4400) near Eastsound on the Horseshoe Highway.

HIKING With more than 30 miles of hiking trails, Moran State Park offers hikes ranging from short, easy strolls alongside lakes, to strenuous, all-day hikes. South of the community of Olga, on the east arm of the island, you'll also find a $1/2$-mile trail through **Obstruction Pass Park.** This trail leads to a quiet little cove that has a few walk-in, paddle-in campsites. The park is at the end of Obstruction Pass Road.

HORSEBACK RIDING Guided trail rides ($40 per person) can be arranged through **Walking Horse Country Farm** (☎ 360/376-5306).

SEA KAYAKING The best way to see the Orcas Island coast is by sea kayak. Guided tours are offered by **Shearwater Adventures** (☎ 360/376-4699), **Spring Bay Inn's Kayak Tours** (☎ 360/376-5521), and **Osprey Tours** (☎ 360/376-3677), which uses traditional, hand-built Aleutian-style kayaks. Expect to pay around $25 for a 2-hour paddle and $35 to $40 for a 3-hour tour. If you're an experienced paddler, you can also rent a sea kayak from **Orcas Kayak Rentals,** Madrona Street, Eastsound (☎ 360/376-3767) and head out on your own.

WHALE WATCHING If you want to see some of the orca whales for which this island is named, you can take a whale-watching excursion ($45 for adults and $30 for children) with **Deer Harbor Charters** (☎ 800/544-5758 or 360/376-5989) or **Orcas Island Eclipse Charters** (☎ 800/376-6566 or 360/376-4663).

WHERE TO STAY

Expensive

✪**Chestnut Hill Inn.** P.O. Box 213, Orcas, WA 98280-0213. ☎ **360/376-5157.** Fax 360/376-5283. www.chestnuthillinn.com. 4 rms, 1 suite. May 1–Oct 31, $145 double; $195 suite. Nov 1–Apr 30, $105 double; $145 suite. Rates include full breakfast. AE, DISC, MC, V.

Located in one of the more remote corners of the island and set on a hilltop with a forest in back and pasture in front, this luxurious country B&B is a good choice for anyone searching for a country getaway. The farm setting conjures up visions of the quiet island life for guests, especially those lounging on the veranda over afternoon tea or an evening glass of wine. Guest rooms all have four-poster feather beds and fireplaces, and you'll find an aperitif awaiting you in your room each afternoon. Breakfasts are lavish, multicourse feasts, and in the off-season, dinners can be arranged. Bicycles are available for guests. At press time, there were plans to add a schoolhouse cottage that would rent for $125 (without breakfast).

Deer Harbor Resort. P.O. Box 200, Deer Harbor, WA 98243. ☎ **360/376-4420.** www.thesanjuans.com/deer harbor. 12 rms, 10 cottages, 3 villas. TV. $129–$139 double; $139–$199 cottage; $269–$299 villa. Lower rates off-season. Rates include breakfast. AE, DISC, MC, V.

Located on the spectacular Deer Harbor inlet, this casual resort offers, in our opinion, the best views on the island. Set on an open hillside above the harbor, it looks across the water to a forested rock wall. At the mouth of the harbor are a few small islands. Add to this the marina and sailboats bobbing at anchor, and you have the quintessential island setting. The Deer Harbor is quiet even by Orcas standards. Our favorite accommodations are the restored 1935 cottages, each of which has their own deck (some with whirlpools), wood stove, and minirefrigerator. The view from the cottages is superb. Facilities at the resort include two hot tubs, an outdoor pool, and a restaurant.

✪ Rosario Resort & Spa. 1 Rosario Way, Eastsound, WA 98245. ☎ **800/562-8820** or 360/376-2222. Fax 360/376-2289. 127 rms and suites. Late May–late Sept, $180–$260 double; $200–$400 suite. Lower rates off-season. AE, DC, DISC, MC, V.

Having recently undergone a very thorough renovation, this is now the most luxurious and upscale resort in the San Juan Islands. The centerpiece of the resort remains the 1904 Moran Mansion, an imposing white stucco building on the shore of Cascade Bay. The mansion houses the resort's main dining room, lounge, spa, and library. The larger and more luxurious rooms (with fireplaces, good views, and French country decor) are across the marina and up a steep hill from this main building, so if you aren't keen on walking, request a room in one of the buildings directly adjacent to the Moran Mansion. These have heavy bamboo furniture that might be more appropriate in the tropics but that is still fun here in the San Juans. New owners are in the process of renovating most guest rooms and giving the resort a more contemporary look and feel.

Dining/Entertainment: The resort's restaurant provides water views and serves creative Northwest cuisine, with dishes in the $18 to $23 range. The lounge is a casual little bar overlooking the water and has live piano music on weekend evenings. There are also evening pipe organ and piano recitals in the mansion's music room.

Services: Rental cars, massages, herbal wraps, skin-care services, aerobics classes.

Facilities: Three pools (one indoor and two outdoor), whirlpool, exercise room, beauty shop, tennis courts, playground, marina.

✪ Spring Bay Inn. P.O. Box 97, Olga, WA 98279. ☎ **360/376-5531.** Fax 360/376-2193. 5 rms. $175–$225 double. Rates include continental breakfast, brunch, and daily kayak tour. AE, DISC, MC, V.

Just for being one of the only waterfront B&Bs in the San Juans, this inn would deserve a recommendation. However, innkeepers Sandy Playa and Carl Burger, both retired park rangers, make a stay here both fun and educational, and the setting and inn itself are great for a romantic getaway. You can soak in the hot tub on the beach and watch the sunset, spot bald eagles from just outside the inn's front door, hike on the nature trails, and best of all, go for a guided sea-kayak tour each morning. Before heading out on the water you're served a continental breakfast, and upon returning you get a filling brunch. Four of the five guest rooms have fireplaces, two have views from their tubs, and two have balconies.

✪ Turtleback Farm Inn. Rte. 1, Box 650, Eastsound, WA 98245. ☎ **800/376-4914** or 360/376-4914. Fax 360/376-5329. 11 rms. Apr 1–Oct 31, $80–$210 double (lower rates other months). Rates include full breakfast. Two-night minimum stay May–Oct, weekends, and holidays. DISC, MC, V.

This bright-green restored farmhouse overlooks 80 acres of farmland at the foot of Turtleback Mountain, and nowhere on Orcas will you find a more idyllic setting. Simply furnished with antiques, the guest rooms range from cozy to spacious, and each has its own special view. Our favorite room in the main house is the Meadow View Room, which has a private deck and claw-foot tub. The four rooms in the new orchard house are among the biggest and most luxurious on the island (gas fireplaces, claw-foot tubs and showers, balconies, wood floors). Days here start with a big farm breakfast served at valley-view tables set with bone china, silver, and linen. Finish your day with a nip of sherry by the fire, and you have the perfect Orcas Island country day.

Windsong Bed & Breakfast. P.O. Box 32, Orcas, WA 98280. ☎ **800/669-3948** or 360/ 376-2500. Fax 360/376-4453. 6 rms. $115–$175 double. Rates include full breakfast. MC, V.

Housed in a converted 1917 schoolhouse not far from the ferry landing, this B&B offers large guest rooms, five of which have their own fireplaces. The inn's two most luxurious rooms, with whirlpool tubs, fireplaces, and window seats, are in the carriage house. Owners Kim and Sam Haines have worked hard to turn this building into a comfortable inn and their hard work shows in the many attractive touches throughout. A large lawn surrounds the B&B and deer can often be seen grazing here. Massages are available and there's a whirlpool for warm soaks. The multicourse gourmet breakfasts are among the best in the islands.

Moderate

Cascade Harbor Inn. HC 1, Box 195, Eastsound, WA 98245. ☎ **800/201-2120** or 360/ 376-6350. Fax 360/376-6354. 44 rms and suites. Mid-June to late Sept, $90–$190 double. Late Sept to mid-June, $54–$114 double. Rates include continental breakfast. DISC, MC, V.

Formerly a part of Rosario Resort, this hotel enjoys similar Eastsound views and is adjacent to both the Rosario marina and Moran State Park. Guest rooms range from standard motel rooms to studios with Murphy beds to spacious suites with kitchens. All the rooms have water views, though in some cases it is somewhat hidden by trees. The lodge sits on a steep hillside above the water, and a path leads down to the Rosario marina. Because high-season rates don't start until mid-June here, this is a good choice for a late spring getaway.

Orcas Hotel. P.O. Box 155, Orcas, WA 98280. ☎ **360/376-4300.** 12 rms (2 with private baths, 3 with half baths). $69–$110 double with shared bath, $110 double with half bath, $170 double with private bath. Rates include full breakfast. AE, DISC, MC, V.

Located right at the Orcas ferry landing, this B&B is a good choice for anyone coming over without a car. On the other hand, the proximity of the ferry precludes the tranquil setting available at other island B&Bs. Nonetheless, the Orcas is an attractive old Victorian hotel and has been welcoming guests since 1904. The guest rooms, done in a simple country style, vary in size, but all are carpeted and furnished with antiques and have quilts on the beds. On the first floor of this three-story building you'll find a quiet lounge, bakery, cafe, and restaurant. Lately this hotel has been looking better from the outside than from the inside.

Inexpensive

Doe Bay Village Resort. Star Rte., Box 86, Olga, WA 98279. ☎ **360/376-2291.** 24 cottages, 10 tent-cabins and yurts, 6 hostel beds, 30 campsites. $44.50–$84.50 double; $15.50 hostel bed; $12–$18 campsite. AE, DISC, MC, V.

This funky collection of cottages, tiny cabins, and tent cabins is a sort of counterculture resort popular with Deadheads. The cottages are furnished in early Salvation Army and many have their own kitchens. The dining room serves vegetarian meals. Spring-fed hot tubs and a sauna are among the resort's top attractions. They're set on a big deck overlooking a picturesque little cove. (The tubs, sauna, and beach are clothing optional.) For those on a really tight budget, there are campsites and even a hostel. Kayak tours operate from the resort, and massages are also available. The tubs and sauna are also open to the public for a small fee.

Campgrounds

With 151 sites, **Moran State Park** (☎ **360/376-2326**) is the most popular camping spot on the island. Reservations are recommended April to September and can be made as much as 11 months to the day ahead of time through **Reservations Northwest** (☎ 800/452-5687). Additional campsites are available at the **Doe Bay Village Resort** (☎ 360/376-2291), a sort of Deadhead beach resort. If you enjoy roughing it, there are hike-in or paddle-in sites at **Obstruction Pass State Park** at the south end of the east arm of the island. Keep in mind that there is no water available at this isolated and beautifully situated park.

WHERE TO DINE

For soups, sandwiches, and lattes, you can't beat the **Comet Café**, Eastsound Square, North Beach Road, Eastsound (☎ 360/376-4220). For baked goods, imported cheeses, and other gourmet foodstuffs, stop by **Rose's Bread and Specialties** (☎ 360/376-5805), which is also in Eastsound Square. For great cookies, don't miss **Teezer's Cookies** (☎ 360/376-2913) at the corner of North Beach Road and A Street.

Bilbo's Festivo. N. Beach Rd., Eastsound. ☎ **360/376-4728.** Reservations highly recommended. Main courses lunch $3–$6, dinner $5–$18. MC, V. Apr–Sept, daily 11:30am–2:30pm and 5–10pm; Oct–Mar, shorter dinner hours and closed for lunch. MEXICAN.

This old bungalow has been transformed into a southwestern hacienda with the addition of stucco, tiles, and some rounded concrete walls on the patio, and over the years Bilbo's has developed a reputation for its Mexican food and Southwest/Northwest ambience. Entrees here can at times be lackluster, so you might want to stick to several rounds of appetizers accompanied by tart margaritas. Summers see the crowds lining up to get into the restaurant's patio where the barbecue grill stays fired up with mesquite.

✪ **Café Olga.** Horseshoe Hwy., Olga. ☎ **360/376-5098.** Reservations recommended. Main courses $5–$10; breakfast $2.75–$7. DISC, MC, V. Mar–Dec, daily 10am–6pm. Closed Jan–Feb. INTERNATIONAL.

Housed in an old strawberry-packing plant that dates back to the days when these islands were known for their fruit, Café Olga is the best place on the island for breakfast or lunch. Everything here is homemade, using fresh local produce whenever possible. The menu includes the likes of gado-gado, Sicilian artichoke pie, an Italian sausage torta, and a cashew-chicken salad sandwich. The blackberry pie is a special treat, especially when accompanied by Lopez Island Creamery ice cream. This building also houses Orcas Island Artworks, a gallery representing more than 70 Orcas Island artists.

✪ **Christina's.** Horseshoe Hwy., Eastsound. ☎ **360/376-4904.** Reservations highly recommended. Main courses $12.50–$24.50. AE, CB, DC, MC. Thurs–Mon 5:30–9pm (longer hours in summer). NORTHWEST.

Located on the second floor of an old waterfront building in Eastsound, Christina's has a beautiful view down the sound, just right for sunsets. If the weather is pleasant, the deck is *the* place on the island for sunset dinner. The menu here is short, changes regularly, and features innovative cuisine prepared with an emphasis on local ingredients. For the most part, Christina's showcases its creativity in its appetizers rather than in its entrees, so whether you crave the unusual or the more familiar, you'll likely be satisfied here. Of late, quite a few Asian-influenced dishes have been showing up and a recent menu included salmon with a shoyu butter and mussels in a coconut-curry broth. The desserts can be heavenly. Christina's has a short but very well-chosen wine list.

La Famiglia Ristorante. A St. and Prune Alley. ☎ **360/376-2335.** Reservations recommended. Main courses $7–$17. AE, DISC, MC, V. Mon–Fri 11:30am–2pm and 4:30–9pm, Sun 4:30–9pm (dinner until 10pm in summer). ITALIAN/SEAFOOD.

La Famiglia serves up fresh Italian fare with an emphasis on seafood dishes and pasta. The decor is simple, with a large deck for sunny days and big windows to let in the thin light on gray days. Start your meal with an unusual combination of herbed artichoke with fruit and cheese or perhaps some steamer clams with garlic bread. Be sure to ask about any oyster specials they might have. You'll find an excellent selection of California and Northwest wines here.

Orcas Wine Company & Oyster Bar. Horseshoe Highway, Eastsound. ☎ **360/376-6244.** Main dishes $7–$15. AE, MC, V. Summer, Sun–Thurs 11am–8pm, Fri–Sat 11am–9pm (other months Sun–Thurs 11am–5pm, Fri–Sat 11am–8pm). SEAFOOD.

If you aren't a fan of shellfish, don't even think about eating here (the only nonshellfish offering on the menu recently was a cheese bread meant to accompany oysters on the half shell). However, if you are a fan of the briny bivalves, there is no better place to toss back a dozen Westcott Bay oysters than right here in this old waterfront building downstairs from Christinas in Eastsound. Mussels in wine, steamer clams, oysters on the half shell, and a couple of different baked oyster preparations constitute almost the entire menu here. This is a particularly good place for lunch, and the oyster po'boy, made with house-baked bread, is excellent (although it could use a few more oysters). Be sure to stop in the wine-tasting room before sitting down to eat.

Ship Bay Oyster House. Horseshoe Hwy. ☎ **360/376-5886.** Reservations recommended. Main courses $14–$19. AE, MC, V. Summer, Tues–Sun 5:30–10pm; winter, Tues–Sat 5:30–9pm, closed Nov 15–Mar 15. SEAFOOD.

About midway between Eastsound and the turnoff for the Rosario Resort you'll spot the Ship Bay. This old white house sits in a field high above the water. Should you arrive after dark and be tempted to walk over to the water, be aware that the restaurant's front yard ends in a sheer cliff. Inside, you'll find a traditional maritime decor and plenty of windows to let you gaze out to sea. Since this is an oyster house, you'd be remiss if you didn't have some bivalves with your meal. You can opt for oysters Kilpatrick, panfried yearling oysters, oyster shooters, and of course, fresh local oysters on the half shell. You can make a meal on oysters alone, but the entree menu includes plenty of other tempting seafood and meat dishes as well.

LOPEZ ISLAND
EXPLORING THE ISLAND

Of the three islands with accommodations, Lopez is the least developed. It's flatter (and less spectacular) than Orcas or San Juan, and consequently is the most popular with bicyclists who prefer easy grades over stunning panoramas. Lopez maintains more of its agricultural roots than either of the two previously mentioned islands, and likewise has fewer activities for tourists. If you just want to get away from it all and hole up with a good book for a few days, Lopez may be the place for you. Lopez Islanders are particularly friendly in that they wave to everyone they pass on the road. The custom has come to be known as the Lopez Wave.

Lopez Village is the closest this island has to a town, and here you'll find almost all of the island's restaurants and shops. At **Chimera Gallery,** Lopez Village Plaza (☎ **360/468-3265**), you can see the work of island artists and artisans. Here in the village, you'll also find the **Lopez Historical Museum** (☎ **360/468-2049** or 360/

468-3447), where you can learn about the island's history and pick up a map of historic buildings. In July and August the museum is open Wednesday through Sunday from noon to 4pm and in May, June, and September, it's open Friday through Sunday from noon to 4pm. Admission is $1.

Taste wine made from Lopez-grown grapes (Siegerrebe and Madeleine Angevine) as well as Yakima Valley wines at **Lopez Island Vineyards (☎ 360/468-3644)**, which is located on Fisherman Bay Road between the ferry landing and Lopez Village.

SPORTS & OUTDOOR ACTIVITIES

Eight county parks and one state park provide plenty of access to the woods and water on Lopez Island. The first park off the ferry is **Odlin County Park (☎ 360/ 468-2496)**, which has a long beach, picnic tables, and a campground. Athletic fields make this more of a community sports center than a natural area. For a more natural setting, check out **Upright Channel Park,** which is on Military Road (about a mile north of Lopez Village in the northwest corner of the island). A little farther south and over on the east side of the island you'll find **Spencer Spit State Park (☎ 360/468-2251)**, which also has a campground. Here, the forest meets the sea on a rocky beach that looks across a narrow channel to Frost Island. You can hike the trails through the forest or explore the beach. South of Lopez Village on Bay Shore Road, you'll find the small **Otis Perkins Park**, which is between Fisherman Bay and the open water.

Down at the south end of the island, you'll find the tiny **Shark Reef Sanctuary,** where a short trail leads through the forest to a rocky stretch of coast that is among the prettiest on all the ferry accessible islands. Small islands offshore create strong currents that swirl past the rocks here. Seals and occasionally whales can be seen just offshore. This is a great spot for a picnic.

BICYCLING Because of its size, lack of traffic, numerous parks, and relatively flat terrain, Lopez is a favorite of cyclists. You can rent bicycles from **Lopez Bicycle Works (☎ 360/468-2847)**, at the marina on Fisherman Bay Road, or at **The Bike Shop on Lopez (☎ 360/468-3487)**, in Lopez Village. Expect to pay $5 to $13 per hour and $23 to $47 per day.

GOLF The island even has a nine-hole golf course—the **Lopez Golf Club (☎ 360/468-2679)**.

SEA KAYAKING If you want to explore the island's coastline by kayak, contact **Lopez Kayaks (☎ 360/468-2847)**, which is located at the marina on Fisherman Bay Road and charges $45 for a half-day trip. Kayaks can also be rented here for $10 to $15 per hour, or $30 to $60 per day.

WHALE WATCHING Whale-watching cruises from Lopez Island are operated by **Lopez Isle Cruise (☎ 800/871-2010** or 360/715-2010), which charges $45 for adults and $35 for students (no children under age 5).

WHERE TO STAY

Idlewild Inn. Lopez Road South (P.O. Box 271), Lopez Island, WA 98261. **☎ 360/468-3238.** Fax 360/468-4080. 8 rms. $100–$145 double. Rates include full breakfast. MC, V.

Located right in Lopez Village, this modern Victorian B&B is a good choice if you have come to Lopez by bicycle or if you just want to use your car as little as possible. Within a block of the inn are all the island's best restaurants. Most of the guest rooms here are quite large, and most also have views of the water. All the rooms have interesting antique furnishings and several have wood-burning fireplaces. In summer, colorful gardens surround the inn and guests can breakfast on a large brick patio. The front veranda, overlooking Fisherman Bay is a great place to relax in the afternoon.

✪ The Inn at Swifts Bay. Rte. 2, Box 3402, Lopez Island, WA 98261. ☎ **360/468-3636.** Fax 360/468-3637. www.swiftsbay.com. 2 rms (both with shared baths); 3 suites. $85–$95 double; $145–$175 suite. Rates include full breakfast. AE, DISC, MC, V.

Long the most luxurious accommodation on Lopez Island, the Inn at Swifts Bay is under new ownership and seems to be maintaining its previous high standards. Set on a large wooded lot a few minutes' walk from the water and a private beach, this inn is utterly romantic, and the breakfasts are lavish affairs from which you might not get up until almost lunchtime. Come prepared to be lazy. The decor is comfortably cluttered with a cozy living room and separate library. The suites all have gas fireplaces and two have private entries and their own decks. These upstairs suites are large and private, just right for a special celebration. After a day of exploring the island, you can soak in the hot tub, bake in the sauna, or gather by the fire for a social hour.

✪ Lopez Farm Cottages. Fisherman Bay Road (P.O. Box 610), Lopez Island, WA 98261. ☎ **800/440-3556** or 360/468-3555. Fax 360/468-3558. 4 cottages. $125 double. Rates include continental breakfast. MC, V.

Set on 30 acres of pastures, old orchards, and forest between the ferry landing and Lopez Village, these modern cottages are tucked into a grove of cedar trees on the edge of a large lawn (in the middle of which stand three huge boulders). From the outside the board-and-batten cottages look like old farm buildings, but inside you'll find a combination of Eddie Bauer and Scandinavian design. There are kitchenettes (where a breakfast basket is delivered each evening), plush beds with lots of pillows, and, in the bathrooms, showers with double showerheads. If showering together isn't romantic enough, there's a hot tub tucked down a garden path. For the full farm experience, you can feed the sheep in the pasture. There are plans to add several more cottages (as well as a campground tucked into the forest on the adjacent property).

Lopez Islander. Fisherman Bay Rd. (P.O. Box 459), Lopez Island, WA 98261. ☎ **800/736-3434** or 360/468-2233. Fax 360/468-3382. 30 rms, 2 suites. TV. July–Sept, $79–$129 double; $199–$259 suite. Oct–June, $59–$99 double; $155–$185 suite. AE, MC, V.

Located about a mile from Lopez Village, the Lopez Islander may not look too impressive from the outside, but it's a very comfortable lodging. All the rooms have great views of Fisherman Bay, and the more expensive rooms have coffeemakers, wet bars, microwaves, and refrigerators, and most rooms have balconies. The Islander offers such amenities as a full-service marina with kayak rentals, seasonal restaurant, lounge, outdoor pool, whirlpool, and adjacent bike-rental shop. Camping cabins (with shared bathroom facilities) are also available in summer ($35 to $45 double). Under new ownership, this hotel has been undergoing extensive remodeling and upgrading.

Campgrounds

Although there is currently no water available at **Spencer Spit State Park,** it is nonetheless the island's largest and best campground. This park has 35 campsites set amid tall fir trees. For reservations, contact **Reservations Northwest** (☎ **800/452-5687**). There are also campsites at **Odlin County Park** (☎ **360/468-2496**), which is just south of the ferry landing and has 30 campsites along the water. Athletic fields make this more of a community sports center than a natural area.

WHERE TO DINE

When it's time for coffee, you'll find the island's best in Lopez Village at **Caffé Verdi,** Lopez Plaza (☎ **360/468-2257**), and right next door, you'll find divinely decadent pastries and other baked goods at **Holly B's Bakery** (☎ 360/468-2133). Across the street, in Lopez Island Pharmacy, you'll find the old-fashioned **Lopez Island Soda Fountain** (☎ 360/468-3711). And keep an eye out for **Lopez Island Creamery's** ice cream stand here in Lopez Village. You'll also find this ice cream, as well as locally made Cape St. Mary Ranch beef sausage and pepperoni at the **Lopez Village Market** (☎ 360/468-2266), the island's grocery store.

✪ **Bay Café.** Village Center, Lopez Village. ☎ **360/468-3700.** Reservations highly recommended. Main courses $12–$26. MC, V. Summer, Wed–Mon 5:30–9pm; the rest of the year, Wed–Sun 5:30–8:30pm. NORTHWEST.

Housed in an eclectically decorated old waterfront commercial building with big windows looking out on nothing but parked cars, the Bay Café serves some of the best food in the state. This is the sort of place where people walk through the door and exclaim, "I want whatever it is that I can smell outside," the sort of place where diners animatedly discuss what that other flavor is in the savory cheesecake with macadamia-cilantro pesto, and where the dipping sauces with the pork satay are unlike anything you have ever tasted before. The menu, though short, spans the globe and changes frequently. Come with a hearty appetite; meals include soup and salad, and the desserts are absolutely to die for (imagine velvety pumpkin crème caramel decorated with a nasturtium flower and candied ginger). Accompany your meal with a bottle of wine from Lopez Island Vineyards for the quintessential Lopez dinner.

Bucky's. Lopez Village Plaza. ☎ **360/468-2595.** Reservations recommended in summer. Main courses $6–$8. AE, MC, V. Apr–Sept, Sun–Thurs 9am–9pm, Fri–Sat 9am–10pm (other months Fri–Mon 11:30am–8:30pm). AMERICAN.

With a laid-back island feeling and an outside waterfront deck, this tiny place is where the locals hang out. The food, though simple, is consistently good—nothing fancy, just delicious. The black-and-blue burger with blue cheese and Cajun spices definitely gets our vote for best burger in the islands. If you're feeling more like seafood, there are fish tacos and fish-and-chips.

Gail's. Lopez Village. ☎ **360/468-2150.** Reservations recommended in summer. Main courses $12–$17; lunch $4–$8. DISC, MC, V. Summer, daily 11am–9pm; winter, Mon–Sat 11am–2pm. SEAFOOD.

Gail's, with a big deck that looks out over Fisherman Bay, is in the middle of Lopez Village. Mainstays of the menu include homemade baked goods, vegetable omelettes, handmade pastas, soups, salads fresh from the garden, and dinner entrees such as tiger shrimp in coconut-curry sauce. Choose a Northwest wine from the affordable wine list.

SHAW ISLAND

Shaw Island is the least developed of the four San Juan Islands served by regular ferries. Most San Juan visitors know Shaw Island only as the island where the nuns run the ferry dock. Other than these nuns, the island is home to a few hundred tranquility-loving residents who like the solitude of the island and want to keep it undeveloped. If you enjoy leisurely drives (or bike rides) in the country, Shaw Island makes a good day trip from any of the other three islands. However, there are no hotels, B&Bs, or restaurants, and only one small park down at the south end of the island. This park, **Shaw Island County Park** (☎ 360/468-2867), does, however, have a small campground and is popular with sea kayakers.

THE OTHER SAN JUAN ISLANDS: SEA KAYAK TRIPS & CHARTER BOAT CRUISES

If you want to explore some of the other 168 islands that are not served by the ferries, you'll need a boat. Sailboats, powerboats, and sea kayaks are all popular vessels for exploring these other San Juans. Many of the islands are private property, but a few are, or have on them, state parks with campsites. If you want to find out about these marine parks, contact the **Washington State Parks Information Center** (☎ **800/233-0321**) for information on these marine state parks. Those without their own boat can still visit some of these islands either on a multiday kayak tour or on a charter boat cruise.

See "The Active Vacation Planner" in chapter 3 for information on companies offering multiday sea kayak tours in the San Juan Islands.

Charter boats, both motorboats and sailboats, can be hired for multiday cruises around the San Juan Islands. This is the easiest (though not the cheapest) way to see some of these outer islands. Anchoring in secluded coves, exploring marine parks, scanning the skies for bald eagles, spying on orcas, porpoises, and sea lions; these are the activities that make a charter cruise through the San Juans such a memorable experience.

During the summer, **Viking Cruises** (☎ **360/466-2639**), operates 3-day/2-night San Juan cruises that overnight at Rosario Resort on Orcas Island. Rates are $449 to $499 per person. **Island Junkets** (☎ **360/671-2908**) offers 7- to 14-day San Juans cruises aboard a 46-foot junk-rigged ketch. Boats can also be chartered through Anacortes Yacht Charters (☎ **800/233-3004** or 360/293-4555) and Charters Northwest (☎ **360/378-7196**).

4 Whidbey Island

30 miles N of Seattle, 40 miles S of Bellingham

At 45 miles in length, Whidbey Island is one of the largest islands in the continental United States, and, at only 30 miles from Seattle, it's a popular weekend getaway for Seattleites who come here seeking romance and relaxation. The island is a mix of farms, forests, bluffs, and beaches. Never more than a few miles wide, Whidbey offers views of the water at seemingly every turn of its winding country roads. Two historic towns, Langley and Coupeville, offer such urban amenities as excellent restaurants, unique shops, and art galleries—without sacrificing their village atmosphere. Charming bed-and-breakfast inns and one of the state's most luxurious small hotels pamper visitors to the island and provide the romantic surroundings that are so much a part of the Whidbey experience.

What is there to do on Whidbey? Next to nothing, and that's the island's main appeal. You don't have to do anything—other than sitting back and relaxing.

Lest you get the impression that Whidbey Island is heaven on earth, let us make you aware of the Whidbey Island Naval Air Station, which, with its thundering jets, has considerably altered the idyllic atmosphere of the island's northern half. Oak Harbor, the island's largest community, is located just outside the base and is characterized by the sort of strip-mall sprawl that surrounds most military bases. For this reason, the island's bed-and-breakfast inns are located mostly in the island's southern half. It's partly because of what has happened to Oak Harbor that Ebey's Landing National Historic Reserve was created. When people who had moved to the island because of its tranquil atmosphere saw what was happening around Oak Harbor, they acted quickly to preserve some of the island's rural beauty, the very essence of Whidbey Island.

ESSENTIALS

GETTING THERE   From I-5, take Wash. 20 west at Burlington. The highway turns south before you reach Anacortes and crosses over the Deception Pass Bridge to reach the north end of Whidbey Island.

Washington State Ferries (☎ **800/84-FERRY** or 206/464-6400) operate between Mukilteo and Clinton at the south end of the island and from Port Townsend to Keystone near Coupeville.

Harbor Airlines (☎ **800/359-3220**) has regular service between Oak Harbor Airport and Seattle and San Juan Island.

The **Airporter Shuttle** (☎ 800/235-5247 or 360/679-0600) offers daily service from Sea-Tac International Airport. The one-way fare is $30.

VISITOR INFORMATION   Contact **Island County Tourism** (☎ **888/ 747-7777;** www.whidbey.net/islandco); **Central Whidbey Chamber of Commerce,** 302 S. Main St. (P.O. Box 152), Coupeville, WA 98239 (☎ **360/678-5434**); or the **Langley Chamber of Commerce,** P.O. Box 403, Langley, WA 98260 (☎ **360/ 221-6765**).

GETTING AROUND   Car rentals are available from **Budget** in Oak Harbor. **Island Transit** (☎ **360/678-7771**) offers free public bus service on Whidbey Island.

FESTIVALS   Each year in mid-July, Langley celebrates the visual and performance arts with the **Choochokam** street festival. In early August, there's the **Coupeville Arts and Crafts Festival.**

EXPLORING THE ISLAND

If you're coming from the south and take the ferry from Mukilteo, then the best place to start exploring Whidbey Island is in the historic fishing village of **Langley**, which is reached by taking Langley Road off Wash. 525. Before you ever reach town, you'll get to **Whidbey Island Vineyard & Winery,** 5237 S. Langley Rd. (☎ **360/ 221-2040**), where you can taste a few wines before heading into town.

Langley today is a compact little village with a mix of sophisticated shops, interesting art galleries, and good, moderately priced restaurants occupying the restored wooden commercial buildings along the waterfront. First Street Park, right in downtown, provides access to a rocky beach and offers views of Saratoga Passage and the distant Cascades. Also here in Langley is the **Whidbey Island Center for the Arts,** 115 E. Sixth St. (☎ **360/221-8268**), which stages a wide range of performances throughout the year.

Four miles northwest of Freeland, the narrowest point of the island, you'll find **South Whidbey State Park** (☎ **360/331-4559**), with 2 miles of shoreline, hiking trails, and a campground. Continuing north you come to **Whidbey Greenbank Farm** (☎ **360/678-7700**), on Wonn Road in Greenbank. This huge loganberry farm is now a park and for many years was the source of Whidbeys, a loganberry liqueur. Gourmet foods and Washington state wines are sold in the gift shop here. Also in Greenbank is **Meerkerk Rhododendron Gardens,** 3531 S. Meerkerk Lane (☎ **360/678-1912**), which was originally a private garden but is now operated by the Seattle Rhododendron Society as a display and test garden. It's open daily from 9am to 4pm (peak bloom is in April and May); admission is $2.

Coupeville, located in Central Whidbey Island just north of the turnoff for the ferry to Port Townsend, is another historic waterfront village. This town was founded in 1852 by Capt. Thomas Coupe, and the captain's 1853 home is among those in town that have been restored. Several other of the town's Victorian homes have also been restored and turned into B&Bs. The quiet charm of yesteryear is Coupeville's greatest appeal, and many of its old commercial buildings now house antiques stores.

Here in Coupeville, you'll find the **Island County Historical Society Museum,** 902 NW Alexander St. (☎ 360/678-3310), which is the best place to learn about the island's seafaring, farming, and military history. It's open daily from 10am to 5pm (closed Tuesday through Thursday in winter). Between April and September, keep an eye out for the horse-drawn carriage of **Whidbey Island Percherons Carriage Co.** (☎ 360/678-6897), which charges $5 per person for a quick tour of town.

Much of the land around Coupeville is now part of the **Ebey's Landing National Historic Reserve.** The reserve, one of the first of its kind in the nation, was created "to preserve and protect a rural community which provides an unbroken historic record from the nineteenth century exploration and settlement of Puget Sound to the present time." There is no visitor center for the reserve, but there is an information kiosk near the dock in Coupeville and the adjacent museum has copies of an informative brochure about the reserve.

Three miles south of Coupeville is **Fort Casey State Park** (☎ 360/678-4636 or 360/678-5632), a former military base that was built in the 1890s to guard Puget Sound and still has its gun batteries. In addition to the fort, the park includes the 1897 Admiralty Head lighthouse, beaches, hiking trails, a campground, and an underwater reserve for scuba divers. Just south of Fort Casey State Park near the Keystone Ferry landing (Port Townsend ferries) is **Keystone State Park,** which is an underwater park for scuba divers. A few miles north of Fort Casey is the smaller **Fort Ebey State Park** (☎ 360/678-4636 or 360/678-3195), another former military site built to protect the sound. Here there are excellent views of the Strait of Juan de Fuca, as well as a campground, hiking trails, a lake for swimming and fishing, and a scuba-diving area.

Between Coupeville and Oak Harbor, you can make a detour to **Hummingbird Farm,** 2319 N. Zylstra Rd. in Oak Harbor (☎ 360/679-5044), which is an herb and dried-flower farm with a display garden, shop, and fields of herbs and flowers. **Oak Harbor,** at the north end of the island, was settled by Dutch immigrants, and here, at City Beach Park, which has a swimming lagoon, you'll find a large Dutch windmill. As the largest town on the island, Oak Harbor lacks the charm of Langley and Coupeville. At **Joseph Whidbey State Park,** west of Oak Harbor, there are great westerly views and a long sandy beach. North of Oak Harbor, **Lavendar Heart Botanicals,** 4233 N. DeGraff Rd. (☎ 360/675-3987), offers everything from indoor topiary to candles to soaps and lotions.

Deception Pass State Park (☎ 360/675-2417), at the northern tip of the island, is the most popular state park in Washington. What draws the crowds are miles of beaches, quiet coves, freshwater lakes, dark forests, hiking trails, camping, and the views of Deception Pass, the churning channel between Whidbey Island and Fidalgo Island. A high bridge connects these two large islands by way of a smaller island in the middle of Deception Pass, and overlooks at the bridge allow you to gaze down on the tidal waters that surge and swirl between the islands.

SPORTS & OUTDOOR ACTIVITIES

BICYCLING   The country roads of Whidbey Island are perfect for exploring by bicycle. If you don't have your own bike, you can rent one from **The Pedaler,** 5603¹/₂ Bayview Rd., Langley (☎ **360/321-5040**).

BOAT CHARTERS   The *Cutty Sark,* which is operated by Aeolian Ventures, 2072 W. Captain Whidbey Inn Rd. (☎ **360/678-4097**), offers scheduled day-sail cruises for $37.50 per person, or you can charter the boat for $65 an hour with a two-hour minimum. If you'd like to sail the waters off Whidbey Island, you can charter the *Sea Fever III,* a 36-foot sailboat, through **North Isle Sailing** (☎ **360/675-8360**) for anywhere from 2 hours to 2 weeks. A 2-hour charter runs $90.

SEA KAYAKING   If you'd like to get out on the waters surrounding Whidbey Island, you can rent sea kayaks at the **Captain Whidbey Inn,** 2072 W. Captain Whidbey Inn Rd. (☎ **800/505-3800** or 360/678-9301) for $18.50 to $23.50 per hour, and at **Adventure Marine** (☎ **360/675-9395**) in Oak Harbor for $30 per day.

WHERE TO STAY

IN LANGLEY

✪ **The Inn at Langley.** 400 First St. (P.O. Box 835), Langley, WA 98260. ☎ **360/221-3033.** 24 rms. TV TEL. $179–$269 double. Rates include continental breakfast. AE, MC, V.

Quite simply, this is one of the most luxurious and romantic inns in the Northwest. With its weathered cedar shingles, exposed beams, works of contemporary art, and colorful garden, this lodge evokes all the best of life in the region, and the guest rooms have a Zen-like quality that soothes and relaxes. The inn's four floors jut out from a bluff overlooking Saratoga Passage, and with 180° views from every room, you'll have plenty of opportunities to spot orca whales and bald eagles. While the bedrooms and balconies are luxurious enough, it's the bathrooms that are the star attractions here. Each comes with an open shower and a double whirlpool tub that looks out over the water. Pull back an opaque sliding window and you also get a view of the room's fireplace. The inn's dining room serves a five-course fixed-price dinner focusing on Northwest flavors every Friday and Saturday night for $62.50.

✪ **Log Castle.** 4693 Saratoga Rd., Langley, WA 98260. ☎ **360/221-5483.** 4 rms. $95–$120 double. Rates include full breakfast. DISC, MC, V.

A mile and a half outside of Langley, on a hillside overlooking Saratoga Passage and distant Mount Baker, stands another of Whidbey Island's unique inns. Designed and constructed by the owners, this sprawling log home isn't exactly a castle, but it certainly is grand in concept and construction. Everywhere you look inside this fascinating home are logs—the walls, the beams, the tables, the shelves, the door handles. Of the four rooms, the two turret rooms are the most popular, and the third-story octagonal turret room is the inn's favorite. From the room's five picture windows there are superb views of water and hills.

The Whidbey Inn. 106 First St. (P.O. Box 156), Langley, WA 98260. ☎ **360/221-7115.** 3 rms, 3 suites. Apr–Oct, $110–$120 double; $130–$160 suite. Nov–Mar, $85–$95 double; $110–$145 suite. Rates include full breakfast. AE, MC, V.

Located right on the waterfront in downtown Langley, this inn is so low-key, you'd hardly know it was there (especially since it's in back of a pizza parlor). However, the rooms are beautifully decorated with antiques, great beds (with down comforters), and have unobstructed water views. The three suites all have fireplaces, and the Gazebo Suite has a bridge to its private gazebo. Breakfast is served in your room, and sherry, afternoon snacks, and evening truffles are all part of a stay here.

IN GREENBANK

○ **Guest House Bed and Breakfast Cottages.** 3366 South Wash. 525, Greenbank, WA 98253. ☎ 360/678-3115. 6 cabins and cottages, 1 suite. TV. Mar 16–Oct 31, $160–$285 cabin/cottage; $110 suite. Nov 1–Mar 15, $125–$285 cabin/cottage; $110 suite. AE, DISC, MC, V.

Feeling more like a rustic mountain resort than a Whidbey Island lodging, this woodsy farm is a little fantasyland for city-dwellers searching for the good life in the country. There are log cabins tucked into the woods, a carriage house, a farm cottage, and a huge lodge with a deck overlooking a pond that is home to the farm's ducks and geese. The ultimate splurge here is the Lodge, which has two whirlpool tubs, a stone fireplace, and big skylights. In fact all the cabins and cottages have double whirlpool tubs. All these have TVs and VCRs For recreation there's a small swimming pool, a hot tub, and an exercise room.

IN COUPEVILLE

○ **The Captain Whidbey Inn.** 2072 W. Captain Whidbey Inn Rd., Coupeville, WA 98239. ☎ 800/366-4097 or 360/678-4097. Fax 360/678-4110. 25 rms, 13 with bath; 2 suites; 4 cottages; 3 houses. $95–$105 double without bath; $135 double with bath; $155 suite; $160 cabin; $185–$225 cottages. Rates include full country breakfast. AE, DC, DISC, MC, V.

Three miles west of Coupeville off Madrona Way stands one of the Northwest's most unique inns. Shady, quiet grounds offer a tranquil setting that has revived flagging spirits for almost a century. Built in 1907 of small madrona logs, the historic inn is architecturally fascinating, a bit of American folk art. The rooms in the main building are small and lack private bathrooms, but they manage to capture the feel of the island's seafaring past. Suites, cottages, and even a few houses are available for those who need more space. The inn's dining room and adjacent bar both overlook Penn Cove; the dining room has a reputation for being very uneven in quality.

The Colonel Crockett Farm. 1012 S. Fort Casey Rd., Coupeville, WA 98239. ☎ 360/678-3711. 5 rms. $75–$105 double. Rates include full breakfast. MC, V.

Built in 1855, this stately farmhouse is surrounded by rolling meadows and looks out over Crockett Lake to Admiralty Bay. The views are some of the best on the island, and no other inn on Whidbey better captures the island's idyllic rural feel. The guest rooms are furnished with antiques, and there is a beautiful, wood-paneled library where guests can peruse the extensive book collection. The Crockett Room, with its canopied four-poster bed and claw-foot tub, is our favorite. A huge red barn with a stone foundation dwarfs the house itself.

The Coupeville Inn. 200 NW Coveland St., Coupeville, WA 98239. ☎ 800/247-6162 in Washington and British Columbia or 360/678-6668. Fax 360/678-3059. 24 rms. TV TEL. $59.50–$105 double. Rates include continental breakfast. AE, DISC, MC, V.

Located right in the heart of Coupeville's historic district, and designed to fit in with the surrounding historic architecture, this modern motel offers large, comfortable rooms overlooking Coupeville and Penn Cove. All the rooms have small balconies.

Fort Casey Inn. 1124 S. Engle Rd., Coupeville, WA 98239. ☎ 360/678-8792. 9 apts. $125 apt for two. Rates include full breakfast. AE, MC, V.

Built in 1909 as officers' quarters for Fort Casey, this row of four Georgian revival houses now serves as a bed-and-breakfast inn offering spacious two-bedroom accommodations. Eagles, military memorabilia, and a red, white, and blue color scheme reflect the houses' history, and Fort Casey State Park and the beach are just a short walk away. The grand old homes are each divided into two apartments that have farm kitchens and spacious living rooms on the first floor and two bedrooms and a bathroom with a claw-foot tub on the second floor. Big front porches overlook Crockett Lake.

The Inn at Penn Cove. 702 N. Main St. (P.O. Box 85), Coupeville, WA 98239. ☎ **800/ 688-COVE** or 360/678-8000. 6 rms (4 with private bath). $60–$65 double with shared bath, $75–$125 double with private bath. Rates include full breakfast. AE, DISC, MC, V.

Housed in two Victorian homes that stand side by side, this inn offers rooms for those seeking romantic Victorian luxuries (fireplaces, antiques, antique or whirlpool tubs) and those seeking a more casual place to stay. The latter rooms are in the Coupe-Gillespie House, which was moved to this site in 1990. The most expensive room here has a gas fireplace, double whirlpool tub, a separate seating area, and views of both the water and Mount Baker, while another room has an interesting antique double pedestal sink. Asian antiques throughout the two houses give these two inns an interesting character.

WHERE TO DINE

At the far north end of the island, 1 mile south of the Deception Pass Bridge, you can get good smoked salmon at **Seabolt's Smokehouse** (☎ **800/574-1120** or 360/ 675-6485).

IN LANGLEY

The **Country Kitchen** at the Inn at Langley serves what most people agree are the finest meals on the island. However, these five-course, fixed-price dinners are only available on Friday and Saturday evenings. See "Where to Stay," above for details. For baked goods and espresso, drop by the **Langley Village Bakery,** 221 Second St. (☎ **360/221-3525**), and for decadent pastries, check out **P.S. Suisse,** 221 Second St. (☎ **360/221-9434**). A few blocks from downtown, you'll find **Whidbey Island Brewing Co.,** 630-B Second St. (☎ **360/221-8373**), where you can get locally brewed beers and pub grub.

✪ **Café Langley.** 113 First St. ☎ **360/221-3090.** Reservations recommended. Main courses $13.75–$17. AE, MC, V. Mon and Wed–Thurs 11:30am–2:30pm and 5–8pm, Tues 5–8pm, Fri–Sat 11:30am–3pm and 5–9pm, Sun 11:30am–3pm and 5–8pm. GREEK/MEDITERRANEAN.

This diminutive cafe conjures up sunnier climes with its flavorful dishes. Though many of the offerings are faithfully Greek, some of the most popular offerings display a Northwest flare. The Dungeness crab cakes might be served with a lime-chipotle aioli and red-pepper concasse and the local Penn Cove mussels might be sautéed in olive oil, garlic, and saffron vermouth. These latter are available as either an appetizer or an entree. Weekly specials add yet another dimension to the reliable menu.

Star Bistro. 201¹/₂ First St. ☎ **360/221-2627.** Reservations recommended. Main courses $7.25–$19. AE, MC, V. Tues–Thurs 11:30am–9pm, Fri–Sat 11:30am–9:30pm, Sun noon–9pm. NORTHWEST.

You'll find this casually chic little place up on the second floor of one of Langley's old commercial buildings. Big black-and-white floor tiles and bold splashes of color everywhere make the decor here lively. Creamy pasta dishes, flavorful salads, creative sandwiches, and fresh seafoods are all reliable choices, and in addition there are nightly specials. On sunny days everyone heads out to the rooftop patio.

IN COUPEVILLE

Christopher's. 23 Front St. ☎ **360/678-5480.** Reservations recommended. Main courses $10–$13. AE, CB, DC, DISC, MC, V. Wed–Thurs and Sat–Sun 5–9pm, Fri 11:30am–2pm and 5–9pm. NORTHWEST.

Located in a warehouselike building in downtown Coupeville, Christopher's is no longer the upscale place it once was but is still a reliable choice in this corner of the island. The menu these days sticks mostly to familiar fare such as shrimp scampi and cioppino, but you'll also find grilled salmon with raspberry barbecue sauce. However, it would be foolish to pass up the Penn Cove mussels and clams, which are steamed with chardonnay, lemon juice, and basil.

Rosi's Garden Restaurant. 606 N. Main St. ☎ **360/678-3989.** Reservations recommended. Main courses $15–$17. MC, V. Daily 5–10pm. NORTHWEST/ITALIAN.

Located a few blocks from the water, this little Victorian cottage dates from 1906. On the front porch and inside the old house you'll find a few tables and a quiet setting for a romantic dinner. The short menu offers both traditional Italian fare such as osso buco and more creative preparations such as pesto scallops or chicken with a mascarpone-marsala sauce. You'll also find prime rib on the menu.

5 Bellingham & Environs

90 miles N of Seattle, 60 miles S of Vancouver

In large part because of the presence of Western Washington University, Bellingham is a vibrant little city. Still an active shipping port, Bellingham enjoys excellent views across Puget Sound to the San Juan Islands, and at Squalicum Harbor there's a large commercial and private boat marina and promenade that provides residents and visitors a chance to enjoy the bay. Bellingham is also the southern terminus for Alaska ferries and cruise ships.

Whatcom County, which extends from the coast to the top of 10,778-foot Mount Baker and beyond, is still, however, primarily a rural area. Near the coast farming predominates, and several nearby farm towns are worth visiting for a glimpse of local history and a chance to explore the countryside. Mount Baker itself is a popular downhill skiing area in winter, while in summer hiking trails lead through meadows and forest. South of the city the mountains dip down to the sea and a drive along scenic Chuckanut Drive provides glimpses of spectacular coastline and the San Juan Islands.

ESSENTIALS

GETTING THERE   I-5 connects Bellingham with Seattle to the south and Vancouver to the north. Wash. 542, the North Cascades Scenic Highway, connects Bellingham with eastern Washington by way of Winthrop.

Bellingham International Airport, 5 miles northwest of downtown Bellingham, is served by Horizon Airlines, and United Express.

The **Airporter Shuttle** (☎ 800/235-5247 or 360/733-3600) runs between Sea-Tac Airport, Bellingham, and Blaine (fare: $29 one way).

In summer, **San Juan Island Shuttle Express** (☎ 800/373-8522 or 360/671-1137), which departs from Fairhaven Station & Cruise Terminal, 335 Harris St., offers passenger ferry service between Bellingham and San Juan and Orcas islands (fares: $20 one way, $33 round-trip).

Both **Amtrak** trains and **Greyhound** buses also stop in Bellingham at the Fairhaven Station & Cruise Terminal on Harris Avenue in the Fairhaven district.

VISITOR INFORMATION   Contact the **Bellingham/Whatcom County Convention & Visitors Bureau,** 904 Potter St., Bellingham, WA 98226 (☎ **800/487-2032** or 360/671-3990).

GETTING AROUND   If you need a taxi, contact **City Cab** (☎ 360/733-8294). Public bus service around the Bellingham area is provided by the **Whatcom Transportation Authority** (☎ 360/676-7433).

WHAT TO SEE & DO

The **Whatcom Museum of History and Art,** 121 Prospect St. (☎ 360/676-6981), is a striking example of Victorian architecture. Inside you'll find reconstructions of old stores from turn-of-the-century Bellingham. Special exhibits focus on Northwest artists and local history, while up on the third floor you'll find old toys, tools, and fashions. An adjacent building contains an excellent collection of Northwest coast Native American artifacts that are beautifully displayed. The museum is open Tuesday through Sunday from noon to 5pm. Admission is by donation.

Two doors down from the Whatcom Museum is the **Whatcom Children's Museum,** 227 Prospect St. (☎ 360/733-8769), which, though small, offers lots of fun hands-on experiences for kids. It's open on Sunday, Tuesday, and Wednesday from noon to 5pm, and Thursday through Saturday from 10am to 5pm; admission is $2.

If you're interested in maritime history, you'll want to visit the **Whatcom Maritime Museum,** 1000 C St. (☎ 360/384-3622). Located on the waterfront off Chestnut Street, this museum houses exhibits on the maritime heritage of the Bellingham area. Hours are Thursday through Saturday from 10am to 4pm; admission is by donation.

Another major landmark in downtown Bellingham is the **Mount Baker Theatre,** 104 N. Commercial St. (☎ 360/734-6080), the city's premier performing arts venue. The theater's 110-foot-tall lighthouse tower is visible from all over the city, and though the exterior decor is quite subdued, inside you'll find an extravagant lobby designed to resemble a Spanish galleon.

At the tiny **Marine Life Center,** 1801 Roeder Ave. (☎ 360/671-2431), which is located in an office plaza on Squalicum Harbor, aquariums and a touch tank provide a brief introduction to the local sea life. The center is open daily from 8am to 9pm and admission is free.

If your interest is art, you shouldn't miss the **Western Washington University Outdoor Sculpture Collection,** off the Bill McDonald Parkway south of downtown. The collection includes more than 20 pieces including a piece by Isamu Noguchi. You can pick up a guide and audiophone tour of the collection at the Visitor's Information Center or at the university's **Visitor's Center** or **Western Gallery** (☎ 360/650-3963), which features exhibits of contemporary art.

Though downtown Bellingham has a fair number of restaurants and a few galleries, the **Fairhaven district** is the most interesting neighborhood in town. Fairhaven was once a separate town and many of its brick buildings, built between 1880 and 1900, have now been restored and house unusual shops and several good restaurants. Also in Fairhaven is the Fairhaven Station & Cruise Terminal, the southern terminal for ferries to Alaska and also the Amtrak and Greyhound station. **Artwood,** 1000 Harris St. (☎ 360/647-1628), one of the most interesting shops in Fairhaven, is a cooperative gallery filled with beautiful woodcraft.

If you're a fan of riding the rails, check the schedule of the **Lake Whatcom Railway** (☎ 360/595-2218), which operates a historic steam-train excursion from the town of Wickersham southeast of Bellingham. There are weekend trips in July and August as well as Saturday runs on various holidays throughout the year. Although this old steam engine doesn't go very fast, it passes through a tunnel, along the shore of a lake, and through the woods, with occasional glimpses of Mount Baker. The trips last 1¹/₂ hours and the fare is $10 for adults and $5 for children under age 18.

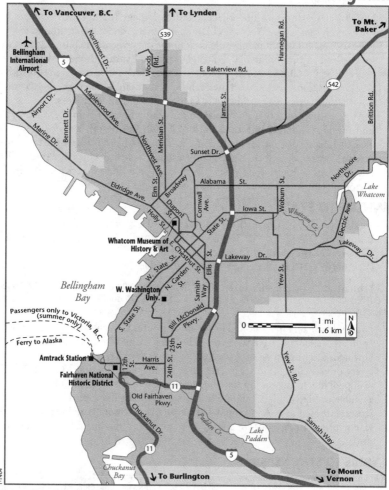

To Vancouver, B.C.

To Lynden

To Mt. Baker

Bellingham International Airport

539

E. Bakerview Rd.

Hannegan Rd.

542

Britton Rd.

Northwest Dr.

Maplewood Ave.

Airport Dr.

Bennett Dr.

Marine Dr.

Woods Rd.

Meridian St.

James St.

Sunset Dr.

Northshore Dr.

Lake Whatcom

Eldridge Ave.

Elm St.

Broadway

Dupont

Holly St.

Alabama St.

Cornwall Ave.

State St.

Iowa St.

Woburn St.

Whatcom Cr.

Electric Ave.

Lakeway Dr.

Whatcom Museum of History & Art

W. State St.

Chestnut St.

N. Garden St.

Ellis St.

Lakeway Dr.

Yew St.

Bellingham Bay

W. Washington Univ.

Samish Way

Bill McDonald Pkwy.

S. State St.

Passengers only to Victoria, B.C. (summer only)

Ferry to Alaska

0   1 mi
     1.6 km

N

Amtrack Station

12th St.

Harris Ave.

24th St.

25th St.

Fairhaven National Historic District

11

Old Fairhaven Pkwy.

Chuckanut Dr.

Yew St. Rd.

Padden Cr.

Lake Padden

Samish Way

11

5

Chuckanut Bay

To Burlington

To Mount Vernon

1-1404

CHUCKANUT DRIVE

Chuckanut Drive, a scenic 10-mile road along Chuckanut and Samish bays, begins in Fairhaven and winds its way south through the Chuckanut Mountains, which rise straight out of the water. Though most of the way is through dense woods, there are pull-offs where you can gaze out to the San Juan Islands or up and down this rugged section of coastline. Chuckanut Drive is particularly popular at sunset and there are several very good restaurants along the way. At the start of the drive, be sure to stop in at the **Chuckanut Bay Gallery and Garden Shop,** 700 Chuckanut Dr. (☎ 360/734-4885), which is full of interesting artworks by Northwest artists and craftspeople. Toward the south end of the drive, you'll come to Larabee State Park, which has a pretty little beach and miles of hiking trails.

LYNDEN: A DUTCH THEME TOWN

Located on Wash. 539 off I-5, Lynden is a self-styled Dutch theme town. The most convincing pieces of Dutch architecture are the four-story windmill that houses the

Dutch Village Inn and the adjacent Dutch Village Mall, which replicates an Amsterdam canal scene. You'll find Dutch restaurants and bakeries around town.

For a look at Lynden pioneer life back in the days when Dutch immigrants were settling in the surrounding rich farmlands, visit the **Lynden Pioneer Museum,** 217 Front St. (☎ 360/354-3675). Among the museum's collections are restored buggies, wagons, carts, and horse-drawn vehicles. Hours are Monday through Saturday from 10am to 4pm, and admission is $3 for adults and $2 for seniors.

More pioneer history is on display in the nearby town of Ferndale, where you'll find the **Hovander Homestead Park** (☎ 360/384-3444), a historic farm, on Neilsen Road. Adjacent to this park is the **Tennant Lake Natural History Interpretive Center,** where there is good bird-watching, as well as a fragrance garden. Take exit 262 off I-5. Right in downtown Ferndale, you'll find Pioneer Park, which has one of the largest collections of historic log buildings in the state.

WHERE TO STAY

Chain motels in town include **Motel 6,** 3701 Byron St. (Exit 252 off I-5), Bellingham, WA 98225 (☎ 360/671-4494), charging $40 to $46 double; and **Best Western Lakeway Inn,** 714 Lakeway Dr. (Exit 253 off I-5), Bellingham, WA 98226 (☎ 360/671-1011), charging $59 to $120 double.

✪ **Schnauzer Crossing.** 4421 Lakeway Dr., Bellingham, WA 98226. ☎ 800/562-2808 or 360/733-0055. Fax 360/734-2808. 3 rms. TV TEL. $115–$190 double. Rates include full breakfast. DC, MC, V.

Located less than 4 miles from downtown, Schnauzer Crossing is set in a quiet neighborhood overlooking Lake Whatcom. The living room, with its Asian decor and wall of windows, looks out on the lake, huge old trees, green lawns, and a garden. There's a very private cottage with a private deck, gas fireplace, TV and VCR, and double whirlpool tub. In the equally appealing master suite you'll find a skylit bathroom with a double whirlpool tub, a king-size bed, a wood-burning fireplace, TV and VCR, and separate sitting room. And should you stay in the one room that doesn't have a private whirlpool tub, you can simply step outside to the hot tub in the Japanese garden.

WHERE TO STAY NEARBY

✪ **The Inn at Semiahmoo.** 9565 Semiahmoo Pkwy., Blaine, WA 98230. ☎ 800/770-7992 or 360/371-2000. 198 rms, 14 suites. A/C TV TEL. Early May–late Oct, $189–$419 double; $269–$499 suite. Late Oct–early May, $129–$319 double; $209–$399 suite. AE, DC, DISC, MC, V.

Located at the end of a long sandy spit that reaches almost to Canada, the Inn at Semiahmoo is Washington's premier golf resort and health spa. Gables and gray shingles give the resort a timeless look, and throughout the classically styled interior of the main lodge are numerous lounges overlooking the water. Artwork abounds, with Native American and nautical themes prevailing. Not all guest rooms have views, but those that do have beds facing out to sea.

Dining: The main dining room overlooks the water and offers excellent Northwest-style meals and an extensive wine list. An oyster bar and lounge in an old salmon-packing plant, and a more casual pier-side restaurant provide other dining options.

Services: Concierge, room service, San Juan Island cruises, bicycle rentals, spa programs, full spa services.

Facilities: Golf course, indoor tennis courts, racquetball, squash, indoor/outdoor pool, whirlpools, sauna, steam room, exercise room, indoor track, marina, bike and running paths.

WHERE TO DINE

For great coffee, stop in at **Tony's Coffee House,** 1101 Harris Ave. (☎ 360/ 738-4710), a classic Fairhaven hangout for many years now. For local microbrews and pub fare, try the **Archer Ale House,** 1212 Tenth St. (☎ 360/647-7002), in a basement in Fairhaven; or **Boundary Bay Brewery & Bistro,** 1107 Railroad Ave. (☎ 360/647-5593), in downtown Bellingham.

Colophon Café & Deli. In Village Books, 1208 11th St. ☎ 360/647-0092. Most items $3–$8. DISC, MC, V. Mon–Sat 9am–10pm, Sun 10am–8pm (summer 10am–10pm). SOUPS/ SANDWICHES/DESSERTS.

Northwesterners spend a lot of time in bookstores hiding from the rain, so, of necessity, bookstores often provide sustenance. Here at the Colophon, you can chill out with some ice cream in summer, warm up with an espresso in winter, or make a filling meal of the star attractions here—homemade soups. You'll always find African peanut soup on the menu, as well as quiches, salads, and great homemade desserts.

☼ Il Fiasco. 1309 Commercial St. ☎ 360/676-9136. Reservations highly recommended. Main courses $9–$24.50. AE, DISC, MC, V. Mon–Fri 11:30am–2:30pm and 5–10pm, Sat–Sun 5–10pm. ITALIAN/ECLECTIC.

Named for those straw-covered Chianti bottles, this restaurant mixes contemporary art, classic decor, and creative Italian dishes; and is Bellingham's premier outpost of urban chic. The menu changes regularly, but you're likely to find such appetizers as fried calamari with artichoke aioli or crispy duck wontons. If pasta is your passion, decision making will be difficult. Entrees might include a tower of prawns with grilled fish, black bean-garlic butter, papaya salsa, and saffron risotto or a classic osso buco. Service is friendly and prompt, and there's an extensive list of Italian wines.

☼ Oyster Creek Inn. Chuckanut Dr. ☎ 360/766-6179. Reservations recommended. Main courses $14.50–23. AE, MC, V. Daily noon–9pm. SEAFOOD.

There may be better views on Chuckanut Drive, but because there's an oyster farm only a few feet downhill, you aren't going to find fresher bivalves. The Oyster Creek Inn is almost in Oyster Creek, and with walls of windows wrapping around the dining room, there's a good view of the tumbling waters. The fried oyster po'boy with jalapeño tartar sauce is a tasty creation, and the creamy oyster stew is extremely satisfying on a rainy day. Sandwiches are pricey, but most are made with seafood. To go with your seafood, there's a long list of vintage and rare wines.

Pacific Café. 100 N. Commercial St. ☎ 360/647-0800. Reservations recommended. Main dishes $13–$20. AE, MC, V. Mon–Thurs 11:30am–2pm and 5:30–9pm, Fri 11:30am–2pm and 5:30–10pm, Sat 5:30–10pm. NORTHWEST.

Located just in the Mount Baker Theater building, this romantic little cafe is, of course, the perfect spot for dinner before the show, but it's also a good choice for a flavorful lunch or dinner even if you aren't on your way to a show. A recent menu ranged from fried brie with apple slices to passion fruit sweet-and-sour chicken. Lunches are among the most creative in the city (crab cakes with ginger black beans, Punjabi chicken curry, ginger marmalade chicken).

7

South Puget Sound & West Sound

Water, water everywhere. That sums up the South Puget Sound and West Sound areas. It seems you are never out of sight of saltwater for very long in this region of convoluted waterways, inlets, bays, harbors, and passages. Past glacial activity gave this region the look of Scandinavian fjords, and is that very similarity that a century ago attracted Scandinavian fishermen who founded what are today two of the region's quaintest little towns: Poulsbo and Gig Harbor.

Today, the waterways of this region are both its chief asset and, sometimes, its greatest liability. The people who choose to live here, as well as those who visit, tend to do so for the water. Quaint fishing villages turned yacht havens, a naval shipyard, the romance of living on an island; these are the aspects of life that attract people to this area. However, when water and automobiles collide, problems often arise. This region is at the mercy of its waterways when bad weather strikes. Vashon and Anderson islands are only accessible by ferry, and for commuters who work in Seattle, Bainbridge Island could just as soon not have the Agate Pass Bridge. Two other ferries, one at the north end of the Kitsap Peninsula and one at Bremerton, serves as the most efficient, though often frustratingly time-consuming, links to Seattle and the east side of the sound. Two of the region's bridges—the Tacoma Narrows Bridge and the Hood Canal Bridge—provide their own particular problems to getting around this region. The former is a major commuter bottleneck while the latter, a floating bridge, is sometimes shut down by high winds.

However, it is these transportation problems that provide much of the region with its slower pace of life, and that slower pace in turn presents opportunities for Seattleites and others to make quick escapes to the country by simply crossing to the west side of Puget Sound where island time prevails and the views of the Olympic Mountains are just that much better.

Down in the southern reaches of the Sound, however, a very different aesthetic rules. Here are two of Puget Sounds' largest cities, Tacoma and Olympia. The former, once derided as an industrial wasteland, is in the middle of a renaissance that is turning it into a very livable city. The latter, as the capital of the state and home of a very liberal, liberal-arts university, has a mellow, laid-back air and often seems like two small towns on top of one another. When the state legislature and the university shut down, Olympia becomes one of the quietest cities in the Northwest.

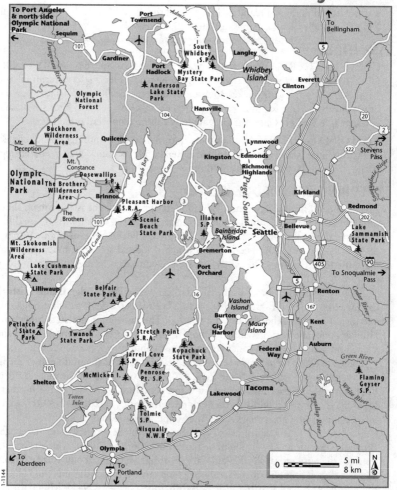

1 Bainbridge Island

10 miles W of Seattle (by ferry), 35 miles NE of Bremerton, 46 miles SE of Port Townsend

Bainbridge Island, popular for its miles of waterfront, sound-and-mountain views, and rural feel, is for the most part an affluent bedroom community for Seattle. However, with its bustling little downtown area (somewhat reminiscent of tony towns in the San Francisco Bay area), excellent restaurants and B&Bs, many parks, and good bicycling and sea kayaking, it is also a great spot for a quick getaway.

Roughly 10 miles long and 3¹/₂ miles wide, Bainbridge Island had long been the home of the Suquamish Indians when the island was first charted by Capt. George Vancouver in 1792. Within less than a century after Vancouver's visit, the island had become the site of the world's largest lumber mill (though this is now long-gone). The island's early settlement centered around mosquito fleet ferry docks, though eventually, when car ferries began using the community of Winslow (now known as downtown Bainbridge Island), that became the island's business center. The island was not linked to the mainland by bridge until the Agate Pass Bridge was opened in 1950. Today the island is home to almost 20,000 people.

ESSENTIALS

GETTING THERE   **Washington State Ferries** (☎ **800/84-FERRY** or 206/464-6400) operates a ferry service between Seattle's Pier 52 ferry terminal and Bainbridge Island. The trip takes 35 minutes and costs $5.90 to $7.10 for a car and driver one way, $3.50 for adult car passengers or walk-ons, and $1.75 for seniors and children ages 5 to 11. Passenger fares are only collected on westbound ferries.

VISITOR INFORMATION   For more information on Bainbridge Island, contact the **Bainbridge Island Chamber of Commerce,** 590 Winslow Way E., Bainbridge Island, WA 98110 (☎ **206/842-3700**).

EXPLORING BAINBRIDGE ISLAND

Just up the hill from the Bainbridge Island ferry terminal is the island's main shopping district where you'll find some interesting shops and restaurants. If you'd like to sample the local wine, drop in at the **Bainbridge Island Vineyards and Winery,** 682 Wash. 305 (☎ **206/842-WINE**), which is located a quarter mile up the hill from the ferry landing. The winery is open Wednesday through Sun from noon to 5pm.

To learn about the history of the island, drop by the **Bainbridge Island Historical Museum,** 7650 NE High School Rd. (☎ **206/842-2773**), which is housed in a restored one-room schoolhouse built in 1908. The museum is located at Strawberry Hill Park one mile west of Wash. 305 not far from downtown Bainbridge Island and is open on Saturdays and Sundays from 11am to 3pm.

There are two state parks on Bainbridge Island. Down at the south end of the island, you'll find **Fort Ward State Park** (☎ **206/842-4041**) on the quiet shore of Rich Passage. The park offers picnicking and good bird watching. At the northern tip of the island, you'll find **Fay Bainbridge State Park** (☎ **206/842-3931**), which offers camping and great views across the Sound to the Seattle skyline.

Garden enthusiasts will want to call ahead and make a reservation to visit the **Bloedel Reserve,** 7571 NE Dolphin Drive (☎ **206/842-7631**), which is 6 miles north of the ferry terminal off Wash. 305 (turn right on Agate Point Road). Expansive and elegant grounds are the ideal place for a quiet stroll amid plants from around the world. Also well worth a visit is **Bainbridge Gardens,** 9415 Miller Rd NE (☎ **206/842-5888**), which is on the west side of the island. These gardens, which today are primarily a plant nursery for garden-crazed Bainbridge Islanders, are also the site of gardens started in 1908 by Zenhichi Harui when he emigrated from Japan. The gardens were abandoned in the 1940s when Harui and his family were forced to leave the island. Today little remains of the original gardens, but the grounds are still quite beautiful.

Bainbridge Island is a favorite of cyclists, who enjoy its quiet, winding roads, occasional hills, and expansive Puget Sound views. If you'd like to rent a bike to explore the island on two wheels, stop in at **B.I. Cycle Rentals,** 195 Winslow Way E. (☎ **206/842-6413**), which is only two blocks from the ferry terminal.

If you'd like to get closer to the water and do a little paddling in a sea kayak, turn left as you get off the ferry and head to Waterfront Park, where you'll find **Bainbridge Island Boat Rentals** (☎ **206/842-9229**), which rents single sea kayaks ($10 per hour) and double kayaks and swan boats ($15 per hour). They also rent canoes and rowboats.

WHERE TO STAY

Island Country Inn. 920 Hildebrand Way NE, Bainbridge Island, WA 98110. ☎ **800/ 842-8429** or 206/842-6861. Fax 206/842-9808. 40 rms, 6 suites. A/C TV TEL. $79–$89 double; $105–$139 suite. Rates include continental breakfast. AE, DC, DISC, MC, V.

Located right in downtown Bainbridge Island, this is the only motel-style lodging on the island, and with its convenient location and its outdoor swimming pool and whirlpool spa, it makes a good choice for anyone coming to the island in summer. Guest rooms are just a cut above your usual motel room. If you're planning a longer stay, the suites, which have kitchens, might be what you need.

WHERE TO DINE

When you need a steaming cup of espresso to warm you and wake you, head to the **Pegasus Coffee House & Gallery,** 131 Parfitt Way (☎ **206/842-6725**), which is located near the marina in Winslow. Soups, salads, sandwiches, and pastries are also available. If you'd prefer a pint of ale in a cozy waterfront pub, drop in at the **Harbour Public House,** 231 Parfitt Way (☎ **206/842-0969**), which overlooks a marina about a block away from Pegasus Coffee. This pub also serves good pub food including burgers, fish-and-chips, and other seafood. To find either of these, follow Winslow Way east through "downtown" Bainbridge Island and turn left onto Madison Avenue.

❖ **The Four Swallows.** 481 Madison Ave. ☎ **206/842-3397.** Reservations recommended. Main dishes $10–$22. MC, V. Tues–Sat 5:30–9pm (longer hours in summer). ITALIAN.

Located less than a block off Winslow way in downtown Bainbridge Island, this casual and unpretentious restaurant is housed in a restored farmhouse that was built in 1889. Out front, under the shade trees, is a big deck for summer al fresco dining. Inside, rustic "primitive" antiques set the tone, and in the main dining room there are old, high-backed wooden booths. The menu changes with the seasons, but any month of the year consider starting with the antipasto for two, which showcases a wide range of seasonal specialties. Pizzas and pastas make up the bulk of the menu, but you might also find beef tenderloin, lamb loin, or grilled Moroccan chicken breast.

Winslow Way Cafe. 122 Winslow Way E. ☎ **206/842-0517.** Reservations for five or more only. Main dishes $6.50–$16. MC, V. Daily 5–10pm; Sun brunch 9am–2pm. MEDITERRANEAN.

Although pasta and pizzas dominate the menu here and prices are very reasonable, this contemporary place oozes Seattle attitude. Sure, the restaurant is housed in the funkiest building in downtown Bainbridge Island (it looks as though it could be on a beach in the Caribbean), but inside all is indirect lighting and contemporary styling. The big bar to one side fairly screams "Have a martini!" The pizzas are just the sort of designer pies you would expect in such a setting and are generally excellent, but it is often hard to ignore the creative dishes on the daily fresh sheet.

2 The Kitsap Peninsula

Poulsbo: 15 miles NW of Bainbridge Island ferry dock, 35 miles S of Port Townsend, 45 miles N of Tacoma

Roughly 45 miles long and confusingly convoluted, this peninsula looks something like an arrowhead wedged between Seattle and the Olympic Peninsula. Tucked amid the folds of its many glacial hills and its fjordlike waterways are an eclectic assortment of small towns, each with a very different character.

For thousands of years this region was home to several tribes of Native Americans, including the Suquamish tribe that once had a 900-foot longhouse on the shores of Agate Pass between the Kitsap Peninsula and Bainbridge Island. Chief Sealth (pronounced *see*-alth), for whom Seattle is named, was a member of the Suquamish tribe and today his grave can be visited near the town of Suquamish.

The region's earliest pioneer history is linked to the logging industry. It was at Port Gamble, on the north end of the peninsula, that Andrew Pope and William Talbot chose to build their sawmill, which went on to become the longest operating mill in the Northwest. Although the mill is now closed, Port Gamble remains a Pope & Talbot company town and looks as if it hasn't changed in 100 years.

The state of Washington seems obsessed with theme towns; there's a Dutch town, a Wild West town, a Bavarian town, and here on the Kitsap Peninsula, a Scandinavian town. Though at first the town of Poulsbo seems merely a contrivance to sell tacky Scandinavian souvenirs, on closer inspection it proves to have much more character than that. The town's waterfront park, marinas, and picturesque setting on Liberty Bay leave no doubt that this town has great appeal for the boating crowd. It also is a magnet for anyone with a sweet tooth; downtown there are at least half a dozen places that prepare excellent sweets of one type or another.

The deep, protected harbors of the Kitsap Peninsula have for more than a century seen the comings and goings of the U.S. Navy, which has naval yards here in the town of Bremerton. Today the Bremerton Naval Yards are also home to a large fleet of mothballed navy ships, and these have become the town's greatest tourist asset in recent years, with two museums and a Vietnam-era destroyer open to the public. Not far away is also a Trident nuclear submarine base.

Across Sinclair Inlet from Bremerton, and accessible via the last privately owned passenger ferry still operating on the Puget Sound, lies the small town of Port Orchard, which is filled with antiques malls.

ESSENTIALS

GETTING THERE   The Kitsap Peninsula lies between Puget Sound and the east side of the Olympic Peninsula and is bound on its west side by Hood Canal (which is not a canal but rather a long fjordlike extension of Puget Sound. Wash. 16 connects the peninsula with I-5 at Tacoma, while Wash. 3 connects the peninsula with U.S. 101 west of Olympia and continues north to the Hood Canal Bridge, a floating bridge that serves as the Kitsap Peninsula's northern link to the Olympic Peninsula. Bainbridge Island is connected to the Kitsap Peninsula by the Agate Pass Bridge on Wash. 305.

The Kitsap Peninsula is connected to the east side of Puget Sound by way of three ferries: the Fauntleroy-Southworth ferry (a 35-minute crossing) from West Seattle, the Seattle-Bremerton ferry (a 60-minute crossing) from downtown Seattle, and the Edmonds-Kingston ferry (a 30-minute crossing) from north of Seattle. Fares are $5.90 to $7.10 for a car and driver one way, $3.50 for adult car passengers or walk-ons, and $1.75 for seniors and children ages 5 to 11. Passenger fares are only collected on westbound ferries.

VISITOR INFORMATION   For information on the Kitsap Peninsula, contact the **Kitsap Peninsula Visitor and Convention Bureau** (☎ 800/416-5615 or 360/297-8200; www.kitsapedc.org). For more information on Poulsbo, contact the **Greater Poulsbo Chamber of Commerce,** 19131 Eight Ave. NE (P.O. Box 1063), Poulsbo, WA 98370 (☎ 360/779-4848).

FESTIVALS   In Poulsbo each May the **Viking Fest** celebrates traditional Scandinavian culture, as do the **Midsommar Fest** and **Yule Log Festival.**

EXPLORING THE KITSAP PENINSULA

Just across the Agate Pass Bridge from Bainbridge Island lies the Suquamish Indian Reservation. Here are two Native American historic sites, a museum, and, of course, a casino. If you take the first right after crossing the bridge from Bainbridge Island, you will see signs for the **grave of Chief Sealth.** To visit the site of the **Old Man House,** which was a large Native American longhouse, return to Wash. 305, continue west, turn left at the Suquamish Hardware building, and watch for the sign. The Old Man House itself is long gone, but you'll find an informative sign and a small park with picnic tables. Continuing a little farther on Wash. 305, you'll see signs for the **Suquamish Museum,** 15838 Sandy Hook Road (☎ **360/598-3311,** ext. 422), on the Port Madison Indian Reservation. The museum houses a compelling history of Puget Sound's native people. May through September, the museum is open daily from 10am to 5pm; October through April, it's open Friday through Sunday from 11am to 4pm. Admission is $2.50 for adults and $1 for children. Just across the Agate Pass Bridge, you'll also find **Suquamish Clearwater Casino & Bingo** (☎ **800/375-6073** or 360/598-6889), which bills itself as Seattle's closest casino.

Continuing north on Wash. 305, you next come to the small town of **Poulsbo,** which overlooks fjordlike Liberty Bay. Settled in the late 1880s by Scandinavians, Poulsbo was primarily a fishing, logging, and farming town until the town decided to play up its Scandinavian heritage. Shops in the Scandinavian-inspired downtown sell all manner of Viking and Scandinavian souvenirs. Between downtown and the waterfront, you'll find Liberty Bay Park, and at the south end of Front Street, you'll find the **Marine Science Center,** 18743 Front St. NE (☎ **360/779-5549**), which houses interpretive displays on the Puget Sound. The center is open Tuesday through Saturday from 10am to 4pm, Sunday and Monday from noon to 4pm. Admission is $2 for adults, $1 for seniors and children ages 2 through 12, $5 for families (free admission on the third Tuesday of each month).

If you'd like to see Poulsbo from the water, you can rent a sea kayak from **Olympic Outdoor Center,** 18971 Front St. (☎ **360/697-6095**), which charges $10 to $15 per hour for kayaks.

If you have time and enjoy visiting historic towns, continue north from Poulsbo on Wash. 3 to **Port Gamble.** This community was established in 1853 as a company town for the Pope and Talbot lumber mill, which was for many years the oldest operating lumber mill on the West Coast. Along the town's shady streets are many Victorian homes that were restored by Pope and Talbot. Stop by the Port Gamble Country Store, which now houses the **Port Gamble Historic Museum** (☎ **360/ 697-6626**) as well as the **Of Sea and Shore Museum** (☎ **360/297-2426**). The former is a collection of local memorabilia, while the latter exhibits seashells from around the world.

From Port Gamble, head south on Wash. 3 toward Bremerton to begin an exploration of the area's naval history. Between Poulsbo and Silverdale, you will be passing just east of the Bangor Navy Base, which is home port for a fleet of Trident nuclear submarines. The base is on Hood Canal, a long narrow arm of Puget Sound. Near the town of Keyport, you can visit the **Naval Undersea Museum,** Garnett Way (☎ **360/396-4148**), which is located 3 miles east of Wash. 3 on Wash. 308. The museum explores all aspects of undersea exploration, with interactive exhibits, models, displays that include a deep-sea exploration and research craft, a Japanese kamikaze torpedo, and a deep-sea rescue vehicle. The museum is open daily from 10am to 4pm (closed on Tuesdays between October and May) and admission is free.

Continuing south, you come to **Bremerton,** which is home to the Puget Sound Naval Shipyard, where mothballed U.S. Navy ships have included the aircraft carriers USS *Nimitz* and USS *Midway* and the battleship USS *Missouri* (which at press time was scheduled to be moved to Hawaii to serve as a floating museum) and USS *New Jersey.* Between May 15 and September 30, **Kitsap Harbor Tours,** 290 Washington Ave. no. 7 (☎ **360/377-8924**), offers boat tours of the mothballed fleet and shipyard hourly between 11am and 4pm. Tours are $8.50 for adults, $7.50 for seniors, and $5.50 for children ages 5 to 12.

One mothballed destroyer, the USS *Turner Joy,* is now operated by the **Bremerton Historic Ships Association** (☎ **360/792-2457**) and is open to the public as a memorial to those who have served in the U.S. Navy and who have helped build the navy's ships. The *Turner Joy* is docked about 150 yards east of the Washington State Ferries terminal. In summer, the ship is open daily from 10am to 5pm; from Oct 1 to May 14, the ship is only open Thursday through Monday from 10am to 4pm. Admission is $5 for adults, $4 for senior citizens and the military, and $3 for children ages 5 to 12. Combination Turner Joy Harbor Tour tickets are also available.

Nearby is the **Bremerton Naval Museum,** 130 Washington Avenue (☎ **360/479-7447**), which showcases naval history and the historic contributions of the Puget Sound Naval Shipyard. The museum is open Monday through Saturday from 10am to 5pm and Sunday from 1 to 5pm; from Labor Day through Memorial Day, the museum is only open Tuesday through Sunday and closes at 4pm daily. Admission is free.

Connecting all of these waterfront attractions is the Bremerton Boardwalk, which provides a pleasant place to stroll along the waters of Sinclair Inlet. Also here in Bremerton, you'll find the **Kitsap County Historical Society Museum,** 280 Fourth St. (☎ **360/479-6226**), which houses an exhibit on the mosquito fleet (dozens of small ferries that operated around the Puget Sound) as well as many other displays of local historical significance.

One of the last remaining private mosquito fleet ferries still operates between Bremerton and **Port Orchard.** If you park your car on the waterfront in Bremerton, you can step aboard the little passenger-only ferry and cross the bay to Port Orchard. In this little waterfront town, you'll find several antique malls that can provide hours of interesting browsing.

WHERE TO STAY

✪ **Manor Farm Inn.** 26069 Big Valley Rd. NE, Poulsbo, WA 98370. ☎ **360/779-4628.** Fax 360/779-4876. 7 rms, 1 cottage. $110–$160 double. Rates include full breakfast. MC, V.

Located between Poulsbo and the Hood Canal Bridge, this inn is a working farm, yet with its luxurious accommodations and gourmet dining, it certainly feels like a manor house as well. Whether you want to hide away in the luxury of your room or hang out with the sheep, geese, horses, cows, and chickens, you're likely to feel content at this retreat from urban stress. Play croquet or horseshoes or go for a spin on the inn's mountain bikes. If you crave lots of space, you might want to opt for the Carriage Room, which has a large picture window. For a large bathroom request The Loft, which is up a flight of stairs and has great views. Food is a major focus of a stay here. Scones at your door in the morning are followed by a full breakfast in the dining room. In the afternoon, sherry and tea are available. Guests can also arrange for gourmet dinners, which run around $45 without wine, although after-dinner drinks are included. Because Manor Farm Inn is so close to Seattle, it books up well in advance for weekends; plan early.

❂ **Willcox House.** 2390 Tekiu Rd. NW, Bremerton, WA 98312. ☎ **800/725-9477** or 360/
830-4492. www.willcoxhouse.com. 5 rms. $119–$189 double. Rates include full breakfast. DISC,
MC, V.

Set on the shore of Hood Canal and with a superb view of the Olympic Mountains,
this 1930s art deco mansion is one of the state's finest inns. Surrounded by lush gardens of rhododendrons and azaleas that erupt into bloom each spring, the inn was
once a private estate. Today guests get the feeling that they have stepped into a
Merchant-Ivory drama. There's a library where you can curl up in a leather chair
beside the fire, a billiard room (also with a fireplace), a pub (for guests only), a home
theater with big-screen TV and an eclectic assortment of videotapes, and of course,
an elegant great room. Guest rooms are similarly elegant. In the Constance Room,
the inn's largest, you'll find a fireplace and an art deco bathroom. Stay in the Clark
Gable Room, and you'll have your own private balcony. Dinners are also served at
the inn by reservation with fixed-price meals ranging in price from $21.50 on week-
nights to $32.50 on Saturday nights. Regional cuisine and an excellent wine list make
this the finest restaurant on the Kitsap Peninsula.

WHERE TO DINE
IN POULSBO

If you have a sweet tooth, don't miss **Sluys Poulsbo Bakery,** 18924 Front St. NE
(☎ **800/69-SLUYS** or 360/779-2798), which bakes mounds of goodies, as well as
stick-to-your-ribs breads. Chocoholics should definitely not miss **Boehm's Chocolates,** 18864 Front St. (☎ **360/697-3318**). When you need a cup of espresso, head
to the **Poulsbohemian Coffeehouse,** 19003 Front St. (☎ **360/779-9199**), which
has an excellent view of Liberty Bay from atop the bluff on the edge of downtown.
If tea's your drink, try **Ye Old Copper Kettle,** 18881 Front St. (☎ **360/697-2999**),
an English tea room where you can get scones and crumpets.

Sheila's Bay Cafe. On the marina, Poulsbo. ☎ **360/779-2997.** Main dishes $7–$10.
MC, V. Mon–Tues 7am–3pm, Wed–Fri 7am–9pm, Sat 8am–9pm, Sun 8am–3pm. NORWEGIAN/
NEW AMERICAN.

Although this place is nothing fancy, just a casual diner where fisherman feel comfortable in their rain gear, it is one of the few places in town that actually serves Scandinavian food. Such dishes as fish cakes with nutmeg are available at dinner
Wednesday through Friday, and on Saturday nights there is a special "Taste of Norway" menu. Lutefisk and sautéed fish pudding will probably never replace Thai food
as our ethnic cuisine of choice, but if you're here in town to soak up the Scandinavian atmosphere, this is definitely the place to eat.

IN SILVERDALE

If you're looking for a pleasant place to heft a pint of fresh craft ale, try the **Silver
City Brewing Co.,** 2799 NW Myre Rd., Silverdale (☎ **360/698-5879**), which,
though located amid the endless shopping plazas adjacent to the Kitsap Mall, has a
lot of character inside.

Yacht Club Broiler. 9226 Bayshore Dr. NW, Silverdale ☎ **360/698-1601.** Reservations recommended. Main dishes $6–$25. AE, DISC, MC, V. Mon–Sat 11am–midnight, Sun 10am–
midnight. AMERICAN.

While it seems easy to dismiss Silverdale as one vast shopping mall, it also happens
to front on Puget Sound. For the best water views in town, head to the Yacht Club
Broiler. Lots of windows ensure that everyone enjoys the surroundings—keep an eye

out for seals and ospreys—and in the dry months, there is outdoor seating with heaters to take the chill off at night. As you'd expect, the menu is long on well-prepared seafood dishes, but also has plenty of other grilled meats as well as lighter meals. The Sunday brunch is very popular and there is a dock you can tie up to if you come by boat.

IN THE BREMERTON AREA

The most elegant meals on the Kitsap Peninsula are served at the Willcox House, a luxurious inn overlooking the Hood Canal. Although it is mostly guests of the inn who dine here, the fixed-price meals are also open to the public by reservation. See above for details.

3 Vashon Island

By ferry: 3¹/₂ miles W of West Seattle, 1 mile E of Southworth (Kitsap Peninsula), 2 miles N of Tacoma

Something of a bedroom community for Seattle, but much less developed than Bainbridge Island, Vashon Island still clings steadfastly to its rural roots. Roughly 13 miles long and 4 miles wide, it actually consists of two islands, Vashon and Maury (although the latter is an island in name only). Maury is connected to Vashon by a narrow causeway known as Portage. Between the two islands lies Quartermaster Harbor, a long narrow bay whose protected waters are popular with sea kayakers. The island is home to some 11,000 people.

Despite the numerous farms, the island is not entirely rural in character. Two of its employers enjoy regional and national recognition. It is here on Vashon that SBC, one of Starbucks' biggest competitors in the Seattle area coffee market, has its headquarters and roasterie. Vashon is also home to famed snow ski manufacturer K2.

Although there aren't too many attractions on the island, the rural atmosphere has an undeniable charm and numerous B&Bs have sprung up on the island to cater to Seattleites looking for a quick and quiet getaway. Far more people simply come out for the day to sample the island's quiet life and then head back to the fast lane.

ESSENTIALS

GETTING THERE   Vashon Island is only accessible by ferry, and is about 25 minutes from Seattle, 10 minutes from Southworth, and 15 minutes from Point Defiance in Tacoma. The northern ferry dock is served by a car ferry that shuttles between Fauntleroy in West Seattle, Vashon, and Southworth on the Kitsap Peninsula. This dock is also served by a passenger ferry from downtown Seattle. The southern ferry terminal at Tahlequah is served by a ferry from Point Defiance in Tacoma. Fares are $7.95 to $9.55 for a car and driver, $2.30 for adult car passengers or walk-ons, and $1.15 for seniors and children ages 5 to 11. These fares are only collected on ferries bound *for* the island.

VISITOR INFORMATION   For more information on Vashon Island, contact the **Vashon-Maury Island Chamber of Commerce,** 17633 Vashon Hwy. SW (P.O. Box 1035), Vashon, WA 98070 (☎ **253/463-6217**).

EXPLORING THE ISLAND

The island likes to play up its rural character and nowhere is this more apparent than at the **Country Store & Gardens,** 20211 Vashon Hwy. SW (☎ **206/463-3655**) and the adjacent **Maury Island Farm General Store,** 20317 Vashon Hwy. SW (☎ **253/463-2635**). At the Country Store, you'll find a classic garden store surrounded by display gardens and a nursery. Cut flowers and U-pick fruits and nuts are the big attraction here in the summer. At Maury Island Farm, you'll find local preserves, fruit toppings, and other Northwest specialty food items, as well as works by island artists and craftspeople. If you're interested in seeing more works by local artists, stop in at the **Blue Heron Art Center and Art Gallery,** 19704 Vashon Hwy. SW (☎ **206/463-5131**), which is roughly across the street from the Country Store. Down in historic Burton, toward the south end of the island, you'll find the **Silverwood Gallery,** 24927 Vashon Hwy. SW (☎ **206/463-1722**), which showcases national and regional artists and is located in an old Masonic Temple. Coffee addicts will certainly want to drop by the **Seattle's Best Coffee (SBC),** 19529 Vashon Hwy. SW (☎ **206/463-3932**) coffee roasterie, housed in a historic building which also contains a coffee museum.

Vashon Island is a favorite of Seattle bicyclists who come across on the ferry, ride the island's quiet country roads and then head back to the big city. If you'd like to see the island by bike, you can rent bikes at **Vashon Island Bicycles,** 17232 Vashon Hwy. SW (☎ **206/463-6225**). If you're interested in paddling the protected waters of Quartermaster Harbor, you can rent a sea kayak from **Vashon Island Kayak Company** (☎ **206/463-YAKS**), which sets up shop between June 1 and September 15 at Burton Acres Park in the historic south island community of Burton.

The island also has a large number of small parks, many of which are on the water. One of the more remote is **Point Robinson Park,** a former coast guard station on the east side of Maury Island, located at the east end of SW Pt. Robinson Road. From here there are great views across the Sound. On Quartermaster Harbor, on SW Burton Drive, you'll find **Burton Acres Park,** a popular sea kayak launching spot. **Dockton Park,** which has a boat launch, is on Dockton Road SW.

WHERE TO STAY

Angels of the Sea B&B. 26431 99th Ave. SW, Vashon, WA 98070. ☎ **800/798-9249** or 206/463-6980. Fax 206/463-2205. www.cimarron.net/usa/wa/angels.html. 3 rms (1 with private bathroom). $75–$85 double with shared bath; $115 double with private bath. Rates include full breakfast. MC, V.

Set on a winding country lane near Dockton Park on the Maury Island part of Vashon, this inn is housed in a renovated 1917 country church. The casual B&B is operated by Marnie Jones, an accomplished harpist, who provides ethereal musical accompaniment during breakfast. Of the three guest rooms, the upstairs room, with its whirlpool tub skylights, TV, and VCR is by far the most comfortable. Because Marnie has a young son, children are welcome here.

Back Bay Inn. 24007 Vashon Hwy. SW, Vashon, WA 98070 ☎ **206/463-5355.** 4 rms. TV TEL. $97.50–$112.50 double. DISC, MC, V.

Although this inn, a sprawling modern Victorian building, sits right on the island's busiest road, it is also in the island's most picturesque community, the historic fishing village of Burton. The inn and guest rooms are furnished with antiques, and the weekend breakfasts are such memorable events that the inn even opens up to the public for these meals. All the guest rooms have views of Quartermaster Harbor.

WHERE TO DINE

For smoothies, fresh-squeezed juices, and creative sandwiches, try the **Dog Day Cafe,** 17530 Vashon Hwy. SW (☎ **206/463-6404**), a popular island hangout tucked into a nondescript shopping plaza adjacent to the island's biggest grocery store (at the corner of SW Bank Road). For breakfast on Saturday or Sunday morning, you just can't beat the **Back Bay Inn** (see above). The island's most interesting espresso place is

Second Wind Cafe (☎ 206/463-4624), at the northern ferry dock. It consists of a romantic little green house.

Sound Food Restaurant & Bakery. 20312 Vashon Hwy. SW. ☎ **206/463-3565.** Main dishes $5–$15. AE, MC, V. Mon–Thurs 7am–8pm, Fri 7am–9pm, Sat 8am–9pm, Sun 8am–8pm. INTERNATIONAL.

Located just about in the middle of the island at Valley Center, this casual restaurant serves a wide variety of familiar and filling meals, but also throws in a bit of unexpected creativity. There are burgers and stir fries, but there are also such dishes as polenta with sun-dried tomatoes in mushroom sauce, tequila scallops, and Jamaican jerk chicken. Sound Foods is particularly popular at breakfast when the excellent baked goodies are a big hit (the perfect place to start a day's exploration of the island).

4 Gig Harbor

45 miles S of Seattle, 30 miles S of Bremerton, 45 miles N of Olympia

On the far side of the Tacoma Narrows Bridge from Tacoma is the quaint waterfront town of Gig Harbor. With its interesting little shops, art galleries, seafood restaurants, fleet of commercial fishing boats, and marinas full of private pleasure boats, this town is the quintessential Puget Sound fishing village. Framing this picture of Puget Sound's past is the snowcapped bulk of Mount Rainier, which lends this town a near story-book quality.

Long the site of a Native American village, Gig Harbor was not discovered by Euro-Americans until 1841 when sailors from an exploratory expedition who were charting the area from a gig (a small boat that had been launched from the expedition's main ship) rowed into the bay. Settlers arrived here in 1867 and soon Gig Harbor was a thriving fishing village of Scandinavians and Croatians.

ESSENTIALS

GETTING THERE   Gig Harbor lies just across the Tacoma Narrows Bridge from Tacoma off Wash. 16.

VISITOR INFORMATION   For more information on this area, contact the **Gig Harbor/Peninsula Chamber of Commerce,** 3125 Judson St., Gig Harbor, WA 98335 (☎ **253/851-6865**).

EXPLORING GIG HARBOR

Connecting Tacoma to the Kitsap Peninsula, the **Tacoma Narrows Bridge** is the fifth-largest suspension bridge in the world and opened in 1950 after a previous bridge had collapsed. This original bridge had been dubbed Gallopin' Gertie for the way it undulated during high winds, and after being completed in 1940, lasted only 4 months before shaking itself apart. Today's bridge, though it, too, often experiences high winds, is far more stable. It is, however, a major transportation bottleneck, with mile-long traffic back-ups daily at rush hour. At press time there were plans to have the area's residents vote on whether to build a new bridge.

On the waterfront you'll find **Rent-a-Boat & Sail Charters,** 8829 N. Harborview Dr. (☎ **253/858-7341**), where you can rent a sailboat, powerboat, pedal boat, or kayak. Rates range from $8 to $55 an hour for the various types of watercraft. Guided sea kayak trips are also available from **Northwest Passages** (☎ **888/42-YAKIT** or 253/851-7987). Tours cost between $20 and $60.

Most visitors to Gig Harbor come because of the boating opportunities, but landlubbers can stroll the town's main street, Harborview Drive, enjoying the view of the harbor and stopping to browse in dozens of interesting little shops and art galleries along the waterfront. Toward the south end of the waterfront, you'll find Jersich Park. At press time, the **Gig Harbor Peninsula Historical Society** was planning to open a historical museum at 4218 Harborview Dr. (☎ **253/858-6722**).

WHERE TO STAY

✪ **Dockside Bed & Boat.** 8829 N. Harborview Dr., Gig Harbor, WA 98335. ☎ **253/ 858-7341.** 7 boats. $95–$250 double. Rates include brunch. No credit cards.

If you've always longed to live the yachting life, here's a great opportunity. Dockside Bed & Boat, which is affiliated with Rent-a-Boat & Sail Charters, will now let you spend the night on a variety of its power and sail yachts. The yachts are moored at various docks around the harbor and the brunch consists of a dining coupon for Le Bistro restaurant in downtown Gig Harbor. You can also charter these same boats so after your night on the water, you can spend the day exploring the area's waterways.

The Maritime Inn. 3212 Harborview Dr., Gig Harbor, WA 98335. ☎ **253/858-1818.** 15 rms. A/C TV TEL. $75–$130 double. AE, DISC, MC, V.

Located across from the waterfront in downtown Gig Harbor, this small hotel is new but manages to conjure up the image of old beach resort cottages with its classic, simple styling. All the guest rooms have gas fireplaces and are romantic without being frilly. Pine furnishings lend a further air of classicism to the rooms. While most rooms have some sort of view of the water, the views are better from those few rooms that are on the second floor. Should you want to sail in instead of driving, you'll find the town's 24-hour public dock is right across the street.

Mary's Bed & Breakfast. 8212 Dorotich St., Gig Harbor, WA 98332. ☎ **253/858-2424.** 3 rms. $75–$95 double. Rates include full breakfast. MC, V.

To stay any closer to the water in Gig Harbor than this charming little inn, you'd have to stay on a boat. This renovated fisherman's home was built in 1915 and is right on the water, with a small yard sloping down to the bay and a pleasant back deck from which you can sit and survey the boats in the harbor. The inn is not fancy but is comfortable and cozy and the locale just can't be beat. Within walking distance are all the town's shops and restaurants.

WHERE TO DINE

When it's time for coffee, head to **Le Bistro Coffee House,** 4120 Harborview Dr. (☎ **253/851-1033**) at the north end of downtown. For great bread, drop by the **Harbor Bread Co.,** 8822 N. Harborview Dr. (☎ **253/851-4181**), which bakes fabulous rustic, wood-oven breads.

✪ **The Green Turtle.** 2905 Harborview St. ☎ **253/851-3167.** Reservations recommended. Main dishes $12–$16. AE, MC, V. Tues–Sat 5–9pm. PAN-ASIAN/INTERNATIONAL.

With the hands-down best view in town (Mount Rainier looming beyond the mouth of the harbor on clear days), this elegant little restaurant is tucked away in an unlikely spot next door to a yacht sales office. Two walls of glass let everyone enjoy the views, and in summer there is a deck under a big old maple tree. The menu is almost entirely seafood, but you will find a few chicken, duck, and steak dishes on the menu. Preparations lean toward the far side of the Pacific, with such dishes as sautéed calamari in spicy black bean sauce, pan-seared ahi with a roasted garlic and ginger sauce, and halibut with artichoke hearts and a creamy basil and curry sauce showing up on a recent menu. The Green Turtles is affiliated with nearby Marco's Ristorante.

Marco's. 7707 Pioneer Way. ☎ **253/858-2899.** Reservations recommended. Main dishes $10–$15. AE, MC, V. Tues–Sat 5–9pm. ITALIAN.

Marco's has long been one of Gig Harbor's best and most popular restaurants and this despite having no view whatsoever. However, the cozy, dark dining room, with its crates and wine bottles everywhere has a great bistro atmosphere that makes up for the lack of a view. The menu, which changes regularly, recently included some surprising twists on Italian classics. How about spaghetti with meatballs that are stuffed with feta cheese or smoked salmon ravioli in a brie sauce? It's these sorts of unexpected creations that keep Marco's so popular, but you're also likely to find more traditional fare such as veal marsala, chicken piccata, and clam linguini. At press time, Marco's was planning to open for lunch several days a week.

Tides Tavern. 2925 Harborview Dr. ☎ **253/858-3982.** Reservations not accepted. Main dishes $4.25–$15. AE, MC, V. Mon–Thurs 11am–10pm, Fri–Sat 11am–10:30pm, Sun 11am–9:30pm. AMERICAN.

This is basically just a tavern with an extensive menu, but because of its great location over the water at the east end of town, it's a great place for lunch or a casual dinner. The building that houses the tavern was originally constructed as a general store back in 1910, but has been the Tides Tavern since 1973. The menu is basic tavern fare—burgers, sandwiches, and pizzas—and if not entirely memorable, it's all tasty. On Friday and Saturday nights there's live music. Because this is a tavern, you must be 21 or older to eat here.

5 Tacoma

32 miles S of Seattle, 31 miles N of Olympia, 93 miles S of Port Townsend

In 1883, Tacoma became the end of the line for the Northern Pacific Railroad and the city's fate as the industrial center of the Puget Sound was sealed. Things have changed a bit since the days when the city's waterfront was lined with smoke-belching lumber and paper mills, but Tacoma, despite incipient gentrification, remains an ugly stepsister to glamorous Seattle. However, with the renovation of Union Station and installation there of impressive Dale Chihuly glass art, the opening of a modern performing arts center (complete with two renovated historic theaters), construction of the huge Washington State History Museum, and the opening of a new University of Washington campus (in renovated buildings), the city is making great strides toward reinventing itself. Future plans include making the Thea Foss Waterway area along the old waterfront more recreation oriented, and construction of an International Museum of Glass Art (with an art glass filled pedestrian bridge over I-705 to connect the new museum with the rest of the downtown). However, jokes about the aroma of Tacoma persist and the city's downtown still becomes something of a ghost town after the office workers head home at the end of the day.

Despite its reputation, Tacoma actually has quite a length of very attractive waterfront. In recent years, the city has reclaimed a major portion of the shoreline along Ruston Way and turned it into a pleasant park lined with restaurants. Sure, you can still stand in downtown's Fireman's Park and look down on an industrial wasteland, but if you then turn around, you'll be facing a new, revitalized Tacoma where the arts are flourishing and historic buildings are being preserved and renovated.

Despite Tacoma's ongoing makeover, Point Defiance Park is still the city's top attraction. With miles of trails, great bicycling and in-line skating, a world-class zoo and aquarium, and numerous other attractions, this is one of the premier parks in Puget Sound.

Tacoma

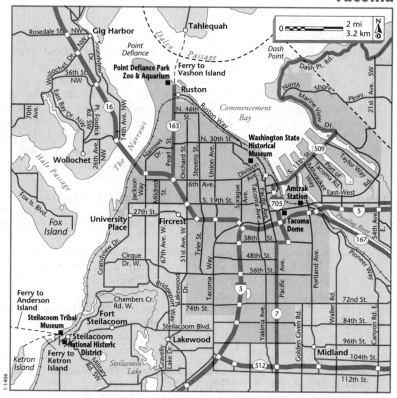

ESSENTIALS

GETTING THERE   Tacoma is on I-5 at the junction of Wash. 16, which is the main route north through the Kitsap Peninsula to Port Townsend and the rest of the Olympic Peninsula. Wash. 7 from the Mount Rainier area leads into downtown Tacoma from the south. Tacoma's city center is accessed by I-705, a short spur that leads from I-5 into the middle of downtown.

Seattle-Tacoma International Airport is located 22 miles north of Tacoma. **Capital Airporter** (☎ 360/754-7113) operates an airport shuttle service; the fare is $13 one way to downtown Tacoma.

Greyhound bus lines serve Tacoma. The station is at the corner of 14th Street and Pacific Avenue.

Amtrak has service to Tacoma. The station is at 1001 Puyallup Ave.

VISITOR INFORMATION   For more information on this area, contact the **Tacoma–Pierce County Visitor & Convention Bureau,** 1001 Pacific Ave., Suite 400 (P.O. Box 1754), Tacoma, WA 98402 (☎ **800/272-2662** or 253/627-2836).

GETTING AROUND   See "Getting Around" in chapter 5 for information on renting cars at Sea-Tac International Airport. If you need a taxi, contact **Yellow Cab** (☎ **253/472-3303**). Public bus service is provided by **Pierce Transit** (☎ **253/581-8000**). Most bus routes start at 10th and Commerce streets downtown.

WHAT TO SEE & DO
POINT DEFIANCE PARK

Point Defiance Park, on the north side of town at the end of Pearl Street, is Tacoma's center of activity and one of the largest urban parks in the country. In the park are many of the city's main attractions, including the Point Defiance Zoo & Aquarium, Fort Nisqually Historic Site, Camp 6 Logging Museum, and Never Never Land. Founded in 1888, the park represents Tacoma's farsightedness in preserving one of the region's most scenic points of land. Winding through the wooded park is **Five Mile Drive,** which connects all the park's main attractions as well as the picnic areas, and hiking and biking trails. Also in the park are a rose garden, a Japanese garden, a rhododendron garden, a dahlia test garden, and a native-plant garden. You can reach the park by following Ruston Way or Pearl Street north.

✪ **Point Defiance Zoo & Aquarium.** 5400 N. Pearl St. ☎ **253/591-5337.** Admission $7 adults, $6.55 seniors, $5.30 children 4–13. Memorial Day to Labor Day, daily 10am–7pm; Labor Day to Memorial Day, daily 10am–4pm. Closed the third Fri in July, Thanksgiving, and Dec 25.

This highly regarded zoo focuses on the wildlife of the Pacific Rim countries, and to that end you'll find animals from such far-flung locations as the Arctic tundra, Southeast Asia, and the Andes Mountains. The Rocky Shores exhibit features marine mammals, including beluga whales. The Jewels of the Sea exhibit sheds a new light on jellyfish. Other exhibits include a northern Pacific aquarium, a tropical coral reef aquarium that's home to more than 40 sharks, and an aquarium of deadly sea creatures. New occupants of the zoo include naked mole rats, snow leopards, and two polar bear cubs. At the farm zoo, kids can pet various animals.

Fort Nisqually Historic Site. 5400 N. Pearl St. ☎ **253/591-5339.** Admission $1.50 adult, 75¢ child from Memorial Day to Labor Day; open daily 11am–6pm. Admission free Labor Day to Memorial Day; open Wed–Sun 11am–5pm (museum and gift shop only).

Fort Nisqually was a trading post founded in 1833 by the Hudson's Bay Company for the purpose of acquiring beaver pelts. However, it was established at a time when the fur trade was in decline and was soon moved to a new location and converted to a commercial farming business. This reconstruction, built in the 1930s, is based on the design of that second fort. Inside the stockade walls are two original buildings and several reconstructed buildings. Once a month there's a living-history day with interpreters dressed in period costumes.

Camp 6 Logging Museum. 5400 N. Pearl St. ☎ **253/752-0047.** Museum, free; logging train rides, $2 adults, $1 seniors and children ages 3–12. Mid-Jan to Mar and Oct, Wed–Sun 10am–4pm; Apr–Memorial Day, Wed–Sun 10am–5pm; Memorial Day–Sept, Wed–Fri 10am–5pm, Sat–Sun 10am–7pm. Closed Nov–mid-Jan.

This museum focuses on the days of steam power in Washington's logging history. Exhibits include plenty of steam equipment as well as old bunkhouses and a railcar camp. The latter was a rolling logging camp with bunkhouses built on railroad cars. On weekends in spring and summer, Camp 6 offers rides on an old logging train.

Never Never Land. 5400 N. Pearl St. ☎ **253/591-5845.** Admission $2.25 adults, $1.75 seniors and children 13–17, $1.25 children 3–12. June–Aug, Wed–Sun 11am–6pm; Mar–Apr and Sept Sat–Sun 11am–5pm; May, Wed–Sun 11am–5pm. Closed Oct–Feb.

The kids will love seeing life-size figures of famous fairy-tale characters such as Humpty Dumpty, the Big Bad Wolf, Mother Goose, Peter Rabbit, Little Red Riding Hood, Hansel and Gretel, and Goldilocks and the Three Bears. Best of all, the park is located amid deep, dark forests that are straight out of the Grimm brothers' fairy tales.

MUSEUMS

Tacoma Art Museum. 1123 Pacific Ave. ☎ **253/272-4258.** Admission $4 adults, $3 seniors and students, free for children 12 and under; free for everyone on third Thurs of each month. Tues–Wed and Fri–Sat 10am–5pm, Thurs 10am–7pm (to 8pm on the third Thurs), Sun noon–5pm.

A small but far-reaching permanent collection features works by such artists as Degas, Renoir, Corot, Pissarro, Edward Hopper, and Roy Lichtenstein. However, the museum's greatest claim to fame is the Dale Chihuly Retrospective Gallery. Chihuly, a Northwest glass artist who grew up in Tacoma, is widely acclaimed as the nation's foremost creator of art glass. This is the only comprehensive permanent public display of his works.

Washington State History Museum. 1911 Pacific Ave. ☎ **888/238-4373.** Admission $7 adults, $6 seniors, $5 students 13–17, $4 children 6–12, $3 children 3–5. Labor Day to Memorial Day, Tues–Wed and Fri–Sat 10am–5pm, Thurs 10am–8pm, Sun 11am–5pm. Memorial Day to Labor Day, Mon–Sat 9am–5pm, Thurs 9am–8pm, Sun 11am–5pm.

This museum opened in its impressive new facility in August 1996 and is now one of the best reasons to pay a visit to downtown Tacoma. This massive archive of Washington state history is like no other history museum in the Northwest and utilizes a full barrage of high-tech displays to make this history both fun and interesting. From a covered wagon to a Boeing B-17, a Coast Salish longhouse to a Hooverville shack, the state's history comes alive through the use of life-sized mannequins, recorded narration, and "overheard" conversations. With loads of interactive exhibits and several films being screened daily, it's obvious that the museum is trying to appeal to the Nintendo generation, but older visitors will have fun, too.

The Children's Museum of Tacoma. 936 Broadway. ☎ **206/627-6031.** Admission $3.75 per person, children under two free. Tues–Sat 10am–5pm, Sun noon–5pm.

With hands-on exhibits, this downtown museum addresses topics of interest to children in the areas of science, the arts, and creative play. Exhibits tend to change every year or two.

TACOMA AREA PUBLIC GARDENS

Lakewold Gardens. 12317 Gravelly Lake Dr. SW ☎ **253/584-3360.** Admission $6 adults, $5 seniors and children under 12. Apr–Sept, Mon, Thurs, Fri–Sun 10am–4pm; Oct–Mar, Mon, Thurs–Fri 10am–3pm.

Formerly a private estate, this 10-acre garden, designed by noted landscape architect Thomas Church, includes extensive collections of Japanese maples and rhododendrons. There are also rose, fern, and alpine gardens that include numerous rare and unusual plants.

Pacific Rim Bonsai Collection. 33663 Weyerhaeuser Way S., Weyerhaeuser Company campus, Federal Way ☎ **253/924-5206.** Admission is free. Mar–May, Fri–Wed 10am–4pm; June–Feb, Sat–Wed 11am–4pm.

Assembled by the Weyerhaeuser Company in 1989 to honor trade relations with Pacific Rim nations, this bonsai collection includes more than 50 miniature trees from Japan, China, Korea, Taiwan, and Canada. This is the most impressive public bonsai collection in the state.

Rhododendron Species Botanical Garden. 33660 Weyerhaeuser Way S., Weyerhaeuser Company campus, Federal Way ☎ **253/661-9377.** Admission $3.50 adults, $2.50 seniors and children under 12. Mar–May, Fri–Wed 10am–4pm; June–Feb, Sat–Wed 11am–4pm.

Covering 24 acres, this garden has one of the most extensive collections of species (wild) of rhododendrons and azaleas in the world. More than 2,100 different varieties of plants put on an amazing floral display from March through May. Also included in these gardens are collections of ferns, maples, heathers, and bamboos. For serious gardeners, this is one of the Northwest's garden musts.

W.W. Seymour Botanical Conservatory. In Wright Park, 316 South G St. ☎ **253/591-5330.** Free admission. Daily 10am–4:30pm.

Constructed in 1908, this elegant Victorian conservatory is one of only three of this kind on the West Coast and is listed on the National Register of Historic Places. More than 500 species of exotic plants are housed in the huge greenhouse, which is built of more than 12,000 panes of glass. The conservatory stands in Wright Park, which has more than 700 trees of 100 species and is a shady retreat from downtown's pavement.

OTHER TACOMA PARKS

Although Point Defiance Park is Tacoma's premier park, the **Ruston Way Parks** rank a close second. Once jammed with smoking, decaying industrial buildings and piers, the Tacoma waterfront was an industrial area of national infamy. However, since the city of Tacoma reclaimed the shore of Commencement Bay and turned it into parkland, it has become one of the most attractive waterfront parks on Puget Sound. With grassy areas, a sandy beach, a public fishing pier, and a paved pathway, the waterfront is popular with strollers, cyclists, and in-line skaters.

Downtown at the corner of A Street and South Ninth, you'll find **Fireman's Park,** which has the world's tallest totem poles as well as a view of the Port of Tacoma below. After gazing down on the port, if you want to have a closer look, stop by the **Port of Tacoma Observation Tower** off East 11th Street. Here you can watch as ships from around the world are loaded and unloaded.

HISTORIC DISTRICTS & BUILDINGS

Tacoma has quite a few historic buildings, the most noticeable of which is **Union Station** at 1717 Pacific Ave. Built in the beaux arts style as the terminal for the first transcontinental railroad to reach the Northwest, the imposing building is now home to the federal courts and is adjacent to the Washington State History Museum. In the lobby of this building you'll find a glass installation by Dale Chihuly.

Stadium High School, at 111 N. E St., is a French château-style structure that was built as a hotel and later converted to a high school. The school is the centerpiece of the historic **Stadium District,** which is at the north end of Broadway and has more than 100 Victorian homes. At the south end of the Stadium District is the **Old City Hall Historic District,** which is the city's main antiques neighborhood. You'll find more than a dozen large antique stores and malls along Broadway just north of Ninth Street. On the east side of town you'll find **Freighthouse Square,** which is near the Tacoma Dome at the corner of 25th and East D streets and is housed in the renovated Milwaukee Railroad freight house. The building is now a public market along the lines of Seattle's Pike Place Market. At the Tacoma-Pierce County Visitor & Convention Center you can pick up brochures on the city's historic buildings.

WHERE TO STAY

Despite its size, Tacoma suffers from a pronounced shortage of hotels. Aside from the Sheraton and a few bed-and-breakfast inns, your only options are chain motels along the Interstate. If you're interested in staying at a bed-and-breakfast, contact the **Bed & Breakfast Association of Tacoma and Mt. Rainier,** P.O. Box 7957, Tacoma, WA 98407 (☎ **253-593-6098**).

In addition to the following accommodations, inexpensive chain motels in the Tacoma area include the following (see the Appendix for a list of toll-free telephone numbers): **Travelodge Tacoma,** 8402 S. Hosmer St., Tacoma, WA 98444 (☎ **253/ 535-2800**), charging $49 to $59 double; **Comfort Inn,** 5601 Pacific Hwy. E., Tacoma, WA 98424 (☎ **253/926-2301**), charging $51 to $69 double; and **Days Inn Tacoma Mall,** 6802 S. Tacoma Mall Blvd., Tacoma, WA 98409 (☎ **253/ 475-5900**), charging $70 to $85 double.

Sheraton Tacoma Hotel. 1320 Broadway Plaza, Tacoma, WA 98402. ☎ **800/845-9466** or 253/572-3200. Fax 206/591-4105. 319 rms, 21 suites. A/C TV TEL. $150–$165 double; $160– $400 suite. AE, CB, DC, DISC, ER, JCB, MC, V. Valet parking $8; self-parking $5.

This 26-story downtown high-rise is Tacoma's biggest, best, and only downtown business hotel, and because it is attached to the Tacoma Convention Center, it stays busy most of the year. A skylit atrium lobby lends both grandeur and character to the lobby, and an espresso cart and cigar store provide all the modern conveniences. Guest rooms are none too large, but are both comfortable and tastefully decorated. For more personal services such as evening turndown, morning newspaper, and a continental breakfast, opt for a room on one of the concierge floors.

Dining/Entertainment: Up on the 26th floor you'll find an Italian restaurant with one of the best views in town. Down on the mezzanine level there's a more casual bistro serving Northwest food. Also on the mezzanine is a lounge featuring live blues and rock music on weekends.

Services: Concierge, room service, valet/laundry service, access to exercise facilities at the adjacent YMCA.

Facilities: Whirlpool, shoeshine stand.

✪ **The Villa Bed & Breakfast.** 705 N. Fifth St., Tacoma, WA 98403. ☎ **888/572-1157** or 253/572-1157. Fax 253/572-1805. 2 rms, 2 suites. $85–$135 double. Rates include full breakfast. AE, MC, V.

From the red roof tiles to the covered portico to the naiad statue in the garden pond, this inn cries out authentic Italianate villa. The only odd thing about this 1920s mansion is that it is in Tacoma and not Santa Barbara. The inn has been lovingly restored and is set amid neatly manicured gardens. For the amount of luxury and attention to details that you get here, the rates are surprisingly reasonable. Even the least expensive room, the former maid's quarters, has a private veranda and the views from this room are the best in the house. However, if it's space you crave, opt for the Bay View Suite, which has views of the Olympic Mountains, a gas fireplace, a private veranda, and a 9-foot-tall four-poster bed.

WHERE TO DINE

When you just have to have a cup of espresso, **Grounds For Coffee,** 764 Broadway (☎ 253/627-7742) is the place to head. This Victorian-inspired coffee house claims the narrow corner space of a flat-iron style building in downtown Tacoma's antiques neighborhood. At press time, there were plans to open an outpost of Seattle's popular Anthony's restaurant chain in the boathouse in Point Defiance Park. With its excellent location and the Anthony's reputation for quality seafood, this restaurant will likely become the city's premier waterfront restaurant.

Harbor Lights. 2761 Ruston Way. ☎ **253/752-8600.** Reservations recommended. Main courses lunch $4.75–$10.50, dinner $12–$36. AE, CB, DC, DISC, MC, V. Mon–Thurs 11am– 11pm, Fri 11am–1am, Sat noon–1am, Sun 2–9pm. SEAFOOD/STEAK.

The oldest restaurant on the Ruston Way waterfront, Harbor Lights has an air of faded elegance about it. The restaurant is quite a bit smaller than the newer dining establishments along this section of waterfront and lacks any outside dining, but the views are the same. A collection of autographed celebrity photos attests to the restaurant's popularity and position as a Tacoma institution. The menu is extensive and portions are large, but try to find room for the clam chowder, which is made from a 1919 family recipe. Though the crab dishes are a bit pricey, there's a good selection. There's also a long list of oyster preparations and several types of fine steaks and chops.

✪ **Harmon Pub and Brewery.** 1938 Pacific Ave. ☎ **253/383-BREW.** Reservations not accepted. Main dishes $5–$14. AE, DISC, MC, V. Sun–Thurs 11am–midnight, Fri–Sat 11am–2am. AMERICAN.

Located in an renovated old commercial building across from the Washington State History Museum, this large pub offers much more than your standard pub fare. Sure there are burgers and sandwiches and pizzas, but you'll also find cedar-plank salmon, ale-lime clam linguine with cilantro-lime butter sauce, and grilled pork loin that has been marinated in pale ale. The pub has adopted an outdoors theme and even serves as meeting point for outdoors excursions by Tahoma Outdoor Pursuits. On weekends there's a wide range of live music.

✪ **The Lobster Shop.** 4015 Ruston Way. ☎ **253/759-2165.** Reservations recommended. Main courses $12–$24. AE, CB, DC, DISC, MC, V. Mon–Thurs 4:30–9pm, Fri–Sat 4:30–10:30pm, Sun 9:30am–1:30pm (brunch) and 3:30–9pm. SEAFOOD.

This is the most upscale of the Ruston Way seafood places and offers outside seating and views, views, views. Starters include a respectable New England–style clam chowder (a rarity in the Northwest) and a good lobster bisque. But the appetizer not to miss is the hot Dungeness crab dip, made with crab, artichoke hearts, onions, and Parmesan. Dishes on the main menu are reliable continental standards, but the daily fresh sheet has more creative dishes. The crab cakes, here served with a red-currant sauce, and the cioppino are always good bets.

Stanley & Seafort's Steak, Chop & Fish House. 115 E. 34th St. ☎ **253/473-7300.** Reservations highly recommended. Main courses $15–$35. AE, DISC, MC, V. Mon–Thurs 11:15am–2pm and 5–10pm, Fri 11:15am–2pm and 5–10:30pm, Sat 4:30–10:30pm, Sun 4:30–9:30pm. AMERICAN.

Perched high on a hill overlooking all of Tacoma, this is the city's favorite special-occasion restaurant and has been for many years. While prices are high, the food is well prepared (if not all that inventive), the service is professional, and the view is fascinating, with the Tacoma Dome in the foreground, the port and downtown in the middle distance, and the Olympic Mountains rising on the horizon. Apple-wood–grilled steaks are the specialty here, but there are also several seafood and chicken dishes, as well as seasonal special theme menus. As with everything else here, wines are a bit overpriced. To reach the restaurant, take Exit 133 east off of I-5, then take the 38th Street exit and follow 38th Street south to Pacific Avenue. Turn right here and then right again on 34th Street. The restaurant is just across the bridge. While most people get dressed up to eat here, you'll still get served if you're in jeans and sneakers.

Trattoria Grazie. 2301 N. 30th St. ☎ **253/627-0231.** Reservations recommended. Main courses $14–$20. MC, V. Sun–Thurs 11am–9pm, Fri–Sat 11am–10pm. ITALIAN.

Located only a block from the Ruston Way Parks in the Old Town neighborhood, this upscale Italian restaurant has the look and feel of an old New England tavern. Huge multipaned windows take in views of the water with the preferred seats being those on the second floor. Upstairs is also where you'll find the restaurant's small lounge, which, with its wood floors and abundance of polished wood, has a very classic feel to it. A wood-burning oven is the centerpiece in the kitchen and turns out such dishes as baked prawns on arugula. For the most part, however, the menu is comfortingly familiar.

TACOMA AFTER DARK
THE PERFORMING ARTS SCENE

Opened in 1983 the **Tacoma Dome,** 2727 E. D St. (☎ **253/272-3663**), which rises beside I-5 on the east side of the city, is Tacoma's most visible landmark and is the world's largest wood-domed arena. With seating for 28,000 people, it is the site of concerts, sporting events, and other large exhibitions. Smaller productions take to the stages at the **Broadway Center for the Performing Arts,** 901 Broadway Plaza (☎ **253/591-5894**), which consists of two historic theaters and a very contemporary third theater. The **Pantages** is a renovated vaudeville theater built in 1918. Its terra-cotta facade is done in a neoclassical style. The **Rialto Theatre,** 310 S. Ninth St., is a classic Italianate movie palace, built the same year as the Pantages. Rounding out the performing arts center's theaters is the modern **Theatre on the Square,** which is home to the Tacoma Actors Guild. Together these three theaters present a wide variety of nationally recognized theater, music, dance, and even an eclectic film series. Other local performing arts companies that appear at these theaters include the **Tacoma Philharmonic,** the **Tacoma Symphony,** the **Tacoma Opera,** and the **Northwest Sinfonietta.** Call the above number for all ticketing and information.

Tacoma supports a lively theater scene that includes the **Tacoma Little Theatre,** 210 North I St. (☎ **253/272-2281**), which claims to be the oldest continuously performing theater west of the Mississippi and has been staging plays for more than 75 years (tickets $14 to $21). The **Tacoma Actors Guild,** 901 Broadway Plaza (☎ **253/272-2145**), is Tacoma's premier professional theater company and presents six productions a year (tickets $25), including both well-known and more experimental plays. Performances are held in the Theatre on the Square right next door to the Pantages Theatre. The **Spirit Theatre,** 891 Pacific Ave. (☎ **253/627-5869**), located downtown near the theaters of the Tacoma Center for the Performing Arts, is a small theater staging award-winning and original plays (tickets $10 to $18). Fans of musicals have the **Tacoma Musical Playhouse,** Narrows Theatre, 7116 Sixth Ave. (☎ **253/565-6-TMP**), which has been growing ever more popular since its founding in 1994 (tickets $11 to $13).

THE BAR, PUB & CLUB SCENE

Although downtown Tacoma has a long way to go before it ever comes close to being as a lively a place as downtown Seattle, there are enough bars, pubs, and clubs down here to keep you busy at night for at least a few nights. For live jazz and blues in a New Orleans atmosphere (with good Cajun food, too), head to **Roof-n-Doofs New Orleans Cafe,** 754 Pacific Ave. (☎ **253/572-5113**). For live jazz with a view of the water, head to **Luciano's Waterfront Italian Ristorante,** 3327 Ruston Way (☎ **253/756-5611**), which has live music Thursday through Saturday nights. For martinis and R&B, try **Elliott's Lounge,** Tacoma Sheraton, 1320 Broadway Plaza (☎ **253/572-3200**). If you're looking to play some pool in a sophisticated setting, check out **Jillian's Billiards Billiard Cafe,** 1114 Broadway (☎ **253/572-0300**). If you're just looking for a comfortable place to try a bit of local ale, head to the **Harmon Pub** and Brewery. 1938 Pacific Ave. (☎ **253/383-BREW**). There's also live music here on the weekends. At the **Antique Sandwich Company,** 5102 N. Pearl St. (☎ **253/752-4069**), the calendar always includes an eclectic blend of acoustic music. **Drake's,** 734 Pacific Ave. (☎ **253/572-4144**), is an old-town saloon that has been around since 1888 and is now Tacoma's hottest dance club with DJ music Wednesday through Saturday.

BETWEEN TACOMA & OLYMPIA: HISTORIC STEILACOOM

Founded in 1854 by a Maine sea captain, Steilacoom is Washington's oldest incorporated town. Once a bustling seaport, the quiet little community is today a National Historic District with 32 preserved historic buildings. To reach Steilacoom, take Exit 127 off I-5 south between Tacoma and Olympia and follow the signs.

Right in town, there's the **Nathaniel Orr Home and Pioneer Orchard,** 1811 Rainier St., which was built between 1854 and 1857 and contains original furnishings. Currently the house is closed to the public due to damage caused to its foundation during recent restoration work, but there are plans to reopen it when repairs can be carried out. The **Steilacoom Town Hall and Museum,** 112 Main St. (☎ 253/584-4133), houses exhibits on the town's pioneer history. It's open March to October, Tuesday through Sunday from 1 to 4pm; in February, November, and December, Friday through Sunday from 1 to 4pm (closed January). At the **Steilacoom Tribal Museum,** 1515 Lafayette St. (☎ 253/584-6308), you'll find a museum with displays on the area's Steilacoom tribe. It's open Tuesday through Sunday from 10am to 4pm; admission is $2 for adults and $1 for seniors and students.

Steilacoom is also the site of the ferry landing for the small ferry that runs to **Anderson Island,** a quiet rural island that is popular with bicyclists. There are several parks on the island, including Lowell Johnson Park on Lake Florence, which is a popular swimming lake. There are also enough scenic Puget Sound vistas to make the island a pleasant place for a leisurely afternoon drive.

WHERE TO DINE

Bair Drug & Hardware Store. 1617 Lafayette St. ☎ **253/588-9668.** Reservations recommended. Main dishes $11–$17. MC, V. Mon–Thurs 9am–4pm, Fri 9am–4pm and 6–9pm, Sat–Sun 8am–4pm. SODA FOUNTAIN/INTERNATIONAL.

Perhaps the best reason to visit Steilacoom is to have a float or milk shake at this historic 1906 soda fountain. While people no longer drop in for nails or tools, they do line up for ice cream sundaes and the like. The interior of the this old wooden building is kept the way it might have looked back when it opened, making the place part museum, part soda fountain. This is the oldest soda fountain we've ever been in, and is one of our favorites. Friday night is the only night dinner is served and the menu might include Dungeness crab cakes, chicken fettuccine, or pork schnitzel.

E.R. Rogers. 1702 Commercial St. ☎ **253/582-0280.** Reservations recommended. Main courses $15–$27. MC, V. Mon–Sat 5–10pm, Sun 10am–2pm (brunch) and 4:30–9:30pm. CONTINENTAL/AMERICAN.

Located in a restored Victorian home that was built in 1891, E.R. Rogers has an excellent view of Puget Sound. The setting and service are quite formal and while prime rib is the specialty, the menu also includes more adventurous dishes, such as Drambuie chicken and halibut in parchment. The appetizer menu sometimes seems even more tempting than the entree menu with the likes of shrimp-stuffed artichoke, salmon cakes with red pepper cream sauce, and seafood wontons with gingery dipping sauces. The Sunday brunch, with its many fish dishes, is an area institution. This is one of the south sound's favorite special occasion restaurants.

6 Olympia

60 miles S of Seattle, 100 miles N of Portland

Located at the southernmost end of Puget Sound, Olympia is the capital of Washington. The city clings to the shores of Budd Inlet's twin bays and is further divided by Capitol Lake, above which, on a high bluff, stands the capitol building. Despite the political importance of being the state capital, Olympia still has the air of a small town. The downtown is compact and low-rise, and when the legislature isn't in session the city can be downright ghostly. Keeping things alive, however, are the ever-progressive students of the liberal-arts Evergreen State College.

The Olympia area has a long history. It was near here, in what is now the city of Tumwater, that the first American pioneers settled in 1844. A historic district and historical park along the Deschutes River preserves a bit of this history. However, it's not history or politics that has given Olympia its greatest fame—it's Olympia beer, a staple of the suds trade throughout the West.

ESSENTIALS

GETTING THERE   Olympia is on I-5 at the junction with U.S. 101, which leads north around the Olympic Peninsula. Connecting the city to the central Washington coast and Aberdeen/Hoquiam is U.S. 12/Wash. 8.

The nearest airport with scheduled service is Seattle-Tacoma International Airport, 54 miles north. **Capital Airporter** (☎ 360/754-7113) provides a shuttle between the airport and Olympia. The one-way fare is $20.

There is **Amtrak** rail service to Olympia; the station is at 6600 Yelm Highway.

Greyhound bus lines also serves Olympia. The station is at 107 Seventh Ave. SE.

VISITOR INFORMATION   Contact the **Olympia/Thurston County Chamber of Commerce,** 521 Legion Way (P.O. Box 1427), Olympia, WA 98507 (☎ 360/357-3362), or the **State Capitol Visitor Information Center,** 14th Avenue and Capitol Way (P.O. Box 41020), Olympia, WA 98504-1020 (☎ 360/586-3460).

GETTING AROUND   If you need a taxi, contact **Capitol City Taxi** (☎ 360/357-4949). Public bus service is provided by **Intercity Transit** (☎ 360/786-1881), which operates free downtown shuttle buses.

THE CAPITOL CAMPUS

Located at 14th Avenue and Capitol Way, the neoclassical **Washington State Capitol** building, constructed between 1911 and 1928, is set amid a large and attractively landscaped campus known for its flowering cherry trees and rose gardens. At 267 feet tall, this is the tallest domed masonry state capitol in the country and bears a surprising resemblance to the Capitol in that other Washington. Around its campus you'll see sculptures, the Tivoli fountain, and a conservatory. The capitol is open daily and the temple of justice, conservatory, and old capitol building are all open Monday through Friday. On Wednesdays, there are guided tours of the Executive Mansion (the governor's home) by reservation only. For more information on tours of the grounds, contact the **State Capitol Visitor Center** (☎ 360/586-TOUR).

OTHER AREA ATTRACTIONS

After the Capitol, the **Olympia Brewing Company,** 100 Custer Way (☎ 360/3754-5212), is the most imposing landmark in this city. A huge sign on the side of the brewery announces to passing motorists on I-5 that visitors are welcome at the brewery, which is now owned by the Pabst Brewing Company. Call ahead for a schedule of tours. The first brewery established on this site was Capital Brewing, which opened in 1896. This brewery's 1906 brick brewhouse, though now abandoned, still stands adjacent to today's brewery.

In downtown Olympia, you'll find the **Olympia Farmers Market,** 700 N. Capitol Way (☎ 360/352-9096), which is the second largest open-air produce market in the state. The market is open Saturday and Sunday from 10am to 3pm in April, November, and December; Thursday through Sunday May through September, and Friday through Sunday in October.

If you'd like to learn more about the area's history, especially that of the Native Americans who have called this region home for thousands of years, stop by the small **Washington State Capital Museum,** 211 W. 21st Ave. (☎ 360/753-2580). However, it is the building itself, an Italian Renaissance mansion built in the 1920s for a former mayor of Olympia, that is the most interesting part of a visit to this museum. Outside, you'll find the Delbert McBride Ethnobotanical Garden. The museum is open Tuesday through Friday from 10am to 4pm and Saturday and Sunday from noon to 4pm. Admission is $2 for adults, $1.75 for seniors, and $1 for children.

PRESERVES, PARKS & GARDENS

Lying at the edge of downtown Olympia, **Capitol Lake** and its surrounding park lands is a favorite of area joggers, canoeists, and anglers. There is an excellent view of the Capitol from the west side of the lake. Also in downtown is the 1 1/2-mile-long **Percival Landing** boardwalk, which wanders along the shore of Budd Inlet past marinas, restaurants, public art, and interpretive panels.

On the north side of Olympia along the East Bay of Budd Inlet, you'll find several miles of hiking trails and nice water views at **Priest Point State Park,** on East Bay Drive. Another spot worth a visit is the **Yashiro Japanese Garden** (☎ 360/753-8380), at the corner of Ninth Avenue and Plum Street, just off I-5 at Exit 105; it's open daily from 10am to 5pm.

Just across I-5 from Olympia, you'll also find **Tumwater Falls Park,** along a rocky stretch of the Deschutes River. Here small waterfalls cascade over rocks and in the autumn, Chinook salmon can be seen as they return to the park's holding ponds. Several historic homes and an old brewery building lend a bit of history to the park, but the presence of the current Olympia Brewery looming overhead detracts quite a bit from the aesthetics of the setting. Still, for the riverside trails and the chance to see salmon in the fall, this park is worth a visit.

Nisqually National Wildlife Refuge (☎ 360/753-9467), located 10 miles north of Olympia, preserves the delta of the Nisqually River, which is a resting and wintering ground for large numbers of migratory birds. Seven miles of trails lead through the refuge. Some 13 miles south of Olympia, near the town of Littlerock, you'll find the **Mima Mounds Natural Area Preserve** (☎ 360/748-2383), which is an area of hundreds of small hills, each around 7 feet high. No one is sure how the mounds were formed, but their curious topography has produced much speculation over the years. The preserve is open daily from 9am to dusk.

TWO NEARBY WILDLIFE ATTRACTIONS

Wolf Haven International. 3111 Offut Lake Rd., Tenino. ☎ 800/448-9653 or 360/264-4695. Admission $5 adults, $2.50 children 5–12; Howl-ins, $6 adults, $4 children 5–12. May–Sept, Wed–Mon 10am–4pm; Oct–Apr, Wed–Mon 10am–3pm. Howl-ins, May–Labor Day only, Fri–Sat 6:30–9:30pm.

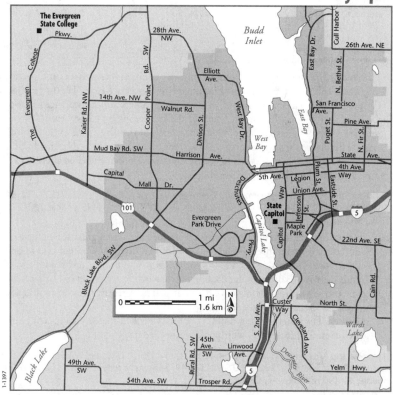

Dedicated to the preservation of wolves and the education of the general public on the subject of wolves, Wolf Haven is a sanctuary for more than 40 wolves. On the hourly tours of the facility, you'll get to meet many of these canines. From May to early September, there are Friday- and Saturday-evening howl-ins that include a tour, a chance to howl with the wolves, and a bit of storytelling and folk singing around a bonfire (reservations are required).

Northwest Trek Wildlife Park. 11610 Trek Dr. E., Eatonville. ☎ **800/433-TREK** or 360/ 832-6117. Admission $8.25 adults, $7.75 seniors, $5.75 children 5–17, $3.75 children 3–4. Hours vary, call for schedule.

The animals of North America are the focus of Northwest Trek, a 635-acre wildlife park 40 miles east of Olympia off Wash. 161. Bison roam, elk bellow, and moose munch contentedly knee-deep in a lake. Visitors are driven through the park in a tram accompanied by a naturalist and learn about the lives of the animals they see along the route. In separate areas, you can see a grizzly bear, a wolf, and such wild cats as cougars, lynx, and bobcats. To reach the park, take Wash. 510 southeast from I-5 (exit 111) to Yelm and continue west on Wash. 702.

WHERE TO STAY

In addition to the hotels listed below, Olympia has several inexpensive chain motels including the following (see the appendix for a list of toll-free telephone numbers): **Super 8 Motel,** 4615 Martin Way, Lacey, WA 98503 (☎ **360/459-8888**), charg-

ing $55 to $66 double; and a **Motel 6**, 400 W. Lee St., Tumwater, WA 98501
(☎ **360/754-7320**), charging $39 to $44 double.

♻ **Harbinger Inn.** 1136 E. Bay Dr., Olympia, WA 98506. ☎ **360/754-0389.** 5 rms. $65–
$95 double. Rates include full breakfast. AE, MC, V.

Located only a short distance from downtown's shops and restaurants and overlooking Budd Inlet and a marina, the Harbinger Inn is a very elegant 1910 stone house.
White pillars and a large balcony give the house an antebellum appearance that would
be right at home in Mississippi. Three of the five rooms have bay views. The nicest
of these is the Innkeepers Suite, which has views of the Olympics, antique furnishings, a fireplace, a sitting room, a private veranda, and a soaking tub. In addition to
a filling breakfast, there are tea and cookies in the afternoon. Pay close attention when
first arriving—the driveway is easy to miss.

Holiday Inn Select—Olympia. 2300 Evergreen Park Dr., Olympia, WA 98502. ☎ **800/
465-4329** or 360/943-4000. 177 rms, 32 suites. A/C TV TEL. $89–$175 double. AE, CB, DC,
DISC, MC, V.

A tranquil setting high on a bluff above Capitol Lake and a great view of the capitol dome itself make this hotel a great choice in Olympia. Though you're only a
5-minute drive from downtown, you'll feel as if you're out in the country. The
grounds display a Northwest landscaping style with plenty of big old fir trees shad-
ing the property. Most rooms have decks or patios. A recent remodeling has added
a number of executive-style suites.

Dining: The hotel's dining room has a nice view and there's an adjacent lounge.

Facilities: Outdoor pool, whirlpool, business center.

Ramada Inn Governor House Hotel. 621 S. Capitol Way, Olympia, WA 98501. ☎ **800/
2-RAMADA** or 360/352-7700. Fax 360/943-9349. 121 rms, 2 suites. A/C TV TEL. $105–$125
double; $140–$160 suite. AE, CB, DC, DISC, MC, V.

Located right downtown, the eight-story Governor House is within walking distance
of the Budd Inlet marina and Percival Landing Waterfront Park, the capitol campus,
and the Washington Center for the Performing Arts, which are several good reasons
to stay here. All the rooms were recently renovated and are looking quite nice these
days, but you'll still want to request a north- or west-facing room on a higher floor
to take advantage of the view of the bay.

Dining: The hotel has a casual restaurant serving three meals a day and an adjacent sports bar.

Services: Room service, valet service.

Facilities: Outdoor pool, whirlpool, sauna, exercise room.

WHERE TO DINE

If you're searching for a good cup of espresso or a quick lunch, check out the **Capitale
Espresso Grill,** 609 Capitol Way S. (☎ **360/352-8007**), which is patterned after
an Italian panini place. Pub food and locally brewed ales are available downtown at
the **Fishbowl Brewpub & Cafe,** 515 Jefferson St. SE (☎ **360/943-3650**), which
is very popular as an after-work gathering spot.

Budd Bay Café. Percival Landing, 525 N. Columbia St. ☎ **360/357-6963.** Reservations recommended. Main courses $7.50–$30; lunch main courses $7–$11. AE, DC, DISC, MC, V. Mon–
Sat 11am–10pm, Sun 10am–9pm (brunch 10am–1pm). SEAFOOD.

Located right in downtown Olympia, the Budd Bay Café, is the city's favorite waterfront restaurant and is a perennial favorite for its lavish Sunday seafood brunch.
The view from both the dining room and large deck takes in the waters of Budd Bay

as well as the state capitol, and outside, the Percival Landing Waterfront Park board-walk stretches for 1 1/2 miles (for that after-dinner stroll). The menu includes such standards as salmon in a white-wine sauce with garlic, butter, and herbs, but you'll also find a Mediterranean-style chicken with black olives and artichoke hearts in an ouzo-cream sauce. There are several good salads, including a hot seafood salad.

✪ **Fifth Avenue Bistro.** 209 Fifth Ave. SE ☎ **360/709-0390.** Reservations recommended. Main courses $9–$20. AE, DISC, MC, V. Mon 11:30am–2:30pm, Tues–Thurs 11:30am–2:30pm and 5:30–9pm, Fri–Sat 11:30am–2:30pm and 5:30–10pm. FRENCH.

With its artfully painted walls and fun little touches (autumn leaves under the glass table tops), this downtown restaurant has the look and feel of a Parisian bistro and the menu to back it up. While the menu is short (and changes almost monthly), you'll likely find everything from a simple meal of quiche and salad to a rich seafood stew with saffron and Pernod. Bistro standards such as a pate and cheese platter and steak with four peppercorn sauce made recent appearances. On weekdays this is a very popular lunch spot for downtown office workers who find good value in the $8 lunch special. The short wine list is reasonably priced and still manages to offer some excellent imported wines.

✪ **The Spar Cafe.** 114 E. Fourth Ave. ☎ **360/357-6444.** Main courses $6–$11. AE, MC, V. Mon–Sat 6am–10pm, Sun 6–8pm. AMERICAN.

In business since 1935, this downtown diner is a Northwest classic. On the walls hang old black-and-white photos of period logging activities (the cafe's name refers to the spar trees that were used for rigging cables and pulleys) and along one wall is the origi-nal cigar counter, which is lined with glass-fronted humidified cabinets full of pre-mium cigars. In back, through a swinging door is a dark bar, but its the cozy old booths out front that are the main attraction. Breakfasts here have been voted the best in town (try the Fourth Avenue Mess). If it's genuine Olympia atmosphere you're looking for, this is the place.

The Urban Onion. 116 Legion Way. ☎ **360/943-9242.** Reservations recommended on weekends. Main courses $6–$13. AE, MC, V. Mon–Fri 7am–10pm, Sat–Sun 8am–11pm. INTER-NATIONAL/VEGETARIAN.

As the site of ultra-progressive Evergreen State College, Olympia has more than its fair share of vegetarians, and for years this simple cafe has been one of their top choices in town. However, the Urban Onion isn't strictly a vegetarian place. There are also burgers, chicken dishes (Mexican, Szechuan, or sautéed with vegetables), and a couple of seafood dishes. Most of the same dishes are available at lunch or dinner, with prices slightly lower at lunch. Meals are always reliable.

OLYMPIA AFTER DARK

Located downtown, the state-of-the-art **Washington Center for the Performing Arts,** 512 Washington St. SE (☎ **360/753-8586**), hosts performances by regional, national, and international performers. The season always features plenty of theater, music, and dance. Various local performing arts companies call this center home. Tickets run $5 to $30.

8 The Olympic Peninsula

The Olympic Peninsula, located in the extreme northwestern corner of Washington and home to Olympic National Park, is a rugged and remote region that was one of the last places in the continental United States to be explored. For decades its nearly impenetrable rain-soaked forests and steep, glacier-carved mountains effectively restricted settlement to the peninsula's coastal regions.

Though much of the Olympic Peninsula was designated a National Forest Preserve in 1897, and in 1909 became a national monument, it was not until 1938 that the heart of the peninsula—the jagged, snowcapped Olympic Mountains—became Olympic National Park. At the time the area was first preserved, it was in order to protect the area's rapidly dwindling herds of Roosevelt elk, which are named for Pres. Theodore Roosevelt (who was responsible for the area becoming a national monument). At the time, these elk herds were being decimated by commercial hunters.

Today, however, Olympic National Park, which is roughly the size of Rhode Island, is far more than an elk reserve. It is recognized as one of the world's most important wild ecosystems. The park is unique in the contiguous United States for its temperate rain forests, found in the west-facing valleys of the Hoh, Queets, Bogachiel, Clearwater, and Quinault rivers. In these valleys, rainfall can exceed 140 inches per year, trees (Sitka spruce, western red cedar, Douglas fir, and western hemlock) grow nearly 300 feet tall, and mosses enshroud the limbs of big-leaf maples.

Within a few short miles of the park's rain forests, the Olympic Mountains rise up to the 7,965-foot peak of Mount Olympus and produce an alpine zone where no trees grow at all. Together, elevation and heavy rainfall combine to form 60 glaciers within the park. It is these glaciers that have carved the Olympic Mountains into the jagged peaks that mesmerize visitors and beckon to hikers and climbers. Rugged and spectacular sections of the coast have also been preserved as part of the national park, and the offshore waters are designated as the Olympic Coast National Marine Sanctuary.

With fewer than a dozen roads, none of which leads more than a few miles into the park, Olympic National Park is, for the most part, inaccessible to the casual visitor. Only two roads penetrate the high country, and only one of these is paved. Likewise, only two paved roads lead into the park's famed rain forests. Although a long stretch of beach within the national park is paralleled by U.S. 101, the park's most spectacular beaches can only be reached by trail.

While the park is inaccessible to cars, it is a wonderland for hikers and back-packers. Its rugged beaches, rain-forest valleys, alpine meadows, and mountain-top glaciers offer an amazing variety of hiking and backpacking opportunities. For alpine hikes, there are the trailheads at Hurricane Ridge and Deer Park. To experience the rain forest in all its drippy glory, there are the trails of the Bogachiel, Hoh, Queets, and Quinault valleys. Of these rain-forest trails, the Hoh Valley has the more acces-sible (and consequently more popular) trails, including the trailhead for the multiday hike to the summit of Mount Olympus. Favorite coastal hikes include the stretch of coast between La Push and Oil City and from Rialto Beach north to Lake Ozette and onward to Shi Shi Beach.

In striking contrast to the wildness of Olympic National Park is the restored Vic-torian seaport of Port Townsend in the northeast corner of the peninsula. Here, doz-ens of stately Victorian homes (many of which are now bed-and-breakfast inns) and a restored historic district filled with shops and restaurants have made Port Townsend one of the most popular destinations in Washington.

The rural community of Sequim (pronounced *skwim*) has also been developing quite a reputation in recent years for a very different reason. The Sequim area lies in the rain shadow of the Olympic Mountains and receives fewer than 20 inches of rain per year, less than half the average of Seattle. Sure, the skies here are still cloudy much of the year, but anyone who has lived very long in the Northwest begins to dream of someplace where it doesn't rain quite so much. In Sequim, these dreamers are building retirement homes as fast as they can.

Long before the first white settlers arrived, various Native American tribes called the Olympic Peninsula home. The Makah, Quinault, Hoh, Elwha, and Skokomish tribes all inhabited different regions of the peninsula, but all stayed close to the coast, where they could harvest the plentiful mollusks, fish, and whales. Today, there are numerous Indian reservations, both large and small, on the peninsula. On the Jamestown S'Klallam Reservation you'll find a casino, and on the Makah Reserva-tion, a fascinating culture and history museum.

While at first it might seem that the entire peninsula is a pristine wilderness, that just isn't the case. When the first white settlers arrived, they took one look at the 300-foot-tall trees that grew on the Olympic Peninsula and started sharpening their axes. The supply of trees seemed endless, but by the 1980s the end was in sight for the trees that had not been preserved within Olympic National Park. Today, U.S. 101, which loops around the east, north, and west side of the peninsula is lined with clear-cuts and second- and third-growth forests for much of its length, a fact that takes many first-time visitors by surprise.

1 Port Townsend: A Restored Victorian Seaport

60 miles NW of Seattle, 48 miles E of Port Angeles, 40 miles S of Anacortes

Named by English explorer Capt. George Vancouver in 1792, Port Townsend did not attract its first settlers until 1851. However, by the 1880s the town had become an important shipping port and was expected to grow into one of the most impor-tant cities on the West Coast. Port Townsend felt that it was the logical end of the line for the transcontinental railroad that was pushing westward in the 1880s; and based on the certainty of a railroad connection, real estate and development boomed. Merchants and investors erected mercantile palaces along Water Street and elaborate

The Olympic Peninsula

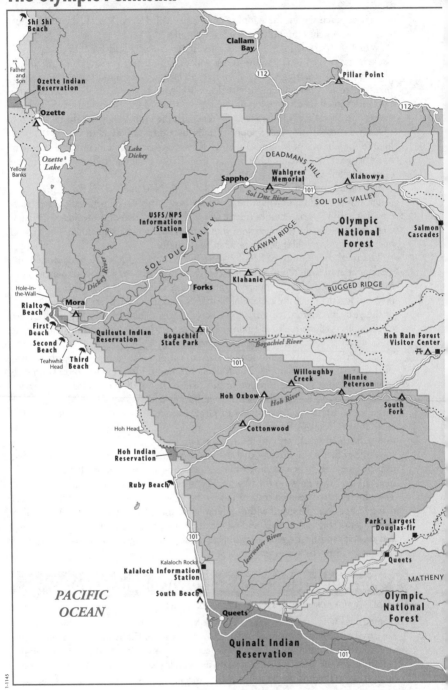

Shi Shi
Beach

Ciallam
Bay

112

Pillar Point

Father
and
Son

Ozette Indian
Reservation

Ozette

DEADMANS HILL

Klahowya

Lake
Dickey

Sappho

Wahlgren
Memorial

Sol Duc River

SOL DUC VALLEY

101

Yellow
Banks

Ozette
Lake

USFS/NPS
Information
Station

Olympic
National
Forest

CALAWAH RIDGE

Salmon
Cascades

SOL DUC VALLEY

RUGGED RIDGE

Klahanie

Forks

Dickey River

Hole-in-
the-Wall

Mora

Rialto
Beach

First
Beach

Quileuto Indian
Reservation

Bogachiel
State Park

Bogachiel River

Hoh Rain Forest
Visitor Center

Second
Beach

101

Teahwhit
Head

Third
Beach

Willoughby
Creek

Minnie
Peterson

Hoh Oxbow

Hoh River

South
Fork

Hoh Head

Cottonwood

Hoh Indian
Reservation

Ruby Beach

Park's Largest
Douglas-fir

Queets

101

Queets

MATHENY

Kalaloch Rocks

Kalaloch Information
Station

PACIFIC
OCEAN

South Beach

Olympic
National
Forest

Queets

Quinalt Indian
Reservation

101

1-1145

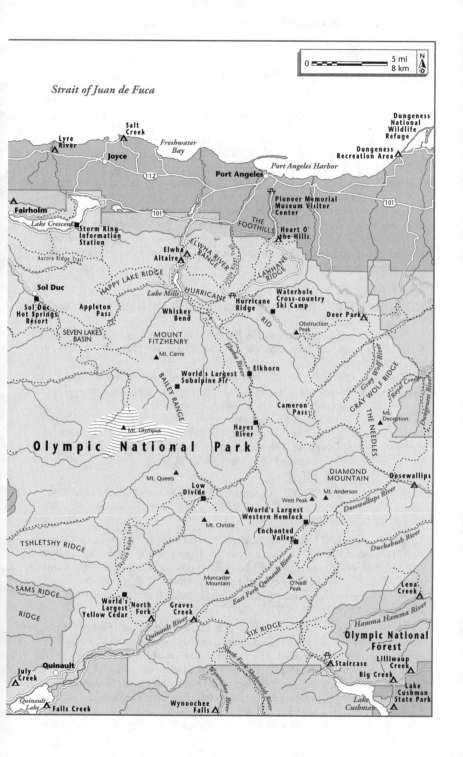

Strait of Juan de Fuca

Dungeness National Wildlife Refuge

Dungeness Recreation Area

Salt Creek

Lyre River

Joyce

Freshwater Bay

Port Angeles

Port Angeles Harbor

112

101

Pioneer Memorial Museum Visitor Center

Fairholm

101

Lake Crescent

Storm King Information Station

THE FOOTHILLS

Heart O' the Hills

Aurora Ridge Trail

Elwha Altaire

ELWHA RIVER RANGE

LAHMANE RIDGE

HAPPY LAKE RIDGE

Sol Duc

Lake Mills

HURRICANE

Hurricane Ridge

Waterhole Cross-country Ski Camp

Sol Duc Hot Springs Resort

Appleton Pass

Whiskey Bend

RIDGE

Deer Park

SEVEN LAKES BASIN

MOUNT FITZHENRY

Obstruction Peak

Mt. Carrie

World's Largest Subalpine Fir

Elkhorn

Elwha River

BAILEY RANGE

Cameron Pass

GRAY WOLF RIDGE

Royal Creek

Dungeness River

Mt. Deception

THE NEEDLES

Mt. Olympus

Hayes River

Olympic National Park

DIAMOND MOUNTAIN

Dosewallips

Mt. Queets

Low Divide

West Peak

Mt. Anderson

Dosewallips River

World's Largest Western Hemlock

Mt. Christie

Duckabush River

TSHLETSHY RIDGE

Enchanted Valley

Skyline Ridge Trail

Muncaster Mountain

O'Neill Peak

Lena Creek

SAMS RIDGE

World's Largest Yellow Cedar

North Fork

Graves Creek

East Fork Quinault River

Hamma Hamma River

RIDGE

Quinault River

SIX RIDGE

Olympic National Forest

Lilliwaup Creek

July Creek

Quinault

South Fork Skokomish River

Staircase

Big Creek

Quinault Lake

Falls Creek

Wynoochee Falls

Wynoochee River

Lake Cushman

Lake Cushman State Park

Impressions

If that not be the home wherein dwell the Gods, it is beautiful enough to be, and I therefore call it Mount Olympus."

—Capt. John Meares, 1788

Victorian homes on the bluff above the wharf district. However, the railroad never arrived. Seattle got the rails, and Port Townsend got the shaft.

With its importance as a shipping port usurped by Seattle and Tacoma, Port Townsend slipped into quiet obscurity. Progress passed it by and its elegant homes and commercial buildings were left to slowly fade away. However, in 1976 the waterfront district and bluff-top residential neighborhood were declared a National Historic District and the town began a slow revival. Today the streets of Port Townsend are once again crowded with people. The waterfront district is filled with boutiques, galleries, and other interesting shops, and many of the Victorian homes atop the bluff have become bed-and-breakfast inns.

ESSENTIALS

GETTING THERE   Port Townsend is on Wash. 20, off U.S. 101 in the northeast corner of the Olympic Peninsula.

There are flights to Port Townsend's Jefferson County International Airport from Seattle and the San Juan Islands on **Port Townsend Airways** (☎ **800/385-6554** or 360/385-6554).

Washington State Ferries (☎ **800/84-FERRY)** operates a ferry between Port Townsend and Keystone on Whidbey Island. The crossing takes 30 minutes and costs $5.90 to $7.10 for a vehicle and driver and $1.75 for passengers.

You might also be able to arrange passenger ferry service from Friday Harbor on San Juan Island through **Puget Sound Express** (☎ **360/385-5288)**, which is headquartered in Port Townsend. The round-trip fare ranges from $45 to $49.

Bus service to Port Townsend from Sequim and Poulsbo is provided by **Jefferson Transit** (☎ **360/385-4777)**.

VISITOR INFORMATION   Contact the **Port Townsend Chamber of Commerce Visitors Information Center,** 2437 E. Sims Way, Port Townsend, WA 98368 (☎ **360/385-2722)**.

GETTING AROUND   Because parking spaces are hard to come by in downtown Port Townsend on weekends and anytime in the summer, **Jefferson Transit** (☎ **360/385-4777)**, the local public bus service, provides a free shuttle into downtown Port Townsend from a park-and-ride lot on the south side of town. Jefferson Transit also operates other buses around Port Townsend. If you need a taxi, call **Peninsula Taxi** (☎ **360/385-1872)**.

FESTIVALS   As a tourist town, Port Townsend schedules quite a few festivals throughout the year. The last week of March, the town celebrates its Victorian heritage with the **Victorian Festival.** The **Jazz Port Townsend** festival is held the fourth weekend in July. The **Wooden Boat Festival,** the largest of its kind in the United States, is on the first weekend after Labor Day. During the **Kinetic Sculpture Race,** held the first weekend in October, outrageous human-powered vehicles race on land, water, and through a mud bog. To see inside some of the town's many restored homes, schedule a visit during the **Historic Homes Tour** on the third weekend in September.

The **Olympic Music Festival,** held in an old barn near the town of Quilcene, is the area's most important music festival. This series of weekend concerts takes place between the fourth weekend in June and the first weekend in September. For information and tickets, call ☎ **206/527-8839.**

EXPLORING THE TOWN

With its abundance of restored Victorian homes and commercial buildings, Port Townsend's most popular activity is simply to walk or drive the historic districts. The town is divided into a waterfront commercial district and residential Uptown Port Townsend, which is atop a bluff that rises precipitously only two blocks from the water. Uptown Port Townsend developed so that proper Victorian ladies would not have to associate with the riffraff that frequented the waterfront. At the Port Townsend Visitor Information Center, you can pick up a **"Historic Tour Map"** that lists the town's many historic homes and commercial buildings.

Water Street is the town's main commercial district and for several blocks is lined with 100-year-old brick buildings, many of which have ornate facades. Within these restored buildings are dozens of interesting shops and boutiques, several restaurants, and a handful of hotels and inns. To learn a little more about the history of this part of town and to gain a different perspective, walk out on **Union Wharf,** which is located at the foot of Tyler Street and was recently rebuilt. Here you'll find interpretive plaques covering topics ranging from sea grass to waterfront history.

Before starting out on an exploration of the town, stop by the **Jefferson County Historical Museum and Maritime Library,** 210 Madison St. (☎ **360/385-1003**), where you can learn about the history of the area. Among the collections here are regional Native American artifacts and antiques from the Victorian era. It's open Monday through Saturday from 11am to 4pm and Sunday 1 to 4pm. Admission is by donation.

The town's noted Victorian homes are to be found in Uptown Port Townsend, atop the bluff that rises behind the waterfront's commercial buildings. Here you'll find stately homes, views and the city's favorite park. To reach Uptown, either drive up Washington Street (one block over from Water Street) or walk up the stairs at the end of Taylor Street, which start behind the Haller Fountain.

At the top of the stairs is an 1890 bell tower that once summoned volunteer firemen and the **Rothschild House,** a Washington State Parks Heritage Site, which is at the corner of Taylor and Jefferson streets. Built in 1868, this is one of the oldest buildings in town and displays a relatively sober architecture compared to other area homes. The gardens contain a wide variety of roses, peonies, and lilacs. It's open April 1 to October 31, daily from 10am to 5pm. Admission is $2 for adults and $1 for children.

However, the most fascinating Uptown home open to the public is the **Ann Starrett Mansion,** 744 Clay St. (☎ **360/385-3205**), which is Port Townsend's most astoundingly ornate Queen Anne Victorian home. Currently operated as a bed-and-breakfast inn, this mansion is best known for its imposing turret, ceiling frescoes, and unusual spiral staircase. The house is open for guided tours daily from noon to 3pm. Tours cost $2.

Also here in Uptown, at the corner of Garfield and Jackson streets, you'll find **Chetzemoka Park,** which was established in 1904 and is named for a local S'Klallum Indian chief. The park perches on a bluff overlooking Admiralty Inlet and has access to a pleasant beach. However, it is the rose garden, arbor, and waterfall garden that attract many visitors.

At the opposite end of town is **Kah Tai Lagoon Park,** which is the best bird-watching spot in the area. The park is across from the Port Townsend Visitor Information Center.

FORT WORDEN STATE PARK

Fort Worden State Park, once a military installation that guarded the mouth of Puget Sound, is north of the historic district and can be reached by turning onto Kearney Street at the south end of town, or onto Monroe Street at the north end of town, and following the signs. Built at the turn of the century, the fort is now a 360-acre state park where a wide array of attractions and activities assure that it's busy for much of the year. Many of the fort's old wooden buildings have been restored and put to new uses.

At the **Fort Worden Commanding Officer's House** (☎ 360/385-4730), you can see what life was like for a Victorian-era officer and his family. The home has been fully restored and is filled with period antiques. It's open April 1 to October 15 (and on a few holidays in other months), daily from 10am to 5pm; admission is $1. More military history is on display at the **Coast Artillery Museum** (☎ 360/385-0373), open daily in summer from 11am to 5pm and on weekends from noon to 4pm in spring and fall. Admission is $1 for adults and 50 cents for children.

Here at the park you can also learn about life below the waters of Puget Sound at the **Port Townsend Marine Science Center** (☎ 360/385-5582), open Tuesday through Sunday from noon to 6pm in summer and Saturday and Sunday from noon to 4pm in spring and fall. Admission is $2 for adults and $1 for students and children.

However, for many people, the main reason to visit the park is to hang out on the beach or one of the picnic areas. Scuba divers also frequent the park, which has an underwater park just offshore. In spring, the Rhododendron Garden puts on a colorful floral display. Throughout the year, there are also a wide variety of concerts and other performances at the **Centrum** (☎ 800/733-3608 or 360/385-3102). Also within the park are two restaurants, campgrounds, a **youth hostel** (☎ 360/385-0655), and restored officers' quarters that can be rented.

PORT TOWNSEND FROM THE WATER (& AIR)

If you'd like to explore the town from the water, there are number of ways to do so. If you're a fan of classic wooden boats, contact **Captain Rolly's Cruises** (☎ 360/379-8829) or **World Wind Ltd.** (☎ 360/301-1555), both of which use classic motor yachts for their tours. If it's sails that you prefer, contact **Brisa Charters** (☎ 360/385-2309). For an educational tour out to nearby Protection Island, contact the **Port Townsend Marine Science Center** (☎ 360/385-5582). Cruises through the San Juan Islands are offered from April through September by **Puget Sound Express,** 431 Water St. (☎ 360/385-5288), which also offers passenger ferry service to Friday Harbor. During the summer you're almost certain to see orca whales on these trips. These cruises cost between $45 and $49.

If you'd like to try your hand at paddling a sea kayak around the area's waters, contact **Kayak Port Townsend** (☎ 360/385-6240), which offers half-day ($39) and full-day tours ($68) and also rents sea kayaks. At the nearby **Port Ludlow Marina** (☎ 360/437-0513), south of Port Townsend, you can rent motorboats, sailboats, sea kayaks, and sea cycles between mid-April and September. Several other places around town also rent boats.

If you'd rather see the area from the air, contact **Port Townsend Airways** (☎ 800/385-6554 or 360/385-6554), which offers three different scenic flights. Rates start as low as $17 for a 30 minute flight (if you have three people in your party).

MARROWSTONE ISLAND

You'll find another old fort turned state park on nearby Marrowstone Island, which is reached by driving south 9 miles to Port Hadlock on Wash. 19 and then turning east on Wash. 116. From Port Hadlock it is another 11 miles to the northern tip of Marrowstone Island and **Fort Flagler State Park.** This large park has a campground, boat ramp, beaches, and hiking trails.

Between Port Hadlock and Marrowstone Island is Indian Island, most of which is an active military base, whose waters are popular with sea kayakers. At the south end of Indian Island is a small park popular with boardsailors.

WHERE TO STAY
IN PORT TOWNSEND
Moderate

✪ **Ann Starrett Mansion.** 744 Clay St., Port Townsend, WA 98368. ☎ **800/321-0644** or 360/385-3205. Fax 360/385-2976. www.olympus.net/starrett/. 11 rms. $65–$225 double. Rates include full breakfast. AE, DISC, MC, V.

The Starrett is about being pampered amid Victorian elegance. Built in 1889 for $6,000 as a wedding present for Ann Starrett, this Victorian jewel box is by far the most elegant and ornate bed-and-breakfast in Port Townsend. A three-story turret towers over the front door of this rose- and teal-green mansion. Inside is a perfectly-preserved museum of the Victorian era. Every room is exquisitely furnished in period antiques. In fact, if you aren't staying here, you can still have a look during one of the afternoon house tours ($2). Breakfast is an extravaganza that can last all morning and will certainly make you consider skipping lunch.

✪ **F.W. Hastings House/Old Consulate Inn.** 313 Walker St., Port Townsend, WA 98368. ☎ **800/300-6753** or 360/385-6753. Fax 360/385-2097. 5 rms, 3 suites (all with private bathrooms). $96–$130 double; $130–$195 suite. Rates include full breakfast. AE, MC, V.

Though not quite as elaborate as the Starrett Mansion, the Old Consulate Inn is another example of the sort of Victorian excess that's so wonderfully appealing today. The attention to detail and quality craftsmanship both in the construction and the restoration of this elegant mansion are evident wherever you look. However, despite its heritage, the Old Consulate avoids being a museum; it's just a comfortable, yet elegant, place to stay. For entertainment, you'll find a grand piano, a billiard table, and VCR, as well as stunning views out most of the windows. A multicourse breakfast is meant to be lingered over, so don't make any early morning appointments. Afternoon tea, evening cordials, and a hot tub add to the experience here.

James House. 1238 Washington St., Port Townsend, WA 98368. ☎ **800/385-1238** or 360/385-1238. Fax 360/385-5551. www.jameshouse.com. 8 rooms (6 with bath), 3 suites, 1 cottage. $65–$75 double without bath, $90–$165 suite or double with bath. Rates include full breakfast. MC, V.

With an eclectic blend of antique and new furnishings, this grand Victorian from 1889 sits atop the bluff overlooking Admiralty Inlet. The entry hall features a parquet floor, and in the two parlors you'll find fireplaces that are the perfect gathering spot on a cool evening. The views from the upper front rooms are some of the best in town. You can even see Mount Rainier on a clear day. Our favorite rooms are the attic rooms, one of which has a brass bed and a futon couch. Another of these rooms has a beautiful sleigh bed and arched windows. If you prefer a bit more space, opt for the bridal suite or one of the garden suites. An additional private bungalow, done in a contemporary style, is adjacent to the James House, and has a water and mountain view.

Manresa Castle. Seventh and Sheridan sts., Port Townsend, WA 98368. ☎ **800/732-1281** or 360/385-5750. Fax 360/385-5883. 32 rms, 8 suites. Summer $75–$85 double; $95–$175 suite; lower rates mid Oct–Apr. Rates include continental breakfast. DISC, MC, V.

Built in 1892 by a wealthy baker, this reproduction of a medieval castle later became a Jesuit retreat and school. Today Manresa Castle is, by far, Port Townsend's most elegant accommodation and also its best deal. A traditional elegance pervades the hotel's lounge and dining room, though currently the food doesn't live up to the setting. The guest rooms have a genuine, vintage appeal that manages to avoid the contrived feeling that so often sneaks into bed-and-breakfast room decor. The best deal in the hotel is the tower suite during the off-season. For $125 a night you'll get a huge room with sweeping views from its circular seating area.

Palace Hotel. 1004 Water St., Port Townsend, WA 98368. ☎ **800/962-0741** or 360/ 385-0773. Fax 360/385-0780. 15 rms (3 with shared bathroom); 3 suites. TV. $69–$79 double without bath, $89–$119 double with bath, $119–$139 suites. Rates include continental breakfast. AE, DISC, MC, V.

Located in the heart of the historic district, the Palace Hotel occupies a building that once served as a bordello. Today Madame Marie's suite is the best room in the house—a big corner room with a kitchenette. Most of the other rooms are named for former working girls. Miss Kitty's room is as nice as the Madame's and includes a cast-iron wood stove and the best views at the Palace. The Crow's Nest room is another interesting space, and features a sleeping loft, nautical theme, and wood stove.

Be forewarned: The hotel is up a steep flight of stairs from the street and some rooms are up on the third floor. The bathroom shared by three rooms has a big clawfoot tub, so you aren't doing too badly if you take one of these rooms.

✪ **Ravenscroft Inn.** 533 Quincy St., Port Townsend, WA 98368. ☎ **800/782-2691** or 360/ 385-2784. Fax 360/385-6724. 8 rms. $67–$175 double. Lower rates off-season. Rates include full breakfast. AE, DC, DISC, MC, V.

If a morning piano concert and lavish gourmet breakfast sound like the perfect way to start the day, then you'll want to book a room at this three-story B&B. Built in 1987 but designed in keeping with Port Townsend's historic homes, the inn offers rooms with distinctively different moods. The Mount Rainier Room, with its gorgeous views, fireplace, and whirlpool tub for two, is a perennial favorite, as is the Fireside Room, which has a fireplace, veranda, and canopy bed. Two other rooms also open onto a veranda, and some rooms on the upper levels have good views of the mountains and water. Pretty gardens surround the house, and there are a couple of Adirondack chairs on the lower veranda.

Inexpensive
The Belmont. 925 Water St., Port Townsend, WA 98368. ☎ **360/385-3007.** 4 rms (all with private bathrooms). $49–$69 double. AE, DC, DISC, MC, V.

Built in 1885, The Belmont is the oldest waterfront restaurant and saloon in town, and on the second floor, you'll find four very spacious, if not exactly luxurious rooms. The two in back open right onto the water and offer one of the best views in town. Exposed brick walls provide character, and three of the rooms have loft sleeping areas. Expect some noise from the saloon downstairs.

Harborside Inn. 330 Benedict St., Port Townsend, WA 98368. ☎ **800/942-5960** or 360/ 385-7909. Fax 360/385-6984. 63 rms. A/C TV TEL. $64–$94 double. Rates include continental breakfast. AE, DC, DISC, MC, V.

This modern motel is south of Port Townsend's historic district, overlooking the town's main marina, and the guest rooms all have balconies that let you enjoy the view of the harbor and Admiralty Inlet. Facilities include an outdoor pool and hot tub, and if you're interested in fishing, you can arrange a charter right across the street.

IN PORT LUDLOW

✪ **Inn at Ludlow Bay.** One Heron Rd. (P.O. Box 65460), Port Ludlow, WA 98365. ☎ **360/ 437-0411.** Fax 360/437-0310. 35 rms, 2 suites. A/C TV TEL. $135–$200 double; $300–$450 suite. Rates include continental breakfast. AE, DISC, MC, V.

Set on a tiny peninsula jutting into Ludlow Bay, this luxurious inn is one of the finest in the Northwest and has helped the Ludlow Bay resort community realize its dream of becoming one of *the* Puget Sound waterfront destinations. The setting rivals anything in the San Juan Islands, and the inn itself conjures up the image of a New England summer home at the shore. Designed for romantic getaways, the guest rooms are spacious and plush, with whirlpool tubs, fireplaces, and down-filled duvets on the beds. Best of all every room has a water view and from some you can see Mount Baker or the Olympic Mountains. Breakfasts are served in a bright sunroom with teak furnishings that evokes a nautical feel.

The dining room here serves superb Northwest cuisine and is the finest restaurant in this neck of the Olympic Peninsula. The Fireside Room provides lighter fare and a small bar. Facilities include privileges at the adjacent 27-hole Port Ludlow Golf Course, paved walking paths through the adjacent resort, a marina, and a croquet lawn.

WHERE TO DINE
IN PORT TOWNSEND

One place on nearly everyone's itinerary during a visit to Port Townsend is **Elevated Ice Cream,** 627 Water St. (☎ **360/385-1156**), which is open daily and scoops up the best ice cream in town.

Moderate

The Belmont. 925 Water St. ☎ 360/385-3007. Reservations recommended. Main courses $9–$18. AE, DC, DISC, MC, V. Summer, daily 11:30am–9pm; winter, daily 11:30am–3pm and 4:30–8:30pm. AMERICAN.

With so much water all around, the most surprising thing about dining in Port Townsend is that there are so few waterfront restaurants. This, the best of them, is also the oldest waterfront restaurant and hotel in town, dating back to 1889. While the interior doesn't really conjure up 1890s, the view out the back, especially from the small deck, is great. The menu delves into some interesting flavor combinations and draws on a lot of different influences (chicken with a pistachio and raspberry-bacon vinaigrette, sautéed prawns with a Philippine sauce, pork tenderloin with black currant-Pinot Noir sauce).

Blackberries. In the Fort Worden State Park Conference Center. ☎ **360/385-9950.** Reservations recommended in summer. Main courses $6–$17. MC, V. Wed–Sat 11am–9pm, Sun 11am–4pm. Closed Sept 15–Apr 30. NORTHWEST.

Located near the historic officers' quarters at Fort Worden (on the right after the Centrum), Blackberries is a simple place with vintage appeal. The menu, however, is anything but old-fashioned. Imaginative Northwest cuisine at very reasonable prices make this place a definite winner. Locally grown ingredients are used as much as possible, and a few vegetarian dishes are always available. A recent menu included eggplant timbales in a pool of basil-tomato concasse, a crab-and-orange salad, and a unique salmon-halibut braid with salal berry buerre rouge. All the profits from this restaurant assist community-action programs. A second Blackberries is located downtown at the Palace Hotel, 1002 Water St. (☎ 360/379-1200).

✪ Lonny's Restaurant. 2330 Washington St. ☎ **360/385-0700.** Reservations recommended. Main courses $11–$19. MC, V. Sun–Mon and Wed–Thurs 5–9pm, Fri–Sat 5–10pm. ITALIAN.

Located at the Boat Haven marina south of downtown Port Townsend, this is a romantic, low-key place that is a welcome alternative to the touristy restaurants downtown. The menu is long and there is always a wide selection of daily specials, including wines available by the glass. Attention to detail is what makes the dishes here stand out. Pork loin is soaked in a juniper brine before being served up as scaloppine. Local oysters and mussels show up frequently and are hard to resist. However, it is the dessert menu, running to 10 luscious offerings, that is the hardest to resist. Not to be missed is the coconut halvah.

Silverwater Café. 237 Taylor St. ☎ **360/385-6448.** Reservations accepted only for six or more. Main courses lunch $4–$9, dinner $8–$14. MC, V. Daily 11:30am–3pm and 5–10pm. NORTHWEST FUSION.

Works by local artists, lots of plants, and New Age music on the stereo set the tone for this casually chic restaurant. Though the menu focuses on Northwest dishes, it includes preparations from around the world. You can start your meal with an artichoke-and-Parmesan pâté and then move on to amaretto chicken, beef bourguignonne, or cioppino. The oysters in a bleu cheese sauce are a favorite of ours.

Inexpensive

✪ The Fountain Café. 920 Washington St. ☎ **360/385-1364.** Reservations not accepted. Main courses $9–$14. AE, MC, V. Sun–Thurs 11:30am–3pm and 4–9pm, Fri–Sat 11:30am–3pm and 4–10pm. INTERNATIONAL.

Housed in a narrow clapboard building, this funky little place is easy to miss. Eclectic hand-painted tablecloths decorate the half dozen or so tables and there are a few stools at the counter. The menu changes seasonally, but you can rest assured that the simple fare here will be utterly fresh and will provide plenty of oysters and pasta. The garlicky oyster stew and Greek pasta are two menu mainstays that are hard to beat, and a wide range of flavors assures that everyone will find something to his liking. This is a local and counterculture favorite.

Khu Larb Thai. 225 Adams St. ☎ **360/385-5023.** Reservations suggested. Main courses $7–$9. MC, V. Sun–Thurs 11am–9pm, Fri–Sat 11am–10pm. THAI.

Located just half a block off busy Water Street, Khu Larb seems a world removed from Port Townsend's sometimes-overdone Victorian decor. Thai easy-listening music plays on the stereo and you're surrounded by cheap souvenirs from Thailand. However, don't let this lack of atmosphere put you off. One taste of any dish on the menu and you'll be convinced that this is great Thai food. Particularly memorable is the tom kha gai, a sour-and-spicy soup with a coconut-milk base. The steamed clams with ginger are another excellent dish, and even the pad Thai is quite good. If you're feeling adventurous, try the black rice pudding for dessert.

The Salal Café. 634 Water St. ☎ **360/385-6532.** Reservations accepted for dinner. Most items $4.50–$9. MC, V. Daily 7am–2pm and 5–9pm. NORTHWEST/NATURAL.

Once upon a time Port Townsend was a counterculture capital, a mecca for folks with alternative lifestyles. Today this isn't so much the case, but some of the restaurants from that time still linger on. Though most of the dishes on the menu at the Salal Café are vegetarian standards—tofu stroganoff, bean burritos, granola with yogurt and fruit—you'll also find ham omelettes, New York steak, and curried scallops. The Salal is best known for its fresh local ingredients including bread, pasta, homemade jam and free-range chicken eggs (on request). Late risers will be glad to know that blintzes, crepes, and omelettes are available on the lunch menu.

IN PORT LUDLOW & PORT HADLOCK

✪ **Ajax Cafe.** Lower Hadlock Road, Port Hadlock. ☎ **360/385-3450.** Reservations recommended. Main courses $9–$17. MC, V. Sun–Thurs 5–9pm, Fri–Sat 5–9:30pm (closed Mon Sept–May). INTERNATIONAL.

With not a matching glass or two chairs the same in the whole restaurant, this longtime local favorite is as eclectic a place as you'll find—and a lot of fun, too. Located on the old waterfront in Port Hadlock in an old wooden storefront, the restaurant is out of the way and funky, and that's exactly why it's so popular. The menu runs the gamut from sesame-peanut noodles, to Moroccan braised lamb, to pan-seared mahimahi with apple-mango chutney. Best of all, there's live music Wednesday through Sunday nights. If you like good times and good food, this is a don't miss.

✪ **Inn at Ludlow Bay Dining Room.** One Heron Rd., Port Ludlow. ☎ **360/437-0411.** Reservations recommended. Main courses $13–$24. AE, DISC, MC, V. Daily 5:30–9:30pm (Fireside Room opens at 3:30pm). NORTHWEST.

With its water views, immaculately set tables, and superb cuisine, this is the finest restaurant in the area these days, which is in keeping with the luxurious surroundings of this waterfront lodge south of Port Townsend. The menu, which changes seasonally, is short, with creative flavor combinations as the keynote. A recent menu included a starter of rabbit confit and mushroom polenta cakes with a blackberry relish and white truffle oil. Among the entrees were a grilled salmon served with a mango-poppy seed sauce and Walla Walla potato cakes. Want to enjoy the atmosphere but can't afford the prices? Most of the appetizers and salads, as well as some simple bar entrees (trout cakes, beef satay, individual pizzas), are served in the adjacent Fireside Room lounge.

PORT TOWNSEND AFTER DARK

After dark, you can catch live music (everything from jazz to country to classical to rock) at **Lanza's,** 1020 Lawrence St. (☎ **360/379-1900**), an Italian restaurant with live music on Friday and Saturday nights; the **Back Alley Tavern,** 923 Washington St. (☎ **360/385-2914**), one block off Water Street at Tyler, with live R&B on Friday and Saturday nights; and the **Public House,** 1038 Water St. (☎ **360/385-9708**), which books an eclectic range of music and has the feel of a 19th-century tavern. If you're lucky, you might catch a performance by Port Townsend's own **Flying Karamazov Brothers,** though they spend most of their time on the road. Check with the Visitors Information Center for a schedule of area events.

HIKING OLYMPIC PENINSULA EAST

South of Port Townsend, U.S. 101 follows the west shore of Hood Canal. Off this highway are several dead-end roads that lead to trailheads in Olympic National Forest. These trailheads are the starting points for many of the best day hikes on the Olympic Peninsula and lead into several different wilderness areas, as well as into Olympic National Park. Many of these hikes lead to the summits of mountains with astounding views across the Olympic Mountains and Puget Sound.

Two miles south of Quilcene, you'll find Penny Creek/Big Quilcene River Road, which leads to the trailheads for both **Marmot Pass** and **Mount Townsend**—two of the best day-hike destinations on the peninsula. Both of these trails are between 10- and 11-mile round-trip hikes. Up the Dosewallips River Road west of Brinnon, you'll find the trailhead for the very popular 4-mile round-trip hike to **Lake Constance.** Up the Hamma Hamma River Road, just north of Eldon, you'll find trailheads for trails to the beautiful **Lena Lakes** area. West of Hoodsport, you'll find popular **Lake Cushman** and the trailheads for the 2-mile round-trip hike along the scenic **Staircase Rapids**, the 4¹/₂-mile round trip hike to the summit of **Mount Ellinor**, and 16-mile round-trip hike to the **Flapjack Lakes**, which are a very popular overnight destination. For information contact Quilene Ranger Station, 20482 U.S. 101 S (P.O. box 280), Quilcene, WA 98376 (☎360-765-2200).

2 The Sequim & Dungeness Valley

17 miles E of Port Angeles, 31 miles W of Port Townsend

Located in the rain shadow of the Olympic Mountains, Sequim is an anomaly that has attracted a great deal of attention in recent years. The rain shadow makes this the driest region west of the Cascade Range and, consequently, sodden, moss-laden Northwesterners have taken to retiring here in droves. While the rains descend on the rest of the region, the fortunate few who call Sequim home bask in their own personal microclimate of sunshine and warmth.

The nearby town of Dungeness is set at the foot of Dungeness Spit, which, at 7 miles in length, is the longest sand spit in the world. However, it is for lending its name to the Northwest's favorite crab, that this region is most famous. The Dungeness crab is as much a staple of Washington waters as the blue crab is in the Chesapeake Bay region.

ESSENTIALS

GETTING THERE   The Sequim-Dungeness Valley lies to the north of U.S. 101 between Port Townsend and Port Angeles. **Jefferson Transit** (☎ 360/385-4777) has service from Port Townsend to Sequim, and **Clallam Transit** (☎ 800/858-3747 or 360/452-4511) operates west from Sequim and around the peninsula to Lake Crescent, Neah Bay, La Push, and Forks.

VISITOR INFORMATION   For more information contact the **Sequim-Dungeness Valley Chamber of Commerce,** U.S. 101 E (P.O. Box 907), Sequim, WA 98382-0907 (☎ 360/683-6197).

EXPLORING THE AREA

The biggest attraction is Dungeness Spit, which is protected as the **Dungeness National Wildlife Refuge** (☎ 360/457-8451). Within the refuge there is a ¹/₂-mile trail to a bluff-top overlook, but it is the spit, where you can hike for more than 5 miles to the lighthouse, that is the favorite hiking area. Along the way you're likely to see numerous species of birds as well as harbor seals. Near the base of the spit, you'll find the **Dungeness Recreation Area** (☎ 360/683-5847), which has a campground, picnic area, and trail leading out to the spit. The waters inside the Dungeness Spit are popular with boardsailors who launch from Cline Spit off Marine Drive. More camping and water access is available at **Sequim Bay State Park** (☎ 360/683-4235) about 4 miles east of Sequim.

If you'd like to tour the area's waters, contact **Sequim Bay Tours** (☎ 360/681-7408), which operates out of the John Wayne Marina, 2577 W. Sequim Bay Rd. on the east side of Sequim. Tours cruise the waters of the Dungeness National Wildlife Refuge and circle Protection Island, also a national wildlife refuge and home to 70% of Washington's nesting seabirds.

While in the area, don't miss an opportunity to visit the **Museum & Arts Center,** 175 W. Cedar St., Sequim (☎ 360/683-8110), which houses a pair of mastodon tusks that were found near here in 1977. The mastodon had been killed by human hunters, a discovery that helped establish the presence of humans in this area 12,000 years ago. The museum also has an exhibit on the much more recent culture of the region's Clallam Indians. Open Monday through Saturday from 9am to 4pm; admission is free.

If you've got the kids with you, Sequim's **Olympic Game Farm,** 1423 Ward Rd. (☎ **800/778-4295** or 360/683-4295), is a must. As actors in Walt Disney films, the animals here have become international celebrities. More than 80 theater and television features have been made with animals from this farm. Among the animals are tigers, jaguars, lions, grizzly bears, polar bears, and many others. There are drive-through and walking tours as well as a petting farm. The farm is open daily from 9am; admission is $7 for adults, $6 for seniors and children ages 5 to 12, and free for children 4 and under.

Its dry climate makes Sequim an almost perfect place to grow wine grapes. If you'd like to taste some local wine, stop by **Olympic Cellars Winery,** 255410 U.S. 101. (☎ **360/452-0160**), or **Lost Mountain Winery,** 3174 Lost Mountain Rd. (☎ **360/683-5229**), about 6 miles south of U.S. 101 on the west side of town. Another interesting place to visit is the **Cedarbrook Herb Farm,** 1345 Sequim Ave. S. (☎ **360/683-7733**), where you can buy herb plants as well as herb vinegars, potpourris, dried flowers, lavender wands, garlic braids, and the like. Sequim's climate is also ideal for growing lavender, and you'll likely pass numerous large fields of this fragrant Mediterranean plant as you tour the area.

Just east of Sequim on U.S. 101, you'll find the **7 Cedars Casino,** 270756 U.S. 101 (☎ **800/4-LUCKY-7** or 360/683-7777), which is operated by the Jamestown S'Klallam Tribe and is designed to resemble a traditional longhouse, with several large totem poles out front. You can see and buy other Native American arts and crafts nearby at the **Native Art Gallery,** 1033 Old Blyn Hwy. (☎ **360/681-4640**), where quality and prices are high.

The Sequim-Dungeness Valley is one of the best areas in the state for **bicycle touring.** The roads are flat, there are great views, and you don't have to worry as much about getting rained on.

WHERE TO STAY

Juan de Fuca Cottages. 182 Marine Dr., Sequim, WA 98382. ☎ **360/683-4433.** 7 cottages. Summer, $110–$210 double; other months, $105–$200 double. DISC, MC, V.

Located across the street from the water and surrounded by wide green lawns, these well-tended cottages have excellent views. While most face the water, the best views are actually from the one cottage that faces the Olympic Mountains to the south. This cabin has skylights and a long wall of windows. Other cottages also have skylights, some have whirlpool baths, and all have kitchenettes. The cottages also have their own little private beach and there is a whirlpool spa on the premises. Although prices seem high for what you get, these cottages can all sleep at least four people. With Cline Spit just across the road, these cabins are a good choice for boardsailors.

WHERE TO DINE

The Original Oyster House. 280417 U.S. 101. ☎ **360/385-1785.** Reservations recommended. Main dishes $11–$27. CB, DC, DISC, MC, V. Mon–Sat 4–9pm, Sun noon–8pm. SEAFOOD.

Located on the shore of Discovery Bay east of Sequim, this restaurant is hidden from the highway, down a winding driveway through an associated condominium complex. The restaurant has a cozy little dining room with big windows that offer a pristine view of the bay and hills on the far side. In summer, the deck is the place to dine. Not surprisingly, the menu is heavy on oyster dishes. Our favorite being those baked with brandy, garlic, pine nuts, and Parmesan. For those who don't eat oysters, there are coconut-almond prawns, cioppino, and salmon. Monday through Friday, there are $9.95 early bird dinners between 4 and 6pm.

The Three Crabs. 11 Three Crabs Rd., Dungeness. ☎ **360/683-4264.** Reservations recommended. Main courses $6–$18. DISC, MC, V. Daily 11:30am–9pm (until 8pm in winter). SEAFOOD.

The Three Crabs is an Olympic Peninsula institution. Folks drive from miles around to enjoy the fresh seafood and sunset views at this friendly waterfront restaurant overlooking the Strait of Juan de Fuca. For 40 years the Three Crabs has been serving up Dungeness crabs in a wide variety of styles. You can order your crabs as a cocktail, a sandwich, cracked, and as crab Louie salad. Clams and oysters also come from the local waters and are equally good.

3 Olympic National Park North & the Northern Olympic Peninsula

Port Angeles park entrance: 48 miles W of Port Townsend, 57 miles E of Forks

The northern portions of Olympic National Park are both the most accessible and most heavily visited. It is here, south of Port Angeles, that the only two roads leading into the high country of the national park are found. Of these the Hurricane Ridge area is the more easily reached—the Deer Park area is at the end of a harrowing gravel road. West of Port Angeles and within the national park lie two large lakes, Lake Crescent and Lake Ozette, that attract boaters and anglers. Also in this region are two hot springs—the developed Sol Duc Resort and the natural Olympic Hot Springs.

Outside the park boundaries, along the northern coast of the peninsula, are several campgrounds, and a couple of small sport-fishing ports, Sekiu and Neah Bay, that are also popular with scuba divers. Neah Bay, which is on the Makah Indian Reservation is also the site of one of the most interesting culture and history museums in the state. This reservation also encompasses Cape Flattery, which is the northwesternmost point in the contiguous United States. Along the coastline between Port Angeles and Neah Bay are also several spots that are popular with sea kayakers.

Port Angeles, primarily a lumber-shipping port, is the largest town on the north Olympic Peninsula and serves both as a base for people exploring the national park and as a port for ferries crossing the Strait of Juan de Fuca to Victoria, British Columbia. It is here that you will find the region's greatest concentration of lodgings and restaurants.

ESSENTIALS

GETTING THERE   U.S. 101 circles Olympic National Park, with main park entrances south of Port Angeles, at Lake Crescent, and at the Hoh River south of Forks.

Fairchild International Airport in Port Angeles is served by Horizon Airlines. Rental cars are available in Port Angeles from Budget Rent A Car.

There is **bus service** to Port Angeles from Seattle on Olympic Bus Lines (☎ **800/ 550-3858** or 360/452-3858). **Jefferson Transit** (☎ **360/385-4777**) has service from Port Townsend to Sequim, where you can transfer to service on **Clallam Transit** (☎ **800/858-3747** or 360/452-4511), which operates from Sequim around the peninsula to Lake Crescent, Neah Bay, La Push, and Forks.

Two **ferries,** one for foot passengers only and the other for vehicles and foot passengers, connect Port Angeles and Victoria, British Columbia. The ferry terminal for both ferries is at the corner of Laurel Street and Railroad Avenue. **Victoria Rapid**

Transit (☎ **800/633-1589** in Washington, 360/452-8088, or 250/361-9144 in Victoria) is the faster of the two ferries (1 hour between Victoria and Port Angeles) and carries foot passengers only. This ferry operates only between May and October. Fares are $20 to $25 round-trip for adults and $10 for children 5 to 11. The **Black Ball Transport** (☎ **360/457-4491** or 250/386-2202 in Victoria) ferry operates year-round except for 2 weeks in late January and early February and carries vehicles as well as walk-on passengers. The crossing takes slightly more than 1 1/2 hours. The one-way fares are $6.75 for adults, $3.40 for children 5 to 11; $27.25 for a car, van, camper, or motor home and driver. Note that Black Ball Transport does not accept personal checks or credit/charge cards.

VISITOR INFORMATION   For more information on the national park, contact the **Olympic National Park,** 600 E. Park Ave., Port Angeles, WA 98362 (☎ **360/452-0330**). For more information on Port Angeles and the rest of the northern Olympic Peninsula, contact the **North Olympic Peninsula Visitor and Convention Bureau,** P.O. Box 670, Port Angeles, WA 98362 (☎ **800/942-4042** or 360/452-8552; www.northolympic.com); or the **Port Angeles Chamber of Commerce,** 121 E. Railroad Ave. (☎ **360/452-2363**).

PARK ADMISSION   Park admission is $10 per vehicle and $5 per pedestrian or cyclist.

EXPLORING THE PARK'S NORTH SIDE

Port Angeles is the headquarters for the park, and it's here that you'll find the **Olympic National Park Visitor Center,** 3002 Mount Angles Rd. (☎ 360/452-0330). Mount Angeles Road is on the south edge of town and leads up to Hurricane Rigde. In addition to having lots of information, maps and books about the park, the center has exhibits on the park's flora and fauna, old-growth forests, and whaling by local Native Americans. It's open daily from 9am to 4pm, with longer hours in the summer.

From the visitor center, continue another 17 miles on this road to **Hurricane Ridge,** which on clear days offers the most breathtaking views in the park. In summer the surrounding subalpine meadows are carpeted with wildflowers. Several hiking trails lead into the park from here. In winter Hurricane Ridge is a popular cross-country skiing area and also has a rope tow for beginners' downhill skiing. The Hurricane Ridge Visitor Center has exhibits on alpine plants and wildlife. In summer, you're likely to see deer grazing in the meadows here and marmots, relatives of squirrels, lounging on rocks or nibbling on flowers.

A few miles east of Port Angeles another road heads south into the park to an area called **Deer Park.** This narrow, winding gravel road is a real test of nerves and consequently is not nearly as popular a route as the road to Hurricane Ridge. However, the scenery once you reach the end of the road is just as breathtaking as that from Hurricane Ridge. As the name implies, deer are common in this area.

Impressions

If the exploiters are permitted to have their way with the Olympic Peninsula, all that will be left will be the outraged squeal of future generations over the loss of another national treasure.

—Harold Ickes, secretary of the interior under Pres. Franklin Delano Roosevelt, who was responsible for creating Olympic National Park

West of Port Angeles a few miles, up the Elwha River, you'll find the short trail (actually an abandoned road) that leads to **Olympic Hot Springs**. These natural hot pools are in a forest setting and are extremely popular and often crowded, especially on weekends. For more developed hot springs soaking, head to Sol Duc Resort, west of Lake Crescent.

West of Port Angeles on U.S. 101 lies **Lake Crescent,** a glacier-carved lake sur-rounded by steep forested mountains that give the lake the feel of a fjord. This is one of the most beautiful lakes in the state and has long been a popular destination. Near the east end of the lake, you'll find the **Storm King Information Station** (open sum-mer only) and the 1-mile trail to 90-foot-tall Marymere Falls. On the north side of the lake, you'll find the **Spruce Railroad Trail,** which parallels the shore of the lake, crosses a picturesque little bridge, and is one of the only trails in the park that is open to mountain bikes. As the name implies this was once the route of the railroad built to haul spruce out of these forests during World War I. Spruce was the ideal wood for building biplanes because of its strength and light weight. However, by the time the railroad was completed, the war was over and the demand for spruce had dwindled.

Between late May and early October, you can cruise the lake on the **paddlewheeler Storm King** (☎ 360/452-4520), which has its ticket office at the Shadow Moun-tain General Store, milepost 233 on U.S. 101. The fare is $15 for adults, $14 for se-niors, $10 for children 17 and under. There are also several places on the lake where you can rent various types of small boats. At **Lake Crescent Lodge,** you can rent row-boats for $5 per hour. At the **Fairholm General Store** (☎ 360/928-3020), at the lake's west end, rowboats, canoes, and motorboats are available. Canoes and rowboats go for $7 per hour or $24 per day, and motorboats go for $12 per hour or $60 per day. The store is only open between April and October. On the north side of the lake at the **Log Cabin Resort,** rowboats, canoes, and pedal boats can be rented year-round for $9 per hour.

Continuing west from Lake Crescent, watch for the turnoff to **Sol Duc Hot Springs** (☎ 360/327-3583). For 14 miles the road follows the Soleduck River, pass-ing the Salmon Cascades along the way. Sol Duc Hot Springs were for centuries con-sidered healing waters by local Indians, and after white settlers arrived in the area, the springs became a popular resort. In addition to the hot swimming pool and soaking tubs, you'll find cabins, a campground, a restaurant, and a snack bar. The springs are open daily from May to September, and on Saturday and Sunday from October to April; admission is $6.50 for adults. A 6-mile loop trail leads to **Sol Duc Falls,** which are among the most photographed falls in the park.

EXPLORING THE PENINSULA'S NORTHWEST CORNER

Continuing west on U.S. 101 from the junction with the road to Sol Duc Hot Springs brings you to the crossroads of Sappho. Heading north at Sappho will bring you to Wash. 112, which is an alternative route from Port Angeles. About 40 miles west, Wash. 112 reaches the community of **Neah Bay** on the Makah Indian Reser-vation. Neah Bay is a busy commercial and sport-fishing port, and is also home to the impressive **Makah Cultural and Resource Center** (☎ 360/645-2711), which displays artifacts from a Native American village that was inundated by a mud slide 500 years ago. This is the most perfectly preserved collection of Native American ar-tifacts in the Northwest; part of the exhibit includes reproductions of canoes the Makah once used for hunting whales. There's also a longhouse that shows the tra-ditional lifestyle of the Makah people. The museum is open June 1 to September 16, daily from 10am to 5pm, and September 17 to May 31, Wednesday through Sunday from 10am to 5pm; admission is $4 for adults, $3 for students and seniors.

The reservation land includes Cape Flattery, which is the northwesternmost point of land in the contiguous United States. Just off the cape lies Tatoosh Island, site of one of the oldest lighthouses in Washington. Cape Flattery is a popular spot for a bit of hiking and ocean viewing, but car break-ins are not uncommon here. Each year in late August, **Makah Days** are celebrated with canoe races, Indian dancing, a salmon bake, and other events.

A turnoff 16 miles east of Neah Bay leads south to **Ozette Lake,** where there are boat ramps, a campground, and, stretching north and south, miles of beaches that are only accessible on foot. A 3.3-mile trail on a raised boardwalk leads from the Ozette Lake trailhead to **Cape Alava,** which is the westernmost point in the contiguous United States. The large rocks just offshore here are known as haystack rocks and are common all along the rocky western coast of the Olympic Peninsula, which is characterized by a rugged coastline. Aside from five coastal Indian reservations, almost all this northern coastline is preserved as part of the national park.

GUIDED TOURS, EDUCATIONAL PROGRAMS & OUTDOOR ADVENTURES

GUIDED TOURS

If you'd like to see the park on a guided tour, contact **Olympic Van Tours** (☎ 800/ 550-3858 or 360/452-3858), which offers tours to Hurricane Ridge, the Hoh River rain forest, and ocean beaches. Tours range from a few hours to all day and cost $13 to $45.

EDUCATIONAL PROGRAMS

The **Olympic Park Institute,** 111 Barnes Point Rd., Port Angeles, WA 98363 (☎ 360/928-3720), which is located in the Rosemary Inn on Lake Crescent, offers a wide array of summer field seminars ranging from painting classes to bird-watching trips to multiday backpacking trips.

OUTDOOR ADVENTURES

Bicycling   If you're interested in exploring the region on a bike, you can rent one at **Pedal 'n' Paddle,** 120 E. Front St., Port Angeles (☎ 360/457-1240), which can recommend good rides in the area and also offers bicycle tours. Bikes are $22 per day or $8 per hour.

Fishing   The rivers of the Olympic Peninsula are well known for their fighting salmon, steelhead, and trout. In Lakes Crescent and Ozette you can fish for such elusive species as Beardslee and Crescenti trout. No fishing license is necessary to fish for trout on national park rivers and streams or in Lake Crescent or Lake Ozette. However, you will need a state punch card—available wherever fishing licenses are sold—to fish for salmon or steelhead. Boat rentals are available on Lake Crescent at Fairholm General Store, the Log Cabin Resort, and at Lake Crescent Lodge.

If you want to hire a guide to take you out, try **Four Seasons Guide Service** (☎ 360/327-3380), which can take you fishing for steelhead, salmon, and trout on the region's rivers (rates $180 per day for one person, $225 for two people). **Olympic Raft & Guide Service** (☎ 888/452-1443 or 360/452-1443) can also get you out where the big ones are biting.

If you're more interested in heading out on open water to do a bit of salmon or deep-sea fishing, there are numerous charter boats operating out of Port Angeles,

Sekiu, and Neah Bay. In Port Angeles, contact **Lucky Strike** (☎ 360/683-2416), or **Port Angeles Charters** (☎ 360/457-7629). In the Sekiu/Clallam Bay area, contact **Herb's Charters** (☎ 360/963-2346) or **Olson's Charters** (☎ 360/963-2311). In Neah Bay, contact **Big Salmon Fishing Resort** (☎ 800/959-2374 or 360/645-2374) or **Far West Fishing Resort** (☎ 360/645-2270).

Hiking & Backpacking   For several of the most popular backpacking destinations in Olympic National Park (the Ozette Coast, Grand Valley, Flapjack Lakes, and Lake Constance), advance-reservation hiking permits are now required between Memorial Day and Labor Day. Reservation can be made by calling the **Wilderness Information Center** (☎ 360/452-0300). Both a permit fee and a nightly camping fee are charged. For most other overnight hikes you can pick up a permit at the trailhead. If in doubt, check with a park ranger before heading out to a trailhead for a backpacking trip.

Most of the best backpacking trips in Olympic National Park are long and aren't easily turned into loop trips. If you want to do a one-way backpacking trip, you can arrange a shuttle through **Olympic Van Tours** (☎ 800/550-3858 or 360/452-3858).

Llama Trekking   If you want to do an overnight trip into the backcountry of the national park but don't want to carry all the gear, consider letting a llama carry your stuff. **Wooley Packer Llama Co.,** 5763 Upper Hoh Rd., Forks, WA 98331 (☎ 360/374-9288), offers overnight trips of up to 7 days within Olympic National Park (rates start at $75 per person per day; two-person minimum).

Mountaineering & Rock Climbing   More adventurous tours ranging in length from half a day to 5 days are offered by **Olympic Mountaineering,** 140 W. Front St., Port Angeles (☎ 360/452-0240). Prices range from $50 for a half day of rock climbing to $695 for a 5-day guided hike through the Hoh rain forest to Mount Olympus. This company's most popular tour is its climb to the summit of Mount Olympus, the highest peak on the Olympic Peninsula.

Scuba Diving   The waters off the town of Sekiu are the Olympic Peninsula's favorite dive site. Divers will want to stop in at the **Sekiu Dive Center** (☎ 360/963-2281), on the main road through town.

Sea Kayaking & Canoeing   Sea kayaking trips on Lake Crescent, Lake Adlwell, and Freshwater Bay, all of which are west of Port Angeles, are offered by **Olympic Raft & Guide Service** (☎ 888/452-1443 or 360/452-1443), which charges between $36 and $66 per person. Sea kayaking tours are also offered by **Pedal 'n' Paddle,** 120 E. Front St., Port Angeles (☎ 360/457-1240).

White-Water Rafting   The steep mountains and plentiful rains of the Olympic Peninsula are the source of some great whitewater rafting on the Elwha, Queets, and Hoh rivers. Contact **Olympic Raft & Guide Service** (☎ 888/452-1443 or 360/452-1443). Rates start at $39 for a 2–2¹/₂-hour rafting trip.

EXPLORING AROUND PORT ANGELES

If you're curious about the general history of this area, you may want to check out the **Clallam County Museum,** 223 E. Fourth and Lincoln streets (☎ 360/417-2364). It's open Monday through Friday from 10am to 4pm, and also on Saturday in summer; admission is by donation. The **Port Angeles Fine Art Center,** 1203 Lauridsen Rd. (☎ 360/457-3532), is the town's only other museum and hosts changing exhibits of contemporary art. It's open Thursday through Sunday from 11am to 5pm; admission is free.

If you'd like to get a close-up look at some of the peninsula's aquatic inhabitants, stop by the **Arthur D. Feiro Marine Lab,** Port Angeles City Pier, Lincoln Street and Railroad Avenue, (☎ **360/417-6254**). In the lab's tanks, you may spot a wolf eel or octopus, and there's a touch tank where you can pick up a starfish or sea cucumber. It's open in summer, daily from 10am to 8pm; other months, on Saturday and Sunday from noon to 4pm. Admission is $2 for adults, $1 for seniors, and children under 5 are free.

WHERE TO STAY

Beyond Port Angeles, accommodations are few and far between, and those places worth recommending tend to be very popular. Try to have room reservations before heading west from Port Angeles.

IN PORT ANGELES

As the biggest town on the northern Olympic Peninsula and a base of operations for families exploring Olympic National Park, Port Angeles abounds in budget motels. You'll find dozens including the **Super 8 Motel,** 2104 E. First St. (☎ **360/ 452-8401**); and the **Best Wester Olympic Lodge,** 140 Del Guzzi Dr. (☎ **360/ 452-2993**), along the section of U.S. 101 east of downtown.

✪ **Domaine Madeleine.** 146 Wildflower Lane, Port Angeles, WA 98362. ☎ **360/457-4174.** Fax 360/457-3037. www.northolympic.com/dm. 5 rms. TV TEL. $135–$165 double. Rates include full 5-course breakfast. AE, DISC, MC, V.

Located 7 miles east of Port Angeles, this B&B is set at the back of a small pasture and has a very secluded feel. Combine this with the waterfront setting and you have a fabulous weekend hideaway—you may not even bother exploring the park. The guest rooms are in several different buildings that are surrounded by colorful gardens, and all have views that take in the Strait of Juan de Fuca and the mountains beyond. There are also fireplaces and VCRs in the rooms, and whirlpool tubs in all but one. The breakfasts are superb.

Doubletree Hotel Port Angeles. 221 N. Lincoln St., Port Angeles, WA 98362. ☎ **800/ 222-TREE** or 360/452-9215. Fax 360/452-4734. 187 rms, 3 suites. A/C TV TEL. $99–$129 double; $165 suite. Lower rates off-season. AE, CB, DC, DISC, MC, V.

If you're on your way to or from Victoria, there's no more convenient hotel than the Doubletree. Located on the waterfront, it's only steps from the ferry terminal. Most rooms have balconies and large bathrooms, and the more expensive rooms overlook the Strait of Juan de Fuca. There's a seafood restaurant adjacent to the hotel. Laundry/valet service is available, and an outdoor pool and hot tub provide recreational options.

The Tudor Inn. 1108 S. Oak St., Port Angeles, WA 98362. ☎ **360/452-3138.** 5 rms. Summer, $85–$125 double; other months, $75–$110 double. AE, DISC, MC, V.

Located in a quiet residential neighborhood 13 blocks from the waterfront, this 1910 Tudor home is surrounded by a large yard and pretty gardens. On the ground floor you'll find a lounge and library, both with fireplaces that get a lot of use. Upstairs there are five rooms furnished with European antiques. Several rooms have good views of the Olympic Mountains.

WEST OF PORT ANGELES

Elwha Ranch Bed & Breakfast. 905 Herrick Rd., Port Angeles, WA 98363. ☎ **360/ 457-6540.** www.northolympic.com/elwharanch. 3 rms. $85–$144 double. Rates include full breakfast. No credit cards

Although it isn't located within the national park, this cedar-log inn, on a 72-acre ranch high above the Elwha River valley, has a superb view up the valley into the park. Two of the rooms are in the main house, which has a casual Western ranch feel and lots of windows to take in the views. If you're traveling with friends or family, opt for the two-bedroom suite. However, the nicest and most comfortable room here is a sort of modern cabin outside the front door of the main house. Be sure to get directions to the inn. Fresh pies are a specialty of innkeeper Margaret Mitchell.

✪ **Lake Crescent Lodge.** 416 Lake Crescent Rd., Port Angeles, WA 98363-8672. ☎ **360/ 928-3211.** 52 rms and cabins, 48 with bath. $67 double without bath, $99–$117.50 double with bath; $105–$126 cottage. AE, CB, DC, DISC, MC, V.

This historic lodge is located 20 miles west of Port Angeles on the south shore of picturesque Lake Crescent and is the lodging of choice for national park visitors wishing to stay on the north side of the park. Wood paneling, hardwood floors, a stone fireplace, and a sun room make the lobby a popular spot for just sitting and relaxing. The guest rooms in this main lodge building are the oldest and all have shared bathrooms. If you'd like more modern accommodations, there are a number of standard motel-style rooms, but these lack the character of the lodge rooms. If you have your family or some friends along, we recommend reserving a cottage. Those with fireplaces are the most comfortable (and are also the only rooms available between October 31 and late April), but the others are nice as well. All but the main lodge rooms have views of either the lake or the mountains. With a view across the lake, the Lodge Dining Room serves a limited menu of continental cuisine with an emphasis on local seafood. Prices are moderate. A lobby lounge provides a quiet place for an evening drink. Rowboat rentals are available.

Log Cabin Resort. 3183 E. Beach Rd., Port Angeles, WA 98363. ☎ **360/928-3325.** Fax 360/ 928-2088. 4 rms; 24 cabins, 8 with bath; 1 chalet. $49 cabin for two without bath, $76–$90 cabin for two with bath; $106 double; $121 chalet. DISC, MC, V. Closed Christmas–Valentines Day.

This log-cabin resort on the north shore of Lake Crescent first opened in 1895 and still has buildings that date back to the 1920s. The least expensive accommodations are rustic one-room log cabins in which you provide the bedding and share a bathroom a short walk away (basically this is camping without the tent). More comfortable are the 1928 cabins with private bathrooms, some of which also have kitchenettes (you provide the cooking and eating utensils). The lodge rooms and a chalet offer the greatest comfort and best views. The lodge dining room overlooks the lake and specializes in local seafood. The resort also has a general store and RV sites.

Sol Duc Hot Springs Resort. Sol Duc Rd., U.S. 101 (P.O. Box 2169), Port Angeles, WA 98362. ☎ **360/327-3583.** Fax 360/327-3593. www.northolympic.com/solduc. 32 cabins. $85–$95 cabin for two. AE, DISC, MC, V. Closed Oct–mid-May.

The Sol Duc Hot Springs have for years been a popular family vacation spot. Campers, day trippers, and resort guests all spend the day soaking and playing in the hot-water swimming pools. The grounds of the resort are grassy and open, but the forest is kept just at arm's reach. The cabins are done in modern motel style and are comfortable if not spacious. There's an excellent restaurant here, as well as a poolside deli, espresso bar, and grocery store. Three hot spring–fed swimming pools are the focal point, and the pools are open to the public for a small fee. Massages are available.

CAMPGROUNDS

The six national park campgrounds on the northern edge of the park are some of the busiest in the park due to their proximity to U.S. 101. **Deer Park Campground**

Look Out: Banana Slugs Crossing

If you happen to be a gardener who lives where summers are humid, you probably curse slugs, which can do immense damage to a vegetable patch. Now, imagine that those slimy little slugs chomping on your tomatoes are not an inch long, but a foot! Sound like a late-night monster movie? Think again. And if you go out in the woods today, be sure to watch your step.

The banana slug (*Ariolimax columbianus*), which can grow to be a foot in length and live for up to 5 years, is the only slug native to the Pacific Northwest. Making its yellowish, elongated way through the region's lowland forests, these slugs dine on plants, mushrooms, and decaying vegetable matter. Though slugs may seem to wander aimlessly, they have two eyes on the ends of long stalks and two olfactory organs on short stalks. The eyes detect light and dark and help them find cool dark places to sleep away the day, while the olfactory organs are used to locate food. A slug eats by shredding organic matter with a tonguelike structure called a radula, which is covered with thousands of tiny teeth.

Aside from their repulsive appearance and annoying habit of devouring gardens, slugs get a bad rap for sliming anyone unlucky enough to grab one accidentally. Slug slime, if you take the time to study it instead of just rubbing your fingers furiously to remove it, is amazing stuff. It's at once as slippery as soap and as sticky as glue, an unusual combination of properties that allows slugs to use their slime as a sort of instant highway on which to travel. Secreting the slime from their chin like so much drool, slugs coat the surface of whatever they're crawling on and then just slide along.

Slug slime may also serve as a defense mechanism. Lacking the protective shell of their close relatives the snails, slugs defend themselves by secreting copious amounts of slime, rendering them unpalatable to predators such as shrews, beetles, crows, and garter snakes.

Think slugs are sluggish? Think again. One of these babies can do 0.007 miles per hour (3 to 4 inches per minute) on the straightaway as the muscles along its foot constrict in waves and move it forward.

It's hard to believe that something as soft and slow moving as a slug could ever be a threat to anything, but slugs are real scrappers. That same serrated tongue that shreds lettuce so efficiently can also be used as a weapon against other slugs. If you start checking slugs closely, you're likely to find a few with old battle scars on their backs.

We know that birds do it and bees do it, but how do slugs do it? With themselves. Slugs are hermaphroditic, and it only takes one to tango. And what this means is that each one of those slugs out in your garden is going to lay eggs! Now that's a nightmare.

And how did banana slugs get their name? No one is quite sure whether it's because they so closely resemble bananas, right down to the brown spots, or because when stepped on, they have an effect similar to that of a banana peel. Either way, it's appropriate.

(18 campsites) is the easternmost of these campgrounds (take Deer Park Road from U.S. 101 east of Port Angeles) and the only high-elevation (5,400 feet) campground in Olympic National Park. Deer Park is reached by a winding one-lane gravel road. The national park's **Heart O' the Hills Campground** (105 campsites), on

Hurricane Ridge Road 5 miles south of the Olympic National Park Visitor Center, is also very popular. On Olympic Hot Springs Road up the Elwha River, you'll find **Elwha Campground** (41 campsites) and **Altaire Campground** (30 campsites).

West of Port Angeles along Wash. 112, there are three campgrounds on the shore of the Strait of Juan de Fuca. **Salt Creek County Park** (80 campsites), 13 miles west of Port Angeles, is among the most scenic spots on this whole coast. About 20 miles west of Port Angeles is the Washington Department of Natural Resources' **Lyre River Campground** (11 campsites, seasonal). About 40 miles west of Port Angeles is **Pillar Point County Park** (37 campsites), which perches atop a bluff overlooking the strait.

The only campground on Lake Crescent is at **Fairholm** (87 campsites) at the west end of the lake. The nearby **Sol Duc Campground** (80 campsites), set amid impressive stands of old-growth trees, is adjacent to the Sol Duc Hot Springs.

Heading west from Lake Crescent on U.S. 101, there are several campgrounds along the banks of the Sol Duc River.

The national park's remote **Ozette Campground** (14 campsites), on the north shore of Lake Ozette, is a good choice both for sea kayakers/canoeists and people wanting to day hike out to the beaches on either side of Capa Alava.

National parks and other campgrounds don't take reservations, however, for general information, contact **Olympic National Park** (☎ **360/452-0330** or 360/956-2300.

WHERE TO DINE
IN PORT ANGELES

Bella Italia. 117-B E. First St. ☎ 360/457-5442. Main dishes $7–$16. AE, DISC, MC, V. Mon–Sat 11am–11pm, Sun 11am–10pm. ITALIAN.

Located in the basement of a natural foods store in downtown Port Angeles, this restaurant has a sort of rathskeller feel, with heavy wood beams overhead. The menu, however, is strictly Italian and starts with a basket of delicious bread accompanied by an olive oil, balsamic vinegar, garlic, and herb dipping sauce. Local seafood makes it onto the menu in a few places, including a Dungeness crab ravioli, a smoked salmon fettucine, and steamed mussels and clams. There's a good selection of wines as well as an espresso bar and the Italian desserts are excellent. With its individual pizzas, and crayons and paper place mats, this is a good choice for families.

✪ **C'est Si Bon.** 23 Cedar Park Rd. ☎ **360/452-8888.** Reservations recommended. Main courses $20–$25. AE, CB, MC, V. Tues–Sun 5–11pm. FRENCH.

Located 4 miles south of town just off U.S. 101, C'est Si Bon is painted a striking combination of turquoise, pink, and purple that gives the restaurant a sort of happy elegance. Inside, the nontraditional paint job gives way to more classic decor—reproductions of European works of art, crystal chandeliers, and old musical instruments used as wall decorations. Most tables have a view of the restaurant's pretty garden. The menu is limited, which just about insures that each dish has been perfected. Desserts are limited, but rich and creamy.

The Coffee House Restaurant. 118 E. First St. ☎ **360/452-1459.** Main courses $9–$13. MC, V. Mon–Sat 8am–9pm. INTERNATIONAL.

Before you can take a seat in this casual café in downtown Port Angeles, you'll have to walk past the pastry case, which should prompt you to not eat too much before it's time for dessert. Though the menu here draws on the cuisines of the world (Thai peanut stir-fry, jerked chicken, teriyaki salmon), the emphasis is on Mediterranean and Middle Eastern. There are always plenty of vegetarian offerings as well as lots of fresh local seafood.

✪ **Toga's International Cuisine.** 122 W. Lauridsen Blvd. ☎ **360/452-1952.** Reservations recommended. Main dishes $14–$27. MC, V. Tues–Sun 5–10pm. INTERNATIONAL/GERMAN.

Located on the west side of Port Angeles, this restaurant is an unexpected treat and serves some very unusual dishes the likes of which are not to be found anywhere else in the state. Chef Toga Hertzog apprenticed in the Black Forest and has brought to his restaurant the traditional *Jagerstein* style of cooking in which diners cook their own meat or prawns on a hot rock. With 24 hours notice you can also have traditional Swiss cheese fondue or a lighter seafood fondue. To start your meal, you might try the crabmeat Rockefeller or the sampler of house-smoked salmon, scallops, oysters, and prawns. For dessert nothing hits the spot like the black forest cake.

WEST OF PORT ANGELES

Outside of Port Angeles, the restaurant choices become exceedingly slim. Your best choices are the dining rooms at Lake Crescent Lodge (open late April to late October) and the Log Cabin Resort (open Valentines Day to Christmas), both of which are on the shores of Lake Crescent. One other dining option on this lake is the **Fairholm General Store & Cafe,** 221121 U.S. 101 (☎ **360/928-3020**), which is at the west end of the lake and is open between April and October. Although all you'll get here are burgers, sandwiches, and breakfasts, the cafe has a deck with a view of the lake.

4 Olympic National Park West

Forks: 57 miles W of Port Angeles, 50 miles S of Neah Bay, 77 miles N of Lake Quinault

The western regions of Olympic National Park can be roughly divided into two distinct sections—the rugged coastal strip and the famous rain-forest valleys. Of course, these are the rainiest areas within the park, and many a visitor has called short a vacation here due to the rain. Come prepared to get wet.

The coastal strip can be divided into three segments. North of La Push, which is on the Quileute Indian Reservation, the 20 miles of shoreline from Rialto Beach to Cape Alava is accessible only on foot. The northern end of this stretch of coast is accessed from Lake Ozette off Wash. 112 in the northwest corner of the peninsula. South of La Push, the park's coastline stretches for 17 miles from Third Beach to the Hoh River mouth and is also accessible only on foot. The third segment of Olympic Park coastline begins at Ruby Beach just south of the Hoh River mouth and the Hoh Indian Reservation and stretches south to South Beach. This stretch of coastline is paralleled by U.S. 101.

Inland of these coastal areas, which are not contiguous with the rest of the park, lie the four rain-forest valleys of the Bogachiel, Hoh, Queets, and Quinault rivers. Of these valleys, only the Hoh and Quinault are penetrated by roads, and it is in the Hoh Valley that the rain forests are the primary attraction.

Located just outside the northwest corner of the park, the lumber town of Forks serves as the gateway to Olympic National Park's west side. This town was at the heart of the controversy over protecting the northern spotted owl, and is still struggling to recover from the employment bust after the logging boom of the 1980s.

ESSENTIALS

GETTING THERE The town of Forks is the largest community in this northwest corner of the Olympic Peninsula and is on U.S. 101, which continues south along the west side of the peninsula to the town of Hoquiam.

Bus service to this area is provided by **Clallam Transit** (☎ 800/858-3747 or 360/ 452-4511), which operates from Sequim and around the peninsula to Lake Crescent, Neah Bay, La Push, and Forks. Bus service between Forks and Lake Quinault is provided by **West Jefferson Olympic Connection** (☎ 800/436-3950). There is service to Lake Quinault from Olympia and Aberdeen on **Grays Harbor Transit** (☎ 800/562-9730 or 360/532-2770).

VISITOR INFORMATION   For more information on this western section of Olympic National Park, see "Visitor Information" above in the "Olympic National Park North" section of this chapter. For more information on the Forks area, contact the **Forks Chamber of Commerce,** P.O. box 1249, Forks, WA 98331 (☎ 800/ 44-FORKS or 360/374-2531).

EXPLORING THE PARK'S WEST SIDE

If you want to learn more about the area's logging history, stop by the **Forks Timber Museum,** south of town on U.S. 101 (☎ 360/374-9663). The museum chronicles the history of logging in this region, but it also has displays on Native American culture and pioneer days. It's open May to October only, daily from 10am to 4pm; admission is by donation. Also in the Forks area, there are quite a few artists' studios and galleries. You can pick up **Olympic West Arttrek** guide and map to these studios and galleries at the Forks Chamber of Commerce (see above for address and phone number).

West of Forks lie miles of pristine beaches and a narrow strip of forest that are part of the national park, though not connected to the inland, mountainous section. The first place where you can actually drive right to the Pacific Ocean is just west of Forks. At the end of a spur road you come to the Quileute Indian Reservation and the community of **La Push.** Right in town there's a beach at the mouth of the Quillayute River; however, before you reach La Push, you'll see signs for **Third Beach** and **Second Beach,** which are two of the prettiest beaches on the peninsula. Third Beach is a 1.6-mile walk and Second Beach is just over half a mile from the trailhead. **Rialto Beach,** just north of La Push, is another great beach; it's reached from a turnoff east of La Push. From here you can walk north for 24 miles to Cape Alava, although this is also a very popular spot for day hikes. One mile up the beach is a spot called Hole in the Wall, where ceaseless wave action has bored a large tunnel through solid rock. On any of these beaches, keep an eye out for bald eagles, seals, and sea lions.

Roughly 8 miles south of Forks is the turnoff for the Hoh River valley. It's 17 miles up this side road to the **Hoh Visitor Center** (☎ 360/374-6925), campground, and trailheads. This valley receives an average of 140 inches of rain per year, making it the wettest region in the continental United States. At the visitor center you can learn all about the natural forces that cause this tremendous rainfall. To see the effect of so much rain on the landscape, walk the three-quarter-mile **Hall of Mosses Trail** where the trees, primarily Sitka spruce, western red cedar, and western hemlock, tower 200 feet tall. Here you'll see big-leaf maple trees with limbs draped in thick carpets of mosses. If you're up for a longer walk, try the **Spruce Nature Trail.** If you've come with a backpack, there's no better way to see the park and all its habitats than by hiking the **Hoh River Trail,** which is 17 miles long and leads past Blue Glacier to Glacier Meadows on the flanks of Mount Olympus. A herd of elk calls the Hoh Valley home and can sometimes be seen along these trails.

Continuing south on U.S. 101, but before crossing the Hoh River, you'll come to a secondary road that heads west from the Hoh Oxbow campground. From the end of the road it's a hike of less than a mile to a rocky beach at the **mouth of the Hoh River.** You're likely to see sea lions or harbor seals feeding just offshore here, and to the north are several haystack rocks that are nesting sites for numerous sea birds. Primitive camping is permitted on this beach, and from here hikers can continue hiking for 17 miles north along a pristine wilderness of rugged headlands and secluded beaches.

U.S. 101 finally reaches the coast at **Ruby Beach.** This beach gets its name from its pink sand, which is comprised of tiny grains of garnet. For another 17 miles or so the highway parallels the wave-swept coastline. Along this stretch of highway there are turnoffs and short trails down to six beaches that have only numbers for names. At low tide, the northern beaches offer lots of tide pools to be explored. Near the south end of this stretch of road, you'll find Kalaloch Lodge, which has a gas station, and the **Kalaloch Information Station,** (☎ 360/962-2271) which is only open during the summer.

Shortly beyond Kalaloch the highway turns inland again passing through the community of **Queets** on the river of the same name. The Queets River valley is another rainy valley, and if you'd like to do a bit of hiking away from the crowds, head up the gravel road to the Queets campground, from which a hiking trail leads up the valley. A little more than 2 miles up this trail is one of the world's largest Douglas firs.

A long stretch of clear-cuts and tree farms, mostly on the Quinault Indian Reservation, will bring you to **Quinault Lake.** Surrounded by forested mountains, this deep lake is the site of the rustic Lake Quinault Lodge and offers boating and freshwater fishing opportunities, as well as more rain forests to explore on a couple of short trails. This is also a good area in which to spot Roosevelt elk.

For more information on guided tours and other outdoor recreational possibilities throughout the park's west side, see "Guided Tours, Educational Programs & Outdoor Adventures" in the "Olympic National Park North" section above.

WHERE TO STAY
IN THE FORKS AREA

The town of Forks has several inexpensive motels and is a good place to look for cheap lodgings if you happen to be out this way without a reservation. These include **The Forks Motel**, 351 Forks Ave. S. (☎ **800/544-3416** or 360/374-6243).

Eagle Point Inn. 380 Stormin' Norman Rd. (P.O. Box 546), Beaver, WA 98305. ☎ **360/ 327-3236.** 3 rms (all with private bathrooms). $75–$85 double. Rates include full breakfast. No credit cards.

Located 10 miles north of Forks at milepost 202 on U.S. 101, this rustic B&B is housed in two log homes, one old and one new. Although the inn's five acres are surrounded by recently planted forest, the inn itself is in a beautiful parklike setting on the bank of the Sol Duc River. The guest rooms are everything the rooms in a log house should be—rustic, romantic, rugged—yet with antiques, down comforters, and private baths. Out in the yard you'll find a hot tub and a covered barbecue area should you want to fix your own meal.
across the hall. For greater privacy, there's a cabin out behind the main house. Meals are available at additional cost, and fishing and hunting packages can be arranged.

Manitou Lodge. Kilmer Rd. (P.O. Box 600), Forks, WA 98331. ☎ **360/374-6295.** 7 rms. $75–$80 double. Rates include full breakfast. AE, MC, V. Take Wash. 110 west from north of Forks; turn right on Spur 110 and then right on Kilmer Rd.

This secluded B&B is set on 10 private acres and is only minutes from some of the most beautiful and remote beaches in the Northwest. The best room in the house is the Sacajawea, which has a marble fireplace and king-size bed. A separate cabin houses two of the rooms. Guests tend to gravitate to the comfortable living room, where a huge stone fireplace is the center of attention. Fires help chase away the chill and damp of this neck of the woods. Breakfasts are hearty and sometimes include huckleberry-apple-walnut pancakes. There's also a Native American art gallery on the premises.

Miller Tree Inn. 654 E. Division St. (P.O. Box 953), Forks, WA 98331. ☎ **360/374-6806.** Fax 360/374-6807. 6 rms, 3 with full bath. $60–$65 double without full bath, $70–$90 double with bath. Rates include full breakfast. MC, V.

Located just a few blocks east of downtown Forks, this large B&B is on the edge of the country and is surrounded by large old trees and pastures, with a hot tub on the back deck. There's nothing fussy or pretentious about this place—it's just a comfortable, friendly inn that caters primarily to outdoors enthusiasts and, during the winter months, anglers. Dinner is available if requested when you make your reservation.

Along the Park's West Side, South of Forks

✪ **Kalaloch Lodge.** 157151 U.S. 101, Forks, WA 98331. ☎ **360/962-2271.** Fax 360/962-3391. 18 rms, 2 suites, 40 cabins. $56–$80 double; $99–$150 cabin for two. Lower rates weekdays Nov–May. AE, MC, V.

This rustic, cedar-shingled lodge and its cluster of cabins perch on a grassy bluff. Below, the Pacific Ocean thunders against a sandy beach where huge driftwood logs are scattered like so many twigs. The breathtaking setting makes this one of the most popular lodges on the coast, and it's advisable to book rooms at least four months in advance. The rooms in the old lodge are the least expensive, but the ocean-view bluff cabins are the most in demand. The log cabins across the street from the bluff cabins don't have the knockout views. For comfort you can't beat the motel-like rooms in the Sea Crest House. A casual coffee shop serves breakfast and lunch while a more formal dining room serves dinner with an emphasis on salmon dishes. Dinner entree prices range from $10 to $18. The lodge also has a general store and gas station.

✪ **Lake Quinault Lodge.** P.O. Box 7, Quinault, WA 98575. ☎ **360/288-2900,** or 800/562-6672 in Washington and Oregon. 92 rms, 2 suites. June–Oct, $99–$140 double; $190–$220 suite. Oct–June, $65–$115 double; $150–$175 suite. AE, MC, V.

Located on the shore of Lake Quinault in the southwest corner of the park, this imposing grande dame of the Olympic Peninsula wears an ageless tranquillity. Huge old firs and cedars shade the rustic lodge, and Adirondack chairs on the deck command a view of the lawn. The accommodations range from small rooms in the main lodge to modern rooms with wicker furniture and little balconies to rooms with fireplaces. The annex rooms are the least attractive, but they do have huge bathtubs. None of the rooms has a TV or telephone.

Dining/Entertainment: The dining room here is a large dark place as befits such a lodge, and the menu reflects the bounties of the Olympic Peninsula, with seafood a specialty. A lounge provides big-screen TV for those who just can't give up the big game or music videos.

Services: Rain-forest tours.

Facilities: Indoor pool, whirlpool, croquet, badminton, canoe and paddle-boat rentals.

Campgrounds

If you want to say you've camped at the wettest campground in the contiguous United States, head for the national park's **Hoh Campground** (95 campsites) in the

Hoh River valley. Almost as wet is the national park's **Queets Campground** (20 campsites). This campground is 14 miles up the Queets Road from U.S. 101. On Quinault Lake there are three campgrounds. On the north shore is the walk-in **July Creek Campground** (29 campsites). On the south shore are two national forest campgrounds—**Willaby** (22 campsites) and **Falls Creek** (31 campsites). East of Lake Quinault, up the Quinault River valley, are two more national park rain-forest campgrounds—**North Fork** (7 campsites) and **Graves Creek** (30 campsites) that provide access to a couple of the park's long-distance hiking trails.

Campsites at **Bogachiel State Park** (41 campsites), on the Bogachiel River 6 miles south of Forks on U.S. 101, are set under huge old spruce trees. On the banks of the Hoh River, the Washington Department of Natural Resources operates four primitive campgrounds for tenters. **Hoh Oxbow Campground** (8 campsites) is right on U.S. 101 and is the most convenient. Heading upriver on the Hoh Rain Forest Road are **Willoughby Creek** (3 campsites) and **Minnie Peterson** (8 campsites). Down river on Oil City Road is **Cottonwood Campground** (9 campsites), which is a good place to camp if you want to explore the national park coast north of the Hoh River. An alternative here is to hike 0.5 mile to the beach and camp there.

Along the peninsula's west side, there are also several beach campgrounds. These include the national park's **Mora Campground** (91 campsites) on the beautiful Rialto Beach at the mouth of the Quillayute River west of Forks. If you're prepared to hike in with your gear, you can also camp on Second Beach (0.5-mile hike) and Third Beach (1.5-mile hike). South of the Hoh River, along the only stretch of U.S. 101 that is right on the beach, you'll find **Kalaloch Campground** (177 campsites), which is the national park's largest campground. For general information on national park campgrounds, contact **Olympic National Park** (☎ **360/452-0330** or 360/956-2300). Bogachiel State State Park reservations can be made by calling Reservations Northwest (☎ **800/542-5687**).

WHERE TO DINE

In the town of Forks, you'll find several basic diners and family restaurants, but nothing really worth recommending, with the exception of the one restaurant listed below. South of Forks, your best bets are the dining rooms at the Kalaoch Lodge and the Lake Quinault Lodge.

The Smoke House Restaurant. U.S. 101 and La Push Rd. ☎ **360/374-6258**. Main dishes $5–$18. DISC, MC, V. Mon–Thurs 11am–9pm, Fri 11am–10pm, Sat 4–10pm, Sun 4–9pm. AMERICAN.

The name says it all here. This place smokes fish, and their salmon is just about the best we've ever had. It's got a good smoky flavor yet is tender and moist. If you're a fan of smoked salmon, don't miss this place. If you don't feel like sitting down for the smoked salmon dinner, smoked salmon salad, or smoked salmon and cheddar cheese tray appetizer, then consider getting some to go. It's great beach picnic food.

9 Southwest Washington

Southwest Washington, which for the purposes of this book is defined as the area west of I-5 and south of U.S. 12, is for the most part sparsely populated and heavily dependent on the timber industry for its economic base. This said, however, the region also contains the state's busiest beach resort areas—the Long Beach Peninsula and the Central Coast area—as well as the often-overlooked city of Vancouver, which shares a name with the far more famous Canadian city to the north. And although Vancouver, Washington these days is little more than a bedroom community for Portland, it abounds in pioneer history.

Aside from two last rocky headlands at the mouth of the Columbia River, the coastline of southwest Washington is a tame strip of sandy beaches and windswept dunes. Grays Harbor and Willapa Bay divide this stretch of coast into three distinct strips of sand: North Beach, South Beach, and the Long Beach Peninsula. These three strands, however, have far more in common with one another than they do with the wild, rock-strewn beaches to the north. Although far less spectacular than those to the north, their abundance of tourist accommodations makes them the favored beach vacation areas of the state.

Summers along the coast also tend to be short and often wet or foggy, and the coastal waters are too cold and rough for swimming (although surfing is fairly popular). Consequently, the traditional beach pursuits of swimming and sunning aren't high on vacation priority lists around these parts. Instead, these beaches have come to rely on other activities to attract visitors. All up and down this coast, digging for razor clams is a popular pastime, though open seasons are now short and as closely regulated as the salmon-fishing seasons. The towns of Westport, at the north end of the South Beach area, and Ilwaco, at the south end of the Long Beach Peninsula, have become the region's charter fishing boat ports, with Westport charter boats also doing double duty as whale-watching excursion boats. South Beach and the Long Beach Peninsula are also among the few region's in the country where cranberries are grown commercially. Long Beach, a beach resort town for more than 100 years, bills itself as the kite-flying capital of America and boasts of having the longest drivable beach in the world. While vacationing families drive the local economy, oysters still reign supreme in Willapa Bay, one of the cleanest estuaries on the West Coast. However, an invasive,

1-1398

nonnative marsh grass called spartina has taken hold in this estuary and is slowly crowding out native salt marsh plants and turning this bay into unproductive mudflats.

While most of this region's development has taken place around fishing and shipping ports both along the coast and up the Columbia River, the heart of the region is the Willapa Hills. These forested hills are almost entirely privately owned, mostly by large lumber companies. Consequently the forests of the Willapa Hills are among the hardest working forests in the region. Much of the region's forests have already been cut twice since the first settlers arrived in the area.

However, despite the lack of publicly held or otherwise protected forests, this coast still has its pockets of wildness. The Willapa National Wildlife Refuge and the Long Beach Peninsula's Leadbetter Point together host a vast number of bird species each year. These areas, when combined with the Grays Harbor National Wildlife Refuge to the north, offer the best bird watching in the entire Northwest. Sea kayakers also are attracted to Willapa Bay, where the paddle around Long Island is as rewarding as any paddle in the Puget Sound or San Juan Islands.

1 Grays Harbor & the Central Coast

67 miles W of Olympia, 67 miles S of Lake Quinault, 92 miles N of Long Beach

Washington's central coast, consisting of the North and South Beach areas and the Grays Harbor towns of Aberdeen and Hoquiam is something of an anomaly. Though far from being the most scenic stretch of Washington coast, it contains the state's most popular beach destination, Ocean Shores, a modern beach development that now consists of numerous oceanfront hotels and vacation homes. Although not as scenic as the Olympic Peninsula coastline, this area is popular for its easy access to the cities of Puget Sound. Located less than an hour east of Olympia; this is a popular weekend vacation spot.

The most scenic stretch of this coastline is the area known as North Beach, which consists of the beach north of the mouth of Grays Harbor. The farther north you go on this stretch of coast the more spectacular is the scenery, even rivaling the beauty of the Olympic Peninsula's shoreline in some places. The South Beach area is so named because it occupies the south side of Grays Harbor. The 18-mile stretch of flat beach is bordered on the south by Willapa Bay, across which lies the Long Beach Peninsula. At the north end of South Beach is the town of Westport, which is Washington's busiest sportfishing and whale watching port. Dividing North Beach and South Beach is the large bay known as Grays Harbor, on whose shores are the two lumber-mill towns of Aberdeen and Hoquiam. These towns were once some of the most prosperous in the state, as attested to by the stately Victorian mansions and imposing commercial buildings in the downtown of each. Unfortunately, these towns have yet to benefit from the prosperity that has overtaken the Puget Sound region and historic commercial buildings stand empty and abandoned. Still, there is history to be seen in these towns, though it is for the beaches, the fishing, and the clamming that most people visit this region.

ESSENTIALS

GETTING THERE   U.S. 12 connects Aberdeen with Olympia to the east, and U.S. 101 connects Aberdeen with Forks and Port Angeles to the north, and Long Beach and Astoria to the south. Ocean Shores and the North Beach area are 20 miles west of Aberdeen on Wash. 109. The South Beach area is 20 miles west of Aberdeen on Wash. 105.

There is bus service from Olympia to Aberdeen, Hoquiam, Westport, and Ocean Shores on **Grays Harbor Transit** (☎ 800/562-9730 or 360/532-2770). This same company also has buses that run north to Lake Quinault, where there are onward connections on other bus lines on around the Olympic Peninsula.

VISITOR INFORMATION   For more information on this area, contact the **Grays Harbor Chamber of Commerce,** 506 Duffy St., Aberdeen, WA 98520 (☎ 800/321-1924 or 360/532-1924), **Tourism Grays Harbor,** P.O. Box 225, Aberdeen, WA 98520 (☎ 800/621-9625), **Ocean Shores Chamber of Commerce,** P.O. Box 382, Ocean Shores, WA 98569 (☎ 800/76-BEACH or 360/289-2451), or the **Cranberry Coast Chamber of Commerce,** P.O. Box 305, Grayland, WA 98547 (☎ 800/473-6018 or 360/267-2003).

LEARNING ABOUT THE REGION'S HISTORY

Aberdeen and Hoquiam together comprise the largest urban area on the Washington coast and have long been dependent on the lumber industry, which once made this a very prosperous part of the state. If you're at all interested in the history of this region, there are several places here worth visiting. Don't miss **Hoquiam's Castle,** 515 Chenault Ave., Hoquiam (☎ 360/533-2005) if you like elegant old homes. This stately Victorian mansion was built in 1897 by a local timber baron and is an amazing assimilation of turrets and gables, balconies and bay windows. Restored in 1973, the "castle," as it came to be known by locals, is furnished with period antiques. It's open mid-June to Labor Day, daily from 11am to 5pm; the rest of the year, on

Saturday and Sunday from 11am to 5pm (closed in December). Admission is $4 for adults, $1 for children 15 and under.

The **Arnold Polson Museum,** 1611 Riverside Ave., Hoquiam (☎ **360/ 533-5862**), contains rooms full of antique furnishings and houses various collections including dolls, vintage clothing, Native American artifacts, and logging memorabilia. It's open in summer, Wednesday through Sunday from 11am to 4pm; other months, on Saturday and Sunday from noon to 4pm. Admission is $2 for adults, 50¢ for children.

The **Aberdeen Museum of History,** 111 E. Third St. (☎ **360/533-1976**), has similar displays and is open the same hours; admission is free.

If maritime history floats your boat, stop by the **Grays Harbor Historical Seaport,** 813 E. Heron St. (☎ **800/200-LADY** or 360/532-8611), where you can tour the *Lady Washington* when it is in the harbor ($3 adults, $2 seniors and students, $1 children ages 6 and under). This vessel is a replica of one of the ships Capt. Robert Gray sailed when he first explored the Northwest coast in 1788. The *Lady Washington* isn't always in port, but when it is, sailing excursions are available ($25 per person).

If you aren't here during the whale-watching season, you can at least have a look at a couple of whale skeletons at the **Westport Maritime Museum,** 2201 Westhaven Dr., Westport (☎ **360/268-0078**). Housed in a 1939 Coast Guard station, the museum contains Coast Guard exhibits, displays on early pioneer life in the area, and, in a glass-enclosed building outside, the skeletons of a minke whale, a gray whale, and part of a blue whale. The museum is open Wednesday through Sunday from noon to 4pm, and admission is $2 for adults and $1 for children.

FISHING, CLAMMING, WHALE WATCHING & OTHER OUTDOOR ACTIVITIES

The stretch of coast known as North Beach begins in the vacation and retirement community of Ocean Shores and stretches north for 30 miles to Taholah, on the Quinault Indian Reservation. In the southern section of North Beach, in Ocean Shores, low windswept dunes covered with beach grass back the wide, sandy beach. Kite flying and horseback riding are among the favorite activities here. Horses can be rented at the north end of Ocean Shores from **Chenois Creek Horse Rental,** which is located on the beach at the end of Damon Road (beside the Best Western Lighthouse Suites Inn) and charges $15 for a 1-hour ride. On the beach near the Shilo Inn on Ocean Shores Boulevard, you'll find **Rising Star Horse Rentals** (☎ **360/532-3273**), which charges similar rates. Also in Ocean Shores are 23 miles of canals and interconnecting lakes that are fun to explore. Canoes can be rented at **Summer Sails** (☎ 360/289-2884), which is located 1/2 mile north of the marina on Grand Canal Street. The flat roads of Ocean Shores are also good for bicycling, and bikes of various types can be rented from **This & That,** 748 Ocean Shores Blvd. NW (☎ **360/289-0919**); **Olympic Outdoors,** 773 Pt. Brown Ave. NW (☎ **360/ 289-3736**); or **Mac's Rentals,** 662 Ocean Shores Blvd. NW (☎ **360/289-9303**). If you're looking for a game of golf, head to the **Ocean Shores Golf Course,** Albatross and Canal Drive NE (☎ **360/289-3357**), an 18-hole course that charges $25 for a round of golf in the summer.

North of Ocean City, high bluffs, haystack rocks, secluded beaches, and dark forests create a more dramatic coastline. Along this stretch of coast there is **beach access** at Ocean City, Griffiths-Priday, and Pacific Beach state parks. **Razor clamming** is one of the most popular activities on the secluded beaches of this area. To try your hand at clamming, you'll need a license, a shovel, and a tide table. With all three in hand, head out to the beach at low tide and start looking for clam holes. When you spot one, dig fast. Good luck! Also, before heading out to the beach, find out if clamming season is open by calling the Westport Chamber of Commerce (☎ **800/345-6223**).

The 18 miles of coastline between Westport and Tokeland is called the South Beach or the Cranberry Coast, and along this stretch of beach, there are plenty of places to access the sand and surf. Four state parks provide the best facilities and easiest access. **Twin Harbors State Park** is 2 miles south of Westport and is the largest of the four, with more than 3 miles of beach. **Grayland Beach State Park** is just south of the town of Grayland and has less than a mile of beach. Both of these parks have nature trails, picnic areas, and campgrounds. Just outside the marina area of Westport is **Westhaven State Park** and just south of town is **Westport Light State Park,** where you'll find the popular Dune Trail, a paved 1-mile-long path that parallels the beach. These latter two parks are day-use areas only.

In the South Beach area, charter fishing, clamming, and whale watching are the big attractions, and most of the activity centers around the marina at Westport. Boats head out daily in summer in search of salmon, tuna, and bottom fish. If you'd like to try your luck at reeling in a big one, try **Bran Lee Charters** (☎ **800/562-0163** in Washington, or 360/268-9177), **Neptune Charters** (☎ **800/422-0425** or 360/268-0124), or **Deep Sea Charters** (☎ **800/562-0151** or 360/268-9300). Rates are between $50 and $100 for a day of fishing. In the fall, salmon fishing is also popular right off the docks in the Westport Marina.

Crabbing is another favorite area activity. To give crabbing a try, you'll need a crab trap (they can be bought or rented at the Westport Marina) and some bacon or chicken necks for bait. Find a spot on Westport's 1,000-foot-long pier, toss your trap over the side, and sit back and wait for the crabs to come to you—it's that easy. Clamming is also popular on the beaches along this stretch of coast.

Each year between February and May, gray whales migrating to the calving grounds off Baja California, Mexico, pass by the Washington coast. The whales sometimes come so close to the mouth of Grays Harbor that they can be seen from the observation tower at the marina in Westport. However, for a closer look, you might want to head out on a **whale-watching** boat trip. Contact one of the charter boat companies mentioned above if you're interested. Rates are between $20 and $25 for adults and between $12.50 and $17.50 for children.

All along the South Beach area between Grayland and Tokeland, you'll see **cranberry bogs** beside the highway. The cranberry harvest begins around Labor Day and continues on through October. To harvest the tart berries, the bogs are flooded, which causes the ripe berries to float on the surface of the water, where they can be easily scooped up mechanically.

Each year in late April and early May, Bowerman Basin in **Grays Harbor National Wildlife Refuge** becomes a staging ground for tens of thousands of Arctic-bound shorebirds. This is one of the largest gatherings of such birds on the West Coast and is also one of the state's biggest annual events for bird watchers. If you're a birder, you won't want to miss this impressive gathering. The wildlife refuge is adjacent to the Aberdeen/Hoquiam Airport on the west side of Hoquiam. For more information, contact the refuge headquarters (☎ **360/532-6237**).

Between mid-April and Labor Day, the **Westport Ocean Shores Passenger Ferry** (☎ **360/268-0047** in Westport or 360/289-3386 in Ocean Shores) connects Westport Marina with Ocean Shores (using the marina at the Silver King Motel, 1070 Discovery Ave. SE). The ferry leaves every $1^1/_2$ hours and charges $8 for a round-trip ticket. Service is offered on weekends between mid-April and mid-June and daily between mid-June and Labor Day.

WHERE TO STAY
OCEAN SHORES & THE NORTH BEACH AREA

If you can't get a room at any of the hotels listed below, contact the **Ocean Shores Reservations Bureau** (☎ **800/562-8612** or 360/289-2430), which handles reservations at nearly 20 hotels, motels, resorts, and condominiums. If you're looking to rent a vacation home that can accommodate the entire family, contact **Beach Front Vacation Rentals,** 759 Ocean Shores Blvd. (P.O. Box 685), Ocean Shores, WA 98569 (☎ **800/544-8887**).

The Caroline Inn. 1341 Ocean Shores Blvd. SW, Ocean Shores, WA 98569. ☎ **360/ 289-0450.** 4 suites (all with private bathrooms). TV. Summer, $125–$140 double; other months $99–$125 double. MC, V.

This modern rendition of an antebellum southern plantation home seems utterly incongruous on the windswept shore of the Washington coast, but its *Gone With the Wind* theme makes this inn both fun and luxurious. The four suites (each of which is named for a character from the movie) all have two floors, with a kitchen and living room on the lower floor and a bedroom and bathroom on the upper. In each bedroom you'll find a whirlpool tub for two that looks out on the crashing waves. All the suites also have fireplaces and VCRs (*Gone With the Wind* tapes are available).

✪ **Iron Springs Ocean Beach Resort.** P.O. Box 207, Copalis Beach, WA 98535. ☎ **360/ 276-4230.** Fax 360/276-4365. 28 cottages and apts. $66–$104 cottage or apt for two, $76– $130 cottage or apt for four. Three-night minimum stay in summer. AE, DISC, MC, V.

It's hard to imagine a more picture-perfect little cove than the one on which this rustic resort is set. Steep wooded hills surround the tiny cove, and at the mouth, a sandy beach begins. This is an isolated and little-developed stretch of beach, so even in summer you won't be bothered by crowds. The cottages here are scattered through the woods on a bluff overlooking the ocean and vary quite a bit in design, decor, and size. However, they're all modestly comfortable and have fireplaces and complete kitchens. Facilities include an indoor pool, hiking trail, playground, and an art gallery.

✪ **Ocean Crest Resort.** Sunset Beach, Moclips, WA 98562. ☎ **800/684-VIEW** or 360/ 276-4465. 45 units. TV TEL. $58–$129 double. Lower midweek rates Oct–Feb. AE, DISC, MC, V.

Perched high on a forested bluff and straddling a forested ravine, this hotel seems poised to go plummeting into the ocean below. You simply won't find a more spectacular location anywhere on the Washington coast. The accommodations vary from small studios with no view to two-bedroom apartments with full kitchens and fireplaces. However, our vote for best rooms goes to the large third-floor ocean-view studios. These have cathedral ceilings, fireplaces, and balconies. The hotel's restaurant has one of the best views at the resort, and is decorated in a Northwest motif. Steaks and seafood are the staples of the menu. The adjacent lounge is a great spot for a sunset drink. Facilities here include an indoor pool, whirlpool, sauna, exercise room, aerobics room, and playground. A wooden staircase winds down through the ravine to the beach.

The Sandpiper. P.O. Box A, Pacific Beach, WA 98571. ☎ **800/567-4737** or 360/276-4580. Fax 360/276-4464. 25 suites, 5 cabins. $80–$100 suite for two, $55–$85 cabin for two. Larger accommodations available. Two-night minimum for advance registration. MC, V.

Set into a steep slope and towered over by big firs, the buildings of the Sandpiper fit comfortably into this Northwest landscape. Their cedar shingles, weathered wood, and pier-like pilings all give the hotel a very beachy feel. What immediately grabs your attention is the dizzying view from the upper rooms, all of which are large suites. Far below you the ocean waves crash on the beach, and the distant roar lulls you to sleep at night. All the suites have kitchens, and all but one have fireplaces, so there's no need to leave this idyllic spot. What you won't find in any of the suites are TVs or phones, a big selling point at the Sandpiper—this is a place to relax.

IN HOQUIAM

✪ **Lytle House.** 509 Chenault St., Hoquiam, WA 98550. ☎ **800/677-2320** or 360/533-2320. Fax 360/533-4025. 8 rms (2 with shared bath), 2 suites. $75–$135 summer, $65–$105 winter. Rates include full breakfast. AE, MC, V.

If a tour of Hoquiam's Castle had you wishing you could stay there, walk right next door and ring the bell on the Lytle House. Equally grand and elegant, this Victorian painted lady was built by the brother of the man who built Hoquiam's Castle. The Lytle House offers antique-filled rooms, bathrooms with claw-foot tubs and heated towel racks, and a full breakfast, as well as an evening dessert. There are no fewer than four parlors where you can sit and relax with other guests, read a book, or even watch a classic movie on the VCR. Our favorite room is the Balcony Suite, which has, of course, a private balcony, as well as a private bathroom and separate claw-foot tub in the room. If you'd like to be able to look out your window at Hoquiam's Castle, opt for the Castle Room.

IN THE SOUTH BEACH AREA

Château Westport Motel. 710 Hancock St., Westport, WA 98595. ☎ **800/255-9101** or 360/268-9101. Fax 360/268-1646. 108 rms, 30 suites. TV TEL. $67–$76 double, $139–$220 suite. Rates include continental breakfast. Lower rates Oct–May. AE, DC, DISC, MC, V.

Though the use of *château* and *motel* in the same name may seem like a contradiction in terms, this is indeed a pleasant lodging. Attractively landscaped grounds and a location right on the beach make this a good place to park yourself for a few days of hanging out or exploring the region. Some rooms have their own fireplaces while others have kitchens; an indoor swimming pool and hot tub make this a good choice any time of year.

✪ **Tokeland Hotel.** 100 Hotel Rd., Tokeland, WA 98590. ☎ 360/267-7006. 18 rms, none with bath. $65 double. Rates include full breakfast. MC, V.

Located on the north shore of Willapa Bay, the Tokeland Hotel has been welcoming guests, though not continuously, since 1889. This area was once a popular summer resort, but when the steamers quit running from South Bend the hotel became too inaccessible. Today the Tokeland still feels remote. Lawns surround the inn, and beyond these lies the water. The first floor is taken up by a large open lobby and dining room, off which is a small library with a fireplace. Antique furnishings lend an air of authenticity to the inn. The rooms are arranged on either side of a long hall as they were at the turn-of-the-century and have painted wood floors. The shared bathrooms all have claw-foot tubs. The inn's moderately priced dining room is the most popular restaurant for miles around and is particularly noteworthy for its Sunday dinner, which includes a delicious cranberry pot roast.

CAMPGROUNDS

On Wash. 109 north of Ocean Shores are two state park campgrounds. **Pacific Beach State Park** (138 campsites) is a small, exposed, and crowded patch of sand with little to recommend it other than good razor clamming nearby. More appealing is **Ocean City State Park** (178 campsites), which at least has trees for protection against the wind. This is a good choice if you plan to bicycle along this stretch of coast.

WHERE TO DINE

IN THE OCEAN SHORES & NORTH BEACH AREA

The best restaurant in this region is the dining room at the Ocean Crest Resort (see above for details).

IN ABERDEEN

Billy's. 322 E. Heron St., Aberdeen. ☎ **360/533-7144.** Reservations not accepted. Main courses $6–$13. AE, MC, V. Mon–Thurs 6:30am–11pm, Fri 6:30am–midnight, Sat 7am–midnight, Sun 7am–9pm. AMERICAN.

Named for an infamous local thug, Billy's evokes Aberdeen's rowdier days as a lawless, Wild West timber town. There's a bar down the length of the room, a pressed-tin ceiling, and enough old paintings and prints to give this bar and grill just the right dance-hall atmosphere. The menu features everything from burgers to fresh oysters to T-bone steaks.

○ **Parma.** 116 W. Heron St., Aberdeen. ☎ **360/532-3166.** Reservations recommended. Main courses $9–$18. AE, DISC, MC, V. Tues–Thurs 4:30–9:30pm, Fri–Sat 4:30–10pm. ITALIAN.

This friendly little place is located in downtown Aberdeen and serves excellent northern and southern Italian dishes. Vol au vent (puff pasty filled with little raviolis) and polenta served with wild boar or rabbit are just two of the specialties here. There are also interesting daily specials, but surprisingly little seafood.

IN HOQUIAM

○ **Levee Street Restaurant.** 709 Levee St. ☎ **360/532-1959.** Reservations recommended. Main courses $12–$26; lunch main dishes $6–$11. AE, DISC, MC, V. Tues–Fri 11am–2pm and 4:30–9:30pm, Sat 4:30–9:30pm. CONTINENTAL/SEAFOOD.

Perched out over the river, the Levee is the antithesis of what you'd expect in a working port town like Hoquiam. The restaurant is tastefully decorated in subdued colors, and a big picture window takes in a view of the lazy river rolling by—it's a great spot for a romantic dinner. As you would expect in a coastal town, the menu revolves around seafood which shows up in fettuccine, on chicken, in bouillabaisse, and paired with steaks. Portions are both generous and well prepared. While creative sandwiches dominate the lunch menu, you can also get the likes of Parmesan-crusted rock fish.

IN THE SOUTH BEACH AREA

In addition to the restaurant listed here, another area favorite is the dining room at the historic Tokeland Hotel (see above for details).

Constantin's of Westport. 320 Dock St., Westport. ☎ **360/268-9353.** Reservations recommended. Main courses $10–$19. DISC, MC, V. Daily 7am–10pm. CONTINENTAL.

Located only half a block from the marina, Constantin's started out as a Greek restaurant, but when Greek didn't go over so well with the locals, the owner switched to a menu he calls European. However, there are still plenty of Greek dishes and daily specials available, and in my book these are still the meals to choose.

DRIVING ON TO LONG BEACH

Though it's only about 5 miles across the mouth of Willapa Bay to the northern tip of the Long Beach Peninsula, it's about 85 miles around to the town of Long Beach by road. Along the way you'll be skirting the shores of Willapa Bay. There aren't too many towns on this bay, which is why it's such a great place to raise oysters. Punctuating the miles of unspoiled scenery are oyster docks and processing plants. As you pass through the town of Raymond, keep an eye out for the 200 steel-plate sculptures that comprise the **Raymond Wildlife-Heritage Sculpture Corridor.** The majority of these sculptures are silhouettes that can be seen along U.S. 101 in the most unexpected places. Included are sculptures of Native Americans, modern sea kayakers, bicyclists, and dozens of wild animals.

The town of **South Bend,** where oystering reaches its zenith, claims to be the oyster capital of the world and holds its annual **Oyster Stampede** festival each year on Memorial Day weekend. South Bend's other claim to fame is its county **courthouse.** Though South Bend is the county seat today, back in 1892 it took a possibly rigged vote and armed force to wrest the title of county seat from Oysterville, across the bay on the Long Beach Peninsula. Construction of the new courthouse began 18 years later, and upon completion the imposing structure was dubbed a "gilded palace of extravagance." The majestic courthouse, seeming quite out of place in such a quiet backwater, stands on a hill overlooking the town. The copper dome is lined inside with stained glass, and there are murals decorating the interior walls. It's definitely worth a look.

If you're interested in a boat tour of Willapa Bay, contact **Willapa Discovery Tours** (☎ **360/875-5357** or 360/875-6641), which offers four different tours of the bay ranging in price from $15 to $28 per person.

WHERE TO STAY

The Russell House. 902 E. Water St. (P.O. Box F), South Bend, WA 98586. ☎ **888/484-6907** or 360/875-5608. 3 rms (all with private bathrooms). $60–$65 double. Rates include full breakfast. AE, MC, V.

Located high on a hill at the east end of town, this restored Victorian home was built in 1891 by a local architect. Consequently, it abounds in interesting details, including some of the most amazing interior woodwork you'll find in any B&B in the state. The Emerald Suite is the inn's largest and best room and comes with a cute bathroom with a claw-foot tub and a tiny, enclosed sunporch. Wicker furniture and a four-poster bed complete the picture. The Rose Room, decorated with lace and shades of pink, has its private bathroom across the hall.

WHERE TO DINE

Boondocks Restaurant. 1015 W. Robert Bush Dr., South Bend. ☎ **360/875-5155.** Main dishes $7.25–$19. MC, V. Summer, daily 8am–9pm, shorter house in other months. SEAFOOD.

Willapa Bay is Washington's most important oyster-farming area and even claims to be the "Oyster Capital of the World." If such boasts have you curious to taste some local oysters, the Boondocks is the place to stop. Whether it's the hangtown fry at breakfast, the pan-fried oysters at lunch, or barbecued oysters at dinner, this place gives you plenty of oyster options. You'll find Boondocks right on the highway, with windows overlooking the bay.

2 The Long Beach Peninsula

110 miles NW of Portland, 180 miles SW of Seattle, 80 miles W of Longview/Kelso

For more than 100 years folks have been flocking to these sandy shores to frolic in the sun, fly kites, and chow down on the local oysters and razor clams—and today the Long Beach Peninsula, a long narrow strip of low forest and sand dunes, is Washington's most developed stretch of beach. There are dozens of resorts, motels, rental cabins, vacation homes, and campgrounds up and down the peninsula.

Each of the peninsula's towns has its own distinct personality. In Seaview, there are restored Victorian homes. In Long Beach, go-cart tracks and family amusements hold sway. Klipsan Beach and Ocean Park are quiet retirement communities, while Nahcotta is still an active oystering port, albeit in a very attractive setting. Last and least is the tiny community of Oysterville, which is a National Historic District.

With 28 uninterrupted miles of sand, the Long Beach Peninsula claims to be the world's longest beach open to vehicles. With this much beach, it isn't surprising that the spring and summer razor-clamming season is one of the most popular times of year. This season is strictly regulated, with specific dates, times, and areas for clamming. Beaches are often closed to clamming because of "red tides," which cause shellfish to store large quantities of a toxin that causes amnesic shellfish poisoning. Always check at a local fishing supply store or motel to find out about restrictions.

Bivalves aren't the only seafoods that attract folks to the south coast. In Ilwaco, south of Long Beach, there is a fleet of charter fishing boats that can take you out in search of salmon, tuna, or bottom fish.

Long Beach is one of the few beaches on the West Coast that still allows vehicular traffic, so if you're of a mind to go for a drive on the beach, feel free. Just remember that the beach is a state highway and a 25-mph speed limit is enforced. There are beach access roads up and down the peninsula, and once you're on the beach, be sure you stay above the clam beds (sand nearest to the low-tide area) and below the dry sand.

ESSENTIALS

GETTING THERE The Long Beach Peninsula begins just off U.S. 101 in southwest Washington. U.S. 101 leads north to Aberdeen and south to Astoria, Oregon. Wash. 4 leads to Long Beach from Longview.

The Astoria Airport, across the Columbia River in Oregon, is served by Alaska Airlines.

VISITOR INFORMATION Contact the **Long Beach Peninsula Visitor's Bureau,** P.O. Box 562, Long Beach, WA 98631 (☎ **800/451-2542** or 360/642-2400), which operates a visitor center at the intersection of U.S. 101 and Pacific Avenue in Seaview.

GETTING AROUND **Pacific Transit System** (☎ **360/642-9418**) operates public buses that serve the area from Astoria in the south to Aberdeen in the north.

FESTIVALS Annual events in Long Beach include the **Ragtime Rhodie Dixieland Jazz Festival** in April; the **Sand-Sations** sand-sculptures tournament in July; the **Washington State International Kite Festival** in mid-August; the **Rod Run to the End of the World** in late August; the **Cranberrian Fair** in mid-October; and the **Water Music Festival** (chamber music) in late October.

SEEING THE SIGHTS

Nine miles east of Ilwaco on Wash. 103 near the Astoria-Megler Bridge, a 4^1/$_2$-mile-long span that connects Washington with Oregon, is **Fort Columbia State Park** (☎ **360/642-3078** or 360/642-3029), a former military base that guarded the mouth of the Columbia River from 1896 until the end of World War II. The park's wooded bluff has some picnic tables and a few short hiking trails past the old bunkers. The views from here are breathtaking. Today the 1903-vintage buildings have been restored and house historical displays and a youth hostel.

To learn more about the history of the area, stop by the **Ilwaco Heritage Museum,** 115 SE Lake St., Ilwaco (☎ **360/642-3446**). This modern museum houses displays on the history of southwest Washington with exhibits on Native American culture, exploration and development of the region, and a working model of the Columbia River estuary. The museum is open Monday through Saturday from 9am to 5pm and Sunday from noon to 4pm (Monday through Saturday from 10am to 4pm between October and April). Admission is $3 for adults, $2.50 for seniors, $2 for youths 12 to 17, and $1 for children 6 to 11.

Also in Ilwaco is the historic **Colbert House,** which is operated by the Washington State Parks and Recreation Commission. You'll find this restored home at the corner of Elizabeth and Lake streets. It's open Friday through Sunday from noon to 4pm between Memorial Day and Labor Day.

Anchoring the south end of the peninsula is forested **Fort Canby State Park** (☎ 360/642-3078), at the mouth of the Columbia River. The park is a former military installation used to guard the river mouth, and many of the bunkers and batteries are still visible. Also within the boundaries of the park are the North Head and Cape Disappointment lighthouses. The former is the windiest lighthouse on the West Coast and has sustained winds as high as 160 miles per hour. The latter lighthouse was built in 1856 and is the oldest lighthouse on the West Coast. The park is also home to the **Lewis and Clark Interpretive Center,** which chronicles the 1805–06 journey of the two explorers; it's open daily from 10am to 5pm and admission is free. Cape Disappointment, here in the park, was the end of the westward trail for Lewis and Clark. Also within the park are several picnic areas, hiking trails, a campground, and **Waikiki Beach,** the prettiest little beach between here and Moclips. This tiny cove backed by steep cliffs is named for several Hawaiian sailors who lost their lives near here. The park is open from dawn to dusk, and admission is free.

In the past 300 years more than 2,000 vessels and 700 lives have been lost in the treacherous waters at the mouth of the Columbia River, and consequently, the U.S. Coast Guard has its **National Motor Life Boat School** here. Lifeboat drills can be observed from observation platforms on the North Jetty. This jetty, completed in 1917, was built to improve the channel across the Columbia Bar. A side effect of the 2-mile-long jetty was the creation of a much wider beach to the north. This widening of the beach accounts for Long Beach's current distance from the waves.

If you're a kite flyer, or even if you're not, you may want to stop by the **World Kite Museum and Hall of Fame,** Third Street NW, Long Beach (☎ 360/642-4020), where you can see displays on kites of the world. It's open daily from 11am to 5pm in summer, Friday through Monday in September and October, and on Saturday and Sunday only November to May; admission is $1.50 for adults, $1 for seniors and children.

Up toward the north end of the peninsula, you'll find the historic village of **Oysterville,** an old oystering community that is a National Historic District and is by far the quaintest little village on the peninsula. Old homes with spacious lawns cling to the edge of the marsh. In the days of the California gold rush, Oysterville was shipping tons of oysters to San Francisco, where people were willing to pay as much as $50 a plate for fresh oysters. Today Oysterville is a sleepy little community of restored homes. In the town's white clapboard church there are occasional music performances.

Willapa Bay, which is one of the cleanest estuaries on the West Coast, is still known for its **oysters.** Up and down the peninsula there are oyster farms and processing plants. If you're interested in learning more about the history of the area's oystering industry, drop by the **Willapa Bay Interpretive Center** (☎ 360/665-4547) on the breakwater beside The Ark Restaurant in Nahcotta. The interpretive center is open Friday through Sunday from 10am to 3pm between May 1 and Oct 30, and admission is free. The peninsula is also a major producer of cranberries, and if you take a drive down almost any side road north of Long Beach, you'll pass acres of **cranberry bogs.** If you have an overwhelming curiosity about cranberries, be sure to stop in at the **Pacific Coast Cranberry Museum,** 2500 Sandridge Rd., Ilwaco (☎ **360/642-4938**). The museum, which is on a demonstration cranberry farm, features exhibits on all the stages of cranberry growing both past and present and is open May 1 through December 15, Friday through Sunday from 10am to 3pm. Admission is free.

Fans of the bizarre won't want to miss **Marsh's Free Museum,** 400 S. Pacific Ave., Long Beach (☎ **360/642-2188**), a beachy gift shop filled with all manner of antique arcade games, oddities à la Ripley's Believe It or Not!, and best of all Jake the alligator man, who has been made famous by tabloids that rank this half-man, half-alligator creature right up there with aliens, Bigfoot, and the latest Elvis sighting. Across the street from Marsh's, you'll find one of the world's largest skillets, which is used for summer oyster feeds here in Long Beach. This skillet is actually a replacement for the town's original giant skillet which had grown rusty after too many years exposed to the elements. On this same corner is another park that has a kiosk filled with historic photos, most of which are of ships that wrecked along this stretch of coast. This corner gets our vote for Washington's weirdest intersection.

AREA ACTIVITIES: KITE FLYING, BIRD WATCHING & CLAMMING

Active vacations are the norm here on the Long Beach Peninsula, and there are plenty of activities to keep you busy. However, one activity you won't be doing much of is swimming in the ocean. Though it gets warm enough in the summer to lie on the beach, the waters here never warm up very much. Add to this unpredictable currents, rip tides, undertows, and heavy surf and you have an ocean that's just not safe for swimming.

Instead of swimming, the beach's number-one activity is **kite flying.** Strong winds blow year-round across the Long Beach Peninsula, and with its 28 miles of beach, you won't have to worry about kite-eating trees. You'll find several kite shops in Long Beach. Another very popular Long Beach activity is beachcombing. The most sought after treasures are hand-blown glass fishing floats used by Japanese fishermen.

Beach access is available up and down the peninsula, but the best beaches are at the peninsula's various state parks. The beaches of **Fort Canby State Park,** at the south end of the peninsula are the most dramatic, while those at **Leadbetter Point State Park** at the north end of the peninsula are among the most secluded. Just north of Ocean Park there is beach access at the small **Pacific Pines State Park,** and south of Ocean Park, there is additional beach access at the west section of **Loomis Lake State Park.** This latter park is named for a popular fishing lake that is in the park's east section.

If you've ever dreamed of riding a horse down the beach, you can make your dream come true here in Long Beach. At the corner of South Ninth Street and Boulevard, you'll find **Skipper's Horse & Pony Rentals** (☎ 360/642-3676), and at South Tenth Street, you'll find **Back Country Wilderness Outfitters** (☎ 800/665-6929 or 360/642-2576). A 1-hour ride will cost you $11.

Bicyclists will find that the flat roads of the Long Beach Peninsula are perfect for cycling, and with the numerous state parks up and down the peninsula, there are plenty of good places to stop. Bike rentals are available from **Long Beach Bike Shop,** 11th Street North and Pacific Highway, Long Beach (☎ 360/642-7000). There is also a 2-mile-long gravel biking and walking path called the **Dune Trail** right in the town of Long Beach. This trail parallels the beach from 17th Street South to 16th Street North.

If you'd just like to get away from the crowds and find a piece of isolated shoreline to call your own, head to Leadbetter Point at the peninsula's northern tip. Here you'll find both **Leadbetter Point State Park Natural Area** and a portion of the **Willapa National Wildlife Refuge.** This area is well known for its variety of birds. More than 100 species have been seen here, including the snowy plover, which nests at the point. Because the plovers nest on the sand, a portion of the point is closed to all visitors from April to September. During these months you can still hike the trails, use the beach, and explore the marshes.

Because all the oysters are privately owned, you aren't allowed to collect them. However, you can **dig for razor clams,** in season, up and down the peninsula. These long, narrow clams are best harvested on a low, or minus, tide, when it's easy to spot the holes made by the clams. All you'll need to go clamming is a clamming license, a clam shovel (available at hardware stores throughout the area), and a tide table. Keep in mind that there are seasons, hours, and limits for clamming, so check with a local before heading out.

At Ilwaco, you'll find charter boats that will take you out fishing for salmon, halibut, sturgeon, or bottom fish. Try **Pacific Salmon Charters** (☎ **800/831-2695** or 360/642-3466), **Sea Breeze Charters** (☎ **360/642-2300**), or **Coho Charters** (☎ **360/642-3333**).

Long Island, in the middle of Willapa Bay, is part of the Willapa National Wildlife Refuge, which has its headquarters about 9 miles up U.S. 101 from Seaview. The island is known for its grove of huge old red cedars and is popular with sea kayakers. There are a few campsites and some hiking trails. During the summer months, **Willapa Bay Excursions** (☎ **360/665-5557**) operates a boat tour around Long Island. These 3¹/₂-hour trips leave from Nahcotta and cost $38 for adults and $19 for children under age 12.

WHERE TO STAY

If you're heading down this way with the whole family and need an entire vacation home, contact **Pacific Realty Property Management,** 102 Bolstad St. N. (P.O. Box 397), Long Beach, WA 98631 (☎ **888/879-5479** or 360/642-4549), which handles about 20 vacation homes. Alternatively, you can contact the Long Beach Peninsula's Visitors Bureau (see above), which maintains a list of most of the vacation homes in the area.

✪ **Boreas Bed & Breakfast.** 607 N. Boulevard (P.O. Box 1344), Long Beach, WA 98631. ☎ **888/642-8069** or 360/642-8069. 5 rms (3 with private bathrooms). $95–$100 double with shared bath, $105–$125 double with private bath. Rates include full breakfast. AE, DISC, MC, V.

Although this inn is housed in a renovated 1920s beach house, you would never guess it from the contemporary styling both outside and within. The inn is only a few blocks from downtown Long Beach and is separated from the beach by only the grassy dunes between you and the beach. The upstairs rooms have the best views, but, with their spaciousness and private decks, the two downstairs rooms are also very comfortable. One of these downstairs rooms was formerly a sunroom and has two walls of windows. This room also has a whirlpool tub in the bathroom. On the grounds, there is an enclosed gazebo housing a whirlpool spa.

✪ **Caswell's on the Bay Bed & Breakfast Inn.** 25204 Sandridge Rd., Ocean Park, WA 98640. ☎ **888/553-2319** or 360/665-6535. www.site-works.com/caswells. 5 rms (all with private bathrooms). $95–$115 double; $115–$150 suite. Rates include full breakfast. MC, V.

With its secluded setting on three acres of estate-like grounds heavily planted with rhododendrons, this modern Victorian inn is a tranquil retreat from the everyday world. While there is a porch that meanders around most of the house, it is not nearly as inviting as the Adirondack chairs on the lawn. From these you can gaze across the bay at the distant mountains. Inside the inn, you'll find a comfortable parlor with a fireplace, as well as a sunroom. Guest rooms are all furnished with antiques, but only two have bay views. Of these the Terrace Suite is the more spacious and has its own terrace. Of the garden view rooms, the Turret Suite is the best choice.

Chick-a-Dee Inn at Ilwaco. 120 Williams St. NE, Ilwaco, WA 98624. ☎ **800/CHICKAD** or 360/642-8686. Fax 360/642-8642. 10 rms. $69–$150 double. Rates include full breakfast. MC, V.

Built on a wooded hilltop on the outskirts of tiny Ilwaco at the south end of the Long Beach Peninsula, this inn is a former Presbyterian church. Though the church itself now serves as a theater and dining room (open to guests only), an attached building, which once served as Sunday school and minister's home, now houses the inn's guest rooms. The decor is simple, with plenty of nautical decor. Ilwaco makes a good base for exploring both the Long Beach Peninsula and Astoria.

Klipsan Beach Cottages. 22617 Pacific Hwy., Ocean Park, WA 98640. ☎ **360/665-4888.** 9 cottages. Summer, $80 double. Lower rates Oct–May. MC, V.

Set under the trees on the edge of the dunes that lead to the beach, these renovated beach cottages capture the less hectic spirit of turn-of-the-century seaside vacations. You can sit in your comfortable one-, two-, or three-bedroom cottage and gaze out over the dunes at glorious sunsets. The cottages have fireplaces and kitchenettes.

Moby Dick Hotel. Sandridge Rd. and Bay Ave., Nahcotta, WA 98637. ☎ **360/665-4543.** Fax 360/665-6887. 10 rms, 1 with bath. $60–$80 double without bath, $70–$90 double with bath. Rates include full breakfast. AE, MC, V.

Though it looks a bit like a big yellow bunker from the outside, the Moby Dick is actually a comfortable, though eclectically furnished, bed-and-breakfast inn. Built as a hotel back in 1930, the year before the train stopped running, the hotel quickly fell on hard times. Today it's a casual place that captures the spirit of small historic hotels. The location, up at the north end of the peninsula, is removed from the beach strip of Seaview and Long Beach, and is convenient to Leadbetter Park and its wild dunes and beaches. You'll also be within walking distance of the Ark Restaurant & Bakery (see below). Low rates, friendly atmosphere, and a tranquil setting make this a great choice. There is a sauna for taking off the chill, and each year in August, dinners are available in the dining room.

✪ Our House in Nahcotta. P.O. Box 33, Nahcotta, WA 98637. ☎ **360/665-6667.** 2 suites. $85–$95 suite for two. Rates include full breakfast. MC, V. In Nahcotta, turn west on 268th St. and then right onto Dell Rd.

This romantic little shingle-sided cottage, a cross between a forest cottage and a beach bungalow, is set at the end of a quiet lane and is surrounded by colorful gardens. The setting is light-years away from the bustle of Long Beach, which makes this a great spot for a relaxing weekend getaway. Part of the inn used to be the Nahcotta Schoolhouse, but it has since been added onto and updated. Today the house wears a Victorian look both inside and out.

✪ Shelburne Country Inn. 4415 Pacific Hwy., Seaview, WA 98644. ☎ **800/INN-1896** or 360/642-2442. Fax 360/642-8904. 13 rms, 2 suites. $99–$145 double; $175 suite. Rates include full breakfast. AE, MC, V.

Though it isn't exactly in the country, the Shelburne Inn might just as well be surrounded by acres of pastures and woods. At least that's the feeling you get the moment you walk through the door. Traffic noises disappear and a pale light, filtered by walls of stained-glass windows salvaged from a church in England, suffuses the entry. To your right is the inn's Shoalwater Restaurant, one of the best on the peninsula, and to your left is the Heron and Beaver Pub, which serves delicious food and Northwest microbrews. Through the second door, dark fir-paneled walls, a big oak table, and a fire crackling on the hearth all extend a classic country welcome. Most guest rooms are on the second floor, but there are a couple of suites on the ground floor. These overlook the gardens and have their own decks. Other rooms vary in size and decor, and those that are on the street side of the inn have stained-glass or frosted windows to screen your view of the street.

Sunset View Resort. P.O. Box 399, Ocean Park, WA 98640. ☎ **800/272-9199** or 360/665-4494. Fax 360/665-6528. 52 rms. TV TEL. May–Sept $65–$99 double; seasonal discounts from Oct–Apr. AE, CB, DC, DISC, MC, V.

About midway up the peninsula, you'll find this attractive motel set back in the woods a bit on the far side of a little bridge. Tall fir trees and attractive gardens surround the resort, and out back, dunes stretch for 100 yards to the beach. Many of the rooms come equipped with kitchens, which makes this a good choice for families; some rooms also have fireplaces and balconies. Though there isn't a pool here, you'll find a sauna, a whirlpool, a volleyball court, horseshoes, a playground, and a picnic area.

CAMPGROUNDS

The only campground in this area worth recommending is **Fort Canby State Park** (254 campsites), which is at the southern end of the Long Beach Peninsula at the mouth of the Columbia River. This park has campsites on a small lake, as well as some at the foot of North Head. Some of the sites in the latter area are tucked in amid massive boulders. For reservations call **Reservations Northwest** (☎ **800/452-5687**).

WHERE TO DINE

If you're struck with an espresso craving while in Long Beach, head for **Pastimes,** Oceanic Building, South Fifth Street and Pacific Avenue (☎ **360/642-8303**), where you can do a little shopping while you sip a tall skinny half-caf latte and enjoy a pastry, salad, or sandwich. You'll know the moment you see the pies at **My Mom's Pie Kitchen,** 4316 Pacific Ave. (☎ **360/642-2342**), that they're the real McCoy—flaky and simply oozing fruit filling. For smoked salmon and oysters, fresh fish and crab, and fresh clam chowder, stop in at **P&K Crab & Seafood Market,** 25312 Vernon St. (☎ **800/519-3518** or 360/665-6800).

✪ The Ark Restaurant & Bakery. Peninsula Rd., Nahcotta. ☎ **360/665-4133.** Reservations highly recommended. Main courses $10–$20. DC, DISC, MC, V. July to mid-Sept, Tues–Sat 5–10pm, Sun 11am–3pm and 4–9pm; other months shorter hours. NORTHWEST.

Located at the north end of the Long Beach Peninsula in what's called "little old Nahcotta," the Ark is a gustatory sanctuary in the wilderness. Set at the foot of a working dock and surrounded by oyster canneries and huge piles of oyster shells, the Ark has its own oyster beds, as well as its own herb and edible-flower garden. You can be sure that whatever you order here will be absolutely fresh, and that's exactly what has kept the Ark afloat since 1981. The Ark's all-you-can-eat oyster feed ($18) is the all-time favorite here, if you love oysters, this meal is definitely one not to miss. Garlic lovers will also find Nirvana here. If you have a sweet tooth, however, you might want to opt for one of the light meals so you can save room for one of the Ark's excellent desserts.

✪ **Cheri Walker's 42nd Street Cafe.** 42nd St. and Pacific Highway, Seaview. ☎ **360/ 642-2323.** Reservations recommended. Main dishes $8–$20. MC, V. Summer, Sun–Thurs 7am– 2pm and 4:30–9pm, Fri–Sat 7am–2pm and 4:30–9:30pm; other months shorter hours. AMERICAN/NORTHWEST.

Cheri Walker used to be the chef at the acclaimed Shoalwater Restaurant just up the street, and since taking over the much more casual 42nd Street Cafe, she has been cooking up a storm. Housed in a cozy little cottage, this restaurant is open for three meals a day, much to the delight of visitors in search of a good breakfast or lunch. At dinner the menu ranges from classic comfort foods such as meat loaf and skillet-fried chicken to great pastas and steaks.

Sanctuary Restaurant. U.S. 101 and Hazel St. ☎ **360/777-8380.** Reservations highly recommended. Main courses $10–$20. AE, MC, V. Summer, Wed–Sat 5–9pm, Sun 5–8pm; other months Thurs–Sun only. CONTINENTAL/SCANDINAVIAN.

Located in the community of Chinook, between Long Beach and the Astoria-Megler Bridge, and built in 1906, the Sanctuary was once the town's Methodist Episcopal Church. In 1983, the church was converted into a restaurant, and people have been flocking to the doors ever since. The church has changed very little since its days as a house of worship. Pews are used for bench seating at the tables, though if you manage to get a table on the altar, you may wind up in the minister's thronelike chair. The menu includes such staples as pan-fried oysters, as well as more creative preparations, but the Scandinavian dishes are the real specialty here.

✪ **The Shoalwater Restaurant/Heron and Beaver Pub.** In the Shelburne Country Inn, Wash. 103 and 45th St., Seaview. ☎ **360/642-4142.** Reservations highly recommended. Main courses $15–$25; pub entrees $7–$12. AE, CB, DC, DISC, MC, V. Restaurant, daily 5:30–9pm. Pub, daily 11:30am–3pm and 5:30–9pm. NORTHWEST.

Not only is the Shoalwater one of the best restaurants on the Long Beach Peninsula, it's one of the best restaurants in the Northwest. Stained-glass windows salvaged from a church in England suffuse the elegant dining room with a soft light, while oak furnishings and deep forest-green wallpaper evoke the Victorian era during which the Shelburne Inn was built. The menu changes frequently but you can be sure you'll find creative dishes perfectly prepared with the freshest Northwest ingredients. Since this is cranberry country, you might want to start your meal with an appetizer of pâté with cranberry chutney and roasted garlic aioli.

Across the entry from the Shoalwater, you'll find the more casual Heron and Beaver Pub, which serves equally creative but lighter fare. Prices are considerably lower than they are at the Shoalwater, and both lunch and dinner are served.

UP THE COLUMBIA RIVER

Between the Long Beach Peninsula and I-5 at Longview lies one of the state's most enjoyable and little known scenic drives. Wash. 4 passes through several small historic riverfront communities and between Cathlamet and Longview runs right alongside the Columbia River, often at the base of steep hillsides or basalt cliffs. The quiet backwaters along this stretch of the river seem little changed by the passing of time.

Heading east from Long Beach on U.S. 101, you first skirt the south end of Willapa Bay, which is the site of the Willapa National Wildlife Refuge. Each year in late April and early May, this area becomes a rest stop for thousands of birds heading north to summer breeding grounds in the Arctic. Roughly 20 miles east of the junction of U.S. 101 and Wash. 4, you'll come to the **Grays Harbor covered bridge,** which was erected in 1905 and is the only covered bridge in Washington. The bridge is a short distance off the highway.

East of Grays River, watch for the turn-off for Wash. 403, which leads 7 miles south to the community of **Altoona,** where a cannery built in 1903 still stands on piling just off shore. This is one of the only such canneries still standing along the lower Columbia River.

Another 15 miles east, you'll come to the tiny community of **Skamokawa** (pronounced Skuh-*mah*-kuh-way), which is one of the only remaining fishing villages from the early 20th century, when salmon canneries abounded along the Columbia River. Here you can visit the **River Life Interpretive Center,** which is housed in Redmen Hall, a restored 1894 schoolhouse. Just east of Skamokawa lies the Julia Butler Hansen National Wildlife Refuge, which protects the rare Columbia River white-tailed deer.

East of the refuge, you come to Cathlamet, which was settled in 1846 and is the largest town on this stretch of road. Here you can visit the **Wahkiakum Historical Museum** and learn about the early pioneer history of the region and see old fishing exhibits. June through September, the museum is open Tuesday through Sunday from 1 to 4pm; other months Thursday through Sunday only. Admission is $1. Cathlamet is connected by bridge to **Puget Island,** which was settled by Scandinavian fishermen in the late 1800s. Today the island is covered with farms and is a popular spot with bicyclists. The flat, uncrowded roads and river views make for an ideal day's bicycle tour. The island is connected to Oregon by the last ferry on the Columbia River.

East of Cathlamet begins the most picturesque portion of this drive, with the cliffs of Little Cape Horn marking the start of this scenic stretch of road. Due to its strong winds, the Little Cape Horn area is popular with boardsailors.

WHERE TO STAY

Bradley House/Country Keeper Bed & Breakfast. 61 Main St. (P.O. Box 35), Cathlamet, WA 98612. ☎ **800/551-1691** or 360/795-3030. 4 rms (2 with private bathrooms). $75–$90 double. Rates include full breakfast. MC, V.

Cyclists wishing to spend a day exploring Puget Island and not wanting to drive home at the end of the day can stay the night in downtown Cathlamet in this restored Eastlake Victorian home overlooking the Columbia River. The house, which was built in 1907 by a local lumber baron, sits high above the main road through town and abounds in beautiful polished woodwork inside. Cathlamet's modest downtown is less than a block away.

3 Vancouver & Vicinity

6 miles N of downtown Portland; 120 miles SE of Long Beach; 40 miles S of Longview

Because Vancouver, Washington, is part of the Portland metropolitan area, and because it bears the same name as both a large island and a city in Canada, it is often overlooked by visitors to the Northwest. However, the city has several historic sites and other attractions that make it a good day-long excursion from Portland. The first three attractions listed here are all in the one-square-mile Central Park, which is located just east of I-5 (take the East Mill Plain Boulevard exit just after you cross the bridge into Washington).

It was here, at the Hudson's Bay Company's Fort Vancouver, that much of the Northwest's important early pioneer history unfolded. The HBC, a British company, came to the Northwest in search of furs and for most of the first half of the 19th century was the only authority in this remote region. Fur trappers, mountain men, missionaries, explorers, and settlers all made Fort Vancouver their first stop in Oregon.

ESSENTIALS

GETTING THERE   Vancouver is located on I-5 just north across the Columbia River from Portland, Oregon. I-205 bypasses the city to the east, while Wash. 14 heads east up the Columbia Gorge.

The city is served by both Amtrak trains and Greyhound buses. With the Portland International Airport just across the river, Vancouver is also well connected to the rest of the world via numerous airlines.

VISITOR INFORMATION   For more information on this area, contact the **Vancouver/Clark County Visitors & Convention Bureau,** 404 E. 15th St., Suite 11, Vancouver, WA 98663 (☎ **800/377-7084** or 360/693-1313).

VANCOUVER'S HISTORICAL ATTRACTIONS

Today the **Fort Vancouver National Historic Site,** 1501 E. Evergreen Blvd. (☎ **360/696-7655**), houses several reconstructed buildings that are furnished as they might have been in the middle of the 19th century (open daily 9am to 5pm, until 4pm in the winter; admission $2 in summer, free in winter).

After the British gave up Fort Vancouver, it became the site of the Vancouver Barracks U.S. military post, and stately homes were built for the officers of the post. These buildings are now preserved as the Officers' Row National Historic District. You can stroll along admiring the well-kept homes, and then stop in at the **Grant House Folk Art Center** (☎ **360/694-5252**), which is named for Pres. Ulysses S. Grant, who was stationed here as quartermaster in the 1850s. Open Tuesday through Sunday from 10am to 5pm in summer (shorter hours other months), this building was the first commanding officer's quarters. In addition to the art center, there is a cafe that serves good lunches. Further along Officers' Row, you'll find the **George C. Marshall House** (☎ **360/693-3103**), which is also open to the public. This Victorian-style building replaced the Grant House as the commanding officer's quarters. The Marshall House is open Monday through Friday from 9am to 5pm. You'll find the tree-shaded row of 21 homes just north of Fort Vancouver.

A very different piece of history is preserved at **Pearson Air Museum,** 1115 E. Fifth St., (☎ **360/694-7026**) on the far side of Fort Vancouver from Officers' Row. This airfield was established in 1905 and is the oldest operating airfield in the United States. Dozens of vintage aircraft, including several World War I–era biplanes and the plane that made the first trans-Pacific flight, are on display in a large hangar. The museum is open Wednesday through Sunday from noon to 5pm, and admission is $4 for adults, $3 for seniors, and $1.50 for students.

EXPLORING OUTSIDE OF TOWN

In the town of Washougal, 16 miles east of Vancouver on Wash. 14, you can visit the **Pendleton Woolen Mills and Outlet Shop,** 217th St., Washougal (☎ **360/835-2131**), and see how the famous wool blankets and classic wool fashions are made. The store is open Monday through Friday from 8am to 5pm and Saturday from 9am to 5pm, with free mill tours offered Monday through Friday at 9, 10, and 11am, and 1:30pm.

Railroading buffs may want to drive north 10 miles to the town of Battle Ground and take a ride on the diesel-powered **Lewis River Excursion Train,** which has its depot at 1000 E. Main St. in Battle Ground (☎ **360/687-2626**). The 2-hour excursions run from Battle Ground to Moulton Falls County Park, where there is a 20-minute stop for passengers to view the falls. There are also dinner train excursions. Call ahead for the days and hours of scheduled trips. Tickets for the regular excursion are $10 for adults and $5 for children.

North of Vancouver 23 miles in the town of Woodland are the **Hulda Klager Lilac Gardens,** 115 S. Pekin Rd., Woodland (☎ 360/225-8996). Between late April and Mother's Day each year, these gardens burst into color and the fragrance of lilacs hangs in the air. The gardens are open daily from dawn to dusk and admission is $1.

Ten miles east of Woodland off NE Cedar Creek Road, you'll find the **Cedar Creek Grist Mill,** Grist Mill Road (☎ 360/225-9552), the only remaining 19th-century grist mill in Washington. Built in 1876, the mill was restored over a 10-year period, and in 1989 once again became functional. When the mill is open, volunteers demonstrate how wheat is ground into flour. Hours of operation are Saturday from 1 to 4pm and Sunday from 2 to 4pm. Admission is by donation.

WHERE TO STAY

Doubletree Hotel at the Quay. 100 Columbia St., Vancouver, WA 98660. ☎ **800/ 222-TREE** or 360/694-8341. Fax 360/694-2023. 160 rms, 3 suites. $85–$120 double; $185–$339 suite. AE, CB, DC, DISC, MC, V.

This aging convention hotel is Vancouver's only waterfront lodging, which alone makes it recommendable. However, it is also at one end of the 4-mile-long Waterfront Trail, a paved walkway along the river. Guest rooms are comfortable if nothing special. Rooms with two queens are cramped; those with a single king feel roomier.

Dining: The Pacific Grill & Chowder House features an interesting nautical decor that includes all sorts of ship's rigging, including furled sails. This nautical theme continues in the lounge.

Services: Room service, valet/laundry service.

Facilities: An outdoor swimming pool.

Vintage Inn Bed & Breakfast. 310 W. 11th St., Vancouver, WA 98660. ☎ **888/693-6635** or 360/693-6635. 4 rms (all with shared bathroom). $70–$75 double. Rates include full breakfast. MC, V.

Although Vancouver is long on history, it is short on B&Bs in old homes. This is the only B&B option in downtown Vancouver, but even if it weren't, it would still be a pleasant place to stay. Located only two blocks from downtown shops and restaurants, the inn is a 1903 home that abounds in leaded glass and polished woodwork. The two parlors are tastefully decorated with antiques and there is a fireplace in the formal dining room. One of the rooms has a sunporch, though the former master bedroom is the largest room. In the shared bathroom, you'll find the original claw-foot tub.

WHERE TO DINE

When it's time for a pint of craft ale, the place to head in Vancouver is **McMenamins on the Columbia,** 1801 SE Columbia River Dr. (☎ **360/699-1521**), a brew pub with a view.

Beaches Restaurant & Bar. 1919 SE Columbia River Dr. ☎ **360/699-1592.** Reservations recommended. Main dishes $6.50–$20.50; lunch main courses $6.50–$12.50. AE, DISC, MC, V. Mon 11am–9pm, Tues–Fri 11am–10pm, Sat noon–10pm, Sun noon–9pm. INTERNATIONAL.

Sure it's a long way to the beach, but why let that stop you having a good time. That seems to be the attitude of this waterfront restaurant. The gardens are full of sand and a party atmosphere prevails most of the time (there are early and late happy hours). The menu is long and includes everything from burgers to taco pizza to smoked salmon ravioli with rock shrimp. A wood oven produces some of the better items on the menu, including the flaming wings and baby back ribs. With big walls of glass overlooking the river, sunset dinners are very popular. Despite the large size, service is usually good. To reach the restaurant from I-5, take Wash. 14 east and then take exit 1.

✪ **Sheldon's Cafe at the Grant House.** 1101 Officers' Row. ☎ **360/699-1213.** Reservations recommended. Main dishes $12–$17. MC, V. Tues–Thurs 11am–2pm and 5–9pm, Fri 11am–2pm and 5–10pm, Sat 5–10pm. REGIONAL AMERICAN.

If you're only in town for the day and are exploring the historic buildings that surround Vancouver's Central Park, this is the ideal place to stop for lunch or dinner. Located in the Grant House, the oldest building still standing at Vancouver Barracks, Sheldon's Cafe shares space with a crafts center, and together both establishments place a heavy emphasis on early American style. The menu features dishes from different regions of the U.S. including a New England fisherman's stew, a southern chicken bourbon John, midwestern hickory-smoked pork and chicken, and panfried Northwest oysters. In the summer, there are tables on the building's veranda and on the garden patio out back. A sunroom provides a cheery setting even when the weather isn't.

✪ **Hidden House.** 100 W. 13th St. ☎ **360/696-2847.** Reservations recommended. Main dishes $14–$23. AE, MC, V. Mon 11am–2pm, Tues–Thurs 11am–2pm and 5–9pm, Fri 11am–2pm and 5–10pm, Sat 5–10pm. CONTINENTAL/NORTHWEST.

In business for 22 years, the Hidden House, located right in downtown, has long been Vancouver's main special-occasion restaurant. The restaurant is housed in a brick home that was built in 1884, and inside, all is dark and cozy, with antique touches that conjure up the 19th century. The menu has a little bit for almost every taste, with steaks, oysters Rockefeller, and shrimp scampi for traditionalists, and the likes of Cuervo prawns, halibut with lemon thyme–apple salsa, and pork tenderloin with peach salsa for more adventurous palates. If you're searching for the very best Vancouver has to offer, this is it.

10 The Washington Cascades

Cloaked in places by dark forests of old-growth trees and stripped bare by logging clear-cuts in others, the Washington Cascades are a patchwork quilt of narrow valleys, rolling foothills, snow-capped volcanic peaks, and rugged mountain ranges. Lakes of the deepest blue are cradled beneath emerald forests. Glaciers carve their way inexorably from peaks that experience some of the heaviest snowfalls in the nation. (It's possible to drive or hike almost to the edge of several of these glaciers and listen to their cracking and rumbling as gravity pulls at their centuries-old ice.) And the appropriately-named Cascades send countless waterfalls cascading from the heights.

From the Canadian border south more than 150 miles to Olympia, along the shores of Puget Sound, lies the most densely populated region of the state, yet for the millions of people who live here, gazing upon mountain wilderness merely requires a look eastward on a clear day. Dominating the eastern skyline of northern Puget Sound are volcanic Mount Baker and the North Cascades. In the southern regions of the sound, Mount Rainier, another dormant volcano, looms grandly on the horizon. It's the easy accessibility of these mountains that helps make the cities of Puget Sound so livable. With two national parks, a national volcanic monument, a half dozen major ski areas, one of the largest networks of cross-country ski trails in the country, hundreds of lakes (including the third-deepest lake in the United States), a Bavarian village, and a false-fronted Wild West frontier town, these mountains offer a diversity of recreational and sightseeing activities. Whatever the season, in good weather and bad, active Washingtonians head for the hills whenever they get the chance. In spring they come for the wildflowers, in summer for the hiking, in autumn for the leaf changes, and in winter for the skiing.

1 Mount Baker & the North Cascades Scenic Highway

Diablo Lake: 66 miles E of Burlington (I-5), 65 miles W of Winthrop
Mount Baker Ski Area: 62 miles E of Bellingham

Wolves and grizzly bears still call this wilderness home, and names such as Mount Fury, Mount Terror, and Forbidden Peak are testament to the rugged and remote nature of this terrain. Much of the region is preserved within the two units of North Cascades National

The Washington Cascades

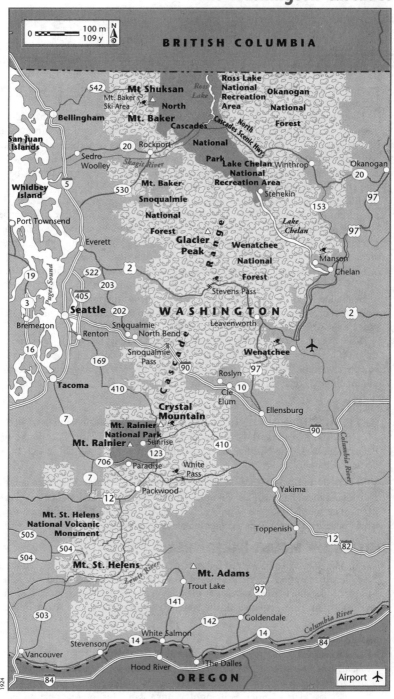

BRITISH COLUMBIA

Ross Lake
National
Recreation
Area

Okanogan
National
Forest

Mt Shuksan

Mt. Baker
Ski Area

North
Cascades

Bellingham

Mt. Baker

Cascades

National

Park

542

San Juan
Islands

Sedro
Woolley

Rockport

20

Skagit River

Lake Chelan
National
Recreation Area

Winthrop

Okanogan

20

97

Whidbey
Island

5

530

Mt. Baker-
Snoqualmie

National

Forest

Stehekin

153

97

Lake
Chelan

Port Townsend

Everett

Glacier
Peak

Wenatchee

National

Forest

Manson

Chelan

19

522

2

Stevens Pass

405

203

WASHINGTON

Leavenworth

2

Seattle

202

Snoqualmie

North Bend

Bremerton

Renton

Snoqualmie
Pass

Wenatchee

16

169

90

Roslyn

97

Tacoma

410

Cle
Elum

10

Ellensburg

90

Columbia River

7

Crystal
Mountain

Mt. Rainier
National Park

Mt. Rainier

Sunrise

706

123

410

7

Paradise

White
Pass

Yakima

Packwood

12

Mt. St. Helens
National Volcanic
Monument

505

504

Toppenish

12

82

504

Mt. St. Helens

Lewis River

Mt. Adams

Trout Lake

97

503

141

142

Goldendale

Columbia River

84

Stevenson

14

White Salmon

14

Vancouver

Hood River

The Dalles

84

OREGON

Airport ✈

0   100 m
    109 y

N

1924

Park, one of the least visited national parks in the country. This lack of visitors is easy to understand when you realize there is but one gravel road within the boundaries of the park, and this road originates in the community of Stehekin on the north shore of Lake Chelan. Stehekin can only be reached by hiking trail, floatplane, or boat, which has severely limited the number of vehicles that use this road. However, passing between the two units of the national park is the North Cascades Scenic Highway.

Though numerous attempts were made over the years to build a road through the craggy, glacier-sculpted North Cascade mountains, it was not until 1972 that Wash. 20 finally connected the Skagit Valley and the communities of northern Puget Sound with Winthrop on the east side of the North Cascades. Today the road is known as the North Cascades Scenic Highway, and it's one of the most breathtakingly beautiful stretches of road anywhere in the United States.

Unfortunately, because of heavy winter snows and avalanches, the road is only open from April to November (depending on the weather). The scenic highway begins east of Sedro Woolley, and along its length you'll find more than a dozen campgrounds. Backpackers can head off on hundreds of miles of trails through wilderness areas, national forest, national park, and national recreation areas.

Lying just outside the northwestern corner of North Cascades National Park is 10,778-foot Mount Baker, which, on a clear day dominates the skyline to the east of Bellingham and the San Juan Islands. This is the northernmost of Washington's Cascade Range volcanoes, and as such rises high above the surrounding North Cascade peaks, which are geologically unrelated to Mount Baker.

While it is the North Cascades Scenic Highway, with its mountain vistas and excellent hiking, that attracts most people to this area, the slopes of Mount Baker are equally rewarding both for hikers and those who simply want to gaze out at rugged mountain peaks or stroll through a mountain meadow.

ESSENTIALS

GETTING THERE   To reach Mount Baker ski area (and, in summer, Heather Meadows and Artist Point), head east from Bellingham on Wash. 542 (the Mount Baker Highway). The North Cascades Scenic Highway is Wash. 20, which leaves I-5 at Burlington.

VISITOR INFORMATION   For information on the Mount Baker area and the North Cascades National Park Complex, contact **North Cascades National Park,** 2105 Star Route 20, Sedro Woolley, WA 98284 (☎ **360/856-5700**, ext. 310), which operates an information center in conjunction with the U.S. Forest Service.

VISITING THE MOUNT BAKER AREA

Wash. 542, known as the Mount Baker Highway, is a dead-end road that climbs to 5,140 feet in elevation at a ridge between 10,778-foot Mount Baker and 9,038-foot Mount Shuksan. The road's end is at the aptly named Artist Point, an area of rugged beauty nearly unequaled in the state. Rising directly above Artist Point is

---

Impressions

No where do the mountain masses and peaks present such strange, fantastic dauntless and startling outlies as here.
            —Henry Custer, assistant of reconnaissance for International Boundary
                        Commission 1859, in reference to the North Cascades

flat-topped Table Mountain, up which there is a short but precipitous trail. Below Artist Point (3 miles by road) lie Heather Meadows and Picture Lake, in which the reflection of Mount Shuksan can be seen when the waters are still. Each year in July and August the meadows of this area burst into bloom and attract crowds of weekend hikers who tramp the many miles of trails that radiate out from here. Between mid-July and September, you'll also find a visitor center here with trail maps for the area and information on this region's unusual geology.

Two of the most popular and most rewarding hikes in the Mount Baker area actually originate not in the Heather Meadows/Artist Point area but off side roads 1 mile east of the town of Glacier. These are the **Heliotrope Ridge Trail** (off Forest Service Road 39) and the **Skyline Divide Trail** (off Forest Service Road 37). Both of these trails climb up through meadows with excellent views of Mount Baker and, from the Heliotrope Ridge Trail, impressive glacier views. Also near Glacier, at milepost 41, is a short trail that leads to 100-foot Nooksack Falls.

As of 1997, **parking permits** were required to park at national forest trailheads throughout most of Washington state. These permits cost $3 per day ($25 for an annual pass) and can be purchased at ranger stations and national forest visitor centers.

While Kodak-moment meadows of colorful wildflowers are a big attraction throughout the summer, Mount Baker is better known as the place where it snows more than 500 inches each winter. Consequently, **Mount Baker Ski Area** (☎ 360/ 671-0211 or 360/734-6771), located at Heather Meadows and one of the nation's snowboarding meccas, is well known throughout the region as being the first ski area to open and the last to close each year. Lift tickets range from $18 to $29.50. Snowboard rentals are available in the town of Glacier at **Mt. Baker Snowboard Shop,** 9996 Forest St. (☎ 360/599-2008), and ski and snowboard rentals are available at the ski area. Cross-country skiers will find a few kilometers of groomed trails at Mount Baker ski area, as well as many more miles at the **Salmon Ridge Sno-Park** further down the mountain. Telemark skiers and backcountry snowboarders will find lots of great terrain adjacent to Mount Baker ski area.

En route to or from Mount Baker, you can sample local wines at **Mount Baker Vineyards,** 4298 Mt. Baker Hwy., Deming (☎ 360/592-2300); and stock up on gourmet picnic foods at the unexpectedly hip **Everybody's Store,** Hwy. 9, Van Zandt (☎ 360/592-2297).

THE NORTH CASCADES SCENIC HIGHWAY

North of Concrete, which was named for the cement it once produced, lie Lake Shannon and Baker Lake, the latter being a popular summer camping and boating destination. From the road leading to **Baker Lake,** you can also access the **Mount Baker National Recreation Area,** which lies on the south side of Mount Baker. Several trails here lead through the beautiful alpine meadows on the south side of the mountain. The Railroad Grade–Paul Scott Trail is particularly breathtaking.

Between Concrete and Marblemount, the highway parallels the Skagit River, and from December to February each year, hundreds of bald eagles descend on this stretch of the river to feed on dying salmon. Highway turnouts at the prime eagle-watching sites along this stretch of road provide opportunities to observe the eagles. To learn more about the eagles, stop by Rockport's **Eagle Interpretive Center** (☎ 360/853-7009), which is located in the Rockport Fire Hall. The center is staffed Friday through Sunday during eagle-watching season. This center can also provide information on the annual Upper Skagit Eagles Festival, which takes place each year in late January or early February. The best way to do your eagle watching is from a raft floating slowly down the river (no white water here). Companies offering **eagle-watching float trips** include **Chinook Expeditions** (☎ 800/241-3451), **Alpine Whitewater** (☎ 800/926-RAFT), and **Downstream River Runners** (☎ 800/234-4644), all of which charge between $60 and $70 for a three-hour trip.

Right in the middle of the eagle-viewing area, you'll come to the town of Rockport, on the west side of which is **Rockport State Park** where you can take a hike through a stand of old-growth Douglas-firs, some of which are more than 300 years old. Three miles east of Rockport keep an eye out for **Cascadian Farm Roadside Stand** (☎ 360/853-8173), which sells organic berries during the summer months.

In Marblemount, the next town you come to, you'll find the **Wilderness Center** of the Ross Lake National Recreation Area (☎ 360/873-4500, ext. 37 or 39), which provides backcountry permits and information.

In the town of Newhalem, a picturesque Seattle City Light company town at the foot of the Gorge Dam, you'll find the **North Cascades Visitor Center** (☎ 206/386-4495), the main visitor center for the North Cascades National Park Complex, which includes North Cascades National Park, Ross Lake National Recreation Area, and Lake Chelan National Recreation Area. The visitor center is filled with interesting exhibits on this remote national park. There are several short hikes in the area, and in the autumn, you can see spawning salmon at the base of the hydro-power plant on the edge of town. There is also an attractively landscaped garden (reached by a swinging footbridge) surrounding this powerhouse. Continuing east from Newhalem, the road passes through a deep, narrow gorge, where you can glimpse **Gorge Creek Falls,** before reaching **Gorge Dam,** the first and smallest of the dams along this stretch of the Skagit River.

Beyond the Gorge Dam, you soon come to Diablo, another Seattle City Light company town, which stands at the base of Diablo Dam. Diablo is the starting point for one of the most fascinating excursions in this corner of the state—the 4-hour **boat tour of Diablo Lake.** The tours start with a trip up an incline railway to the top of 389-foot-tall Diablo Dam. From there you board a boat for the 5-mile cruise to Ross Lake Dam, where you get a tour of the powerhouse. At the end of all this, you get a chicken or vegetarian spaghetti dinner. Tours are offered Thursday through Monday between mid-June and late September and cost $25 for adults, $22 for seniors, $12.50 for children 6 to 11. There are also 1¹/₂-hour tours of **Diablo Dam,** for $5, not including the boat ride or dinner. For information, or to make a reservation (highly recommended), call **Seattle City Light** (☎ 206/233-2709).

Continuing on past Diablo, you cross the Thunder Arm of Diablo Lake and climb up to the spectacular **Diablo Lake Overlook.** When the sun shines, the glacier-fed lake displays an astounding turquoise color due to the suspended particles of silt in the water. High above the lake you can see glaciated Colonial and Pyramid peaks.

At the **Ross Lake Overlook,** several miles farther east, the dammed waters of this huge reservoir come into view. The lake, and in fact this entire stretch of highway from east of Marblemount to east of Ross Lake, is designated the **Ross Lake National Recreation Area.** The lake itself extends 24 miles north, with its northern shore lying 1¹/₂ miles inside Canada. The only access to the lake from the United States is by trail or water, and with its many shoreline backcountry campsites and East Bank Trail it is a popular backpacker destination. Sea kayakers also frequent these remote waters. See "Where to Stay," below, for information on the Ross Lake Resort, which offers both a water taxi service and shuttle that will haul your kayak or canoe around Ross Dam. Trails lead down to the lake both at the dam (before the Ross Lake Overlook) and east of the overlook (access to the East Bank Trail).

Natural History Seminars

Want to track radio-collared mountain caribou? Stalk newts, frogs, and salamanders in Heather Meadows? Learn about Lummi Indian basketry? Delve into the mysteries of mycology? Hang with some bats? You can do any of these things if you sign up for the right class through the North Cascades Institute. Offering more than 70 natural history field seminars each year, the **North Cascades Institute,** 2105 Star Route 20, Sedro Woolley, WA 98284-9394 (☎ **360/856-5700,** ext. 209) is a non-profit educational organization that offers a wide range of courses each year. While these seminars, many of which involve camping out, focus on the North Cascades region, there are programs throughout the state. The institute has plans to open a North Cascades Environmental Education Center in 1999.

However, hikers in search of mountain vistas and wildflower-filled meadows should hold out for **Rainy Pass** (and hope that the pass is not living up to its name). Here you'll find an easy paved trail to **Rainy Lake,** which can be combined with the strenuous, but astoundingly soul-satisfying, **Maple Pass Loop.** The view from Maple Pass is one of the finest in the Northwest. The Pacific Crest Trail also crosses the highway at Rainy Pass. If you head north along the Pacific Crest Trail, you will climb to Cutthroat Pass, with more superb views. A few miles farther east, you'll find the trailhead for the short, but steep, hike to picturesque **Blue Lake.**

Roughly 20 miles before reaching the Wild West town of Winthrop, you come to the most breathtaking stretch of the North Cascades Scenic Highway. Here, at **Washington Pass** (5,447 feet in elevation), the granite peak of Liberty Bell Mountain rises 2,200 feet above. Across the valley are the jagged Early Winter Spires, a full 200 feet taller than Liberty Bell Mountain. Below the pass the road has been blasted out of a steep cliff face in one huge switchback. At the pass, the Washington Pass Overlook, with its short walking trail, provides an opportunity to enjoy these last awesome vistas of the North Cascades. With its in-your-face view of craggy peaks, this is the North Cascade Scenic Highway's big payoff—this alone is worth the drive over the mountains.

WHERE TO STAY
IN THE MOUNT BAKER AREA

The best accommodations at the foot of Mount Baker are to be had through **Mt. Baker Lodging,** 7500 Mt. Baker Hwy., Maple Falls, WA (Mailing address: P.O. Box 5177, Glacier, WA 98244) (☎ **800/709-7669** or 360/599-2453), which rents out around 20 cabins. Rates range from $125 to $245 per night.

ALONG THE NORTH CASCADES SCENIC HIGHWAY

Clark's Skagit River Cabins & Resort. 5675 Wash. 20, Rockport, WA 98283. ☎ **800/ 273-2606** or 360/873-2250. Fax 360/873-4077. www.northcascades.com. 23 cabins. TV. $47– $107 double. AE, DISC, MC, V.

The first thing you notice when you turn into the driveway to Clark's Skagit River Cabins are the rabbits. They're everywhere—hundreds of them in all shapes and sizes, contentedly munching the lawns or just sitting quietly. Today the bunnies are one of the main attractions at Clark's, but it's the theme cabins that keep people coming back. Western, nautical, Victorian, Native American, Adirondack, hacienda, and mill are the current choices of interior decor in these cabins. There are other cabins that are equally comfortable, but the theme cabins are what make Clark's just a bit different. These cabins are especially popular in winter when folks flock to the area to watch the bald eagles that congregate on the Skagit River. There's also a restaurant on the property.

Ross Lake Resort. Rockport, WA 98283. ☎ **206/386-4437.** 15 cabins. $61–$147 cabin for two. MC, V. Drive to Diablo Dam on Wash. 20, then take a tugboat to the end of Diablo Lake where a truck carries you around the Ross Dam to the lodge; or hike in on a 2-mile trail from Milepost 134 on Wash. 20.

Unique in the Northwest, all 15 of this resort's cabins are built on logs floating in Ross Lake. Two newly-built "peak" cabins with vaulted ceilings have up-to-the-minute modern amenities. If you're looking to get away from it all, this place comes pretty close—there's not even a road to the resort. There's no grocery store or restaurant here, so be sure to bring enough food for your stay. What do you do once you get here? Rent a boat and go fishing, rent a kayak or canoe, do some hiking, or simply sit and relax.

CAMPGROUNDS

In the Mount Baker Area

There are several campgrounds in the forests along the banks of the Nooksack River along the Mount Baker Highway. **Silver Fir Campground** (30 campsites) 13 miles east of Glacier is the closest campground to the Heather Meadows area. **Douglas Fir Campground** (50 campsites) 2 miles east of Glacier is the next best choice in the area. The most developed campground in the area is at **Silver Lake County Park** (78 campsites) north of Maple Falls.

Along the North Cascades Scenic Highway

Heading over the North Cascades Highway from the west side, you'll find a very nice campground, with walk-in sites, at **Rockport State Park** (62 campsites) just west of Rockport. This campground is set amid large old-growth trees. Right in Rockport itself, there are campsites in a large open field at **Howard Miller Steelhead Park** (59 campsites). Outside the town of Newhalem are the **Goodell Creek Campground** (21 campsites) and the **Newhalem Creek Campground** (111 campsites), which is the site of the North Cascades Visitor Center. The next campground east is at **Colonial Creek** (162 campsites) on the bank of Diablo Lake. This campground has some very nice sites right on the water.

East of Marblemount, there are a couple of small campgrounds on the Cascade River Road, which leads to the trailhead for the popular hike to Cascade Pass. **Marble Creek** (24 campsites) is 8 miles east of Marblemount, and **Mineral Park Campground** (4 campsites) is 15 miles east of Marblemount. Reservations at state park campgrounds can be made by calling **Reservations Northwest** (☎ 800/452-5687). Some National Forest campgrounds also accept reservations. For more information call the **National Forest Reservation Service,** (☎ **800/280-CAMP**.)

WHERE TO DINE
IN THE MOUNT BAKER AREA

Milano's Market & Deli. 9990 Mt. Baker Hwy., Glacier. ☎ **360/599-2863.** Main dishes $5–$12. MC, V. Mon–Fri 10am–8pm, Sat 9am–9pm, Sun 7am–8:30pm. ITALIAN.

This casual deli and Italian eatery has long been a favorite of snowboarders and skiers coming down off the mountain after a day on the slopes. There's a good variety of pasta dishes made with fresh pasta. Ravioli can be had with a choice of smoked salmon, porcini mushrooms, cheese, or meat. The desserts, including tiramisu, cappuccino chocolate torte, and polenta cake, are all big hits with the hungry down-hill crowd.

Mountain Laurel Café. 9393 Mt. Baker Hwy., Glacier. ☎ **360/599-1002.** Main dishes $5–$12. DISC, MC, V. Tues–Sun 11am–9pm. INTERNATIONAL.

Located just west of the tiny town of Glacier, the Mountain Laurel Café (formerly Innisfree) serves a fairly simple menu that includes vegetarian and seafood dishes, free-range meats, and organic produce. However, the menu leans heavily toward fish and fowl, with sautéed salmon and trout, duck with Zinfandel, chicken rosemary, shrimp stir-fry, and bouillabaisse. There are also regional wines and microbrews to accompany meals, and home-baked desserts and breads.

ALONG THE NORTH CASCADES SCENIC HIGHWAY

In addition to the restaurant listed here, you can get decent, simple meals at the restaurant at Clark's Cabins, which are also in Marblemount.

Buffalo Run Restaurant. 5860 Hwy. 20 (Milepost 106), Marblemount. ☎ **360/873-2461.** Main dishes $9.50–$30. AE, DISC, MC, V. Sun–Thurs 8am–9pm, Fri–Sat 8am–10pm. AMERICAN.

From the outside this looks like any other roadside diner, but once you see the menu, it's obvious this place is unique. The restaurant's owners have a buffalo ranch and feature buffalo meat on the menu. There are buffalo burgers, buffalo chili, and buffalo T-bones. You'll also find venison and ostrich on the menu, as well as salmon and mussels. Of course there's a buffalo head (and skin) on the wall. You'll find the restaurant right in Marblemount.

2 Winthrop & the Methow Valley

193 miles (summer) or 243 miles (winter) E of Seattle, 53 miles N of Chelan

Driving into Winthrop you may think you've driven onto a movie set. A covered wooden sidewalk lines the town's main street which includes a trading post and a saloon. If it's a Saturday in summer, you might even see a shoot-out. But where are the cameras? No, this isn't a Hollywood set—it's the real Winthrop.

Well, not *exactly.* Winthrop needed a way to stop a few of the cars that started crossing the North Cascades when the scenic highway opened in 1972. Someone suggested that they cash in on their Wild West heritage and put up some old-fashioned cow-town false fronts (based on old photos of the town). This rewriting of history worked and now Winthrop gets plenty of cars to stop. In fact it has become a destination in its own right, known for its cross-country skiing in winter and mountain biking, hiking, and horseback riding in summer.

Winthrop and the Methow River valley in which it is located really do have a Wild West history. Until 1883 there were no white settlers in this picturesque valley. The only inhabitants were Native Americans who annually migrated into the valley to harvest camas bulbs and fish for salmon. The Native Americans felt it was just too cold to live in the Methow Valley, but when the first white settlers showed up, they refused to listen to the Native Americans' weather reports and built their drafty log cabins anyway. Gold was discovered in the late 1800s and fueled a short-lived boom, but it was agriculture in the form of apples that kept the valley alive until the advent of tourism in the 1970s.

Why an Old West theme town? Possibly because Owen Wister, author of *The Virginian,* a Western novel that became a popular television series, was inspired to write his novel after coming to Winthrop to visit his former Harvard University roommate who ran a trading post here.

ESSENTIALS

GETTING THERE   In summer you can take Wash. 20, the North Cascades Scenic Highway, from I-5 at Burlington. However, in winter this road is closed and it's necessary to cross from north of Seattle on U.S. 2 to Wenatchee and then drive north on U.S. 97. to Wash. 153 at Pateros. If you're coming from north-central or eastern Washington, head east on Wash. 20 at Okanogan.

VISITOR INFORMATION   For more information on the Methow Valley, contact the **Winthrop Chamber of Commerce,** P.O. Box 39, Winthrop, WA 98862 (☎ **888/4-METHOW** or 509/996-2125).

FESTIVALS   Each year in mid-July the **Winthrop Rhythm & Blues Festival** brings a variety of national and regional R&B acts to town for a 3-day music binge.

SPORTS AND OUTDOOR ACTIVITIES

If you're here for the outdoors, then sooner or later you're going to need the **Mazama Store,** 50 Lost River Rd. (☎ **509/996-2855**), which is a general store for the multisport crowd. Not only are outdoor gear and clothing for sale, but there are gourmet groceries, Washington wines and microbrews, an espresso bar, and a deli.

FISHING   Fly-fishing is particularly popular in the Methow Valley, and the valley's fly-fishing headquarters is **Mazama Troutfitters,** 50 Lost River Rd. (☎ **509/ 996-3674**), which has all manner of gear, can give you tips on where the fish are biting, and also offers a guide service ($195 per day for one or two people).

HIKING   Hikers will find miles of trails, including the **Pacific Crest Trail,** within a few miles of Winthrop, although the best hiking trails are farther west off the North Cascades Scenic Highway. For information, contact the **Okanogan National Forest,** Winthrop Ranger District, P.O. Box 579, Winthrop, WA 98862 (☎ **509/ 996-2266**).

   If you want to head for the hills for a few days but don't want to carry a pack, consider a llama trek. These can be arranged through **Deli Llama Wilderness Adventures** (☎ 360/757-4512) or **Pasayten Llama Packing** (☎ 509/996-2326).

HORSEBACK RIDING   If you've come to Winthrop because you're a cowboy at heart, you'll probably be interested in doing some horseback riding. **Early Winters Outfitting** (☎ 800/737-8750 or 509/996-2659) in Mazama offers rides ranging from an hour ($18) to overnight ($135) or longer. **North Cascade Outfitters** (☎ 509/997-1015) in Twisp also offers a variety of rides.

HOT-AIR BALLOONING   If you'd like to see the Methow Valley from the air, you can arrange a hot-air balloon flight through **Morning Glory Balloon Tours** (☎ 509/997-1700).

MOUNTAIN BIKING   In the summer and fall, many of the MVSTA trails become mountain-bike routes. Together with the areas many miles of gravel and dirt roads and national forest trails that are open to bikes, the Methow Valley ranks as the best mountain biking area in the state. Mountain-bike rentals and trail recommendations are available from **Winthrop Mountain Sports,** Riverside Drive (☎ 509/996-2886), which is located in downtown Winthrop.

ROCK CLIMBING   The best rock climbing in the state surrounds the Methow Valley and if you'd like to hire a guide to lead you or are interested in taking some climbing lessons, contact **Mazama Mountaineering,** 42 Lost River Rd. (☎ **509/ 996-3802**).

WHITE-WATER RAFTING   May to August is white-water rafting season on the Methow River. If you're interested, contact **Osprey River Adventures** (☎ **800/ 997-4116** or 509/997-4116). Trips are $50 to $65 per person.

WINTER SPORTS   With its sunshine and winter snows, the Methow Valley is legendary in the Northwest for its cross-country skiing. The **Methow Valley Sport Trail Association** (☎ **800/682-5787** or 509/996-3287) maintains more than 109 miles of groomed ski trails ($13 for daily trail passes), which makes this the second most extensive groomed trail system in the country. The greatest concentration of trails for all skill levels are in the vicinity of Sun Mountain Lodge, while the trails around Mazama offer plenty of easy miles for distance skier. The Rendezvous area trails are long and strenuous, but include huts that can be rented for overnight stays from Rendezvous Outfitters. Call **Central Reservations** (☎ **800/422-3048** in Washington, or 509/996-2148) for information.

You can pick up trail maps and rent equipment at **Sun Mountain Ski** (☎ **800/ 572-0493** or 509/996-2211), located at Sun Mountain Lodge; **Winthrop Mountain Sports,** 275 Riverside Ave. (☎ **509/996-2886**), in downtown Winthrop; or in the Mazama area at either **Mazama Mountaineering,** 42 Lost River Rd. (☎ **509/ 996-3802**), or **Jack's Hut at Wilson Ranch,** 17798 Wash. 20 (☎ **509/996-2752**). All of these also offer a variety of lessons.

If you happen to be out here with downhill skis or maybe want to do a little telemark skiing, try the small ski hill at **Loup Loup Ski Bowl** (☎ **509/826-2720**), 20 minutes east of Twisp on Wash. 20. It's open Wednesday and Friday through Sunday, and lift passes are $10 to $18. Experienced downhill skiers in search of virgin powder can, if they can afford it, do some heli-skiing with **North Cascade Heli-Skiing** (☎ **800/494-HELI**). A day of skiing that includes 10,000 vertical feet of slopes will cost $540 per person.

Snowmobiles can be rented from **Winthrop Snowmobile Rentals** (☎ **800/ 488-3857** or 509/996-3267). You can also go dog-sledding with **Malamute Express** (☎ **509/997-6402**), which offers half-day ($112.50 for one person) and full-day trips for ($225 for one person).

EXPLORING THE METHOW VALLEY

Though Winthrop is primarily a base for skiers, hikers, and mountain bikers, it also has a few interesting shops. If you're interested in the town's history, visit the **Shafer Historical Museum,** Castle Avenue (☎ **509/996-2712**), which consists of a collection of historic buildings from around the area. It's open in May, Saturday and Sunday from 10am to 5pm; and June to September, daily from 10am to 5pm; admission is by donation. To find the museum, go up Bridge Street from the junction of Wash. 20 and Riverside Drive and turn right on Castle Avenue.

WHERE TO STAY

If you're interested in renting a cabin or vacation house, contact **Methow Valley Central Reservations** (☎ **800/422-3048**). Mazama Ranch House and Brown's Farm are two noteworthy properties that can be booked through this service.

IN WINTHROP

Hotel Rio Vista. P.O. Box 815, Winthrop, WA 98862. ☎ **509/996-3535.** 16 rms. A/C TV TEL. $65–$85 double. MC, V.

As with all the other buildings in downtown Winthrop, the Rio Vista looks as if it had been built for a Hollywood western movie set. Behind the false front you'll find modern rooms with pine furnishings and an understated country decor. Step out onto your balcony and you'll have a view of the confluence of the Chewuch and Methow rivers. Guests often see deer, bald eagles, and many other species of birds. A hot tub overlooks the river.

River Run Inn. 27 Rader Rd., Winthrop, WA 98862. ☎ **800/757-2709** or 509/996-2173. 17 rms (15 with private bathrooms). A/C TV TEL. $50–$55 B&B double with shared bath, $55–$70 B&B double with private bath, $65–$90 motel double. MC, V.

Located only a few hundred yards from downtown Winthrop, this combination motel and B&B on the bank of the Methow River feels as if it is miles from town. The motel rooms all have balconies overlooking the river, with the mountain visible across the valley. Rustic peeled-log furniture made by a local craftsman gives the large motel rooms a Western feel. If you'd like your breakfast included, opt for one of the smaller rooms in the main house, which now serves as a casual B&B. Aside from the riverside location, the best reason to stay here is the small indoor swimming pool and hot tub.

✪ **Sun Mountain Lodge.** P.O. Box 1000, Winthrop, WA 98862. ☎ **800/572-0493** or 509/996-2211. Fax 509/996-3133. 102 rms, 13 cabins. Summer, $145–$250 double; $145–$285 cabins. Winter, $105–$205 double; $105–$240 cabins. Spring/fall, $105–$230 double; $105–$280 cabins. AE, MC, V.

If you're looking for resort luxuries and proximity to hiking, cross-country skiing, and mountain-biking trails, the Sun Mountain Lodge should be your first choice in the region. Perched on a mountaintop with grand views of the Methow Valley and the North Cascades, this luxurious lodge captures the spirit of the West in both its breath-taking setting and its rustic design. In the lobby, flagstone floors, stone fireplaces, and wagon-wheel tables all combine for a classically Western style. Most guest rooms feature rustic Western furnishings and views of the surrounding mountains. The rooms in the Gardiner wing have balconies and slightly better views than those in the main lodge. The newest rooms are those in the Mt. Robinson wing. If seclusion is what you're after, opt for one of the less luxurious cabins down on Patterson Lake.

Dining: A superb menu that focuses on Northwest cuisine makes the lodge's dining room the region's best restaurant, and the views will definitely take your breath away. Prices range from $18 to $25 for entrees.

Services: Concierge, ski rentals and ski school, horseback and sleigh rides, guided hikes, boat rentals, mountain-bike rentals, ice-skate rentals.

Facilities: Outdoor heated pools, three whirlpools, tennis courts, exercise room, ski shop, children's playground, ice-skating pond, lawn games.

The Virginian. 808 N. Cascades Hwy. (P.O. Box 237), Winthrop, WA 98862. ☎ **800/854-2834** or 509/996-2535. 40 rms, 7 cabins. A/C TV. $55–$85 double; $75 cabin. AE, DISC, MC, V.

Located just east of downtown Winthrop, the Virginian is a collection of small cabins and motel rooms on the banks of the Methow River. The deluxe rooms overlooking the river are our favorite rooms. These have high ceilings, balconies, and lots of space. Though quaint, the cabins don't have river views. The rooms and cabins are all lined with cedar which gives them a rustic feel. A heated swimming pool, hot tub, horseshoe pit, and volleyball court provide recreational options. There's a restaurant and a bar popular with bicyclists.

WolfRidge Resort. 412-B Wolf Creek Rd., Winthrop, WA 98862. ☎ **800/237-2388** or 509/996-2828. 17 rms, suites, and townhouses, 1 cabin. TV TEL. $59–$74 double; $98 suite for two; $144 townhouse for two; $149 cabin. MC, V. Head south out of Winthrop, cross the bridge, and turn right on Twin Lakes Rd.; after 1¹/₂ miles, turn right onto Wolf Creek Rd. and drive for 4 miles to the lodge (the road turns to gravel after 3 miles).

Set on 60 acres at the edge of a pasture on both the Methow River and the cross-country ski trails, this lodge is a great choice in winter or summer. Accommodations are in modern log buildings. The town houses and suites are big enough for families, and the smaller rooms are fine for couples. The lodge has an outdoor pool, indoor whirlpool, a recreation room with a pool table, and a children's playground. The wide-open ranch feel and proximity to the ski trails are the best reasons to stay here.

In Mazama

✪ **Freestone Inn.** 17798 Wash. 20, Mazama, WA 98833. ☎ **800/639-3809** or 509/996-3906. Fax 509/996-3907. 12 rms, 15 cabins, 2 lodges. TEL. Summer, $130–$225 double; $100–$195 cabin; $190–$300 lodge. Winter, $110–$220 double; $90–$175 cabin; $170–$270 lodge. Lower rates in spring and fall. AE, DC, DISC, MC, V.

Located at the upper end of the Methow Valley outside the community of Mazama, the Freestone Inn is giving Sun Mountain Lodge some stiff competition. The inn's main building is a huge new log structure complete with massive stone fireplace in the cathedral-ceilinged great room that serves as lobby and dining room. The lodge sits on the shore of small Freestone Lake and has a superb view of the mountains rising beyond the far shore of the lake. Guest rooms are thoughtfully designed with gas fireplaces and double whirlpool tubs that open to the bedroom so you can lie in the tub and still see the fireplace. All in all these are some of the most memorable rooms in the state. For more privacy, you can opt for one of the renovated Early Winters Cabins (attractively furnished but dark) or one of the newly constructed cabins. Families may want to go all the way and rent one of the large lakeside lodges.

Dining: Meals here are every bit as memorable as the rooms and setting. Northwest cuisine is the focus with prices in the $13 to $20 range.

Services: Tour arrangements, cross-country ski lessons, ski rentals, mountain-bike rentals, sleigh rides.

Facilities: Fly-fishing and swimming lake (ice skating in winter); ski trails adjacent.

The Mazama Country Inn. 42 Lost River Rd., Mazama, WA 98833. ☎ **800/843-7951** or 509/996-2681. Fax 509/996-2646. www.mazama-inn.com. 14 rms. Summer, $70–$95 double. Winter (including all meals), $150–$175 double. DISC, MC, V.

Set on the flat valley floor but surrounded by rugged towering peaks and tall pine trees, this modern mountain lodge is secluded and peaceful and offers an escape from the crowds in Winthrop. If you're out here to get some exercise, be it hiking, mountain biking, cross-country skiing, or horseback riding, the Mazama Country Inn makes an excellent base of operations. After a hard day of having fun, you can come back and soak in the hot tub and have dinner in the rustic dining room with its massive freestanding fireplace and high ceiling. The guest rooms are medium-sized and simply furnished, but modern and clean. The inn also rents out six cabins ranging in size from one to five bedrooms.

Campgrounds

Lone Fir (27 sites) is the first real campground below Washington Pass, but there are a few campsites at the **Cutthroat Pass trailhead** that can used for a single night. Continuing eastward on Wash. 20, you come to **Klipchuck** (46 campsites) and **Early Winters** (13 campsites) campgrounds. There are also several campgrounds west of Early Winters on the Harts Pass Road. **Harts Pass** (5 campsites) and **Meadows** (14 campsites), a little bit farther on this rough road are both at high elevations and provide access to the Pacific Crest Trail.

In the Winthrop area, **Pearrygin State Park** (113 campsites) is a good choice if you are in need of a hot shower. There are also more than half a dozen Forest Service campgrounds north of here on the Chewuch River and Eightmile Creek. Of these **Falls Creek** (7 campsites) beside a 75-foot waterfall and **Buck Lake** (9 campsites) are two of the best. There are also five campgrounds up the Twisp River Road from Twisp. For reservations at **Pearrygin State Park,** call Reservations Northwest (☎ 800/452-5687). For information on all other campgrounds, contact **Winthrop Ranger District,** P.O. Box 579, Winthrop, WA 98862 (☎ 509/996-2266). For national forest campground reservations, contact the **National Forest Reservation Service** (☎ 800/280-CAMP.

WHERE TO DINE
IN THE WINTHROP AREA

The best meals in the Winthrop area are to be had at the dining rooms of **Sun Mountain Lodge,** where you'll also enjoy one of the most spectacular views in the state. See "Where to Stay," above, for details. Down valley from Winthrop, in the town of Twisp, you'll find great baked goodies at **Cinnamon Twisp Bakery,** 116 N. Glover St. (☎ 509/997-5030).

The Duck Brand. Wash. 20 (Riverside Ave.) ☎ **509/996-2192.** Reservations recommended in summer. Main courses $6–$16. AE, MC, V. Daily 7:30am–9pm. MEXICAN.

Located across the street from the gas station and partially hidden by trees, the Duck Brand is a casual restaurant with a big, multilevel deck that's a great spot for a meal on a warm summer day. In cold or rainy weather, you can grab a table in the small dining room and order a plate of fajitas or ribs and a microbrew to wash it all down. The Duck Brand's muffins and cinnamon rolls make great trailside snacks.

✪ **Winthrop Brewing Company.** 155 Riverside Ave. ☎ **509/996-3183.** Main courses $5–$18. DISC, MC, V. Daily noon–midnight (shorter hours in winter). AMERICAN.

Located in a tiny, wedge-shaped building in downtown Winthrop, this local watering hole is by far the most fun restaurant/bar in town. The walls are covered with the owner's cigarette lighter collection, as well as old rifles and beer coasters from around the world. There's a deck out back overlooking the river and in summer, a beer garden. On weekends there's usually some kind of live music going on. The menu is typical pub fare—burgers, fish-and-chips, steaks, sandwiches, chicken, fish, and ribs.

IN MAZAMA

The best meals at the Mazama end of the valley are to be had at **Freestone Inn,** which serves meals and views that rival those at Sun Mountain Lodge. See "Where to Stay," above, for details. Also in Mazama, you'll find **Mazama Store,** 50 Lost River Rd. (☎ 509/996-2855), which sells gourmet groceries, espresso, simple deli meals. Or you can get lunch at the **Mazama Country Inn** if you happen to be skiing up this way around noon.

3 Lake Chelan

166 miles E of Seattle, 37 miles N of Wenatchee, 59 miles S of Winthrop

A rare land-locked fjord, formed when a glacier-carved valley flooded, Lake Chelan is 1,500 feet deep, 55 miles long, and less than 2 miles wide in most places. It's the third-deepest lake in the United States (reaching 400 feet below sea level) and the longest natural lake in Washington. Only the southern 25 miles of the lake are accessible by road, yet at the northern end, the community of Stehekin (reachable only by boat, plane, or on foot) has managed to survive for more than 100 years despite not being connected to the outside world by road. Plenty of summer sunshine, clear water, and blue skies have made the lake the number one destination in eastern Washington and today the town of Chelan has the feel of a beach town despite the rugged mountain views all around. At the southern end of the lake, apple orchards cover the foothills, while at the northern end, forests and rugged slopes that are home to mountain goats and black bears come right down to the waters edge.

ESSENTIALS

GETTING THERE Chelan is on U.S. 97, the main north-south highway in central Washington. From Seattle, take U.S. 2 to Wenatchee and then head north.

The Link bus system (☎ **800/851-LINK** or 509/662-1155) is free and provides service between the Lake Chelan, Leavenworth, and Wenatchee areas.

VISITOR INFORMATION For more information on this area, contact the **Lake Chelan Chamber of Commerce,** 102 E. Johnson St. (P.O. Box 216), Chelan, WA 98816 (☎ **800/4-CHELAN** or 509/682-3503).

EXPLORING CHELAN & LOWER LAKE CHELAN

Lake Chelan history is on display at the **Chelan Museum,** 204 E. Woodin Ave. (☎ **509/682-5644**), open June 1 to October 1 Monday through Saturday from 1 to 4pm. If you're looking for something to do at night, you can drop some cash at the **Mill Bay Casino** (☎ **509/687-2102**), which is on Wash. 150 in Manson and offers poker, blackjack, craps, and slot machines. You might also consider catching a film at the historic **Ruby Theatre,** 135 E. Woodin Ave. (☎ **509/682-5016**), which has been lovingly renovated over the past few years.

UP THE LAKE TO STEHEKIN

If you have time for only one activity while in the Lake Chelan area, it should be an all-day boat ride up the lake to Stehekin, a community accessible only by boat, floatplane, or hiking trail, and within the Lake Chelan National Recreation Area part of the North Cascades National Park Complex. This remote community has been a vacation destination for more than 100 years and is set amid rugged, glacier-clad mountains at the far north end of Lake Chelan.

The **Lake Chelan Boat Company,** South Shore Road (☎ **509/682-2224**), operates the two-passenger ferries—*Lady of the Lake II* and the faster *Lady Express*—that make the trip from Chelan to Stehekin. The *Lady of the Lake II* takes 9¹/₂ hours for the round-trip (including layover) and charges $22 per person, while the *Lady Express* takes about 6 hours (including layover) and charges $41. Unless you plan to stay overnight, you won't have more than 90 minutes to look around Stehekin unless you book a combination ticket that allows you to go up on the *Lady Express,* spend 3 hours in Stehekin, and return on the *Lady of the Lake II.* This combination ticket is only available in summer. The trip encompasses some of the most spectacular scenery in the Northwest as you travel from gentle rolling foothills to deep within the rugged North Cascades mountains. Wildlife, including deer, mountain goats, and even bears, are frequently seen from the boats.

If you want to get to Stehekin in a hurry, you can make the trip by floatplane on **Chelan Airways** (☎ **509/682-5065** or 509/682-5555), which leaves from the dock next to the ferries. The fare is $120 round-trip. This company also offers flightseeing trips for between $80 and $150.

A variety of day trips are also operated in conjunction with the two passenger ferries of the **Lake Chelan Boat Company** (☎ **509/682-4584**). Tours include the popular bus ride to 312-foot Rainbow Falls ($6 adults, $4 children ages 6 to 11), a bus ride up the valley and a bike ride back down ($12), and a narrated bus trip up the valley to High Bridge and then a picnic lunch ($20 adults, $10 children ages 6 to 11).

Although a road (paved for the first 4 miles) once led 23 miles up the Stehekin Valley to Cottonwood Campground, a flood in 1995 damaged much of the road toward the upper end of the valley. As of 1997, the road was only open as far as Bridge Creek (16 miles up valley). Transportation up the Stehekin Valley Road is provided by two different buses. One of these is operated by the National Park Service and costs between $5 and $10 depending on how far up the valley you go (currently Bridge Creek is the end of the bus route). Reservations for this bus should be made at least 2 days ahead of time (preferably much farther in advance) by calling the **Golden West Visitor Center** (☎ 360/856-5700, ext. 340, then 14). Between mid-June and the end of September, another bus runs several times a day between Stehekin Landing and High Bridge. No reservations are required for this bus, and the cost is $4. If you just want to ride as far as the Stehekin Pastry Company, the fare is only $1. Taxi service is also available from the North Cascades Stehekin Lodge at the boat landing.

A wide range of recreational activities can also be arranged in Stehekin through the **Courtney Log Office** (☎ 509/682-4677), which is located 150 yards up the road from the boat landing. These include all of the following activities. Horseback rides are offered through **Cascade Corrals** at Stehekin Valley Ranch. A 2^1/$_2$-hour ride costs $32.40. Horse-drawn wagon rides are operated by **Stehekin Valley Wagon Tours**. Rides are $10 for adults and $5 for children ages 5 to 12. White-water rafting trips on the Stehekin River are operated by Stehekin Valley Ranch and cost $40 per person.

Along the length of the Stehekin Valley, there are many miles of excellent hiking trails ranging from easy strolls along the river to strenuous climbs high into the mountain wilderness that surrounds the valley. Many of the valley's trailheads can be accessed from the bus that runs up the valley, which makes this an excellent place for doing a variety of day hikes over several days. There are also many longer trails originating here in Stehekin, which makes this a popular starting point for backpacking trips. For information on hiking trails and to pick up permits for overnight backpacking trips, stop by the **Golden West Visitor Center,** which is operated by the National Park Service and is located near the boat landing. It's open daily between mid-March and late September or mid-October. Fly-fishing on the Stehekin River is also very popular and usually very productive. In winter there is excellent cross-country skiing and snowshoeing at Stehekin, with 10 kilometers of groomed ski trails and many miles of good snowshoeing. Skis and snowshoes can be rented from **North Cascades Stehekin Lodge** (☎ 509/682-4494).

SPORTS & OUTDOOR ACTIVITIES

FISHING   Fishing is one of the top recreational activities at Lake Chelan, and in this deep lake's clear waters you'll find chinook and kokanee salmon, lake trout, rainbow trout, smallmouth bass, and freshwater lingcod. Although there is bank fishing for stocked rainbows in the lower lake, most other fishing requires a boat. Up in Stehekin there is good fly fishing for native cutthroat and rainbow trout. If you want to hire a guide to take you where the fish are biting, try **Fish'n Lake Chelan** (☎ 800/626-RUSH or 509/682-2802) or Graybill's Guide Service (☎ 509/682-4294).

GOLF   Right on the edge of town, golfers will find the municipal **Lake Chelan Golf Course,** 1501 Golf Course Dr. (☎ 509/682-5421). However, anyone out this way with golf clubs is probably headed to **Desert Canyon Resort,** 1201 Desert Canyon Blvd., Orondo (☎ **800/258-4173** or 509/682-2697), which is located 17 miles south of Chelan and has been voted the best public course in Washington.

HANG GLIDING & PARAGLIDING   In recent years, Chelan has become one of the nation's hang gliding and paragliding meccas. Strong winds and thermals allow flyers to sail for a hundred miles or more from the Chelan Sky Park atop Chelan Butte, which is located on the outskirts of town. The top of Chelan Butte is now the Chelan Sky Park. Paragliding lessons are available here through **Chelan Paragliding School** (☎ **509/682-7777**).

HIKING   Beyond the end of the roads at the south end of Lake Chelan lie thousands of acres of unspoiled forests and many miles of hiking trails. Access to the trails is from roadside trailheads or from flag stops along the route of the *Lady of the Lake II.* However, the best trails begin in the Stehekin area. For more information on hiking and biking opportunities, contact the **Chelan Ranger Station,** 428 W. Woodin Ave. (P.O. Box 189), Chelan (☎ **509/682-2576**).

WATER SPORTS   Opportunities for aquatic activities abound at Lake Chelan. Good places to swim include **Lakeside Park** on the South Shore Road, **Don Morse Memorial Park** on the edge of downtown Chelan, and at **Manson Bay Park** in Manson. **Lake Chelan State Park** and **25-Mile Creek State Park,** both on South Shore Road, offer swimming, picnicking, and camping.

   You can rent a personal watercraft ($35 an hour to $250 per day), a wide variety of power boats ($15 to $85 per hour), and canoes and paddleboats ($10 per hour) from **Chelan Boat Rentals,** 1210 W. Woodin Ave. (☎ **509/682-4444**). Boats and personal watercraft are also available from **Shoreline Watercraft Rentals** (☎ **800/ 682-1561** or 509/682-1515) and **RSI Sports** (☎ **509/669-4779**).

   If you want to check out the water from above, call **Chelan Parasailing** (☎ **509/ 687-SAIL**), which charges $39 for a ride.

   If you've got the kids along, you'll find it impossible not to spend some time at **Slidewaters,** 102 Waterslide Dr. (☎ **509/682-5751**), which has 10 water slides, an inner-tube river ride, a 60-person hot tub, and a swimming pool. Admission is $10.95 for adults, $7.95 for children. You'll find this water park just outside town off the South Shore Road.

WINTER SPORTS   The Lake Chelan area also offers both cross-country and downhill skiing opportunities at **Ski Echo Valley** (☎ **509/687-3167** or 509/ 682-4002), a small ski area just north of Chelan. With only one poma lift and three rope tows, this isn't much of a downhill area. A lift ticket is $15 for the day. Cross-country skiers, on the other hand, will find miles of groomed trails, many of which have great views, at Echo Ridge, which is a short distance past the downhill area. Trail passes are $5 per day. Ski rentals are available at Ski Echo Valley from **Lakeland Ski** (☎ **509/687-3204**). Stehekin is also a great spot for cross-country skiing and has several miles of marked trails.

   Snowmobile rentals are available through **Back-Country Adventure** (☎ **509/ 670-0877**) and **Shoreline Snowmobile Rentals** (☎ **800/682-1561** or 509/ 682-1515).

WHERE TO STAY
IN CHELAN

Campbell's Resort on Lake Chelan. 104 W. Woodin Ave., Chelan, WA 98816. ☎ **800/ 553-8225** or 509/682-2561. Fax 509/682-2177. 170 rms, 7 cottages, 4 suites. A/C TV TEL.

Summer, $132–$162 double; $154–$222 cottage; $168–$308 suite. Lower rates off-season. AE, DISC, MC, V.

The first Campbell Hotel opened in 1901 and has remained Chelan's most popular lodging ever since. Located on the banks of the lake right in downtown Chelan, Campbell's is now a small convention hotel with acres of lawns, beaches, and boat docks. Many of the guest rooms, though updated, have an older feel about them. However, several wings have been recently updated (one was even completely rebuilt) and now feature furnishings and styling the equal that of any Seattle luxury hotel. For these newer rooms, through, you'll have to spend quite a bit extra. Fortunately, every room here has a lake view, and many, including several of the cottages, have a kitchen or kitchenette.

Dining/Entertainment: The Campbell House Restaurant is located in the original 1901 Campbell Hotel, and offers the most elegant dining on the lake, albeit without a lake view. There's a pub upstairs from the restaurant and, in summer, a beach bar.

Facilities: 1,200-foot beach, two outdoor swimming pools, indoor and outdoor hot tubs, boat docks.

Darnell's Resort Motel. 901 Spader Bay Rd. (P.O. Box 506), Chelan, WA 98816. ☎ **800/ 967-8149** or 509/682-2015. Fax 509/682-8736. 40 units. A/C TV TEL. Summer, $77 double; $144 one-bedroom unit; $190–$220 two-bedroom unit; $295 penthouse. Lower rates off-season. AE, DISC, MC, V.

Located just a couple of blocks from downtown Chelan, Darnell's is set back from the road and surrounded by wide green lawns. The combination of proximity and attractive landscaping makes this our top choice in Chelan itself. Families make up the bulk of the guests here, and when you see the wealth of activities available at no extra cost, you'll understand why. However, couples, too, will enjoy the numerous amenities. Rooms vary from a humongous so-called penthouse suite to one- and two-bedroom units, which have kitchens, decks, and views of the lake. These rooms sleep up to six people.

Services: Complimentary use of rowboats, canoes, pedal boats, bicycles.

Facilities: Outdoor swimming pool, hot tub, sauna, tennis courts, nine-hole pitch-and-putt course, children's play area, boat launch and docks, shuffleboard, volleyball, badminton.

✪ Kelly's Resort. Route 1, Box 119, Chelan, WA 98816. ☎ **800/561-8978** or 509/ 687-3220. Fax 509/687-3320. 10 cottages, 4 apts. A/C TV. Summer, $100–$150 one-bedroom; $120–$170 two-bedroom. Other months, $60–$130 one-bedroom; $80–$150 two-bedroom. MC, V.

Located 14 miles from Chelan on the South Shore Road, this small family cottage resort has been in business for almost 50 years. Set on a steep hillside, Kelley's includes 10 cabins in the trees across the road, but for the best views, try to get one of the four apartments that are built right on the water. Two of these apartments have fireplaces. Facilities include a sunbathing area, swimming area, playground, volleyball court, a boat dock, cozy lobby with a fireplace, and a general store. There are also sailboats, rowboats, and canoes for the use of guests.

Westview Resort Motel. 2312 W. Woodin Ave., Chelan, WA 98816. ☎ **800/468-2781** or 509/682-4396. Fax 509/682-2043. 20 rms, 5 suites. A/C TV TEL. Summer, $115 double; $145–$165 suite. Off-season, $54–$89 double; $85–$110 suite. AE, CB, DC, DISC, MC, V.

With lake views from every room, an outdoor pool, a whirlpool, and a public park with an adjacent beach, this comfortable motel on the south shore of the lake is a good choice, especially for families. The guest accommodations range from standard motel rooms to suites that feature complete kitchens. Some of the rooms have VCRs, and all have coffeemakers, microwaves, refrigerators, and balconies or patios.

IN STEHEKIN

If you're heading up to Stehekin and plan to do your own cooking during your stay, bring your own food. Only limited groceries are available here.

North Cascades Stehekin Lodge. P.O. Box 457, Chelan, WA 98816. ☎ **509/682-4494.** Fax 509/682-8206. 28 units. $71–$95 unit for two. DISC, MC, V.

Located right at Stehekin Landing, the North Cascades Lodge is shaded by tall conifers and overlooks the lake. A variety of accommodations range from basic rooms with no lake view to spacious apartments. The studio apartments, which have kitchens, are the best deal and all have lake views. The lodge's restaurant serves three meals a day but is only open from May 1 to October 15. Boat and bicycle rentals are available, and after a long day of pedaling, paddling, hiking, or riding you'll appreciate the hot tub.

✪ Silver Bay Lodging & Resort. 10 Silver Bay Rd. (P.O. Box 85), Stehekin, WA 98852. ☎ **800/555-7781** or 509/682-2212. 2 rms, 3 cabins. $85–$150 double or cabin for two. Additional person $20 extra. Lower rates off-season. Rates include continental breakfast. Minimum stay 2 nights (5 nights for cabins in summer). MC, V.

Situated right on the banks of both the lake and the Stehekin River, Silver Bay offers both bed-and-breakfast rooms and self-catering cabins. The views are superb, and should you stay in the master suite, you'll find antiques, a soaking tub, and decks with a view of the river. Breakfast is included if you stay in one of the two rooms, but if you plan to stay in a cabin you'll need to bring your own food to cook. Bicycles and canoes are available to guests free of charge, and there's an outdoor hot tub for soaking away your aches and pains. A nearby restaurant serves meals year-round and in winter there are groomed cross-country ski trails.

Stehekin Valley Ranch. P.O. Box 36, Stehekin, WA 98852. ☎ **509/682-4677.** 3 cabins, 9 tent cabins. $60 per adult, $50 per child 7–12, $35 per child 4–6, $20 per child 3 and under. $10 more for cabins. Rates include all meals and transportation in lower valley. $5 off if you bring sleeping bag or sheets. No credit cards.

If you're a camper at heart, then the tent cabins at the Stehekin Valley Ranch should be just fine. With canvas roofs, screen windows, and no electricity or plumbing, these "cabins" are little more than permanent tents. Bathroom facilities are in the nearby main building. For slightly more comfortable accommodations, opt for one of the permanent cabins. Activities available at additional cost include horseback riding, river rafting, and mountain biking.

CAMPGROUNDS

On Lake Chelan, there are two state park campgrounds at the southern end of the lake—**Lake Chelan State Park** (46 campsites) and **Twenty-Five Mile Creek State Park** (85 campsites)—both of which tend to be very crowded and noisy. At the north end of the lake, near Stehekin, there are nine campgrounds, most of which are served by the shuttle bus from Stehekin. **Purple Point Campground** is right in Stehekin and is the most convenient to the boat landing.

For reservations at the two state parks, call **Reservations Northwest** (☎ **800/ 452-5687**). For information on campgrounds in the Stehekin Valley, contact the **Golden West Visitor Center,** P.O. Box 7, Stehekin, WA 98852 (☎ **360/856-5700,** ext. 340, then 14). For national forest campground reservations, contact the **National Forest Reservation Service** (☎ **800/280-CAMP.**)

WHERE TO DINE
IN CHELAN

If you're looking for a good cup of coffee, try **Latte Da Coffee Stop Cafe,** 303 E. Wapato Ave. (☎ **509/682-4196**), which is housed in an old house on the edge of downtown Chelan.

Campbell House Restaurant. 104 W. Woodin Ave. ☎ **509/682-4250.** Main courses $8.50–$18. AE, DISC, MC, V. Mon–Thurs 6:45am–11am, 11:30am–2pm, and 5:30–8pm; Fri–Sat 6:45am–11am, 11:30am–2pm, and 5:30–9pm; Sun 6:45am–1pm and 5:30–8pm. AMERICAN.

Housed in the original 1901 Campbell Hotel, this is the most elegant restaurant in the area, and as such stays pretty busy in the summer months. While the menu is not overly creative, you'll find more imaginative offerings here than anywhere else in town. In addition to the regular menu and the weekly specials, there are special wine dinners a few times a year. If you prefer burgers to snow crab-stuffed prawns, then you'll be better off upstairs at the casual pub.

Goochi's. 104 E. Woodin Ave. ☎ **509/682-2436.** Reservations recommended. Main courses $9.50–$17. AE, DISC, MC, V. Daily 11am–9pm (longer hours in summer). INTERNATIONAL.

Despite its cavernous proportions, this popular restaurant and tavern can be packed to overflowing in summer, so be prepared for a wait. Eclectic in both decor and menu, Goochi's offers up everything from basic burgers to steak-and-prawn combos. The asbestos-mouthed won't want to miss the fire pasta, a combination of chicken, linguine, cream, and chiles. To accompany any dish, there are more than two dozen microbrewery ales on tap in the summer. A long list of appetizers offers plenty to snack on if you just happen to be whiling away a few hours here. We like the Louisiana black-bean chili and tortilla chips. Late nights see live or recorded rock music as well as a weekly comedy night in summer, making this the number-one nightspot in town.

IN STEHEKIN

The dining options in Stehekin are slim, and if you plan to stay in a cabin or camp out, be sure to bring all the food you'll need. Otherwise, simple meals are available at **North Cascades Stehekin Lodge** (☎ **509/682-4494**), which is located right at the boat dock in Stehekin. When you just have to have something sweet, you're in luck, the **Stehekin Pastry Company** (☎ **509/682-4677**), which is located 2 miles upvalley from the boat landing serves pastries and ice cream, as well as pizza and espresso.

4 Wenatchee: Apple Capital of the World

20 miles E of Leavenworth, 37 miles S of Chelan, 75 miles N of Ellensburg

Apples are the single largest agricultural industry in Washington, and more than 50% of the apples sold in the United States come from central Washington. The combination of warm, sunny days and abundant irrigation water from both the Columbia and Wenatchee rivers have made Wenatchee the center of this apple-growing region. While Wenatchee, which lies at the base of the eastern Cascade slopes on the bank of the Columbia River, isn't exactly a tourist destination in its own right, anyone exploring this region of the state passes through the city sooner or later. Skiers, on the other hand, are familiar with the city as the closest town to the slopes of Mission Ridge ski area.

ESSENTIALS

GETTING THERE   Wenatchee is at the junction of U.S. 2, which connects to I-5 by way of Stevens Pass, and U.S. 97, the main north-south route along the east side of the Cascades. Wash. 28 connects the city to the eastern part of the state.

Wenatchee's Pangborn Memorial Airport is served by Horizon Air. Amtrak trains stop in Wentachee en route between Spokane and Seattle, and Wenatchee is also served by Greyhound buses.

VISITOR INFORMATION   For more information on the Wenatchee area, contact the **Wenatchee Area Visitor & Convention Bureau,** 2 S. Chelan Ave. (P.O. Box 850, Dept. A), Wenatchee, WA 98807 (☎ **800/57-APPLE** or 509/662-2116).

GETTING AROUND   The Link bus system (☎ **800/851-LINK** or 509/662-1155) is free and services the Lake Chelan, Leavenworth, and Wenatchee areas.

FESTIVALS   The city celebrates its apples each year with the **Washington State Apple Blossom Festival,** which includes three weeks of festivities in late April and early May.

EXPLORING WASHINGTON'S APPLE CAPITAL

At the **Washington Apple Commission Visitor Center,** 2900 Euclid Ave. (☎ **509/663-9600** or 509/662-3090), on the northern outskirts of town just off U.S. 97, you can learn all about apples and how they're grown and stored. May through December, it's open Monday through Friday from 8am to 5pm, Saturday from 9am to 5pm, and Sunday from 11am to 5pm; January to April, it's open Monday through Friday from 8am to 5pm. Admission is free.

More apple-industry displays are part of the focus of the **North Central Washington Museum,** 127 S. Mission St. (☎ **509/664-5989**), but there are also interesting exhibits on local Native American cultures and the first trans-Pacific flight. Model-railroading buffs will enjoy the HO-scale Great Northern Railroad. The museum also hosts concerts, lectures, and traveling exhibitions, and a 1919 Wurlitzer organ is often played during concerts and as accompaniment to classic silent films. The museum is open Monday through Friday from 10am to 4pm and Saturday and Sunday from 1 to 4pm; closed weekends in January. Admission is $2 for adults, $1 for children 6 to 12.

Though it's only a dozen or so miles from the lush forests of the Cascades, Wenatchee is on the edge of central Washington's high desert. To bring a bit of the mountains' greenery into the desert, Herman Ohme and his family spent 60 years creating **Ohme Gardens,** 3327 Ohme Rd. (☎ **509/662-5785**), a lush alpine garden covering 9 cliff-top acres north of Wenatchee. The gardens wind along the top of a rocky outcropping that overlooks the Wenatchee Valley, Columbia River, and Cascade peaks. Rock gardens, meadows, fern grottos, and waterfalls give the gardens a very naturalistic feel similar to that of a Japanese garden.

The gardens are open April 15 to October 15, daily from 9am to 6pm (until 7pm in summer). Admission is $5 for adults, $3 for children 7 to 17.

Only a few miles outside town is **Mission Ridge** ski area (☎ **800/374-1693** or 509/663-7631 for a snow report), which is known for its powder snow (a rarity in the Cascades) and its sunny weather. Lift ticket prices range from $20 on weekdays to $30 on weekends.

CASHMERE: AN EARLY AMERICAN TOWN

West of Wenatchee a few miles, you'll find the town of **Cashmere,** which has adopted an Early American theme. The town's main attraction is the **Aplets &**

Cotlets Candy Factory and Country Store, 117 Mission Ave. (☎ **509/782-4088**), where you tour the kitchens that produce these unusual fruit-and-nut confections. It's open April through December, Monday through Friday from 8am to 5:30pm and Saturday and Sunday from 10am to 4pm; January through March, Monday through Friday from 8:30am to 4:30pm.

Also worth a visit in Cashmere are the **Chelan County Historical Museum and Pioneer Village,** 600 Cottage Ave. (☎ **509/782-3230**). Nearly 20 old log buildings have been assembled here and are filled with period antiques. Inside the main museum building you'll find exhibits on the early Native American cultures of the region, pioneer history, and natural history. The museum is open March 1 to October 31, Tuesday through Sunday from 9:30am to 5pm; call for winter hours. Admission is $3 for adults, $2 for students and seniors, $1 for children 5 to 12.

WHERE TO STAY

Westcoast Wenatchee Center Hotel. 201 N. Wenatchee Ave., Wenatchee, WA 98801. ☎ **800/426-0670** or 509/662-1234. Fax 509/662-0782. 147 rms, 4 suites. A/C TV TEL. $79–$95 double; $175–$195 suite. AE, CB, DC, DISC, MC, V.

With Wenatchee's convention center across a sky bridge from the lobby, the Westcoast Wenatchee caters almost exclusively to convention business, but it's also the city's most comfortable hotel. A moderately priced and casual rooftop dining room and lounge provide the best view in town. Room service is also available. Facilities include an indoor/outdoor pool, whirlpool, and exercise room.

WHERE TO DINE

John Horan's Steak & Seafood House. 2 Horan Rd. ☎ **509/663-0018.** Reservations recommended. Main courses $15–$24. AE, DISC, MC, V. Sun–Thurs 5–10pm, Fri–Sat 5–10pm. Cross the Wenatchee River bridge from downtown, take your first right, the next right, and then, at the end of the road, turn right a third time; at the end of this road, turn left onto the restaurant driveway. CONTINENTAL.

Though it's in a rather unlikely spot surrounded by industrial complexes, the Horan House, where the wealthy of Wentachee dine, is well worth searching out. Secluded in its own little apple orchard, the 1899 Victorian farmhouse is a world apart. The menu these days is heavy on steaks and traditional preparations, although you'll find more daring creations on the appetizer list. For those with less disposable cash or a desire for a more casual atmosphere, the Carriage House Pub and Cafe is adjacent to the main restaurant. Meals here are in the $6 to $8 range.

5 Leavenworth: Washington's Own Bavarian Village

108 miles E of Everett, 22 miles W of Wenatchee, 58 miles SW of Chelan

You're out for a Sunday drive through the mountains, just enjoying the views, maybe doing a bit of hiking or cross-country skiing, when you come around a bend and find yourself in the Bavarian Alps. Folks in lederhosen and dirndls are dancing in the streets, a polka band is playing the old oompah-pah, and all the buildings look like alpine chalets. Have you just entered the Twilight Zone? No, it's just Leavenworth, Washington's Bavarian village.

Many an unsuspecting traveler has had just this experience, but if you're reading this, you'll be prepared for the sight of a Bavarian village transported to the middle of the Washington Cascades. Whether you think it's the most romantic town in the state, a great place to go shopping, the perfect base for hiking and skiing, or just another example of *über* kitsch, there's no denying that Leavenworth makes an impression.

ESSENTIALS

GETTING THERE   From I-5, take U.S. 2 from Everett, or, if you're coming from the south, take I-405 to Bothell and then head northeast to Monroe, where you pick up U.S. 2 heading east. From U.S. 97 in the central part of the state, head west on U.S. 2.

There is bus service to Leavenworth on Northwest Trailways.

VISITOR INFORMATION   For more information on this area, contact the **Leavenworth Chamber of Commerce & Visitor Center,** P.O. Box 327, Leavenworth, WA 98826 (☎ **509/548-5807**). You'll find the visitor center in the clock tower at the corner of U.S. 2 and Ninth Street.

GETTING AROUND   The Link bus system (☎ **800/851-LINK** or 509/ 662-1155) is free and services the Leavenworth, Lake Wenatchee, Lake Chelan, and Wenatchee areas.

FESTIVALS   During the annual **Maifest** (early May) and **Autumn Leaf Festival** (late September) Leavenworth rolls out the barrel and takes to the streets and parks with polka bands, Bavarian dancing, and plenty of craft vendors. In August, more music hits town with the **Leavenworth International Accordion Celebration.** In mid-September, the **Wenatchee River Salmon Festival** celebrates the annual return of salmon to the river. In December, the whole town gets lit up in one of the most impressive **Christmas Lighting** shows in the Northwest.

EXPLORING LEAVENWORTH

Leavenworth's main attraction is the town itself. Thirty-some years ago this was just another mountain town struggling to get by on a limited economy. Sure the valley was beautiful, but beauty wasn't enough to bring in the bucks. A few years after a motel with alpine architecture opened in town, Leavenworth decided to give itself a complete makeover. Today nearly every commercial building in town, from the gas station to the Safeway, looks as if it had been built by Bavarian gnomes. What may come as a surprise is that they did a good job! Stroll around town and you'll convince yourself that you've just had the world's cheapest trip to the Alps. People here even speak German.

Any time of year the town's most popular tourist activity seems to be shopping for genuine Bavarian souvenirs in the many gift shops—you'll find cuckoo clocks, Hummel figurines, imported lace, and nutcrackers. In fact, if nutcrackers are your passion, don't miss the **Leavenworth Nutcracker Museum,** 735 Front St. (☎ **509/ 548-4708**), which has more than 2,000 nutcrackers of all shapes and sizes. The museum is open May through October from 2 to 5pm daily and November through April on weekends only.

Classical music fans should be sure to see what's happening at the **Icicle Creek Music Center** (☎ **509/548-6347**), which is located at the Sleeping Lady resort and has programs throughout the year. There are also many musical performances and festivals in the small Front Street Park in downtown Leavenworth, where a large gazebo serves as a bandstand.

Just east of Leavenworth begin the apple and pear orchards of the Wenatchee Valley, in summer and fall, you can taste the fruits of the valley at farm stands along U.S. 2. **Smallwood's Harvest Fruit & Antiques** (☎ **509/548-4196**) and **Prey's Fruit Barn** (☎ **509/548-5771**), are the biggest and best farm stands along this stretch of road.

OUTDOOR ACTIVITIES: FROM HORSEBACK RIDES TO DOGSLEDDING

If your interests tend toward hiking rather than Hummel figurines, you'll still find plenty to do around Leavenworth. Leavenworth is on the valley floor at the confluence of the Wenatchee River and Icicle Creek and rising all around are the steep, forested mountainsides of the Stuart Range and Entiat Mountains. Spring through fall, there is rafting, hiking, mountain biking, and horseback riding, and in winter, there is downhill and cross-country skiing and snowmobiling.

North of town 25 miles, you'll find **Lake Wenatchee,** a year-round recreation area with hiking and cross-country ski trails, horseback riding, canoe rentals, windsurfing, swimming, fishing, mountain biking, camping, and snowmobiling. **Lake Wenatchee State Park (☎ 509/763-3101)** is the center of recreational activity here.

If you need to rent some gear, contact **Leavenworth Outfitters Outdoor Center,** 21312 Wash. 207 (☎ 800/347-7934 or 509/763-3733), which rents mountain bikes, cross-country skis, kayaks, and canoes.

FISHING Icicle Creek, which runs through Leavenworth, has a short summer salmon season for fish headed upstream to the Leavenworth Fish Hatchery. Lake Wenatchee, at 5 miles in length, is the biggest lake in the area and holds kokanee, as well as Dolly Varden and rainbows. To fish for kokanee, you'll need a boat. Several of the rivers and streams in the Leavenworth area are open to fly fishing only. If you want to take a fly-fishing class while you're in the area, contact **English Flyfishing School of Leavenworth** (☎ 509/548-5218 or 509/763-3429). A one-hour class is $30.

GOLF Golfers can play 18 holes at the Leavenworth Golf Course (☎ 509/548-7267), on the outskirts of town, or north of Leavenworth near Lake Wenatchee at **Kahler Glen Golf Course,** 20700-A Club House Dr. (☎ 509/763-3785). Greens fees range from $20 to $25 for 18 holes. If you want to practice your putting, check out the **Enzian Falls Championship Putting Course** (☎ 509/548-5269), which is located across from the Enzian Motor Inn and is a beautiful bent-grass 18-hole putting course (not to be confused with your usual tacky miniature golf course).

HIKING Right in town, you'll find a pleasant paved walking path in **Waterfront Park.** Out at the **fish hatchery** on Icicle Road, there is also a mile-long interpretive trail with information on the hatchery. In winter, both of these areas have cross-country ski trails. In Tumwater Canyon, the narrow gorge that serves as something of a gateway to Leavenworth as you approach from the west, there's an easy hiking trail along the banks of the Wenatchee River.

Just outside Leavenworth, in the Alpine Lakes Wilderness, lies some of the most spectacular mountain scenery in the state, and the trails that lead into this wilderness are among the most popular. So popular in fact, that backpackers must reserve camping permits months in advance to overnight in such heavily visited areas as the Enchantment Lakes basin. Most of the trails in the area are best suited for overnight trips because they climb steeply and steadily for many miles before reaching the more scenic areas. For information on hiking trails in Wenatchee National Forest, contact the **Leavenworth Ranger Station,** 600 Sherbourne St. (☎ 509/782-1413). To apply for a backpacking permit (reservations are taken starting in late February), call **Reservations Northwest** (☎ 888/953-7677).

HORSEBACK RIDING If you'd like to go horseback riding, contact **Eagle Creek Ranch** (☎ 800/221-7433 or 509/548-7798), which offers everything from 1¹/₂-hour-long rides to overnight pack trips and wagon rides; or **Icicle Outfitters &**

Guides (☎ **509/763-3647** or 509/669-4909), which offers a similar variety of rides and has stables both at Lake Wenatchee State Park and in Leavenworth on Icicle Road near the fish hatchery. In the summer, try a carriage ride around town with **Carriage Services of Leavenworth** (☎ **509/548-6825**), which charges $25 for a 20-minute tour of town for four people.

MOUNTAIN BIKING From easy rides on meandering dirt roads to grueling climbs to mountaintops with spectacular views, the Leavenworth area has some of the best mountain biking routes in the state. Mountain bikes can be rented at **Der Sportsmann,** 837 Front St. (☎ **509/548-5623**), and the Leavenworth Ski & Sports Center, Icicle Junction at U.S. 2 and Icicle Road (☎ **509/548-7864**). Ask at either of these shops for ride recommendations. You can also put your bike on the free Link bus and go as far as Lake Chelan or Lake Wenatchee to start biking.

ROCK CLIMBING Two miles west of Cashmere on U.S. 2, you'll find **Peshastin Pinnacles State Park,** Washington's only state park created exclusively for rock climbing. There are also plenty of other good climbing spots around the area. For information, ask at Leavenworth Ski & Sports (see below).

WHITE-WATER RAFTING The Wenatchee River flows right through Leavenworth and just downstream from town becomes one of the best whitewater rafting rivers in the state. Rafting season runs from April to July. If you're interested, contact **All Rivers/Wenatchee Whitewater & Company** (☎ **800/74-FLOAT** or 509/782-2254), **Osprey Rafting Co.** (☎ **800/743-6269** or 509/548-6800), or **Leavenworth Outfitters** (☎ **800/347-7934** or 509/763-3733). A day trip costs about $65 per person.

WINTER SPORTS Some of the best downhill skiing and snowboarding in the state is available 40 miles west of Leavenworth at **Stevens Pass** (☎ **360/634-1645** for general information, or 206/634-0200 for snow conditions). Lift tickets range in price from $12 to $34. A little more than half the runs are for intermediate skiers. Here you'll also find the groomed trails of **Stevens Pass Nordic Center** (☎ **360/973-2441**), which has mostly intermediate and expert level trails. These trails are open Friday through Sunday and on holidays, and a trail pass costs $7.50 for adults.

About 30 miles of **cross-country ski trails** around Leavenworth are maintained by the Leavenworth Winter Sports Club (☎ **509/548-5115**). There are even 1¹/₄ miles of lighted trails for night skiing. This ski club also operates the beginner-level **Leavenworth Ski Hill,** a mile outside of town.

Skis can be rented at **Leavenworth Ski & Sports,** Icicle Junction Theme Park (☎ **509/548-7864**), on U.S. 2 at Icicle Road. At this family fun park, you'll also find an ice skating rink in the winter.

Dog sledding isn't just an Alaskan sport, and if you'd like to find out what it's like, you've got a couple of options in the Leavenworth area. **Enchanted Mountain Tours** (☎ **800/521-1694** or 360/856-9168) offers dog-sledding tours. A 1-hour ride (weekdays only) costs $85 for one person or $140 for two, and a half-day excursion costs $135 for one or $$240 for two. Dog sled rides are also offered by **Alaska Dreamin' Sled Dog Company** (☎ **509/763-8017**), which has rides as short as 30 minutes ($55 adults, $45 children 8 to 12, and $35 children 4 to 7).

If you'd rather experience the snow from a horse-drawn sleigh, you can do that, too. Sleigh rides are offered by **Red-Tail Canyon Farm,** 11780 Freund Canyon Rd., Leavenworth (☎ **800/678-4512** or 509/548-4512); **Eagle Creek Ranch,** Eagle Creek Road (☎ **800/221-RIDE** or 509/548-7798); and **Mountain Springs Lodge,** 19115 Chiwawa Loop Rd. (☎ **800/858-2276** or 509/763-2713). Rides cost between $12 and $15 per person.

At Mountain Springs Ranch, you can also arrange a guided **snowmobile tour** for between $55 and $125.

WHERE TO STAY

EXPENSIVE

✪ **Mountain Home Lodge.** P.O. Box 687, Leavenworth, WA 98826. ☎ **800/414-2378** or 509/548-7077. Fax 509/548-5008. www.mthome.com. 9 rms, 1 suite. Summer (rates include full breakfast), $95–$145 double, $175 suite. Winter (rates include three meals daily), $195–$275 double, $265–$305 suite. DISC, MC, V.

Set 2¹/₂ miles up a very steep, narrow road that is only paved in its lower stretch, this mountain lodge is surrounded by a 20-acre meadow and has a spectacular view of the craggy Stuart Range. In winter, the road up here is not plowed and guests are brought to the lodge by Snowcat. At this time of year, miles of cross-country ski trails are the main attraction. In summer, hiking and mountain biking are the big draws. Guest rooms vary in size and each is individually decorated with themes that reflect the area's activities (Mountain Trout, The Harvest, The Ranch, The Mountain View), however, The Hide Away, atop the lodge, is the best room in the house (excluding the suite). If you're looking to get away from it all, this is the place!

Dining: During the summer, when rates include only breakfast, gourmet lunches ($12) and dinners ($24.95) are available.

Services: Guided snowmobile tours, massages, tour arrangements.

Facilities: Heated outdoor swimming pool, hot tub, tennis court, 40 miles of cross-country ski trails. Cross-country skis and snowshoes are available for guests.

✪ **Sleeping Lady.** 7375 Icicle Rd., Leavenworth, WA 98826. ☎ **800/574-2123** or 509/548-6344. Fax 509/548-6312. 46 rms, 3 cabins. www.sleepingladyresort.com. $130 double, $180–$250 cabin. Rates include continental breakfast. AE, DISC, MC, V.

Although ostensibly a conference resort, Sleeping Lady (the name comes from a nearby mountain) is one of the most luxurious and best-designed mountain retreats in the state. Set on the outskirts of Leavenworth amid ponderosa pines and granite boulders, the small resort looks much like the summer camp it once was with red-roofed green cabins tucked amid the pines. Guest rooms and cabins, all of which are done in a rustic contemporary style, abound in natural wood and have high ceilings with exposed beams. The grounds, including a meadow on the bank of Icicle Creek, a rocky knoll, and a pond, are beautifully landscaped and a delight to wander.

Dining/Entertainment: Meals, with produce from the resort's large organic vegetable garden, are primarily for conference attendees, although other guests can arrange to have meals as well. Throughout the year there are classical music performances and plays staged here; there's even a resident string ensemble. The Grotto is an evening gathering spot serving beer and wine.

Services: Massages.

Facilities: A boulder-lined swimming pool is one of the most memorable in the state. There's also a sauna (with cold plunge), a dance studio, and nearby cross-country ski trails.

MODERATE

✪ **Abendblume Inn.** 12570 Ranger Rd. (P.O. Box 981), Leavenworth, WA 98826. ☎ **800/669-7634** or 509/548-4059. Fax 509/548-9032. www.rightathome.com/~abendblm. 6 rms. $77–$159 double. Rates include full breakfast. AE, DISC, MC, V.

This alpine chalet is a luxurious and romantic B&B overlooking Leavenworth and the valley. An eye for detail is apparent throughout the inn, from the hand-carved front door to the wrought-iron stair railing. In the living room, the fireplace is a popular gathering spot in winter. Although there are a couple of smaller rooms, the large rooms with balconies overlooking the valley are the best. In these you'll find fireplaces, VCRs, and wonderfully luxurious beds and linens, but it's the bathrooms that are the real attractions. Our favorite has a triangular tub for two, plush terry robes and towels, two sinks, and heated marble floors. Nowhere in Leavenworth is there a more romantic room. Buffet breakfasts include enough variety to keep everyone happy. Guests also have use of an outdoor spa.

Blackbird Lodge. 305 Eighth St., Leavenworth, WA 98826. ☎ **800/446-0240** or 509/548-5800. Fax 509/548-7134. 16 rms. A/C TV TEL. $69–$125 double. Rates include full breakfast. AE, DISC, MC, V.

Located right in downtown Leavenworth overlooking the Icicle River, this new hotel offers the convenience of being within walking distance of all the town's shops and restaurants but with the feel of a country inn. The guest rooms are large, but otherwise are standard motel-style rooms. However, the lobby, with its slate floor and dark, woodsy decor, sets this lodge apart from other moderately priced lodgings in town.

Enzian Inn. 590 U.S. 2, Leavenworth, WA 98826. ☎ **800/223-8511** or 509/548-5269. 104 rms, 7 suites. A/C TV TEL. $90–$140 double; $160–$170 suite. Rates include full breakfast. AE, DC, DISC, MC, V.

Located on the highway just outside downtown Leavenworth, the Enzian offers both convenience and amenities. Of course, it has an alpine exterior, complete with half-timbering, steep roofs, and turrets, and inside you'll find an attractive lobby with a high ceiling and a stone fireplace. To continue the Bavarian theme, the guest rooms are decorated with reproduction antique furniture imported from Germany. If you feel like splurging, the tower suite is richly appointed with burgundy carpets, a heavy carved-wood canopy bed, and a double whirlpool tub in the sitting room. Facilities here include a large indoor swimming pool, an outdoor swimming pool, hot tubs, racquetball court, table tennis, and an 18-hole putting golf course. Guests also have complimentary use of cross-country ski equipment.

✪ Haus Lorelei. 347 Division St., Leavenworth, WA 98826. ☎ **800/514-8868** or 509/548-5726. Fax 509/548-6548. 10 rms (all with private bathrooms). $89–$99 double. Rates include full breakfast. No credit cards.

Although it is located only a few blocks from downtown Leavenworth, this 1903 home feels like a secluded mountain estate. From the setting atop a bluff overlooking the Wenatchee River you have a splendid view of the mountains and can hear the river tumbling over the rocks below. Rocks also play an integral part in this home's construction. The stone foundation wall has a decidedly European feel, and the massive river-rock fireplace took three years to build and cost more than the house itself. The guest rooms on the main floor are romantic retreats designed for couples, while the larger rooms on the second floor are set up to accommodate families.

Haus Rohrback Pension. 12882 Ranger Rd., Leavenworth, WA 98826. ☎ **800/548-4477** or 509/548-7024. 5 rms (3 with private bathrooms); 5 suites. A/C. $75 double with shared bath; $95–$125 double with private bath; $145–$160 suite. Rates include full breakfast. AE, DISC, MC, V.

Located a mile out of town on a hillside overlooking the valley and mountains, the Haus Rohrbach is a copy of a lodge near Innsbruck, Austria. The big chalet has balconies stretching across the front on all three floors, and in the living room there's a wood stove for cozy winter nights. The decor is simple to the point of being rustic— with a Bavarian flare, of course. One main lodge suite is a bilevel unit with a private balcony, while two others are housed in a separate building and have cathedral ceilings. Three of the suites have gas fireplaces and double whirlpool tubs. The swimming pool (in summer) and hot tub (year-round) make a stay here particularly pleasant.

⚙ **Run of the River Bed & Breakfast.** 9308 E. Leavenworth Rd. (P.O. Box 285), Leavenworth, WA 98826. ☎ **800/288-6491** or 509/548-7171. Fax 509/548-7547. 6 rms. $95–$150 double. AE, DISC, MC, V.

Rustic yet contemporary, this log house on 2 acres outside of town is one of the Northwest's most tranquil bed-and-breakfast inns. You can almost feel the weight fall from your shoulders as you drive through the alpine rock garden that lines the driveway. Step through the front door and you enter a house full of bare wood, hand-hewn log furniture, and exposed stones (in both the fireplaces and entry floor). This extensive use of natural materials gives the inn a timeless mountain-lodge atmosphere that's complemented by contemporary architecture. Upstairs, the guest rooms have lofts that are great spaces for a bit of quiet reading, but for a quiet moment the log porch swings just can't be beat. Novice bird watchers will appreciate the binoculars in every room.

INEXPENSIVE

Inexpensive rooms are also available at Lorraine's Edel House (see "Where to Dine" below).

Hotel Pension Anna. 926 Commercial St. (P.O. Box 127), Leavenworth, WA 98826. ☎ **800/509-ANNA** or 509/548-6273. www.pensionanna.com. 12 rms, 3 suites. A/C. $80 double; $150–$175 suite. Rates include full breakfast. AE, DISC, MC, V.

Though the guest rooms in the Pension Anna's main building are attractively appointed with pine furniture, including a four-poster bed in the honeymoon suite, the annex building contains the inn's two most outstanding rooms. This annex is a renovated church built in 1913, and the Old Chapel Suite is a grand space that includes part of the old choir loft (now a sleeping loft) and the old baptismal font. Ceilings 20 feet high give the room an expansive feel, and in the bedroom you'll find an ornately carved headboard framed by draperies that reach to the ceiling. Though considerably smaller, the Parish Nook Room has an ornate king-size bed, marble-top bedside stands, and the original arched windows. Only slightly more expensive than a regular room, the Parish Nook is the inn's best deal.

Mrs. Anderson's Lodging House. 917 Commercial St., Leavenworth, WA 98826. ☎ **800/829-5311** or 509/548-6173. 9 rms, 7 with bath. TV. $47–$51 double without bath, $65–$73 double with bath. Rates include continental breakfast. AE, DISC, MC, V.

Housed in the oldest wooden building in Leavenworth, Mrs. Anderson's is a former boarding house that now doubles as an attractive bed-and-breakfast inn and a quilting supply shop. The decor is simple, and a few of the rooms have mountain views out the windows, with the best view from Room 5. There's a long front porch and two parlors if you want to just sit and relax or play a game, and some rooms have their own balconies. With economical rates and cozy rooms, this makes an excellent budget choice.

CAMPGROUNDS

Tumwater Campground (80 campsites) is the biggest campground in the Leavenworth area, yet is always full on summer weekends. Up Icicle Road on the west side of Leavenworth, there are six campgrounds.

The Lake Wenatchee area is one of the most popular summer camping destinations in the state and there are lots of choices in the area. If you want creature comforts (hot showers) stay at **Lake Wenatchee State Park** (197 campsites), which is at the south end of the lake. This campground has a sandy beach and a great view up the lake. Farther up the south shore of the lake, the Forest Service's **Glacier View Campground** (20 campsites) provides a similar lakeside atmosphere with walk-in campsites. Right outside the entrance to the state park, you'll find the **Nason Creek Campground** (68 campsites), which has some nice sites right on this large creek. Northwest of Lake Wenatchee, there are several campgrounds along both the White River and the Little Wenatchee River.

For reservations at Lake Wenatchee State Park, call **Reservations Northwest** (☎ 800/452-5687). For information on all other campgrounds, contact the **Lake Wentachee Ranger Station,** 22976 Wash. 207, Leavenworth, WA 98826 (☎ 509/763-3103); or the **Leavenworth Ranger Station,** 600 Sherbourne St., Leavenworth, WA 98826 (☎ 509/782-1413). For national forest campground reservations, contact the **National Forest Reservation Service** (☎ 800/280-CAMP).

WHERE TO DINE

In addition to the restaurants listed below, the **Danish Bakery,** 731 Front St. (☎ 509/548-7514), downtown makes a wonderful Danish pastry, and of course, German chocolate and Black Forest cakes. For more delectable baked goods, drop by the **Homefires Bakery,** 13013 Bayne Rd. (☎ 509/548-7362), which is housed in an old log cabin off Icicle Road near the fish hatchery.

Andreas Keller. 829 Front St. ☎ **509/548-6000.** Reservations recommended. Full dinner $7.25–$15. MC, V. Daily 11am–9pm. GERMAN.

Down in a cellar (*Keller*) opposite the gazebo on Front Street, you'll find one of Leavenworth's true German experiences. From the waitresses shouting across the restaurant in German to the accordionist who plays on the weekends, everything about this place is Bavarian. Take a seat and you'll be surrounded by *Gemütlichkeit.* Rotisseried chicken and wursts are the staples here, washed down with Bavarian beer.

Cafe Mozart Restaurant. 829 Front St. ☎ **509/548-0600.** Reservations recommended. Main courses $11–$18. MC, V. Daily 11am–9pm. GERMAN.

Located upstairs from and under the same management as the ever-popular Andreas Keller, this restaurant serves more refined German meals in a more refined atmosphere. The camembert Amadeus, served with a lingonberry sauce, and the smoked trout with horseradish sauce both make interesting starts to a meal here. Follow this up with Bavarian onion steak or Munich-style sauerbraten for a gourmet German meal. Yes, Mozart is played on the stereo, and on Friday and Saturday nights, there is live harp music.

✪ **The Leavenworth Brewery Restaurant & Pub.** 636 Front St. ☎ **509/548-4545.** Main courses $7–$11. MC, V. Sun–Thurs 11am–10pm, Fri–Sat 11am–midnight. AMERICAN.

With its interesting variety of seasonal beers, this brew pub stays packed throughout the year. However, more often than not people here are dining as well as drinking. All the usual pub foods are on the menu, but since this is Leavenworth, the huge Bavarian dinner (German sausages, German potato salad, sauerkraut, and brewery bread) and the Bavarian pork cutlet are the dinners of choice. The brewery keeps eight of its beers on tap, and makes a dynamite root-beer float with its own root beer.

✪ **Lorraines's Edel House.** 320 Ninth St. ☎ **509/548-4412.** Reservations recommended. Main courses $9–$22. DISC, MC, V. May–Oct, Sun–Thurs 11:30–2:30 and 5–8:30pm, Fri–Sat 11:30–2:30 and 5–9pm; no lunch served Dec–Apr. INTERNATIONAL.

This restaurant, a simple small house on the Wenatchee River in the center of town, is Leavenworth's premier non-Bavarian restaurant (although you can get schnitzel) with most of the menu offerings drawing on Asian and Mediterranean influences. There are always several pasta dishes such as puttanesca and mezzaluna (lemon thyme pasta filled with prawns and roasted elephant garlic mousse), as well as such substantial entrees as Asian-influenced roast duck or grilled salmon. The restaurant also has a rooms and a cottage for rent at reasonable rates ($60 to $105), and if you stay here, you get 50% off a lunch or dinner.

6 The Snoqualmie Pass Route

Snoqualmie Pass: 50 miles E of Seattle, 53 miles W of Ellensburg

While Seattle has become a sprawling city of congested highways and high housing prices, there is a reason so many put up with the city's drawbacks. Less than an hour east of the city lie mountains so vast and rugged that you could hike for a week without ever crossing a road. In winter, The Summit at Snoqualmie Pass ski area is so close to the city that people head up after work for a bit of night skiing.

Between the city and this wilderness lies the Snoqualmie Valley, the Seattle region's last bit of bucolic countryside. Here you'll find small towns, pastures full of spotted cows, U-pick farms, and even a few unexpected attractions, including an impressive (and familiar) waterfall and, in summer, a medieval fair. While driving the back roads of the Snoqualmie Valley, keep an eye out for historic markers that include old photos and details about the valley's past.

ESSENTIALS

GETTING THERE   Snoqualmie Pass is on I-90 between Seattle and Ellensburg. In winter, **The Summit** at Snoqualmie Pass ski area (☎ **206/232-8182**) offers bus service to the ski area.

VISITOR INFORMATION   For more information on the area, contact the **Snoqualmie Pass Visitor Center** (☎ **425/434-6111**), which is located just off I-90 at Snoqualmie Pass and is operated by the National Forest Service. Information is also available through the **Cle Elum/Roslyn Chamber of Commerce,** P.O. Box 43, Cle Elum, WA 98922 (☎ **509/674-5958**).

EXPLORING THE SNOQUALMIE VALLEY

Snoqualmie Falls, the Snoqualmie Valley's biggest attraction, plummet 270 feet into a pool of deep blue water. The falls are surrounded by a park owned by Puget Power, which operates a hydroelectric plant inside the rock wall behind the falls. Built in 1898, the plant was the world's first underground electric-generating facility. Within the park you'll find two overlooks near the lip of the falls and a half-mile-long trail leading down to the base of the falls. The river below the falls is popular both for fishing and for white-water kayaking. To reach the falls, take I-90 east from Seattle for 35 to 45 minutes and get off at exit 27.

Snoqualmie Falls are located just outside the town of Snoqualmie, which is where you'll find the restored 1890 railroad depot used by the **Puget Sound and Snoqualmie Railroad** (☎ **425/746-4025**). On weekends between April and October, 40-minute railway excursions, using steam or diesel trains, run between here and the town of North Bend. The fares are $6 for adults, $5 for seniors, and $4 for children ages 3 to 12. Be sure to call ahead for a current schedule.

In North Bend, you can learn more about the history of this valley at the **Snoqualmie Valley Historical Museum,** Gardiner-Weeks Park, Park Street (☎ **425/888-3200**), which is only three blocks from the railroad depot.

Down the Snoqualmie Valley from the falls, you'll come to the town of Fall City, which is home to one of the Northwest's best loved farms, ☻ **The Herbfarm,** 32804 Issaquah–Fall City Rd. (☎ **206/784-2222**). Started in 1974 with a wheelbarrow full of potted herbs, The Herbfarm has since blossomed into a farm, country store, school, theme gardens, mail-order business, and the region's most famous (and most expensive) restaurant (see below under "Where to Dine"), which at press time was still rebuilding after a devastating fire.

Between Fall City and the town of Carnation, you'll pass several U-pick farms, where you can pick your own berries during the summer or pumpkins in the fall.

On weekends between late July and early September, the Snoqualmie Valley is also the site of the **Camlann Medieval Faire** (☎ **425/788-1353**), which is located off Wash. 203 north of Carnation. This reproduction of a medieval village is home to knights and squires, minstrels, and assorted other costumed merry-makers. There are crafts stalls, food booths, and, the highlight each day, jousting matches. Medieval clothing is available for rent if you don't happen to have any of your own. There are also evening banquets. Admission is $8 for adults, $5 for seniors and children ages 6 to 12, free for children 5 and under. Admission to both the faire and the banquet is $35.

To the east of Snoqualmie Pass 30 miles, you'll find the remote town of **Roslyn,** which was just a quietly decaying old coal-mining town until television turned it into Cicely, Alaska, for the hit TV show *Northern Exposure.* Although Cicely is but a fading memory now, visitors still wander up and down the town's two-block-long main street soaking up the mining-town atmosphere. To learn more about the town's history, pay a visit to the **Roslyn Museum** on Pennsylvania Avenue, the town's main street ($1 suggested donation). About the only other activity in town is wandering through the town's 25 cemeteries, which are up the hill from the museum. These cemeteries contain the graves of miners who lived and died in Roslyn.

SPORTS & OUTDOOR ACTIVITIES

HIKING   Outside of North Bend rises **Mount Si,** one of the most frequently hiked mountains in the state. This mountain, carved by glaciers long ago, rises abruptly from the floor of the valley outside North Bend and presents a dramatic face to the valley. If you are the least bit athletic, it is hard to resist the temptation to hike to the summit (take lots of water—it's a strenuous 8-mile round-trip hike), where awesome views are the payoff. To reach the trailhead, drive east of downtown North Bend on North Bend Way, turn left on Mount Si Road, turn right after crossing the Snoqualmie River, and continue another 2.5 miles.

Farther east on I-90, at Snoqualmie Pass and before you reach it, there are several trailheads. Some trails lead to mountain summits, other to glacier-carved lakes, and still others past waterfalls deep in the forest. Due to their proximity to Seattle, these trails can be very crowded, and you will need a parking permit (available at the ranger station in North Bend) to leave your car at national forest trailheads (though not at the Mount Si trailhead, which is on state land). For more information, contact the **North Bend Ranger District** (☎ **206/888-1421**).

HORSEBACK RIDING   If you're looking to spend a few hours or a few days in the saddle, there are several options in the Cle Elum area on the east side of

FACTOID

The town of Cle Elum, east of Roslyn, was the last town in the country to get dial phones and last in the country to get Touch-Tone phones.

Snoqualmie Pass—**High Country Outfitters** (☎ 888/235-0111 or 425/392-0111), **3 Queens Guide Service** (☎ 509/674-5647), and **Hidden Valley Ranch** (☎ 509/ 857-2087).

MOUNTAIN BIKING Iron Horse State Park, a railroad right-of-way that has been converted to a gravel path stretching 113 miles, provides one of the most unusual mountain biking routes in the Northwest. The trail passes under Snoqualmie Pass by way of the $2^1/2$-mile-long Snoqualmie Tunnel, which is open to bicycles from May 1 to October 31. To ride the tunnel you'll need good lights, warm clothes and rain gear (water constantly drips from the ceiling of the tunnel). To access the trail from the west side, take exit 38 off I-90. From the east side, take exit 62 off I-90.

SKIING While much of the terrain is not that interesting and the snow can be frustratingly unreliable, **The Summit at Snoqualmie Pass** (☎ 206/232-8182 or 206/ 236-1600 for snow conditions), which consists of the former Alpental, Ski Acres, Snoqualmie, and Hyak ski areas is right on I-90 and is the closest ski area to Seattle. Together, the four ski areas offer more than 65 ski runs, rentals, and lessons. Adult lift ticket prices range from $15 to $18 for midweek night skiing to $32 for a weekend all-day pass. Call for hours of operation.

At Snoqualmie Pass, there are many miles of both groomed and ungroomed crosscountry ski trails. **Ski Acres/Hyak Nordic Center** (☎ 206/434-6646) offers rentals, instruction, and many miles of groomed trails, some of which are lighted for night skiing. Trail fees run $6 to $8.

There are also several sno-parks along I-90 at Snoqualmie Pass. Some of these have groomed trails while others have trails that are marked but not groomed. **Sno-Park permits,** which are required for parking at these areas, are available at ski shops.

WHERE TO STAY
ON THE WEST SIDE

In addition to the Salish Lodge, you may be able to book a room at The Herbfarm (see below under "Where to Dine"), which, having suffered a devastating fire, was at press time planning to rebuild and add a B&B.

✪ **Salish Lodge & Spa.** 6501 Railroad Ave. SE (P.O. Box 1109), Snoqualmie, WA 98065. ☎ **800/826-6124,** 800/2SALISH, or 425/888-2556. 91 rms, 4 suites. A/C TV TEL. $129–$269 double; $450–$599 suite. AE, CB, DC, DISC, MC, V.

Set at the top of 270-foot Snoqualmie Falls and only 35 minutes east of Seattle on I-90, Salish Lodge is a popular weekend getaway spot for folks from Seattle. With its country lodge atmosphere, the Salish aims for casual comfort and hits the mark. Guest rooms are furnished with wicker and Shaker furniture and have down comforters. With fireplaces and whirlpool baths in every room, this lodge is made for romantic weekend getaways. To make it even more attractive, a full-service spa was added in 1996, making this the only resort hotel in the Northwest with a spa. Anyone who was a fan of Twin Peaks should immediately recognize the hotel.

Dining: The lodge's country breakfast is a legendary feast that will likely keep you full right through to dinner when you can dine on creative Northwest cuisine in the Salish Dining Room. The dining room also has one of the most extensive wine lists in the state. In the Attic Lounge, you can catch a glimpse of the falls through the window.

Services: Room service, concierge, valet/laundry service, complimentary morning coffee and afternoon tea and cookies, baby-sitting.

Facilities: Full-service spa offering a wide range of body treatments and massages, exercise room, whirlpools, general store.

ON THE EAST SIDE

Hidden Valley Guest Ranch. 3942 Hidden Valley Rd., Cle Elum, WA 98922. ☎ **800/ 5-COWBOY** or 509/857-2322. Fax 509/857-2130. 13 cabins. May 1–Oct 15, $198 double (rate includes all meals); Oct 16–Apr 30, $120 double (rate includes full breakfast). MC, V.

If you're looking to get away from it all but don't have the time or inclination to head to the wilds of Montana, this 700-acre guest ranch is as good a substitute as you'll find in Washington. The setting, on a grassy ridge above Swauk Creek, is the absolute epitome of a mountain ranch setting, and the cabins are suitably rustic yet have comfortably modern amenities (microwaves, refrigerators, coffeemakers). The Appletree Cabin is the best. While horseback riding ($32.50 for 1¹/₂ hours) is the favorite activity most of the year, when the snow falls, this is a great place to do some cross-country ski or snowshoe exploring. A swimming pool, tennis court, and recreation center with pool table provide other recreational options. Although there is a 2-night minimum during the high season, last-minute calls can sometimes get you in for just 1 night. The ranch is 15 minutes east of Cle Elum off Wash. 970, which connects to U.S. 97 (the route over Blewett Pass to Leavenworth and Wenatchee).

The Moore House. P.O. Box 629, South Cle Elum, WA 98943. ☎ **800/22-TWAIN** or 509/ 674-5939. 9 rms (3 with private bathrooms), 1 suite, 2 cabooses. $45–$65 double with shared bath, $70–$80 double with private bath; $115 suite; $105–$115 caboose. Rates includes full breakfast. AE, DISC, MC, V.

Railroad buffs won't want to miss an opportunity to stay at this restored Chicago, Milwaukee, St. Paul and Pacific Railroad bunkhouse. The inn is filled with railroading memorabilia and each of the guest rooms is named for a railroad worker who once lived here. The rooms vary in size and are simply furnished with antiques. However, the most popular rooms here are the two cabooses on short lengths of track beside the inn. These are large enough to sleep four or five people.

CAMPGROUNDS

Along the I-90 corridor, there are only a couple of campground choices on the west side of Snoqualmie Pass. **Tinkham Campground** (47 campsites) at exit 42 off I-90 is the closest Forest Service campground to Seattle. It is set on the bank of the South Fork Snoqualmie River. **Denny Creek Campground** (39 campsites), is so close to the freeway that campers are lulled to sleep by the roaring of trucks.

Kachess Campground (180 campsites), near the north end of Kachess Lake, is the biggest campground in the area. Powerboating and fishing are the most popular activities here, but there are also some nearby trailheads providing access to the Alpine Lakes Wilderness. The Cle Elum Lake area offers the I-90 corridor's greatest concentration of campgrounds including **Wish Poosh** (39 campsites), **Cle Elum River** (35 campsites), **Red Mountain** (9 campsites), and **Salmon la Sac** (112 campsites), which is this area's biggest and busiest campground.

For information on campgrounds in this area, contact the **Snoqualmie Pass Visitor Center** (☎ 425/434-6111). For national forest campground reservations, contact the **National Forest Reservation Service** (☎ 800/280-CAMP).

WHERE TO DINE
IN THE SNOQUALMIE VALLEY

Because ✪ **The Herbfarm**, 32804 Issaquah-Fall City Rd., Fall City (☎ 206/ 784-2222), one of Washington's finest restaurants, was, at press time, still recovering from a devastating fire, the dining room at the **Salish Lodge** (see above) is the best restaurant in the area. Made famous by the hit TV show "Twin Peaks" as a place to get "damn good pie, North Bend's **Mar-T Cafe** (☎ 425/888-1221), on the town's main intersection, is still a great place to get a slice of pie."

DINING & NIGHTLIFE IN ROSLYN

For fresh-baked bread and pastries, check out **Roslyn Bakery,** 30 N. First St., Roslyn (☎ 509/649-2521). If you're heading to the hills and want to pack some great jerky, stop by **Carek's Market,** 510 S. A St., Roslyn (☎ 509/649-2930). For nightlife, don't miss **The Brick Bar & Grill,** 1 Pennsylvania Ave., Roslyn (☎ 509/649-2643), which claims to be the oldest operating saloon in Washington and has a unique flowing-water spittoon under the bar. This place is an absolute classic. Good pizzas can be had at **Village Pizza,** 105 Pennsylvania Ave. (☎ 509/649-2992). At Pennsylvania Avenue and Second Street you'll also find the ever-popular **Roslyn Cafe** (☎ 509/649-2763). If it's good microbrews that you crave, wander up the street to the **Roslyn Brewing Company,** 208 Pennsylvania Ave. (☎ 509/649-2232), which is a much more modern place.

7 Mount Rainier National Park & Environs

Paradise: 110 miles SE of Seattle, 70 miles SE of Tacoma, 150 miles NE of Portland, 85 miles NW of Yakima

At 14,410 feet high, Mount Rainier is the highest point in Washington, and to the sun-starved residents of Seattle and south Puget Sound, the dormant volcano is a giant weather gauge. When the skies clear over Puget Sound, the phrase "The Mountain is out" is often heard around the region. And when the Mountain is out, all eyes turn to admire its broad slopes.

Those slopes remain snow-covered throughout the year due to the region's infamous moisture-laden air, which has made Mount Rainier one of the snowiest spots in the country. In 1972, the mountain set a record when 93 1/2 feet of snow fell in one year. Such record snowfalls have created numerous glaciers on the mountain's flanks, and one of these, the Carbon Glacier, is the lowest-elevation glacier in the continental United States.

Snow and glaciers notwithstanding, Rainier has a heart of fire. Steam vents at the mountain's summit are evidence that, though this volcanic peak has been dormant for more than 150 years, it could erupt again at any time. However, scientists believe that Rainier's volcanic activity occurs in 3,000-year cycles—and luckily we have another 500 years to go before there's another big eruption.

Known to Native Americans as Tahoma, Mount Rainier received its current name in 1792 when British explorer Capt. George Vancouver named the mountain for a friend (who never even visited the region). The first ascent to the mountain's summit was made in 1870 by Gen. Hazard Stevens and Philemon Van Trump, and it was 14 years later that James Longmire built the first hotel on the mountain's flanks. In 1889, Mount Rainier became the fifth national park. Today the park covers 235,612 acres and is visited by more than two million people a year.

ESSENTIALS

GETTING THERE   If you're coming from Seattle and your destination is Paradise (the park's most popular destination), head for the southwest (Nisqually) park entrance. Take I-5 south to Exit 127 and then head west on Wash. 512. Take the Wash. 7 exit and head south toward Elbe. At Elbe, continue east on Wash. 706.

If you're coming from Seattle and are heading for the northeast (White River) park entrance en route to Sunrise or Crystal Mountain, take I-90 to I-405 south. At

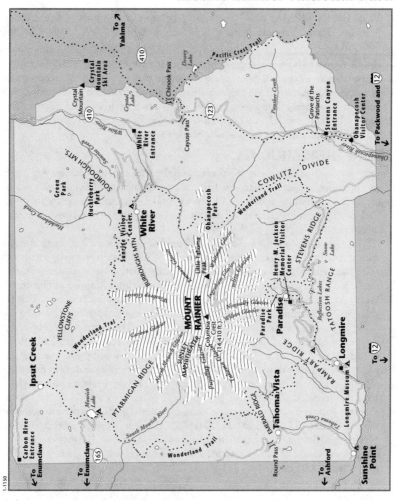

Renton, take Wash. 169 south to Enumclaw, where you pick up Wash. 410 heading east.

Note that in winter only the roads from the Nisqually entrance to Paradise and from U.S. 12 to the Ohanapecosh Visitor Center are kept open.

From Portland, head north on I-5 to Exit 68 and then take U.S. 12 east to the town of Morton. From Morton, head north on Wash. 7 to Elbe and then turn east on Wash. 706, which will bring you to the Nisqually (southwest) park entrance.

From May 1 to mid-October, **Grayline of Seattle** (☎ 800/426-7532) operates one bus daily between Seattle and Mount Rainier; the fare is $25 each way. Between May 15 and October 1, the **Rainier Shuttle** (☎ 360/569-2331) operates between Seattle-Tacoma International Airport and Mount Rainier National Park ($34 each way between the airport and Paradise; $26 each way from the airport to the town of Ashford). This company also operates a shuttle between the town of Ashford and Paradise ($8).

VISITOR INFORMATION For more park information, contact **Mount Rainier National Park,** Tahoma Woods, Star Route, Ashford, WA 98304 (☎ **360/ 569-2211**).

PARK ADMISSION The park entrance fee is $10 per vehicle and $5 per person for pedestrians or cyclists. Another option, if you plan to visit several national parks in a single year, is the Golden Eagle Passport, an annual pass good at all national parks and recreation areas. The pass costs $50 and is available at all national park visitor centers. If you're over 62, you can get a Golden Age Passport for $10, and if you have a disability, you can get a free Golden Access Passport.

SEEING THE HIGHLIGHTS

Just past the Nisqually (southwest) entrance, the park's main entrance, you'll come to **Longmire,** site of the National Park Inn, the Longmire Museum (with exhibits on the park's natural and human history), a hiker-information center that issues backcountry permits, and a ski-touring center where you can rent cross-country skis in winter.

The road then continues climbing to **Paradise** (elevation 5,400 feet), the aptly named mountainside aerie from which you get a breathtaking close-up view of the mountain. Paradise is the park's most popular destination, so expect crowds. During July and August the meadows here are ablaze with wildflowers. The circular **Henry M. Jackson Memorial Visitor Center** (☎ 360/569-2211, ext. 2328) provides 360° panoramic views, and includes exhibits on the flora, fauna, and geology of the park, as well as a display on mountain climbing. The visitor center is open daily from early May to mid-October and on weekends and holidays from mid-October to early May. A 1.2-mile walk from the visitor center will bring you to a spot from which you can look down on the Nisqually Glacier. It's not unusual to find plenty of snow at Paradise as late as July, and it was here that the world-record snowfall of 1972 was recorded.

In the summer months you can continue beyond Paradise to the **Ohanapecosh Visitor Center** (☎ 360/569-2211, ext. 2352), which is open weekends from late May to mid-June and daily from mid-June to early October. Nearby, you can walk through the **Grove of the Patriarchs,** a forest of old-growth trees, some of which are more than 1,000 years old.

Continuing around the mountain, you'll come to the turnoff for **Sunrise.** At 6,400 feet, Sunrise is the highest spot accessible by car. A beautiful old log lodge serves as the **Sunrise Visitor Center** (☎ 360/569-2211, ext. 2357). From here you get a superb view of Mount Rainier and **Emmons Glacier,** which is the largest glacier in the 48 contiguous states.

If you want to avoid the crowds and see a bit of dense old-growth forest, or do a bit of uncrowded hiking, head for the park's **Carbon River entrance** in the northwest corner. This is the least visited region of the park because it only offers views to those willing to hike several miles uphill. Carbon River has another distinction as well. It's formed by melt water from the Carbon Glacier, a glacier that descends lower than any other glacier in the continental United States.

OUTDOOR ACTIVITIES IN & NEAR THE NATIONAL PARK

If, after a long day of taking advantage of the outdoor activities available in the park, you'd like to soak in a hot tub or get a massage, contact the little woodland spa called **Wellspring** (☎ 360/569-2514). You'll find Wellspring in Ashford not far from the Nisqually park entrance. An hour in the hot tub costs $10 per person, while an hour massage costs $45. Alternatively, you can soak in a hot tub and get a massage at

Factoid

On August 10, 1890, Fay Fuller became the first woman to climb Mount Rainier.

nearby **Stormking** (☎ 360/569-2964). Both of these places also have cabins available for overnight guests.

HIKING & BACKPACKING   Hikers have more than 240 miles of trails to explore within the park. Paradise offers many excellent day hikes. The 5-mile **Skyline Trail** is the highest trail at Paradise and climbs through beautiful meadows above the tree line. Unfortunately, the meadows here, which are among the park's most beautiful, have been heavily damaged by hikers' boots over the years and now there are signs everywhere telling hikers to stay on the trails. Along the way there are views of Mount Adams, Mount St. Helens, and the Nisqually Glacier. The **Lakes Trail,** of similar length, heads downhill to the Reflection Lakes, which have picture-perfect views of the mountain reflected in their waters.

At Sunrise there are also numerous trails of varying lengths. Among these, the 5-mile **Burroughs Mountain Trail** and the 5.6-mile **Mount Fremont Trail** are both very rewarding—the latter even offers a chance to see mountain goats. The **Summerland Trail,** which starts 3 miles from the White River park entrance (the road to Sunrise), is another very popular day hike. This trail starts in forest and climbs up into meadows with a great view of the mountain.

The 95-mile-long **Wonderland Trail,** which circles the mountain, is the quintessential Mount Rainier backpacking trip. This trail takes 10 days to two weeks to complete and offers up spectacular scenery. However, there are also many shorter overnight hikes. Before heading out on any overnight backpacking trip, **you'll need to pick up a permit** at the Longmire Hiker Information Center, the White River Hiker Information Center, or the Carbon River Ranger Station.

For the less adventurous, there are naturalist-led programs and walks throughout the spring, summer, and fall. Check the park newspaper for schedules.

HORSEBACK RIDING   If you'd like to do some horseback riding, you've got a couple of choices in the area. In Elbe, you'll find **EZ Times Outfitters,** 18703 Wash. 706 (☎ 360/569-2449), which leads rides into the Elbe State Forest. Over on the east side of the park, 19 miles east of Chinook Pass on Wash. 410, you'll find **Susee's Skyline Packers,** Bumping River Road (☎ 206/472-5558). East of White Pass on U.S. 12, you'll find **Indian Creek Corral** (☎ 509/672-2400) near the shore of Rimrock Lake. Horse-rental rates start around $15 per hour.

MOUNTAIN BIKING   At both Crystal Mountain ski area (off Wash. 410 north of the park) and White Pass ski area (off U.S. 12 east of the park), you'll find lift accessed mountain-bike trails in the summer. Within the national park all trails are closed to mountain bikes, but cyclists can ride the West Side Road, a gravel road that has long been closed to cars due to mudslides that have repeatedly washed out one short stretch of the road. Off this road are several little-used hiking trails if you want to combine a ride with a hike.

MOUNTAINEERING   Climbers will know of Mount Rainier's reputation as a training ground for making attempts on higher peaks, such as Mount Everest. If you're interested in taking a mountain-climbing class, contact **Rainier Mountaineering,** 535 Dock St. Suite 209, Tacoma, WA 98402 (☎ 360/569-2227 in summer, or 253/627-6242 in winter). Alternatively, you can try the new **Mount Rainier**

Impressions _____

Every one of these parks, great and small, is a garden filled knee-deep with fresh, lovely
flowers of every hue, the most luxuriant and the most extravagantly beautiful of all
the alpine gardens I have beheld.
　　　　　　　　　　　　—John Muir, after a visit to Mount Rainier in 1888

Alpine Guides, P.O. Box T, Ashford, WA 98304 (☎ **360/569-0977**), which offers similar services.

WHITE-WATER RAFTING　The Tieton River, which flows down the eastern
slopes of the Cascades to the east of the national park is one of the state's most popular rafting rivers. However the rafting season lasts for only 3 weeks during the annual
September drawdown of water from Rimrock Reservoir. Rafting companies offering
trips on this river include **All Rivers Adventures** (☎ **800/74-FLOAT** or 509/782-
2254), **Alpine Adventures** (☎ **800/926-RAFT** or 509/548-4159), and **River Riders**
(☎ **800/448-RAFT** or 206/448-RAFT).

WINTER SPORTS　In winter, there is excellent cross-country skiing at Paradise.
At Longmire, you'll find a ski touring and rental shop (☎ **360/569-2411**). There
are also **guided snowshoe walks** at Paradise, and snowboarding is popular throughout the year, though there is no lift to get you up the slope.

　　Outside the park, near the town of Packwood, you can ski cross-country from hut
to hut on an 88-mile trail system. For more information, contact the **Mount Tahoma
Trails Association,** P.O. Box 206, Ashford, WA 98304 (☎ **360/569-2451**).
Unfortunately, many of these trails are at such low elevations that snow cover is
unreliable.

　　Just outside the northeast corner of the park, off of Wash. 410, you'll find **Crystal Mountain Resort** (☎ **206/663-2265** for general information, or 206/634-3771
for snow conditions), which most Washingtonians agree is the state's best all-around
ski area due to the variety of terrain. Lift ticket prices range from $15 for night ski-
ing to $35 for a weekend all-day pass. Call for hours of operation. Experienced back-
country skiers will also find some challenging cross-country skiing here at Crystal
Mountain.

　　You'll find downhill and cross-country skiing less than 20 miles from the southeast corner of the park on U.S. 12 at the small **White Pass ski area** (☎ **509/
672-3100**). Rental equipment is available. Lift rates range from $16 for an adult half-
day midweek ticket to $31 for a full-day weekend ticket. Nordic track passes are $7.

OTHER ACTIVITIES & ATTRACTIONS OUTSIDE THE PARK

　　Between Memorial Day and Labor Day, the **Mt. Rainier Scenic Railroad** (☎ **360/
569-2588**) operates vintage steam locomotives and both enclosed and open passenger cars along a 14-mile stretch of track between Elbe and Mineral Lake, just west
of the park's Nisqually entrance. The trips last 1¹/₂ hours and cost $8.50 for adults,
$7.50 for seniors, $6.50 for youths 12 to 17, and $5.50 for children under 12.

WHERE TO STAY
INSIDE THE PARK

National Park Inn. P.O. Box 108, Ashford, WA 98304. ☎ **360/569-2275**. Fax 360/569-
2770. 25 rms, 18 with bath. $64 double without bath; $88–$119 double with bath. AE, CB,
DC, DISC, MC, V.

　　Located in Longmire in the southwest corner of the park, this rustic lodge was opened
in 1920 and fully renovated in 1990. With only 25 rooms and open all year, the

National Park Inn makes a great little getaway or base for exploring the mountain. The inn's front verandah has a view of Mount Rainier, and inside there's a guest lounge with a river-rock fireplace that's perfect for winter-night relaxing. The guest rooms vary in size, but come with rustic furniture, new carpeting, and coffeemakers. In winter, this lodge is popular with cross-country skiers; rentals are available. The inn's restaurant has a limited menu that nevertheless manages to have something for everyone. There's also a small bar.

✪ **Paradise Inn.** P.O. Box 108, Ashford, WA 98304. ☎ **360/569-2275.** Fax 360/569-2770. 126 rms, 95 with bath; 2 suites. $68 double without bath, $95–$121 double with bath; $127 suite. AE, CB, DC, DISC, MC, V. Closed early Oct to mid-May.

Built in 1917 high on the flanks of Mount Rainier in an area aptly known as Paradise, this rustic lodge offers breathtaking views of the mountain and the nearby Nisqually Glacier. Miles of trails and meadows make this the perfect spot for some relatively easy alpine exploring. Cedar-shake siding, huge exposed beams, cathedral ceilings, and a gigantic stone fireplace all add up to a quintessential mountain retreat. A warm and cozy atmosphere prevails. The guest rooms vary in size and amenities, so be sure to specify which type you'd like. The inn's large dining room serves three meals a day, and the Sunday brunch, served from 11am to 2:30pm, is legendary. There's also a lounge and a snack bar.

OUTSIDE THE SOUTHWEST (NISQUALLY) ENTRANCE

Alexander's Country Inn. 37515 Wash. 706 E., Ashford, WA 98304. ☎ **800/654-7615** or 360/569-2300. Fax 360/569-2323. 7 rms; 5 suites. May 1–Oct 31, $89–$95 double; $115–$135 suite. Nov 1–Apr 30, $75 double; $85–$95 suite. Rates include full breakfast. Lower rates Nov–Apr. MC, V.

Located just outside the park's Nisqually entrance, this large bed-and-breakfast first opened as an inn back in 1912. Today, as then, it is one of the preferred places to stay in the area, offering not only comfortable rooms but some of the best food for many miles around. Much care has been taken in restoring the interior. The first floor is taken up by the dining room, but on the second floor, you'll find a big lounge where you can sit by the fire on a cold night. By far the best room in the house is the tower suite, which is in a turret and has plenty of windows looking out on the woods. After a hard day of playing on the mountain, there's no better place to relax than in the hot tub overlooking the inn's trout pond. The inn also rents two three-bedroom houses.

The Hobo Inn. P.O. Box 921, Elbe, WA 98330. ☎ **360/569-2500.** 8 rms. May–Oct, $70–$85 double. Oct–May, $50–$60 double. MC, V.

If you're a railroad buff, you won't want to pass up this opportunity to spend the night in a remodeled caboose. Each of the eight cabooses is a little bit different (one even has its own private hot tub). Though the oldest of the cars dates from 1916, they have all been outfitted with comfortable beds and bathrooms. Some have bay windows while others have cupolas. For the total railroad experience, you can dine in the adjacent Mount Rainier Dining Co. dining car restaurant and go for a ride on the Mount Rainier Scenic Railroad.

Mountain Meadows Inn Bed & Breakfast. 28912 Wash. 706 E, Ashford, WAS 98304. ☎ **360/569-2788.** 5 rms (all with private bathrooms). $55–$95 double. Rates include full breakfast. MC, V.

Set beneath tall trees beside a small pond, this B&B was built in 1910 as the home of the superintendent for the lumber mill in the town of National, which was the site of the largest sawmill west of the Mississippi. When the mill shut down, much of the town was moved up the road to become present-day Ashford, but this impressive old home still stands and is today filled with antiques. The big front porch overlooks the pond, and there is room to roam on nearby trails through the National townsite. An extensive model railroad collection is on display throughout the inn.

Stormking. P.O. Box 126, Ashford, WA 98304. ☎ **360/569-2964.** 1 cabin. $85–$105 double. MC, V.

Stormking started out as another hot tub and massage facility similar to the long-established Wellspring, and people enjoyed the setting and experience so much that they kept telling co-owner Deborah Sample that she should build a cabin and take overnight guests. That's just what she and co-owner Steven Brown did, and it's a gorgeous cabin. Set on the far side of a footbridge over a tiny pond, the modern cabin has a slate-floored entry hall, parquet floors, a woodstove, stereo system with plenty of relaxing music, and a high ceiling. In the big bathroom, which has a flagstone floor and is filled with plants, you'll find a double shower amid the greenery. There's also a hot tub on the back deck. This place appeals primarily to young, active travelers.

Wellspring. 54922 Kernahan Rd., Ashford, WA 98304. ☎ **360/569-2514.** 4 rms, 3 log cabins, 1 cottage. $75–$125 double. MC, V.

Billing itself a woodland spa, this rustic and relaxing hideaway more than lives up to its name and is an excellent choice for anyone wanting pampering and the chance to visit the national park. Private hot tubs and wood-fired saunas will take the chill off even the coldest night, while sore muscles will benefit from a massage by co-owner Sunny Thompson-Ward. Accommodations are an eclectic and fanciful mix. In the modern log cabins, which are tucked up against the edge of the forest, you'll find feather beds, woodstoves, and vaulted ceilings. In The Nest, you'll find a queen-size bed under a skylight and suspended from the ceiling by ropes. In the Three Bears Cottage, you'll find rustic log furniture and a full kitchen. In the Tatoosh Room, you'll find a large stone fireplace, a whirlpool tub and a waterfall shower. You can even sleep in a greenhouse with a cedar hot tub and wood-fired sauna, but you can't have the room to yourself until 9pm.

Several of the rooms and the cabins come with a daily breakfast basket. Hot tubs and saunas are an additional $5 per person per hour for guests. This New Age retreat isn't for everyone, but it is certainly the most unique accommodation in the area.

OUTSIDE THE NORTHEAST (WHITE RIVER) ENTRANCE

Alta Crystal Resort at Mt. Rainier. 68317 Wash. 410 E., Greenwater, WA 98022. ☎ **800/277-6475** or 360/663-2500. Fax 360/663-2500. 24 chalets and log cabins. $89–$159 chalet for one to four. AE, MC, V.

This is the closest lodging to the northeast (White River) park entrance and the Sunrise area. Though this condominium resort with wooded grounds is most popular in winter when skiers flock to Crystal Mountain's slopes (just minutes away), there's also plenty to do in summer, with an outdoor pool and nearby hiking trails. A hot tub is set in the woods. Accommodations are in one-bedroom and loft chalets. The former sleep up to four people and the latter have bed space for up to eight people. No matter what size condo you choose, you'll find a full kitchen and fireplace.

OUTSIDE THE SOUTHEAST (STEVENS CANYON) ENTRANCE

Hotel Packwood. 104 Main St., Packwood, WA 98361. ☎ **360/494-5431.** 9 rms, 2 with bath. TV. $30 double without bath, $38 double with bath. MC, V.

Two stories tall with a wraparound porch and weathered siding, this renovated 1912 hotel looks like a classic mountain lodge even though it's right in the middle of a small town. The tiny rooms aren't for the finicky, but most guests spend their days traipsing around on park trails and come back to the hotel thoroughly exhausted.

Though the hotel lacks much in the way of character, there are iron bed frames in some rooms, a fireplace in the lobby, and a hot tub. Packwood is about 10 miles from the southeast entrance to the park.

CAMPGROUNDS

There are five main campgrounds within Mount Rainier National Park, all of which are available on a first-come, first-served basis and stay full on summer weekends. Arrive early. The fees range from $10 to $12 per campsite per night. No electrical or water hookups are available. Only the Sunshine Point Campground stays open all year. The rest are open only from late spring through late fall.

The **Ohanapecosh Campground** (205 campsites), located in the southeast corner of the park, is the largest but is a long way from the alpine meadows that are what most visitors want to see. The closest campground to Paradise is **Cougar Rock** (200 campsites), where you can camp under huge old-growth trees. The **White River Campground** (117 campsites) is close to Sunrise, which is one of the most spectacular spots in the park. The **Sunshine Point Campground** (18 campsites), is near the Nisqually entrance. Up in the northwest corner of the park, there is **Ipsut Creek Campground** (29 campsites).

In addition to drive-in campgrounds, and the many backcountry camps, there are two walk-in campgrounds that often have spaces available, even on weekends. **Mowich Lake Campground** (10 campsites) is in the northwest corner of the park not far from Ipsut Creek Campground and the sites are only 100 yards from the parking lot. If you're prepared for a longer walk in, consider the **Sunrise Campground** (8 campsites) which is about a mile from the Sunrise parking lot.

When the park campgrounds are full, try **La Wis Wis** (100 campsites), a national forest campground on U.S. 12 and the Cowlitz River near the Ohanapecosh entrance. There are also numerous unremarkable National Forest Service campgrounds along U.S. 12 east of White Pass and along Wash. 410 east of the park.

For information on campgrounds in the national park, contact **Mount Rainier National Park,** Tahoma Woods, Star Route, Ashford, WA 98304 (☎ 360/569-2211). For those outside the park, contact the **Naches Ranger District**, 10061 U.S. 12, Naches, WA 98937 (☎ 509/653-2205); the **Packwood Ranger District**, 13068 U.S. 12, Packwood, WA 98361 (☎ 360/494-0600); or the **Randle Ranger District**, 10024 U.S. 12 (P.O. Box 670), Randle, WA 98377 (☎ 360/497-1100). For national forest campground reservations, contact the **National Forest Reservation Service** (☎ 800/280-CAMP).

WHERE TO DINE

In the park there are dining rooms at Paradise Inn, open from May to October, and the National Park Inn, open year-round. As the only formal dining options within the park, these restaurants tend to stay busy. For quick meals, there are snack bars at the Henry M. Jackson Memorial Visitor Center, at Paradise, and at Sunrise Lodge.

In Ashford you'll find a couple of places that bake great pies including the **Wild Berry Restaurant,** 37720 Hwy. 706 E., Ashford (☎ **360/569-2628**), which is one of the closest restaurants to the park entrance, and, a bit farther west, the **Copper Creek Restaurant,** Wash. 706 E., Ashford (☎ **360/569-2326**).

One other interesting dining option in the area is the **Cascadian Dinner Train** (☎ **888/RRDINER**), which leaves from the town of Elbe, west of the park's Nisqually entrance, and spends four hours meandering through the foothills. A vintage steam locomotive pulls the restored passenger cars, which include an observation lounge car. The dinner train costs $55 per person, and passengers have the option of prime rib, salmon, or ground ostrich steak.

Alexander's. 37515 Wash. 706 E., Ashford. ☎ **360/569-2300.** Reservations recommended. Full dinners $16–$19, à la carte $11–$14. MC, V. AMERICAN.

Alexander's, which is also a popular B&B, is the best place to dine outside the Nisqually entrance to the park. Fresh trout from the inn's pond is the dinner of choice here, but you'll also find beef stew, pork ribs, and pasta on the menu. Whatever you order, just be sure to save room for the wild blackberry pie.

Mt. Rainier Railroad Dining Co. Wash. 7, Elbe. ☎ **360/569-2505.** Main courses $10– $17; lunch main courses $6–$11. DISC, MC, V. Mon–Fri 11am–7pm, Sat–Sun 8am–8pm. AMERICAN.

You can't miss this unusual restaurant in Elbe—just watch for all the cabooses of the adjacent Hobo Inn. Meals are basic, with steaks and fried seafoods the staples of the dinner menu, but the surroundings make this place worth a stop. You'll be dining in an old railroad dining car. Your car won't go anywhere, but you'll still get a sense of being on a rail journey.

8 Mount St. Helens National Volcanic Monument

Coldwater Ridge Visitor Center: 90 miles N of Portland, 168 miles S of Seattle

Named in 1792 by Capt. George Vancouver for his friend Baron St. Helens, Mount St. Helens was once considered the most perfect of the Cascade peaks, a snow-covered cone rising above lush forests. However, on May 18, 1980, all that changed when Mount St. Helens erupted with a violent explosion previously unknown in modern times.

The eruption blew out the side of the volcano and removed the top 1,300 feet of the peak, causing the largest landslide in history. This blast is estimated to have traveled at up to 650 miles per hour, with air temperatures of up to 800°F. The eruption also sent more than 540 million tons of ash nearly 16 miles into the atmosphere. This massive volume of ash rained down on an area of 22,000 square miles and could be measured as far away as Denver.

ESSENTIALS

GETTING THERE Mount St. Helens National Volcanic Monument is accessed by three different routes. The one with all the major information centers is Wash. 504, the Spirit Lake Highway, which heads east from I-5 at Castle Rock. The southern section of the monument is reached via Wash. 503 from I-5 at Woodland. The east side of the monument is reached via U.S. 12 from I-5 at exit 68.

VISITOR INFORMATION For more information on the national monument, contact **Mount St. Helens National Volcanic Monument,** 42218 NE Yale Bridge Road, Amboy, WA 98601 (☎ **360/247-3900**).

ADMISSION Admission is $8 per person at any developed area within Mount St. Helens National Volcanic Monument. However, once paid, this admission will get you into all the other monument visitor centers and allow you to park at any of the important monument sites.

EXPLORING THE NATIONAL MONUMENT
MOUNT ST. HELENS WEST

The best place to start an exploration of Mount St. Helens National Volcanic Monument is at the **Mount St. Helens Visitor Center at Silver Lake** (☎ **360/274-2100**), which is located at Silver Lake, five miles east of Castle Rock on Wash. 504. The visitor center houses extensive exhibits on the eruption and its effects on the region. Sum-

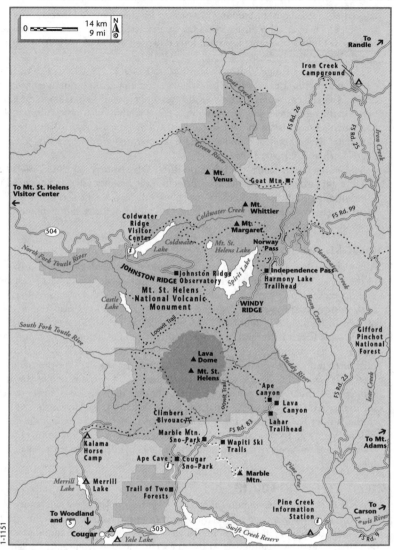

mer hours at are daily from 9am to 5pm. Before even reaching this center, you can stop and watch a 25-minute, 70mm film about the eruption at the **Mount St. Helens Cinedome Theater** (☎ 360/274-8000), which is located at exit 49 off of I-5 (tickets $5 adults, $4 seniors and children).

Continuing east from the visitor center, you'll come to the **Hoffstadt Bluffs Visitor Center** (☎ 800/752-8439) at milepost 27 (open daily 9am to 9pm in summer; daily 10am to 4pm in winter), which has a snack bar and is the take-off site for helicopter flights over Mount St. Helens ($69).

A few miles farther, just past milepost 33, you'll come to the **Forest Learning Center** (☎ 360/414-3439), which is open May to October daily 10am to 6pm. This is primarily a promotional center for the timber industry but does show a short but fascinating video about the eruption in a theater designed to resemble an ash-covered landscape. There are also displays on how forests destroyed by the blast have been replanted. Outside the center you can look down on a herd of elk that live in the Toutle River valley far below.

The **Coldwater Ridge Visitor Center** (☎ 360/274-2131), which is at Milepost 47 on Wash. 504, only 8 miles from the crater is the second monument visitor center. This center features interpretive displays on the events leading up to the eruption and the subsequent slow regeneration of life around the volcano. Hours are May to September daily 10am to 6pm, and October to April daily 9am to 5pm. Here at Coldwater Ridge, you'll also find a picnic area, interpretive trail, a restaurant, and a boat launch at Coldwater Lake.

The newest visitor center, the **Johnston Ridge Observatory** (☎ 360/274-2140), is a little bit farther up this same road. Built into the mountainside and designed to blend into the landscape, this observatory houses the equipment that is still used to monitor activity within Mount St. Helens. This view from here is stupendous. The observatory is open daily from 9am to 6pm.

MOUNT ST. HELENS EAST

Although the three visitors centers on the monument's west side can give you an idea of the power of the Mount St. Helens eruption, it is on the monument's east side that the power of this explosion really sinks in. Here you can see the forest that was blown down by the eruption. For the best views, take U.S. 12 east from exit 68 off I-5. In Randle, head south on Local Route 25 and then take Local Route 26. The **Woods Creek Information Center,** on Route 25 just before the junction with Route 26, has information on this part of the monument. Route 26 travels through mile after mile of blown-down trees, and though the sight of the thousands of trees that were felled by a single blast is quite bleak, it reminds one of the awesome power of nature. Almost two decades after the eruption, life is slowly returning to this devastated forest. At Meta Lake, Route 26 joins Route 99, which continues to the **Windy Ridge Viewpoint,** where visitors get their closest look at the crater. Below Windy Ridge lies Spirit Lake, which was once one of the most popular summer vacation spots in the Washington Cascades. Today the lake is desolate and lifeless.

MOUNT ST. HELENS SOUTH

On the south side of the monument, you can explore the **Ape Cave,** a lava tube that was formed 1,900 years ago when lava poured from the volcano. When the lava finally stopped flowing, it left a 2-mile-long cave that is the longest continuous lava tube in the Western Hemisphere. At the Ape's Headquarters, you can rent a lantern for exploring the cave on your own, or join a regular ranger-led exploration of the cave. This center is open daily from late May through September.

Hikers who aren't doing the climb to the summit will find many other hiking trails within the monument, some in blast zones and some in forests that were left undamaged by the eruption. Of the trails on this side of the monument, the **Lava Canyon Trail** is the most fascinating. It follows a canyon that was unearthed by a mudflow that swept down this side of the mountain after the eruption.

On Wash. 503, the road leading to the south side of the monument, you'll find, in the town of Ariel, the **Lelooska Gallery and Museum,** 165 Merwin Village Rd. (☎ 360/225-9735 or 360/225-8828), which features Native American art and crafts from around the country. This is one of the finest Native American galleries in the state.

Bigfoot: Lost Primate or Tabloid Hoax?

The legend of Bigfoot is firmly entrenched in the Northwest, and though there aren't too many people around who have seen one of its footprints, the reports have been steady enough over the years to keep the belief alive.

Variously described over the years as being anywhere from under 5 feet tall to over 8 feet tall, most Bigfoots share the common traits of being hairy and very shy of humans. In a few instances they have displayed aggressive behavior, but for the most part they have simply seemed curious about human activities. More frequent than actual sightings have been discoveries of Bigfoot tracks, and it was just such tracks, found north of the Klamath River in California, that prompted a reporter for the *Humboldt Times* newspaper to coin the term Bigfoot in 1958. This beast's other common name, Sasquatch, is derived from a Native American name used in the Fraser River valley of British Columbia.

Though Bigfoot reports have come from all over the country, and all over the world for that matter, the region from Northern California to southern British Columbia has produced by far the most incidents. Since the first settlers began arriving in this region, there have been hundreds of reports of giant footprints and handprints, as well as actual sightings of these large apelike creatures.

Among the most famous reports are that of "Jacko," a wild man captured in British Columbia in 1884. However, after the first newspaper report of this curious beast, there were no more reports. The single most famous sighting was that of two Sasquatch hunters who, in 1967, spotted Bigfoot and managed to film it on their movie camera.

If you'd like to do a bit of searching for Sasquatch, you should pick up a copy of the *Field Guide to Sasquatch* by David George Gordon (Sasquatch Books, 1992). This little book details the history of Bigfoot in the Northwest and cites various sightings over the years. It even gives tips on how to recognize Sasquatch footprints and what to do if you should have a Bigfoot encounter.

CLIMBING THE MOUNTAIN

If you are an experienced hiker in good physical condition, you may want to consider climbing to the top of Mount St. Helens. It is an 8- to 10-hour, 10-mile hike and can require an ice ax. The trailhead is on the south side of the monument and permits ($15 per person) are required between May 15 and October 31. Because this is a very popular climb it is advisable to request a permit in advance (summer weekends book up months in advance). However, you can also try your luck at getting an unreserved permit on the day of your climb. These are issued at **Jack's Restaurant and Store** on Wash. 503 5 miles west of Cougar. To request a climbing permit, phone ☎ **360/247-3900**.

A FEW UNIQUE WAYS TO SEE THE NATIONAL MONUMENT

If you'd like a bird's-eye view of the volcano, you can take a **helicopter flight** from the Hoffstadt Bluffs Visitor Center (☎ **800/752-8439**), $69 per person, or go up in a **small plane** with C&C Aviation (☎ **800/516-6969** or 503/760-6969), which flies out of the Evergreen Airport in Vancouver, Washington ($70 per person). **Mountain-bike tours** just outside the monument are offered by **Volcano View Mountain Bike Tours** (☎ **360/274-4341**) for $60 per person. **Mount St. Helens**

Adventure Tours (☎ 360/274-6542) offers van tours that are narrated by survivors of the big blast.

WHERE TO STAY

If you'd like to spend the night at a camp inside the blast zone (though outside the national monument), **Mount St. Helens Adventure Tours,** 980 Schaffran Rd., Castle Rock (☎ 360/274-6542; fax 360/274-8437), offers a tent-and-breakfast tour that includes a night in a large tent, plus dinner and breakfast for $125 for one person or $220 for two. This company also rents out five log cabins ($52.80 double) at its Eco-Park on Wash. 504 (the Spirit Lake Highway).

Blue Heron Inn Bed & Breakfast. 2846 Spirit Lake Hwy., Castle Rock, WA 98611. ☎ **800/ 959-4049** or 360/274-9595. www.blueheroninn.com. 6 rms (all with private bathrooms). $95 double. Rates include full breakfast. MC, V.

Although this modern inn on the road to the Coldwater and Johnston Ridge visitor centers calls itself a bed-and-breakfast, it also serves dinner (for an extra $15 per person), which makes it an excellent choice if you're searching for comfort and convenience in this area. Set on five acres of land beside Silver Lake and Sequest State Park, the inn has an excellent view of Mount St. Helens. Lots of decks provide plenty of places for relaxing and soaking up the view, and during cooler weather, you can sit by the fire in the parlor. This inn is by far the best bet for accommodations in the area and is close to the Mount St. Helens Visitor Center. There are plans to operate a barbecue stand on the premises in upcoming summers.

Timberland Inn & Suites. 1271 Mt. St. Helens Way, Castle Rock, WA 98611. ☎ **360/ 274-6002.** Fax 360/274-6335. 40 rms and suites. A/C TV TEL. $66.60–$119.60 double or suite. AE, CB, DC, DISC, MC, V.

This newer motel is right off I-5 at Exit 49 and is adjacent to the Cinedome Theatre. The guest rooms are for the most part standard-issue motel rooms, but the suites have separate sitting areas. Some suites also have whirlpool tubs.

CAMPGROUNDS

West of the monument, **Sequest State Park** (92 campsites), set amid impressive old-growth trees on Wash. 504 about 5 miles off I-5, is the closest public campground to Coldwater Ridge. This campground is set on Silver Lake adjacent to the Mount St. Helens Visitor Center. For reservations, call **Reservations Northwest** (☎ **800/ 452-5687**).

East of the monument, **Iron Creek Campground** (98 campsites), a Forest Service campground, is the closest to Windy Ridge. This campground is set amid old-growth trees on the bank of the Cispus River.

South of the monument, there are a couple of conveniently located campgrounds on Yale Lake—**Cougar** (45 campsites) and **Beaver Bay** (63 campsites)—and another near the east end of **Swift Reservoir** (93 campsites). For more tranquillity, try the little **Merrill Lake Campground** (11 campsites), which is operated by the Washington Department of Natural Resources. Although a bit out of the way for exploring the monument, the **Lower Falls Campground** (43 campsites) on the Lewis River is a beautiful spot set beside the waterfalls for which it is named. For information on national forest campgrounds in the area, contact the **Randle Ranger District,** 10024 U.S. 12 (P.O. Box 670), Randle, WA 98377 (☎ **360/497-1100**). For national forest campground reservations, contact the **National Forest Reservation Service** (☎ **800/ 280-CAMP**).

9 The Columbia Gorge & the Mount Adams Area

Stevenson: 45 miles E of Vancouver, 25 miles W of White Salmon

The Columbia Gorge, which begins a few miles east of Vancouver, Washington, and extends eastward for nearly 70 miles, cuts through the Cascade Range and connects the rain-soaked west-side forests with the sagebrush scrublands of eastern Washington. This change in climate is caused by moist air condensing into snow and rain as it passes over the crest of the Cascades. Most of the air's moisture falls on the western slopes, so that the eastern slopes and the land stretching for hundreds of miles beyond lie in what's called a rain shadow. Perhaps nowhere else on earth can you witness this rain-shadow effect so clearly. Between the two extremes lies a community of plants that's unique to the Columbia Gorge. Springtime in the gorge sees colorful displays of wildflowers, many of which exist only here.

The Columbia River is older than the hills. It's older than the mountains, too. And it's this great age that accounts for the river's dramatic gorge through the Cascades. The mountains have actually risen up *around* the river. Though the river's geologic history dates back 40 million years or so, it was a series of recent events, geologically speaking, that gave the Columbia Gorge its very distinctive appearance. About 15,000 years ago, toward the end of the last Ice Age, huge dams of ice far upstream burst and sent floodwaters racing down the Columbia. As the floodwaters swept through the Columbia Gorge, they were as much as 1,200 feet high. Ice and rock carried by the floodwaters helped the river to scour out the sides of the once gently sloping valley, leaving behind the steep-walled gorge that we know today. The waterfalls that attract so many oohs and aahs are the most dramatic evidence of these great floods. As early as 1915 a scenic highway was built through the gorge and in 1986 much of the area was designated the **Columbia Gorge National Scenic Area** to preserve its spectacular and unique natural beauty.

While the Oregon side of the Columbia Gorge has the spectacular waterfalls and tends to get all the publicity, it is actually from the Washington side, along Wash. 14, that you get the best views. From this highway the views take in both the southern wall of the Columbia Gorge and the snow-capped summit of Mount Hood. It is also on the Washington side of the Gorge, in Stevenson, that you'll find the informative Columbia Gorge Interpretive Center.

Roughly 45 miles north of White Salmon, lying directly across the Columbia from Hood River, rises Mount Adams, which, at 12,276 feet in elevation, is the second highest peak in Washington. However, because it is so inaccessible from Puget Sound and can't be seen from most of Portland (the nearest metropolitan area), it remains one of the least visited major peaks in the state. Though few get to this massive peak, those who do often make the relatively easy, nontechnical climb to the mountain's summit.

ESSENTIALS

GETTING THERE   Wash. 14 parallels the Columbia River from Vancouver through the Columbia Gorge and into eastern Washington. Mount Adams lies to the north of the Gorge and is accessed via Wash. 141 from White Salmon.

VISITOR INFORMATION   For more information on the Columbia Gorge, contact the **Skamania County Chamber of Commerce,** P.O. Box 1037, Stevenson, WA 98648 (☎ **509/427-8911**).

AN INTRODUCTION TO THE GORGE

✪ Columbia Gorge Interpretive Center. 990 SW Rock Creek Dr., Stevenson. ☎ **509/ 427-8211.** Admission $6 adults, $5 seniors and students, $4 children 6–12, free for children 5 and under. Daily 10am–5pm. Closed: Easter, Thanksgiving, Christmas, and New Year's.

This museum on the Washington side of the Gorge is your best introduction to the Gorge and focuses on early Native American inhabitants and the development of the area by white settlers. Exhibits contain historical photographs by Edward Curtis and other photos that illustrate the story of portage companies and paddlewheelers. Period quotations and explanations of Gorge history put the museum's many artifacts in their proper context. One relic that you can't miss is a 37-foot-high replica of a 19th-century fish wheel, which gives an understanding of how salmon runs have been threatened in the past as well as in the present. Displays also frankly discuss other problems that the coming of civilization brought to this area. A slide program tells the history of the formation of the Gorge, and when the volcanoes erupt, the floor in the theater actually shakes from the intensity of the low-volume sound track. When it's not cloudy, the center has an awesome view of the south side of the Gorge.

EXPLORING THE GORGE

Heading east from Vancouver, Wash. 14 passes through the industrial towns of Camas and Washougal before finally breaking free of the Portland/Vancouver metropolitan area. For much of the way, the highway stays close to the river, but at Cape Horn, an area where basalt cliffs rise straight out of the water, the highway climbs high above the river providing one of the best views along this stretch of the highway.

Roughly 35 miles east of Vancouver, you come to **Beacon Rock,** an 800-foot-tall monolith that has a 1-mile trail to its summit. The trail, which for much of the way consists of metal stairways and catwalks, was built between 1915 and 1918 by Henry Biddle, who saved Beacon Rock from being blasted into rubble for a jetty at the mouth of the Columbia River. Continuing east, you'll come to Stevenson, which is the site of the above-mentioned Columbia Gorge Interpretive Center.

Beyond Stevenson, is the town of Carson, where you can avail yourself of the therapeutic waters of the **Carson Hot Springs Resort** (☎ **509/427-8292**), located just north of town. It's open daily from 8:30am to 7pm; charges are $10 for a soak that includes a postsoak wrap, and $32 for an hour's massage. The resort has been in business since 1897 and looks every bit its age. However, it's just this old-fashioned appeal that keeps people coming back year after year to soak in the hot mineral springs (separate men's and women's soaking tubs) and get massaged. There are also some very basic hotel rooms ($30 to $35) and cabins ($40 to $50) available. If you're looking for natural hot springs, the folks here can give you directions to some that are nearby.

If you're up for a strenuous but rewarding hike, the 3-mile trail to the summit of 2,948-foot **Dog Mountain** provides ample views up and down the Gorge. In spring, the wildflower displays in the meadows on Dog Mountain's slopes are some of the finest in the Gorge. You'll find the trailhead on Wash. 14, 12 miles east of the Bridge of the Gods, a bridge that now spans the river at a site where a huge landslide once blocked the Columbia creating a natural "bridge" across the river.

THE MOUNT ADAMS AREA

While Mount Adams' summit is popular with mountain climbers, at lower elevations, there are also excellent trails for hikers and backpackers. The favorite summer spot for a hike is Bird Creek Meadows on the Yakama Indian Reservation north of the town of Trout Lake. These meadows are ablaze with wildflowers in July. Eight miles west of Trout Lake, you can explore several **ice caves.** The caves were formed by lava flows centuries ago. For more information on hiking on Mount Adams, contact the **Gifford Pinchot National Forest,** Mt. Adams Ranger District, 2455 Hwy. 141, Trout Lake, WA 98650 (☎ **509/395-2501**).

SPORTS & OUTDOOR ACTIVITIES

The Columbia Gorge is one of the nation's top boardsailing spots, and if you're here to ride the wind, or just want to watch others as they race back and forth across the river, head to the **fish hatchery,** west of the mouth of the White Salmon River, or **Swell City,** a park about 3 miles west of the Hood River Bridge. **Bob's Beach,** in downtown Stevenson, is another popular spot.

When there isn't enough wind for sailing, there's still the option to go **rafting** on the White Salmon River. Companies offering raft trips on this river include **Phil's White Water Adventure** (☎ **800/366-2004** or 509/493-3121), **AAA Rafting** (☎ **800/866-RAFT** or 509/493-2511), and **Renegade River Rafters** (☎ **509/ 427-RAFT**). The river-rafting season runs from March to October and a half-day trip will cost around $45 per person. White-water kayaking is also popular on the White Salmon River.

If you're interested in a bit of horseback riding, contact **Northwestern Lake Riding Stable** (☎ **509/493-4965**), which is at Northwestern Lake off Wash. 141 north of White Salmon.

WHERE TO STAY
IN STEVENSON

✪ **Skamania Lodge.** 1131 Skamania Lodge Way (P.O. Box 189), Stevenson, WA 98648. ☎ **800/221-7117** or 509/427-7700. Fax 509/427-2547. 195 rms, 5 suites. A/C TV TEL. $135–$210 double; $240 suites (lower rates in winter). AE, DC, DISC, MC, V.

Located on the Washington side of the Columbia Gorge, Skamania Lodge has the most spectacular vistas of any area hotel. It has the distinction of being the only golf resort in the Gorge, but is equally well situated whether you brought your sailboard, hiking boots, or mountain bike. The interior decor is classically rustic with lots of rock and natural wood and Northwest Indian artworks and artifacts on display. In the cathedral-ceilinged lobby, where big wicker chairs are set by the stone fireplace, huge windows take in the Gorge panorama. If you should opt for a fireplace room, you won't have to leave your bed to enjoy a fire. The river-view guest rooms are only slightly more expensive than the forest-view rooms (which also happen to look out over the huge parking lot).

Dining/Entertainment: The casual Northwest cuisine in the lodge's dining room is excellent (and the view of the Gorge is amazing). Adjacent to the dining room is a lounge with a large, freestanding stone fireplace.

Services: Room service, concierge.

Facilities: 18-hole golf course, tennis courts, swimming pool, whirlpool, exercise facility, nature trails, volleyball court.

IN BINGEN & WHITE SALMON

The Bingen School Inn. Humboldt and Cedar sts., Bingen, WA 98605 (just east of the turnoff for White Salmon). ☎ **509/493-3363.** Fax 509/493-3321. www.gorge.net/lodging/cgoc. 6 rms (none with private bathrooms), 3 dorm rooms. $29 double; $11 dorm bed. AE, DISC, MC, V.

Bingen is a lumber mill town just across the river from Hood River, and the Bingen School Inn, as its name implies, is an old schoolhouse that has been turned into a hostel. The folks who stay here come from all over the world, but share a love of the outdoors. Sailboarding is the main topic of conversation around the hostel in the summer, but when there aren't any winds, guests usually head off on their mountain bikes, catch a raft trip, hike, or practice their rock-climbing skills on the hostel's indoor climbing wall. In winter, skiing and snowboarding are the raison d'être of guests. Accommodations, in old school rooms, are very basic (beds are banged together from two-by-six lumber). There's a lounge and a laundry. This place is very basic, but if you're traveling the Northwest on a backpacker's budget, you'll appreciate the atmosphere. Mountain bikes and sailboards can both be rented at the hostel.

IN GLENWOOD

Flying L Ranch. 25 Flying L Lane, Glenwood, WA 98619. ☎ **888/MT-ADAMS** or 509/364-3488. Fax 509/364-3634. 11 rms (8 with private bathrooms), 2 cabins. $70–$80 double with shared bath, $85–$110 double with private bath; $110–$120 cabin. Rates include full breakfast. AE, MC, V.

With its meadows and ponderosa pines, this 160-acre ranch in a wide valley at the foot of Mount Adams is the ideal base for exploring this area. In summer, you can head up to the alpine meadows on the slopes of the mountain, and in winter, there are cross-country ski trails on the ranch and also nearby. While the two cabins, tucked under the pine trees, offer lots of room and privacy, the rooms in the old 1940s lodge have a classic ranch feel. Other rooms are in a separate guest house with a rooftop observation deck. The hot tub has a view of the mountain.

WHERE TO DINE

The dining room of **Skamania Lodge** (see above for details) is by far the best restaurant on the Washington side of the Gorge. There are also quite a few good restaurants across the river in Hood River, Oregon, including the following:

The Mesquitery. 1219 12th St. ☎ **541/386-2002.** Main courses $9–$16. AE, MC, V. Wed–Fri 11:30am–2pm and 4:30–9:30 or 10pm, Sat–Tues 4:30–9:30 or 10pm. STEAK/SEAFOOD.

Located in the uptown district of Hood River, the Mesquitery is a small and cozy grill with a rustic interior. As the name implies, mesquite grilling is the specialty of the house. Chicken and ribs are most popular, but you can also get a sirloin steak or grilled fish. At lunch there are sandwiches made with grilled meats. If you aren't that hungry, this is a good place to put together a light meal from such à la carte dishes as shrimp burritos, fish tacos, and fettuccine pesto.

✪ **Sixth Street Bistro.** 509 Cascade St. ☎ **541/386-5737.** Reservations recommended. Main courses $8–$13. MC, V. Daily 11:30am–10:30pm. AMERICAN/INTERNATIONAL.

Just a block off Oak Street toward the river, the Sixth Street Bistro has an intimate little dining room and patio on the lower floor and a lounge with a balcony on the second floor. Each has its own entrance, but they share the same menu so there's a choice of ambience. There are numerous international touches such as chicken satay appetizers and a grilled-chicken salad with sesame-ginger dressing, and plenty of interesting pasta dishes such as Cajun fettuccine and pad Thai. You'll also find seasonal specials and a good list of burgers.

PETROGLYPHS, RODINS & STARGAZING EAST OF THE GORGE

Between The Dalles Dam and the town of Goldendale (north of Wash. 14 on U.S. 97), there are a few unusual attractions that are well worth a visit if you are exploring down at this eastern end of the Gorge.

Horsethief Lake State Park. Wash. 14. ☎ **509/767-1159.** Free admission. Apr–Oct, daily 9am–dusk. Closed Nov–Mar.

Located between The Dalles Dam and Wishram on Wash. 14, Horsethief Lake is a popular fishing area and campground. However, long before the area was designated a state park, this was a gathering ground for Native Americans. The park lies not far from the famous Celilo Falls, which were, before being inundated by the waters behind The Dalles Dam, the most prolific salmon-fishing area in the Northwest. Each year for thousands of years Native Americans would gather here from as far away as present-day Northern California and southern British Columbia. These Native Americans left signs of their annual visits, in the form of petroglyphs, on rocks that are now protected within Horsethief Lake State Park. Petroglyphs abound here, the most famous of which is Tsagaglalal ("she who watches"), which is a large face that gazes down on the Columbia River. Due to past vandalization, the only way to see this and other park petroglyphs is on ranger-led walks held on Friday and Saturday mornings (reservation highly recommended).

✪ **Maryhill Museum of Art and Stonehenge.** 35 Maryhill Museum Dr., Goldendale, WA. ☎ **509/773-3733.** Admission $5 adults, $4.50 seniors, $1.50 children 6–16. Mar 15–Nov 15, daily 9am–5pm. Closed Nov 16–Mar 14.

Atop a windswept bluff overlooking the Columbia River, at a spot more than 100 miles from the nearest city, eccentric entrepreneur Sam Hill built a grand mansion he called Maryhill. Though he never lived in the mansion, he did turn it into a museum that today is one of the finest, most eclectic, and least visited major museums in the Northwest. Exhibited here are an internationally acclaimed collection of sculptures and drawings by Auguste Rodin; an extensive collection of Native American artifacts, including rock carvings, beadwork, and baskets; the personal collection of Queen Marie of Romania; and vintage miniature French fashion mannequins. A few miles farther east from Maryhill, you'll come to Hill's concrete reproduction of Stonehenge, which he had built as a memorial to local men who died in World War I.

Goldendale Observatory State Park Interpretive Center. 1602 Observatory Dr., Goldendale. ☎ **509/773-3141.** Free admission. Apr–Sept, Wed–Sun 2–5pm and 8pm–midnight; Oct–Mar, Sat 1–5pm and 7–9pm, Sun 1–5pm.

If you happen to be an amateur astronomer, you won't want to miss a visit to the Goldendale Observatory. The central 24$^1/_2$-inch reflector is one of the largest public telescopes in the country—large enough for scientific research. But instead, it's dedicated to sharing the stars with the general public. The observatory is out in this remote part of the state because this region's dry weather and distance from city lights almost guarantees that every night will be a good night for stargazing.

11 Central & Eastern Washington

For many people who live on the wet west side of the Cascades, life in Washington would be nearly impossible if it were not for the sunny east side of the mountains. Eastern Washington lies in the rain shadow of the Cascades and, with many areas receiving less than 10 inches of rain per year, is considered a high desert. The lack of rain is accompanied by plenty of sunshine—an average of 300 days per year. Statistics like these prove irresistible to folks from Puget Sound, who regularly head over to the Yakima Valley to dry out.

Though there's little rainfall, rivers such as the Columbia, which meanders through much of this region, have provided, with the assistance of several dams (including the huge Grand Coulee Dam), sufficient irrigation water to make the region a major agricultural area. Apples, pears, cherries, wine grapes (and wine), wheat, and potatoes have become the staple crops of a land that once grew little more than sagebrush and bunchgrass. The Columbia River was also responsible thousands of years ago for creating the region's most fascinating geological wonders—a dry waterfall that was once four times larger than Niagara Falls and abandoned riverbeds known as coulees.

Down in the southeastern corner of the state, near the college and wheat-farming town of Walla Walla, the desert gives way to the Blue Mountains. It was near here that the region's first white settlers, Marcus and Narcissa Whitman, set up a mission in order to convert Native Americans to Christianity. They were later massacred by Cayuse Indians angered by the Whitmans' inability to cure a measles epidemic. To the north of Walla Walla lie the Palouse Hills, a scenic region of rolling hills that are now blanketed with the most productive wheat farms in the United States.

Though Yakima attracts sunseekers from the western part of the state, it is Spokane, at the far eastern end of the state only a few miles from Idaho, that is the region's largest city. With its proximity to forests and mountains and its setting on the banks of the Spokane River, it appeals to those who value outdoor activities. The city's far easterly location, however, makes it seem less a part of the Northwest and more a part of the Rocky Mountain states. Thus it forms an eastern gateway both to Washington and to the Northwest.

Eastern Washington

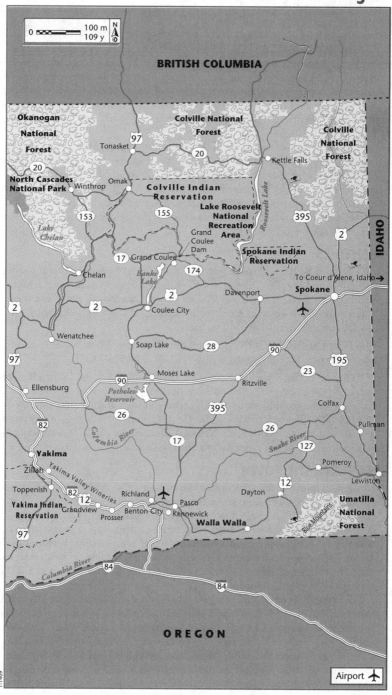

BRITISH COLUMBIA

Okanogan
National
Forest

Colville National
Forest

Colville
National
Forest

Tonasket

97

20

Kettle Falls

North Cascades
National Park

20

Winthrop   Omak

Colville Indian
Reservation

153

155

Lake Roosevelt
National
Recreation
Area

395

2

IDAHO

Lake
Chelan

Grand
Coulee
Dam

17   Grand Coulee

174

Spokane Indian
Reservation

Chelan

Banks
Lake

2

Davenport

To Coeur d'Alene, Idaho →

Spokane

2

2

Coulee City

Wenatchee

Soap Lake

28

90

195

Ellensburg

90

Potholes
Reservoir

Moses Lake

Ritzville

23

Columbia River

26

395

17

26

Colfax

Pullman

82

Yakima
Zillah

Yakima Valley Wineries

127

Pomeroy

Lewiston

Toppenish

82

12

Richland

Dayton

12

Umatilla
National
Forest

Yakima Indian
Reservation   Grandview
Prosser

Benton City
Pasco
Kennewick

Walla Walla

Snake River

Blue Mountains

97

Columbia River

84

84

OREGON

Airport ✈

1-1-1409

307

1 Ellensburg: A Glimpse of the Wild West

110 miles SE of Seattle, 36 miles N of Yakima, 75 miles S of Wenatchee

In Ellensburg, which lies on the edge of cattle- and sheep-ranching country just east of the last Cascade foothills, the Wild West lives on. Best known as the site of the annual Ellensburg Rodeo, this town clings to its cowboy image despite its current incarnation as a college town. Although the town isn't really a destination per se, its proximity to Seattle and its sunny climate make it a quick escape from the Puget Sound rains.

The town's downtown historic district, one of the most attractive in the state, is full of buildings dating from 1889, the year in which most of the town's commercial buildings were destroyed in a fire on the Fourth of July. Had it not been for this fire, the town would likely have become the state capital. But with only one commercial building remaining, how could the government set up business in Ellensburg? Instead of becoming the capital, the town became the site of a state college that's now Central Washington University.

ESSENTIALS

GETTING THERE   Ellensburg is on I-90. Just east of town, I-82 leads southeast to Yakima and the Tri-Cities area (Wash. 821 provides a scenic route south to Yakima). U.S. 97 leads north over Blewett Pass to Leavenworth and Wenatchee.

Greyhound bus lines has service to Ellensburg. The station is at Eighth Avenue and Okanogan Street.

VISITOR INFORMATION   Contact the **Ellensburg Chamber of Commerce,** 436 N. Sprague St., Ellensburg, WA 98926. (☎ **509/925-3137**).

FESTIVALS   The annual Ellensburg Rodeo, held each year on Labor Day weekend, is the town's biggest event and is one of the top 10 rodeos in the United States. For more information, contact the **Ellensburg Rodeo and Kittitas County Fair** (☎ **800/637-2444** or 509/962-7831). The third weekend of May each year sees the annual Western Art Association's **National Western Art Show & Auction,** which features works by some of the nation's finest western artists.

EXPLORING THE TOWN

Ellensburg's most unusual attraction can be experienced at the university's **Chimpanzee and Human Communication Institute,** Nicholson Boulevard and D Street (☎ **509/963-2244**), a research facility that stages what it calls **"Chimposiums."** At these programs, visitors learn about the primate communication project and get to observe several chimpanzees that have learned to use American Sign Language (ASL). Among these chimps is the famous Washoe, which was the first chimpanzee to learn ASL. The programs, held on Saturday and Sunday, cost $10 for adults and $7.50 for students; reservations are recommended.

The Western art of Ellensburg native John Clymer is displayed at the **Clymer Art Museum,** 416 N. Pearl St. (☎ **509/962-6416**). A member of the prestigious Cowboy Artists of America, Clymer is best known for producing more than 80 *Saturday Evening Post* covers. The museum is open Monday through Friday from 10am to 5pm and on Saturday and Sunday from noon to 5pm; admission is $3. Also here in town is the **Kittitas County Historical Museum,** 114 E. Third St. (☎ **509/925-3778**), which has an interesting collection of Native American artifacts, as well as a large rock and mineral collection that focuses on petrified wood. The museum is open Tuesday through Saturday from 10am to 4pm; admission is by donation.

If you're interested in art, you may also want to drop by **Gallery One,** 408$^{1}/_{2}$ N. Pearl St. (☎ **509/925-2670**), which features works by regional, national, and international artists. If you want to shop for some of the region's rare Ellensburg blue agate, stop by the **Ellensburg Agate Shop,** 201 S. Main St. (☎ **509/925-4998**). Be forewarned: This pale blue semiprecious stone can be quite pricey.

It's partly because of the rodeo and John Clymer that Ellensburg likes to present itself as a Western town. However, the city has much more of a college town feel, with a youthful population and a cosmopolitan atmosphere that's much more urban than cowboy. For a look at some unique local art, cruise by **Dick & Jane's Spot** at 101 N. Pearl St. The house and yard here are decorated with hundreds of colorful objects. However, the town's most famous work of art is *The Ellensburg Bull,* which sits on a bench in a plaza in the downtown historic district.

Some 4$^{1}/_{2}$ miles southeast of town you'll find **Olmstead Place State Park** (☎ **509/925-1943**), a heritage site that preserves a pioneer homestead of the 1870s. Northwest of Ellensburg at Exit 101 off I-90, in the town of Thorp, is the **Thorp Mill** (☎ **509/964-9640**), an 1880s gristmill that now houses a museum; it's open Wednesday through Sunday from 1 to 4pm from Memorial Day weekend to September 30.

Although Ellensburg lies more than 30 miles west of the Columbia River along I-90, it is the closest major town to the famed amphitheater called The Gorge. Each summer, this remote natural amphitheater overlooking the Columbia near the community of George, Washington (no kidding), hosts numerous major rock concerts that attract people from all over the Northwest. For more information, contact the **George Visitor Information Center** (☎ **509/785-3831**).

While most outdoors enthusiasts head west of Ellensburg to the mountains, lakes, and rivers around Cle Elum, Roslyn, and Snoqualmie Pass (see chapter 10, "The Washington Cascades," for details), anyone wanting to cool off on a hot summer day makes for the waters of the nearby Yakima River. **Rill Adventures,** 10471 Thorp Hwy. North (☎ **509/964-2520**), offers guided rafting and fishing trips on the Yakima River west of Ellensburg. Raft rentals are also available through **River Raft Rentals,** 9801 Wash. 10 (☎ **509/964-2145**), on the west side of town. The section of this river south of town, through Yakima Canyon, is a popular stretch of river with tubers and canoeists; and is a favorite of fly anglers as well.

WHERE TO STAY

Unfortunately, the accommodations situation in Ellensburg isn't too good. The **Super 8 Motel,** 1500 Canyon Rd., Ellensburg, WA 98926 (☎ **509/962-6888**), charging $50 to $66 double, is as good a place as you'll find here.

WHERE TO DINE

If you're in need of some espresso, pull up a saddle at the Cowboy Espresso Bar inside **Jaguar's,** 423 N. Pearl St. (☎ **509/962-6081**), a Western-clothing store.

✪ **Valley Café.** 105 W. Third St. ☎ **509/925-3050.** Main courses $7–$17. AE, DC, MC, V. Mon–Thurs 11am–8:30pm, Fri–Sat 11am–9 or 10pm. INTERNATIONAL.

Behind the shining black glass facade of this easily overlooked vintage cafe, you'll find a classic 1930s diner straight out of an Edward Hopper painting. Take a seat in one of the wooden booths and you'll swear you've stepped back in time. The menu, however, is quite contemporary and features such dishes as blackened salmon, chicken with spicy peanut sauce, and tortellini. At lunch, meals are likely to range the globe and might include chimichangas or a chicken Dijon sandwich.

The Yellow Church Cafe. 111 S. Pearl St. ☎ **509/933-2233.** Main dishes $4–$6. MC, V. Daily 7am–2pm. AMERICAN.

Though basically just a cheap college breakfast and lunch place, this restaurant is worth checking out for its setting in a renovated little yellow church that was built back in 1923. Breakfast is the big meal here, especially on weekends, and the baked goods are hot items. There are always interesting specials on the blackboard. If you can't find a table on the main floor, check up in the choir loft.

2 Yakima & the Wine Country

150 miles SE of Seattle, 92 miles NW of Richland, 195 miles SW of Spokane

Located only 3 hours from Seattle, Yakima is in another world—the sunny side of the Cascades, which receives only about 8 inches of rain a year. Despite this lack of rainfall, the area has become one of Washington's main apple-growing regions. Hops, used in making beer, is another important crop in the Yakima Valley, but it is grapes and the wines produced from those grapes that have been bringing the valley international attention in recent years. On a visit to Yakima, you can sample the area's bounties at fruit stands, wineries, and microbreweries.

All the land around Yakima was once the homeland of the Yakama people. The first white settlers, Catholic missionaries, arrived in 1847 and set up their mission south of present-day Yakima, and by the 1850s growing hostilities between settlers and Native Americans had led to the establishment of Fort Simcoe, 38 miles west of Yakima. In 1880, when residents of Yakima City refused to sell land to the Northern Pacific Railroad, the railroad built North Yakima 4 miles away and proceeded to move 50 buildings from Yakima City to the new town site, which grew into the Yakima of today.

ESSENTIALS

GETTING THERE Yakima is on I-82 at the junction with U.S. 12, which connects to I-5 south of Centralia. U.S. 97 connects to I-84 east of The Dalles, Oregon.

The Yakima Municipal Airport, on the southern outskirts of town, is served by Horizon Airlines and United Express. There is also **Greyhound** bus service to Yakima; the station is at 602 E. Yakima Ave.

VISITOR INFORMATION Contact the **Yakima Valley Visitors & Convention Bureau,** 10 N. Eighth St., Yakima, WA 98901 (☎ **800/221-0751** or 509/575-3010), or for information on Toppenish, the **Toppenish Chamber of Commerce,** P.O. Box 28, Toppenish, WA 98948 (☎ **509/865-3262**).

GETTING AROUND If you need a taxi, contact **Diamond Cab** (☎ **509/453-3113**). Public bus service in the Yakima area is provided by **Yakima Transit** (☎ **509/575-6175**).

FESTIVALS The annual **Spring Barrel Tasting** in late April is Yakima's biggest wine festival. During this festival, the previous year's vintages are tasted before being bottled. **Thanksgiving weekend** is another big wine-tasting weekend. Each year over the Fourth of July weekend the **Toppenish Pow Wow and Rodeo** brings crowds of people to Toppenish to watch broncobusters and Native American dances. Late September sees the skies over Prosser fill with hot-air balloons in the **Great Prosser Balloon Rally.**

A WINE COUNTRY TOUR

Located on the same latitude as France's main wine regions, the **Yakima Valley** is Washington's premier wine region. The valley sees sunshine on about 300 days of the year, which, combined with the rich volcanic soil, provides near-perfect grape-growing conditions. The only thing missing here is rain. Central Washington is virtually a desert, but irrigation long ago overcame this minor inconvenience and today the area produces award-winning Chardonnay, Riesling, Chenin Blanc, Sauvignon Blanc, Semillon, Gewürztraminer, Cabernet Sauvignon, Merlot, Lemberger, and muscat wines. You can get a guide and map of the region's wine country from the Yakima Valley Visitors & Convention Bureau or the **Yakima Valley Wine Growers Association,** P.O. Box 39, Grandview, WA 98930. However, even without a map, signs throughout the valley point the way to various vineyards and wineries, and you can just choose to wander the back roads between Zillah and Benton City, dropping in at whichever winery strikes your fancy. Most are open from 10 or 11am to 5pm daily. Though there are more than 20 wineries in the valley, we suggest picking no more than four or five to visit during an afternoon of wine tasting. It's also advisable to have a designated driver.

Actual wine country starts about 20 miles southeast of Yakima near the town of **Zillah.** The first winery you come to is the **Staton Hills Winery,** 71 Gangl Rd. (☎ 509/877-2112), which is just off I-82 at Exit 40 and has a panoramic view of the valley and Mount Adams.

Because so many wineries have picnic areas and panoramas, you might want to pick up ingredients for your own picnic. In **Donald,** there's the **Donald Fruit and Mercantile,** 4461 Yakima Valley Hwy. (☎ 509/877-3115), which is housed in a restored 1911 general store and sells local and Northwest gourmet foods.

In Zillah, right off the freeway, you'll find the **Zillah Oakes Tasting Room,** 1001 Vintage Valley Pkwy. (☎ 509/829-6990), which offers wines from several different wineries in the area. Zillah wineries include the **Bonair Winery,** 500 S. Bonair Rd. (☎ 509/829-6027), with its Tudor-style home surrounded by vineyards; **Wineglass Cellars,** 260 N. Bonair Rd. (☎ 509/829-3011), a small family winery; the **Hyatt Vineyards,** 2020 Gilbert Rd. (☎ 509/829-6333), which has great views of the valley and is a good place for a picnic; **Covey Run Winery,** 1500 Vintage Rd. (☎ 509/829-6235), where you can observe the cellar operations through large windows; and the **Portteus Vineyards,** 5201 Highland Dr. (☎ 509/829-6970), which has a stupendous view.

While in Zillah, don't miss the opportunity to see the **Teapot Dome gas station,** a national historic building built in 1922 in the shape of a giant teapot to call attention to a scandal in the administration of President Warren G. Harding. You'll find the teapot on the south side of I-82.

From Zillah, get back on I-82 and take Exit 54 to get to **Horizon's Edge Winery,** 4530 E. Zillah Dr. (☎ 509/829-6401), which takes its name from the tasting-room view of the valley and mountains, and the **Eaton Hill Winery,** 530 Gurley Rd. (☎ 509/854-2220), which is housed in the restored Rinehold Cannery building. East of this winery you'll find **Tefft Cellars,** 1320 Independence Rd. (☎ 509/837-7651), which makes excellent Cabernet Sauvignon and Merlot, as well as an unusual Cabernet port. Continuing on I-82 to Exit 58 and then heading south past the town of Granger will bring you to the **Stewart Vineyards,** 1711 Cherry Hill Rd. (☎ 509/854-1882), which sits atop Cherry Hill.

Getting back on the interstate and continuing to Exit 67 and the town of Sunnyside, you'll find the **Washington Hills Cellars,** 111 E. Lincoln Ave. (☎ 509/839-9463), housed in a historic Carnation building. At Exit 69, you'll find the **Tucker Cellars,** 70 Ray Rd. (☎ 509/837-8701), which has an adjacent produce market. At Exit 73, near Grandview, is the **Château Ste. Michelle,** 205 W. Fifth St. (☎ 509/882-3928), which was Washington's pioneer winery and is today the state's largest winery. Here in Grandview they produce their red wines—Cabernet Sauvignon, Merlot, and port.

At Exit 80, you can stop in at **Chukar Cherries,** 320 Wine Country Rd. (☎ 509/ 786-2055), and sample dried cherries and lots of other dried fruits and candies. Nearby is the **Yakima River Winery,** 143302 N. River Rd. (☎ 509/786-2805), which is across the river from downtown Prosser. At this same exit, but on the opposite side of the interstate, you'll find **Pontin del Roza,** 35502 N. Hinzerling Rd. (☎ 509/786-4449). Continuing north, you'll come to **Willow Crest Winery,** 135701 Snipes Rd. (☎ 509/786-7999), which is one of the newer wineries in the area. Prosser wineries include the **Hinzerling Winery,** 1520 Sheridan Rd. (☎ 509/ 786-2163), the oldest family owned winery in the valley; **Chinook Wines,** Wine Country Road (☎ 509/786-2725), which has a pretty garden that's perfect for an afternoon picnic; **Hogue Cellars,** Wine Country Road (☎ 509/786-4557), one of Washington's largest wineries; and, right next door, **Thurston Wolfe,** 3800 Lee Rd. (☎ 509/786-3313), which moved here from downtown Yakima in 1996 and produces zinfandel, grenache, and port among other wines.

At Exit 96, in the Rattlesnake Hills near Benton City, you'll find the two wineries along De Moss Road, which is on the south side of the Yakima River east of town—**Oakwood Cellars,** 40504 N. De Moss Rd. (☎ 509/588-5332), with its 100-year-old European oak wine barrel; and **Terra Blanca Vintners,** 34715 N. De Moss Rd. (☎ 509/588-6082), one of the region's newest wineries. Continuing a little farther east you'll come to Sunset Road along which there are three wineries— **Seth Ryan Winery,** 353006 Sunset Rd. (☎ 509/588-6780), which is the most convenient; **Kiona Vineyards,** 44612 N. Sunset Rd. (☎ 509/588-6716); and **Blackwood Canyon** (☎ 509/588-6249), which is near the north end of Sunset Road and produces some of the most outstanding wines in the state. From Benton City, it's 70 miles back to Yakima.

THE TOPPENISH MURALS

Before or after visiting wineries around Zillah, you might want to drive into the town of **Toppenish.** Toppenish was just a quiet little cow town until someone got the great idea of enlivening a few town walls with historical murals. Today, there are almost 50 **murals** depicting aspects of Toppenish history. You'll see these murals on walls all over town, and if you stop in at almost any store in town you can pick up a map to the murals. Though some murals have taken as much as a month to paint, each year on the first Saturday in June, Toppenish gets a mural in a day. On this day crowds descend on the town to watch a new mural created in just one day. One of the best ways to see the murals is on a horse-drawn trolley tour with **Conestoga Wagon Tours** (☎ 509/865-2898), which leaves several times a day from the corner of Toppenish and Division. Tours last 1¹/₂ hours and cost $7.50 for adults and $5 for children.

Toppenish is within the boundaries of the Yakama Indian Reservation, which operates the **Cultural Heritage Center** on U.S. 97 (☎ 509/865-2800), just outside town. This large building, designed to resemble the traditional Yakama winter lodge, contains a museum, library, gift shop, and restaurant serving salmon, buffalo, and fry bread.

Exhibits in the museum present the history and culture of the Yakama people. The Yakama are well known for their beadwork and you'll find pieces for sale in the gift shop. The center is open Monday through Saturday from 8am to 6pm and Sunday from 9am to 5pm; admission is $4 for adults, $2 for seniors and students.

Several other attractions in town provide glimpses into the town's and the region's history. The most fun of these is the **Yakima Valley Rail & Steam Museum,** 10 S.

Asotin Ave. (☎ 509/865-1911), which has its museum in the town's 1911 railway depot and also operates, on weekends, 21-mile scenic railway excursions on the Toppenish, Simcoe & Western Railroad. Excursions are $18 for adults and $13 for children. At the **Toppenish Historical Museum,** 1 S. Elm St. (☎ 509/865-4510), you can see more Native American artifacts, including baskets and beadwork. The museum is open Tuesday through Thursday from 1:30 to 4pm and Friday and Saturday from 2 to 4pm; admission is $1.50. The Yakima Valley is one of the world's top hops-growing regions, and it is here that you will find the **American Hop Museum,** 22 S. B St. (☎ 509/865-HOPS), where you can learn all about this crucial beer ingredient. March through September, the museum is open daily from 11am to 4pm; admission by donation.

MUSEUMS & OTHER ATTRACTIONS

Local history is chronicled at the **Yakima Valley Museum,** 2105 Tieton Dr. (☎ 509/248-0747), where a collection of restored horse-drawn vehicles is on display. There are also displays on the Yakama tribe and on former Supreme Court justice and environmentalist William O. Douglas, who was a Yakima resident. The museum is open Monday through Friday from 10am to 5pm and Saturday and Sunday from noon to 5pm; admission is $3 for adults, $1.50 for seniors and students. The museum also operates the **Gilbert House,** an 1898 Victorian farmhouse, at 2109 W. Yakima Ave.

The **Capitol Theatre,** 19 S. Third St. (☎ 509/575-6267), was built in 1920 and was the largest vaudeville theater in the Northwest at the time. A hand-painted mural on the inside of the theater's dome and ornate plasterwork make this a classic well worth seeing should there be a performance going on during your visit. The Yakima Symphony Orchestra performs here.

On weekends and holidays from May to October you can ride the vintage electric trolleys of the **Yakima Interurban Lines Association** (☎ 509/575-1700), which operates between Yakima and the nearby town of Selah. The trolleys depart from the corner of Third Avenue and West Pine Street and the round-trip takes less than 2 hours. The fare is $4 for adults, $3.50 for seniors, and $2.50 for children.

Fort Simcoe, 27 miles west of Toppenish in the Cascade foothills, was established in 1856 because of conflicts between Indians and settlers. Today, the fort is preserved as **Fort Simcoe State Park** (☎ 509/874-2372) and is the site of surprisingly elegant quarters that were used for only a few years before becoming the Indian Agency headquarters and school. It's open April through September daily 6:30am to dusk (buildings open Wednesday through Sunday from 9am to 4:30pm); other months weekends from 8am to dusk (buildings open by request only).

SPORTS & OUTDOOR ACTIVITIES

Extending for 10 miles between Union Gap and Selah Gap, the **Yakima Greenway** follows the banks of the **Yakima River,** with a paved path along 5 miles of the greenway. The easiest place to access the path is at Sherman Park on Nob Hill Boulevard. In summer, **kayaking, rafting, and tubing** are popular on this section of the river, and the **bird watching** is good year-round.

If you'd like to see another scenic stretch of the river, head north to Selah and then take Wash. 821 north through the **Yakima River Canyon.** The river has been around for longer than the surrounding hills, which have risen concurrent with the river slicing through them. You can rent rafts, kayaks, and bikes from **Richie's River Rentals** (☎ 509/453-2112), which also offers a shuttle service.

Golfers will enjoy playing a round at the **Apple Tree Golf Course,** 8804 Occidental Ave. (☎ 509/966-5877), where the green on the 17th hole is an apple-shaped island. If you're a fan of horse racing, you can play the ponies at **Yakima Meadows, Central Washington State Fairgrounds** (☎ **509/248-3920**). The season runs from November to March with races starting at noon on Wednesday and Friday through Sunday. Feeling like a game of croquet or some lawn bowling? Check out **The Lawns at Hollow Way Meadows,** 1017 S. Euclid Rd., Grandview (☎ **509/882-3150**).

WHERE TO STAY

For a list of bed-and-breakfast inns in the wine country, contact the **Yakima Valley Wine Growers Association,** P.O. Box 39, Grandview, WA 98930 (☎ **800/ 258-7270**).

IN YAKIMA

Best Western Oxford Inn. 1603 Terrace Heights Dr., Yakima, WA 98901. ☎ **800/528-1234** or 509/457-4444. Fax 509/453-7593. 96 rms. A/C TV TEL. $62–$72 double. AE, MC, V.

Located east of I-82 on the banks of the Yakima River, this is Yakima's most pleasant and popular budget accommodation. As such it regularly books up on weekends. The rooms are spacious, and many have balconies overlooking the river. Most also have refrigerators. Walkers and joggers will be pleased to find a 5-mile walking-and-biking path running past the motel. Facilities include an outdoor pool, an indoor whirlpool, and an exercise room. A courtesy airport shuttle is available.

✪ **Birchfield Manor Country Inn.** 2018 Birchfield Rd., Yakima, WA 98901. ☎ **800/ 375-3420** or 509/452-1960. Fax 509/452-2334. 11 rms. $80–$175 double. AE, DC, MC, V.

Located 2¹/₂ miles east of Yakima, Birchfield Manor is surrounded by pastures and is well known for its elegant dinners. Upstairs from the dining room in the 1910 Victorian farmhouse and in a new building constructed to resemble a vintage home, you'll find antique-filled guest rooms, most of which have good views out over the countryside. Four of these rooms have fireplaces, whirlpool tubs and decks to take in the view. Breakfasts here are nearly as legendary as the dinners and are a great start for a day of wine touring.

Cavanaugh's at Yakima Center. 607 E. Yakima Ave., Yakima, WA 98901. ☎ **800/ 325-4000** or 509/248-5900. Fax 509/575-8975. 153 rms, 4 suites. A/C TV TEL. $60–$95 double, $150–$200 suites. AE, CB, DC, DISC, ER, MC, V.

Located adjacent to the convention center and tourist information office, this is the most convenient of Yakima's downtown convention hotels. The rooms are of average size, though if you opt for a corporate room, you'll enjoy a few more amenities. We like the first-floor poolside rooms, which have patios within steps of the pool. The hotel's restaurant serves reasonably priced dishes of seafood, steak, and pasta. For evening entertainment, there's live or recorded Top 40 dance music in the lounge. Room service is available and there are two outdoor pools.

IN SUNNYSIDE

Sunnyside Inn Bed & Breakfast. 800 E. Edison Ave., Sunnyside, WA 98944. ☎ **800/ 221-4195** or 509/839-5557. 8 rms. TV TEL. $59–$89 double. Rates include full breakfast DISC, MC, V.

Located right in downtown Sunnyside, which, unfortunately, is not one of the valley's most attractive towns, this inn offers large rooms, most of which come with double whirlpool tubs. The home was built in 1919 and guest rooms are decorated in a simple, country style.

IN PROSSER

Wine Country Inn. 1106 Wine Country Rd. ☎ **509/786-2855.** 3 rms (2 with private bath). $65–$75 double. Rates include full breakfast. AE, MC, V.

Located at the foot of the Yakima River bridge in Prosser, this inn backs onto the river and has a casually elegant restaurant on the ground floor. Guest rooms in this old farmhouse-style home are furnished in simple country style, with hardwood floors and quilts. These rooms are nothing fancy, but the riverside location, big shade trees in the front yard, and convenience of having a restaurant on the premises, make this a good choice for wine touring.

WHERE TO DINE

IN YAKIMA

If you're looking for a convivial place to hoist a pint of microbrew ale, ✪ **Grant's Brewery Pub,** 32 N. Front St. (☎ **509/575-2922**), housed in Yakima's restored train station, is the place. This is the oldest brew pub in the country.

Birchfield Manor Country Inn. 2018 Birchfield Rd. ☎ **509/452-1960.** Reservations required. Three-course dinner $20–$30. AE, DC, MC, V. Seatings Thurs–Fri at 7pm, Sat at 6 and 8:45pm. CONTINENTAL.

Birchfield Manor, a grand old home surrounded by shade trees, doubles as a B&B and Yakima's best restaurant. The restaurant's dining room looks as if a wealthy family had cleared out the regular furniture and brought in a few extra tables for a holiday dinner. The menu changes with the season and includes a choice of five or six entrees. The house specialty is salmon in puff pastry with a Chardonnay sauce. The dinner includes fresh-baked bread, an appetizer, and salad.

✪ **Deli de Pasta.** 7 N. Front St. ☎ **509/453-0571.** Reservations recommended. Complete meals $9–$21. AE, MC, V. Mon–Sat 11:30am–9pm, Sun 5–8pm. ITALIAN.

It's small and inconspicuous, but Deli de Pasta has made a big impression on Yakima. All the pastas and sauces are made fresh on the premises (the owner is also the chef) and the menu lets you mix and match the two. You can combine black-pepper fettuccine with a creamy lemon sauce or herb linguine with pesto or rotelli with white clam sauce or whatever. However, it's the smoked-salmon ravioli with a basil-cream sauce that has been the restaurant's biggest hit. A good wine list offers both local and Italian wines.

Gasperetti's. 1013 N. First St. ☎ **509/248-0628.** Reservations recommended. Main courses $16.50–$24.50. AE, DISC, MC, V. Tues–Fri 11:30am–2:30pm and 5:45–10:30pm, Sat 5:45–10:30pm. ITALIAN/INTERNATIONAL.

Though this restaurant is very nondescript from the outside, the owners have done much to create a feeling of elegance inside. The menu changes every other week and, though primarily Italian in flavor, often includes inspiration from around the globe. The rack of lamb, a regular on the menu, comes with different sauces at different times of year (a soy-cilantro vinaigrette recently). A fine selection of local wines complements the menu offerings, and the extensive dessert list is, in itself, worth the visit. This restaurant is a favorite of Yakima's wealthier residents and has a very formal atmosphere.

✪ **The Greystone Restaurant.** 5 N. Front St. ☎ **509/248-9801.** Reservations recommended. Main courses $12–$25. AE, MC, V. Tues–Sat 6–10pm. CONTINENTAL/NORTHWEST.

Located in Yakima's restored Front Street district, The Greystone takes its name from the stone walls inside and outside the building. A high pressed-tin ceiling, an old mirrored side bar with marble counter, and antiques help capture the feel of Yakima's past. If you prefer lighter fare, there are excellent salads and homemade pasta dishes. Lamb, steak, and pork tenderloin are mainstays of the menu and come with flavorful sauces. There is, of course, an extensive selection of local wines. This casually elegant restaurant is the town's chief alternative to Gasperetti's.

IN ZILLAH & TOPPENISH

At the **Yakama Nation Cultural Center,** 280 Buster Rd., Toppenish (☎ **509/ 865-2551**), there's a casual restaurant that serves barbecued salmon, buffalo, Indian fry bread, and wild huckleberry pie.

El Ranchito. 1319 E. First Ave., Zillah. ☎ **509/829-5880**. Main dishes $3.75–$5.55. No credit cards. Summer, daily 8am–7pm; winter, daily 8am–6pm. MEXICAN.

This near-legendary tortilla factory and restaurant in Zillah has a very authentic Mexican feel and prices that will let you spend more money buying bottles of wine at area wineries. The food is simple but tasty and the tortillas are as fresh as they come.

IN GRANDVIEW

✪ **Dykstra House Restaurant.** 114 Birch Ave. ☎ **509/882-2082.** Reservations highly recommended. Main courses $13–$22.50. AE, DISC, MC, V. Tues–Thurs 9:30am–4pm, Fri 9:30am–4pm and 6–9pm, Sat 11am–2pm and 6–9pm. ITALIAN/CONTINENTAL.

This eclectic eatery, housed in a historic building that dates back to 1914, is primarily a lunch spot, but on Friday and Saturday nights dinners are also served. The menu changes every week, but a recent Saturday night featured salmon in puff pastry and chicken with béarnaise sauce and tart cherries. Friday night menus are a bit simpler and might include lasagna, ravioli, or chicken Dijon. Lunches are equally unpredictable—you never know what might show up on the menu, which makes a meal here all the more fun. There's a good selection of local wines to accompany meals.

IN PROSSER

Wine Country Inn. 1106 Wine Country Rd. ☎ **509/786-2855.** Reservations recommended. Main dishes $10–$25. AE, MC, V. Mon–Tues 11:30am–2pm, Wed–Sat 11:30am–2pm and 5:30–8:30pm, Sun (Easter–Dec 1) 9am–2pm.

Set on the bank of the Yakima River at the foot of the bridge leading into downtown Prosser, this restaurant is a favorite of people touring the wine country. The dining rooms are in the ground floor rooms of an old farmhouse-style home that now doubles as a B&B, and out back there is a deck overlooking the river. While lunches of sandwiches and salads are fairly simple, at dinner, the menu displays much more creativity. Recent selections included duck breast with a ginger-blueberry sauce, chicken Chardonnay with blue cheese and fresh basil, and an orange-ginger halibut.

3 Walla Walla

50 miles E of Richland/Pasco/Kennewick, 155 miles S of Spokane, 39 miles NE of Pendleton

Walla Walla is a quiet college town with three schools of higher learning: Walla Walla College, Whitman College, and Walla Walla Community College. Due in large part to these colleges, the town wears a rather cultured air, though the downtown is still not a very lively place. Instead, it is the town's residential streets, lined with stately old homes and large shade trees, that are the town's biggest attraction. A stroll or drive through these neighborhoods conjures up times past when the pace of life was slower.

Walla Walla is also one of the oldest communities in the Northwest and was the site of both an early mission and one of the region's first forts. Before white settlers arrived, the area was home to several Indian tribes, and it is from these tribes that the town's name, which means "many waters" or "small, rapid streams" has come. However, despite the area's regional historic importance, onions are what have made Walla Walla famous. The Walla Walla onion is a big sweet variety, similar to the Vidalia onion of Georgia, and owes its sweetness not to sugar but to a high water content and a low sulfur content. These onions, which can weigh as much as 2 pounds, are legendary around the Northwest as the very best onions for putting on burgers at summer barbecues. Between June and August each year, produce stands all over the valley sell big bags of these sweet onions. There's even a Walla Walla Sweet Onion Festival at harvest time.

ESSENTIALS

GETTING THERE   Walla Walla is on U.S. 12, 45 miles east of I-82/I-182 in the Tri-Cities area. From I-82 west of Richland, take I-182 to Pasco and continue south and then west on U.S. 12. From Pendleton, Oregon, and I-84, take Ore. 11 north. From Spokane, take U.S. 195 south to Colfax, continuing south on Wash. 26 and then Wash. 127. In Dodge, you pick up U.S. 12 and continue south to Walla Walla.

Walla Walla Regional Airport is served by Horizon Airlines and United Express. **Greyhound** bus lines also has service to Walla Walla.

VISITOR INFORMATION   Contact the **Walla Walla Area Chamber of Commerce,** 29 E. Sumach St. (P.O. Box 644), Walla Walla, WA 99362 (☎ **509/ 525-0850**).

FESTIVALS   In early May there is the Walla Walla Balloon Stampede, and in mid-July there is the Walla Walla Sweet Onion Festival.

EXPLORING THE TOWN

The **Whitman Mission National Historic Site** (☎ **509/522-6360**), 7 miles west of Walla Walla just off U.S. 12, is dedicated to a tragic page in Northwest history. Missionaries Marcus and Narcissa Whitman arrived in this area in 1836 and were some of the very first settlers to travel overland to the Northwest. Although the Whitmans had come here to convert the local Native Americans, Marcus Whitman was also a doctor and often treated the local Cayuse people. During the mid-1840s a wagon train brought a measles epidemic to the area, and the Cayuse, who had no resistance to the disease, began dying. Though Whitman was able to save his own family, most of the Cayuse who contracted the disease died from it. Supposedly, the Cayuse had a tradition of killing medicine men who could not cure an illness, and on November 29, 1847, several Cayuse attacked and killed the Whitmans and 11 other residents of the mission. The massacre at the Whitman mission prompted a war on the Cayuse and a demand for territorial status for what was at that time the Oregon country. In 1848, in response to pleas brought about by the Whitman massacre, Oregon (which at that time included present-day Washington state) became the first territory west of the Rocky Mountains.

Today nothing remains of the mission, but a trail leads through the mission site and the locations of buildings are outlined with concrete. An interpretive center provides historical background on the mission and includes numerous artifacts from the days when the Whitmans worked with the Cayuse. The site is open daily: in summer from 8am to 6pm and in winter from 8am to 4:30pm; the park is open until dusk. Admission is $2.

In town, you'll find the **Fort Walla Walla Complex,** 755 Myra Rd. (☎ **509/ 525-7703**). The museum is a collection of pioneer-era buildings, including log cabins, a one-room schoolhouse, an old railway station, and several other buildings. It's open April through October, Tuesday through Sunday from 10am to 5pm. Admission is $4 for adults, $3 for seniors and students, and $1 for children ages 6 to 12. In addition to the displays on pioneer life, there's a large collection of horse-era farming equipment.

For a glimpse inside one of the town's elegant mansions, visit the **Kirkman House Museum,** 29 N. Colville St. (☎ **509/529-4373**), a brick Victorian home that's open Monday through Friday from 1 to 3pm.

Walla Walla, because of its colleges, has become something of an art town, with numerous art galleries. At the **Carnegie Art Center,** 109 S. Palouse St. (☎ **509/ 525-4270**), which is housed in a former Carnegie library, you'll find monthly exhibits and a gift shop that features Northwest artists and craftspeople.

AREA WINERIES

Although Washington's main winery region lies to the west of the Tri-Cities area, the climate and soils around Walla Walla are also good for wine grapes and you'll find several wineries in the area. These include **Woodward Canyon Winery,** U.S. 12 (☎ **509/525-4129**); **L'Ecole No. 41,** 41 Lowden School Rd. (☎ **509/525-0940**); and **Waterbrook Winery,** off McDonald Road (☎ **509/522-1918**), all of which are located in or near the town of Lowden. In Walla Walla, you'll find **Canoe Ridge Vineyard,** 1102 W. Cherry St. (☎ **509/527-0885**), **Glen Fiona,** Mill Creek Road (☎ **509/522-2566**), and **Patrick M. Paul Vineyards,** 1554 School Ave. (☎ **509/ 522-1127**). This latter is open by appointment only, but the others are open on a regular basis.

SPORTS & OUTDOOR ACTIVITIES

Though the land immediately surrounding Walla Walla is rolling farm country, less than 20 miles to the east, the **Blue Mountains** rise to more than 6,000 feet. Hiking, mountain biking, fishing, and hunting are all popular in these little-visited mountains. For more information, contact the **Walla Walla Ranger District,** 1415 W. Rose St., Walla Walla, WA 99362 (☎ **509/522-6290**).

WHERE TO STAY

In addition to the bed-and-breakfast inns listed below, you'll find a few inexpensive chain motels in Walla Walla. These include the following (see the Appendix for toll-free telephone numbers): **Comfort Inn Walla Walla,** 520 N. Second St., Walla Walla, WA 99362 (☎ **509/525-2522**), charging $65 to $99 double; and the **Super 8 Motel,** North Wilbur Avenue and Eastgate Street, Walla Walla, WA 99362 (☎ **509/525-8800**), charging $50 to $59 double.

Green Gables Inn, 922 Bonsella St., Walla Walla, WA 99362. ☎ **888/525 5501** or 509/ 525-5501. 5 rms, 1 carriage house. A/C TV. $85–$105 double; $165 carriage house for four. Rates include full breakfast. AE, MC, V.

Located on a quiet, shady street, this large 1909 home, with its three large front gables, is located only a block from the Whitman College campus. Two sitting rooms downstairs are furnished with antiques and have fireplaces at each end that make it quite cozy on a chill evening. Guest room names are from the book *Anne of Green Gables.* Dryad's Bubble is filled with Maxfield Parrish prints and has a claw-foot tub, while in the master suite, you'll find a fireplace, whirlpool tub, a deck, and mahogany furniture. The carriage house easily sleeps four and has 1 1/2 baths and a kitchen.

✪ **Stone Creek Inn.** 720 Bryant Ave., Walla Walla, WA 99362. ☎ **509/529-8120.** 4 rms (2 with private bathrooms). $95–$115 double with shared bath, $110–$125 double with private bath. Rates include full breakfast. MC, V.

From the moment you turn into the driveway of this secluded inn, you know that this place was once the home of someone very wealthy and very important. Wide lawns are shaded by hundred year old trees, and the driveway leads to a covered portico attached to the front porch. Built in 1883 for Washington's last territorial governor, this huge Eastlake Victorian mansion sits on a four-acre estate only a few minutes from downtown and epitomizes the Walla Walla of the late 19th century. With its high ceilings and large rooms, this inn is decidedly less cramped than most Victorian inns. Two rooms have their own fireplaces and all have large windows. Breakfasts are large and often include a few Walla Walla onions, and in the afternoon there is lemonade and cookies or wine and cheese set out. Guests also have use of both a swimming pool and a hot tub.

WHERE TO DINE

Jacobi's Café. 416 N. Second Ave. ☎ **509/525-2677.** Main courses $5.50–$15. AE, DC, DISC, MC, V. Sun–Thurs 11am–10pm, Fri–Sat 11am–11pm. ITALIAN/AMERICAN.

Housed in Walla Walla's renovated railroad depot, Jacobi's is a local favorite as much for its atmosphere as for its food. The railroad theme is carried so far as to include a restored dining car attached to the main dining room. During the summer there's patio dining, and there's an espresso bar for cappuccino fixes any time of year. The menu includes burgers and steaks as well as plenty of pasta dishes. Be sure to try the deep-fried Walla Walla onions. Plenty of local wines are available. There is also an attached lounge, which seems to be the preferred place to eat.

Paisano. 26 E. Main St. ☎ **509/527-3511.** Reservations recommended. Main dishes $10–$18. AE, DISC, MC, V. Mon–Sat 11am–9pm. ITALIAN.

This is currently Walla Walla's most upscale downtown restaurant, with creatively folded napkins on the tables, olive oil for your bread, and a welcome small-town sophistication. There's even a sidewalk cafe area complete with low fence topped with flower boxes. The menu includes well-prepared Italian classics as well as plenty of more contemporary fare, including some originals such as smoked-duck cappelini. The wine list focuses on local wines, and at lunch there is a buffet.

Pastime Café. 215 W. Main St. ☎ **509/525-0873.** Main courses $3–$14.25. No credit cards. Mon–Sat 5:30am–10:30pm. ITALIAN.

Walla Walla may be a college town, but it's also small-town America, so if you suddenly have a craving for old-fashioned comfort food, this vintage diner/bar should fit the bill. From the neon sign and green tile facade out front to the pink vinyl booths and neon wall clock inside, this place, which has been in business since 1920, is a classic. The food is good old-fashioned American-Italian diner fare, with lots of spaghetti and ravioli as well as steaks, fried chicken, and even liver and onions. The bar side of the restaurant is as popular for meals as the diner side.

4 The Palouse: A Slice of Small-Town Rural Washington

Dayton: 33 miles NE of Walla Walla, 62 miles E of Tri-Cities, 129 miles SW of Spokane

Between Walla Walla and Spokane lie the rolling Palouse Hills, some of the most productive wheat country in the nation. Before the settlement of the region by whites, the Native American peoples had discovered that the Palouse, as it's known, offered ideal grazing land for horses, which reached the Northwest sometime after the Spanish conquered the southern regions of North America. By the time Lewis and Clark passed through the Palouse, the local Native Americans had become well known for their horses, which they had bred for stamina and sure-footedness. On the site of present-day Dayton, there was even a Native American horse racing track. Today these native-bred horses are known as Appaloosas for the Palouse Hills from which they came.

Although the Lewis and Clark expedition passed through this area in 1806, it was not until the 1850s that the first pioneers began settling in the area. By the 1880s, the region was booming as a major wheat and barley-growing region. Throughout the Palouse, small towns that have long been out of the mainstream of Northwest development are nestled along creek banks below rolling hills. The region's roads wind up hill and down, through a zebra-striped landscape. This distinctive striping is due to the farming practice of alternating sections of wheat with land left untilled to reduce erosion on the steep hills.

ESSENTIALS

GETTING THERE   U.S. 12, which runs from Walla Walla to Clarkston is the main route through the southern part of the Palouse. From Lewiston, Idaho, across the Snake River from Clarkston, U.S. 195 runs north through the heart of the Palouse to Spokane.

VISITOR INFORMATION   For more information on the Dayton area, contact the **Dayton Chamber of Commerce,** 166 E. Main St. (P.O. Box 22), Dayton, WA 99328 (☎ **800/882-6299** or 509/382-4825). For more information on the Pullman area, contact the **Pullman Chamber of Commerce,** 415 N. Grand Ave., Pullman, WA 99163 (☎ **800/365-6948** or 509/334-3565).

EXPLORING THE PALOUSE

Among the many little towns along the route from Walla Walla to Spokane, **Dayton** is by far the prettiest. Its old-fashioned small-town American feel is as genuine as it gets. Dayton was once one of the most important towns in this region and is still the county seat of Columbia County. Its 1887 **Columbia County Courthouse** is the oldest county courthouse still in use as such in the state of Washington. It's open Monday through Friday from 8:30am to 4:30pm. Here you'll find the **Dayton Depot,** Commercial Street (☎ **509/382-2026**), the oldest railway depot in the state (built 1881), which is open for tours Tuesday through Friday from 12:30 to 6pm and on Saturday from 10am to 6pm. Admission is $1. All in all, Dayton has 90 buildings on the National Historic Register. On the second Sunday in October each year there is a historic homes tour. In nearby Waitsburg, where there are more Victorian homes, you can also tour the **Bruce Memorial Museum** (☎ **509/337-6582**), which is open Friday and Saturday from 1 to 4pm and is filled with Victorian era furnishings.

About 44 miles northwest of Dayton, you'll find **Palouse Falls State Park.** The spectacular falls here cascade 198 feet into a rock-walled canyon. South of town 21 miles, you'll find **Ski Bluewood** (☎ **509/382-2877**), a small ski area in the Blue Mountains.

Northwest of Dayton 37 miles, you'll pass through **Pomeroy,** which, with its historic county courthouse, old flour mill, small historical museum, and turn-of-the-century buildings, is another Palouse town worth a closer look.

Pullman is the largest town in the region and is the home of Washington State University, which sent its football team to play (and lose) against the University of Michigan in the 1998 Rose Bowl. The university's **Museum of Art,** Stadium Way (☎ **509/335-1910**), is worth a visit. It's open Monday and Wednesday through Friday from 10am to 4pm, Tuesday from 10am to 10pm, and on Saturday and Sunday from 1 to 5pm; admission is free. Also on the WSU campus, you'll find the **Museum of Anthropology,** College Hall (☎ **509/335-3441**), which has human evolution and Bigfoot exhibits. The museum is open Monday through Thursday from 9am to 4pm, Friday from 9am to 3pm (closed June 16 through August 15); admission is free.

In **Colfax** you can take a look at the largest chain-saw sculpture in the world. It's called the **Codger Pole,** and it depicts the members of two football teams who got together in 1988 to replay their 1938 game. Some 18 miles north of Colfax, **Kamiak Butte County Park** provides the ideal vantage point for surveying the vast Palouse. Nearby is **Steptoe Butte State Park,** which also offers good views of the surrounding landscape.

WHERE TO STAY

The Purple House. 415 E. Clay St., Dayton, WA 99328. ☎ **800/486-2574** or 509/382-3159. 3 rms (1 with private bathroom). $85–$125 double. Rates include full breakfast. MC, V.

Well, it isn't quite purple, more a tasteful plum, but this 1882 Queen Anne Victorian home certainly does stand out from the other houses in the neighborhood. With its backyard pool and antique-filled rooms, it is the most distinctive accommodation in the Palouse. German hostess Christine Williscroft takes great pride in her cooking and is sometimes willing to prepare dinners as well as breakfast. The inn is located a block off Dayton's main street.

✪ **The Weinhard Hotel.** 235 E. Main St., Dayton, WA 99328. ☎ **509/382-4032.** Fax 509/382-2640. 15 rms. A/C TV TEL. $65–$110 double. AE, MC, V.

Constructed in 1889 to house a saloon operated by Jacob Weinhard, the nephew of Portland, Oregon, brewer Henry Weinhard, this brick building is now a comfortable and generally inexpensive Victorian inn. In the large lobby, you'll find a grand piano and, off in one corner, board games and magazines. Guest rooms have high ceilings with overhead fans and in each room there is at least one piece of antique furniture. The best room in the house has a whirlpool tub in the bathroom. Up on the roof, you'll find a terrace garden where you can enjoy a cup of espresso.

WHERE TO DINE
IN DAYTON

✪ **Patit Creek Restaurant.** 725 Dayton Ave. ☎ **509/382-2625.** Reservations recommended. Main courses lunch $5.75–$11, dinner $16–$36. MC, V. Tues–Thurs 11:30am–1:30pm and 4:30–8pm, Fri 11:30am–1:30pm and 4:30–8:30pm, Sat 4:30–8:30pm. FRENCH.

This little green cottage beside the road on the north side of Dayton alone is worth the trip to this small Palouse town. Stained-glass front windows hide the passing traffic from diners and allow guests to immerse themselves in enjoying their food. Though lunches include everything from burgers to veal piccata, all at reasonable prices, dinners are on a very different level. You might start a meal with pâté maison or baked Danish herb cheese in phyllo pastry. The entree menu includes such dishes as filet mignon poivre verte with green peppercorns, cognac, and cream; and lamb chops Provençal with a reduction of cognac, garlic, and Provençal herbs.

5 Spokane

284 miles E of Seattle, 195 miles NE of Yakima, 155 miles N of Walla Walla

Until the 1974 World's Fair focused the eyes of the nation on Spokane and its reno-vated waterfront and downtown area, the city was little more than an eastern gate-way to the Pacific Northwest. Today, however, Spokane is the second-largest city in Washington, the largest city between Seattle and Minneapolis, and a center for both commercial and cultural pursuits.

For thousands of years Native Americans lived along the Spokane River, and it was at Spokane Falls that the Spokan-ee tribe congregated each year to catch salmon. When the first explorers and fur traders arrived in 1807, it was near these falls that they chose to establish a trading post where they could barter with the Native Ameri-cans for beaver pelts. Spokan House (the original spelling had no letter *e*), established in 1810 downriver from Spokane Falls, became the first settlement in the area, but it was not until 1872 that a settlement was established at the falls themselves. When the Northern Pacific Railroad arrived in 1881, the town of Spokan Falls became the most important town in the region. However, in the summer of 1889 the city's downtown commercial district was destroyed by fire. Within 2 years the city had fully recovered from the fire and also changed the spelling of its name.

Today the city isn't really a destination as such, but its proximity to Lake Coeur d'Alene and several Idaho ski areas makes it something of a jumping-off point for explorations of the northern Idaho Rocky Mountains.

ESSENTIALS

GETTING THERE   Spokane is on I-90, Washington's east-west Interstate. U.S. 2 is an alternative route from western Washington. U.S. 395 is the main route from Canada south to Spokane. U.S. 195 connects to Lewiston, Idaho.

Spokane International Airport is located 10 miles west of downtown and is served by Air Canada, Alaska Airlines, Delta, Horizon, Northwest, Southwest, and United.

Amtrak passenger trains provide service to Spokane. The station is at 221 W. First Ave. Greyhound buses also stop in Spokane at the same station.

VISITOR INFORMATION   Contact the **Spokane Area Convention & Visitors Bureau,** 801 W. Riverside Ave., Spokane, WA 99201 (☎ **509/624-1341**) or the **Visitor Information Center,** 201 W. Main Ave., Spokane, WA 99201 (☎ **800/ 248-3230** or 509/747-3230).

GETTING AROUND   **Rental cars** are available from Alamo, Avis, Dollar, Na-tional, and Thrifty. If you need a taxi, contact **Yellow Cab** (☎ **509/624-4321**). Public bus service is provided by the **Spokane Transit System** (☎ **509/328-7433**); the fare is 75¢.

FESTIVALS   Spokane's nickname is the Lilac City, and the city's biggest annual event is the **Lilac Festival,** which is held each year in the third week of May. On the first Sunday in May, the city holds its annual **Lilac Bloomsday Run,** the largest timed race in the world (more than 55,000 runners participate).

WHAT TO SEE & DO

Spokane has made it very easy for visitors to get a sense of what the city is all about by mapping out a Spokane City Drive that takes in all the city's highlights. The well-marked route meanders through Spokane and passes by all the city attractions listed below. The drive also takes in some great vistas from the hills to the south of the city.

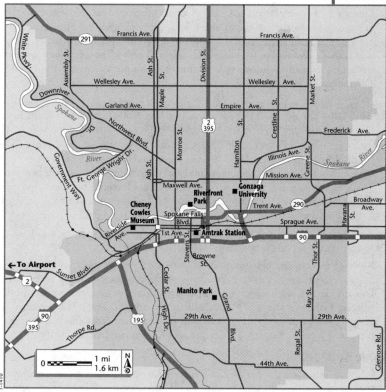

RIVERFRONT PARK

Created for the 1974 World's Fair Expo and set on an island in the middle of the Spokane River, 100-acre **Riverfront Park** (☎ **800/336-PARK** or 509/456-4-FUN) is the city's pride and joy. The land on which the park stands was once a maze of railroad tracks and depots, and the polluted river was nearly inaccessible to the public. The creation of the park helped rejuvenate downtown Spokane, and today crowds flock here to enjoy everything from summertime concerts to ice skating in the winter. Activities for both adults and children abound. The restored 1909 Looff Carrousel, with its hand-carved horses, is one of the most beautiful in the country. More contemporary entertainment is offered at the **IMAX Theatre** (☎ **509/625-6686**), where 70mm films are shown on screens five stories high. A family fun center includes kiddie rides, miniature golf, and arcade games. Throughout the summer there are lunchtime and evening concerts, special events, and a weekend arts-and-crafts market.

Serving as a spectacular backdrop for the park is the Spokane River, which here cascades over Spokane Falls. The best view of the falls is from the Gondola Skyride that swings out over the falls; rides cost $3.

MORE ATTRACTIONS

Cheney Cowles Museum and Campbell House. W. 2316 First Ave. ☎ **509/456-3931.** Admission $4 adults, $3 seniors, $2.50 students and children 6–16 (half price on Wed 10am– 5pm and free 5–9pm). Tues and Thurs–Sat 10am–5pm, Wed 10am–9pm, Sun 1–5pm.

Though it's not very large, the Cheney Cowles Museum does an outstanding job of presenting the history of the Spokane area. Beginning with a display on Native American culture and artifacts, the museum moves through the fur-trading and pioneer years. In addition to the historical displays, there's a fine-arts gallery in the museum. Adjacent to the museum is the historic Campbell House, a restored 1898 Tudor-style home.

Crosbyana Room. In the Crosby Student Center of Gonzaga University, 502 E. Boone Ave. ☎ **509/328-4220,** ext. 3847. Free admission. Sept–May, Mon–Fri 7:30am–midnight, Sat–Sun 11am–midnight; June–Aug, Mon–Fri 8:30am–4:30pm.

Bing Crosby got his start here in Spokane, where he spent most of his youth. When young Bing's aspirations soared beyond the bounds of Spokane and he made his name in Los Angeles, the members of his band who chose to stay safely at home must have long regretted their decision. All of Crosby's gold records, his Oscar, and plenty of other memorabilia (including a Bing-endorsed mousetrap and a Bing Crosby Ice Cream box) are on view.

Manito Park and Botanical Gardens. 4 W. 21st Ave. ☎ **509/625-6622.** Free admission. Daily 8am–dusk. Japanese Garden closed Nov–Mar.

Among the rocks and pine forest of this park are several of the most beautiful public gardens in the Northwest. Foremost of these is the classically proportioned Duncan Garden, a formal garden patterned after those of 17th-century Europe. The adjacent Gaiser Conservatory brims with exotic tropical plants. The perennial garden and rose garden are at their exuberant peaks in June and should not be missed. A separate Japanese Garden is a tranquil spot for contemplation.

WINE TOURING

In the Spokane area there are several wineries that you can visit. Right downtown in the historic Broadview Dairy Building you'll find **Caterina,** 905 N. Washington St. (☎ 509/328-5069). **Arbor Crest Wine Cellars,** 4705 N. Fruithill Rd. (☎ **509/ 927-9894**), is housed in the historic Cliff House atop a bluff overlooking the Spokane River. To reach Arbor Crest, take the Argonne North exit off I-90. The **Worden Winery,** 7271 W. 45th Ave. (☎ **509/455-7835**), has its tasting room in a log cabin. You'll find the winery off I-90 at Exit 276. The **Latah Creek Wine Cellars,** 13030 E. Indiana Ave. (☎ **509/926-0164**), is housed in a Spanish mission-style building. To reach this winery, take Exit 289 off I-90.

SPORTS & OUTDOOR ACTIVITIES

Walkers, joggers, and cyclists will want to get in some exercise on the **Spokane River Centennial Trail.** The paved trail starts at the Spokan House historic site west of the city and parallels the river for 39 miles to the Idaho state line, where it connects to the Idaho Centennial Trail for a final leg into Couer d'Alene. Bicycle rentals are available at Riverfront Park.

    Riverside State Park (☎ 509/456-3964), which follows the meandering Spokane River on the west edge of the city, has hiking trails, picnic areas, and campgrounds.

    For a great view of the region, head northwest 30 miles to **Mount Spokane State Park** (☎ 509/238-4258), where you can drive to the top of the mountain. Hiking trails wander for miles through the forest here.

GOLF   Golf courses in Spokane include **Downriver Municipal Golf Course,** 3225 N. Columbia Circle (☎ 509/327-5269); **Esmeralda Municipal Golf Course,** 3933 E. Courtland Ave. (☎ 509/487-6291); and **Indian Canyon Municipal Golf Course,** 4304 W. West Dr. (☎ 509/747-5353).

SKIING Within an hour of Spokane are two small downhill ski areas—**Mt. Spokane** (☎ **509/443-1397**), 30 miles northwest of the city; and **49 Degrees North Ski Area,** 52 miles north on U.S. 395 (☎ **509/935-6649**). Cross-country skiers will find great trails at **Mount Spokane State Park** (☎ **509/238-4258**).

WHITE-WATER RAFTING Downstream from the falls, the Spokane River produces some good whitewater. Rafting trips on this stretch of river are offered by **Wiley E. Waters** (☎ **888/502-1900** or 208/777-1826). The 1¹/₂-hour trips cost $35.

SHOPPING

Two renovated downtown buildings, the **Bennet Block** on the corner of Main Avenue and Stevens Street, and the **Flour Mill,** 621 W. Mallon St. (just across Riverfront Park from downtown), now house specialty shops and restaurants. Housed in an old mill that was built beside Spokane Falls, the Flour Mill, has, in addition to its many interesting shops and restaurants, displays on the mill and Spokane history.

WHERE TO STAY

✪ **Angelica's Mansion Bed and Breakfast.** 1321 W. Ninth Ave., Spokane, WA 99204. ☎ **509/624-5598.** 4 rms (2 rms with private bath). $75 double with shared bath, $85–$95 double with private bath. Rates include full breakfast. DISC, MC, V.

Located in an elegant tree-shaded neighborhood on a hillside above downtown Spokane, this 1907 Craftsman brick home is filled with elegant period touches including hardwood floors, a tiled fireplace, and lots of built-in cabinetry. Off the landing of this two-story house, there is a small sunporch and out front there is a long veranda. Guest rooms are very tastefully furnished and have down comforters on the beds. In one room you'll find a wicker bed and in another there is a four-poster.

✪ **Cavanaugh's Inn at the Park.** 303 W. North River Dr., Spokane, WA 99201. ☎ **800/325-4000** or 509/326-8000. Fax 509/325-7329. 402 rms, 25 suites. A/C TV TEL. $99–$159 double; $199–$900 suite. AE, DC, DISC, ER, MC, V.

There is no more conveniently located hotel in Spokane. In addition to the fun that can be had in the adjacent park, the hotel offers a resort-like pool and a sunny atrium lobby. A wide variety of rooms accommodate all types of travelers. Anyone wishing a bit more luxury than the standard rooms afford may want to opt for the executive rooms, which come with balconies overlooking the pool or the river.

Dining/Entertainment: You have a choice of continental cuisine served in a room overlooking the river, or less expensive meals in an atrium cafe. The lounge on the seventh floor provides drinks with a view, and down at ground level there is another lounge.

Services: Concierge, room service, airport shuttle.

Facilities: Outdoor pool, indoor lap pool, exercise room, sauna, whirlpools.

✪ **The Fotheringham House.** 2128 W. Second Ave., Spokane, WA 99204. ☎ **509/838-1891.** Fax 509/838-1807. 4 rms, 1 with bath. $75–$95 double. Rates include full breakfast. DISC, MC, V.

Located in the historic Browne's Addition neighborhood, this pretty, blue Queen Anne Victorian home is right across the street from Patsy Clark's Mansion, Spokane's most elegant restaurant. Most of the furnishings are period antiques, and in the large shared bathroom you'll find the original claw-foot bathtub.

The Ridpath. 515 W. Sprague Ave., Spokane, WA 99201-0367. ☎ **800/426-0670** or 509/838-2711. Fax 509/747-6970. 350 rms, 35 suites. A/C TV TEL. $85–$135 double; $175–$350 suite. AE, CB, DC, DISC, MC, V.

Popular with conventions because of its size, the Ridpath has undergone extensive renovations over the past few years and is now a very attractive place to stay. In the lobby, you'll find travertine walls and Asian accents. The hotel consists of a high-rise and an adjacent motel, both of which have been thoroughly updated. This latter wing holds the more spacious executive rooms and also overlooks the pool. For convenience and value, it's hard to beat the Ridpath.

Dining: Ankeny's, up on the top floor, provides decent meals and great views of the city, while down in the lobby is the more casual Silver Grill.

Services: Concierge, room service, airport shuttle.

Facilities: Outdoor pool, fitness center.

WHERE TO DINE

For espresso and creative sandwiches, try **Romeo's Cafe,** 221 N. Wall St. (☎ 509/455-5594), in downtown. If you've just had a hard afternoon of having fun at Riverside Park and you need a cold ale to cool you off, just head across the street to the **Fort Spokane Brewery,** 401 W. Spokane Falls Blvd. (☎ **509/838-3809**). Alternatively, you can check out the nearby **Bayou Brewing Company,** 1003 E. Trent Ave. (☎ **509/484-4818**) or **Big Horn Brewing Company,** 908 N. Howard St. (☎ **509/326-3745**), across the street from the Arena.

✪ **The Elk.** 1931 W. Pacific Ave. ☎ **509/456-0454.** Sandwiches/salads $7–$16. No credit cards. Mon–Fri 7am–9pm, Sat 8am–9pm, Sun 9am–3pm. AMERICAN/NORTHWEST.

The Elk has been around since the early 1900s when it was the Elk Drug Company, supplying medicines and soda fountain treats to neighborhood residents. Today it has been restored, complete with the original soda fountain, vintage advertising, and pharmaceutical paraphernalia, and not only do they serve milkshakes, malts, and floats, but also interesting sandwiches, soups, salads, and pizzas that appeal to contemporary tastes. In the evening, you'll even find the likes of apple-almond pork scallops, seafood trinity risotto, and grilled lavender chicken breast.

✪ **Fugazzi.** 1 N. Post St. ☎ **509/624-1133.** Reservations recommended. Main courses $13–$18. AE, MC, V. Tues–Sat 11am–2:30pm and 5–9pm. INTERNATIONAL.

With its contemporary art, exposed brick walls, and counter full of rustic breads, this place is brazenly hip. It also happens to serve some of the best food in town. Using the freshest seasonal ingredients, Fugazzi assembles menus that cater to the city's adventuresome palates. How about a smoked salmon egg roll with Thai dipping sauce or shoestring fries sprinkled with rice wine vinegar and chili flakes to start things out? There are always a few pastas, such as wild mushroom ravioli in a basil and red wine broth. Heartier appetites might opt for something such as Moroccan chicken with a grilled vegetable, pine-nut, and currant couscous, or Tuscan lamb shanks. Just don't eat too much of that great bread or you won't have room for dessert.

Milford's Fish House and Oyster Bar. 719 N. Monroe St. ☎ **509/326-7251.** Reservations recommended. Main courses $13–$25. MC, V. Sun–Mon 4–9pm, Tues–Sat 5–10pm. SEAFOOD.

Over on the north side of the river near the Veterans Memorial Arena, you'll find Spokane's best seafood restaurant. With its moosehead, old, worn carpets and overstuffed chairs, pressed-tin ceiling, and walls covered with old ads, Milford's manages to look as if it's been around since the Great Fire of 1889. Sidle up to the bar and peruse the day's oyster menu, then take a seat in one of the back rooms. The menu changes regularly, but plenty of local favorites such as crawfish and shrimp pie and the New England–style shell bake are usually available.

⚙ **Patsy Clark's Mansion.** 2208 W. Second St. ☎ **509/838-8300.** Reservations recommended. Main courses lunch $7–$12, dinner $14–$26. AE, DC, DISC, MC, V. Mon–Fri 11:30am–1:45pm and 5–9pm, Sat 5–9pm, Sun 10am–1:30pm (brunch) and 5–9pm. INTERNATIONAL.

Built in 1895 to be the grandest mansion in Spokane, Patsy Clark's is still just that. There are 26 rooms, each with a different style, nine fireplaces, and Tiffany stained-glass windows and lamps. The menu changes frequently, but might include such creative and complexly flavored dishes as an ahi tuna fillet with a toasted sesame seed crust, a grilled Angus New York steak with a sour mash whisky demiglaze, or tequila-lime marinated duck with orange-pepper barbecue sauce. Patsy Clark's tends to attract a very well-heeled clientele, so we suggest dressing for dinner or lunch.

Rock City Grill. 505 W. Riverside Ave. ☎ **509/455-4400.** Reservations recommended. Main courses $6–$16. AE, CB, DC, DISC, MC, V. Sun–Thurs 11:15am–10pm, Fri–Sat 11:15am–11pm. MEDITERRANEAN/INTERNATIONAL.

The Rock City Grill, an outpost of contemporary urban chic, has taken up the challenge of satisfying jaded palates in Spokane. Though Mediterranean flavors predominate on this inexpensive eatery's menu, entrees also include the likes of wood-oven roasted prawns, creative pizzas, and New York steak with Jack Daniels sauce (once served by the owners to Pres. George Bush). If you're in the mood for an espresso and a pastry, you won't do much better anywhere in town.

SPOKANE AFTER DARK

To find out what's going on around Spokane, pick up a copy of *The Inlander,* a free weekly arts-and entertainment newspaper. You'll find copies in restaurants, record stores, and bookstores.

6 The Grand Coulee Dam Area

85 miles W of Spokane, 92 miles NE of Wenatchee

When construction was completed on the Grand Coulee Dam in 1941, it was the largest man-made structure in the world. The 5,223-foot-long dam turned the Columbia River into 150-mile-long Roosevelt Lake and was used to fill the formerly dry Grand Coulee with a reservoir 27 miles long (Banks Lake).

Grand Coulee, formerly a wide, dry valley, is a geologic anomaly left over from the last Ice Age. At that time, a glacier dammed an upstream tributary of the Columbia River and formed a huge lake. When this prehistoric lake burst through the ice dam, massive volumes of water flooded across central Washington, spilling out of the normal channel of the Columbia River and carving out deep valleys as it flooded southward, eventually merging once again with the main river to roar through the Cascade Range forming the Columbia Gorge. With the end of the Ice Age, the Columbia returned to its original channel and the temporary flood channels were left high and dry. Early French explorers called these dry channels *coulées,* and the largest of them all was Grand Coulee, which is 50 miles long, between 2 and 5 miles wide, and 1,000 feet deep.

The dam is built across the Columbia River at the northern end of Grand Coulee, which has been filled once again with water pumped from Roosevelt Lake. The waters of both Roosevelt Lake and Grand Coulee's Banks Lake have been used to irrigate the arid lands of eastern Washington, turning this region into productive farmlands.

ESSENTIALS

GETTING THERE   The towns of Grand Coulee, Coulee Dam, and Electric City are at the junction of Wash. 155, which runs south to Coulee City and north to Omak, and Wash. 174, which runs west to Wash. 17 and east to U.S. 2.

VISITOR INFORMATION   Contact the **Grand Coulee Dam Area Chamber of Commerce,** P.O. Box 760, Grand Coulee, WA 99133-0760 (☎ **800/COULEE-2**).

WHAT TO SEE & DO

You can learn the history of the dam by stopping in at the **Grand Coulee Dam Visitor Arrival Center,** which is open daily. There are guided and self-guided tours of the dam. Every night during the summer, the **world's largest laser-light show** is projected onto the face of the dam. The accompanying narration is broadcast over the AM radio and tells the history of Grand Coulee and the dam. There is also a self-guided walking tour through historic Coulee Dam, the government town built to house workers during the construction of the dam.

Lake Roosevelt, with its 600 miles of shoreline, provides ample opportunities for water sports and fishing and comprises the **Lake Roosevelt National Recreation Area,** 1008 Crest Dr., Coulee Dam, WA 99116-1259 (☎ **509/633-9441**). Along the shores of the lake are more than 30 campgrounds. About 22 miles north of Davenport, at the confluence of the Spokane and Columbia rivers, stands **Fort Spokane,** which was built in 1880. Four of the original buildings are still standing. An 1892 brick guardhouse here now serves as a visitor center, though the main visitor center is the Grand Coulee Dam Visitor Arrival Center right at the dam.

Much of the land bordering Roosevelt Lake lies within the Colville Indian Reservation. In the town of Coulee Dam, you can visit the **Colville Confederated Tribes Museum,** 516 Birch St. (☎ **509/633-0751**), a small museum with interesting displays of baskets and tribal regalia, as well as historical photos. From May to September, the museum is open daily from 10am to 6pm; October to December, it's closed on Sunday; and January to April, it's closed Sunday and Monday. Admission is by donation. The Colville tribes also operate a casino next door to the museum.

Some 30 miles down the Grand Coulee, just south of Coulee City on Wash. 17, you can have a look at a natural wonder that's as impressive as the dam. **Dry Falls** are the remains of a waterfall created by the same flood of water that scoured out the Grand Coulee. At their peak flow, the waters cascading 400 feet over Dry Falls stretched 3^1/$_2$ miles wide, making this the largest waterfall of all time. An interpretive center stands beside the highway at the Dry Falls Overlook, and if you're interested in going to the base of the falls, continue south 2 miles to **Sun Lakes State Park,** which has a road leading back to the falls.

Ten miles south of Coulee City on Pinto Ridge Road are the impressive Summer Falls at **Summer Falls State Park.**

Another 20 miles or so will bring you to **Soap Lake,** an alkaline lake named for the soap suds that gather on its shores. For centuries the lake has attracted people who believe the waters have medicinal properties. Once a busy health spa, Soap Lake today is a quiet little town. However, it does have a couple of good lodges where you can soak in the lake's waters. A public town beach also provides access to the lake.

WHERE TO STAY

In addition to the accommodations listed below, you can also stay on a houseboat and cruise up and down Lake Roosevelt. Houseboats are available from **Roosevelt**

Recreational Enterprises, P.O. Box 5, Coulee Dam, WA 99116-0005 (☎ **800/ 648-5253** or 509/633-0136), which charges between $1,080 and $2,060 for a weekly houseboat rental (depending on time of year and size of boat).

IN COULEE DAM

Columbia River Inn. 10 Lincoln St., Coulee Dam, WA 99116. ☎ **800/633-6521** or 509/ 633-2100. 35 rms. A/C TV TEL. Summer, $72–$95 double; winter, $49–$75 double. AE, DISC, MC, V.

Located right across the street from Grand Coulee Dam Visitor Center, this remodeled motel is convenient for viewing the laser light show (just cross the street to the park). Guest rooms have attractive pine furnishings and small balconies with partial dam views, and some have their own whirlpool tubs. There's an outdoor pool, as well as a hot tub.

Four Winds Guest House. 301 Lincoln St., Coulee Dam, WA 99116. ☎ **800/786-3146** or 509/633-3146. 10 rms (1 with private bath). $62 double with shared bath, $74 double with private bath. Rates include continental breakfast. AE, MC, V.

Located in the picture-perfect company town that was built to house engineers and laborers working on the dam, this inn is in a former engineers dorm where Pres. Franklin D. Roosevelt once held a meeting during his visit to the dam site. The guest rooms are simply furnished and there's a bathroom for every two rooms.

IN SOAP LAKE

✪ **The Notaras Lodge.** P.O. Box 987, Soap Lake, WA 98851. ☎ **509/246-0462.** 20 rms. TV TEL. $55–$110 double. MC, V.

A modern log building only steps from the lake offers the most interesting lodgings in Soap Lake. Each room at the lodge is decorated differently and many commemorate local and national celebrities. Unusual woodworking, log beds, Native American artifacts, and Western trappings are all part of the fantasy world at the Notaras Lodge. Eight rooms have whirlpool tubs, and all the rooms have lake water piped into them so you can soak in the therapeutic waters.

Useful Toll-Free Numbers

MAJOR AIRLINES

Alaska Airlines	800/426-0333
Aero México	800/237-6639
America West	800/235-9292
American	800/433-7300
Continental	800/525-0280
Delta	800/221-1212
Northwest	800/225-2525
Southwest	800/435-9792
TWA	800/221-2000
United	800/241-6522
US Airways	800/428-4322

CAR-RENTAL COMPANIES

Alamo	800/327-9633
Avis	800/331-1212
Budget	800/527-0700
Dollar	800/800-4000
Hertz	800/654-3131
National	800/227-7368
Thrifty	800/367-2277

MAJOR CHAIN MOTELS

Best Western	800/528-1234	
Comfort Inns	800/228-5150	
Days Inns	800/329-7466	(800/DAYS-INN)
Econo Lodges	800/424-4777	
Embassy Suites	800/362-2779	(800/EMBASSY)
Hampton Inns	800/426-7866	(800/HAMPTON)
Hilton	800/445-8667	
Holiday Inns	800/465-4329	(800/HOLIDAY)
La Quinta Inns	800/531-5900	
Marriott	800/228-9290	
Marriott Residence Inn	800/331-3131	
Motel 6	505/891-6161	(no 800 number)
Quality Inns	800/228-5151	
Radisson	800/333-3333	

Ramada	800/272-6232
Rodeway Inns	800/424-4777
Sheraton	800/325-3535
Super 8 Motels	800/800-8000
Travelodge	800/578-7878
Wyndham	800/996-3426

Index

FROMMER'S® COMPLETE TRAVEL GUIDES

*(Comprehensive guides to destinations around the world, with
selections in all price ranges—from deluxe to budget)*

Acapulco, Ixtapa &
  Zihuatenejo
Alaska
Amsterdam
Arizona
Atlanta
Australia
Austria
Bahamas
Barcelona, Madrid &
  Seville
Belgium, Holland &
  Luxembourg
Bermuda
Boston
Budapest & the Best of
  Hungary
California
Canada
Cancún, Cozumel & the
  Yucatán
Cape Cod, Nantucket &
  Martha's Vineyard
Caribbean
Caribbean Cruises & Ports
  of Call
Caribbean Ports of Call
Carolinas & Georgia
Chicago
China
Colorado
Costa Rica
Denver, Boulder &
  Colorado Springs
England

Europe
Florida
France
Germany
Greece
Hawaii
Hong Kong
Honolulu, Waikiki & Oahu
Ireland
Israel
Italy
Jamaica & Barbados
Japan
Las Vegas
London
Los Angeles
Maryland & Delaware
Maui
Mexico
Miami & the Keys
Montana & Wyoming
Montréal & Québec City
Munich & the Bavarian Alps
Nashville & Memphis
Nepal
New England
New Mexico
New Orleans
New York City
Northern New England
Nova Scotia, New
  Brunswick
  & Prince Edward Island
Oregon
Paris

Philadelphia & the Amish
  Country
Portugal
Prague & the Best of the
  Czech Republic
Provence & the Riviera
Puerto Rico
Rome
San Antonio & Austin
San Diego
San Francisco
Santa Fe, Taos &
  Albuquerque
Scandinavia
Scotland
Seattle & Portland
Singapore & Malaysia
South Pacific
Spain
Switzerland
Thailand
Tokyo
Toronto
Tuscany & Umbria
USA
Utah
Vancouver & Victoria
Vienna & the Danube
  Valley
Virgin Islands
Virginia
Walt Disney World &
  Orlando
Washington, D.C.
Washington State

FROMMER'S® DOLLAR-A-DAY GUIDES

(The ultimate guides to comfortable low-cost travel)

Australia from $50 a Day
California from $60 a Day
Caribbean from $60 a Day
Costa Rica & Belize
  from $35 a Day
England from $60 a Day
Europe from $50 a Day
Florida from $50 a Day
Greece from $50 a Day
Hawaii from $60 a Day
India from $40 a Day

Ireland from $50 a Day
Israel from $45 a Day
Italy from $50 a Day
London from $60 a Day
Mexico from $35 a Day
New York from $75 a Day
New Zealand from $50 a Day
Paris from $70 a Day
San Francisco from $60 a Day
Washington, D.C., from
  $60 a Day

FROMMER'S® PORTABLE GUIDES

(Pocket-size guides for travelers who want everything in a nutshell)

Bahamas	Dublin	Puerto Vallarta, Manzanillo
California Wine Country	Las Vegas	& Guadalajara
Charleston & Savannah	London	San Francisco
Chicago	Maine Coast	Venice
	New Orleans	Washington, D.C.

FROMMER'S® NATIONAL PARK GUIDES

(Everything you need for the perfect park vacation)

Grand Canyon	Yosemite & Sequoia/
National Parks of the American West	Kings Canyon
Yellowstone & Grand Teton	Zion & Bryce Canyon

FROMMER'S® IRREVERENT GUIDES

(Wickedly honest guides for sophisticated travelers)

Amsterdam	Manhattan	San Francisco	Walt Disney World
Chicago	New Orleans	Santa Fe	Washington, D.C.
London	Paris		

FROMMER'S® BY NIGHT GUIDES

(The series for those who know that life begins after dark)

Amsterdam	Los Angeles	Miami	Prague
Chicago	Madrid	New Orleans	San Francisco
Las Vegas	& Barcelona	Paris	Washington, D.C.
London	Manhattan		

THE COMPLETE IDIOT'S TRAVEL GUIDES

(The ultimate user-friendly trip planners)

Cruise Vacations	New York City	San Francisco
Las Vegas	Planning Your Trip	Walt Disney World
New Orleans	to Europe	

SPECIAL-INTEREST TITLES

Arthur Fommer's New World of Travel	Outside Magazine's Adventure Guide
The Civil War Trust's Official Guide to	to New England
the Civil War Discovery Trail	Outside Magazine's Adventure Guide
Frommer's Caribbean Hideaways	to Northern California
Frommer's Complete Hostel Vacation	Outside Magazine's Adventure Guide
Guide to England, Scotland & Wales	to the Pacific Northwest
Frommer's Europe's Greatest	Outside Magazine's Adventure Guide
Driving Tours	to Southern California & Baja
Frommer's Food Lover's Companion	Outside Magazine's Guide to Family Vacations
to France	Places Rated Almanac
Frommer's Food Lover's Companion to	Retirement Places Rated
Italy	Washington, D.C., with Kids
Israel Past & Present	Wonderful Weekends from New York City
New York City with Kids	Wonderful Weekends from San Francisco
New York Times Weekends	Wonderful Weekends from Los Angeles

WHEREVER
YOU TRAVEL,
*H*ELP IS NEVER
FAR AWAY.

From planning your trip to providing travel assistance
along the way, American Express® Travel Service Offices
are always there to help you do more.

Washington State

Travel Source International (R)
1882 136th Place N.E.
Suite 105
Bellevue
425-747-1900

American Express Travel Service
Plaza 600 Building
600 Stewart Street
Seattle
206-441-8622

Select Travel (R)
32020 First Avenue South
Federal Way
253-874-6033

House of Travel (R)
1322 N. Monroe #105
Spokane
509-326-4212

Kennewick Travel (R)
100 North Morain, Suite #102
Kennewick
509-735-6494

Adventure in Travel (R)
12929 E. Sprague
Spokane
509-928-7961

Travel Professionals (R)
3051 78th Avenue, S.E.
Mercer Island
206-236-0990

do more AMERICAN EXPRESS
®
Travel

http://www.americanexpress.com/travel
**American Express Travel Service Offices
are located throughout the United States.
For the office nearest you, call 1-800-AXP-3429.**